VICTORIA

B

To Jean

VICTORIA

The Young Queen

MONICA CHARLOT

BLACKWELL
Oxford UK & Cambridge USA

Copyright © Monica Charlot 1991

English edition first published 1991
The French language edition of this book was first published in 1989 by Flammarion

Monica Charlot is hereby identified as author of this work in accordance with Section 77 of the Copyright, Designs and Patents Act 1988.

Basil Blackwell Ltd
108 Cowley Road, Oxford, OX4 1JF, UK

Basil Blackwell, Inc.
3 Cambridge Center
Cambridge, Massachusetts 02142, USA

Library of Congress Cataloging in Publication Data

Charlot, Monica.
Victoria: the young queen/Monica Charlot.
p. cm.
Includes bibliographical references and index.
ISBN 0-631-17437-0
1. Victoria, Queen of Great Britain, 1819–1901—Childhood and youth. 2. Great Britain—History—Victoria, 1837–1901. 3. Great Britain—Kings and rulers—Biography. I. Title.
DA555.C48 1991
941.081'092—dc20
[B] 90-24757 CIP

British Library Cataloguing in Publication Data

A CIP catalogue record for this book is available from the British Library.

Typeset in 10 on 12 pt Baskerville
by Best-set Typesetter Ltd., Hong Kong
Printed in Great Britain by T. J. Press Ltd., Padstow, Cornwall
This book is printed on acid-free paper.

Contents

List of Plates		vi
Acknowledgements		viii
1	The Lost Heir	I
2	The Line of Succession	16
3	A Solitary Childhood	36
4	The Kensington System	55
5	Victoria Regina	81
6	The First Six Months	101
7	The Coronation	115
8	Scandals and Political Crises	128
9	Courtship	148
10	The Royal Wedding	167
11	Conflicts of Roles	188
12	Albert's Search for Power	209
13	Royal Travels	234
14	A Neutral Crown?	258
15	Domestic Life	274
16	Foreign Affairs	299
17	Mid-century Grandeur	325
18	The Crimean War and the Indian Mutiny	345
19	Family Affairs	376
20	Death in the Family	406
Family Trees of Victoria and Albert		426
Notes		428
Index		475

Plates

PLATES BETWEEN PAGES 152 AND 153

Kensington Palace, birthplace of Victoria

HRH The Duchess of Kent with the Princess Victoria, painted by Sir W. Beechey, RA, etched by W. Skelton

The Princess Victoria, engraved by Dean

Princess Victoria at the age of seventeen, by H. Collen

Princess Victoria, by Count D'Orsay

Coronation of Queen Victoria, 1838, by Sir George Hayter

Baroness Lehzen, sketched by Queen Victoria

Leopold I of Belgium

The mother and father of Prince Albert with views of his birthplace, The Rosenau

The marriage of Queen Victoria and Prince Albert, by Sir George Hayter

Albert, sketched by Victoria

PLATES BETWEEN PAGES 312 AND 313

Lord Melbourne, sketched by Queen Victoria

Lady Flora Hastings

Windsor Castle in Modern Times, by Sir Edwin Landseer

Sir John Conroy

The Duchess of Kent, by Sir George Hayter

Windsor Castle, engraved by A. Willmore after Birket Foster

The Royal Family, 1846, by Winterhalter

State procession to the opening ceremony of the Crystal Palace, 1851, lithograph by Butler

Funeral of the Duke of Wellington, by Haghe

Group on the lower terrace, Osborne, August 1853

Queen Victoria and Prince Albert, 30 June 1854

Entry of Queen Victoria into Paris, by Bajot and Daurats. The visit to Emperor Napoleon III, 1855

Arrival of the Queen at Eu, by Charlotte Canning

Drawing room in the private apartments at Eu, by Eugène Lami

The Emperor Napoleon III and Empress Eugénie, Queen Victoria and Prince Albert visit the Hall of Mirrors at the Palace of Versailles, 20 August 1855, by Victor Chavet

Queen Victoria and Prince Albert inspecting the sick and wounded Grenadier guardsmen from the Crimea War, 20 February 1855, by G. H. Thomas

The Royal residence at Balmoral, by Fripp

The Royal Family at Osborne, 26 May 1857

Victoria, The Princess Royal, on her wedding day, 25 January 1858, with her parents Queen Victoria and the Prince Consort, from a daguerreotype of T. R. Williams

Queen Victoria and the Prince Consort

The Mausoleum, Frogmore

Queen Victoria, with Victoria, Princess Royal, 25 June 1857

Acknowledgements

My grateful thanks go first to Her Majesty the Queen, who graciously allowed me access to the Royal Archives at Windsor Castle. I am also grateful to Sir Robin Mackworth Young, former director of the Royal Library for his advice and encouragement. Miss Jane Langton, former Registrar of the Royal Archives at Windsor, was extremely helpful and a wise counsellor. I am very much indebted to her successor Lady de Bellaigue for her advice and suggestions, and for her very careful reading of the text both in French and in English. I owe her more than I can say. I would also like to thank Miss Frances Dimond of the Royal Photographic Department, Jane Roberts of the Royal Drawings Department and Lady Millar for her kind and generous help with the illustrations.

I am under a great obligation to Asa Briggs, who has read the text and given me invaluable advice. John Davey, my English editor, has been a source of great encouragement and support. Ms Ann Bone has done an excellent job as copy editor.

I must also express my thanks collectively to all those who have helped me in the British Library, the Bodleian and the Library of Balliol College.

I add a special thank you to my father who helped me with the German translations and who sadly will never see the finished work; to my daughter Claire who has typed and retyped the manuscript in French and English; to my husband who encouraged me to embark on this biography – but for him, this book would never have been finished.

1
The Lost Heir

On the night of Monday 3 November 1817 Princess Charlotte, heir to the throne of Britain, experienced the first symptoms of approaching labour, including 'the dreadful sickness that accompanies these occasions'.[1] She had been married some eighteen months and had already had two miscarriages. This pregnancy had not gone smoothly either. Lady Holland had noted in a letter in September, 'Princess Charlotte is going on in her *grossesse*, but there are some strange awkward symptoms.'[2]

The Princess was only twenty-two, but her short life had been tempestuous. She had grown up with no family life and little affection. Her birth had signalled the end of all marital contact between her parents. Her father – the future George IV – had conveyed this decision to her mother in the spring of 1796: 'Our inclinations are not in our power nor should either of us be held answerable to the other, because nature has not made us suitable to each other. Tranquil and comfortable society is, however, in our power . . .'[3] In fact the relationship between her parents was to be anything but tranquil. After their formal separation the Prince resumed his connection with the beautiful, twice-widowed Maria Fitzherbert, whom he had secretly married earlier. Charlotte's mother, Princess Caroline, went her own way and rumours of her infidelity trickled back to her husband and were duly taken to the King. Caroline was submitted to the humiliation of a 'delicate investigation' of her morals in 1806. Charlotte was dispatched at the age of twelve to the safe keeping of her grandmother and namesake Queen Charlotte. Her mother was allowed to see her only once a week.

Starved of affection Charlotte was attracted to men from an early age. She had her first liaison at sixteen with a certain Captain Hesse, a womanizer whose acquaintance she made in Windsor when he rode by the side of her carriage. The liaison was encouraged, even engineered, by her mother. 'The Princess of Wales [Caroline] used to let him into her own apartment by a door that opens into Kensington Gardens and then left them together in her own bedroom, and turned the key upon them saying, "A présent, je vous laisse, amusez-vous." '[4] Correspondence between them went through her mother's hands. Whether it was in fact a liaison or simply an imprudent flirtation is uncertain. When she told her father the whole miserable story on Christmas Day 1814, after her mother had left England, she declared of her suitor: 'God knows what would have become of me if he had not behaved with so much respect to me.'[5] Her father accepted this version of things.

He cared little for his daughter. When he was displeased with her he refused to see her for weeks on end. Nevertheless, he kept her continually under his surveillance and he even seemed to fear her popularity, which contrasted with the low opinion the public had of him. Lord Brougham noted in 1813: 'Young P. and her father have had frequent rows of late, but one pretty serious one. He was angry with her for flirting with the Duke of Devonshire and suspected she was talking politics.' Perspicaciously Brougham continued: 'It signifies nothing how they go on this day or that – in the long run, quarrel they must. *He* has not equality of temper, or any other kind of sense, to keep well with her, and she has a spice of her mother's spirit.'[6] When at the age of seventeen Charlotte was given a separate residence, Warwick House, near her father's palace, Miss Knight her companion was warned that 'Charlotte must lay aside the idle nonsense of thinking that she has a will of her own; while I live she must be subject to me as she is at present, if she were 30 or 40 or even 45.'[7] Her only means of escape lay in marriage. The Prince Regent – as her father had become in 1812 – wanted her to marry the hereditary Prince of Orange, a solution which would have reinforced the links between England and Holland and got his wayward daughter safely off his hands. The idea did not appeal to her: 'I think him so ugly that I am sometimes obliged to turn my head away in disgust when he is speaking to me. Marry I will, and that directly, in order to enjoy my liberty; but not the Prince of Orange.'[8]

She feared her father, however, and shortly before her eighteenth birthday she became engaged to the Prince. Her fiancé was dissolute, unstable and self-indulgent, given to gambling, gaming and womanizing. Charlotte had accepted his suit in November 1812 and the Dutch Ambassador to the Court of St James made the formal demand for her hand in the following March. By June, however, it was all over. The reasons for the breaking off of the engagement were complex. The first stumbling block had been Charlotte's refusal to spend half the year in Holland. Her mother and Henry Brougham, a Whig Member of Parliament who was politically hostile to the royal family and for this reason had become her mother's legal adviser, convinced her that her father's insistence on this marriage stemmed from his desire to see her leave the country. Charlotte therefore made it a condition of the marriage that she must be mistress of her own actions and never leave England unless she so desired. The Prince of Orange's father gave way, so did the Regent. Preparations for the wedding went ahead. Brougham, however, continued to put pressure on Charlotte, who had now become a pawn in his game against the Regent. A squabble between the Prince and Charlotte over whether he should go out riding with her or go to the Mint as he had planned was a pretext for calling the wedding off. She had never really wanted him and when he left for the Mint she despatched a note breaking off their engagement. Creevey, writing to his wife, was jubilant:

> Well, my pretty, ... we have now, however, a new game for Master Prinny [the Prince Regent] which must begin tomorrow. Whitbread has formal authority from young Prinny [Princess Charlotte] to state that the marriage is broken off, and that the reasons are – first, her attachment to this country, which she cannot and will not leave; and above all her attachment to her mother, whom in her present distressed situation she likewise cannot leave ... What think you of the effect of this upon the British publick?[9]

Creevey gives us a glimpse in this letter of the manner in which Charlotte was used by the Regent's enemies. 'And now what do you suppose has produced this sudden attachment to her mother? It arises from the profound resources of old Brougham, and is, in truth one of the most brilliant movements in his campaign.'[10] Lord Brougham had led the Princess to believe that she would lose the throne if her mother went abroad – as she was always threatening to do on account of the way she was used in England, and as she would most certainly do if her daughter were no longer there to keep her in the country: 'then a divorce will inevitably take place, a second marriage follow, and thus the young Princess's title to the throne be gone. This has had an effect upon the young one,' Creevey noted, 'almost magical.'[11]

The Prince of Orange left for Holland, a rather pathetic figure. Charlotte's eyes turned to the Byronic figure of Prince Frederick, nephew of the King of Prussia – but her days of freedom were over.

Three weeks after the engagement had been broken, the Regent decided to show his daughter who was master. She was removed first to her father's palace, Carlton House, and from there a few days later to Cranbourne Lodge in Windsor Forest, where she was placed entirely under the care of new attendants. All her old friends and acquaintances were kept at bay. The Regent was much criticized for the treatment of his daughter, but perhaps his decision was not unwise. According to the Duke of Buckingham, Charlotte 'possessed also a nature susceptible of every generous impression; unsuspicious and trusting, she readily became the dupe of persons who sought for their own objects to influence her through her sympathies, but when the influence was removed, the natural good sense of the Princess suggested a line of conduct becoming her sex and position.'[12]

The breaking off of the Dutch connection was greeted with relief. As Madame d'Arblay wrote to Viscountess Keith:

> Certainly, *between ourselves*, my residence in *Les Pays bas* did not add to my regrets at the breach of the Dutch alliance for though the young Prince is really worthy, as well as heroically brave, and all his family merits esteem, the Court is too new and *ordinaire* for our brilliant Princess. There is a total want both of dignity and ease, and a kind of timid obsequiousness to the People that lets down Royalty, and yet would have made our Princess so surrounded, a pattern of ungenial haughtiness.[13]

Once Charlotte's engagement had been broken off another suitor came forward – Prince Leopold of Saxe-Coburg – third son of the Duke. A younger son of small means he was determined to make his way in the world. He became a friend of Mercer Elphinstone, Charlotte's friend and confidante, and persuaded her to give the Princess a good impression of him. Once Charlotte's engagement to the Prince of Orange was broken, Prince Leopold took to riding in the park when Charlotte drove there, saluting her from a distance. He played his cards with tact – and calculation. Having made it obvious that he was interested in her, he then went abroad for a whole year, during which time Charlotte's eagerness to see him gradually increased.

In February 1816, therefore, the Regent invited him officially to England. He was to meet the Princess at the Pavilion in Brighton. The court was agog with expectation by the time he arrived. 'I lose no time in telling you', the Countess Dowager of Ilchester wrote to a friend, 'that Prince Leopold is enchanting as far as appearance and manner, and imagination cannot picture a countenance more justifiable of love at first sight. There is a particularly soft and gentle expression blended with positive manliness of cast.'[14] The Prince was applauded for his knowledge of English, his fondness for reading, his business head and his taste for music. A really superior being, 'like an Englishman in all but the ease, elegance and deference of his manners'.[15]

Charlotte herself was neither graceful nor elegant. At sixteen she already had 'all the fulness of a person of five and twenty . . . her bosom full, but finely shaped; her shoulders large, and her whole person voluptuous, but of a nature to become soon spoiled, and without much care and exercise, she will shortly lose all her beauty in fat and clumsiness.' But she did, however, 'have style and the prestige that comes with royalty and power'.[16] Lady Campbell feared she was 'capricious, self-willed, and obstinate. I think she is kind-hearted, clever and enthusiastic. Her faults have evidently never been checked, nor her virtues fostered.'[17]

Leopold determined to do both. The Regent, who had nicknamed his future son-in-law the '*Marquis peu à peu*', had greeted him coldly. He warned Leopold of his daughter's obstinacy and of his own determination to have the marriage solemnized at the earliest possible moment. It was said at Court that the Prince Regent 'was quite nervous with impatience to get Princess Charlotte married, as otherwise the Opposition might clamour for her being treated as an heir apparent'. The young couple were from the first popular. Leopold was highly spoken of, and many would have agreed with Madame d'Arblay that as for Charlotte: 'Her early youth had been spent with so little happiness' that one could 'doubly rejoice at her apparently good destiny.'[18] The couple were married on 2 May 1816, two months after their meeting in Brighton. Charlotte wore a dress of silver lamé on net, over a silver tissue slip embroidered at the hem with silver lamé in shells and flowers. Her cloak was also of silver tissue lined with white satin. On her head she wore a sparkling circlet in the form of leaves and rose-buds.[19] Leopold was decked out in a British General's embroidered uniform coat, white cashmere waistcoat and breeches and a jewelled sword and belt presented to him by the Regent.[20] They were married at Carlton House – it was the last time an heir to the English throne was married in a private house. The altar was placed near one of the fireplaces in the crimson stateroom. The ceremony was short. It began at nine in the evening and was performed by the Archbishop of Canterbury assisted by the Bishop of London. By nine thirty it was over. After a honeymoon at Oatlands, the Yorks' house at Weybridge, they went to London, and finally at the end of the summer to their home – Claremont near Esher, sixteen miles from London. The house and its park of two hundred acres had been bought by Parliament and given to the royal couple as a 'gift from the nation'.[21] A Palladian edifice of cream brick with stone dressings, the house was built by Lancelot Brown, better known as Capability Brown, the landscape gardener.

The couple had married for reasons little concerned with love. She sought freedom, he prosperity. But they did in fact temper one another. Her spontaneity made him less calculating, his gentleness awakened her sensibility. What had been a marriage of convenience became a love match. 'Our mutual affection', the Princess wrote to Mercer, 'has grown by degrees, and with the more intimate acquaintance and knowledge of each other's dispositions and characters.'[22]

Leopold did not, for it was not in his nature, give up the idea of reforming his bride. He tried to restrain her, to make her give up her boisterous ways. When she raised her voice or slapped her thighs, he would murmur, 'Doucement ma chère, doucement.' She took it in good part from this man she acknowledged her superior, poking fun at him, nicknaming him 'doucement' – but restraining her manners as he suggested. Their life was simple: walking or riding together, singing duets or reading in quiet domesticity. Charlotte sat to Lawrence who had come to Claremont to do her portrait, Leopold went out shooting. Gradually she changed.

As Stockmar noted 'Intercourse with her husband has, however, had a markedly good effect upon her, and she has gained surprisingly in calmness and self-control, so that one sees more and more how good and noble she really is.'[23] She herself acknowledged the change: 'It is quite certain that he [Leopold] is the only being in the world who would have suited me and who could have made me happy and a good woman. It is his celestial character, his patience, his kindness, and nothing else would have succeeded.'[24] Only one thing remained to crown their married bliss – an heir. In early 1817 Charlotte was pregnant for the third time – and this time she hoped her pregnancy would run its full course.

Dr Mathew Baillie – Charlotte's physician in ordinary – had recommended a specialist, Sir Richard Croft, an obstetrician who had come into residence at Claremont on 11 October. He was 'a long, thin man, no longer very young, fidgety and good natured'.[25] A nurse, Mrs Griffiths, had been with her since the beginning of the month. The birth was expected round about the middle of the month. The days came and went, the Princess's health deteriorated but the birth did not take place. The expectant mother was bled regularly, given aperients and advised to eat as little solid food as possible.

During the last weeks of her pregnancy the young Princess underwent a deep fit of depression. All the deprivations that she had suffered, in particular the lack of motherly warmth and closeness, came to the surface. She took up her pen and poured out her heart to the mother who had deserted her.

> Why is not my mother allowed to pour cheerfulness into the sinking heart of her inexperienced and trembling child? I have but one mother and no variation of place or circumstance can remove her from my mind.

She seemed to see the shadows of death enveloping her.

> Believe me, my adored mother, I fear less to die than to live, the prospect of protracted existence is so blended with dangers and difficulties, so shadowed with clouds and uncertainties, so replete with anxieties and apprehensions that I must shrink from the contemplation of it, and fly for refuge even to the probability of my removal from so joyless an inheritance.[26]

It is difficult to unravel the causes of such gloom. Leopold was as attentive as a young husband could be, her father was not due to arrive until 16 October. She must have felt the lack of an older woman in whom to confide her hopes and fears as the birth approached. Her heartrending cry for help went unheeded. At the beginning of the month after taking Communion she told the chaplain, Dr Short, 'I have not now a wish ungratified. Any change must be for the worse.'[27]

The birth was some fifteen days overdue when labour began. At three o'clock on the morning of Tuesday 4 November it was thought necessary to assemble the members of the group who traditionally attended the birth of an heir to the throne. Throughout the night the dignitaries continued to arrive: Lord Bathurst, Viscount Sidmouth, the Archbishop of Canterbury and the Bishop of London, the Chancellor of the Exchequer . . .

At the same hour Croft declared optimistically that nothing could 'be going on better'. The symptoms he said had become 'more violent' and he had recommended Her Royal Highness to go to bed.[28] Croft declared he had never witnessed such resolution and firmness as that of the Princess – 'not a murmur or complaint uttered and the Prince Leopold certainly shows a mind most extraordinary. He keeps up his own firmness – and supports the Princess in her suffering. He scarcely quits her.'[29] So modern an attitude on the part of a husband was not typical of the period – nor were the old-fashioned ideas of her obstetrician. His complacency was only gradually shaken. After the Princess had been in labour for twenty-seven hours and the contractions had become weaker instead of stronger he finally decided that some artificial assistance might become necessary. To this effect he had Dr Sims summoned from London.

On the Wednesday morning the assembled council was informed that the 'labour of Her Royal Highness the Princess Charlotte has made a considerable though very gradual process throughout the night'[30] and that it was therefore hoped that 'the child may be safely born without artificial assistance.'[31] They could not however say when. Throughout the day the process continued. To begin with the Princess had 'walked about the rooms and was very little in her bed';[32] on the Wednesday afternoon tiredness overtook her and she was 'at times inclined to doze'.[33] Still Croft believed that affairs should be left to nature – the Princess remained cheerful and her pulse was good.

At nine o'clock on the evening of the fifth Charlotte gave birth to a still-born male child after forty-six hours of pain and fatigue. 'The child had been born dead but appeared not to have been dead long.'[34] Strenuous efforts were made to revive it – in particular it was plunged into hot water – but they were unavailing. 'When informed that her child was dead she [Charlotte] said she was sorry for the Prince, and added, "I hope we may be more fortunate another time", and certainly showed no sign of fear the whole time.'[35] On examination Croft and Sims discovered 'an hour-glass contraction of the uterus'.[36]

Leopold sent off a rather cold letter to the King.

> I write only a few lines to your Royal Highness to tell him that Charlotte was delivered, after over forty-eight hours of suffering, of a dead male child. She is as well as can be expected in these circumstances.[37]

Leopold, too, was tired – he had hardly left his wife's room for three days. He swallowed his bitter disappointment – after all, they were still young, he twenty-six and she only twenty-two, the years ahead would bring other births. He comforted his wife. Then, convinced that the state of the Princess was satisfactory, he retired to his room to take some rest.

It was not until midnight that it became obvious that all was not well with the Princess. Nurse Griffiths brought her some broth and a little gruel, but the Princess found it difficult to swallow. She complained of 'singing in her ears'[38] and was sick. She then became, her physicians say, a little irritable and began to talk somewhat too much.

Sir Richard Croft found the Princess's body had grown cold and had flannels and hot water bottles administered to the exterior, and when this proved ineffective she was given port wine. All to no effect. By this time Croft and Baillie were seriously alarmed. The Prince would have to be told.

There was in the house at the time another physician – Baron Stockmar. He had practised medicine in Coburg under his uncle and had later acted as head of the military hospital in the town. It was there that he had met Prince Leopold, who had offered him an appointment as his physician in ordinary. Although he soon became the confidante of both husband and wife, Stockmar refused from the commencement of her pregnancy to attend the Princess professionally, in view of the 'danger that must necessarily accrue to me if I arrogantly and imprudently pushed myself into a place in which a foreigner could never expect to reap honour but possibly plenty of blame.'[39]

His prudent consideration of his own future was to cost his master and his young wife dear. From the beginning Stockmar was convinced that the treatment Charlotte was receiving was not all it should be. He told Leopold of this and entreated him to make his observations known to the official physicians. But he himself continued to steer clear of any direct intervention. On the night when the Princess went into labour Stockmar did not go to see her until he was actively induced to by the Princess's obstetrician.

When Croft realized that the Princess's life was in danger he hurried to Stockmar's bedside to entreat him to arouse the Prince and inform him of the state of things. Stockmar found Leopold in bed, exhausted. After so much strain the reaction had set in and he seemed unable to grasp the fact that the state of the Princess was very serious. Stockmar returned to his own room. A quarter of an hour later Baillie sent to say that he wished the Baron would see the Princess. After some hesitation Stockmar did go to see Charlotte. He found her in a state of great suffering and disquiet, tossing about incessantly, speaking now to Baillie, now to Croft. Stockmar relates that as he entered, Baillie said to her:

> "Here comes an old friend of yours." She stretched out her left hand eagerly to me, and pressed mine twice vehemently. I felt her pulse which was very quick; the beats now full, now weak, now intermittent.[40]

Baillie administered wine to her constantly and she, turning to Stockmar, said: 'They have made me tipsy.' For about a quarter of an hour he went in and out of the room.

Then the rattle in the throat began. I had just left the room when she called out loudly, "Stocky! Stocky!" I went back; she was quieter, but the rattle continued. She turned more than once over on her face, drew her legs up and her hands grew cold. At two o'clock in the morning of 6 November 1817 – thereafter about five hours after the birth of the child – she was no more.[41]

Cornelia Knight noted in her diary: 'The faculty of mind never abandoned her. She asked about an hour previous to death, whether there was any danger: the difficulty of breathing from about that time prevented her speaking much.'[42]

It was Stockmar who went to Leopold to tell him of his wife's death. They went to her room together and the Prince let loose his grief, kneeling by the bed, kissing her cold hands for over an hour.[43] Then he pressed Stockmar to him and said: 'I am now quite desolate. Promise me always to stay with me.'[44] The Baron promised that he would indeed remain with the Prince as long as he confided in him and loved him. Stockmar's sceptical nature can be seen from the comment he made in a letter to his sister: 'I did not hesitate to promise what he may perhaps claim for ever, perhaps even next year may find no longer necessary to him.'[45] Leopold was in fact to keep the Baron to his promise all through his life – for the next thirty-six years the Baron spent less than six months a year with his wife and his three children in Coburg. The rest of the time he was with Leopold or on some mission for him: accompanying his nephew Albert on his educational journeys; helping his niece Victoria as a sort of private secretary; or again taking the role of familiar and confidential friend to them both.

In the days following Charlotte's death, Stockmar was Leopold's mainstay. He dined with the Prince, slept in his room, got up when Leopold woke in the night and sat by his bedside till he fell asleep again. In a curious way the Baron enjoyed being useful in times of stress. 'I feel increasingly', he wrote to his sister, 'that unlooked for trials are my portion in life, and that there will be many more of them before life is over. I seem to be here more to care for others than for myself and I am well content with this destiny.'[46]

The dramatic death of Princess Charlotte thus bound Baron Stockmar to Prince Leopold for life. It was also to change the young Prince's prospects – and his character. He had been the husband of the future Queen of England – a Prince Consort in the making, perhaps even a King, so great was her devotion to him. He was now a widower at the mercy of his royal father-in-law and a foreign Parliament. In fact both treated him handsomely, so great was the sympathy felt for him.

The Regent gave him as he requested[47] the title of Royal Highness and gave him authority to bear the arms of Princess Charlotte. He also made him a Field Marshal and a privy councillor. Parliament decided to continue his annual grant of 50,000 pounds and Claremont was given him for life – but all this was, however generous, so much less than he had thought his.

His regrets were not, however, only material. At a time when it was rare in court circles, Leopold had established a real domestic happiness. His prospects were shattered and at the same time some deep capacity in him to love was destroyed. He was not far from the truth when he wrote to the Prince Regent on 1 January 1818, two months after his wife's death: 'For me all happiness has gone, nothing can ever repay me for what has been taken from me, for the loss of that life of conjugal felicity which alone can make one truly happy.'[48] Baron Hardenbrock saw this clearly when he wrote: 'The Prince is, thank God, in good health but he is in great distress and as to the genuine feeling he had for the Noble Dear Departed it seems to be that this wound will remain open throughout his life; never was there nor will there be such an exemplary couple.'[49]

Years later he wrote to Victoria that he had never recovered the feeling of happiness which had blessed his short married life with Charlotte.

The Regent had last seen Charlotte when he visited her on 16 October. Since the date of the confinement was still uncertain he had gone off to shoot at the Hertfords' country estate at Sudbourne in Suffolk. It was there that he received the message that his daughter's labour had begun. He set out for London and the messenger bringing him the news that his grandchild was still-born passed him in the night. He arrived at Carlton House at three o'clock on the Thursday morning. Here it was that he learnt that the baby was dead. At such an hour, thinking no doubt that his daughter was resting, he himself retired to bed. A little later he was roused by the Duke of York who told him that the Princess had died.

His grief was seen by some as insincere. After all, it was well known that his affection for his daughter was not unbounded. The physical impact of the shock cannot, however, be denied. When he learnt what had happened he was in such a state that he had to be bled twice and cupped. He retired to the Pavilion in Brighton where he lived in retirement for some months. Was his grief occasioned by affection for his daughter or by bitter disappointment that there was no longer an heir to the throne, the only justification for his disastrous marriage?

Charlotte's mother received the news of her only child's death on the shores of the Adriatic. Three years earlier, in 1814, she had found her situation in England intolerable. Her husband refused to attend any public occasion at which she was present, her daughter was kept from her, and George III, who had to a certain extent protected her from his son, had been declared insane. She had asked and obtained permission to go abroad. She went first to visit her brother at the Court of Brunswick and then proceeded to Italy, spending the winter in Naples.

As she travelled round Europe, the Old Continent rang with stories of her scandalous conduct. In Geneva she had appeared at a fancy-dress ball as a half-naked Venus, later she figured as a half-dressed Muse of History. 'Poor Princess!' sighed her former lady in waiting, 'I fear she will come to no good end; and there is so much good in her, it is doubly to be regretted there should not be one grain of prudence to guide her right.'[50] By seeking voluntary exile, she had in fact played into the Regent's hands. Was the outrageous conduct she now adopted her way of avenging herself on her regal husband? If so, she harmed herself more than she harmed him. She became the mistress first of Napoleon's brother-in-law Joachim Murat and then of an Italian quartermaster in the Hussars, her gigolo Bartolomeo Bergami. They had in common a swashbuckling virility far removed from the Regent – 'Prinny' as he was called – whose 'belly . . . now reaches his knees.'[51] One by one her retainers brought from England left her. In 1815 she set out with a motley crew for the Holy Land via Tunis and Algiers, Athens and Syria – then on to Constantinople and Acre. In her wake stories of her conduct flowered. Back in Italy in 1817 she settled down in Pesaro and it was here the messenger arrived with the news of her daughter's death. The Prince Regent had not informed her officially of her daughter's engagement, nor of her marriage, and when she died it was a common messenger on his way round Europe with printed bills announcing the Princess's death who brought her – in December – a letter from Leopold's private secretary.

The Regent was blamed for not having had her brought back during their daughter's pregnancy and much has been made of Charlotte's own judgement on her mother, noted down by Stockmar: 'My mother was bad, but she would not have become as bad as she was if my father had not been infinitely worse.'[52] In fact the judgement is harsh. When the Regent had given his consent to his marriage with Caroline, in 1794 after King George III's first bout of insanity, he had not yet even seen his future consort. He did not know then that she would be physically repulsive to him. Not only was she rather plain and gauche but she washed little and, as the diplomat Malmesbury noted when he first accompanied her from Brunswick to England, she smelt. The pair was ill-assorted, the honeymoon a catastrophe. After the separation she might have assumed the role of Princess of Wales, but this she refused to do. She threw in her hand with the opposition extreme sections of which wanted not only to overthrow the Regent but with him the monarchy.

As to her devotion to her daughter, it can certainly be questioned. She knew she was compromising Charlotte in the Hesse affair and it rather looks as if she were using her daughter as a means of squaring accounts with her husband. Once abroad she never wrote to Charlotte and the pathetic letter her daughter sent her three weeks before her death remained unanswered.

News of the still-born baby reached the Queen in Bath on 6 November, the day after her granddaughter's death. She had been ill on and off for a whole year and had finally decided to take the waters at Bath. It was the first time that she had visited any part of the kingdom by herself. She had prepared to come with the King – who still had lucid moments – but he had been suddenly afflicted with blindness and the visit had been put off. When she had arrived on the third she had found the town illuminated in her honour. The sad news of the still-birth reached her just as she was preparing for the reception of the Mayor and Corporation of Bath. 'Her first thought', says Alexander d'Arblay charitably, 'was to issue orders for deferring this Ceremony':

but when she considered that all the Members of the Municipality must be assembled, and attired; and that the great dinner they had prepared to give to the Duke of Clarence for celebrating the Festival, could only be postponed at an enormous and useless expense, she composed her spirits, and finished her regal decorations, and admitted the Citizens of Bath.[53]

A less charitable pen might have hazarded that she was more eager to see honour done to the Duke of Clarence, 'the smallest and least good looking'[54] of her sons, than to mourn for the daughter of her detested daughter-in-law. She was not, however, able to keep up the pretence. The news of Charlotte's death was sent more speedily and the Duke of Clarence received an express with the terrible tidings just as they had sat down to dinner: 'all were dispersed in a moment, and she [the Queen] shut herself up, admitting no one but His Royal Highness.'[55] The Queen, on her doctor's advice, remained in Bath for a further day and then set off for Windsor Castle.

The letter the ageing Queen addressed to the Prince Regent undoubtedly shows more feeling for him than for his daughter.

> I need not I am sure tell you that as I always share in Your Prosperity most sincerely so do I most deeply feel your present life and misery upon this melancholy event and pray most anxiously to the Almighty that Your Health may not suffer from it. You must allow me to add to this that I rejoice in the comfort you must find of having had it in your power to make your child completely happy by granting Her to marry the man she loved and wished to be united to and who made her happy as also the bestowing upon her a place she did enjoy with every possible gratitude in which she spent to the very last almost complete felicity. These reflexions I do hope will aledge your grief in some respects as much as they give me real comfort upon your account.[56]

The cause of Charlotte's death has been much discussed. Leopold writing to Queen Victoria thirty-five years later laid responsibility clearly at the door of her obstetrician. 'Charlotte also had taken a dislike to the good physicians of those days, and had taken a fancy for Sir Richard Croft who was half mad.'[57] In fact Charlotte does not seem to have had much choice. As to Croft's insanity it is certainly true that he died insane, but Charlotte's death was probably a cause not a consequence. After the death of the Princess he was in a state of melancholy, unable to go about his business normally and unable to pay his personal respects to Leopold since he could not, as he wrote to Stockmar, 'support the painful feelings which a view of Claremont would revive.'[58] His depression continued and in the following February, when he was attending the wife of a clergyman in her confinement and labour was protracted, fearing another death on his conscience, he shot himself in his patient's house. Shortly afterwards she was safely confined.

Of Croft's incompetence there seems little doubt. Charlotte was from all accounts about two weeks overdue when labour began and the baby was big – too big to be delivered without assistance. At the time, however, the dangers of postmaturity were not fully realized. In fact instruments should have been used to speed up the birth and limit the risk of death from the lessening efficiency of the placenta. The instruments were there. They could have been used. Small wonder that Croft found the burden of Charlotte's death unbearable.

Was her death a catastrophe for the kingdom she might one day have governed? The Duke of Wellington held that 'her death was a blessing to the country.'[59] But death magnifies virtues and the nation mourned its Princess.

2

The Line of Succession

When Charlotte died, her grandfather George III was still alive – but blind and insane. He was thus spared the spectacle of his offspring's behaviour. He had had fifteen children, of whom twelve were still alive – five daughters and seven sons – with not a legitimate heir between them. His eldest son, the future George IV, had had only one daughter, the Charlotte that the country mourned. Frederick, Duke of York, the second son, was married to Princess Frederica of Prussia, but had no children. The picture we have of them gives the impression that this was really just as well.

The Duke was tall and like all the brothers suffered from an immense stoutness and, says Stockmar, 'not proportionately strong legs; he holds himself in such a way that one is always afraid he will tumble over backwards; very bald, and not a very intelligent face: one can see that eating, drinking and sensual pleasure are everything to him.'[1]

Charles Greville, Clerk of the Privy Council and diarist, confirms this: 'He delights in the society of men of the world and in a life of gaiety and pleasure. He is very easily amused, and particularly with jokes full of coarseness and indelicacy; the men with whom he lives most are *très-polissons* and *la polissonerie* is the *ton* of his society.'[2] The Duke's amusements were going to the races, sitting at table and playing for hours at whist. His talents were not rated high but he had a certain warmth and steadiness in his attachments and a sincerity lacking in his elder brother.

His wife was: 'A little animated woman, talks immensely and laughs still more. No beauty. Mouth and teeth bad. She disfigures herself still more by distorting her mouth and blinking her eyes.'[3] Her husband was notorious for his infidelities and the Duchess shut herself in a world of her own:

The Duchess seldom goes to bed, or, if she does, only for an hour or two; she sleeps dressed upon a couch, sometimes in one room, sometimes in another. She frequently walks out very late at night, or rather early in the morning, and she always sleeps with open windows. She dresses and breakfasts at three o'clock, afterwards walks out with all her dogs, and seldom appears before dinner-time.[4]

The Duchess's life was indeed, as Croker says, 'an odd one; she seldom has a female companion, she is read to all night and falls asleep towards morning and rises about three; feeds her dozens of dogs and her flocks of birds, etc., comes down two minutes before dinner and so round again ... '[5] The Duchess disliked all form and ceremony. Her mind was not perhaps of the most delicate, showing 'no dislike to coarseness of sentiment or language'.[6] The Duchess rarely went to Court and she and the Regent cordially disliked one another.

The third son, William, Duke of Clarence, had ten children – five boys and five girls born alternately. They were known as the Fitzclarences for all ten were born illegitimate to Mrs Jordan, with whom the Duke lived for twenty years. Mrs Jordan was born illegitimate of an Irish father and Welsh mother, had been seduced and 'ruined' by her employer in Dublin before she was twenty. She had fled to England pregnant, had lived there with the son of a court physician, Richard Ford, and had borne him three children. Employed as an actress she rose to the top of her profession: 'She was all gaiety, openness and good nature. She rioted in her fine animal spirits and gave more pleasure than any other actress, because she had the greatest spirit of enjoyment in herself.'[7] Her liaison with the Duke of Clarence began in 1790. Soon a definite understanding was reached and by 1791 they were established as man and wife. They went everywhere, save to Court, together. Mrs Jordan continued to work and to contribute to the expenses of the household, for the Duke was riddled with debts. William was a kind, if over-indulgent father and the ménage was considered harmonious and respectable for some twenty years.

By 1811, however, the level of the Duke's debts had risen, the beauty of Mrs Jordan had declined and William decided to look elsewhere. In 1811 the terms of a separation were drawn up: Mrs Jordan was to receive 1,500 pounds for her own use each year, 800 pounds for her children by earlier liaisons, 1,500 pounds for her four younger daughters and 600 pounds for their house and carriage.[8] This may at first seem generous, but she was to be separated from her sons and given no status. Her children gradually abandoned her, even the girls preferring the advantages of paternal care, and she fled the country to escape her creditors. She died at St Cloud on 5 July 1816. Thus when Charlotte died, William was already in search of a wife.

The fourth son, Edward, Duke of Kent, was living with his mistress of twenty-seven years, known as Mme Julie de St Laurent. He had met her in Gibraltar but she was, in fact, a bourgeoise from Besançon whose real name was Alphonsine Thérèse Bernadine Julie de Montgenet. The Duke's financial affairs were in such a lamentable state that in August 1816 he went abroad, leaving his yearly income in the hands of his creditors, who allowed him under half of it as living expenses, using the rest to gradually pay themselves off. He moved to Brussels, a town popular with foreigners with slender purses. There he rented a large mansion at a very modest price and set about renovating and innovating.

Both the Duke and his mistress were forty-nine when Charlotte died. Like his brother, the Duke of Kent was by now ready to discard his faithful companion of over a quarter of a century. He had in fact been actively engaged on seeking a suitable wife since 1815, when the pressure of his debts had become unbearable. He had thought of Princess Katherine Amelia of Baden, sister of the Tsarina of Russia, and the Tsar had paid the expenses of a journey to Darmstadt so that he might meet her and make up his mind. He did so and found her – an old maid of forty-one – most unsuitable. The Dowager Princess of Leiningen, Princess Victoire, who lived in the pocket principality of Amorbach, he found much more attractive. A young widow of thirty, cheerful, friendly and well-dressed in bright silks and satins, Victoire was the sister of Leopold of Saxe-Coburg. In 1816 he proposed to her – and was rejected.

While he continued to live with Mme de St Laurent in Brussels, he did not give up his courtship of Victoire, encouraged by both Leopold and Charlotte, whose favourite uncle he was. Once the succession was thrown open by Charlotte's death he decided to intensify his courtship.

The fifth son, Ernest, Duke of Cumberland, had married Princess Frederica, daughter of the Duke of Mecklenburg-Strelitz, in 1815. He was her third husband – she had married first Prince Ludwig of Prussia and then the Prince of Solms-Braunfels. Between her first and second marriage she had been engaged to the Duke of Cambridge – her third husband's younger brother – and had jilted him without warning. When she married the Duke of Cumberland, with the Prince Regent's consent, her mother-in-law Queen Charlotte refused to receive her and advised her son not to bring his wife to England. Parliament refused to grant the Duke the customary marriage allowance.

The Duke was almost universally disliked. He was 'a tall, powerful man, with a hideous face: can't see two inches before him, one eye turned out of its place.'[9] At the Regent's receptions in the Pavilion, Creevey noted with satisfaction that he wore 'the regimentals of his own Hussars', a German volunteer regiment which disgraced itself at Waterloo by deserting the field at the very crisis of the French cavalry attack, and that he 'looked really hideous, everybody trying to be rude to him – not standing when he came near them.'[10] Ernest was an active member of the ultra-Tory party but it was his face not his politics that people took the most objection to. When Charlotte died, the Duke and his wife had as yet no offspring.

Augustus Frederick, Duke of Sussex, sixth son of George III, was by all accounts the most amiable of the brothers. Princess Charlotte referred to him as a 'sincere and true hearted creature with a great deal of good sound sense'.[11] But, for Creevey, his amiableness stemmed from a lack of personality: 'He has every appearance of being a good-natured man, is very civil and obliging, never says anything that makes you think him foolish; but there is a *nothingness* in him that is to the last degree fatiguing.'[12] This seems rather unfair as the Duke did have genuine liberal sympathies. He had married Lady Augusta Murray in 1793 and had two children by her. But since the marriage had not received the sovereign's consent and thus violated the Royal Marriages Act, the children were illegitimate and not in the line of succession. The couple broke up in 1801, the Duke of Sussex retaining the custody of the children. He continued to maintain his former wife, allowing her 4,000 pounds a year out of his own income. The Duke took up with Lady Cecilia Buggin, the daughter of the second Earl of Arran and the widow of an alderman of the City of London. Once again the Sovereign refused to give his consent to the union so any children the Duke might have would once again be illegitimate. The Duke was to spend his energies under Victoria trying to secure official recognition for his wife.

The youngest son, the Duke of Cambridge, was unmarried. He was a good-looking man with a blond wig, who had never kept a mistress and was the only solvent duke. It was to be expected that he would be first off the mark in the race to provide an heir to the throne. Seven brothers – four married and three single – with not a legitimate child between them! No wonder the prestige of the monarchy was low. Shelley described the royal family thus:

> An old, mad, blind, despised and dying King,
> Princes, the dregs of their dull race, who flow
> Through public scorn – mud from a muddy spring
> Rulers who neither see nor feel nor know,
> But leech-like to their fainting country cling.[13]

After Charlotte's death the monarchy declined still further, not least on account of the manner in which the brothers strove to make capital out of the country's need for an heir.

The royal dukes bargained hard before agreeing to endeavour to provide an heir to the throne. The unmarried brothers were determined to sell their bachelor freedom dearly. The nearest to the succession, William, Duke of Clarence, set this out clearly in a letter to his mother:

> If the Cabinet consider the measure of my marrying one of consequence they ought to state to me what they can and will propose for my establishment: for without previously being acquainted with their intentions as to money matters I cannot and will not make any positive offer to any Princess. I have ten children totally and entirely dependent on myself: I owe forty thousand pounds of funded debt for which of course I pay interest, and I have a floating debt of sixteen thousand pounds.[14]

The Duke of Kent was convinced that the terms his brother asked from the Ministers were

> terms that no Ministers can accede to. Should the Duke of Clarence not marry, the next prince in succession is myself; and altho' I trust I shall be at all times ready to obey any call my country may make upon me, God only knows the sacrifice it will be to make, whenever I shall think it my duty to become a married man.[15]

The 'sacrifice' was certainly not to be given for nothing:

> As to my own settlement, as I shall marry (if I marry at all) for the succession, I shall expect the Duke of York's marriage to be considered the precedent. That was a marriage for the succession and 25,000 pounds for income was settled, in addition to all his other income, purely on that account. I shall be contented with the same arrangement, without making any demands grounded upon the difference of the value of money in 1792 and at present. As for the payment of my debts, I don't call them great. The nation, on the contrary, is greatly my debtor.[16]

The Prince Regent took up his brothers' cause in 1818. On 13 April he sent a message to both Houses of Parliament declaring how essential it was in the best interests of the country that a suitable provision should be made for such of his royal brothers as had contracted marriage with the consent of the Crown. The message ended with the words

> His Royal Highness has received so many proofs of the affectionate attachment of this House to His Majesty's person and family, as leave him no room to doubt of the concurrence and assistance of this House in enabling him to make the necessary arrangements for this important purpose.[17]

On 15 April the Foreign Secretary Lord Castlereagh, put his own proposals before the House. It would be right, he thought, to give the Duke of Clarence what had been given to the Duke of York twenty-six years earlier – an additional income of 25,000 pounds – and as for the junior branches of the royal family, 12,000 pounds should be added to their existing income if they married with the royal consent. There was, however, a determined effort on the part of the Opposition to make the royal dukes lower their demands. Negotiations took place and the Prime Minister announced that the royal dukes would settle for half of the original proposals and moved that a grant of an additional 10,000 pounds be given to Clarence. More and more Members had meantime decided that even this sum was overgenerous and that 6,000 pounds would be sufficient. Mr Holme Sumner, for instance, declared that the Duke of Clarence was in no sense heir to the throne and should get no more than 6,000 pounds. First, however, he wanted to know whether the House was assured that such an increase would be used to 'uphold the splendour and dignity of that illustrious personage'.[18]

In committee, there was a division on the amendment proposing a reduction to 6,000 pounds: for the amendment 193, against 184. The House then voted a grant of 6,000 pounds only to the Duke of Clarence and also to the Duke of Cambridge and the Duke of Kent. The Duke of Cumberland, however, saw his grant refused by 143 to 136 votes. It was felt that Parliament was not fairly treated by hooking the Duke of Cumberland into the proposed grants for the other dukes – he had after all married three years earlier. During the debate it was also held that the money should come from a transfer from the Windsor establishment of their stricken father and not be an additional charge on the people. So fierce was the debate that observers were excluded from the House for almost an hour.

The repeated defeats sustained by the government on the marriage grants worried many for it was the authority of the State that was held up to ridicule, yet at the same time there was much sympathy with those who refused to accept the proposals to augment the Princes' establishments. As the Duke of Wellington put it:

> By God! There is a great deal to be said about that. They [the Princes] are the damnedest millstone about the necks of any Government that can be imagined. They have insulted – *personally* insulted – two thirds of the gentlemen of England and how can it be wondered at that they take their revenge upon them when they get them in the House of Commons? It is their only opportunity, and I think by God! they are quite right to use it.[19]

The three unmarried brothers had not waited for the marriage grant question to be settled before seeking their new partners. The Duke of Cambridge had sent off his proposal of marriage to Augusta, Princess of Hesse-Cassel, before Princess Charlotte had been dead ten days. She accepted him and they were duly married.

The Duke of Clarence resumed his arduous quest for a wife. First he wanted to marry an heiress – Catherine Tylney-Long, who refused and married Wellington's nephew. Margaret Mercer Elphinstone, Charlotte's confidante, and Lady Charlotte Lindsay both turned him down, as did the Dowager Lady Downshire and the Earl of Berkeley's widow. The Tsar's sister, the Grand Duchess of Oldenburg, refused because she found him vulgar and unpleasant, and the Duke of Gloucester's sister, Princess Sophia, preferred to remain single. Then the Duke turned to Germany, but neither the eldest daughter of the Landgrave Frederick of Hesse nor the eldest daughter of the Electoral Prince of Hesse-Cassel found him to their taste. He then turned to Miss Wyckham of Thame Park, an Oxfordshire heiress. She was attracted by the prospect of becoming Queen, he by her fortune, but there was undoubtedly some sentiment between them. The Regent however would not hear of such a misalliance nor would the House of Commons and reluctantly the Duke abandoned his suit. He did not forget Miss Wyckham, however, and four years after his accession to the throne, as William IV, he secured her a peerage, no doubt to make up for the taunts her lack of title had provoked; she became Baroness Wenman. No wonder that the Duke of Kent noted, 'The Duke of Clarence, I have no doubt, will marry if he can.'[20] The Duke's protracted search finally found him a wife at fifty-two in the person of Princess Amelia Adelaide of Saxe-Meiningen, a home-loving woman of twenty-five ready to welcome her husband's ten children.

Charlotte's death made the Duke of Kent even more eager to conclude matters promptly with Princess Victoire of Leiningen. Her reluctance had little to do with the person of the Duke. He was a man of forty-nine, of a military bearing that reflected the military training he had had as a young man. His fleshy underlip and flamboyant whiskers gave him a self-satisfied air. He was immensely fat and smelled of garlic and tobacco. But he had a certain charm, a capacity for quietness rare among the Hanoverians and he was kind and courteous. He was a fine man for his age and combined 'a simple soldierlike manner with the refinement of a man of the world'.[21] Victoire's doubts came from different considerations. First, she was loath to give up her independence. She had been married at seventeen to a widower twenty-three years older than she was, and after eleven years of married life had been left a widow with two children – Prince Charles of Leiningen, her husband's heir, and Princess Feodora. Her son had been nine when his father died so a regency had been inevitable. This was under the control of the Grand Duke of Baden. Victoire feared that if she married and left the country she might endanger her son's succession. She was not eager either to give up her independence and her power – even if it only consisted in acting as a broker for petty disputes and minor problems.

Another drawback was that she spoke no English. Under pressure from her brother Leopold, she did, however, withdraw her negative answer to the Duke and ask for time to reconsider the matter. When Charlotte died her final reply was still pending.

The Duke, while hoping for a union with Victoire, was still living with Julie de St Laurent. His sisters nicknamed him 'Joseph Surface', after Sheridan's smooth hypocrite. Events were precipitated when Mme de St Laurent learnt of his duplicity. The Duke himself recounted the scene to Creevey:

> You saw, no doubt, that unfortunate paragraph in the *Morning Chronicle*, which appeared within a day or two after the Princess Charlotte's death; and in which my marrying was alluded to. Upon receiving the paper containing that article at the same time with my private letters, I did as is my constant practice, I threw the newspaper across the table to Madame St Laurent and began to open and read my letters.

He heard a strange noise and found his companion in the throes of a fit and 'entertained serious apprehensions for her safety'.[22]

He continued his duplicity, however, by persuading the Brussels newspapers to keep all articles on the subject of his marriage out of their columns, and at the same time endeavoured to ensure her a decent livelihood when he should abandon her. He insisted that she was 'of very good family and has never been an actress, and I am the first and only person who ever lived with her'; remarks which were no doubt intended to show how much worthier she was than his brother Clarence's former mistress, Mrs Jordan.[23]

In the event, Madame de St Laurent left Brussels to take up residence in Paris as the Comtesse de Montgenet, a courtesy title granted by Louis XVIII. The Duke continued to write to her. After their separation he wrote to Baron de Mallet:

> our unexpected separation arose from the imperative duty I owed to obey the call of my family and my Country to marry, and *not* from the least diminution in an attachment which had stood the test of 28 years and which, but for *that* circumstance, would unquestionably have kept up the connexion, until it became the lot of one or other of us to be removed from this world.[24]

This did not prevent him from having a genuine affection for the woman he wanted to marry. He wrote to Victoire on 10 January 1818 asking for a definite answer to his proposal. On 25 January she accepted. 'I am', she wrote, 'leaving an agreeable, independent position in the hope that your affection will be my reward.'[25] In order to prevent doubts as to the validity of the marriage, and succession problems in either country, the couple married twice over. First on 30 May 1818 in the Ehrenburg Palace in Coburg and then on 11 July in England.

The English marriage was a double marriage. On the same day, William, Duke of Clarence, and Adelaide of Saxe-Meiningen and Edward, Duke of Kent, and Princess Victoire of Leiningen were married by the Archbishop of Canterbury, assisted by the Bishop of London. Both brides were given away by the Prince Regent and the marriages were formally witnessed by the Queen, the Prince Regent and all those members of the royal family who were present. The ceremony took place in the late afternoon at Kew Palace and lasted a bare three-quarters of an hour. After the scant ceremony came an enormous banquet, such were the priorities of the brothers.

At seven in the evening the Kents drove away in Prince Leopold's coach, accompanied by Leopold himself, to his mansion near Esher, Claremont, and it was there they spent their first months as a married couple. There was no doubt that the Duke of Kent had made himself popular by marrying a descendant of the Coburgs. *The Times* itself had commented favourably on the possibility of their union: 'We can wish the Duke no higher felicity than the possession of a woman who may prove herself akin in virtue as in birth to her excellent and illustrious brother.'[26] Croker had long thought that popularity had been the sole reason for the match. 'The lady', he wrote to Peel in 1817, 'in the Duke of Kent's eye is not ill-chosen for popular effect. She is the sister of Prince Leopold.'[27]

The marriage caused some surprise, however, because it was an instant success. The Prince Regent found the couple two days after the wedding 'sitting by the fire exactly like Darby and Joan'.[28] They were both home-loving, neither had much interest in society and from the outset they were happy in their own company.

Marriage had not, however, put an end to the Duke's financial difficulties. He had indeed added to his debts by borrowing to pay for the presents he offered his future wife, including a magnificent wedding dress. The Prince Regent refused to help his brother and his mother urged him to leave the country since living abroad was cheaper. In September the Duke and Duchess returned to Amorbach near Darmstadt.

By mid 1818 all the brothers save the Duke of Sussex had legitimate spouses and there seemed little doubt that 1819 would see the succession ensured. By November 1818 the Duchess of Clarence, the Duchess of Kent, the Duchess of Cumberland and the Duchess of Cambridge were all pregnant. The Duke of Kent was convinced that his robust constitution and the irregular lives of his elder brothers signified that his children would one day rule over England. It was therefore of paramount importance that Victoire should give birth to her child in England, so that there could be no question of the infant's parentage. Since he was as usual in straitened circumstances, the Duke appealed to his brother, the Prince Regent, for help in resettling in England. The situation was delicate. Since his daughter's death the Regent had become very sensitive on the subject of the succession and his brother's request met with irritation – and a flat refusal.

The Duke of Kent had written to his brother in November and it was painfully obvious that the possibility of a refusal had not occurred to him. He had set down all that he needed: money for the journey, a yacht to cross over to England, an apartment in Kensington Palace, and the possibility of a house by the sea after the confinement.[29] He had simply forgotten that he was only the fourth son and that the Clarences (higher up in the succession than he) were awaiting the arrival of their baby in Hanover, as were the Cambridges.

The Duke of Kent's friends however pressed him to return to England. They warned that it must not be thought that the Duchess sought to frustrate the nation of an English-born heir. A small committee of five or six close friends clubbed together to find the necessary money and on 15 March 1819 the Duke informed the Prince Regent that he would arrive at Calais on 18 April. He asked for the royal yacht to come and collect him and take him to Dover. Reluctantly the Prince Regent agreed.

The Duchess, by now seven months pregnant, journeyed 427 miles in primitive conditions to allow the future Queen Victoria to be born on English soil. Conditions were indeed uncomfortable, to say the least. The Duke drove the Duchess himself in a cane phaeton to save the expense of a coachman, the suite came behind – a shabby procession consisting of the phaeton followed by a landau, a barouche and two large post-chaises, a cabriolet and a caravan. Once in Calais the party waited a full week for the wind to be favourable, and it was not until 24 April that Victoire and her precious burden were safely on English soil. They drove straight to Kensington Palace. Exactly a month later, on Monday 24 May 1819, after just over six hours labour, the Duchess was delivered of 'a pretty little Princess, as plump as a partridge'.[30] Her father had seen to it that the Duke of Wellington, the Archbishop of Canterbury and the Bishop of London, the Chancellor of the Exchequer and others had assisted at the birth. Her grandmother had no doubt about her future. 'The English like Queens and the niece of the ever lamented beloved Charlotte will be most dear to them.'[31] But when Victoria came into the world it was by no means evident that she would be heir to the throne. Not only George III and the Prince Regent, but the Duke of York and the Duke of Clarence and their possible heirs stood between Victoria's father, the Duke of Kent, and the throne. Victoria's parents themselves might have a boy – and in that case he would take precedence over her. Fate was, however, on her side.

On 29 January 1820 the long reign of George III came to a close. For ten years he had been King in name only and now the Prince Regent became King George IV, and his dissolute wife Caroline legally became the Queen of England. If she would give up her title and remain abroad, the new King promised her 50,000 pounds a year. The Queen, encouraged by Brougham and the more radical wing of the Whigs, declined the offer and returned to England, where popular sympathy was dangerously in her favour. As George IV was hated, so his Queen was revered.

The whole affair was to take a most unsavoury turn. In 1818 – perhaps with the idea at the back of his mind of producing another heir – the Prince Regent had appointed a commission which went to Germany and Italy to collect evidence for a divorce. This seemed quite a simple matter as the rumours concerning the Queen and her male servant Bergami had reached every corner of Europe. Infidelity on the part of a Queen Consort, or the wife of the heir apparent, was considered high treason and was indeed punishable by death. All George IV wanted was the right to remarry.

When he learnt that his wife was in England he sent a message to the House of Lords stating that he thought it necessary to communicate to the House of Lords 'certain papers respecting the conduct of her Majesty since her departure from This Kingdom', which he recommended to the 'immediate and serious attention of the House'. The battle was on. Throughout the country meetings were held to protest against 'the persecution' of the Queen. The King had exercised his prerogative in having the Queen's name removed from the liturgy and in forbidding her to be named in the public prayers of the Established Churches. On 19 June 1820 the decision was debated in the House of Commons.

On 5 July 1820, urged on by the King, Lord Liverpool introduced in the Lords a Bill 'to deprive her Majesty Queen Caroline Amelia Elizabeth of the title, prerogative, rights, privileges and exemptions of Queen Consort of this realm and to dissolve the marriage between his Majesty and the said Caroline Amelia Elizabeth'. The King's brothers were divided on the subject.

> When the Duke of Sussex's name was called, the Chancellor read his letter, begging to be excused on the ground of consanguinity; upon which the Duke of York rose, and in a very marked and angry tone said: "*I* have much stronger ground for asking leave of absence than the Duke of Sussex, and yet I should be ashamed not to be present to do my duty!"[32]

The whole affair dragged on through September and October and amounted to a trial of the Queen. During that time 32,000 daily news sheets were printed in London each day and there was a spate of cartoons. Feeling against the King ran high. The Bishops, as one would have expected, were soon joined by other members of the King's party and finally – aware that he was heading for defeat – the King said through the person of Lord Liverpool: 'If it was the wish of the religious part of the House and of the community that this clause [the dissolution of marriage] should be withdrawn, his Majesty had no personal wish in having it made part of the bill.'[33] An obvious untruth showing the weakness not of the King's case, but of his prestige. Many agreed in substance with Creevey's acid remarks: 'the title of the Bill ought to be – "A Bill to declare the Queen a w-, and to settle her upon the King for life, because from his own conduct he is not entitled to a divorce".'[34]

As the debate in parliament continued, the prestige of the monarchy decreased. There were tales, and indeed evidence, of bribery and corruption in order to produce witnesses against the Queen. There were stories of adultery and infamy, witnesses who brought 'much dirt and some damage certainly'[35] and much mighty rhetoric was wielded – especially by Brougham – and a brilliant parallel was made with Nero and his wife Octavia. Queen Caroline herself did nothing to help the image of the monarchy. One of her neighbours described her as very disagreeably dirty in her person and her establishment and commented on her style of life, which was comfortless and unbecoming to her situation. She added 'I hope she will be disquieted sufficiently to set off to dear Bergami, but the radical party will not suffer her to depart till a little more mischief is completed.'[36]

Finally, after the King's name had been dragged through the mire for many weeks, the Bill had its second reading on 6 November 1820. There were 123 for the Bill, 95 against: a majority for the Bill of only 28. Tantamount to a defeat. This was reduced to nine (108 for, 99 against) on the third reading. Prudently, on 10 November, Lord Liverpool moved that his own Bill be read this day six months – in other words the Bill was abandoned.

After these abortive proceedings against Queen Caroline there was little danger of George IV producing an heir to the throne – at least as long as his wife lived. His domestic affairs continued, however, to bring the monarchy into disrepute, with the Marchioness Conyngham reigning as his recognized mistress. The Queen bought Cambridge House in South Audley Street in February 1821 and decided to affirm her rights. The first real occasion was the King's Coronation. Brougham advised a memorial to the King claiming the right of the Queen to attend the ceremony. This was referred to the Privy Council, which informed the Queen that no arrangements would be made for her attendance and that she should not be allowed to be present at the Coronation. It would have been wise to let the matter rest. But Caroline was not renowned for her wisdom. She determined to assert her rights by demanding access to the Abbey on the day. She set off at a quarter-past five on the morning of 19 July. Brougham told Creevey:

> I followed on foot and found she had swept the crowd after her; it was very great, even at that hour. She passed thro' Storey's Gate, and then round Dean's Yard, where she was separated from the crowd by the gate's being closed. The refusal was peremptory at all the doors of the Abbey where she tried, and one was banged in her face. . . . About half

past six (a.m.) she had finished her walks and calls at the doors and got
into the carriage to return. . . . A vast multitude followed her home, and
then broke windows. But they soon (in two or three hours) dispersed or
went back.[37]

The sparring between the Queen and the King might have turned
into something more serious – Brougham was making plans to rouse
the North in the Queen's favour – but death intervened. The Queen
made her last public appearance at Drury Lane on 30 July 1821, but
she was already in great pain. Her doctor announced she was suffering
from obstruction attended by inflammation. The remedies applied no
doubt hastened her end. Creevey noted:

> On Friday last she lost sixty-four ounces of blood; took first of all 15
> grains of calomel, which they think she threw up again in the whole or in
> part; and then she took 40 grains more of calomel which she kept entirely
> in her stomach; add to this a quantity of castor oil that would have
> turned the stomach of a horse.[38]

Viscount Hood announced her death to Henry Brougham in these
terms: 'Her Majesty has quitted a scene of uninterrupted persecution,
and for herself I think her death is not to be regretted . . . She died in
peace with all her enemies. "I do not die without pain but I die without
regret" – was frequently expressed by Her Majesty.'[39]

Even while she was dying she was being maligned. Croker, in Dublin
where the King was on a visit, wrote in his diary two days before her
death: 'The Queen's disorder is said to be unabated. Some people think
it is all a hoax and others more charitable say that she is poisoned.'[40]
The Queen wanted her coffin to bear the inscription 'Caroline, the
injured Queen of England' and, said Croker, 'It is observed that she
says injured, not innocent.'[41] As was to be expected, the King did not
mourn. He even astounded his visitors by his total neglect of mourning.
Soon after his wife's death he greeted them in a bright blue coat with
bright, yellow buttons. Not a month after her death, Creevey noted:
'His mind is clearly made up, according to Lauderdale, to have another
wife, and all his family are of that opinion. He goes straight to Vienna
after his Irish trip, so probably he will pick up something before his
return at Christmas.'[42] This was counting without the influence of the
King's mistress, the Marchioness Conyngham, and without his declining health.

Lady Conyngham was the daughter of a wealthy City banker. She
had married Viscount Conyngham in 1794 and in 1816 he had been
created a Marquess. The King fell violently in love with her in 1820

when he was fifty-eight and she fifty-one. A true Hanoverian, the King's passion for this middle-aged woman was equal to that he had felt forty years earlier for Mrs Fitzherbert. Quite why she pleased him so must remain a mystery. She was a plump matron with five grown-up children. She was lacking in conversation, intelligence and beauty. The Princess Lieven echoed the thoughts of many when she wrote to Metternich: 'Love which allows nothing to interfere with it is all very fine; but how extraordinary when its object is Lady Conyngham! Not an idea in her head; not a word to say for herself; nothing but a hand to accept pearls and diamonds with, and an enormous balcony to wear them on.'[43]

Later on the Princess found an explanation for the King's attachment which persisted despite the fact that in her opinion he realized that she was grasping: 'Here is a lover whose eyes are wide open; if he sees as clearly as that, I do not understand how his love can last long. But it does last, simply because he needs a habit.'[44] In fact George IV could not live without a favourite. Mrs Fitzherbert, Lady Hertford, Lady Conyngham were in turn in constant attendance. As he grew older and sicker, domesticity took the place of passion. The situation was not, however, always agreeable for Lady Conyngham, as Creevey learnt from Lauderdale in 1825.

> There has been a blow-up again between Prinny and Lady Conyngham, but matters are all settled again thro' the kind and skilful negotiation of Lauderdale. She has become of late very restless and impatient under what she calls her terrible restraint and confinement, and about ten days ago announced her fixed determination to go abroad.[45]

Lauderdale managed to convince her that however blameworthy it was to have got into the situation she was in, it was now her bounden duty to bear the consequences. Countess Grey tells one of her correspondents: 'I hear from those who have been that the Cottage is more dull than ever: that Lady C. throws herself back on the sofa and never speaks; and the opinion is (which I don't believe) that she hates Kingy.'[46]

The poor state of the King's health during the last ten years of his life did not improve matters. When she went to the Pavilion in 1822, Princess Lieven found him in a sorry state. 'He is tortured by gout and employs the most violent remedies to get rid of it. He looks ghastly; he is plunged in gloom; he talks about nothing but dying. I have never seen him so wretched; he did everything he could to pull himself together, but in vain.'[47] Eight months later, Lady Charlotte Greville told the same story: 'His irritability of temper is becoming quite intolerable; his prevailing subject of complaint is his *old age* at which he feels, of course, the most royal indignation.'[48]

The King's health deteriorated in 1822 after another severe attack of gout. From then on he could walk only with difficulty. He became more and more of a recluse and it was obvious that there would be no direct heir to the throne.

The Duke of York had lost his wife on 6 August 1820 of dropsy of the chest. She had been ill for six months and in a coma for two days when she died. Before she was even buried, the Minister from the Elector of Hesse requested an audience of Lauderdale to inform him – since the Duke would no doubt marry again – that the Elector had a daughter whom he thought well qualified to be his second wife. 'About a week after the Duchess's funeral, Lauderdale mentioned this to the Duke, who immediately said: "This is the *second* application to me, for the King has communicated to me his wishes that I should marry again; but my mind is quite made up to do no such thing, and so I have given the King to understand."'[49] The Duke at fifty-seven was in fact enamoured of the Duchess of Rutland – who was already provided with a husband.

In November 1818 the Duke and Duchess of Clarence had lost their first child, Charlotte Augusta, born prematurely after only a few hours. Four months later the Duchess was pregnant again, but she miscarried. On 10 December 1820 she finally gave birth to a live daughter – Adelaide Georgina Elizabeth. She had been born six weeks premature but seemed to be in good health. Less than four months later, on 4 March 1821, the infant princess died unexpectedly, from an inflammation in the bowels. Victoria, who had been heir presumptive from her birth until her father's elder brother, the Duke of Clarence, had a child, was now reinstated in that position. The Crown would only devolve on Victoria if her uncle, the Duke of Clarence, later King William IV, had no legitimate issue and her father, the Duke of Kent, had no son. But the Duchess of Clarence was only twenty-seven; and since the Duke had already fathered ten children by his mistress it was thought more than probable that the Clarences would yet have a family.

The Duke and Duchess of Kent – Victoria's parents – had established a happy relationship. They were, however, little appreciated by the Regent and the royal family. King Leopold, writing to Queen Victoria after her succession, told her that the Regent hated the Duke of Kent 'most sincerely'[50] and his attitude towards the couple – and their daughter – certainly bore this out. He had refused to help the couple financially before Victoria's birth. Once she was born, his attitude if anything hardened. He decided her christening was to be a private and not a state affair and that evening dress could not be worn. His younger brother was not to be given the publicity of a grand ceremony.

The christening was performed at Kensington Palace, where the Kents were living. The baby had four sponsors. The first two were close relatives of her parents – Charlotte, the Duke of Kent's sister, widow of the King of Württemburg, and the Duchess of Kent's mother, Augusta, the Dowager Duchess of Saxe-Coburg-Saarfeld. The third sponsor, Tsar Alexander, was by far the most illustrious for he was heralded as the most powerful man in Europe. He himself had conveyed his desire to be godfather to the child to the Kents through the Russian Embassy in London. None of these sponsors were, however, present at the christening. They were represented respectively by Princess Augusta, the Duchess of Gloucester and the Duke of York. The Prince Regent was also to be the child's godfather, even if somewhat reluctantly.

It was the Prince Regent who chose the date of the ceremony – 24 June 1819; the time – three o'clock; and the guests, eight in all, including himself. The other seven were the Duke and Duchess of Gloucester, the Duke and Duchess of York, Princess Augusta and Princess Sophia, and Prince Leopold. Although he lived in the Palace, the Duke of Sussex did not attend the ceremony for he was in the middle of one of his frequent rows with his eldest brother. He came, however, to the dinner party, which the Regent did not attend! A gilded font was placed in the centre of the Cupola Room and the walls were hung with crimson velvet. The service was conducted by the Archbishop of Canterbury and the Bishop of London. When the time came to pronounce the child's name, the Archbishop turned to her parents. They had intended to call her Victoire Georgiana Alexandrina Charlotte Augusta, the name of her mother and those of her four sponsors, feminized in the case of George and Alexander. The Prince Regent had been asked to approve. The Kents considered this a mere formality. But on the eve of the christening, a message came from the Prince Regent informing them that the name Georgiana could not be used since: 'He did not choose to place his name before the Emperor's of Russia and he could not allow it to follow.'[51] As for the other names, he would indicate them at the christening. What he did, in fact, was tell the child's parents that neither the name of Charlotte nor that of Augusta could be used. There was too much presumption in the use of the name of the Regent's own dead daughter, too much majesty in that of Augusta. So at the font the Archbishop paused, looking enquiringly from father to uncle. Into the silence the Regent dropped the name 'Alexandrina' and paused again. The Duke of Kent urged a second name – Elizabeth perhaps? The Regent opted for Victoria, an anglicized form of her mother's name. 'Give her the mother's name also then, but it cannot precede that of the Emperor.' So Alexandrina Victoria it was.

The Regent's animosity to his brother did not stop at spoiling Victoria's christening. He proceeded to ignore his brother at official ceremonies, actually turning his back on him at a reception given by the Spanish Ambassador in August 1819. It was clear that no support would be given to the Kents by the royal family. Yet help was desperately needed. The Duke's financial situation had once again deteriorated. He was incapable, so it seemed, of cutting his coat according to his cloth. Debts were mounting up and more loans were out of the question. The only solution open to him was to find a cheaper place than London to live. He was determined not to return to Leiningen, for he was convinced his daughter would one day be Queen and must therefore be brought up in England.

Thus it was that in October 1819 the Duke of Kent went off to Devonshire, with his equerry Captain Conroy in attendance, to find a house for his family. He wanted a house by the sea, which would enable him to save face and present his departure as necessary for the health of the infant Victoria. He visited Torquay, Teignmouth and Dawlish and found nothing to suit his taste – or his pocket. It was finally at Sidmouth that he found a small white house, Woolbrook Cottage. After delays due to the Duke's appeasing of his creditors, the Duke and Duchess reached Sidmouth on the afternoon of Christmas Day. They were accompanied by the little Princess, now nearly six months old, and her half-sister Feodora. Her half-brother Prince Charles of Leiningen was at school in Geneva.

The cottage was some 150 yards from the sea and exposed to the glacial cold and fierce gales. The air was keen, the nights bitterly cold. In early January, Victoria had a sore throat, the Duke of Kent a bad cold. The Duchess tended her daughter but her husband shook off any idea that he was ill. He was fifty-two, healthy, robust and convinced he would outlive his brothers and secure the throne. He therefore treated his cold with long walks, coming in soaked to the bone and chilled to the marrow. He was finally obliged on 10 January to remain in bed, running a fever.

Once again, as for Charlotte, a battle now began 'between the magnificent constitution of the Duke and the medical treatment of the period'.[52] The Duke had a high fever and pains in his chest and vomited constantly. He was therefore bled twice. He had great difficulty in breathing and was therefore kept in a recumbent position. He had a bad headache, so his head was cupped (a cut was made on his head, a heated cup placed over it and as the cup cooled a vacuum was created and blood ran into it. Some 125 grammes were removed by each cup). By the time a court physician was summoned, the Duke had already lost by bleeding and cupping some three litres of blood. The Duchess had sent a messenger to London begging the royal physician Sir David Dundas to come and attend the Duke. But he was tending the old sick King George III, whose state was critical and whose status was superior. In his place he dispatched Sir William Morton, physician to the late Queen Charlotte.

He, too, was unfortunately convinced that bleeding and cupping were essential and so the disastrous treatment continued. The Duchess watched her husband tormented by the new physician and wrote to her old friend Polyxene von Tubeuf, 'I cannot think it can be good for the patient to lose so much blood.'[53] The Duke became more and more exhausted and ten days after he had taken to his bed it was thought wise to inform his relatives that he was dangerously ill. The Regent sent a letter expressing his anxious solicitude, but only Prince Leopold, attended by faithful Stockmar, came to Sidmouth. Stockmar was consulted as a physician by the Duchess when he arrived on 22 January and declared that the Duke would probably not survive the night. The Duke managed to summon up enough strength to sign his will – a last defiant effort in favour of his wife and child. In it he appointed the Duchess sole guardian of their only child, the Princess Alexandrina Victoria, and left his property to his executors in trust for the Duchess, to be disposed of at her pleasure for the sole use and benefit of herself and her infant daughter.

The Duke died of pneumonia at ten o'clock on the following morning, 23 January 1820, less than a week before the death of his father George III. Within the week, the infant Princess moved from fifth in the line of succession to third.

The death of the Duke was totally unexpected and diversely commented on. 'He was strongest of the strong,' Croker wrote. 'Never before ill in all his life, and now to die of a cold when half the kingdom have colds with impunity. It was very bad luck indeed. It reminds me of Aesop's fable of the oak and the reed.'[54] The Countess Lieven was crueller:

> That Hercules of a man is no more, while I – a slip of a creature – am still alive and well; from which I deduce that the weak go farther than the

strong. No-one in England will mourn the Duke. He was false, hard and greedy. His so-called good qualities were only for show, and his last public appeal to the charity of the nation had lost him the support of the only friends he had – prisoners and City men. His wife kills all her husbands, though. She would cut an interesting figure now if she had it in her to do so; but . . . she is the most mediocre person it would be possible to meet.[55]

He was buried by night in the family vault at Windsor on 12 February. The Duchess of Kent had wished to be present but etiquette forbade it.

On her husband's death, the Duchess of Kent was in great distress, both moral and material. Still no mistress of the English language she had lost the husband who had shielded her from the harsh realities of the world of debts and promises in which he lived. The Duchess did, however, have a protector – in the person of her brother Prince Leopold. He it was who persuaded her to resist the temptation of returning to Amorbach, where she had lived with her first husband. He it was who begged Princess Mary, Duchess of Gloucester, one of the Prince Regent's sisters, to persuade her brother, soon to be King, to allow the Duchess to return to Kensington Palace and to be able to use the Duke's apartments there. The Prince Regent agreed and the Duchess of Kent duly returned to Kensington Palace.

3

A Solitary Childhood

The Duchess of Kent and Princess Victoria were now back in London. London, the great Leviathan, had over a million inhabitants in 1811 and almost a million and a half in 1831. The other growing towns were fairly easy to characterize – Manchester with its cotton manufacturers was the 'chimney of the world', Liverpool was the sea-gate to America and the Atlantic, Birmingham was a town of small craftsmen next to the Black Country. London was different.[1] It lacked economic identity. Its huge growth was partly due to the fact that it had cheap sea communications with the rest of the country. In 1824, the first year of official records, more than three-quarters of the total tonnage arriving by sea came from other parts of the United Kingdom. London's lack of unity in fact preserved it to a certain extent from any large-scale riots. The diversity of its economic life flattened the effects of slumps and booms, limiting unrest.

As towns grew in the nineteenth century, segregation of classes into different residential areas became the rule, and here London was no exception. The rising middle classes were beginning to move out from the centre, creating the characteristic suburban zones. Kensington Palace, where Victoria was to grow up, was at this time cut off from London by market gardens and rural lanes.

The situation in which the Duchess of Kent found herself at Kensington Palace was singularly inglorious. In a suite of rooms on the ground floor lived Augustus, Duke of Sussex, now in his late forties. At twenty he had married Lady Augusta Murray, first privately in Rome, then at St George's, Hanover Square. King George III had refused to consent to the marriage and had had it annulled. Yet notwithstanding, Augustus remained with his wife and had two children by her before leaving her some eight years later in 1801. He did, however, provide for her, giving her 4,000 pounds of the 12,000 pounds Parliament granted him. Now he was firmly ensconced in his low-ceilinged ground-floor rooms, where he would sit in a violet satin dressing gown and black velvet skull cap surrounded by his library of 50,000 books, while the innumerable timepieces he had collected ticked the time away.

Another middle-aged relative of the Regent's was also installed in the Palace – Princess Sophia. She had had an affair with George III's elderly equerry Colonel Garth and had had a son by him in August 1800. Kensington was considered secluded enough for her to hide her guilt there. This did not prevent her from becoming, later, the object of cruel rumours. In 1829 the rumour spread that her son was in fact the result not of an affair with Garth but of incest. The 'devil' Cumberland was quite unjustly accused of having seduced his sister. 'The poor woman', Creevey noted, 'had always said this business would be her death.'[2]

Accompanying the Duchess were two men who were to play major roles in Victoria's childhood – her uncle, the Duchess's brother Prince Leopold, and Captain John Conroy, the late Duke's equerry. Leopold saw himself as protector of the future Queen of England. He himself lived at Marlborough House – in a luxury in sharp contrast to the rigour of Kensington Palace. One of his visitors wrote in 1819:

> The Prince has laid out a great deal of money on Marlborough House in painting and cleaning it, very handsome carpets to the whole range of apartments, and silk furniture, and on my asking if the silk on one sofa was foreign, he seemed quite to reproach me, and said I should never see anything that was not English in his house, that he could avoid. . . . He has also purchased a large collection of fine paintings, which are coming over, and though that is giving money out of the country, it brings a value back.[3]

Leopold's anxiety to be adopted as an English gentleman was now reinforced by the fact that he saw himself as the ideal Regent if the young Victoria were to be called too soon to the throne.

Leopold, however, managed his affairs badly – socially speaking at least. He antagonized George IV by paying a visit to Queen Caroline during her trial. The Queen sent him away without seeing him, but this did not prevent him from being permanently out of the King's favour. At a reception in January 1821, 'the King turned his back upon Prince Leopold in the most pointed manner; upon which the said Leopold, without any alteration on a muscle of his face, walked up to the Duke of York, – and in hearing of every one near him said – "The King has thought proper at last to take his line, and I shall take *mine*" – and so, with becoming German dignity, marched out of the house.'[4] When he was in London, Leopold went regularly to Kensington to see his sister and his niece. But his visits were frequently interrupted by long tours abroad. Indeed during the reign of George IV he was more often abroad than in England, a wandering Prince, biding his time, aspiring ardently to power, which always seemed just out of his reach.

He gave his sister support but he was in no sense a joyous companion. Princess Lieven considered him: 'Wearing ... with his slow speech and his bad reasoning. Leopold is a jesuit and a bore'[5] and the word that comes most easily to Creevey's pen when describing him is 'humbug'.[6]

Small wonder then that his sister should find Captain Conroy more entertaining and listen to his advice as well. He was of the same age as the Duchess, a good-looking man of Irish descent gifted with the traditional blarney. His father had come from Connaught but had left his native land for Wales, where his son John was born. John joined the army at seventeen and soon obtained a commission. At twenty-two he made an advantageous marriage, marrying Elizabeth Fisher, niece of the Bishop of Salisbury. She gave him six children – four sons and two daughters.

A few months after his marriage Conroy was attached to the service of his father-in-law Major-General Fisher, and three years later became his aide-de-camp. When his father-in-law died in 1814, he was looking for a new position in the army: his non-participation in the Waterloo campaign in 1815 shows he had little desire for active service. In 1817, through his wife's connections, he entered the household of the Duke of Kent as Equerry. After the Duke's death he remained with the Duchess and accompanied her to Kensington. He was undoubtedly an ambitious man, ready to grasp any opportunity. He thought, with much shrewdness, that as director and counsellor of the Duchess he could become a power behind the throne – to the Duchess in the case of a Regency, to Victoria when she became Queen. He was naturally pleasing to women and the Duchess fell an easy prey to his Irish charm.

The struggle for influence between Leopold and Conroy was, as we shall see, to be waged on two fronts, with very different results. Conroy had an insidious growing influence over the Duchess; Leopold relied on the power he had over her daughter.

Apart from the two men, the Duchess had about her two women who had come from Germany: her lady-in-waiting, the Baroness Spaeth, and her older daughter's governess, Louise Lehzen. The first was later referred to by Victoria as 'Old Baroness de Spaeth, the devoted lady of my mother'.[7] She had been with the Duchess since her first marriage to Prince Leiningen and had thus seen her through two marriages and two widowhoods. For Creevey, Spaeth was an 'old, ugly German female companion'.[8] She was in fact a middle-aged woman totally devoted to the Duchess and her daughter.

Louise Lehzen was a more formidable figure. She had come into the Duchess's service in December 1819 to act as governess to Princess Feodora. She was then thirty-five. The daughter of a Lutheran clergyman of Hanover, she was a woman of character with a fair share of good looks and a great capacity for devotion.

The Duchess also had with her, of course, her two daughters: the younger, still a mere baby, Alexandrina Victoria – sometimes known in her infant years as 'Drina'; and the older, Princess Feodora of Leiningen, some twelve years Victoria's senior and the daughter of the Duchess's first husband.

When the Duchess arrived in Kensington not only did she not have the house to herself. She also had very little money to live on. Although the Duke of Kent had made a will, he left no property to which his creditors had not a first claim. As his estate was insolvent the Duchess prudently renounced all interest in it on behalf of herself and her daughter.

Prince Leopold has often been praised for financing his sister, the Duchess. He did indeed give her an allowance of 3,000 pounds a year from his own income, but since he was receiving 50,000 pounds a year from the British Parliament, as the widower of Charlotte, he was in fact giving her a mere 6 per cent of what he was given on the civil list. In practice, his meagre gift merely allowed the House of Commons to wriggle out of paying the Duchess and her daughter anything. When the continuation of parliamentary allowances to the offspring of the late King was considered by the House of Commons on 3 July 1820, the Leader of the House, Lord Castlereagh, declared that although it might well be up to Parliament to support the Duchess of Kent and the infant Princess, he would not propose any vote to them 'as the Prince Leopold with great liberality, had taken upon himself the charge of the support and education of the infant Princess.'[9] So apart from Leopold's 3,000 pounds the Duchess had only the 6,000 pounds a year settled on the Duke on his marriage, which reverted to her. The new King George IV refused to give his brother's wife a penny. He hoped this would drive her back to Amorbach.

When one considers the social structure in Britain at the time, the Duchess's straits become even more obvious. Basically there were two tiers in the social structure – the upper and lower classes, between which the middle classes were struggling to emerge. The upper classes comprised the titled aristocracy and the gentry and counted some 4,000 families, making up no more than 5 per cent of the population. Their power, however, was immense. Since 1688 they had dominated the political life of the nation. They controlled both Houses of Parliament and governed the rural areas through grand juries and quarter sessions. The top of the social pyramid was composed of just over 300 peers. Social status was largely bound up with land ownership. No rank was formally closed – one could rise in the social scale by making money, by marriage or by the help of influential friends. A complicated system of entail, settlement and primogeniture ensured the non-division of estates.

The Duchess had no land, no estate. She had had to beg a home in Kensington Palace from the King. Alongside the non-royal dukes the future Queen's family cut a poor figure. The Duke of Devonshire, for instance, was the richest in the land, with an income of 150,000 pounds a year, not to mention the 86,000 acres he owned in Bedford, Cambridgeshire and Devon, his mines in Devon and the 119 acres of real estate he owned in London.[10]

Was there no one to comfort the Duchess in this difficult situation? She certainly had the sympathy of her late husband's unmarried sisters, Sophia and Augusta, and the friendship of the Duchess of Clarence, Adelaide, who came to see her every day. Adelaide and the Duchess of Kent were both German princesses and they could talk away in German, an undoubted advantage since the Duchess of Kent never really mastered the English language. The Duchess of Clarence was a very kind woman and the two might have become friends. The Duchess of Kent was, however, prickly and difficult – she feared that the Clarences would produce a child that would do Victoria out of a throne and her mother out of a seat of power! The birth of a daughter to Adelaide in 1820 did not improve relations. George IV was delighted and allowed the child to be christened Elizabeth Georgina Adelaide. As Conroy wrote in his own cheap fashion, 'We are all on the kick and go. Our little woman's nose has been put out of joint.'[11] Less than three months later the infant Princess Elizabeth died suddenly and Victoria was again second in line to the throne. Relations between the Duchesses did not, however, ease, for Adelaide was not yet thirty and might still give birth to an heir to the throne. The possibility of her having a further child remained until her husband's death in 1837.

George IV treated the Duchess of Kent extremely badly, mainly because he had disliked her husband and, being of a vindictive turn of mind, visited the sins of the husband on the wife. In any case he was mortified that it was not his own descendants that would sit on the throne of England and this alone made him little inclined to welcome the newcomers to Kensington Palace. It was thus in comparative seclusion that the Princess spent most of the first eighteen years of her life.

The Queen's childhood falls into two parts, corresponding to the reigns of her two uncles. For the first eleven years of her life the ruler was George IV, and while he was alive the Duchess of Kent made no real attempt to push her own and her daughter's claims for recognition. Perhaps this was because the reactions of the King were all too predictable; perhaps, too, because these years were the ones during which Leopold's ascendancy over his sister was the greatest. When he was in London he went every Wednesday evening to Kensington, where a family concert was held round the drawing-room piano. He also had a weekly record of Victoria's educational progress sent to him. It was during this period that he won the child's heart, the first father figure in her long life.

Leopold was, however, very far from the paragon of virtue his young niece took him for. His sexual appetites were large and, a widower in his twenties, he assuaged his desires with a string of amorous relationships. They included Jane, Lady Ellenborough, whom Balzac was to picture as Lady Dudley in *The Lily in the Valley*. The relationship between Leopold and Caroline Bauer, a young and beautiful actress in the Prussian state company, was even more extraordinary. The story has been detailed by Caroline herself. Leopold saw her act the Höttentot in Potsdam in a popular musical comedy *Die Höttentottin* and completely lost his customary self-control. He wrote to Caroline's mother: 'All the long years since the death of my consort I have been living alone. Now I believe I have found the sympathetic creature I seek. At the very first glance my heart inclined to her, because she looks so wondrously like my departed Charlotte.'[12] He persuaded her to leave the theatre and to come to England with her mother, making her vague promises of marriage. No doubt at the time he was sincere. But when mother and daughter arrived in London eight months later, they found they were to be set up in a Georgian love-nest. The Prince himself was not even there to welcome them and they waited for him all day. Finally,

Muffled up like an Arctic explorer or a light-shunning highwayman, my knight alighted, consideringly, from his carriage, and softly approached the glass door of the salon. I heard the heavy, slow footsteps, one by one, on the creaking ground. My heart beat loud and high as if it would burst. In my nervous agitation I plucked to pieces the rose my mother had with such fond hopefulness inserted in my hair in the morning, and which the long, long weary day had withered. Softly the glass door opened – then three, slow, heavy footsteps, and the tall form of the prince stood before me, while trembling and deprived of all composure I leant against the chimney awaiting in silence the prince's address.

The prince, too, kept silent, nor did he stretch out any arm to embrace me, nor any hand to shake with mine. The prince's eyes surveyed me consideringly, then slowly there came from his lips:

"O, how the spring sun has burnt your cheeks!"[13]

The Potsdam actress no longer seemed to him the physical replica of his dead wife. He no longer found her touching. For six months he visited her daily – never arriving without his drizzling box. Drizzling was the fashionable pastime of the day. Gold and silver tassels or epaulets were put through a machine which converted them into their original gold or silver powder, from which objects might be made – gold rings or silver dishes, for instance. While Leopold operated the box, Caroline played the piano or read aloud to him. She pictures him, 'an inch over six feet tall, sat bent in the most solemn earnestness over his elegant tortoise-shell drizzling-box, and thoughtfully picking thread after thread out of old silver galloons, a task apparently of no less moment than that of unravelling the threads of fate'.[14] During the year he drizzled out enough silver to make a stately soup tureen, which on 24 May 1830 he presented to his niece Victoria!

Caroline was Stockmar's first cousin and he it was who decided to put an end to this anomalous situation. Leopold was told that unless he made up his mind to marry the girl, Stockmar would take her back to Germany. Why did Leopold not let her go? Probably because, in a very egotistical manner, he found in her a sort of mental repose. On 2 July 1829 they were according to Caroline married – but the ceremony was singular. 'No priest laid his hand to invoke a blessing on my head. No bridal garland adorned my hair,' Caroline complained.[15] The girl received the title of Countess Montgomery and an allowance was settled on her. The marriage, if marriage it was, lasted only twenty-eight days. Days that marked, according to his new wife, the last expiring flush of romance in his life. In late July Leopold went to take the waters in Carlsbad and it was arranged that his wife and her mother should go to Paris, where the Prince would join them later. He did not join them until November, and when he did booked rooms in another hotel, paying his wife frosty visits with the ominous drizzling box. Yet he would not release Caroline, whose only wish was to return to Germany and forget this parody of a marriage. He insisted mother and daughter return to England with him and established them in a 'lonely, desolate and mournful villa near Claremont House, fourteen English miles from London'. The drizzling and the long melancholy visits began again. 'There is no denying', Caroline wrote, 'that I had myself nearly unlearned laughing.'[16]

Finally in June 1830 Caroline's brother Karl arrived, threatened to make a scandal and finally returned to Germany with his mother and sister. Caroline had wasted two years of her life. History does not tell us what, if any, material compensation she received. We do know, however, that she resumed her theatrical career and never saw Leopold or cousin Stockmar again.

This discreditable episode shows a very different Leopold from the man Victoria looked up to as a father. Creevey's 'humbug' is nearer the mark. One wonders whether the child was really ignorant of all that was going on around her. One passage in Caroline's accounts of her life at Claremont leads to speculation. She and her mother were walking through the grounds when:

> A clear girlish voice and a child-like laugh came ringing to our ears. On a silver-grey pony, accompanied by a large, white, long-haired dog, a young girl of eleven years came trotting up, fresh and round like a red rosebud with flying curls and large luminous eyes. These eyes looked at me so astonished and with such a gaze of inquisitive questioning in them, while the little hand securely held in the pony. And then all at once the little Amazon curved round, and presently returned with a stately round lady. She too started, and her eye glided all over us not without scrutiny, and I felt how I grew red with shame under this glance. Then the lady called to her little daughter a word in English, and both disappeared in the shrubbery leaving us behind in a deep sense of shame.
>
> We had recognized each other. It was the Duchess of Kent, sister of Prince Leopold, with her little daughter, Victoria.[17]

We do not know what the Duchess told her daughter on this occasion, nor what Victoria guessed or surmised. The admiration she felt for her uncle is evident in her diary. 'To hear dear Uncle Leopold speak on any subject is like reading a highly instructive book.'[18] The earliest letter preserved of the long series written by Victoria to Prince Leopold shows how affectionate their relationship was.

Kensington Palace, 25 November 1828

My dearest Uncle, – I wish you many happy returns of your birthday; I very often think of you, and I hope to see you soon again, for I am very fond of you. I see my Aunt Sophia often, who looks very well, and is very well. I use every day your pretty soup-basin. Is it very warm in Italy? It is so mild here that I go out every day. Mama is tolerably well and I am quite well. Your affectionate niece

Victoria

P. S. I am very angry with you, Uncle, for you have never written to me once since you went, and that is a long while.[19]

The tone of gentle admonition in the postscript is not a tone that a child would use in a letter that was merely written at an adult's bidding.

Perhaps the clearest proof of the happy relationship lies in the fact that Leopold and the Princess would open their hearts to one another all down the years much as father and daughter might do. She might disagree, she might even rebel, but she always replied in detail and never took lightly any recommendation, any piece of advice, any counsel coming from her uncle.

Over fifty years later Queen Victoria wrote down some of her earliest recollections of her early childhood.[20] They included 'crawling on a yellow carpet', being told that if she was naughty her Uncle Sussex on the floor below would hear her and punish her, 'for which reason I always screamed when I saw him!' She remembers that she had a great horror of Bishops on account of their wigs and aprons but got over this in the case of Dr Fisher, then Bishop of Salisbury, because he knelt down and allowed her to 'play with his badge of Chancellor of the Order of the Garter'. Dr Fisher – the royal family aptly nicknamed him 'the Kingfisher' – was rather tedious and over-anxious to be welcomed in royal drawing rooms. He owed his invitations to Kensington to a rather tenuous link with the Duchess – his niece had married Captain Conroy.

As any child, Victoria particularly appreciated one uncle – the Duke of York – who 'always gave me beautiful presents'. Among them was the donkey she first rode on. He it was, too, who introduced her to Punch and Judy, which he organized for her in a friend's garden 'when he was already very ill'. The Queen looked back with pleasure on her numerous visits to Ramsgate, by steamer, and to Tunbridge Wells. But her fondest memories were of Claremont, which 'remains as the brightest epoch of my otherwise rather melancholy childhood'.

Victoria's contacts with her royal uncle, George IV, were extremely limited and this suited her mother well. When Greville asked Wellington why the Duchess of Kent was in such opposition to the Court, the Duke told him that George IV was always talking of taking her child from her, and would have done so but for the Duke of Wellington himself, who did all in his power to deter his royal master. He never openly opposed the King, since this would have been the surest way of precipitating events; he simply put the thing off as best he could.[21] Victoria remembered one visit to Carlton House, the King's London residence, as 'quite a little child'. She went there before a dinner the Queen gave, and then again in 1826, when George IV asked her mother, her sister and Victoria herself down to Windsor for the first time. His interest in his brother's widow and her child can be gauged by the fact that he had by then been King for six whole years. Perhaps he would have been kinder more often had he known the impression her first visit to Windsor was to make on the little girl of seven.

She spent three delightful days at Windsor, living not in Royal Lodge where the King lived but at Cumberland Lodge close by. When the Kensington party arrived at Royal Lodge, the King took her by the hand saying: 'Give me your little paw.' Her impression of him tallies with those of many who knew him well. 'He was large and gouty but with a wonderful dignity and charm of manner.' The child saw, with a perception children often have, beyond the bodily infirmities of her uncle. There is no doubt that he was a cultured man, had an elegant taste and the manners of a Prince. When Victoria arrived at Windsor, George IV presented her with his picture set in diamonds – it was worn by the Princess attached to a blue ribbon as if it were a decoration. 'I was', she later noted, 'very proud of this, – and Lady Conyngham pinned it on my shoulder.' The little Princess knew instinctively how to please the King. One day, for instance, as they came into the drawing room, hand in hand, an orchestra was playing. 'Well, Victoria,' George IV said, 'the orchestra is in the next room and will play whatever you like. What is it to be?' She replied, 'God Save the King.'[22] She was taken on a drive about the park in a pony carriage and four – 'with four grey ponies (like my own)'. She was also taken to Sandpit Gate, where the King had a menagerie with wapitis, gazelles, chamois, etc. On the second day the party went to Virginia Water and met the Duchess of Gloucester.

'Pop her in', he said and I was lifted in and placed between him and Aunt Gloucester who held me round the waist. (Mama was much frightened.) I was greatly pleased and remember that I looked with great respect at the scarlet liveries, etc. [In those days the Royal Family had crimson and green liveries and only the King scarlet and blue.] We drove round the nicest part of Virginia Water and stopped at the Fishing Temple. Here there was a large barge and every one went on board and fished, while a band played in another.

The King paid great attention to Feodora and, the Queen remembers, 'some people fancied he might marry her!' She was a very lovely eighteen-year-old and had charming manners, 'about which the King was extremely particular'. It is interesting to note that the Duchess of Kent was not at all pleased by the King's attentions to her elder daughter. At the first opportunity she sent her off to Germany to stay with her grandmother, well out of the King's way. Was this because the idea of her young daughter marrying this sixty-year-old shocked her? That seems doubtful, given her own life history. Perhaps she believed her own influence would be greater as the mother of a Queen in her own right which Victoria would be, rather than as the mother of the King's wife, which Feodora might have been.

Feodora remained in Germany and towards the end of 1827 her betrothal to Prince Ernest Christian Charles of Hohenlohe-Langenburg was announced. Another mediatized, pauper prince, as her father, the Prince of Leiningen, had been. As Cecil Woodham-Smith rightly notes, 'Though devoted to Prince Ernest, her beauty, intelligence and charm, combined with her close connection with the powerful English Court, fitted her for a more brilliant existence than the economy, the dullness and isolation of life at Schloss Langenburg, an immense building, sparsely furnished and celebrated for the icy cold of its corridors "like caves".'[23] The bond between Victoria and Feodora was not shattered by absence, they wrote to one another throughout their lives. Feodora's letter to the Princess on her tenth birthday, the first without her sister, shows her affection.

> If I had wings and could fly like a bird I should fly in at your window like the little robin to-day, and wish you many very happy returns on the 24th and tell you how I love you, dearest sister, and how often I think of you and long to see you. I think if I were once with you again I could not leave you so soon. I should wish to stay with you, and what would poor Ernest [her husband] say if I were to leave him so long? He would perhaps try to fly after me, but I fear he would not get far; he is rather tall and heavy for flying.[24]

Victoria's infancy might at first seem like that of any upper-class child of the period with two exceptions: she was breast-fed by her own mother and not by a wet nurse, and at ten weeks old she was vaccinated. She breakfasted at eight o'clock on bread, milk and fruit put on a little table by her mother's side. Then came an hour's walk or drive, followed by two hours, from ten to twelve, during which her mother instructed her. The Duchess would then retire to her private sitting room and leave Mrs Brock – the homely, affectionate nurse Victoria called 'dear, dear Boppy' – to watch over the child as she ran to and fro and played with her toys – carriages, horses, dolls, dolls' houses, models of ships and the like.

At two, came lunch with the Duchess. Then lessons again with her mother till four. Then came a visit or a drive to see some favoured friend or member of the royal family, or simply to take the air. On returning, the Princess would ride or walk in Kensington Gardens and on very fine evenings the whole family would sit on the lawn under the trees. At the time of her mother's dinner, the Princess had her bread and milk supper laid at her side. She was allowed to leave the table as soon as she had finished, and played with 'Boppy' in her room until the Duchess had finished her dinner. Victoria returned at dessert – and this was always the case, whether the Duchess had company or not. At nine o'clock the Princess would retire to her bed, which was placed alongside that of her mother. Princess Feodora slept in a third bed on the other side of her mother's. The nurse slept in a small adjoining room. Victoria tells us 'I was brought up very simply – never had a room to myself till I was nearly grown up – always slept in my mother's room till I came to the throne.'[25]

Victoria's formal education began when she was four. Most biographers have stressed that she disliked learning.[26] To back up this view of things authors use her own statement: 'I was not fond of learning as a little child – and baffled every attempt to teach me my letters up to five years old – when I consented to learn them by their being written down before me.'[27] But this was Victoria's reconstruction years after the event. Nor does it take into account the manner in which she was taught. Cecil Woodham-Smith seems to think Fraulein Lehzen taught her until she was eight, when the Reverend George Davys, an evangelical clergyman, was engaged.[28] In fact a journal kept by the Reverend Davys between 1823 and 1825 tells us that he was introduced to the Duchess of Kent by Captain Conroy and attended the Princess for the first time on Wednesday 6 April 1823. She was not yet four years old. 'Her first lesson', Davys tells us, 'was the alphabet, which the Princess had learned before. Then the following line, b-a, b-e, b-i, b-o, b-u, b-y, which we did not quite conquer.'[29] So before she was four she knew her alphabet and was learning to read syllabically – a phenomenon she did not quite master in one lesson! The method of teaching her to read was singular. Davys noted, 'I wrote some short words on cards for Princess Victoria, and endeavoured to interest her by making her bring them to me from a distant part of the room as I named them.'[30] Just after her fourth birthday her tutor wrote, 'The Princess Victoria improves in reading, but is still not fond of keeping her eyes long together on the book.'[31] On the first of July, for instance, he tells us that the two princesses, Victoria and Feodora, had a lesson of two hours and a quarter together, and that 'The little Princess improves in attention. She attended well for an hour. I was glad that the Duchess asked me to go half an hour sooner than usual, as before there was scarcely time enough to do much.'[32]

To these two hours with Davys were added hours of work with Fraulein Lehzen, whom Davys tells us was very zealous. Queen Victoria told Lord Melbourne later that her mother was tyrannical, 'always having insisted on being at my lessons'.[33]

In 1825 Parliament unanimously voted the Duchess an additional 6,000 pounds a year 'for the purpose of making an adequate provision for the honourable support and education of her Highness Princess Alexandrina Victoria of Kent.'[34] And accordingly the teaching became diversified. Writing lessons were now given by Thomas Steward, the writing master of Westminster. Davys had, however, found it necessary 'for the sake of fixing the attention of the Princess'[35] to teach her to write short sentences on a slate. Victoria is at this point 'quick of comprehension and takes an interest in the accounts which she reads; but there is still a great reluctance in giving that attention which is required to master difficulties.' The Princess is, however, under six years of age 'and, consequently much cannot be expected. I have endeavoured to teach the Princess a little arithmetic. She can now read with tolerable facility.'[36]

We are here far from the traditional picture of a rather slow starter who was most reluctant to learn. She was in fact a quick learner. Two specimens of her writing, one in December 1825, the other in August 1826, show rapid improvement in less than a year. She also had a good ear and with Davys's help got rid of a somewhat Germanized accent. When he first came to her, 'She confused the sound of "v" with that of "w", and pronounced *much* as *muts*.'[37]

In 1829 other specialists were recruited in French and German, and in the arts – drawing, music, and dancing.[38] Her day was now distributed according to a strict timetable six days a week, Saturday included.[39] Lessons from half-past nine to half-past eleven, then walk-

ing or playing from half-past eleven to one, followed by dinner from one
to two and another hour's walking or playing afterwards. Lessons
began again at three and ended at six. In any week there were thus
thirty one-hour periods for lessons. Of these the last hour of each day
and Saturday mornings were devoted to repetitions of work done.
Within the timetable an hour was set aside for the learning of poetry by
heart and another – which was to stand her in good stead – to learning
the art of letter-writing. In 1830, when the Princess was almost eleven,
her mother decided the time had come to show the wider world how
well she had brought up the heir presumptive. She therefore sent off a
letter to the Bishops of London and Lincoln asking them to test the
results of Victoria's education by personal examination. They were to
examine the Princess with a view to telling the Duchess:

> First   If the course hitherto pursued in her education has been the best,
> if not, where it was erroneous?
>
> Second   If the Princess has made all the Progress she should have done?
>
> Third   And if the course I am to follow is that you would recommend
> and if not, in what respect you would desire a change and on what
> grounds?[40]

With mock humility the Duchess told the bishops

> I allowed no attempt to be made, to push the Princess intellectually
> beyond her years: on this point I was firm, satisfied, as far as my poor
> judgement could direct me, that it was the safest and surest course,
> although not the most brilliant.[41]

The Duchess, albeit unwittingly, thus fed the idea that her daughter
was something of a plodder.

However the diverse appreciations of her masters showed how
untrue this was. Steward, who also taught her arithmetic, told the
Duchess that 'the Princess Victoria has a peculiar talent for arithmetic;
her correctness in working sums and her quickness in comprehending
the explanation of her rules are excellent.'[42] His judgement was all the
less suspect as he was not satisfied with the manner in which she copied
writing examples. Her German teacher credited her with a good
vocabulary in German and praised her pronunciation, 'which is particularly remarkable for its softness and distinction'.[43] On her French,
M. Grandineau declared: 'The Princess can now hold a conversation in
French but she does not write it as well as she speaks it. . . . I have every
reason to believe that her pronunciation will be perfect. I think I can

say that the Princess is much more advanced than children of her age usually are.' And, as he was eager to encourage the use of French, he went on, 'Would it be possible for me to ask your Royal Highness very humbly to devote a little more time to the study of the French language.'[44] Davys himself thought the Princess had made considerable progress. 'The Princess is better informed in history than most young persons of the same age. . . . The same remark is applicable to geography. The Princess can read Poetry extremely well; and I think understands what she reads, as well as, at her age, could possibly be expected.' Only in Latin is she 'not far advanced'.[45]

The Bishops duly examined the Princess and gave their entire approbation of that course both as to the choice of subjects and the arrangement of her studies:

> In answering a great variety of questions proposed to Her, the Princess displayed an accurate knowledge of the most important features of Scripture, History and the leading truths and precepts of the Christian Religion as taught by the Church of England; as well as an acquaintance with the chronology and principal facts of the English History remarkable in so young a person.[46]

Victoria was a naturally good linguist and later, fascinated as she was by opera, studied Italian. Throughout her childhood she was not allowed to read novels, though later on she and her eldest daughter were to exchange titles of novels to be read and impressions of them. Nor was her literary taste formed by her tutors – her first volumes of poetry to commit to memory were *The Infant Minstrel*, *Poetry without Friction* by a Mother, and *The Keepsake*, in a word moralistic sentimentality.

Although not exceptionally gifted, the Princess delighted in music. She had a sweet, reliable voice – but it was not very strong – and played the piano to good effect. Victoria was also a keen artist. She was taught first by Richard Westall, the Academician, and later by Landseer. Sketching in pencil or watercolours was a lifelong hobby. With a rather attractive modesty she continued to study under various masters both music and art long after she was married and a mother.

The lessons she enjoyed most were those in riding and she became an excellent horsewoman. Here at last was an occasion to break free from constraint, to shake off surveillance as she galloped fast through Windsor Park to the terror of many of her ladies-in-waiting. Dancing, which she was first taught by a French demoiselle, Mademoiselle Bourdin, she was devoted to. On the dance floor she both showed exceptional grace and energy and was, right into middle age, untiring.

On 28 May 1829, four days after her birthday, she danced in public for the first time. It was also her first acquaintance with the ceremony of a Court. The occasion was a Juvenile Ball given by the King at St James's Palace in honour of the child-Queen of Portugal Donna Maria II. The young Queen of Portugal was only a month older than Victoria and had already been Queen for three years. The two young ladies danced in the same quadrille and Greville noted:

> I saw for the first time the Queen of Portugal and our little Victoria. The Queen was finely dressed with a ribbon and Order over her shoulder, and she sat by the King. She is good-looking, and has a sensible Asturian countenance.... Our little Princess is a short, plain-looking child, and not near so good-looking as the Portuguese. However, if Nature has not done so much, Fortune is likely to do a great deal more for her.[47]

Victoria was certainly not, at ten or later, a beauty, but she had appealing dark blue eyes, a good-tempered mouth and a small but graceful figure. Donna Maria was not a beauty either – indeed Victoria in her journals as Queen continually refers to her as 'the little fat queen'. Even at ten she was podgier than Victoria and indubitably less childlike.

On the second count, of course, Greville was right. Victoria's reign was to exceed Donna Maria's not only in length but in tranquillity and in grandeur. But as she danced her quadrille how conscious of her future was she? Did she at eleven, as the well-worn account put abroad by Lehzen would have it, suddenly discover her proximity to the throne? If so, was it as her mother claimed by chance, or as Lehzen declared by design – by agreement between the mother and the governess?

Lehzen's version, communicated to the Queen in 1867, thirty-seven years after the supposed scene had taken place, has become part of the Queen's legend. A genealogical table was slipped into Victoria's history book. On discovering it she is said by Lehzen to have declared:

> "I see I am nearer the throne than I thought." "So it is", I [Lehzen] said. After some moments the Princess resumed, "Many a child would boast, but they do not know the difficulty. There is much splendour, but more responsibility." The Princess, having lifted up the forefinger of her right hand before she spoke, gave me her little hand, saying, "I will be good."[48]

The language is stilted and unchildlike and the Princess does not seem from other accounts such a prig. The account is in any case a reconstruction after the event. It is more than probable that the question of the succession could not have escaped the young child's ears, cooped up as she was with adults to whom the question was all-important. As Sir Walter Scott put it, 'This Lady [Victoria] is educated with much care, and is watched so closely that no busy maid has a moment to whisper "You are heir of England." I suspect, if we could dissect the little heart, we should find some pigeon or other bird of the air had carried the matter.'[49]

Stories of her happy contented childhood abound. Lord Albermarle in his autobiography pictures her 'a bright pretty little girl of seven years of age', watering her plants immediately under the window. 'It was amusing to see how impartially she divided the contents of the water-pot between the flowers and her own little feet.'[50] She was dressed simply in a large straw hat and a suit of white cotton, a coloured scarf round her neck her only ornament. The note is one of carefree happiness. Charles Knight plays on the same theme when he shows her getting up from her outdoor breakfast table to go and pick a flower in the adjoining field, her merry laugh 'as fearless as the notes of the thrush in the groves around her'.[51]

This is the conventional image. The real story has a much darker side. Victoria was brought up under ceaseless surveillance. Never was she left in a room without a servant, never was she allowed to go downstairs without someone holding her hand. Not only did she sleep in her mother's bedroom but a guard was kept over her in her bedroom till the Duchess came up to undress. The child saw no one apart from the Kensington set; her only consolation was her half-sister Feodora, full twelve years older than herself. Writing to Victoria later on in life Feodora says

> Not to have enjoyed the pleasures of youth is nothing but to have been deprived of all intercourse, and not one cheerful thought in that dismal existence of ours was very hard. My only happy time was going or driving out with you and Lehzen; then I could speak and look as I liked. I escaped some years of imprisonment, which you, my poor darling sister, had to endure after I was married.[52]

In 1830–1 two events were to make Victoria's life at Kensington even harder. The death of the King and the departure of Uncle Leopold. George IV's health deteriorated suddenly at the beginning of 1830, when he began to have violent attacks of coughing. 'The ossification of the heart could have no other than a mortal termination, though that termination was hastened by the bursting of a blood-vessel during a violent fit of coughing.'[53] Early on the morning of Saturday 26 June,

George IV died. During the latter years of his reign he had lived in relative seclusion and he had never been dear to his people. He was, however, a man of character and the Duchess of Kent had been careful not to antagonize him. She made the mistake of believing, as did John Conroy, that the Duke of Clarence, who now became William IV, was much more malleable. Over the next seven years the Duchess and Conroy were to realise how completely they had misjudged the new King.

The second major event that was to change Victoria's situation at Kensington Palace was the turn in the fortunes of her uncle Leopold. He had been offered, and accepted, the throne of Greece in 1830 but had finally declined it on the grounds that England would not grant Greece satisfactory financial help. There seems little doubt that Victoria's proximity to the throne was an element in favour of his remaining in England. When a few months later the Belgians offered him their throne, the thought that here was an opportunity really too good to be missed caused him to overcome his tendency to be irresolute.

Revolution had come to Paris on 29 July 1830 and Louis Philippe, ex-Duke of Orléans, had agreed to become not King of France but King of the French. Repercussions on Belgium were almost immediate. After the July revolution in France came the August days in Belgium. The Belgians, united with the Dutch whom they detested at the Congress of Vienna in 1815, decided to free themselves from them. In September the Belgian National Congress voted the separation of Belgium from Holland, and in October Belgium was declared an independent state. In December, despite Metternich's opposition, the London Conference confirmed the principle of Belgian independence. But what sort of regime was Belgium to adopt? A monarchy, a republic or again a French dependency? The Belgians favoured a monarchy and the Belgian National Congress duly elected Louis Philippe's son, the Duke of Nemours, to the Belgian throne. Belgium and Holland had been united in 1815 as a bulwark against French ambition; England could not brook a virtual annexation of Belgium by the French and Palmerston threatened France with war. Louis Philippe refused the offer for Nemours and Palmerston brought forward his own candidate – Leopold.

Did he want to rid Britain of a possible power behind the throne in future years? Was he simply looking for a candidate whose links with England were sufficiently strong? Be that as it may, the Belgians who had wanted a French Catholic King found themselves with a German

Protestant. And one who hummed and hawed into the bargain. First Leopold told Belgian envoys that he could not accept the throne unless he were to be clearly elected by the Belgian Congress. This was done by 155 votes to 44. And still Leopold did not give his final answer. Finally he accepted and in July 1831 set out for Belgium – not however without doubts. 'It seems', Greville says, 'that desirous as he had been to go, when the time drew near he got alarmed, and wanted to back out, but they brought him (though with difficulty) to the point.'[54] So he sailed for Belgium and moreover: 'He has proposed to the Princess Louise, King Louis Philippe's daughter.'[55]

Leopold's representation of his new wife to Princess Victoria in reply to a letter from her asking for a description reinforces the idea that this was indeed a marriage of convenience – for the portrait is rather cold and gives a rather daunting picture of a woman who was virtuous but not joyful.

> She is extremely gentle and amiable, her actions are always guided by principles. She is at all times ready and disposed to sacrifice her comfort and inclinations to see others happy. She values goodness, merit and virtue much more than beauty, riches, and amusements. With all this she is highly informed and very clever; she speaks and writes English, German and Italian; she speaks English very well indeed. In short, my dear Love, you see that I may well recommend her as an example for all young ladies being princesses or not.[56]

So Victoria's 'dear uncle' was now a King and as such in future years was to talk to her as one sovereign to another. But for the moment his departure was mourned by his young niece. Captain Conroy on the other hand was delighted. With George IV dead and Leopold out of the way, his star was rising. The Kensington system was about to be operated to the full.

4

The Kensington System

The aim behind the Kensington plan was in the first instance to secure the Regency for the Duchess; in later years it was to ensure the authority of the Duchess over her daughter once she was Queen.

Several years later, when she had ascended the throne, Victoria's half-brother, Charles of Leiningen, set out for the benefit of the royal couple: 'A complete History of the Policy followed at Kensington, under Sir John Conroy's guidance.'[1] This version of events seeks to explain why he, Charles, should have gone along with the system when he was in England, and also seeks to 'free' his mother from any blame. But this story reduces the Duchess of Kent to a mere cipher who is led astray by her 'evil servant'. Things must, however, have been more complicated. The twice-widowed Duchess was a woman of experience still possessed of great attractions. Captain Conroy was an attractive man of her own age, a man whose panache appealed to her. The precise nature of their relationship is uncertain – even if they were not lovers, they must have flirted and the Duke of Wellington puts Victoria's animosity to Conroy down to her witnessing 'familiarities' between her mother and Conroy.[2] Conroy became the Duchess's counsellor and he was probably the stronger figure of the two, but there is nothing to show that his desire to cut her daughter off from the Court, to use her as a means for his own advancement, did not fit in perfectly with the Duchess's own views of things.

Prince Charles tells us that the Duchess was brought to agree with Conroy's plans after lengthy discussions and disputes – this strengthens the idea of a partnership rather than a submission. The Prince, no doubt in an attempt to please Victoria and Albert in later years, insists that even Fraulein Lehzen was chosen as governess as part of the plan – for she had no influential friends. The simpler explanation was that, having been governess to Feodora and having done her job most satisfactorily, she was simply transferred to Victoria as a natural choice, and this seems more convincing. Charles also claimed that Princess Sophia, who lived in Kensington Palace, was 'considered by him [Conroy] to be very favourably disposed towards the Kensington system and was used by him whenever necessary and in various ways, for the carrying out of his plan.' But Charles also says that the Duchess of Kent thought Sophia very difficult and rather unbalanced. Conroy may have taken pity on her, forced as she was to live far from Court with an unhappy past, and advised the Duchess to treat her with 'indulgence or toleration', not in itself a bad thing.

The major aim of Victoria's family in later years was to prove the innocence – even if misguided innocence – of the Duchess. Prince Albert for his part blames his uncle: 'Mama here would never have fallen into the hands of Conroy, if Uncle Leopold had taken the trouble to guide her.' What is not explained is why, up to the time he left England in 1830, Prince Leopold allowed the Princess to be secluded. He was certainly not ignorant of it. Indeed he probably encouraged his sister, so poor were his own relations with George IV. According to Cecil Woodham-Smith all the blame should fall on Conroy, who had made himself a dictator at Kensington. He ordered every detail of life, even choosing the little Princess's tutors. He decided what policy the Duchess should adopt and what actions she should take and his plans were then sanctioned by the Duchess; not always without difficulty.[3] The Duchess of Clarence had a more nuanced view of things. Hearing the whispers about Conroy's relations with the Duchess of Kent, she wrote her a letter of warning, noting that the family realized she was cutting herself off more and more from them with Victoria. 'This they attribute to Conroy. Whether rightly or wrongly I cannot judge.' In the same note she spoke of Conroy 'as a man of merit' but insisted that his family was 'not of so high a rank that they *alone* should be the entourage and companions of the future Queen of England'.[4] The Duchess of Clarence believed that responsibility did not lie with Conroy alone. Conroy was undoubtedly a schemer, an ambitious man pursuing his own devices. But the Duchess was a harder headed woman than biographers of Victoria would have us believe. She had in fact found herself in a similar position after the death of her first husband. The Prince of Leiningen had appointed as his Master of the Horse a commoner, Captain Schindler, who thereafter prefixed the noble 'von' to his name. He was, as Conroy, a man of little education and of great skill with women. After Leiningen's death he soon became the Master of the Household and before long was acting as co-Regent with the Dowager Princess. The Conroy–Duchess of Kent relationship was history repeating itself.

Nor does the fact that the Duchess wrote to Stockmar in 1834 for advice on how to handle Victoria, Lehzen and Conroy tally with the picture of a Duchess completely under the control of Conroy, unable to exercise her faculty of criticism. Stockmar, incidentally, saw Conroy as 'an excellent business man and absolutely devoted to your Royal Highness', even if he was also 'vain, ambitious, most sensitive and most hot tempered'. Stockmar, always more conscious of the risks he ran himself than of the help he might be to others, concluded that he did not wish to run the risk of any charge of tampering with the Princess being brought against him as it had been against his master, King Leopold: 'to tamper means intrigue, I don't know any other word for it.'[5] The Duchess of Kent was certainly no Lady Macbeth, but neither was Conroy the 'Mephistopheles' Leopold described in later years.

The Kensington pair were to make several mistakes in the operation of their 'system'. The first was a complete misreading of the character of William IV, who was perhaps weak but also extremely obstinate. The second was a total incomprehension of the character of Victoria.

William IV was a man of plain habits and plain manners. He was given to rambling, incongruent speeches but he was not devoid of common sense. He had passed the greater part of his life before his accession in obscurity and neglect. He had been not far from poverty, surrounded by his numerous children by his first companion – all, officially bastards. Small wonder that his grief on his brother's passing was not strong. Princess Lieven commented: 'A quaint King indeed. A *bon enfant* – with a weak head. At times I think he is likely to lose it, so great is his pleasure at being King.'[6]

He was indeed extraordinarily active, after the lethargic George. He developed a real passion for inspecting soldiers. Not the least surprising feature of the new King was that he appeared to love and respect his wife. Queen Adelaide was undoubtedly a good wife. In her quiet way she had as Duchess of Clarence won the affection of most of the royal family. As a child, Victoria was very fond of her aunt. It was from her aunt that the Princess received her very first letter. It came in May 1821 when she was three, just two months after the Duchess had lost her baby, who had for a few months been heir to the throne. Queen Adelaide was devoid of envy and jealousy.

My dear little Heart, – I hope you are well and don't forget Aunt
Adelaide, who loves you fondly.

Loulou and Wilhelm [the Duchess's nephew and niece] desire their
love to you, and Uncle William also.

God bless and preserve you is the constant prayer of your most truly
affectionate Aunt, Adelaide.[7]

The Duchess of Kent's girl was indeed a great favourite with the new
King and Queen. Perhaps now she would become really part of the
royal family. But the Duchess of Kent was to think otherwise . . .

The day after William's accession the Duchess of Kent sent the
Prime Minister, the Duke of Wellington, a letter spelling out her
claims.[8] She wanted to be placed on the footing of a Dowager Princess
of Wales, in other words to be accorded the equivalent status – and
income. The Princess Victoria should, she claimed, be treated as
Heiress Apparent and the allowance given her should be controlled by
her mother. The Duke of Wellington wrote back[9] that the Duchess
would be wise not to have her letter laid before the King. She should
wait for the King and his Ministers to propose a settlement, as they
were bound to in due course. She might, the Duke told her, rely upon it
that no measure which affected her in any way should be considered
without being imparted to her and the fullest information given her.
She had intended to dictate her conditions. She was told that she would
be informed of the decisions taken. At this she took great offence 'for
she did not speak to him for a long time after.'[10]

Meanwhile, on 29 June, the King had sent a Message to Parliament
announcing that, as was customary after the demise of the Crown, he
would call, with as little delay as possible, a new Parliament. The
Whigs resolved to insist that Parliament should continue to sit, until a
Bill could be carried through, appointing a Regency, in case the new
King should die before the new Parliament could meet. Their aim was
to irritate the King but they did have a point – the law recognizes no
minority. If a Regency bill were not voted, all the regal rights and
functions would at the very moment of demise of the Crown descend on
the young Princess. The Government claimed there was no pressing
necessity, given William IV's strong constitution and temperate habits.
On the division in the Lords, the Government had a majority of 44 –
100 against 56 – but the debate was a declaration of war.[11]

When the new Parliament assembled in the autumn, the new Whig
Prime Minister, Lord Grey, framed a Regency Bill. Princess Victoria
was named, apart from possible offspring of William IV, as heir to the
throne. Should William IV leave an heir, Queen Adelaide would be

Regent; if the heir was still Victoria, the Duchess of Kent would be Regent. Should William IV die leaving Queen Adelaide pregnant, Victoria, if of age, would occupy the throne till her uncle's heir arrived. The Lord Chancellor, introducing the Bill on 15 November, had declared:

> The manner in which Her Royal Highness, the Duchess of Kent, has hitherto discharged her duty in the education of her illustrious offspring – and I speak upon the subject not from vague report, but from accurate information – gives us the best ground to hope most favourably of Her Royal Highness's future conduct. Looking at the past, it is evident we cannot find a better guardian for the time to come.[12]

On hearing the news that the longed-for idea of herself as Regent had become a constitutional possibility, the Duchess burst into tears and proclaimed that this was really her first happy day since she lost the Duke of Kent.

On 3 August 1831 William IV sent a message to Parliament recommending an increased allowance for the Duchess of Kent and the Princess Victoria, to support her as became a presumptive heiress to the Crown. An additional income of 10,000 pounds a year was voted them. The Duchess engaged the Duchess of Northumberland to be the Princess's constant companion, to accompany her on all public occasions and to teach her Court etiquette.

Was the Princess going to take up her place at Court and familiarize herself with its workings – helped by a kindly uncle and a loving aunt? On 26 July 1830 she walked behind Queen Adelaide at a Chapter of the Order of the Garter held at St James's Palace and on 24 February 1831, the day appointed by Queen Adelaide for the celebration of Her Majesty's birthday, she had made her first appearance at a drawing room. Drawing rooms were ceremonial receptions presided over by the Sovereign. There were several every year. Ladies, often débutantes, could only obtain the honour of being presented through someone who had already been presented. In addition, both had to be of unblemished character. This particular drawing room had been the most magnificent since that which had taken place when Princess Charlotte had been presented on the occasion of her marriage. Victoria wore a dress which was simple, modest and becoming. 'She was the object of interest and admiration on the part of all assembled, as she stood on the left of Her Majesty on the throne. The scene was one of the most splendid ever remembered and the future Queen of England contemplated all that passed with much dignity, but with evident interest.'[13] The Duchess saw such events and read such comments with alarm. If she were not careful the projected isolation of the child would break down, Victoria would become the King's heir rather than her mother's daughter. Attendance at Court must be limited and the King must understand that he could not dispose of his young niece as he wished. What better occasion to make this clear than the King's Coronation?

William IV and Queen Adelaide were to be crowned at Westminster Abbey on Thursday 8 September 1831. The King dreaded the occasion. He had tried to persuade his Government that he might well do without the ceremony, but the Prime Minister would not hear of it. William was indeed in the throes of a constitutional revolution. The Parliament elected in 1830 had had to be dissolved following a Cabinet crisis over the Reform Bill, which aimed at widening the franchise. The authority of Parliament had been eroded by half a century of reform agitation; many among the wealthy and powerful rising middle classes were excluded from the benefits of the system; and at the bottom end of society severe economic depression had led to increasing rural rioting and industrial agitation. In March 1831, the first Reform Bill had passed its second reading by a majority of one vote in the best-attended House within living memory, but in April the Tories had defeated the Whig Government in committee and the King, after some hesitation, finally agreed to dissolve Parliament. A second Bill was introduced in June after an election fought on the direct issue of reform. The Bill passed the House of Commons in September – and everyone knew a clash with the Lords was inevitable.

In the middle of all this came the Coronation, and not unnaturally William feared demonstrations. He decided that, given the state of the nation, he would make his Coronation as economical as possible. It cost roughly ten times less than that of his brother George IV. No Coronation banquet was given – though the King did entertain a large party of the royal family and nobility. All this displeased the Tories and the Coronation was derided as the 'half Crown-ation'.

At a time when the King felt he needed support, the Duchess of Kent decided, two days before the event, that neither she nor her daughter would attend the ceremony. *The Times* carried the news and asserted with iteration that the Duchess of Kent had 'refused to attend, yes, refused to attend'. The paper reproved the Duchess, stressed her impertinence and claimed she was unfit to be the guardian of the future Queen. An angry and prolonged discussion arose among the daily newspapers as to the cause of this extraordinary conduct. There were those who, like *The Times*, saw the Duchess as entirely responsible, seeking to spurn the King. Another interpretation was that the refusal rested on the Coronation arrangements: In ordering the Coronation procession on paper, Princess Victoria had been placed after the brothers of the King instead of directly after the King and Queen, which might indicate that the new King sided with the 'salic set' (the party which had been active against Princess Charlotte on the grounds that a woman on the throne would cause severance between the kingdoms of England and Hanover). It was also said that William IV had given precedence to Princess Victoria over her mother, saying she was to be led by the hand by her new lady, the Duchess of Northumberland.[14]

The official explanation given in the House of Commons in reply to an oral question was the delicate state of Victoria's health. The real motives which led to the course adopted by the Duchess are still uncertain. It was not in the interest of King William at such a time to show rifts within his family in public. It seems therefore unlikely that he provoked the Duchess by not giving her daughter her rightful place under the Regency Bill.[15] It is far more likely that the Duchess saw this as an admirable occasion to sever, as much as it lay in her power, the links between Victoria and the King.

Although she refused to allow her daughter to go to Court, the Duchess kept Victoria – and herself – in the public eye by a series of tours. The first took place shortly after George IV's death in the summer of 1830. The Duchess and her suite spent two months at Hollymount in the Malvern hills. On the way there, visits were paid to the famous house of the Marlboroughs at Blenheim, to Stratford, Kenilworth and Warwick, and to Birmingham where several of the big factories were visited. While at Malvern excursions were made to Earl Beauchamp's seat at Madresfield, to Hereford and to Worcester, where the Princess visited the porcelain works. On the return journey she stopped at Badminton and Gloucester, Bath and Stonehenge. Everywhere the Princess was received with great enthusiasm. On 23 October 1830 the Princess opened the Royal Victoria Park at Bath and later the Victoria Drive at Malvern – the first associations of her name with English topography. The Duchess denied she had any other ambition than to show her daughter historic English sites.

From 1832 onwards these tours became more extended. It was on the occasion of one of them that the Duchess gave her daughter a plain-leaved book so that she might record her impressions. The book is dated 31 July 1832 and inscribed, 'This Book Mamma gave me that I might write the journal of my journey to Wales in it. Victoria.' Thus began, at thirteen, the habit of a lifetime. Every day, the child, then the young girl, then the woman recorded her impressions of the day. By the end of her life the Queen had filled well over a hundred volumes. Today we only have the journal intact, as it was written, up to the Queen's accession in 1837. For the following years we have a truncated version of the diary. In 1901, on Victoria's death, her diaries passed into the hands of the Queen's youngest daughter, who was her literary executor. On her mother's instructions she copied out the journal into a series of copy books, omitting anything which might cause pain. As soon as the transcription had been carried out the corresponding manuscript by Queen Victoria was burnt. The copied diary still remains an important source of information but how one wishes the original still existed!

For her younger years we do have the original but the Princess's diary was at this time submitted to her governess and no doubt read by her mother, so it contains impressions of her visits rather than more personal reflections. But these 'progresses', as the King called them, did not please him. Greville tells us that, 'The King has been (not unnaturally) disgusted at the Duchess of Kent's progresses with her daughter through the kingdom, and amongst the rest with her sailings at the Isle of Wight, and the continual popping in the shape of gun salutes to Her Royal Highness!'[16] Since she had the Royal Standard on board, every time the Duchess of Kent passed the navy was obliged to salute her. Lord Grey opened negotiations with the Duchess of Kent to persuade her to waive the salutes of her own accord, and send word to the navy that as she was sailing about for her amusement she would rather they did not salute her whenever she appeared. The negotiations failed, for the Duchess insisted on her right to be saluted. Greville was told 'that Conroy (who is a ridiculous fellow) . . . had said, "that as Her Royal Highness's *confidential adviser*, he could not recommend her to give way on this point." '[17] The King therefore decided to change the regulations. An Order in Council on 3 July provided that the Royal Standard should only be saluted when the King or Queen was on board.

The next subject of dissent concerned the necessity of a country residence for Her Royal Highness the Princess Victoria. The Duchess wrote to the Prime Minister that 'the first rangership or suitable House that may be vacant or could be vacated should be assigned to our use.'[18] The King offered the Palace at Kew as 'a temporary retreat during the present summer'.[19] The Duchess replied that her request concerned a permanent residence – and that for the coming summer she was going to Tunbridge Wells. Lord Melbourne tried to calm things down. The offer of Kew, he said, had not been intended to supersede her request for a permanent residence and His Majesty had a strong desire 'to effect your Royal Highness's object with all convenient speed and in a manner which may be agreeable to your Royal Highness'.[20] In July 1836 the King finally offered the Duchess Kew Palace and told her she might 'make any arrangements she pleases' and that her instructions would be carried out.[21] The Duchess replied that having visited the Palace she found it 'an old house quite unfit for the Princess Victoria and me to occupy, being very inadequate in accommodation and almost destitute of furniture'.[22] She enclosed a letter from Dr Clark declaring the residence most unfit for the maintenance of Her Royal Highness the Princess Victoria. The King expressed his concern, told her that he could offer no other accommodation and recollected that Kew was for many years the summer residence of his 'royal father and mother and of their numerous family'.[23]

Next it was the King the Prime Minister had to pacify. The Duchess of Kent decided to get rid of Victoria's companion, the Duchess of Northumberland, because she was too independent of Conroy and herself. She would be replaced by Flora Hastings, who had become the Duchess of Kent's lady-in-waiting in 1834 and was part of the Conroy set. The Duchess also decided to send away Victoria's governess, Louise Lehzen.

The King was not of this mind. He would communicate only with the Duchess of Northumberland concerning Victoria's imminent confirmation. The Duchess of Kent refused to use this channel. Viscount Melbourne tried to reason with the King. 'Dissensions in the Royal Family', he wrote, 'are always to be deplored; they cannot always be averted, but it appears to Viscount Melbourne that it will be more particularly unfortunate, if discord should arise or betray itself upon a question relating to the Sacred Offices of Religion.'[24] The King replied that he could not yield to the Duchess of Kent without surrendering his authority[25] and would show 'a very bad example to his niece and presumptive successor to the Throne by yielding on this occasion to Her ill advised mother'.[26]

In a fury at the Duchess of Kent's persistant refusal to comply, the King wrote a letter in his own hand to the Bishop of London forbidding the Bishop, as Dean of the Chapels Royal, to allow the Princess to be confirmed in any of them. The Duchess gave in:

under the circumstances in which I am placed by the King, I feel that
although I have been treated in a manner I was quite unprepared to
expect, yet that I owe so much to my child not to delay the confirmation
and also to avoid making the matter a subject of public observation
which in these times, could not fail to be injurious to the Royal Family.'[27]

The confirmation accordingly was to take place in the Chapel Royal of
St James at twelve o'clock on 30 July. The King then wrote to the
Duchess of Kent.

His Majesty trusts if the weather shall continue to prove fair, that the
Duchess of Kent, with her young and *then* perfectly received Christian,
will finish the auspicious day at Kew, with a dinner; and on Saturday,
the first of August, accompany their Majesties to Greenwich Hospital
that the King may show his truly beloved niece the magnificence of the
Thames and the Retreat of those who have bled for their Sovereign and
Country in the British Navy.[28]

But the Duchess would not be disarmed. She refused the invitation on
the grounds that she had lost a beloved sister and that Victoria shared
in her grief for her late aunt. 'Their feelings could not allow them in
such deep mourning to mix in company.'

The confirmation duly took place. The Princess was confirmed by
the Archbishop of Canterbury, assisted by her tutor Dr Davys who had
become Dean of Chester in 1831. Conroy came into the chapel but was
ordered out by William IV – a spurning Conroy never forgave the
King.

The Princess was much affected – by the embarrassment, by the
religious emotion, no doubt, and by the fear that her dear Lehzen, her
bulwark, was to be taken away from her. In a long letter written on the
day of her confirmation, the Duchess told Victoria that her attitude
towards Lehzen must change – in future she was to be treated with
'dignity' and not with friendship. What did this signify if not that
Victoria's will was to be broken? This interpretation was all the more
convincing as Victoria's mother had written: 'Until you are at the age
of either 18 or 21 years . . . you are still confided to the guidance of your
affectionate mother and friend.'[29] But royalty comes of age at eighteen
– so what was the Duchess preparing? Victoria was soon to know.

Meanwhile, however, the Duchess was planning for September a
new and lengthy tour in the north Midlands and the east of England –
first to the ancestral home of the Cecils at Hatfield then to Stamford,
Grantham, Newark, Doncaster and York. After that to Leeds,
Wakefield and Barnsley. Finally to Belvoir Castle and Wentworth

House. The King was against these perambulations, in particular the visit to the musical festival at York where the Princess would be 'exposed to the reception of addresses and counter addresses embodying sentiments of an opposite tendency and would necessarily become the object of party jealousy'.[30] Lord Melbourne tried to dissuade the King from vetoing the visit, on the grounds that the King would be powerless if the Duchess disobeyed. The Duchess, indeed, when told of the King's desire to see her abandon her objectionable intention, replied:

> On what grounds can I be prevented making these visits? I have for years done the same thing – even on a greater scale – and my journeys have been attended with the happiest results to the Princess. ... It requires but one step more to assign the Princess and myself, a limit as to residence to be prisoners at large.

And then came the thinly disguised threats.

> I must therefore entreat your Lordship to consider well that unkindness to us, will only give us additional interest, and the odium will fall back on that Person, who it is no less my duty than my inclination to see shielded from being supposed capable of acting so.[31]

The King decided, since the Duchess would not listen, to appeal to the Princess herself. On 22 August 1835 he addressed her a letter in which he declared:

> I hope the newspapers will not inform me of your travelling this year – I cannot and therefore do not approve of your flying about the Kingdom as you have done the last three years, and which if attempted I must and shall prevent in future. It is your real good and permanent happiness I have really at heart and I therefore write these my sentiments as being the best advice I can give.[32]

Caught in the middle of a great struggle between her uncle the King and her mother, Victoria who was only sixteen tried to convince her mother that they should not go on the great tour of 1835. After a terrible scene on the evening before her departure, Victoria received a long letter from her mother full of reproaches:

> You may imagine that I feel very much disappointed and grieved, that the journey we are to commence tomorrow is not only disagreeable to you, but that it makes you even unhappy; that the fatigue of it will make you ill, that you dislike it.

She went on to explain to her daughter that it was her duty to go on such journeys, to get to know her country and be known by all classes. And, according to her habitual method, after the Duchess's admonitions came the threat.

> I must tell you dearest love, if your conversation with me could be known, that you had not the energy to undertake the journeys or that your views were not enlarged enough to grasp the benefits arising from it, then you would fall in the estimation of the people of this country.[33]

The journey took place and was, as Greville says, a great success. At Burghley there were 'vast crowds of people to see the Princess Victoria'. At Stamford, 'the civil authorities' turned out to escort them, along with 'a procession of different people all very loyal'. The address read to the Duchess talked of the Princess as 'destined to mount the throne of these realms' and 'Conroy handed the answer [to the Duchess], just as the Prime Minister does to the King.' In the evening, on 27 September, there were three hundred people at Burghley at the ball opened by the Princess and Lord Exeter.[34]

Behind the brilliant façade, Victoria was in a state of emotional tension. Throughout the journey she was poorly. On the very first day she 'felt very tired'.[35] This state of exhaustion continued throughout the visit – she could not eat, suffered from backache, had headaches and was generally worn out.

At the end of September the Kensington set repaired to Ramsgate and Uncle Leopold crossed over the water to see his niece and introduce his wife to her. But all through their visit the Princess's health gave trouble. Just after her uncle's departure on 7 October she took a turn for the worse. Her mother thought she was exaggerating her illness to annoy her. No doctor was called, despite the insistence of Lehzen who was simply thought to be on the Princess's side against her mother. The result was a five-week-long illness during which she seems to have been in real danger. Whether the illness was typhoid, tonsilitis or simply collapse from strain has not been elucidated. What is certain is that not only was she not treated, she was also tormented.

During her illness Sir John Conroy tried to get her to sign a paper making him her private secretary. She was, later, to tell Lord Melbourne about it. 'They (Mamma and John Conroy) attempted (for I was still very ill) to make me promise beforehand, which I resisted in spite of my illness and their harshness, my beloved Lehzen supporting me alone.'[36]

The Duchess's conduct, her popularity hunting, her progresses and, above all, the addresses which she received and replied to exasperated the King more and more. On his birthday he told Melbourne:

> I cannot expect to live very long, but I hope that my successor may be of full age when she mounts the throne. I have great respect for the person upon whom, in the event of my death, the Regency would devolve, but I have great distrust of the persons by whom she is surrounded.[37]

His steadfast attachment to Victoria and the manner in which he publicly recognized her on several occasions are much to his credit. When his fourth daughter by his first marriage, Lady Augusta Fitzclarence, was married from Windsor in August 1836 he gave the Princess Victoria's health.

> And now, having given the health of the oldest, I will give that of the youngest member of the Royal Family. I know the interest which the public feel about her, and although I have not seen so much of her as I could have wished, I take no less interest in her, and the more I do see of her, both in public and in private, the greater pleasure it will give me.[38]

Despite these gracious words the Princess, who was sitting opposite, hung her head. The tensions between her mother and the King caused her anxiety and grief.

In the same month, August 1836, things came to a head between them. The King invited the Duchess to Windsor to celebrate the Queen's birthday on the thirteenth and to stay there till his own birthday, which was to be kept privately on the twenty-first and publicly the following day. The Duchess, with studied insolence, declared she wanted to keep her own birthday at Claremont on the fifteenth, made no reference at all to the Queen's birthday but said she would go to Windsor on the twentieth. The King did not reply. On the twentieth he was in London to prorogue Parliament – but sent instructions that they not wait dinner for him at Windsor. After leaving Parliament he went to Kensington Palace and found that the Duchess of Kent had taken over seventeen rooms for which she had applied the preceding year and which he had refused her. He returned to Windsor in a fury. He entered the drawing room at about ten in the evening, the whole party being already assembled there. He went up to Victoria and taking both her hands expressed his joy at seeing her there and his regret that he did not see her more often. Then, turning to the Duchess, he made a low bow and informed her 'that he had just come from Kensington, where he found apartments had been taken possession of not only without his consent, but contrary to his commands, and that he neither understood nor would endure conduct so disrespectful to him. This was said loudly, publicly, and in a tone of serious displeasure.'[39]

This was, however, only the first affront. After dinner on the following day much worse was to come. His Majesty's health was drunk and the King replied in a long speech, including the following tirade.

> I trust in God that my life may be spared for nine months longer, after which period, in the event of my death no regency would take place. I should then have the satisfaction of leaving the royal authority to the personal exercise of that young lady (pointing to the Princess), the heiress presumptive of the Crown, and not in the hands of a person now near me, who is surrounded by evil advisers and who is herself incompetent to act with propriety in the station in which she would be placed. I have no hesitation in saying that I have been insulted – grossly and continually insulted – by that person, but I am determined to endure no longer a course of behaviour so disrespectful to me. Amongst many other things I have particularly to complain of the manner in which that young lady has been kept away from my Court; she has been repeatedly kept from my drawing-rooms, at which she ought always to have been present, but I am fully resolved that this shall not happen again. I would have her know that I am King, and I am determined to make my authority respected, and for the future I shall insist and command that the Princess do upon all occasions appear at my Court, as it is her duty to do.[40]

The effect of this philippic was electrifying. The Queen looked distressed and embarrassed, Princess Victoria burst into tears, the company was aghast. The Duchess announced her immediate departure and ordered her carriage – but she was finally prevailed on to remain until the following day. The King, by choosing to rebuke his sister-in-law in public, before a hundred people, undoubtedly put himself in the wrong. He insulted her grossly and publicly – and in the presence of her daughter. He insulted her in *his* house where she was his guest.

The King did, however, have some excuse. It was he and not Uncle Leopold who first realized that the Kensington system was weighing heavily on the young girl. Leopold had advised his niece to be very wary of the King and his Court.

> I hope you were very prudent; I cannot disguise from you, that though the inhabitants are good-natured people, still that I think you want all your natural caution with them. Never permit yourself to be induced to tell them any opinion or sentiment of yours which is beyond the sphere of common conversation and its ordinary topics. Bad use would be made of

it against yourself, and you cannot in that subject be too much guarded. I know well the people we have to deal with. I am extremely impartial, but I shall also always be equally watchful.[41]

In April of the following year – with a view to her majority – Leopold told Victoria what she should do about her establishment. 'Your position, having a Mother with whom you very naturally remain, would render a *complete* independent establishment perhaps matter of *real* inconvenience.'[42] He suggested something on the model of what Charlotte had had. But above all he insisted that she not let the King choose the people he put about her. 'Resist mildly but positively any nomination of a Gentleman other than the Dean; it is highly probable that any other would be put about you as a spy, and turn out at all events a great bore, which is better avoided.'[43]

Leopold misjudged the King greatly. On 18 May – her eighteenth birthday was on the 24th – the King wrote his niece a letter which was to be placed in her hands and hers alone. In it the King told the Princess that it was his intention when she came of age to apply to Parliament for 10,000 pounds a year to be 'entirely in her power and disposal'. She was also to appoint her own Keeper of the Privy Purse and to form her own establishment if she wished. This emancipation of the Princess was not to the Duchess's taste. She coerced her daughter into replying. Victoria had at first resisted. 'Felt very miserable and agitated,' she wrote in her journal, 'did not go down to dinner.'[44] On the following morning she copied out the draft prepared by Conroy and her mother. In it she accepted the grant but insisted on her youth and inexperience, which would not allow her to deal with it herself, and asked for the money to be given to her mother. The King on receiving the reply declared, 'Victoria has not written that letter.'[45] This was true, as Victoria declared in a memorandum dictated to Lehzen explaining exactly what had happened.[46] The King later wrote to Lord Melbourne:

> His Majesty wholly acquits His Niece, the Princess Victoria, of having any share in these unbecoming Transactions. He is convinced indeed that she has not been permitted to have a voice in any part of them and that in the Letter she addressed to the King she was made to write that which did not accord with Her own wishes.[47]

As for the Duchess, she wrote to Melbourne declaring that, as she was hostile to any separation of her daughter's pecuniary concerns from hers, she 'begged therefore again most respectfully but most firmly to decline the offer made to us'.[48]

On 24 May the Princess celebrated her eighteenth birthday and attained her legal majority. 'We came home', she wrote in her journal, 'at twenty minutes to two in the morning. The courtyards and the street were crammed when we went to the ball, and the anxiety of the people to see poor stupid me was very great, and I must say I am very touched by it, and feel proud, which I always have done of my country and the English nation.'[49]

Despite the Kensington system and the tiring 'progresses', Victoria's life was not all tears. She had a love of life, a great capacity for love and friendship and an ability to keep her friendships alive through letter-writing. An example of her loyalty and affection can be seen during the visit of Feodora with her husband in 1834. Victoria had not seen her for six years. When she had left England Victoria had been only seven. But through the years the half-sisters had written to one another. Feodora sent her sister dried flowers, little drawings, little books of views, and Victoria sent her paper dolls which Feodora sent back painted. Victoria wrote regularly. 'I am delighted', she noted in 1834, 'to hear that you do not dislike receiving my letters, as in writing them I almost imagine I am speaking to you.'[50] When Feodora had her daughter Eliza in 1830, Victoria was godmother and although she could not go to the christening, Ernest promised his little son would drink her health in milk! From then on Victoria made little things for her niece such as a cashmere frock trimmed with red braiding.

When Feodora came to England the two girls immediately slipped back into their earlier intimacy, even though Feodora now had a husband and two children. 'I must tell you', wrote Feodora once she had gone back to Germany, 'that the thought often tormented me that we two should be strangers to each other; for you were such a child when I left England. . . . but now I can love you as a sister and a friend, for the accordance of heart and mind attaches me much more than the feelings of relationship alone.'[51] When she left, Princess Victoria found the separation quite unbearable. 'I clasped her in my arms, and kissed her and cried as if my heart would break, so did she, dearest Sister. We then tore ourselves from each other in the deepest grief.'[52] For the rest of the morning Victoria sobbed and cried. She continued to write to Feodora regularly – mostly to tell her that she had not much to say, for her life was very dull. In 1837 she wrote typically, 'My letter will, I fear, be short and stupid, as I have literally nothing of the news kind to tell you.'[53] She could only tell her how much she missed her. 'God knows how I wish I could embrace you *en personne* and tell you *de vive voix* how I love you.'[54]

More important for her preparation as Queen was the loving correspondence she kept up with Uncle Leopold. He it was who early on insisted that her proximity to the throne meant she must prepare herself. On her thirteenth birthday he wrote: 'By the dispensation of Providence you are destined to fill a most eminent station; to fill it *well* must now become your study.' And he insisted that she would always find in him 'that faithful friend which he has proved to you from your earliest infancy, and whenever you feel yourself in want of support or advice call on him with perfect confidence.'[55] His first aim was to insist on the qualities a monarch must have. On her fourteenth birthday he noted that the pastimes of childhood must now be mixed with more serious things. 'Now comes the time when the judgement must form itself, when the character requires attention; in short when the young tree takes the shape which it retains afterwards through life.'[56] She must therefore give up some of her time to 'reflection' and 'self-examination'. Every evening she was to examine the events of the day and her own motives. 'Persons in high situations must particularly guard themselves against selfishness and vanity.' The aim was to learn to know oneself, to judge oneself. He insisted, too, on the fact that rulers had less stable situations than before.

> The position of what is generally called great people has of late become extremely difficult. They are more attacked and calumniated and judged with less indulgence than private individuals. What they have lost in this way they have not by any means regained in any other. Ever since the revolution of 1790 they are much less secure than they used to be, and the transition from sovereign power to absolute want has been as frequent as sudden.[57]

The Princess must therefore not be intoxicated by greatness and success, nor unduly cast down by misfortune.

In her studies he insisted on the importance of history – which could in her case replace the practical knowledge it would be difficult for her to have until she was old.[58] But she must guard against party spirit, which ran high and often coloured the writing of history. 'Our times resemble most those of the Protestant reformation; then people were moved by religious opinions as they are now by political passions.'[59] French history was richer than English because more authenticated memoirs were available. He particularly recommended her to study the period from before the accession of Henry IV of France to the throne till the end of the minority of Louis XIV: 'after that period, though interesting, matters have a character which is more personal, and therefore less applicable to the present time';[60] though she could study with profit the intrigues and favouritism, and the role of Madame de Maintenon who was 'nearly the cause of the destruction of France'. He particularly recommended the Memoirs of Sully.

In her reply Victoria asks him to send the Memoirs as he had proposed and tells him what she is at present reading – Russell's *Modern Europe* (which in a series of letters from a nobleman to his son deals in five volumes with the rise of modern kingdoms down to the Peace of Westphalia in 1648) and Clarendon's *History of the Rebellion*. She tells him that she likes 'reading different authors, of different opinions, by which means I learn not to lean on one particular side.'[61] When he sends her a critical account of the political character of Queen Anne, she writes back: 'I am much obliged to you, dear Uncle, for the extract about Queen Anne, but must beg you, as you have sent me to show what a Queen *ought not* to be, that you will send me what a Queen *ought to be*.'[62]

With Uncle Leopold she was already discussing politics. As was to be the case throughout her life, increasingly so as her own children spread out throughout Europe, Victoria tended to see foreign affairs in terms of the personalities she knew and the friends she cherished. The year 1836 was a disturbing one on the continent. The succession in Spain was disputed – on the one hand Isabella, daughter of the late King who had done away with Salic law, on the other Don Carlos, the late King's brother. Victoria's sympathies, as indeed England's and France's, were with Isabella. 'The news were rather better yesterday and the day before. The Christinos had gained a victory over the Carlists. I take a great interest in the whole of this unfortunate affair.'[63]

Events in Portugal also interested her. The country was only just emerging from a war of succession which had opposed Dom Miguel, the younger son of the late King John VI, and Donna Maria, Dom Pedro's daughter. Dom Pedro had abdicated his throne in order to become Emperor of Brazil, but he was expelled from Brazil and had returned to recover the throne for his daughter. Donna Maria, only a few weeks older than Victoria, thus found herself on the throne but surrounded by revolutionary agitation. She had lost her first husband, the Duc de Leuchtenberg, and was married in April 1836 – at seventeen – to Prince Ferdinand of Saxe-Coburg, a great favourite with Princess Victoria. In 1836 the young Queen had appointed her husband, Prince Ferdinand, Commander-in-Chief of the Portuguese army. It was a highly unpopular move which caused the army to mutiny. The Queen was obliged to accept a radical constitution in the place of Dom Pedro's constitutional charter. In November the Queen made a countermove, believing she had popular support – she dismissed her ministers. She had, however, to give up the struggle and accede to revolutionary requirements. Sà da Bandeira became Prime Minister and the Queen was virtually a captive in her own country. Victoria wrote to her uncle:

> I cannot tell you how distressed I was by the late unfortunate *contre-révolution manquée* at Lisbon. . . . [Lord Palmerston] speaks in the highest terms of our beloved Ferdinand, which proves that he becomes daily more and more worthy of his arduous situation, and says the Queen's situation 'is better than it was', less bad than it might have been 'after such an affair', and not so good as it would have been had poor Donna Maria waited patiently till all was ripe for action.[64]

Later Victoria condemned Donna Maria more categorically. 'She is unfortunately surrounded by a *camarilla* who poison her ears, and fetter all her actions; poor soul! she is much to be pitied.'[65] And she added later: 'Poor, good Donna Maria! I feel much for her; her education was one of the worst that could be.'[66]

In this world where thrones were endangered, the future Queen Victoria rejoiced when all went well.

> I cannot say how happy I am that the *entrée publique* into Paris succeeded so well, and that the dear King was so well received; I trust he will now at last be rewarded for all the troubles and anxiety he has had ever since 1830. Lord Palmerston said that the French say that *l'assassinat est hors de mode*. I hope and trust in Heaven that this may be the case, and for ever!'[67]

With regard to internal politics Uncle Leopold's advice can be summed up in a series of precepts. *First* use the Church to consolidate the State. In England the Sovereign is the Head of the Church, Protestantism a state religion.

> In times like the present, when the Crown is already a good deal weakened, I believe that it is of importance to maintain as much as possible this state of affairs, and I believe that you will do well, whenever an occasion offers itself to do so without affectation, to express your sincere interest for the Church, and that you comprehend its position and count upon its good will.

Secondly, that the Crown is ever the loser when violence intervenes. When people act, as they so often do, out of passion they are often injurious to their own interests. The Reform Bill is an excellent

example. 'If the Tory part of Parliament could have brought themselves to act without passion, much in the reform of Parliament might
have been settled much more in conformity with their best interests.'[68]
When matters are difficult to settle, 'the poor Crown is more or less the
loser . . . as it generally ends with the abolition of something or other
which might have proved useful for the carrying on of Government.'[69]

The last precept was that a monarch must proceed with caution for it
is easier to do than to undo. 'In high positions it is excessively difficult
to retrace a false move to get out of a mistake; and there exists very
rarely, except in time of war and civil feuds, a necessity for an
immediate decision.'[70] King Leopold therefore counsels Victoria to
begin by taking everything as the King left it.

All was not, however, politics and counselling. Victoria told Uncle
Leopold how much she enjoyed her singing. 'I sing regularly every
evening, as I think it better to do so every day to keep the voice
manageable. Oh my beloved Uncle, could you join us how delightful
that would be! How I should delight in singing with you all our
favourite things from *La Gazza, Otello, Il Barbiere* etc.'[71] And how eager
she was to return to London after six months at Claremont. 'I am sure
you will stand by me for my having my season fully as you may
understand that my operatic and Terpsichorean feelings are pretty
strong, now that the season is returning . . . '[72]

Victoria's other great pleasure, apart from writing and receiving
letters, was the theatre. Her upbringing was in this respect surprisingly
liberal and not at all 'Victorian'. She saw her first play probably in
1828 – before she was in her teens. It was *Charles XII* by Planché. Her
favourite art, however, was opera. She became acquainted early on
with the greatest singers of the early nineteenth century: Malibran and
Persiani among the ladies, Tamburini and Lablache among the men.
Her favourite singer in her youth was Giulia Grisi, who was only
twenty-two when she first performed in London in 1834. 'She is a most
beautiful singer and actress,' the Princess noted, 'and is likewise very
young and pretty.'[73] The Princess followed her so closely that she noted
when she was tired or changed her hairstyle![74] One of the highlights of
her youth was the day when she was almost sixteen, when she actually
met her heroine. She found her quite beautiful. Grisi was quiet, ladylike
and unaffected and became the idol of the young Princess. Such crushes
of adolescents are not rare – especially among children who do not
receive sufficient affection.

Quite different was her association with Luigi Lablache, the bass
baritone. She begged to study singing with him, and on 19 April 1836

had her first lesson. She was to continue for twenty years. He came every summer season when he was at the King's Theatre, arriving in April. She studied with him until two years before his death in 1858.

Animals were also a great comfort to the young Princess, especially her dogs and her horses. She reproaches Feodora with never enquiring about Dash, who 'was so much attached to you, is greatly improved in beauty; but as for his manners I fear they are not so, for his voice is shriller than ever, and he hunts the sheep dreadfully.'[75] Her interest in horses began in 1831, when she first began to learn to ride at the riding school in her riding habit of dark blue cloth and a cap. Another of her great joys was the day at the Ascot races when she betted with the King and won, and was given a beautiful horse. 'She is a dark chestnut mare, as quiet as a lamb and excessively pretty; she is called Taglioni; I have ridden her three times and her paces are delightful.'[76]

As the Princess grew older so the prospect of her being betrothed became discussed in the press. As early as May 1828, when the Princess was only nine, one newspaper noted:

> It is rumoured and confidently believed in the highest circles, that Prince George, Son of His Royal Highness the Duke of Cumberland, will speedily be betrothed to his royal Cousin, the Princess Victoria, daughter of the late Duke of Kent; the Prince is a fine healthy boy, in his tenth year, and the Princess, a lovely child, within a few days of the same age.[77]

To its credit *The Times* came out, not against this particular match, but against the very idea of such a betrothal.

> In barbarous and brutal times it was not uncommon to unite infants of high birth by what may be called a prenatural, if not a preter-natural marriage; but the age of barbarism, we should suppose, is extinct, and the sacred ritual of our church is totally incompatible with any application to an union such as that which is rumoured or insinuated.[78]

The paper therefore recommended that the whole matter sink into oblivion for some eight or ten years.

In 1829 another suitor was notwithstanding found by the press, an even more unlikely one: the Duke of Orléans. The Duke's visit to England enabled the press to give imaginary substance to the idea.[79] The following year the French newspapers, with a flair for unlikely gossip concerning the English royal family some have not lost, put forward an even more preposterous rumour. 'Several journals have spoken of a plan for a marriage between Prince Leopold of Saxe-Coburg, and his Niece, the daughter of the Duke of Kent.'[80] The

British newspaper reporting on this stressed that marriages between uncles and nieces were not only offensive to English manners but expressly prohibited by law.

When the Princess was fourteen, newspapers in Belgium rumoured that negotiations were afoot for her marriage to the eldest son of the Prince of Orange;[81] while this was contradicted in Britain, it was hinted that a journey of the Duke of Orléans to England was intimately connected with the Princess. The Court journal itself noted, 'One of the flying rumours of the day is that the illustrious guest who honours the capital with his presence is charged to propose a royal hymeneal alliance between his brother the Duke of Nemours and the Princess Victoria.'[82]

The next suitor woven into the tapestry of political romances was the Duke of Brunswick, despite his age: 'to be sure there is some difference between the ages of the Duke and the young Princess; but a few years are counted nothing in affairs of the heart.'[83] More important than his age was that he was the son of the brother of Queen Caroline, George IV's eccentric wife, and seemed to have inherited her eccentricity.

Details of this congress of suitors make frivolous reading down the years. But the question had its serious side. Victoria's husband would not unnaturally play an important role in England should she become Queen. This had been a possibility in 1830, by 1836 it had become a strong probability. King William was over seventy, his health declining fast. The Court party and the Kensington set now each produced their candidates for marriage. For William IV the ideal nephew-in-law would be one of the sons of the Prince of Orange, the eldest son of the King of the Netherlands, England's hereditary ally and of a staunch Protestant branch. The Prince of Orange had the additional advantage of thoroughly disliking Victoria's uncle King Leopold, whom William IV also detested. The Prince of Orange had more reason for, as he used to say, 'Here is a man who has taken both my wife [Charlotte] and my Kingdom [Belgium].'[84]

Lord Melbourne was not in favour of a Dutch marriage. He told Sir Herbert Taylor:

> If the Princess Victoria must marry a Foreign Prince it appears to me very doubtful whether Holland is not the last power, with which Great Britain ought in prudence to connect herself. Holland is too powerful and too important from her situation not to be engaged and compromised in any continental struggle which may arise of any magnitude and she is at the same time too small and too weak to defend herself.

Into the bargain, added Lord Melbourne, if the King imposed such a marriage he would deprive the King of the Belgians of the support of Britain and endanger his throne. As the Coburgs 'appear to act together pretty firmly and unitedly for the furtherance of their general interests', the Duchess would, thought Lord Melbourne, support her brother, and Victoria, who looked on King Leopold as a father, would do likewise.[85] The Duchess of Kent was – as was King Leopold – in favour of a German union.

The two sides began in 1836 to jockey for position. William IV invited the Prince of Orange and his two sons to visit him. The Duchess of Kent urged Ernest, Duke of Saxe-Coburg and Gotha, and his two sons, Princes Ernest and Albert, to visit her in Kensington. After a great tussle, William IV agreed to receive the Duke of Saxe-Coburg with all the attentions due to his high station and his connections with the royal family. Leopold for his part let off steam in a letter to Victoria: 'I am really *astonished* at the conduct of your old Uncle the King; this invitation of the Prince of Orange and his sons, this forcing him upon others is very extraordinary.' One wonders what was so extraordinary in the King inviting his relatives to England. Leopold says that he has had a half-official communication – whatever that may be – from England insinuating that it would be '*highly* desirable that the visit of *your* relatives *should not take place this year – qu'en dites vous?*' Then, really working himself up, and quite forgetting that the King's relatives were also Victoria's, he went on: 'The relations of the Queen and the King, therefore, to the God-knows-what degree, are to come in shoals and rule the land, when *your relations* are to be *forbidden* the country.' Surpassing himself in exaggeration Leopold incited his niece to rebel.

> Really and truly I never saw anything like it, and I hope it will *rouse your spirit*; now that slavery is even abolished in the British Colonies, I do not comprehend *why your lot alone should be kept, a white little slavey* in England, for the pleasure of the Court, who never bought you, as I am not aware of their having gone to any expense on that head, or the King's even having spent *a sixpence for your existence*.[86]

In May 1836 the Princess met all four young men. The first to arrive, with the Prince of Orange, were his sons William and Alexander. Whether because her uncle had put her against them or because they were simply not her style, she wrote to her uncle, 'The boys are both very plain and have a mixture of Kalmuck and Dutch in their faces, moreover they look heavy, dull and frightened and are not at all prepossessing. So much for the Oranges, dear Uncle.'[87] The Coburg princes she found more to her taste. 'They are both very amiable, kind and good. Albert is very handsome, which Ernest is not, but he has a most good natured countenance.'[88]

In fact the visit did not go very well. Prince Albert was not used to Court life. He was invited to balls, dinners and concerts, obliged to remain up till one or two in the morning. For a time he collapsed completely – first of all on 23 May he retired early, then at the ball in honour of the Princess's majority, 'after being but a short while in the ball room and having only danced twice, [he] turned as pale as ashes; and we all feared he might faint.'[89] He had then to keep to his room for the next two days. 'I am sorry to say', Victoria wrote to Leopold on 24 May, 'that we have an invalid in the house, in the person of Albert.'[90] Victoria was delighted with all this dressing up. 'I wore a plume and a train for the first time ... ' she wrote to Feodora. 'There were more than 3,000 people.'[91]

Albert found all these festivities too much for him. 'The climate of this country, the different way of living and the late hours, do not agree with me,' he wrote to his stepmother. He complained that the levées of the King were 'long and fatiguing', that at the first concert he had had to 'stand till two o'clock' in the morning and that another concert on the King's birthday had lasted till one o'clock. 'You can', he added, 'well imagine that I had many hard battles to fight against sleepiness during these late entertainments.' His cousin he mentions in passing, almost as an afterthought. 'Dear Aunt is very kind to us and does everything she can to please us, and our cousin also is very amiable.'[92] Here indeed was no love at first sight.

Victoria was not swept off her feet either. In the week after the great festivities she had sung duets with Albert and found that he loved music, she had conversed with him and found him agreeable. She had, however, been told that Leopold intended her to marry Albert. As a genuinely good niece, convinced of her uncle's wisdom, she accepted his choice, for the moment unquestioningly. When the visit was over she wrote a few telling lines to Leopold.

> I must thank you, my beloved Uncle, for the prospect of great happiness you have contributed to give me in the person of dear Albert. Allow me, then, my dearest Uncle, to tell you how delighted I am with him, and how much I like him in every way. He possesses every quality that could be desired to render me perfectly happy. He is so sensible, so kind, and so good, and so amiable too. He has, besides, the most pleasing and delightful exterior and appearance you can possibly see.[93]

She begged her uncle to take care of the health of one now so dear to her. Albert was pleasing to her, but not to the point of wanting him to stay longer or envisaging an early marriage.

Why then did Victoria acquiesce so easily? One reason no doubt was that Leopold had chosen as his emissary to convey his wishes her good Baroness Lehzen – who had helped her resist the pressure put on her by her mother and the dreaded Conroy. They had tried to make her promise to put him at the head of her affairs when she came to the throne. Another reason no doubt was the fact that when her suitors were there life was all gaiety, parties and dancing – and perhaps she believed marriage would make this quasi-permanent. She was moreover only seventeen, an age when one dreams of romance. What better to dream of than an absent Prince not devoid of qualities? Most important of all, Victoria's pent-up emotions, her lack of love, caused her to centre her affections on Leopold. 'I love him so very very much,' she confided in her journal. 'He is *Il mio secondo padre* or rather *solo padre!* for he is indeed like my real father, as I have none!'[94]

Officially nothing was as yet decided, and suitors from abroad continued to present themselves. In May 1837 came a letter from Berlin from William Russell. He asked whether it would be agreeable to the Duchess of Kent that Prince Adelbert of Prussia, the son of Prince William, 'should place himself on the list of those who pretend to the hand of Her Royal Highness the Princess Victoria', and said what satisfaction her consent would give the Court of Berlin.[95] The Duchess replied that the Princess would not marry until she was much older.[96] Her reply was curt and so incensed the King that he had his private secretary write to Melbourne. 'The King has ordered me to repeat to your Lordship that nothing will induce Him to consent to the marriage of the Princess Victoria to a Prince of Coburg.'[97]

By the spring of 1837 King William's health was failing; he was languid and very weak. He had, however, the satisfaction of seeing Victoria reach her majority. The cares of state had weighed heavily on him and the great change in habits they had entailed had worn him out. In the last months he did everything with great weariness. Too weak to walk, he attended to all matters of state from a wheelchair. When he died on 20 June 1837 at the age of seventy-two he had reigned seven years. He had presided over the greatest nineteenth-century constitutional change – the widening of the franchise – and survived long enough for Victoria to be almost a month past her legal majority.

He was more lamented than his predecessor George IV had been.

His integrity was praised, if not his intelligence; his simplicity, if not his grandeur. *The Times* treated him in death as in life and was perhaps nearest to a just evaluation of the man.

> The events of his life afford no fit material for the biographer; they partake so much of the commonplace of history. The simplicity of William the Fourth's career before his accession to the Crown corresponds with that of his original mind and disposition. There was no involution or complexity in either. He met with no adventures on a grand scale; he displayed no gross, nor great, nor memorable attributes. There was little guile in his nature nor obliquity in his course.[98]

As for Victoria, while the King was almost at the end of his last illness she wrote to Leopold, 'Poor old man! I feel sorry for him; he was always personally kind to me, and I should be ungrateful and devoid of feeling if I did not remember this.' But the prospect of becoming Queen did not daunt her.

> I look forward to the event which it seems is likely to occur soon, with calmness and quietness; I am not alarmed at it, and yet I do not suppose myself quite equal to all.[99]

5

Victoria Regina

King William died at Windsor Castle at twelve minutes past two on Tuesday 20 June 1837. Almost immediately the Archbishop of Canterbury (Dr Howley) and the Lord Chamberlain (the Marquess Conyngham) left Windsor for Kensington Palace to break the news to Victoria, now Queen. Arriving very early, around five o'clock in the morning, they knocked and rang and had great difficulty in rousing the porter at the gate. Once they had been admitted into the courtyard, they were again kept waiting. Then they were admitted to one of the lower rooms and again left to their own devices. After some time they rang the bell and insisted that they had come on business of importance – they were then informed that it was too early to disturb the Princess! They then said:

> We are come on business of State to the Queen and even her sleep must give way to that.

Victoria takes up the story:

> I was awoke at 6 o'clock by Mamma who told me that the Archbishop of Canterbury and Lord Conyngham were here and wished to see me. I got out of bed and went into my sitting-room (only in my dressing-gown) and *alone* and saw them.[1]

Why did the messengers come so speedily? Was it the fear that if the news of the King's death got abroad there might be an attempt not to allow Victoria – a mere girl – to reign? Certainly Uncle Leopold had envisaged opposition but comforted himself with the idea that only Victoria could offer the Whig Government 'any durability'.[2] With the possible exception of the Duke of Sussex no other member of the royal family could offer them half as much. Added to that was the fact that if they refused Victoria, the immediate successor would be the Duke of Cumberland, who, Leopold believed, would be 'enough to frighten them into the most violent attachment' for the young Queen. With the situation in Portugal and Spain so difficult for their young heiresses one can understand King Leopold's anxiety.

The situation in Britain was, however, very different. Within Parliament the Reform Bill of 1832 had led to the reinforcement of a two-party system – for to secure power it was now necessary for both Whigs and Tories to widen their social basis. The aristocratic factions of Whigs and Tories were already giving way to the liberal and conservative parties, and this movement was gradually strengthened throughout Victoria's reign. Perhaps even more important at the moment of the succession was the fact that these British parties were not class parties. The division of opinion was vertical rather than horizontal. Between 1832 and 1846 the Whigs were incarnated by Lord Melbourne, the Tories by Sir Robert Peel.

It was from Lord Melbourne, the Whig Prime Minister, that Victoria received the following note after breakfast:

> Viscount Melbourne presents his humble duty to your Majesty and being aware that your Majesty has already received the melancholy intelligence of the death of his late Majesty, will do himself the honour of waiting upon your Majesty a little before 9 this morning. Viscount Melbourne has desired the Marquis of Lansdowne to name eleven as the hour for the meeting of the Council.[3]

This, her first Privy Council was held in the red saloon. When Melbourne duly arrived at nine the Queen informed him that it was her intention to 'retain him and the rest of the present Ministry at the head of affairs and that it could not be in better hands than his.'[4]

In so doing she was following the precepts so carefully laid down by her uncle, King Leopold, who had written to her three days before her accession, telling her exactly what she should do after the King's death:

> The moment you get official communication of it, you will entrust Lord Melbourne with the office of retaining the present Administration as your Ministers. . . . The fact is that the present Ministers are those who will serve you, personally with the greatest sincerity and, I trust, attachment.[5]

After Melbourne had kissed hands he read the Queen the Declaration which he had written, and she was to read to the Privy Council two hours later.

He then left her but returned before the time of the Council 'to teach her her lesson'[6] which he himself had had explained to him by the diarist Charles Greville – who was also Clerk of the Council. Melbourne asked her if she wanted to enter the Council room accompanied by the great officers of state – but she preferred to go in alone. This was to be Victoria's first great test as Queen. 'Her extreme youth and inexperience, and the ignorance of the world concerning her, naturally excited intense curiosity to see how she would act on this trying occasion, and there was a considerable assemblage at the Palace, notwithstanding the short notice which was given.'[7]

Victoria waited in a room adjoining the Council, to which some 220 Privy Councillors had been summoned. A small delegation – composed of the two Royal Dukes, Cumberland and Sussex, the two Archbishops, Canterbury and York, the Chancellor and the Prime Minister Melbourne – went to the Queen to announce to her, officially, the death of William IV. The Queen received them, alone, in the adjoining room. They then returned to the Council room and the proclamation was read. Then the doors were thrown open and the Queen entered. She was dressed in a plainly made black bombazine dress, drawn in tightly to the waist with a long skirt stiffening out at the feet. She bowed to the Lords, took her seat and then read the declaration which Lord Melbourne had written, 'in a clear, distinct, and audible voice'.[8] It was short, and in Victoria's opinion 'a very fine'[9] declaration. In it, after a brief mention of the loss to the nation of the King and the support she herself would seek from Divine Providence, came the declaration of adherence to the unwritten constitution of parliamentary monarchy:

> I place my firm reliance upon the wisdom of Parliament and upon the loyalty and affection of My People. I esteem it also a peculiar advantage that I succeed to a sovereign whose constant regard for the rights and liberties of his subjects and whose desire to promote the amelioration of the laws and institutions of the country have rendered his name the object of general attachment and veneration.[10]

It only remained for her to uphold the established religion, and religious tolerance, and to declare the monarchy above the class struggle:

> It will be my unceasing study to maintain the reformed religion as by law established, securing at the same time to all the full enjoyment of religious liberty and I shall steadily protect the rights and promote to the utmost of my power the happiness and welfare of all classes of my subjects.[11]

The Queen, once she had read her speech and taken and signed the oath for the security of the Church of Scotland, swore in the Privy Councillors. First came the two royal Dukes by themselves – Cumberland and Sussex. The Duke of Cambridge was not present as he was in Hanover. As these two old men, her uncles, knelt before her, swearing allegiance and kissing her hand, 'I saw her', Greville wrote, 'blush up to the eyes as if she felt the contrast between their civil and their natural relations, and this was the only sign of emotion which she evinced. Her manner towards them was graceful and engaging.'[12] She was perfectly natural, kissed them both and even rose from her chair and moved towards the Duke of Sussex, who was too infirm to reach her.

As the multitude of men were sworn in and kissed her hand one after the other she did not speak to any of them, nor make the slightest difference in her manner to any Councillor of any party. Once again the good advice of Leopold had stood her in good stead. 'Your advice is most excellent', she wrote to him on the eve of her accession, 'and you may depend upon it I shall make use of it; I follow it, as also what Stockmar says. I never showed myself openly to belong to any party and I do not belong to any part.'[13] Not even Greville, who 'particularly watched her when Melbourne and the Ministers and the Duke of Wellington and Peel approached her',[14] could see her preferences reflected in a smile or a gesture. The only thing he noted was that from time to time she looked at Lord Melbourne for instructions. Under those watchful eyes, she behaved altogether 'with perfect calmness and self-possession but at the same time with a graceful modesty and propriety particularly interesting and ingratiating'.[15] Peel told Greville that he was amazed at her manner and behaviour, her deep sense of her situation and her modesty allied to her firmness. While the Duke of Wellington declared that if she had been his own daughter he could not have desired to see her perform her part better. Even the redoubtable Tory Privy Councillor Croker was subjugated:

> Her voice, which is naturally beautiful, was clear and untroubled and her eye was bright and calm, neither bold nor downcast, but firm and soft. There was a blush on her cheek which made her look both handsome and more interesting; and certainly she *did* look as interesting and handsome as any young lady I ever saw.[16]

Creevey, too, thought her 'perfection.'[17] She presided over the Council on the following day with as much ease as if she had been doing nothing else all her life. Greville drew a thumbnail portrait of her:

She looked very well, and though so small in stature, and without much pretension to beauty, the gracefulness of her manner and the good expression of her countenance give her on the whole a very agreeable appearance, and with her youth inspire an excessive interest in all who approach her, and which I can't help feeling myself.[18]

The coming of a woman to the throne did make two changes: one inevitable, the other a reflection of the vision of women in the nineteenth century. First the Salic law, which was the law in Hanover, forbade a woman to mount the throne there. Since 1714 when George, the Elector of Hanover, became King George I of England, British sovereigns had ruled Hanover as well. The kingdom now passed to the Queen's uncle, next heir after her to the English throne – Ernest, Duke of Cumberland. The dissolution of the union was readily agreed in both countries. It was not, however, welcomed by Victoria's youngest uncle, the Duke of Cambridge, who had been Viceroy of Hanover, standing in for the English King for twenty-one years. His brother, the new King of Hanover, out of sympathy with his own family, jealous of his young niece, was to be a reactionary unpopular ruler, revoking constitutional government.

The second change Queen Victoria's accession was to bring is related to the criminal law. When capital sentences were pronounced at the Old Bailey it was the sovereign who, at the close of each session, gave his final judgment. This task was judged repugnant for a woman, and a new law was passed transferring the examination of petitions affecting capital offenders to the Home Secretary.[19]

The proclamation of accession had declared that 'the High and Mighty Princess Alexandrina Victoria is now, by the death of our late Sovereign William the Fourth, of happy memory, become our only lawful and rightful liege Lady Alexandrina Victoria I, Queen of Great Britain and Ireland ... '[20] Her name had long been a sore point. She told Uncle Leopold in 1836, 'You are aware, I believe, that about a year after the accession of the present King there was a desire to change my favourite and dear name Victoria to that of Charlotte.'[21] The idea had first been mooted by the King early in 1831 on the grounds that the name was not English, nor even German, but of French origin and that it had never been known to be used in England. In the course of the parliamentary debate on the Duchess of Kent's income in August 1831, one Member suggested changing the Princess's name to Elizabeth, which it was claimed would be more in accordance with the feelings of the people. The subject gave rise to dissension between King William and the Duchess of Kent – whose Christian name was Victoire, which may well explain King William's desire to change his niece's name.

The Archbishop of Canterbury affirmed that no archbishop or bishop could change at confirmation the name given at baptism, but that it might legally be possible to change it by Act of Parliament. The idea was finally dropped and the Princess remained officially Alexandrina Victoria.

On her first day as Queen she signed the Privy Council register as 'Victoria' and had all the papers which had been prepared with her two names changed. Alexandrina was to be omitted.

On this momentous twentieth day of June, Victoria continued as always throughout her life to write letters and to write her journal. Both are revealing. The first two letters she wrote, straight after breakfast, were to Uncle Leopold and Feodora – they were both very short. To her 'dearest, most beloved Uncle' she addressed 'two words only' at half-past eight in the morning to tell him the King had expired and that she was expecting Lord Melbourne almost immediately. She signed herself 'your devoted and attached Niece, Victoria R.'[22]

To Feodora she wrote, 'Dearest Feodora, two words only to tell you that the poor King died this morning at 12 minutes past 2, that I am well, and that I remain for life your devoted attached sister V. R.'[23] This note not only told her sister the news, it also let her know that the newly acquired situation had done nothing to change their loving, sisterly relationship. Her only other letter was to the Queen Dowager – William IV's widow, who had asked to be permitted to remain at Windsor till after the funeral. Victoria wrote her 'a letter couched in the kindest terms, begging her to consult nothing but her own health and convenience, and to remain at Windsor just as long as she pleases.'[24] Her journal shows a touching mixture of enthusiastic anticipation and humility on this the first day of her reign.

> Since it has pleased Providence to place me in this station, I shall do my utmost to fulfil my duty towards my country; I am very young and perhaps in many though not in all things, inexperienced, but I am sure that very few have more real good will and more real desire to do what is fit and right than I have.[25]

For the first time in her life Victoria was able to do as she wished without the supervision of her mother and her acolyte. Her first act was to decide that what she did she would do *alone*. She saw the emissaries from Windsor 'alone' when they came to tell her of the King's demise. She saw Lord Melbourne on that first morning 'of course quite alone, as I shall always do all my Ministers'; she even took her dinner 'alone'.[26] She was able for the first time to decide whom she spoke to, whom she accepted advice from. In her journal she wrote on the evening of her first day as Queen that 'good, faithful Stockmar' came and talked to her at breakfast and at three times during the day – after the audiences following the Council, when she went downstairs in the evening after dinner and again after her last talk with Melbourne. Melbourne she also saw four times on that first day – twice before the Council, at nine and then eleven, during the Council and the audiences that followed, and again in the evening when he came 'at about twenty minutes to 9' and 'remained till near 10'. She described him as a 'straightforward, honest, clever, and good man' and insisted that she had 'a very comfortable conversation' with him.[27]

Apart from the other dignitaries and officials she gave audiences to, a special mention must be made of Baroness Lehzen. The Queen obviously offered her some important post in her household for she concluded the entry to her journal for 20 June, 'My dear Lehzen will always remain with me as my friend, but will take no situation about me'[28] – a phrase which must be remembered when in the years to come Baroness Lehzen is seen by Prince Albert as a scheming individual, eager for power. Certainly Victoria's attachment to Lehzen may be judged excessive in so far as she regarded her as both a mother figure and her saviour:

> I fear I often plague those I am fondest of, most; I am sure I often plague my mother (for that she ever has been and is) and friend, my angelic dearest, beloved Lehzen; whom I love so very dearly and to whom I owe everything; who is my constant companion and friend and without whom I could not exist. No words can ever do justice to her and what she has done and does.[29]

But faced with this enthusiastic affection the Baroness took no personal advantage from it.

The freedom to see whom one wishes has as a corollary the freedom to avoid those one has no wish to see. The Duchess of Kent spent the day receiving rebuffs. The Queen had received the dignitaries who came to see her, alone without her mother. Then she had asked to be alone and undisturbed for an hour. She had eaten alone and she had had a small bedroom of her own made ready for her so that she could sleep in it alone. The only mention of her mother in her first day's journal comes at the end of the day when she 'went down and said good night to Mamma, etc.'[30] One presumes that the vague 'etc.' includes Sir John Conroy.

Throughout May and June 1837 Conroy and the Duchess had put

increasing pressure on Princess Victoria. The King was dying, the Princess was now of an age to reign. The Regency had slipped from the grasp of those surrounding her. How then was Sir John to obtain the position of wealth and influence he craved? The couple returned to the idea, already tried at Ramsgate, to force the young girl to sign an agreement binding herself to Sir John, by selecting him for instance as her Private Secretary or her Privy Purse. The Duchess of Kent wrote long letters explaining to her daughter that Victoria was nothing and her mother all: 'You are untried, you are liked for your youth, your sex and the hope that is entertained but all confidence in you comes from your mother's reputation.'[31] Victoria was moreover obliged not only from filial duty but also 'public prudential motives' to have her mother live with her once she was Queen. It was necessary for Victoria's safety to have a gentleman of tried honour and ability and no party preference as her personal secretary: 'that person I must repeat to you again your father considered to be Sir John Conroy, I therefore solemnly and on my knees advise you to take Sir John Conroy – this advice I give you only for your own security.' And as always with the pleading comes the veiled threat: 'Mount the throne, only recollecting kindness, throwing oblivion over the past. For God's sake, do not be thought vindicative. Recollect if you can injure, you injure yourself more. The individual may pass away but the stain will remain on you; to attempt to hurt Sir John Conroy as a daughter's first act to her parents would be a very injudicious measure ... '[32] Victoria's reply was unambiguous: 'I declare my firm resolution and determination not to fetter or bind myself by giving any premature promises.'[33]

Victoria had been supported in her resistance by Baroness Lehzen and by Stockmar, whom Leopold had sent to advise the young Queen. Leopold obviously knew little of the battle raging at the palace and admitted as much to the Princess: 'My Dearest Child – You have had some battles and difficulties of which I am completely in the dark.'[34] He did, however, have some inkling of it for in the same letter of May 1837 he told his niece that two things seemed necessary: 'not to be fettered by any establishment other than what will be comfortable to *you*, and then to avoid any breach with your mother'.[35] Clearly Leopold had no concern for Sir John Conroy and was only eager to bring mother and daughter closer together – this was also Stockmar's aim.

The Princess's half-brother Prince Leiningen had also taken part in the attempt to 'persuade' Victoria.

> Allow me, dearest sister to stand up boldly for a man whose doings I have closely watched for fourteen years. . . . Do you think the native hails

your reign with unparalleled joy, calls you their hope, because you will
be a Queen of eighteen years? Oh, no! They expect that you will follow
the path which your mother has gone for many years. Who led her on
this path? Consider if it would be wise to begin your reign by disgarding
the man who has worked hard many a year to create this enormous
popularity for you.[36]

Prince Leiningen's counsels weighed little in the balance. A short note
from the Princess put an end to his interventions. It is cutting in the
extreme: 'as the subject to which you allude is strictly private and only
between my mother and myself I must beg to remain silent about it.
Believe me always my dear brother, your affectionate sister.'[37] If Charles
Leiningen had little influence over the Princess, his intervention raises
two interesting questions. When he insisted that 'Nobody means
that Sir John should stand to you in the position as he did to Mama',
is he referring to more than a personal relationship? When he said
'I know your objections. That Sir John Conroy has offended you
personally',[38] what exactly was the nature of the offence? Victoria's
feelings had, thought Stockmar, 'been deeply wounded by what she
called "his impudent and insulting conduct" towards her'.[39]

There are further clues in a letter the Princess wrote to Lord Liverpool five days before the King's death. The constant battering of
Conroy and the Duchess had not been without effect. Victoria's nerves
had become frayed as the intimidation continued. Lord Liverpool was
a Tory peer whose daughter Lady Catherine Jenkinson was one of
Victoria's friends. She told him she desired to have 'a few words of
private conversation ... in the strictest confidence' with a view to
settling a difference of opinion with her mother. She stated the case
clearly:

> I further beg to know whether you think it right in my mother to force
> upon me an adviser in whose judgement I cannot place the same re-
> liance as she does, and whose conduct moreover has been on many
> occasions personally offensive to me. For the last I refer you to your own
> daughter.[40]

However, it is not clear whether Conroy had made advances to
Victoria, or insulted her in some other way.

Lord Liverpool came to see her at two o'clock on 15 June. He had
already seen Conroy that morning and had indeed told him that he was
in no way suited to becoming Victoria's private secretary and that her
only political advisers were her Ministers 'and in particular Lord
Melbourne'.[41] He also told Sir John Conroy that the position of Private

Secretary that Herbert Taylor had held under William IV was not a normal one and should in any case be done away with. Lord Liverpool told Victoria that there was no need for an adviser, but he insisted that she should remain with her mother as this was the proper thing to do. As to Baroness Lehzen, in answer to a question put by Sir John Conroy, Lord Liverpool said there was no reason why Lehzen should not remain as a friend but that she should not occupy any official position.

Meanwhile, the Duchess was occupied with various stratagems to convince the Government that her daughter was not sufficiently mature to reign. 'The Duchess thinks', Lord Duncannon wrote to Lord Melbourne, 'her daughter not of age or experience to act without her care and she offers the continuation of that care on condition that the person in whom from the death of her husband she has placed her confidence'[42] (in other words Sir John Conroy) ... should be the Private Secretary of the Queen. In a memorandum he wrote in 1840, Prince Leiningen claimed that Conroy had also consulted his friend Abercromby, the Speaker of the House of Commons, who had declared that if Victoria would not listen to reason, 'she must be coerced'. Prince Leiningen showed himself in a good light, saying that it was he who pleaded with his mother not to shut Victoria up.[43]

Hardly had King William IV breathed his last than Conroy hastened to press his claims, using Baron Stockmar as his intermediary. The very morning the Queen ascended the throne, he acknowledged to Baron Stockmar that he was completely defeated and said that, considering his public life at an end, he could do no better than retire into privacy.[44] But he put his conditions. He claimed that the Duke of Kent on his deathbed had made him the Duchess of Kent's servant and that this had led him to give up three professions: 'the artillery where I should have risen to rank and emolument, the army where I should have risen to rank and the civil service where I should have risen to rank and emolument.'[45] Conroy claimed that for thirteen years he had served the Duke and Duchess at his own expense. His services had been recognized by George IV, who had given him the Grand Cross of Hanover and promised him a baronetcy, later refused him by William IV.[46] His claim was now: 'My reward for the Past I conceive should be – a peerage, the red ribbon and a pension from the Privy Purse of £3,000 a year.'[47]

The demand was exorbitant, more than a Minister of the Crown might receive. Furthermore Sir George Couper, when consulted by the Duchess, wrote: ' "Poor Sir John!" His statements are sadly incorrect.'[48] Had Conroy remained in the artillery he would have been when he died a Colonel with 400 pounds a year instead of the 6,200 pounds a year which he acquired in the Duchess's service. His widow would have had a pension after his death of 80 pounds a year for herself and her children. But Victoria was ready to do almost anything to get rid of the man. Melbourne informed Conroy on 26 June 1837 that 'it was Her Majesty's intention to direct that £3,000 annually should be issued to you from her Privy Purse'[49] when the Civil List had been voted by Parliament. On the same day, in a private letter, Melbourne also said that if he should 'continue to be her Majesty's adviser' it was his intention to recommend 'when the state of the Irish peerage shall authorise a new creation'[50] that Conroy become an Irish peer.

Conroy was never in fact made an Irish baron, only a baronet, but although he was given the promised – exorbitant – pension of 3,000 pounds a year, still he did not leave the Palace. Victoria chose to ignore him completely. 'He has never once been invited to the Palace, or distinguished by the slightest mark of personal favour, so that nothing can be more striking than the contrast between the magnitude of the pecuniary bounty and the complete personal disregard of which he is the object.'[51] This it was that so upset the Duchess of Kent. The Duchess had asked her daughter for permission to take Sir John and Lady Flora Hastings, one of her ladies-in-waiting, to the Proclamation ceremony and the Queen had refused, on the advice, she said, of Lord Melbourne. Back came the serpent-like note: 'Take care Victoria, you know your Prerogative! take care that Lord Melbourne is not King . . .'[52] But the Duchess of Kent did not really know her daughter. She had certainly never imagined that behind the facade of filial obedience was a young girl with a will of her own and a deepseated hatred of Sir John Conroy. Nor could the Duchess have imagined that Victoria would ignore her, while preserving a disconcerting veneer of politeness.

The Duchess wrote to her daughter telling her how she should, now that she was Queen 'and her own mistress, treat her mother'.[53] People, claimed the Duchess, could not look into hearts to see affection, they judged from outward signs. Therefore 'for this reason it hurts me more for your sake than for my own, when you are not always quite attentive to me. . . . You see dear love, when you do not look after me, and if you do not stop for me, I am obliged to go with your ladies, which is not my place, as I am your mother.'[54]

The outside world certainly realized very swiftly that mother and daughter were not on the best of terms. 'The Duchess of Kent', the tireless Greville noted, 'never appears at Kensington where the Queen

occupies a separate range of apartments, and her influence is very
slightly exercised if at all.'[55] The Duchess herself made no secret of the
state of affairs. Madame de Lieven had an interview with her and she
told her that she was overwhelmed with vexation and disappointment,
for while her daughter behaved to her with kindness and attention she
had rendered herself quite independent and there was no place at all for
her.[56]

The Duchess continued, however, to plead for Conroy, and Conroy
continued to put pressure on the Duchess. 'To please me,' wrote the
Duchess of Kent to her daughter in July, 'you made Sir John a baronet
and you will give him a pension. With one hand you bestow a kingly
favour, with the other you banish and punish his family. In marking Sir
John as You have done he is branded in the eyes of the world.'[57]

But Victoria stood firm. She would not invite Sir John. She had
thought her mother would not expect otherwise, 'after his conduct
towards me for some years past, and still more so after the unaccount-
able manner in which he behaved towards me, a short while before I
came to the throne.'[58] She had thought her mother would be amply
satisfied by the pension and the baronetcy. She would, however, do
more, she would do what she could for his sons. But receive him at
Court – that she would not do.[59]

In a footnote to a letter to King Leopold in August 1837 she stated
the position, clearly showing her annoyance.

> I wrote to you that a certain shocking person was finally put down, that
> is to say I never see him, nor does he meddle with my affairs but he still
> continues to tease me by ways and underhand means. Stockmar is
> determined to get him away. Lord Melbourne thinks your coming will be
> of great use to send him finally away.[60]

Throughout the winter of 1837–8 Victoria was constantly badgered
by the Duchess. 'Saw Ma and oh what a scene did she make!'[61] and
'Got such a letter from Ma Oh! Oh! – such a letter!'[62] are typical
entries in her journal. Lord Melbourne comforted her, encouraging the
idea that the Duchess was not responsible, that she was simply
misguided and often hardly knew what she was doing – 'a woman',
Lord Melbourne told her, 'will do anything when she has given herself
into someone's hands.'[63] Victoria was highly strung and the tension her
mother created literally made her ill. Her mother's poisonous letters
came frequently and 'they always contrived to give me these torments
just before dinner.'[64]

By March 1838 the Queen was longing for her mother simply to go away. When Lord Melbourne came on the first of March Victoria showed him 'a very strange letter' she had received from her mother the night before.

> He and I both agreed that we must not mind what she does any more; "but that's easier to say than to do", Lord Melbourne observed. Spoke for some time of Ma, how much better it would be if Ma was not in the house and if she would go and visit her family; Lord Melbourne observed that that would be a great thing; for if she were to go away without going to her own family, it would be awkward and we should have to state the cause to the public; and make a cause of it.[65]

There indeed was the rub. The Duchess and Conroy had the upper hand – and both Stockmar and Lord Melbourne realized it.

The question of the Queen's private secretary remained. Both Government and Opposition were in fact relieved that the Queen did not want Sir John Conroy. Not because of what he was, but because the very notion of a private secretary was not to their taste. The office had first come into being in 1805 when King George III, who had become blind, needed someone to write his letters. But the post had been kept under the Prince Regent, who appointed Colonel McMahon as his Private Secretary. This raised a constitutional storm, so fearful was Parliament that the Regent intended to reinstate a form of personal monarchy. The influence a Private Secretary might exercise over the mind of a young, inexperienced girl was even more to be feared. Might not his power exceed that of the Prime Minister himself? Another rumour had it that Baron Stockmar might be offered the job – and this might well mean that King Leopold of the Belgians would become the power behind the throne. Finally the Prime Minister, Lord Melbourne, was to solve the problem by acting as Private Secretary to the Queen himself. And so began the touching encounter of the ageing politician and the young inexperienced Queen.

Lord Melbourne impressed the Queen first of all by his physique. He had been an extremely handsome young man, and now, at fifty-eight, he was still impressive. He had grown portly but he had an elegance and an easiness of manner that were bound to charm the young Queen. Here was breeding and mellowness. Here was a man of the world, a master at handling difficult situations, a brilliant conversationalist. Creevey wrote of him a few years before the accession, 'I am very fond of Melbourne. There is an absence of all humbug about him and a frankness and good humour that, in a Secretary of State, are charming.'[66]

Melbourne was the younger son of a brilliant, fashionable, society mother and of a peer of the realm. William Lamb, as he then was, was born into the wealthy nobility with its palatial town houses and large estates. When he was in his twenties his brother died and William became heir to his father's title. From 1806, when he was twenty-seven, until 1829, when his father died, he had sat in the House of Commons. Thereafter he took his father's title and his seat in the Lords. In the House of Commons he had been a Whig but his temperament inclined him towards conservatism and he even served in 1827 as Irish Secretary in Canning's Tory administration. But he resigned his post after only eleven months and from then on identified himself completely with the Whigs.

His political activity before the age of fifty had been very limited, and he had spent much time away from the House of Commons in his family's country home at Brocket Hall in Hertfordshire. When there, he immersed himself in his private library. He had thus become one of the best-read men of his time and his reading had given him his own specific philosophy of life. Greville noted that

> No man is more formed to ingratiate himself with her [the Queen] than Melbourne. He treats her with unbounded consideration and respect, he consults her tastes and her wishes, and he puts her at her ease by his frank and natural manners, while he amuses her by the quaint, queer, epigrammatic turn of his mind, and his varied knowledge upon all subjects.[67]

In addition the stories Victoria learned of his private life made him even more of a romantic hero. At twenty-six he had married for love. His wife was Lady Caroline Ponsonby, the only daughter of the third Earl of Bessborough. As niece to the Duchess of Devonshire, she had been brought up in the atmosphere of emotional disorder and destabilizing bohemianism associated with the Devonshire House set. She was charming, lighthearted and very provocative. She was a woman of the new generation – with short hair and a boyish manner. Unfortunately for her husband, her highly strung nature exacerbated by her education caused her to totter on the edge of sanity. At her marriage to William she found the ceremony so long that she tore at her dress, fainted and had to be carried out of the church.

The marriage seemed at first happy and a son was born. But William was unaware of her frailty. The more erratic her behaviour became, the more her husband tried to reason with her. He succeeded only in pushing her into the realms of folly and destroying the last shreds of her sanity. She had already had one serious infatuation with another man when, in 1812, Byron came on the scene. He completely overthrew her precarious mental balance. After a year-long tempestuous, flamboyant love affair the poet left her for Lady Oxford. She made scenes, the world gossiped and her husband, with an admirable understanding and tenderness, stood by her unflinchingly. Lord and Lady Melbourne, convinced that she was mad, persuaded their son to agree to a separation – but this did not prevent him from watching over her for the next fifteen years until her death at forty-two. In that time she continued to live at his country home, Brocket, where he constantly paid her visits. Of their three children only the first, Augustus, survived infancy. But even he failed to mature in the normal way and he finally died in 1836 at the age of twenty-nine.

Victoria, who had learnt all this little by little from Court gossip, was full of admiration. 'Talked with Stockmar for some time upon various subjects, but principally about our mutual favourite Melbourne. . . . He praised him. . . . Spoke of the dreadful life his wife had led him and how very admirably he had behaved to her up to the very last.'[68]

In his political ideas Melbourne was a Whig: he was tolerant, believed in government by discussion and had the capacity for adaptation which characterized Whig philosophy. He had become leader of the Whigs when Grey had been forced to retire. Grey had failed to get support within his party for his solution to the maintaining of order in Ireland: a renewal of the Coercion Bill which suspended the right of meeting, partially suspended habeas corpus and applied curfews in selected areas. The King called for Melbourne, who was, Greville tells us, not over-eager for office. When the King sent for him he told Young, his private secretary,

> he thought it a damned bore, and that he was in many minds what he should do – be Minister or no. Young said, "Why damn it such a position never was occupied by any Greek or Roman, and, if it only lasts two months, it is well worth while to have been Prime Minister of England." "By God that's true", said Melbourne; "I'll go."[69]

Melbourne formed his first Government in July 1834. In November of that year, when Althorp – leader in the Commons – was removed by the death of his father to the House of Lords, King William decided to dismiss the Whigs, who still had the confidence of the Commons, and to give the premiership to Robert Peel. This was to be the last time that a King of England censored a policy of which he did not approve by bringing in a Prime Minister of his own choosing. Never again was a Sovereign to dismiss a Prime Minister in this way, for by his action King William IV did more than anything else to help develop the party system he hoped to fight. The dismissal of the Whigs, followed by their losses in the 1835 election, led them to realize that the Reform Bill had not given them a monopoly. Henceforth the Whigs, different brands of Radicals and O'Connell's Irish, combined for the purpose of re-conquering and then remaining in government. It is significant that in 1836 a new London club was created, the Reform Club, which welcomed both Radicals and Whigs.

The ball was now to be for a few years in the Radicals' court. Should they fight the Whigs, who were not prepared to accept their demands, with the risk of returning a conservative Government under Peel; or should they support them (with or without participation?) even if they were not able to get all they wanted?

A hundred days after he had been called to office, Peel, defeated in the House of Commons, resigned. He was in fact given more than a fair trial for he did not resign until the government had been beaten six times in six weeks over how the revenue of the Church of Ireland should be spent. Melbourne returned. But his position was not enviable. The King was, and had proved himself to be, committed to the Tories; the Whigs had only a small majority in the House of Commons and were in a minority in the Lords. In history books Melbourne never figures alongside Peel, Gladstone and Disraeli as a great Prime Minister. He has the reputation of being indolent and his scepticism, together with his frequently proffered suggestion 'Why not let it alone', have often made him appear as an indifferent, even a lazy Prime Minister. On doing business, Melbourne once said to Victoria, 'All depends on the urgency of a thing. If a thing is very urgent, you can always find time for it; but if a thing can be put off, well then you put it off.'[70]

Many observers of the time present Lord Melbourne as already an old man in 1835. In reality he was only fifty-five. But, 'if he was not yet old in age,' wrote Elie Halévy, 'he was and always had been by temperament. A sceptic, he felt to what extent life was short, art difficult, human nature unchanging: reform seemed to this singular leader of the Reform party either impossible or dangerous.'[71] This seems a very harsh judgement. Melbourne was a statesman in the full sense of the word. He kept together for six whole years the extraordinary mix of reforming politicians – Radical, Whig and Irish. He was a man who did not hesitate not to give a position in Government to those he considered impossible to work with – showing undeniable political courage. He did not, for instance, give a place in his second adminis- tration to Lord Brougham, who had been Lord Chancellor in his first. When Brougham demanded an explanation he wrote:

> It is a very disagreeable task to have to say to a statesman that his character is injured in the public estimation; it is still more unpleasant to have to say that you consider this his own fault ... I must, however, state plainly that your conduct was one of the principal causes of the fall of the last Ministry, and that it forms the most popular justification of that step.[72]

Broadly speaking, with the exception of Brougham, Lord Melbourne's second administration was identical to the first. Melbourne was a very tolerant man. His major work during the 1836 session concerned the granting of rights to the Dissenters despite the anticlerical faction and the supporters of the Established Church. His Government saw a charter granted to the University of London, the first secular university in England. This was later criticized as a half-measure because the two great historic universities, Oxford and Cambridge, retained the monopoly of degrees. But this university charter was but one of a series of liberal measures: authorization for Dissenters to celebrate their marriages elsewhere than in the Established Church (The Dissenting Marriages Act); a solution to the problem of the tithe (The Tithe Commutation Act); compulsory registering of births, marriages and deaths ... Lord Melbourne thus passed a certain number of Bills tending towards the separation of the Church and State.

Another major field in which Melbourne's Government had been active was the reform of local government. The Municipal and Cor- porations Reform Bill of 1835 remedied gross abuse and laid the foundations of local government in towns as it remained for over a century. It was a tremendous undertaking, second only in importance to the Reform Bill.

Melbourne's parliamentary action may seem dull but in the context of the nineteenth century it was imperative. Melbourne was a man of compromise, probably a *primus inter pares* Prime Minister, first among equals. He allowed his Ministers freedom of action within the frame- work of collective Cabinet responsibility. His supervision was lightly exercised but it was efficient. He even managed to convince Palmerston that all his actions were not judicious. Greville saw his distinguishing characteristic as a statesman as good common sense. He figured in Lytton's poem, *St Stephen's*:[73]

Sincere, yet deeming half the world a sham.
Mark the rude handsome manliness of Lamb!
None then foresaw his rise; ev'n now but few
Guess right the man so many thought they knew;
Gossip accords him attributes like these –
A sage good-humour based on love of ease,
A mind that most things undisturbed'ly weighed,
Nor deemed the metal worth the clink it made.
Such was the man, in part, to outward show;
Another man lay coiled from sight below –

Which Melbourne did Victoria see? Undoubtedly the man 'coiled from sight below'. He very soon became 'my excellent kind friend Lord Melbourne',[74] a man to whom she confided all her unhappy times at Kensington, her own failings and doubts, and her hopes. The traditional image of the young, eager, inexperienced girl leaning on the wise, experienced yet lively elder statesman is not very far from the truth. She confided in him:

> the great difficulty was to keep my temper when I was very much
> irritated and plagued; he observed that "you must struggle as much as
> you can against that feeling. I dare say you'll find you have much more
> control over yourself now and you can keep that in now very well." I
> replied I could, but still let out my temper towards my servants which I
> was very sorry for: he said that a person who had rather "a choleric
> disposition might conceal it, never wholly got over it, and could not help
> letting it out at times".[75]

He offered her what she had so rarely known – disinterested kindness. She was profoundly grateful. 'He was so kind when I spoke to him of the unhappy scene I had with poor Ma yesterday.'[76] Melbourne's devotion to her was fatherly, her fascination with him was similar to that of a student of philosophy with a guru. She absorbed all he had to teach her – his inimitable table-talk, his epigrams, his unrivalled knowledge of the world he moved in. Melbourne spent some five to six hours a day in the Queen's company. And she wrote to him every day when he was not there, often two or three times a day.

Greville understood what Melbourne felt for this young girl who knew so little of life and letters.

> I have no doubt he is passionately fond of her as he might be of his
> daughter if he had one; and the more because he is a man with a capacity
> for loving without anything in the world to love. It is become his
> province to educate, instruct and form the most interesting mind and
> character in the world.[77]

It is possible, too, that the uniqueness of his situation appealed to him. No Prime Minister since Addington had been on intimate personal terms with the Sovereign. Melbourne could go to Buckingham Palace whenever he wanted. Windsor Castle became his country house. He could get anyone he wanted invited to either place, so people now became extraordinarily affable to him.

Be that as it may, he gave himself wholeheartedly to the job of filling the gaps in the Queen's knowledge of both public affairs and people, past and present. Sometimes he may have been bored, for he retreated from the world of children's games and trivialities into his own thoughts. 'Lord Melbourne is very absent when in company, and talks to himself very often, loud enough to be heard, but never loud enough to be understood. I am now, from habit, quite accustomed to it; but at first I turned round, thinking he was talking to me.'[78] He certainly knew how to charm the young girl. For the first time on 20 February 1838 Victoria noted in her journal, 'Got a beautiful bouquet of flowers from Lord Melbourne. How kind of him to think of sending me flowers.'[79] This was the first of many bouquets of roses and daphnes that were sent from his country home of Brocket to the Queen.

The ceremonies on the accession of a Sovereign follow quickly on one another. On 21 June the Queen had to go to St James's to see herself proclaimed by the heralds. There was a great crowd in the courtyard below. While the heralds recited their announcement she stood in full view of the public – between Lord Melbourne and Lord Lansdowne at the open window of the Privy Council chamber. As the first cheers went up, 'the colour faded from the Queen's cheeks and her eyes filled with tears. The emotion thus called forth imparted an additional charm to the winning courtesy with which the girl sovereign accepted the proffered homage.'[80] It is these tears that Elizabeth Barrett Browning so totally misinterpreted in her poem.

> She saw no purple shine,
> For tears had dimmed her eyes;
> She only knew her childhood's flowers
> Were happier pageantries!
> And while the heralds played their part
> Those million shouts to drown –
> "God save the Queen", from hill to mart –
> She heard, through all, her beating heart,
> And turned and wept;
> She wept to wear a crown.

The poet did not understand how delighted Victoria was to be Queen.

The first great state ceremony which enabled the people to see her as Sovereign was the dissolution of Parliament on 17 July 1837. Here again Lord Melbourne supported her, giving her the confidence she needed. After going to the robing room and putting on the Parliamentary robe, 'which is enormously heavy', she entered the House of Lords preceded by all the officers of state 'and Lord Melbourne bearing the sword of state walking just before me. He stood quite close to me on the left hand of the throne, and I feel always the satisfaction to have him near me on such occasions.' The House was very full and the Queen felt 'somewhat nervous'.[81]

In November came the Lord Mayor's dinner. She reached Guildhall at a little before four. 'Throughout my progress to the city, I met with the most gratifying, affectionate, hearty and brilliant reception from the greatest concourse of people I ever witnessed, the streets being immensely crowded as were also the windows, houses, churches and balconies everywhere.' Victoria's enthusiasm knew no bounds. She wrote to Feodora.

> It is really most gratifying to have met with such a reception in the greatest capital in the world and from thousands and thousands of people. I really do not deserve all this kindness for what I have yet done. I may well, may I not, dearest sister, be proud of my country and my people.[82]

By the end of 1837 – after six months as Queen – Victoria had slipped into her role with ease. On no better note could the New Year begin than on that of the letter sent to Victoria by Lord Melbourne in reply to her best wishes.

> Whatever may happen in the course of events it will always be to Lord Melbourne a source of the most lively satisfaction to have assisted Your Majesty in the commencement of your reign which was not without trouble and difficulty, and Your Majesty may depend that whether in or out of office Lord Melbourne's conduct will always be directed by the strongest attachment to Your Majesty's person and by the most anxious desire to promote Your Majesty's interests, which, from his knowledge of Your Majesty's character and disposition Lord Melbourne feels certain will always be identified with the interests of your people.

When she reported Melbourne's New Year greetings in her journal, Victoria simply added:

> This is so kind, so noble, so like himself, I feel it deeply and it quite touched me.[83]

6

The First Six Months

In the first year of her reign Victoria breathed gaiety and enthusiasm into the task of being a monarch. She was by nature active. Mooning about Kensington Palace, spending long inactive months at Claremont with little real occupation for her mind, her health had deteriorated. The tensions within the Kensington household had not, as we have seen, helped. She had continual headaches and bilious attacks. But within four months of mounting the throne, she was writing: 'Everybody says that I am quite another person since I came to the throne. I look and am so very well, I have such a pleasant life; just the sort of life I like. I have a good deal of business to do, and all that does me a world of good.'[1] Feodora asked her whether she did not find it like a dream to find everything so changed. Yes, indeed, replied Victoria, 'but like a happy one, God knows; it is not the splendour of the thing or the being Queen that makes me so happy, it is the pleasant life I lead which causes my peace and happiness.'[2]

Victoria's Court was at this time held mainly at Buckingham Palace and Windsor Castle. On 13 July, three weeks after her accession, the Queen had moved from Kensington Palace to Buckingham Palace. Buckingham House, when it was bought by George III, had had many advantages. First of all its situation had been well chosen – there was the vista along the Mall and the Chelsea fields. It was also near St James's Palace, which George III had decided to keep for official occasions. In 1775 the house was legally settled on Queen Charlotte by Act of Parliament, in exchange for Somerset House, and was from then on called the 'Queen's House'. There it was that, over the next twenty years, Queen Charlotte gave birth to fourteen princes and princesses – the eldest of her fifteen children, the future George IV, had been born in St James's Palace.

When George IV finally succeeded his father, after over eight years as Regent, he was already known to his people as an excessive spender. When a young man he had incurred his father's ire on account of the money he had spent on altering and decorating Carlton House; after that he had built at no little expense the Pavilion at Brighton; and latterly he had spent a fortune repairing Windsor Castle. It is therefore not surprising that when he put forward the idea of building himself a new Palace on the site of Queen's House, Parliament refused to vote the money necessary for a new building. Not to be outdone by Parliament, George – with the help of his architect, John Nash – put forward a new proposal for repairing the existing building. Between them it was agreed that the modernization would be most extensive. Under the title of improving and repairing Queen's House, over 252,000 pounds was granted him.[3] In the event, the cost was to work out at some 720,000 pounds. The virtually new Palace was not one of Nash's successes – indeed he did not finish it, though he worked on it for five years. When George IV died, Nash, who was by then seventy-eight, retired to the Isle of Wight.

William IV gave orders for Edward Blore to finish the Palace and in early 1833 work recommenced. By October 1834 it was almost completed. On the sixteenth of that month both Houses of Parliament were burnt down, though Westminster Hall and the Abbey were saved. William was so dissatisfied with Buckingham Palace that he offered the building for the use of the Lords and Commons – but they had no desire to inhabit the Palace either. The poor Palace received more hostile criticism than any similar building. Creevey wrote:

> It has lost a million of money and there is not a fault that has not been committed in it. You may be sure there are rooms enough, and large enough, for the money; but for staircases, passages, etc. I observed that instead of being called Buckingham Palace, it should be the "Brunswick Hotel". The costly ornaments of the state rooms exceed all belief in their bad taste and every species of infirmity. Raspberry coloured pillars without end, that quite turn you sick to look at, but the Queen's [Adelaide] paper for her own apartments far exceed everything else in their ugliness and vulgarity.[4]

And the *Quarterly Review* ridiculed Nash's renovation:[5]

> Augustus at Rome was for building renowned,
> And of marble he left what of brick he had found.
> But is not our Nash, too, a very great master?
> He finds us all brick and leaves us all plaster.

It was indeed by this time a mixture of every kind of architecture and decoration. The building was finally completed in May 1837. Within a month, William IV was dead.

It may seem curious that Victoria chose to live in Buckingham Palace. But in fact she had little choice. Kensington Palace was, of course, not grand enough and encumbered with aunts and uncles. Windsor Castle was too far from London to be suitable as a permanent residence. So Buckingham Palace it was.

She did not leave Kensington Palace without a lump in her throat: 'Though I rejoice to go into Buckingham Palace for many reasons,' wrote the Queen, 'it is not without feelings of regret that I shall bid adieu ... to this my birthplace.'[6] Here it was that she had seen her sister married, here it was that she had received so many dear relations. She had been to 'pleasant balls and delicious concerts' in the Palace. Moreover she found the rooms she then occupied, presumably since her accession, 'really very pleasant, comfortable and pretty'. Here, too, she had so recently held her first Council. All this meant that, though she had 'gone through painful and disagreeable scenes' at Kensington, she was still very fond of the place.

As soon as she arrived at Buckingham Palace she walked through her rooms, which were 'high, pleasant and cheerful', and then walked round the garden, 'which is large and very pretty'.[7] She was, however, soon to realize that the Palace was a very difficult place to live in. A month after she had moved in, letters were still being sent to the Lord Chamberlain's departments asking for fittings, conveniences and other alterations to be proceeded with and completed during Her Majesty's absence at Windsor. The list was impressive and included: the opening of a communication from Queen Victoria's bedroom to Baroness Lehzen's room; the conveyance of hot water from the bathroom for the supply of Her Majesty's movable bath and for the bedroom; the water to be immediately laid on and sinks etc. fitted up for the housemaids in the most convenient situation on the bedroom floors; the picture gallery and the Bow Room to be ventilated by opening casements and perforations.[8] The Palace was obviously still not very habitable.

The young Queen brought into the Palace the charm and excitement of youth. She gave life to a Court which had long been slumbering. First she wanted music. 'I have now got a band of my own', she wrote proudly to Feodora, 'who play every evening after dinner and exceedingly well, it is composed only of wind instruments.'[9] Concerts brightened up the Palace. The first was held less than five weeks after she had moved in on 17 August. The Court was allowed for one day to come out of mourning for her uncle. The concert was directed by Signor Costa and many famous singers came to sing, including the Queen's favourites: Madame Grisi, Signor Lablache and Signor Tamburini.

After music came dancing, with the Queen's first ball at Buckingham Palace in May 1838. The Palace was, in the Queen's opinion, remarkably well built for a ball. 'There are no less than five fine large rooms besides the gallery and dining room and they are so high, the doors so large and they lie so well near one another that it makes an ensemble rarely seen in this country.'[10] Even the critical Mary Frampton wrote: 'Although the rooms at Buckingham Palace are not nearly so high or as large (with the exception of the one long picture gallery) as at St James's, yet it is a remarkably good house for a ball if one may so express it.'[11]

The Queen was in a state of exaltation. Just before ten o'clock she entered the ballroom, in which Strauss's band was playing. 'I felt a little shy in going in,' she confided to her journal. Never in her life had she heard 'anything so beautiful as Strauss's band'. Oh how she loved dancing. 'I had not danced for *so* long and was so glad to do so again.' The Queen was a devotee of the dance and enthusiastically engaged in galops and quadrilles. When waltzes were played she retired to a sofa. With great satisfaction she noted afterwards that she had not left the ballroom until ten minutes to four and 'was in bed by half-past four – the sun shining'. Her only regret was 'that my excellent, kind, good friend, Lord Melbourne was not there. I missed him much at this my first ball.'[12]

Although Greville found the ball at the Palace 'a poor affair in comparison with the Tuileries', in particular because the gallery was ill-lit, he nonetheless thought 'The Queen's manner and bearing perfect . . . her manners exceedingly graceful, and blended with dignity and cordiality, a simplicity and good humour, when she talks to people, which are mighty captivating.'[13]

This simplicity was not to everyone's taste. Mary Frampton wrote an account of the ball in which she is scandalized by the fact that the Queen '*stood* to eat her supper. This shocked me dreadfully, and horrifies Grand Mama Ilchester, as there is not sufficient *state* in it. Even William IV who was quite Citizen King enough, always supped with the Queen in his private apartments with a select party.' When Mary Frampton asked for an explanation she was told that the Queen liked to be able to move about and to see and speak – if she so wished – to as many people as she could. This did not satisfy Mary: 'in fact,' she says, 'it arises from her extreme youth, but nevertheless I think it is a great pity. At all events, the multitude ought not to be admitted to the supper room until the Queen has herself finished.'[14] Queen Victoria's balls were, however, very different from those of King William IV – not least because they were in fact more select.

On 22 August 1837 the Queen went to Windsor to assume residence at the Castle for the first time. Like Buckingham Palace, Windsor bore the undeniable mark of George IV. For here, too, he had carried out reconstruction on a lavish scale. The Round Tower of Henry II was doubled in height and given a new flag tower, the carriageway of the Long Walk was carried right up to the Castle and a new monumental entrance was pierced through the south wall. Much work was done inside too – all the rooms on the south and east fronts, including those occupied by the King, were linked by a new connecting corridor running along two of the inner sides of the quadrangle. The apartments on the north front, which had been the King's private quarters for some six hundred years, became a suite for ceremonies and for the entertainment of visitors of state, and the former apartments of the Prince of Wales became those of the King. In addition, George IV had purchased many works of art at a time when the French revolution and the French invasion of the Low Countries had put many magnificent pictures, sculptures and other works of art on the international market. The Castle became enriched with Sèvres vases and services, Gobelin tapestries, clocks, bronzes and French royal furniture. George IV had also commissioned many works of art for Windsor by English artists, notably a series of portraits by Sir Thomas Lawrence of sovereigns, commanders and statesmen who had contributed to the downfall of Napoleon – these were put into a picture gallery especially created in place of an open courtyard and known as the Waterloo Chamber. George IV also finally solved the problem of the lack of garden. He had the ground outside the east front surrounded by a stone structure, the top of which was level with the terraces, thus creating a sunken garden effect.

When Victoria came to the Castle in August 1837 the weather was not clement. It was raining and 'Windsor looked somewhat gloomy' despite the 'remarkably friendly and civil throng' which had crowded into the Long Walk. The young Queen's spirits were low: 'I cannot help feeling as though *I* was not the Mistress of the House and as if I was to see the poor King and Queen. There is a sadness about the whole which I must say I feel.'[15] Her vision of Windsor was soon to change, however. Uncle Leopold and Aunt Louise came to stay and the joy of having them with her was reflected in the place itself. 'It is an inexpressible happiness and joy to me, to have these dearest beloved relations with me and in my own house.'[16]

Melbourne, too, came down on several occasions to stay, as did Lord Palmerston. The long, hot summer, the first of her reign, was one long succession of delights and the Queen fell in love with Windsor. 'I have just spent there the happiest summer of my life', she wrote to Aunt Louise,[17] and to Leopold she enthused, 'Oh! that place, there is nothing like that and the castle too is so comfortable.'[18]

At Windsor her great delight was riding – usually in a cavalcade consisting of twenty-five or thirty equestrians. Promenades of this sort in the Great Park usually lasted about two hours and no formal etiquette was observed. The Queen was an excellent horsewoman, graceful and at ease on horseback. She changed horses as her mood changed and often mounted the fiery Monarch. One highlight of the summer was a military review in the Great Park. The Queen wore a habit of dark blue with red collar and cuffs – the Windsor uniform worn by all her gentlemen. She rode up to the colours and was saluted by her regiments. 'I saluted them by putting my hand to my cap like the officers do, and was much admired for my manner of doing so.'[19] She then cantered up to the lines and rode along them before cantering back. The troops then manoeuvred and, despite the firing and skirmishing, her horse Leopold never moved. 'The whole went off beautifully; and I felt for the first time like a man, as if I could fight myself at the head of my Troops.'[20]

Music was one of the delights at Windsor. The bands of the Grenadiers and the Life Guards often played near the fountain. Victoria often sang, either solo or with her mother or with royal guests. She also talked and listened to Ministers and illustrious guests. So pleasant was the summer that she was sad to leave Windsor and that first perfect summer was one she was never to forget.

The Queen left Windsor on 4 October to go to the third and last of the royal palaces then in occupation – the Pavilion at Brighton. 'The Pavilion itself, which you know I had never seen before, is a strange odd building,' she told Feodora.[21] While in a letter to Aunt Louise, she called it 'the most extraordinary Palace that I have ever seen, you could imagine yourself to be in China.'[22] Nash had transformed the east front into a picturesque fantasy – changing the character of the building. The foreignness of many of its features was striking: the minarets, the battlements, the arches, the delicate tracery and the castellated turrets. . . . It married styles and periods with abandon. Inside, the rooms were rich in colour and originality. In the red drawing room, for instance, the columns needed to enlarge the room were dressed up as brightly coloured palm trees with bamboo trunks and repeated as pilasters around the walls. In the banqueting room, the dome appeared open to a tropical sky almost filled by the leaves of a tree. From the leaves emerged a carved dragon with, hanging from its claws, a great chandelier which descended by way of a mirrored star in cascades of glass flowers to a ring of six silvered dragons spouting lotus-petal bowls.

In surroundings which were so utterly foreign to her, Victoria certainly did not feel at home. They had indeed been devised for a style of life very far removed from her own. Here it was that George IV had held his magnificent parties. They often lasted a full week and bordered on dissipation, if one is to believe Princess Lieven: 'I do not believe that since the days of Heliogabalus there has been such magnificence and such luxury. One spends the evening half-lying on cushions; the lights are dazzling; there are perfumes, music, liqueurs'[23] – and a general air of effeminacy which the Princess said disgusted her, but which does not seem to have kept her away!

The young Queen stayed at the Pavilion for six weeks. She sang operatic airs in the music room – which had the air of a gigantic red lacquer cabinet with enormous Chinese landscapes filling the walls. But she was not enamoured of the place. She was to return at Christmas in 1838, then four years later with her husband and children. Three years after that, when the train put Brighton within reach of the London masses, she and her family sought privacy elsewhere, and the Royal Pavilion was put up for sale.

The Queen was to find that the upkeep of palaces and servants was no mean affair – financially her first years on the throne were not to be without difficulties. On her accession the Queen had been in a difficult financial situation. She inherited nothing and the Crown had lost the royal revenue of Hanover, which now went to the Duke of Cumberland, their new King. The Queen had been obliged to have recourse to Coutts, the bankers, for a loan while waiting for the Civil List to be voted six months later. It was on 23 December 1837 that the Queen went to the House of Lords to thank her Parliament for her Civil List.

The Crown did still have some hereditary revenues coming from Crown Lands. There had originally been a great number, but George III and George IV had yielded a considerable portion in exchange for a fixed revenue from Parliament. Finally William IV had surrendered all such revenues save those coming from the Duchies of Cornwall and

Lancaster. The Duchy of Cornwall, moreover, was the legal appanage of the heir apparent and thus ceased to be the Sovereign's property as soon as there was a lawful heir to the throne – a son in the direct line. William IV, in exchange for the revenues surrendered, had received an agreement that the general expenses of civil government should no longer be charged to the King's Civil List but to the Consolidated Fund. The King conserved, however, two budgetary responsibilities – pensions and the Secret Service Fund. For the first he received 75,000 pounds from Parliament, for the second 10,000 pounds. His total Civil List was 460,000 pounds, just over half of the 850,000 pounds paid to George IV – but his responsibilities were much less great.

The new Bill sought to remove pensions and the Secret Service Fund from the monarch's Civil List. The Crown did in fact retain the right to confer Civil List pensions to the tune of 1,200 pounds a year but this sum was defrayed annually by the Treasury independently of the Queen's annuity. During the debate in the Commons an amendment moved by Sir Robert Peel, Leader of the Opposition, and not opposed by the Government, was carried — it provided that if less than 1,200 pounds was spent on pensions in any one year, the difference might be used in any later year. These pensions were given essentially to those in need who had distinguished themselves in the sphere of literature, art or public service other than politics.

A number of Radicals in the House of Commons made two fundamental criticisms of the Bill as it stood. The first concerned the fact that the two remaining duchies were not brought under the control of Parliament. The second concerned the level of income that was proposed for the Queen. Two amendments were defeated on this score – one aimed to reduce the 385,000 pounds proposed by 50,000 pounds (rejected by 199 votes to 19), the other to reduce it by 10,000 pounds, which would have brought it to the level of the personal income of William IV (defeated by 173 votes to 41). In the House of Lords only Lord Brougham opposed the measure. He presented the same criticisms, but was above all intent on disputing the wisdom of making a definitive arrangement which was valid for the life of the Sovereign.

Lord Melbourne stood firm and refused any modification. Having given a full explanation of the details of the Bill, he called on the peers to support it, 'as they valued the preservation of the monarchy, laws and liberties of England.' He would not say that monarchy was the best form of government that ever existed but he did maintain that 'the attempt to alter it in this country would be the height, not less of insanity than crime.'[24] The Bill was passed and became law before the end of the year. Melbourne told the Queen that 'the Commons had never worked so hard in order to get the list through. He said with tears in his eyes "that the Duke of Wellington and Sir Robert Peel had behaved very well; they have helped us a good deal." '[25]

The 385,000 pounds thus granted was not as large a sum as it may seem since a great part of it was already allocated – 131,260 pounds went to the salaries of her Household, and 172,500 pounds to its expenses. The three remaining allocations, which gave the Queen a little more latitude, were the Privy Purse, 60,000 pounds, the Royal Bounty, 13,200 pounds, and unappropriated funds, 8,040 pounds. The sum was generous, however, as can be seen by the fact that it remained unchanged for the sixty-three years of the Queen's reign, although additional grants for her children were added as the years went by.

The first financial problem the Queen felt herself obliged to settle – it was a question of honour – was that of her parents. The Duke of Kent, her father, had died in considerable debt to the Lords Fitzwilliam and Dundas, who were by this time dead. Their heirs received the amount due, together with a valuable piece of plate from the Queen with a letter thanking them and expressing her pleasure at being able to show her appreciation.[26]

There was also the problem of the debts of the Duchess of Kent. According to the Duchess, Victoria had said to her mother shortly after the accession, 'Mama, I will pay your debts.' This was done 'without even a hint from me. I felt it was most natural that her first feeling should be, to take care of her mother, whose difficulties had risen, in the execution of her duty.'[27] The Queen selected Baron Stockmar to carry out 'her filial and generous feelings'. In November 1837 the Duchess's debts were evaluated at 55,000 pounds. The problem arose as to *how* the debt was to be paid. The Duchess wanted her daughter to pay 30,000 pounds directly out of her Privy Purse, if necessary by instalments, while her unfunded debt of 25,000 pounds should be reimbursed by savings on the civil list. The advantage of the system was that no enquiries would be made as to the nature of the debts. The Queen, on the advice of her Ministers – in particular Thomas Spring Rice, the Chancellor of the Exchequer – refused. Spring Rice was, however, willing to ask Parliament to pay out of public money those debts incurred during the minority of the Queen. The Duchess replied that she felt it due to her honour and her position 'as Mother of the Queen to decline negotiating with her Majesty's servants in the manner you point out'.[28]

After negotiations the Duchess was offered an annual addition to her income of 8,000 pounds – and this went through Parliament in the civil list of December 1837. The Queen, therefore, was surprised and indignant when she received in February 1838 another letter from her mother concerning her debts. She showed Lord Melbourne a letter she had received from the Duchess 'at which he was much shocked and grieved; showed him also a list of the number of things I had paid – which money was owing to tradesmen – about my dress etc. which had never been paid.'[29] In March the problems of the Duchess became public. On 9 March *The Times* published an article which attacked Conroy and claimed that he had mismanaged the Duchess's affairs and misappropriated some of her money. The paper claimed that the Duchess's debts were of the order of 80,000 pounds.

Victoria finally persuaded her mother to appoint an equerry to be in charge of her household and finances. They agreed after much discussion on one Colonel Couper, a man of great integrity and ability. She kept the keys, however, to the commodes containing her former accounts until February 1850, when he was allowed by her to open them. In a long memorandum[30] he explained the frauds carried out by Conroy and his assistant, Rea. Not only had they not kept accounts – 'From 1829–1840 it is not possible to show the expenditure of any quarter of any year' – but large capital sums were missing. Money sent by Leopold had never been credited to the Duchess's account.

Victoria straightened out her mother's affairs. She also found herself, ironically, supporting Sir John Conroy's family when he died insolvent in 1854. She was, in addition, financially generous to more distant relatives, whichever side of the blanket they had been born on. Creevey noted:

> A propos to our little Vic we are all enchanted with her for her munificence to the Fitzclarences. Besides their pensions out of the public pension list, they had nearly £10,000 a year given them by their father out of his privy purse, every farthing of which the Queen continues out of her privy purse, with quantities of other such things.[31]

The difference the Queen made was social, not financial. As Greville noted: 'The Queen has been extremely kind and civil to the Queen Dowager, but she had taken no notice of the King's children [the Fitzclarences], good, bad or indifferent.'[32]

One of the things that pleased her was that she now had the means to bring over to England her dear sister, Feodora. 'I have it now in my power', she writes in October 1837, 'to render it easy for you to come and see me when I like, not when others please and choose.' And with tact and delicacy the general principle was made concrete. 'You shall have £300 at your disposal for your journey hither and you need not feel embarrassment about it for it comes from my Privy Purse with which I may do what I please and this is therefore *entre nous deux seulement*.'[33]

The Royal Household of Queen Victoria, since she was young and unmarried, included a certain number of Ladies. These appointments were considered political and the Queen therefore discussed them with her Prime Minister. Lord Melbourne made the mistake, despite the smallness of his parliamentary majority, of surrounding the Queen entirely with Whig ladies. The Duchess of Sutherland became Mistress of the Robes. She was thirty-one and a really beautiful woman. She became the Queen's greatest friend, not only during the first years, but until the Duchess died in the late 1860s. And there were eight Ladies of the Bedchamber – the Marchioness Tavistock (later the Duchess of Bedford), the Marchioness Lansdowne, the Countess of Charlemont, the Countess of Mulgrave (later Marchioness of Normanby), Baroness Portman, Baroness Lyttleton, Lady Barham (later Countess of Gainsborough) and the Countess of Durham. Two were in their twenties, the others were middle-aged. Each of them received, as did the Duchess of Sutherland, 500 pounds a year. The Queen also had eight Maids of Honour and eight Women of the Bedchamber – only one of whom was resident. The Women of the Bedchamber and the Maids of Honour attended to the personal wants of the Queen for the small sum of 300 pounds a year. During the three months when they were at the Castle or Palace, their lives were hardly their own.

Altogether the Queen's Household consisted of 445 persons. At the top of the pyramid was the Lord Chamberlain, with a salary of 2,000 pounds a year. The list includes, as one would expect, the Gentlemen at Arms, the Heralds, and the Yeomen of the Guard, but also included some more unexpected posts: 'a rat killer (£80 a year), body linen laundress (£170 a year), chimney sweep (£111), fire lighter chapel royal (£10), stove and fire lighter (£64), linen women at Windsor Castle and Buckingham Palace (£60 and £66 respectively).'[34] Not to mention the Poet Laureate (£72) and the principal painter (£39).

There was in addition a considerable medical staff – physicians and surgeons, a chemist and an apothecary – who treated not only the Queen and the royal family but also all the royal servants, a perk well worth having in Victorian times!

The business habits of the Queen were fixed from the very beginning

of the reign and lasted all through it. They owed much to Uncle
Leopold. He wrote to the Queen a week after her accession, telling her:

> The best plan is to devote certain hours to it [business]; if you do that,
> you will get through it with great ease. I think you would do well to tell
> your Ministers that for the present you would be ready to receive those
> who should wish to see you, between the hours of eleven and half-past
> one.[35]

This practice Victoria adhered to and it did enable her to get through a
considerable amount of work with calm and an absence of hurry and
fuss. The Queen set herself a very tight timetable. She got up at eight
and signed despatches till breakfast. Then, with a rather cold formality,
she sent a servant to invite the Duchess of Kent to the royal table.
Indeed the Duchess never approached the Queen unless especially
summoned. Speaking from his own observations Greville remarked:

> In the midst of all her propriety of mind and conduct the young Queen
> begins to exhibit slight signs of a peremptory disposition, and it is
> impossible not to suspect that, as she gains confidence, and as her
> character begins to develop, she will evince a strong will of her own.[36]

The second major precept Victoria obeyed throughout her life was
also deduced from a piece of Uncle Leopold's advice.

> Whenever a question is of some importance it should not be decided on
> the day when it is submitted to you. Whenever it is not an urgent one, I
> make it a rule not to let any question be forced upon my immediate
> decision; it is really not doing oneself justice *de décider des questions sur le
> pouce*.[37]

Victoria even in her youthful years had a remarkable dislike for any
precipitate action: the Minister should bring his box with him, explain
it to the Queen, who should then keep the papers a while before
returning them to the Minister.

Victoria's work as Queen sat lightly on her. When Uncle Leopold
advised her to spend more time at Claremont and less in London she
told him in no uncertain manner that she took her work seriously.
'Respecting Claremont, Stockmar will be able to explain to you the *total*
impossibility of my being out of London as I must see my Ministers
every day. I am very well, sleep well and drive every evening in the
country.'[38] So busy was she that she apologized to Feodora for not
writing at length as before. 'I see my Ministers every day and have a
great deal to write and sign and talk, and as my duty to my country is
my first and greatest wish and pleasure I trust you will forgive me if I

do not just at present write such long letters as usual.'[39] This was in no sense a bore to her. She was, on the contrary, most enthusiastic. 'I have seen almost all my other Ministers and do regular, hard but to me delightful work with them.'[40] She delighted in her work and never felt 'tired or annoyed by it'.[41]

She had from the first a very strong notion of her responsibilities and that they were hers alone. Charles Murray said that whereas all the Queen's private correspondence was carefully copied by Baroness Lehzen before Victoria came to the throne, since her accession she had not shown her

> one letter of Cabinet or State documents, nor has she spoken to her, nor to any woman, about or upon party or political questions. As Queen she reserves all her confidences for her official advisers, while as a woman she is as frank, gay, and unreserved as when she was a young girl.[42]

More than anything else her relations with Uncle Leopold were to show that, despite her years, she was fully aware of what being a Queen was all about. Leopold had spent his time grooming her for her task, seeing himself no doubt as a sort of power behind the throne. Victoria's first reactions, despite the amiable letters, were not entirely to his taste. He saw clearly the growing influence of Lord Melbourne. Five days after the accession the Queen had written to him.

> How fortunate I am to have at the head of the Government a man like Lord Melbourne. I have seen him now every day, with the exception of Friday, and the more I see him, the more confidence I have in him. He is not only a clever statesman and an honest man but a good and kind-hearted man whose aim is to do his duty for his country, and not for a party. He is of the greatest use to me, both politically and privately.[43]

Leopold in his reply praised Melbourne but recommended to her kind attention 'what Stockmar will think it his duty to tell you.'[44]

Leopold himself must have felt that the Queen was liable to forget how much she owed him. It was not until March 1838, however, that their relationship was put to the test. Seven years earlier, in August 1831, before Leopold had been a month on the throne, the new kingdom of Belgium had been invaded by Holland under the Prince of Orange. Belgium called on England and France to carry out their treaty obligations and defend Belgian independence. France rushed to help, only too eager to have occasion to gain Belgian territory. In ten days the Dutch army was routed, essentially by the French, and Talleyrand was proposing a division of Belgium between Prussia, France and Holland. Britain, under Palmerston, threatened the French with war. The result was a London conference which, on 15 November, modified the previous territorial arrangements and provided for part of Luxemburg and Limburg – then held by Belgium — to be given to the Dutch. Leopold forced the Belgian Chamber to accept. It was to prevent new problems with France that Leopold reminded Louis Philippe that he hoped to ally himself to an Orléans princess; in 1832 he married Princess Louise.

Since then six more years had gone by. Six years during which the King of Holland had refused to recognize Belgian independence, and the Treaty of London had therefore not been enforced. Now, on 14 March 1838, King William declared that he was ready to accept the 'twenty-four articles' of the treaty and take over the territories in question. Leopold decided to refuse and to enlist the help of Victoria. On 2 June 1838 he wrote her a long letter on the subject. So far he had by discretion not touched on this affair at all. Now, having been given 'so many proofs of affection', he had something to ask.

> All I want from your kind Majesty, is that you will occasionally express to your Ministers, and particularly to good Lord Melbourne, that, as far as it is compatible with the interests of your own dominions, you do not wish that your Government should take the lead in such measures as might in a short time bring on the destruction of this country, as well as that of your uncle and his family.[45]

Victoria's reply came on 10 June. It was scarcely to her uncle's liking. After having assured him of her 'warm and devoted attachment to him', she told him that her Government would not be party to any measure prejudicial to Belgium that would conflict with 'the interests or engagements of this country'. She came then to the real purpose of the letter. She had had the whole matter of Belgium 'fully explained' to her.

> The Treaty of November 1831 was perhaps not so advantageous to the Belgians as could have been wished, yet it cannot have been thought very advantageous to the Dutch, else they would have most probably urged their Government before this time to accept it.... This Treaty having been ratified, it is become binding and therefore it is almost impossible to consider it as otherwise.[46]

Leopold's task, according to the Queen, was to use his powerful influence over his subjects, 'to strive to moderate their excited feelings on these matters'. For the new Queen, politics and family affections were not to be mixed. British politics were the concern of the Queen and her Ministers – and of them alone.

7

The Coronation

'Thursday, June 28th 1838 . . . I was awoke at 4 o'clock by the guns in the Park and could not get much sleep afterwards on account of the noise of the people, bands etc. etc.'[1]

Queen Victoria's Coronation day had at last arrived. Three months before, in March, Lord Melbourne had told the Queen that the Cabinet had been talking about the Coronation and they all thought that it would be best to have it about the twenty-fifth or twenty-sixth of June, as it would come at the end of the parliamentary session and make a good break. The machinery was set in motion by an Order-in-Council of 7 April 1838 and thereafter the Lord Chamberlain called for estimates of costs from the various tradespeople concerned – the jewellers, robemakers, etc. When the estimates had been submitted and accepted, the great work of preparation began.

One of the major tasks was the modification of the crown the Queen wore. The crown, which had been made for George IV and weighed more than seven pounds, was too large and too heavy for the Queen. A new one was therefore made for the occasion. All the diamonds and precious stones from the old crown were set into the new one – with the addition of diamonds, pearls and a fine sapphire. The new crown was formed of hoops of gold covered with precious stones over a cap of rich blue velvet; it was surmounted by a sphere set with small diamonds. On top of the sphere was a Maltese cross with a sapphire in the centre. The wide gold circlet linking the hoops was set with a ring of diamonds in the shape of fleur-de-lys and Maltese crosses. The Black Prince's large heart-shaped ruby, worn by Henry V, at Agincourt, was in the centre of the circlet, with a large oblong sapphire below it and clusters of dropped pearls, with emeralds, rubies, sapphires and other gems.

The Queen's robes also had to be prepared. She required three. First the parliament robes she would wear on going to the Abbey: a dress of gold tissue over which was fastened a crimson velvet mantle, bordered with gold lace and lined with ermine, with a long ermine cape. Then the Imperial Mantle, with which she would be invested during the service – she was robed in a sort of white muslin shift, trimmed with very fine Brussels lace, and the dalmatic, a robe of cloth of gold, worked with the rose, shamrock and thistle in colours, and lined with crimson. Lastly the purple robes of state in which she was to leave the Abbey at the end of the service.

There were also the robes of the trainbearers to be made – 'all dressed alike and beautifully in white satin and silver tissue with wreaths of silver corn-ears in front, and a small one of pink roses round the plait behind, and pink roses in the trimming of the dresses.'[2] Among other things to be prepared were the coronets, the silver gilt sword and the gold ingot offered to the Queen, and the silver gilt inkstand which the Queen used when she appended her 'royal sign manual' to a transcript of the oath. New uniforms were made for the Yeomen of the Guard and the Warders of the Tower, new trumpet banners, etc. Enough work to keep goldsmiths, seamstresses and embroiderers fully occupied for two months before the great event.

It was the first time in its history that the British people crowned a young and pretty woman as Queen in her own right. None of the three preceding female Sovereigns – Mary, Elizabeth I and Anne – had had the advantages of Victoria. At her Coronation, Victoria was both young and seemly. She also benefited from a great display of unity as neither of the two Kings preceding her had inspired respect. There was thus no organized faction who refused to take part in the general joy or stood aloof. By contrast Mary I had really accumulated difficulties. The Tudors did not make a separation between religion and politics. 'Heresy was a civil as well as an ecclesiastical offence, and treason was both crime and sin.'[3] Since Mary was known to be a Catholic there was no universal rejoicing at her Coronation. Nor did her physique inspire. Soranzo, the Venetian Ambassador, described her as 'of low stature, with a red and white complexion and very thin', and says that despite her 'flattened nose . . . were not her age on the decline, she might be called *bella* rather than the contrary.'[4] But she was already thirty-seven, and in the sixteenth century that was well into middle age. Elizabeth, though near in age to Victoria – since she was only twenty-five and extremely personable, tall with reddish-gold hair and an olive complexion – was looked on with trepidation by those who had supported Mary. As for Queen Anne, at the time of her crowning, she was suffering from gout and had not been able to walk far or stand long.

It was to be expected, therefore, that Victoria's Coronation would be celebrated with befitting pomp. But the Government had had a considerable deficit in their annual budget and had no desire to indulge in the follies of George IV's time. Those had cost the country 243,000 pounds! In the House of Lords, Earl Fitzwilliam took advantage of the Queen's youth to give his opinion that a great deal of show was only suitable to barbarous ages and that the exhibition of a youthful Princess to a staring populace was not consistent with feminine delicacy. But he found no response in the assembly. When asked whether he thought there should therefore be no Coronation, Earl Fitzwilliam replied in the affirmative. The Marquess of Londonderry then remarked, 'I suppose that the Noble Earl is prepared to follow up that proposition by another – that there ought to be no longer an Earl Fitzwilliam.'[5]

At the end of the day the Coronation was to cost only slightly more than that of William IV – 70,000 pounds as against 50,000 pounds (three and a half times less than that of George IV). The Chancellor of the Exchequer would explain to the House that the increase had come about because of the effort made to enable the great mass of the people to participate in the national festivity.

The great desire to see the Queen crowned – the Coronation madness as some called it – led to a congestion such as London had never seen. People travelled from place to place at this time by coach, post-chaise, private carriage or rode on horseback – or if they were poor they walked. By the time of the Coronation, coaches whizzed along the macadamized road at the great speed of nine miles an hour. Railways were just coming into being – in June 1838 there were only some two hundred miles of railway in the country; in another four years there were to be nearly two thousand miles. Mary Frampton gave her mother this graphic description on the eve of the Coronation:

> Stoppages in every street, and hundreds of people waiting on the line of road from Birmingham, to get lifts on the railway in vain. If my brother Charlton had not come by the Mail on Sunday, he could not have got here at all, as the coachman told him that people were waiting at Exeter for places. . . . The Queen herself was stuck for three quarters of an hour in Piccadilly the day before yesterday. . . . Conceive the Lady Elliots not being able to get out of their own house without a Ticket! I suppose on account of the barriers and scaffolding. Not a fly or cab to be had for love or money. Hackney coaches £8 or £12 each, double to foreigners![6]

Certainly the town was full. No less than 400,000 persons were said to have come into the capital. 'Not a mob here and there, but the town all mob, thronging, bustling, gaping and gazing at everything, at anything, at nothing.'[7] The parks were transformed into vast encampments as the Queen herself had seen from her windows. 'Got up at 7. The Park presented a curious spectacle, with crowds of people up to Constitution Hill, soldiers, bands etc.'[8]

Among those who had come especially to London were many foreigners, including the Queen's closest relatives, the Prince of Leiningen and Feodora. Uncle Leopold did not come. On 17 April he had written to his niece.

> When we left England you expressed a wish to see us at the time of the Coronation, which was then believed to take place at the end of May. More mature reflection made me think that a King and Queen at your dear Coronation might perhaps be a hors d'oeuvre, and I think, if it meets with your approbation, that it might be better to pay you our respects at some other period which you might like to fix upon.[9]

The Queen replied: 'It would have made me very happy to see you both at the Coronation, but I think upon the whole it is perhaps better you should not do so.' She suggested he came in August.[10]

It was not at the time habitual for Sovereigns to attend one another's Coronations – travelling was too long and arduous. Ambassadors of note were sent instead – the King of Prussia sent the Prince of Putbus, his wealthiest and most noble subject; the Russian envoy Count Stroganoff had with him the Russian Croesus, Prince Anatole Demidoff; the Queen of Portugal sent the Duke de Palmella and the Queen of Spain the Marquis de Miraflores. There was thus an influx of luxury and of show as each nation sent its greatest and most wealthy representatives. The envoy who was the most cordially received was neither of an old and noble family nor a very rich man. It was the Ambassador Extraordinary of Louis Philippe, the King of the French, Marshal Soult, Duke of Dalmatia – who had fought against the Duke of Wellington in the Peninsula and at Waterloo. At a party given before the Coronation by the Duke of Sutherland at Stafford House, the Marshal met his old opponent. 'The Duke [of Wellington] and Soult', Greville noted, 'have met here with great mutual civilities.'[11] Soult had entered the royal army of Louis XVI but it was the new Emperor, Napoleon, who gave him his *bâton de maréchal*. He fought in Portugal, Spain and France, and was pardoned by Louis XVIII, who recognized his revolutionary dukedom and gave him back his *bâton*. He bore the sceptre when Charles X was crowned at Reims.

The 1830 revolution had not ended Soult's career since here he was, as the envoy of Louis Philippe – a rare example of the continuity of the French State. For the English he was the man who had fought brilliantly against them at Orthez and Toulouse and played a decisive role in the fields of Austerlitz and Friedland. He was cheered along the procession route and applauded in the Abbey. His appearance was 'that of a veteran warrior, and he walked alone, with his numerous suite following at a respectful distance, preceded by heralds and ushers, who received him with marked attention, more certainly than any of the other Ambassadors.'[12] Raikes in his *Journal* confirmed the warmth of his reception. 'Soult was so much cheered, both in and out of the Abbey, that he was completely overcome. He has since publicly said "it was the happiest day of my life. It shows that the English believe that I have always fought loyally." When in the Abbey he seized the arm of his aide-de-camp, quite overpowered, and exclaimed, "This is truly a great people." '[13]

The good people had been up and waiting for hours when at ten in the morning the procession formed near Buckingham Palace. It had been decided to follow the precedents of William IV's reign and to have no walking procession of all the Estates of the Realm and no banquet in Westminster Hall. On the other hand, the procession was increased in splendour and in number, and the route was much longer. Indeed the cavalcade harked back to the last grand procession through the metropolis, that of King Charles II – but it did not go as it had then through the City of London but through Westminster, which was now the most magnificent part of the capital.

Victoria got into the state coach, originally built for the Coronation of George III, with the Duchess of Sutherland and Lord Albemarle. It took an hour and a half to reach the Abbey.

> It was a fine day, and the crowds of people exceeded what I have ever seen; many as there were the day I went to the City, it was nothing, nothing to the multitude, the millions of my loyal subjects, who were assembled in every spot to witness the Procession. Their good humour and excessive loyalty was beyond everything, and I really cannot say how proud I feel to be the Queen of such a Nation. I was alarmed at times for fear that the people would be crushed and squeezed on account of the tremendous rush and pressure.[14]

There was scarcely a house from Hyde Park Corner to the Abbey which did not have galleries or scaffolding to enable a maximum number of people to watch the event. The Chancellor of the Exchequer

said later that it had been estimated that the public had paid no less
than 200,000 pounds for seats commanding a view of the procession.
The streets, which had been gravelled in the night, were lined with
soldiers and policemen – without them the procession itself would not
have been able to pass.

The procession unfurled before the spectators: trumpeters and a
squadron of the Household Brigade; foreign Ambassadors in the order
in which they respectively reported their arrival in Britain; Ministers,
bands and more cavalry; carriages of the branches of the royal family
with their escorts; more mounted bands and the Queen's barge-master
and near fifty watermen; then came twelve royal carriages conveying
the Queen's Household; then more cavalry and music, the staff and
distinguished officers; then, directly preceding the Queen, the Royal
Huntsmen, the Yeomen Prickers and Foresters, the Yeomen of the
Guard and their officers. Then came the Queen's carriage drawn by
eight cream-coloured horses. It was followed by the Captain of the
Royal Archer Guard of Scotland and cavalry who brought up the rear.

Virtually all the accounts of the procession were positive. 'The day
was fine,' Greville commented, 'without heat or rain – the innumerable
multitude which thronged the streets orderly and satisfied.'[15] But there
were some exceptions to the rule, some grumblers. Among them Mary
Frampton, who had been persuaded by Miss Burdett Coutts to remain
in Strutton Street and see the procession return from the Abbey. 'I
confess that taken altogether I was extremely disappointed.' First the
squadrons of Life Guards were small whereas 'what makes the
processions on the continent so splendid are the thousands of troops
who always take part in them.' Then there was the 'line' which was
'being kept by Policemen and Rifles' and which 'took off from the
gaiety extremely'. Finally the carriages followed each other so
'excessively closely' that they were in great danger of 'poling their
neighbour's chasseurs' and into the bargain one could not tell 'which
was which, or rather which was who.' Nothing was to Mary
Frampton's taste – not even the music. 'There was not nearly music
enough, as from the great length of the procession a band was required
much oftener.'[16]

The Queen reached the Abbey amid deafening cheers at a little after
half-past eleven. She went into the robing room, where she found her
eight trainbearers. The Queen had chosen them herself. At the
beginning of May she had sent Lord Melbourne a list of eight names.
They included 'Lady Mary Talbot, as being the daughter of the oldest
Earl in the Kingdom [John, sixteenth Earl of Shrewsbury] and a

Roman Catholic; and Lady Anne Fitzwilliam' as the Queen was anxious 'to show civility to Lord Fitzwilliam who has been very kind to the Queen.'[17] The Duchess of Cleveland was, as Lady Wilhelmina Stanhope, one of the trainbearers.

> We were all dressed alike in white and silver. The effect was not, I think, brilliant enough in so dazzling an assembly, and our little trains were serious annoyances, for it was impossible to avoid treading upon them. We ought never to have had them; and there certainly should have been some previous rehearsing, for we carried the Queen's train very jerkily and badly, never keeping step as she did, evenly and steadily, and with much grace and dignity, the whole length of the Abbey.[18]

The sight in the Abbey was beautiful. On each side of the nave, galleries were erected for the accommodation of some thousand spectators, the fronts covered with crimson cloth fringed with gold. Underneath the galleries were ranged lines of Foot Guards. In front was a platform about twelve foot wide, raised a few inches from the stone floor and matted and covered with purple and crimson carpeting. In the interior of the choir, on a carpet of gold and purple, a platform was raised five steps from the ground. The platform itself was covered with cloth of gold – on it, the chair of homage facing the altar. Within the chancel, near the altar, was St Edward's chair. The altar was covered with massive gold plate. Immediately above the altar was the gallery appointed for Members of the House of Commons.

The Coronation of Victoria occurred at a time when the middle classes were gaining in influence. The year 1832 had seen the enfranchisement of a sizeable part of the middle classes and between 1832 and 1838 there had been no fewer than three general elections. One might therefore have imagined that the Estates of the Realm summoned to Westminster Abbey might have been significantly different from those of preceding Coronations. The elements composing the House of Commons had not, however, had time to change greatly. This might almost be termed the last full-dress parade of the *ancien régime*. In the Lords there were still fourteen members who had been subjects of George II and thus had lived through five reigns. Seven of them – the most vigorous – came to Westminster to pay their antique homage and make obeisance before their Queen.[19]

In the House of Commons, too, were many elderly men, and, of course, no women – they were only allowed to stand for Parliament in 1918. The father of the House of Commons, George Byng, had first been returned to Parliament as Member for Middlesex in 1780 with

John Wilkes. The hereditary element in the lower House was still very strong. Eighty Members were noble lords – Irish peers (who did not sit in the Lords) or eldest sons (lords by courtesy as they were often called); some ninety-odd were untitled sons or brothers of peers, and an additional eighty were baronets – nearly all of whom were country gentlemen with large estates. Many of these titles, however, were so recent that they had been conferred almost within the memory of persons present in the Abbey. The Grosvenors, for instance, had come forward from the ranks of country gentlemen in the mid-eighteenth century, and the Grenvilles had only reached the House of Lords in 1752 by virtue of the death of a peeress in her own right who had borne an heir to one of them. The Greys and the Lascelles, too, had been ennobled less than a century earlier.

The highest honours and dignities were, in fact, open to persons of comparatively modest condition, provided they were landowners. These aristocrats, though of varied ability and opinion, were to all intents and purposes one class – that of the landed interest, whether of ancient or modern origin. The veneer of the elite was not acquired, as in the France of Louis XIV, in a polished Court where fine manners and elegance were learnt, but in the great political houses where the wit was sharpened and politics were of paramount interest. The best known was that of the Duchess of Devonshire, a hostess to the most brilliant society in Britain. The terms 'government' and 'society' were at the beginning of Victoria's reign almost synonymous.

There was, however, a trickle of men who were actively engaged in business. They were not a product of the extension of the franchise but of the redistribution of seats. They tended to be identified with the commercial prosperity of their constituencies.

As the Queen came into the Abbey she was impressed by its red and gold splendour. She found it all most impressive, with 'the bank of Peeresses quite beautiful, all in their robes, and the Peers on the other side.'[20] The array of fine dresses and jewels was no doubt dazzling in the extreme. 'I had never before seen the full effect of diamonds,' Harriet Martineau noted. 'As the light travelled each peeress shone like a rainbow. The brightness, vastness and dreamy magnificence of the scene produced a strange effect.'[21] One Prince was covered with diamonds and pearls, another had a uniform encrusted with turquoises. Greville considered that among all this splendour the young Queen did not stand out well enough. 'The Queen looked very diminuted and the effect of the procession itself was spoilt by being too crowded; there was not interval enough between the Queen and the Lords going before her.'[22] The Queen advanced slowly towards the centre of the choir and excitement or apprehension invaded her. 'I think', said the Duchess of Cleveland, 'her heart fluttered a little as we reached the throne; at least the colour mounted to her cheeks, brow, and even neck, and her breath came quickly.'[23]

Then the magnificent ceremonial began. First the recognition. Greeted by the boys of Westminster School, who enjoyed the historic privilege of shouting 'Vivat Victoria Regina', the new monarch was next recognized by the Archbishop of Canterbury as the 'undoubted Queen of this realm', and by the people there assembled, who cried 'God save Queen Victoria' as she turned to the north, the south and the west. At the recognition the people are, as it were, asked if they wish the ceremony to proceed, and it is made clear that the British monarchy is based upon the people's will and consent. The oath was that of a constitutional monarch who respected the rule of law, the freedom of her subjects and the privileges of the Established Churches.

'Will you solemnly promise and swear', the Archbishop of Canterbury asked the Queen, 'to govern the people of this United Kingdom of Great Britain and Ireland, and the dominions thereto belonging, according to the statutes in Parliament agreed on, and the respective laws and customs of the same.'

'I solemnly promise so to do,' answered the Queen.

'Will you, to your power, cause law and justice, in mercy, to be executed in all your judgements?'

'I will.'

'Will you, to the utmost of your power, maintain the Laws of God, the true profession of the Gospel and the Protestant Reformed religion established by law? And will you maintain and preserve inviolable the settlement of the United Church of England and Ireland, and the doctrine, worship, discipline, and government thereof, as by law established within England and Ireland, and the territories thereunto belonging? And will you preserve unto the bishops and clergy of England and Ireland, and to the churches there committed to their charge, all such rights and privileges as by law do or shall appertain to them or any of them?'

The Queen replied 'All this I promise to do.'

The central moment was the consecration of the Sovereign by the anointing. Victoria sat in the historic chair of Edward I, four Knights of the Garter held a cloth of gold over her head. The Dean of Westminster took the ampulla from the altar and poured some of the oil into the anointing spoon, and the Archbishop anointed the head and hands of the Queen, marking them with the sign of the cross. 'Be thou anointed with holy oil, as kings, priests and prophets were anointed' . . . This was followed by the investiture with the Dalmatic robe, the rendering of the orb and the delivery of the ring and sceptre.

The placing of the crown on the Sovereign's head was the supreme moment. One spectator said that as the Queen knelt and the crown was placed on her brow, a ray of sunlight fell on her face and, being reflected from the diamonds, made a kind of halo round her head.[24] Victoria herself wrote of the ceremony:

> and last . . . the Crown being placed on my head, which was, I must own, a most beautiful impressive moment; *all* the Peers and Peeresses put on their coronets at the same instant.[25]

The Bishops also put on their caps and the Kings-of-Arms their crowns. Loud cheers were echoed from every part of the Abbey and trumpets sounded and drums beat. The guns at the Tower and in the park were fired by signal.

Now came the benediction, the enthroning and the formal rendering of homage. This last had a singularly feudal character. First the Archbishop of Canterbury knelt and did homage for himself and the other Lords Spiritual; then the Queen's uncles removed their coronets and, without kneeling, made a vow of fealty. 'I do become your liege man, of life and limb, and of earthly worship; and faith and truth I will bear unto you, to live and die, against all manner of folks. So help me God!' Having touched the crown on the Queen's head, they kissed her left cheek, and retired. The other peers then performed their homage kneeling, the senior of each rank pronouncing the words. While the Lords were doing homage, the Treasurer of the Household threw silver medals about the choir and lower galleries, which led to a good deal of rather unseemly scrambling!

The ceremony concluded with a Communion service and final blessing.

Supporting the Queen, giving her confidence, were the two people whom she saw at this time as replacing her parents. As the crown was placed on her head: 'My excellent Lord Melbourne who stood very close to me throughout the whole ceremony, was completely overcome at this moment, and very much affected; he gave me such a kind, and I may say fatherly look!'[26] When the Prime Minister came in his turn to do her homage there was loud cheering. 'When my good Lord Melbourne knelt down and kissed my hand, he pressed my hand and I grasped his with all my heart, at which he looked up with his eyes filled with tears and seemed much touched, as he was, I observed, throughout the whole ceremony.'[27] Lord Melbourne it was who, according to the procedure, after she received Communion and then again after she had put on her purple velvet garments helped her to proceed again to the throne, which she ascended leaning on Lord Melbourne's arm.

There was another 'most dear Being' present at the ceremony, 'in the box immediately above the royal box, and who witnessed all; it was my dearly beloved angelic Lehzen, whose eye I caught when on the throne, and we exchanged smiles.'[28]

Support the Queen certainly needed for the Coronation did not go off as a well-oiled ceremony should. 'The different actors in the ceremonial were very imperfect in their parts,' Greville recorded, 'and had neglected to rehearse them.'[29] 'The Queen', wrote Disraeli to his sister, 'performed her part with great grace and completeness, which cannot in general be said of the other performers; they were always in doubt as to what came next, and you saw the want of rehearsal.'[30]

Dr John Ireland, the Dean of Westminster, who had conducted the two preceding Coronations of George IV and William IV, was too infirm to attend – he was seventy-eight. His place was filled by the Sub-Dean Lord John Thynne, who confessed to Greville that 'nobody knew what was to be done except the Archbishop and himself (who had rehearsed), Lord Willoughby (who is experienced in these matters), and the Duke of Wellington, and consequently there was a continual difficulty and embarrassment, and the Queen never knew what she was to do next.'[31]

The Queen confirmed this in her journal. 'The Bishop of Durham stood on the side near me, but he was, as Lord Melbourne told me, remarkably maladroit, and never could tell me what was to take place.'[32] They made her leave her chair and enter into St Edward's Chapel before the prayers were concluded, much to the discomfiture of the Archbishop. When the orb was put into her hands she said to the Dean, 'What am I to do with it?' 'Your Majesty is to carry it, if you please in your hand.' She found it very heavy. In fact it had been given her too early. 'The Archbishop . . . ought to have delivered the Orb to me, but I had already got it and he (as usual) was so confused and puzzled and knew nothing and – went away.'[33]

The most distressing moments for the Queen concerned the putting on of the ring and of the crown. The ruby ring which had been made for her little finger had, according to the rules, to be placed on the fourth finger of her hand. Although she said it was too small, the Archbishop insisted on putting it on the fourth finger, pressing it down and forcing it on. In the robing room after the ceremony she 'had the greatest difficulty to take it off again, which I at last did with great pain.'[34]

The crown had also hurt her a good deal. She complained of a headache, according to the Duchess of Cleveland, 'from having her crown very unceremoniously knocked by most of the peers – one actually clutched hold of it; but she said she had guarded herself from any accident or misadventure by having it made to fit her head tightly.'[35]

Despite these hitches the ceremony was moving. Not least because of the character of the Queen herself. 'It is in fact', noted Greville, 'the remarkable union of naiveté, kindness, nature, good nature, with propriety and dignity, which makes her so admirable and so endearing to those about her, as she certainly is.'[36] Nothing better illustrated this than her attitude towards Lord Rolle, a man of over eighty, who fell down the steps as he was going up to the throne to give homage. With the words 'May I not get up and meet him?' she rose from the throne and went down one or two of the steps to prevent his coming up.

Victoria, despite her youth, was undoubtedly regal. Greville said of her, 'She never ceases to be a Queen, but is always the most charming, cheerful, obliging, unaffected Queen in the world.'[37] The best compliment, however, came from Melbourne. 'You did it beautifully – every part of it, with so much taste; it's a thing that you can't give a person advice upon; it must be left to a person.'[38]

After nearly five hours the ceremonial ended. To the strains of the Hallelujah Chorus the Queen left and went to the robing room where she put on her purple robes of state. And here she waited for at least an hour with all her ladies and trainbearers.[39] Finally, at about half-past four, she set off on her return journey – the crown on her head, the sceptre and orb in her hands. On the return journey the crowds were even more numerous and more enthusiastic. By six she was home. But the evening was not ended. At eight came a small family dinner – with, in addition to her ladies and relatives, Lord Melbourne and Lord Surrey. They talked over the event – the incidents, the foreign emissaries, the number of peers who had attended. Finally at nearly eleven the Queen went out on to her 'Mamma's balcony looking at the fireworks in Green Park which were quite beautiful.'[40] The firework displays began at eleven in both Hyde Park and Green Park.

The public illuminations did not conclude the popular festivities. All London's theatres and most other places of popular amusement were opened free on that memorable evening. At the request of Mr Hawes, Member of Parliament for Lambeth, a fair was allowed to be held in Hyde Park for four days, starting on the day after the Coronation. It covered roughly one-third of the park and within it were theatres, taverns and an endless variety of exhibitions, with stalls at the centre selling fancy goods, sweetmeats and toys. On the second day the Queen herself paid the fair a long visit.

Greville saw it as the great merit of the Coronation 'that so much has been done for the people: to amuse and interest *them* seems to have been the principal object.'[41] Certainly the procession enabled many more people to see the Queen than any former ceremonial. Whereas the traditional banquet, which had been abandoned, was only open to the rich and privileged, anyone could witness the procession – over a million were said to have seen something of the Coronation. Prince Esterhazy, when asked what foreigners thought of it all, replied: 'Stroganoff and the others don't like you, but they feel it, and it makes a great impression on them; in fact nothing can be seen like it in any other country.'[42]

8

Scandals and Political Crises

The year 1839 was to shatter the atmosphere of admiration and contentment surrounding the young Queen. Victoria was to realize all of a sudden that her popularity was not inviolable and that Lord Melbourne would not always be there to protect and guide her. A Court scandal, a political crisis and physical attacks on the Queen darkened these early years of the reign.

The Court scandal broke out in the first months of the year. It was in a sense the culmination of the tensions and animosities between the group surrounding the Queen and the group surrounding her mother, the Duchess of Kent; it was also the fruit, in this context, of Victoria's almost pathological hatred of Sir John Conroy, her mother's confidant. At the centre of the affair was Lady Flora Hastings. Lady Flora, the eldest child of the first Marquess of Hastings, of a strong Tory family, had first come to the household of the Duchess of Kent in the autumn of 1834. She quickly became part of the Conroy faction, sharpening her wit on poor Baroness Lehzen. Despite the Queen's reluctance, on 30 April 1838 Lady Flora replaced Lady Mary Stopford as lady-in-waiting to the Duchess of Kent. The Queen warned Lord Melbourne that this spinster of thirty-two was 'an amazing spy who would repeat everything she heard.'[1]

Lady Flora, after having spent the Christmas holiday at her mother's home in Scotland, came back into waiting on 30 January 1839. On the return journey she had shared a post-chaise with Sir John Conroy. The ladies then in waiting were Lady Charlemont, Mrs Campbell, Miss Spring Rice and Miss Paget. Baroness Lehzen and Miss Davys were in constant waiting. Having been suffering from a 'bilious illness' since the beginning of December, Lady Flora consulted Sir James Clark – the physician of the Queen – and placed herself under his treatment.[2]

Dr James Clark had been Leopold's physician and it was at the latter's suggestion that he had become the physician of first the Duchess in 1834 and then the Princess in 1835. Victoria kept him as her doctor after she became Queen. His competence seems on several occasions to have been questionable – but after all, in the 1830s, medicine was not yet much advanced. In a statement he later made, Clark declared that when Lady Flora consulted him, 'She had derangement of the bowels, and of the general health and she complained of pain low in the left side. There was also considerable enlargement of the lower part of the abdomen.'[3] It was this latter phenomenon which gave rise to Court gossip. On 2 February the Queen noted in her journal that she had acquainted Lord Melbourne with the 'awkward business' connected with Lady Flora.

In her diary she wrote that she and Lehzen 'have no doubt that she is – to use the plain words – with child!! Clark cannot deny the suspicions; the horrid cause of all this is the Monster and demon Incarnate, whose name I forbear to mention, but which is the first word of the second line of this page.'[4] The word was John Conroy. So great was Victoria's hatred of John Conroy that she was ready to believe anything of him. Was she looking back to the non-proven infidelities of her mother? In any case she was only too ready to believe that the young lady's virtue had been ravished by Sir John.

Meanwhile, at the beginning of February, Lord Melbourne had sent for Sir James Clark to have a medical opinion on the rumours brought to him by Lady Tavistock. Clark told him that, while he was of the opinion that such suspicions ought not to be readily listened to, he was at the same time 'bound to admit to him that the appearance of Lady Flora in some degree countenanced them.' Without a more thorough examination he could not give an opinion. Lord Melbourne's advice was to let things ride. Cecil Woodham-Smith considers that 'Worse advice could hardly have been given.'[5]

The gossip continued. Indeed it was encouraged. Not by Baroness Lehzen – who was later to be accused by her enemies of having stirred up the whole matter. Lady Portman asserted that when she returned to waiting in early February the information concerning Lady Flora was not given her by Lehzen.[6] Nor was the culprit Sir John Conroy – although he was to be blamed not only by the Queen but also by the austere Baron Stockmar, who believed that 'with the intriguing spirit of revenge he [Conroy] continued to foment the causes of disagreement between mother and daughter and proved himself almost daily the bitterest enemy to the true interests of both.'[7] No, the man who fomented the gossip seems to have been Lady Flora's doctor himself. When Lady Portman had come into waiting in February he had informed her 'as the lady-in-waiting of his suspicions that Lady Flora Hastings was privately married' and had asked her opinion on the subject, which she gave only as connected with her 'observation of her appearance'.[8] He it was, too, who sowed doubts in Lord Melbourne's mind. In the statement he later made, Clark said that he continued to visit Lady Flora about twice a week between 10 January and 16 February, and he clearly stated that he

> examined the state of the abdomen over her dress; but being unable to satisfy myself as to the nature of the enlargement, I at length expressed to her my uneasiness respecting her size, and requested that at my next visit, I might be permitted to lay my hand upon her abdomen with her stays removed. To this Lady Flora declined to accede.[9]

By the middle of February the Queen's ladies had decided not to obey Lord Melbourne's advice to wait and see. They had worked themselves up into a fury of moral indignation. Greville noted that 'Lady Flora Hastings, the Duchess of Kent's lady, has been accused of being with child. It was first whispered about, and at last swelled into a report, and finally into a charge.'[10] On 16 February Sir James Clark, in his own words, 'found it had been determined that I should acquaint Lady Flora with the suspicions which existed in the palace, and should suggest her calling another physician into consultation with me.' He declared that he had asked Lady Portman if he might use her name as one of the ladies entertaining these suspicions – and he held she had 'at once assented.'[11]

Sir James Clark then went to Lady Flora Hastings and asked her whether she were privately married, 'giving as his reason', wrote Lady Flora, 'that my figure had excited the remarks of the ladies of the palace.'[12] On her emphatic denial he began to bully her – 'he became excited', Lady Flora Hastings later reported, 'urged me to confess' as 'the only thing to save me'; he stated his own conviction to agree with that of the ladies, that it had occurred to him at the first, that 'no one could look at me and doubt it and remarks even more coarse.'

Lady Flora observed that the swelling from which she had been suffering was much reduced and offered him the proof of her dresses. 'Well,' Clark replied, 'I don't think so. You seem to grow larger every day – and so the ladies think.' In Clark's opinion either Lady Flora was pregnant or she had some real disease. He rejected the second alternative on the grounds that she did not seem to be in bad health as she continued to perform her duties without apparent difficulty. Clark went on to say that 'nothing but a medical examination could satisfy the ladies of the Palace, so deeply were their suspicions rooted.' Lady Flora reacted vigorously. 'I said, feeling perfectly innocent, I should not shrink from any examination however rigorous, but that I considered it a most undelicate and disagreeable procedure and that I would not be hurried into it.'[13] This reaction merely served to confirm Clark's suspicions. He was devoid of any delicacy of feeling and could not understand why the girl would not be examined and prove him wrong – if he were!

Clark then went to the Duchess of Kent and gave her an account of the nature of his interview with Lady Flora. 'Her Royal Highness immediately expressed her entire disbelief of anything so injurious to Lady Flora's character.'[14] Meanwhile Lady Portman had also asked the Duchess of Kent for an audience, which her husband finally obtained for her on Sunday 17 February. She told the Duchess 'that Sir James Clark, having expressed his strong suspicion [of Lady Flora being pregnant] . . . it is impossible that the honour, either of the Court, or of the Lady can admit of the least doubt or delay in clearing up the matter.' If Lady Flora was pregnant she should leave the Palace immediately, if she were not then suspicion must be removed. According to Lady Portman, 'Nothing but the opinion of medical men could possibly be satisfactory,' and she asserted that 'it is quite impossible that the Queen should admit the Lady into her presence until her character is cleared.'[15]

Lady Flora was thus forced either to leave the Court under a cloud, dishonoured, or submit to a medical examination. Consequently, on the Monday, Lady Flora sent a note to Clark: 'Sir – By her Royal Highness's command, I have written to Sir Charles Clarke [another physician] this afternoon to come to me. He has answered my note by coming and is now here. Could you come and meet him.'[16]

On receiving this note, Clark went to Lady Flora immediately and found Sir Charles Clarke with her. She asked for Lady Portman to be called in. Sir Charles examined her first and stated there was no pregnancy. He urged James Clark to make a second examination – which he did. The two doctors then issued the following statement: 'We have examined with great care the state of Lady Flora Hastings, with a view to determine the existence or non-existence of pregnancy, and it is our opinion, although there is an enlargement of the stomach, that there are no grounds for suspicion that pregnancy does exist, or ever did exist.'[17] The examination, Lady Flora said, 'took place in the presence of my accuser, Lady Portman and my own maid.'[18]

Before parting with Lady Flora, the two doctors advised her to appear on that day at table as usual. Lady Portman came to see her that very evening

> to express her regret for having been the most violent against me. She acknowledged that she had at several times spoken a great deal to the Queen on the subject, especially when she found it was her Majesty's own idea. She said she was very sorry, but she would have done the same respecting any one of whom she had the same suspicion. I said, my surprise is, that knowing my family as she did, she could have entertained those suspicions.[19]

On the same day the Queen sent Lady Portman to Lady Flora with a message of deep regret at what had happened and an offer to see her that very evening should she so wish. Lady Flora replied that she felt gratitude towards the Queen, but that she was ill and not in a fit state to see the Queen at present. It was almost a week before she felt strong enough to face up to what was by now undoubtedly an ordeal. She finally saw the Queen on 23 February. Lady Flora 'was dreadfully agitated', wrote the Queen, 'and looked very ill, but on my embracing her, taking her by the hand, and expressing great concern at what had happened, – and my wish that all should be forgotten, she expressed herself exceedingly grateful to me, and said, that for Mamma's sake she would suppress every wounded feeling and would forget it etc.'[20] But that was not how it was to be.

Certainly Lady Flora did not incriminate the Queen. She plainly stated to her uncle, 'I am quite sure the Queen does not understand what they have betrayed her into. She has endeavoured to show her regret by her civility to me, and expressed it most handsomely with tears in her eyes.'[21] But excuses so late in the day in the privacy of the Queen's room, when the rumour had been spread wide, could not suffice. Cecil Woodham-Smith is too hard on Lady Flora when he says she 'behaved with duplicity', pretending reconciliation and at the same time writing 'a letter containing the facts and allegations' to her uncle by marriage Hamilton Fitzgerald, who was to make the whole affair public.[22]

Her letter to her uncle was in fact written later, on 8 March, and some time after she had spoken of the whole business to her brother, as any sister in a close-knit family would have done. As soon as her brother received the letter, in which she told him that her honour had 'been most basely assailed',[23] he rushed to London. She had given him no details – that single phrase had sufficed. His sister's honour, and that of the family, must be safeguarded.

To understand this phase of the affair one must recall the role played in society at that time by position, reputation and respect. Society had divided women into two sorts – the Madonnas and the Magdalenes. The latter were the demi-mondaines, the exclusive prostitutes who were sought after as the expensive mistresses of the well-born and fashionable. They lived openly in triumphant sin. Their lives were full of glamour and luxury, variety and insecurity. Outstanding among them was Skittles, who had risen from humble origins and street-walking to become the mistress of a Duke, and have her portrait, by Landseer, in the Academy – even if under an assumed name. These women were invariably beautiful – for their looks were their fortune – and they were very often lively and imaginative as well.

The young girls of good family who hoped for marriage, as the vast majority did, had one treasure which the demi-mondaines did not have – their virginity. Any blemish on a young girl's reputation would leave her definitively on the shelf – and Lady Flora at just over thirty must have been aware of this. It was not duplicity but self-preservation that caused her to want her name well and truly cleared. The no-smoke-without-fire syndrome is not a new one . . .

Lord Hastings went first to see his sister, to hear first hand the details of the whole scandalous business. Lord Melbourne was, he decided, responsible for the whole affair and he would therefore challenge him to a duel. Wisely he went to see Melbourne first and was convinced by him that the Prime Minister's only role had been to try in vain to keep everything quiet. Why was it, Hastings questioned, that a man of experience, a man of the world like Melbourne had not been able to prevent this scandal and keep a bevy of young girls quiet? Unless, of course, Melbourne had been able to do little because the Queen herself had some responsibility in the affair. Hastings determined to see the Queen and to discover from her how this plot had come about and who was responsible. Melbourne prevaricated. He certainly had no desire to see the Queen further mixed up in this regrettable affair. But Lord Hastings would not be put off. 'My Lord,' he wrote to the Prime Minister:

> Having in vain waited for two days, in the hope of having an audience with Her Majesty, which I requested (if not as a matter of right as a Peer, at least as one of feeling), my patience being exhausted, and being anxious to return to the bosom of my afflicted and insulted family I am

forced to resort to the only means now left in my power, of recording my abhorrence and detestation of the treatment which my sister has lately sustained, by addressing myself to you as the organ through which all things are now carried on at Court.[24]

Hastings set down his accusations. He did not think Her Majesty directly responsible, it was 'the baneful influence which surrounds the throne', Baroness Lehzen. With a threat that if he discovered any new elements or particulars he would not hesitate to take the whole affair up again, he declared that he now retired 'from the polluted atmosphere of a Court'[25] in which he hoped his poor sister would no longer remain.

Melbourne wrote a soothing letter, and did in fact arrange an interview with the Queen, believing that only this could calm down the excitable Lord. The visit was not a success. 'All information, or satisfaction on the subject of my inquiries as to who had been the originators of the plot having been denied me at the palace.'[26]

The young Lord, still not satisfied, continued his quest by letter. To Lord Tavistock he wrote: 'May I then ask, was not Baroness Lehzen the first person who originated this foul slander and mentioned it to Lady Tavistock, and if she be not the individual, who was?'[27] To Lord Portman he wrote: 'My purport in now writing to your Lordship is to know whether Lady Portman's [suspicions] were suggested to her, or occurred to herself; and what communication, if any passed between her Ladyship and the Baroness Lehzen.'[28] The correspondence continued throughout March – with the husbands of the ladies-in-waiting both trying to convince Hastings that their wives had only been influenced by the best motives.

By now all this was public knowledge. Greville on 2 March noted that 'the whole town has been engrossed for some days with a scandalous story at Court'; having exposed not only the bare facts but also Lord Hastings's actions and Lord Melbourne's attempts to smother the affair and calm down the young Lord, Greville added: 'The Court, is plunged in shame and mortification at the exposure, that the palace is full of bickerings and heart-burnings, while the whole proceeding is looked upon by society at large as to the last degree disgusting and disgraceful.'[29]

The Duke of Wellington urged conciliation between the Queen and her mother, Lord Melbourne urged an end to the gossiping, but the Hastings family would have none of it for by now the foreign press had got hold of the affair. It is at this precise time that Lady Flora Hastings wrote to her uncle Hamilton Fitzgerald. In this letter she set out the facts as she saw them – true as far as the actual actions were concerned, much more difficult to judge as far as interpretations were concerned. For Lady Flora the whole affair was 'a diabolical conspiracy' against both the Duchess of Kent and herself. She was convinced that 'a certain foreign lady whose hatred to the Duchess is no secret, pulled the strings.' By this she meant, of course, Baroness Lehzen. What angered Lady Flora most was that 'the subject had been brought before the Queen's notice and all this had been discussed and arranged and denounced to me, without one word having been said to my own mistress [the Duchess of Kent], one suspicion hinted, or her sanction obtained for their proposing such a thing to me.' Lady Flora also insisted on the kindness of the Duchess, who had stood by her, 'generous-souled' woman that she was. 'A mother could not have been kinder, and she took up the insult as a personal one' – one can imagine with what satisfaction.[30]

When he received the letter, Lady Flora's uncle, seeing the injurious reports in the papers, the letters that he had read misrepresenting his niece and the infamous stories that were being circulated, went to London. Here he found that public opinion was largely hostile to Lady Flora – so he determined to publish his niece's version of the matter.

Lady Flora's mother was also active. She, too, was determined to obtain reparation for her daughter. So she wrote a letter to the Queen which was one long, subtly composed insult. Her letter opened with an implicit reference to Victoria's inexperience. 'The anguish of a mother's heart, under circumstances such as mine, can only be understood by a mother.' Then she stressed her affection for and attachment to Victoria's mother. 'I am deeply and gratefully attached to your admirable mother.' Next came proof of her family's loyalty to the Crown. 'But I trust a sense of morality is not yet so callous a thing as not to be held in some due respect even in the sight of a thoughtless world.' It was therefore, she claimed, her duty to call the Queen's attention 'to its being not more important for my daughter than essentially consonant to Your Majesty's honour and justice, not to suffer the criminal inventor of such falsehoods to remain without discovery.'[31]

The letter was sent to Melbourne to ensure its immediate delivery and four days later he replied, in the Queen's name, in no uncertain terms. 'The allowance which Her Majesty is anxious to make for the natural feelings of a mother upon such an occasion tended to diminish that surprise which could not be otherwise than excited by the tone and substance of your Ladyship's letter.'[32]

Before Lady Hastings had received the Prime Minister's answer on behalf of the Queen, she had also sent a note to Melbourne himself, explaining exactly what reparation she expected: 'The nature and the manner of the course pursued in this atrocious conspiracy (for it admits of no other name) were unexampled, and yet Sir James Clark remains her Majesty's physician. I claim at your hands, my Lord, as a mark of public justice, the removal of Sir James Clark.' Melbourne's reply was categorical. 'The demand which your Ladyship's letter makes upon me is so unprecedented and objectionable that even the respect due to your Ladyship's sex, rank, family and character would not justify me in more, if indeed it authorises so much than acknowledging the letter for the sole purpose of acquainting your Ladyship that I have received it.'[33]

Here indeed was a blunt refusal. If that was the way the land lay, then so be it. If reparation were refused, why then the Hastings would publish and use public opinion as their court of appeal. In the _Morning Post_ on 9 April 1838 Lady Hastings published both her letter to the Queen and her correspondence with Melbourne. The Queen was furious. 'That wicked foolish old woman Lady Hastings, has', she wrote, 'had her whole correspondence with Lord Melbourne published in the Morning Post.' She had attempted to harm Lord Melbourne and because of this the Queen 'would have wished to have hanged the Editor and the whole Hastings family for their infamy.'[34] The publication of the correspondence had undoubtedly envenomed the whole affair. The hubbub grew. The Duke of Wellington who, although a Tory, was now viewed as something of a sage, an elder statesman, tried to pacify both Victoria and her mother – not to mention Conroy and the Hastings.

What part did Conroy play in all this? There seems little evidence that he played any. Wellington, however, believed that it was he who egged on the Duchess of Kent, persuading her to keep the issue alive. Suddenly, on 1 June 1839, Conroy announced that he intended to resign from the Duchess's service and go abroad within a fortnight! He asked to see Lord Melbourne to inform him of his decision. Lord Wellington, according to Greville, was convinced that he had brought about a change of heart in Conroy by flattering him and appealing to his sense of honour.[35] The explanation does not, however, tally with what we know of Conroy. It is more probable that the Duchess – who was far stronger than she is generally pictured – instigated this utilization of the scandal herself. Lord Holland in his diary clearly saw the Duchess of Kent in charge of the conspiracy. 'The Duchess of Kent', he noted, 'was very active, under colour of asking advice, in spreading the story and complaining to her friends personal or political of the cruelty practised and the plot contrived against a Lady of her household.'[36] Another element which would seem to justify this interpretation is the Duke of Wellington's remark to Melbourne that not only was Conroy going but that he seemed in 'great joy' about it. And Conroy did leave. He left the Duchess and he left the country for Italy. When he returned some time later he lived quietly in retirement in Reading.

His departure did not immediately improve things between the Queen and the Duchess. The rift between mother and daughter was indeed so deep that even the fact that Lady Flora was becoming more and more ill did not seem to touch the Queen at all. She refused to take Lady Flora's illness seriously. Lord Melbourne was now convinced that the lady-in-waiting was dying and that James Clark had made a bad mistake. He told the Queen so, but she refused to be convinced. When her mother came to her in tears to inform her of Lady Flora's state she told Lord Melbourne that she did not believe Lady Flora was as ill as they said she was.[37] Victoria was certainly young and thoughtless, and she was also blinded by her hatred of the whole Conroy faction. There was another factor, however. She herself had an exceptionally strong constitution and always tended to think other people's ailments were half imaginary. She was to adopt exactly the same attitude of disbelief towards her husband in his last illness.

But Lady Flora's health did deteriorate steadily. By 26 June even Victoria had to recognize that the young woman was dying, and the Queen postponed a ball she was to have given that evening. Next day her physician thought Lady Flora's state so bad that he sent to Victoria to say that she should come now if she wished, as she had said, to see her. Victoria's description of the visit is simple but very telling.

> I went in alone; I found poor Lady Flora stretched on a couch looking as thin as anybody can be who is still alive; literally a skeleton, but the body *very* much swollen like a person who is with child; a searching look in her eyes, a look rather like a person who is dying; her voice like usual and a good deal of strength in her hands; she was friendly, said she was very comfortable, and how very grateful for all I had done for her, and that she was glad to see me looking well. I said to her, I hoped to see her again when she was better upon which she grasped my hand as if to say 'I shall not see you again.' I then instantly went upstairs and returned to Lord Melbourne who said 'You remained a very short time.'[38]

There is no real word of compassion in this recital. One can feel the Queen looking at her and saying to herself – yes, she did look like a pregnant woman. Then she met Lady Flora's eyes and their probing, searching look – did Victoria turn her eyes away, was she ashamed of the treatment she had allowed to be inflicted? Did Lady Flora really greet her with such equanimity? Was there no irony in her words? Something of Lady Flora's despair – she was after all dying very young – must have communicated itself to the Queen, who fled. Lady Flora Hastings lingered on her deathbed for nearly a week. At one point the Queen told Lord Melbourne that 'it was disagreeable and painful to me to think there was a dying person in the house.'[39] Was this the callousness of youth or a remorse that she wanted to bury? On Friday, 5 July, Lady Flora died.

While Lady Flora had been spending her last unhappy months at Court, not going home because if she did rumours as to her state would begin to grow again, the public took up her cause. 'On the principle of favouring an injured person, and one who appears to have obtained no reparation for the injuries inflicted on her.'[40] The Queen was beginning by the early summer to be insulted and hissed when she rode out. Coarse expressions were shouted at her as she passed, such as 'whose belly up now?' At Ascot, members of high society hissed her and some even shouted 'Mrs Melbourne'. All this, according to a certain Mr Doyle who wrote to Lord Melbourne, was not to be wondered at. The British Court was becoming as 'depraved and licentious as that of Marie Antoinette'. The two men deemed most responsible for it by Doyle were Melbourne himself, who allowed such people to be placed about the Queen, and 'that beast Clark who deserves to be kicked out of all decent society.'[41]

The Tories began to realize that this tragic affair was a gift to them as Opposition. Here was an opportunity to damage the Whigs. The Queen had made no reparation, she had not even dismissed James Clark, as the Duchess of Kent had. She must therefore be badly counselled. The papers took up the cry. *The Times* defending the Queen, the *Morning Post* condemning her, in its own somewhat lurid style:

> *The Times* ridicules a writer in the *Morning Post* for saying 'the deplorable event of Lady Flora's death is to be inscribed upon the historic page of Queen Victoria's reign.' And so it will. *The Times* may continue to treat the late deep tragedy enacted at the Palace as a farce but we may rest assured that it will be brought forward before Posterity with full effect and that Buckingham Palace will be as famous in future ages as that of Holyrood House for the cruel immolation of its victim, even in the Queen's presence, with this difference, that Mary had no hand in the tragical affair.[42]

On 14 September the *Morning Post* devoted an entire double page to the affair. First came a letter from the Marquis of Hastings to the editor, the aim of which purported to be to 'defeat the many prejudiced statements, gross misrepresentations and unblushing falsehoods of interested persons'. In fact the Marquis was seeking revenge. His appeal was to public opinion since it was the only court of appeal left to him.

> I have been told on high authority, that if I bring this subject before the House of Lords it will be immediately silenced as an attack upon the Throne. Insurmountable technical difficulties prevent my exposing in a court of justice the vile conduct of those who have slandered my sister; and but one course therefore remains open to me and that is to publish the accompanying correspondence.

His desire was to find 'alive in the breasts of the British nation that justice and sympathy which has been denied me in a higher quarter'.[43]

The documents published included Lady Flora's statement, submitted in the form of a case to Sir William Follett and Mr Talbot in March 1839; the correspondence between Lord Hastings and Lord Melbourne; Hastings's correspondence with Lord Portman and Lord Tavistock; Lady Portman's statement; and Lady Flora's letter to her uncle, Hamilton Fitzgerald.

Worse than the daily press was the underground press – pamphlets and booklets printed anonymously and sold for a few pence: *The Dangers of Evil Counsel*, for instance, bearing as a subtitle, 'a voice from the grave of Lady Flora Hastings to Her most gracious Majesty the Queen', which could be bought for one shilling. Its preface claimed:

> the cause here advocated is that of female innocence, slandered and persecuted to death: it is the cause of the weaker party, oppressed by power; it is the cause of British justice and liberty; it is the cause of the character and honour of the Queen's court; it is the cause of our innocent young Queen herself "surprised", "betrayed" by evil suggestions and evil counsel into that which she knew not.[44]

Or again the *Warning Letter to Baroness Lehzen* by 'a voice from the grave', which also sold for a shilling and claimed that 'a certain foreign lady pulled the wires of a diabolical conspiracy of which Lady Flora was to be the first victim.' In this publication the Queen was taken to task for not having repelled the advice of Lehzen and sought the advice and guidance of her mother ... Latent xenophobia was evident when Lehzen was referred to as 'of comparatively mean descent, and so much beneath the ladies in rank and station ... a stranger harboured in our country . . .' The pamphlet ended: 'O may you escape, ere yet it be too late for your own and the Nation's safety, from evil counsel! . . . May you be solaced by the fulfilment of filial duty and the delightful exercise of filial love!'[45]

One satire at least was by a man of rank – that entitled *The Palace Martyr!* by the Honourable *** once again sold at one shilling. This time the accusations were in verse. The attack was directed first against the Court:

> Where arts and luxury are most refined
> And all is fair and polished – but the mind.

and then against the Queen herself:

> Strange destiny that Britain's mighty isle
> Should hang dependent on a school girl's smile
> The court physician, with his cringing back
> And coward sneer, the leader of the pack;
> While titled beldames their assistance brought,
> And the young Queen smiled blithely on the sport.[46]

In the national and provincial papers, and in the underground press, the message was clear. The Court needed to be cleansed. If the young Queen did not change her attitude she would lose the loyalty of her subjects, the people of England. Lord Melbourne, who was maligned and treated as an old rake, had to be tolerated while he was still Prime Minister – but there were others who should be chased from the Court. Sir James Clark came under the severest criticism. For the Glasgow *Constitution* he was an 'unclean functionary', for the *Edinburgh Evening Post* he was 'self convicted of incompetency, on the presumption that he acted from no worse principle', for the *Kentish Observer* 'every line of his letter breathes fear, and cunning and caution', for the *Manchester Caution* he was 'the pliant tool of the courtly conspirators'. The Queen was accused of being too preoccupied with dresses and dances, routes and balls, concerts and fancy fairs, gymnastic exhibitions and the feats of wild beasts. The nation, it was claimed, expected her to set an example . . .

Through these difficult months the Hastings affair was not the only problem Victoria had to face. There was a question of more constitutional moment – the Bedchamber Question.

Lord Melbourne's Government had been gradually losing the confidence of the House of Commons, and on 7 May 1839 it mustered only a majority of five on the Jamaican question. This was an issue of some importance since it concerned the authority of Great Britain over its colonies. The British Parliament had, in 1835, declared that slavery and negro apprenticeship were abolished throughout the British Empire. The sugar planters in Jamaica refused to apply the measure. Faced with their defiance, Melbourne's Government proposed to suspend the constitution of Jamaica for five years and to impose direct rule through a Governor General and Council. The Tories were against the measure – and so were a number of Radicals, who refused the very notion of direct rule. On an issue of such moment Lord Melbourne considered a majority of five too slender. He tendered his resignation to the Queen – for the government 'cannot give up the Bill either with honour or satisfaction to their own consciences, and in the face of such an opposition they cannot persevere in it with any hope of success.'[47] In his letter of resignation Lord Melbourne expressed his fear that his decision would be both painful and embarrassing to the Queen and his confidence that she would 'meet this crisis with that firmness which belongs to your character and with that rectitude and sincerity which will carry your Majesty through all difficulties.'

Melbourne was right to fear the effect his resignation would have on the nineteen-year-old girl still so new to her task. 'The state of agony, grief and despair into which all this placed me may', she wrote, 'be easier imagined than described! All, all my happiness gone! That happy peaceful life destroyed, that dearest, kind Lord Melbourne no more my Minister . . .'[48] Lord Melbourne came to see the Queen at ten minutes past twelve but 'it was some minutes before I could muster up the courage to go in.' When she did the atmosphere was heavy with emotion, as her diary shows.

> I really thought my heart would break; he was standing near the window; I took that kind, dear hand of his, and sobbed and grasped his hand in both mine and looked at him and sobbed out, 'You will not forsake me'; I held his hand for a little while, unable to leave go; and he gave me such a look of kindness and affection, and could hardly utter for tears, 'Oh! no', in such a touching voice.[49]

In the afternoon she saw Lord John Russell who again moved her to tears. Lord Melbourne came again shortly afterwards, this time the bearer of a memorandum advising her what she should do in this crisis. He read the document to her – she should, he said, send for the Duke of Wellington. The Radicals had neither 'ability, honesty nor numbers', she therefore had no choice but to call for the leader of 'that great party which calls itself Conservative.'[50] Should Wellington decline to form a government himself and suggest it be led by Sir Robert Peel, the Queen should accede to his request but press Wellington to take office himself in such a government.

Lord Melbourne thus acted with the greatest rectitude, presenting the Opposition as the only solution. He also counselled the Queen to retain her royal prerogatives by being 'very vigilant that all measures and all appointments are stated to your Majesty in the first instance and your Majesty's pleasure taken thereon previously to any instruments being drawn out for carrying them into effect, and submitted to your Majesty's signature.'[51] Similarly, the Queen should insist that patronage should be disposed of not by the Lord Chamberlain but by herself in consultation with the Prime Minister. The memorandum ended with the advice that 'Your Majesty had better express your hope that none of your Majesty's Household, except those who are engaged in politics may be removed.'[52]

Melbourne's attitude throughout was exemplary. When the Queen said how hard it was to have people forced upon you whom you disliked, he told her, 'It is very hard, but it can't be helped'; when she begged him to come and see her on that evening after dinner he told her it wouldn't be right while her negotiations with the other party were in progress. 'It would create feeling, possibly lead to remonstrance and throw a doubt upon the fairness and integrity of your Majesty's conduct.'[53] He told her that she must 'try and get over [her] dislike for Peel', explaining that he was a 'close, stiff man'.[54] He had for some time tried to create good feeling between the Queen and Peel. 'On one occasion, at a Court Ball, he noticed that Peel stood proudly aloof, and going up to him he whispered with great earnestness "For God's sake go and speak to the Queen."' Peel, however, made no move. An episode, noted Lord Esher, 'characteristic of both men'.[55]

On the morning after Lord Melbourne's resignation the Queen received the Duke of Wellington and told him that 'as his party had been instrumental in removing them [her late ministry], that she must look to him to form a new Government.'[56] The Duke, however, declared that he had no power whatever in the House of Commons and advised her to send for Sir Robert Peel, who was, he said, 'a gentleman and a man of honour and integrity'.[57] Although at first Wellington declared he was too deaf and old even to join the Cabinet, when the Queen pressed him he said he would accept office if she so wished. The Duke advised her to write to Peel herself rather than send a message, and this she did.

Peel came to see her that afternoon, 'embarrassed and put out',[58] and she asked him to form a new ministry. Her impression was that he was 'not happy and sanguine'.[59] He complained that entering the Government in a minority was very difficult and that he felt unequal to the task. He stressed that he felt the task arduous and would require the Queen to demonstrate confidence in the Government. He was clearly on the defensive and the Queen found him 'a cold, odd man'.[60] She did not like his manner: 'how different, how dreadfully different, to that frank, open, natural and most kind warm manner of Lord Melbourne.'[61]

Rhodes James holds that 'even if Peel had possessed formidable resources of personal warmth and charm, nothing could have availed him at this moment with the Queen. He was a Tory; therefore he was her enemy.'[62] Certainly the Queen was at the time suffering from the Tory treatment of the Hastings affair, but Wellington, for instance, was kind and considerate to her and she confided in Melbourne that she liked him far better than Peel. There is no doubt that Peel had a gift for making enemies. Disraeli explained his 'bad manner' as follows: 'He was by nature very shy, but forced early in life into eminent positions, he had formed an artificial manner, haughtily stiff or exuberantly bland, of which, generally speaking, he could not divest himself.'[63] He was very tense in his relationships – especially on a social level – for he was not of the caste of the Melbournes and the Wellingtons. Peel was a professional politician, one of the first to rise to eminence – he was in no sense a courtier.

His manner to the Queen may perhaps also be explained by his own reluctance to take office. The Tories had been taken by surprise when Lord Melbourne resigned – after all he could still command a majority in the House, albeit a majority of only five.[64] At their first meeting the Queen and Peel talked of the new ministry. Peel agreed that Wellington should take office and told the Queen he meant to offer him the Foreign Office. He talked of Lord Aberdeen and Lord Lyndhurst, of Stanley and Graham, and the posts he might offer them. Despite the fact that the Queen had clearly stated that she was against a dissolution of Parliament he insisted on offering the Speaker's Chair to Goulburn even if this were to lead to a 'severe conflict resulting in his resignation or the dissolution of Parliament.'[65] The idea of not being able to govern did not seem to perturb Peel unduly . . .

At this first meeting it was the Queen and not Peel who brought up the question of her Household. The problem concerned those of her ladies whose husbands were amongst Peel's strongest opponents in Parliament. As Prime Minister he would no doubt wish to change them. Asked whether he intended to dismiss her ladies, Peel gave her no answer save to say that nothing would be done without her knowledge and approbation. Lord Melbourne, whom she kept informed of her audiences, advised her to insist on the fact that the choosing of her Household was her own business. He prudently added that if Sir Robert insisted it was otherwise, then she would have to concur.[66] Melbourne strongly advised the Queen to do everything to facilitate the formation of the Government rather than 'run the risk of getting into the situation in which they are in France of no party being able to form a Government and conduct the affairs of the country.'[67]

On the following morning Melbourne wrote to the Queen and told her that if Peel pressed for the dismissal of those of her Household who were not in Parliament, he was creating a precedent and pressing her harder than any Minister had ever pressed a Sovereign before. In 1830, for instance, when the Government was changed, the Grooms and Equerries were not removed. When Peel himself became Prime Minister in 1834 'no part of the Household were removed except those who were in Parliament' – similarly when Melbourne himself became Prime Minister in 1835.[68]

Just after one o'clock the same day, the Queen received Peel again and they spent an hour together. Sir Robert 'insisted on my giving up my Ladies, to which I replied that I *never* would consent, and I never saw a man so frightened.'[69] This was an issue the Queen might use to keep Peel out of office and there was no doubt that she was delighted to see a way to bring back Melbourne. Her note to Melbourne began: 'The Queen writes one line to prepare Lord Melbourne for what *may* happen in a very few hours'; it ended, 'Keep yourself in readiness for you may soon be wanted.'[70] Greville was perhaps not wrong when he saw in Victoria's insistence on this matter a simple pretext. The young girl, 'clever but rather thoughtless and headstrong', was 'secretly longing to get back old Ministers (if she could by any pretext or expedient). She boldly and stubbornly availed herself of the opening which was presented to her.'[71]

It may well be, however, that Victoria was not the only one seeking a pretext. What if Peel were glad of an issue which prevented him from leading a fragile Government? He began by misinterpreting what the Queen said to him. 'I then repeated that I wished to retain about me those who were not in Parliament, and Sir Robert *pretended* that I had the preceding day expressed a wish to keep about me those who *were* in Parliament.'[72] He told the Queen that he had talked the matter over with those who were to have been his colleagues and 'that they agreed that with the probability of being beat the first night about the Speaker, and beginning with a Minority in the House of Commons, that unless there was *some* . . . demonstration of my confidence and if I retained all my Ladies they agreed unanimously they could not go on!'[73]

Peel's argument was that the Ladies were all the wives of the opponents of what would be the new Government. Lady Normanby, whom the Queen particularly wished to keep, was the wife of the former Lord Lieutenant of Ireland; there were also two sisters of the Irish Secretary, Lord Morpeth, the sisters-in-law of Lord John Russell, and the daughter of the Privy Seal. Victoria's argument was that she never talked politics with them and that many of them were related to Tories. When Victoria claimed that it had never been done before, Peel replied that she was a Queen Regnant – not a consort – and that that made the difference. When the Duke of Wellington was called in by Peel to discuss the matter with the Queen, the Duke said, 'the opinions of the Ladies were nothing, but it was the principle whether the Minister could remove the Ladies or not, and that he [the Duke] had understood it was stated in the Civil List Bill, "that the Ladies were instead of the Lords".'[74] But in fact, Wellington was wrong about the Civil List. The Ladies, moreover, were not in the House of Lords and had no votes or political influence.

Since the Tories considered that they could not now form a Government unless the Ladies of the Bedchamber were changed, the Queen sent for Lord Melbourne. She was evidently pleased, not to say elated, at the breaking down of the negotiations with Peel. Melbourne called a Cabinet meeting and, after much discussion, the Cabinet advised the Queen to return the following answer to Peel: 'The Queen having considered the proposal made to her yesterday by Sir Robert Peel, to remove the Ladies of her Bedchamber, cannot consent to adopt a course which she conceives to be contrary to usage and which is repugnant to her feelings.'[75]

Greville considered that this action by the outgoing Cabinet was highly unconstitutional. 'They ought to have explained to her that until Sir Robert Peel had formally and finally resigned his commission into her hands, they could tender no advice.'[76] Peel responded to the Queen's note in a rather laboured letter acknowledging that he must have the power of dismissing the Ladies but suggesting that he would have used it sparingly. The Queen thus considered negotiations at an end and asked Melbourne if the former Cabinet would take up the seals of office again. Lord Holland recounts:

Melbourne, in laying this question before us, observed very pertinently that after we had advised the Queen to answer as she had done, we were bound in honour to do all consistently with our public duty to support her, but at the same time we could not hope to alter that condition in which we stood with the House of Commons, and which had induced us to resign as unsufficient to our purposes, without being prepared to make concessions of a popular nature to reclaim a portion of those who had been estranged from us by the moderation and caution of our policy.[77]

So Melbourne returned and his Government followed its uncertain path for another two years. The Whigs introduced another Jamaica Bill which was less stringent and which was carried with the assistance of the Tories. The Tories were furious that they had been outmanoeuvred. Curiously enough, however, the four-day crisis had subtly changed the relationship between Lord Melbourne and the Queen. Was it because Victoria felt that she had in some sense matured, achieved something on her own? 'I acted', she wrote to Uncle Leopold, 'quite alone, but I have been, and shall be, supported by my country, who are very enthusiastic about it, and loudly cheered me on going to Church on Sunday. My Government have nobly stood by me, and have resumed their posts, strengthened by the feelings of the country.'[78] Uncle Leopold highly approved of his niece's action and considered the affair did her great credit. Was it Melbourne who, having believed himself rid of the burden of office, was not altogether enamoured of taking up the reins again? Whatever the reason, the relationship of the young Queen and her ageing Prime Minister was not to be what it had been.

It was towards the end of the year, in the wake of the other events, that for the first time the Queen's physical security was threatened. Between October and December 1839 three different disturbing events occurred.

At Windsor, one October night, some panes of glass were broken in the window of the Queen's dressing room. An inspector of police on guard at the Castle discovered the offender, who was arrested and confessed that he had secreted himself in the Home Park and had broken the panes with stones flung over the wall. No real harm had been done, but the incident certainly showed that the security of the Queen in her own castle was far from satisfactory.

At the beginning of December, at half-past ten one evening, a respectably dressed man got over the high iron gates leading to the Castle, opposite the Long Walk where no sentries were usually placed. He walked across the park to the grand entrance – without being stopped – and said to the porter, 'I demand admittance into the castle as the King of England.' The porter reacted very calmly, saying, 'Very well your majesty, but be pleased to wait until I get my hat.' He then took the intruder into the Castle, into the professional care of Mr Russell, one of the inspectors of police on duty there. On examination the man was found to be a partner in an extensive wholesale establishment at Manchester and to have been recently released from a lunatic asylum. In reply to one question he declared he was 'like all other men who wanted wives, he was looking after one' and had thus come to see her Majesty. Once again no harm had been done. But Windsor was certainly proving very poorly guarded. What if the man had not gone to the porter's lodge but had managed to slip into the Castle unseen?

That was precisely what the 'Boy Jones' did on Thursday, 13 December. At an early hour in the morning he actually secreted himself in one of the apartments, not at Windsor but at Buckingham Palace. He was found there and handed over to the police. The boy looked about thirteen years old though it transpired that he was sixteen. Although he had the appearance of a chimney sweep he was in fact a tailor's son. At a few minutes before five in the morning, the boy had half-opened the door of the porter's lodge at the equerries' entrance and, when asked by the porter which chimney he had come to sweep, had run away. The porter was suspicious of this conduct and warned the police. They discovered that the boy had been to Sir Charles Murray's rooms, where he had found a pot of bear's grease which he had used liberally to plaster his hair! He had also no doubt rolled on the bed for it was covered in soot. In the corridor was a bundle of things he intended to take away – including a sword and various articles of linen.

Under examination the boy, who was intelligent and appeared to have had some education, revealed that this was not his first night in the Palace. He had been living there since the beginning of December: 'And a very comfortable place I've found it. I used to hide behind the furniture and up the chimneys in the day time; when night came, I walked about, went into the kitchen and got my food. I have seen the Queen and her Ministers in council, and have heard all they have said.' He went on to tell the magistrate that the place he liked best was the drawing room and that he knew his way all over the Palace and had been everywhere, 'the Queen's apartments and all'.[79] In the event, the boy was declared insane and discharged. He came back to the Palace again in March 1841. This time he was condemned to three months on the treadmill in the House of Correction and then sent to sea.

9

Courtship

On 24 May 1839, Victoria was twenty. As she herself put it, 'This day I go out of my teens.'[1] Her two supporters were still Baroness Lehzen and Lord Melbourne. But the happy round of regal duties was beginning to pall. 'It was a most beautiful bright day', she noted three days later, 'yet the first impression, I know not why, beautiful as it looked and green and bright – is always a triste one.'[2] Not that she was idle. That very day the Grand Duke Alexander of Russia, eldest son of Tsar Nicholas I, arrived and a great dinner was given in St George's Hall. The young Victoria was by now full of emotional stirrings and very much attracted by the opposite sex. 'I really am', she noted, 'quite in love with the Grand Duke; he is a dear, delightful young man.' When he danced a Mazurka with her, she felt his masculinity very strongly. 'The Grand Duke is so very strong, that in running round, you must follow quickly and after that you are whisked round like in a *Valse*, which is very pleasant.'[3] She also danced a folk dance,

> which begins with a solemn walk round the room and comprises many different figures including one in which the lady and gentleman run down holding their pocket handkerchief by each end, and letting the ladies on one side go under it, and the gentlemen jump over it. This concluded our little Ball at near two o'clock. I never enjoyed myself more. We were all so merry.[4]

In bed by a quarter to three she was so over-excited that she could not sleep till five.

When the time came for the Grand Duke to say goodbye at the end of his stay, he pressed her hand and told her he would never forget the fine reception she had given him and the days he had spent there, adding, 'These are not mere words I can assure you Madame.' He looked pale and his voice faltered as he said, 'Words fail me to express all I feel.'[5] Victoria kissed his cheek, upon which he kissed hers 'in a very warm affectionate manner'. With a touching naiveté Victoria noted that she felt more as if she were taking leave of a relative than of a stranger. She had nothing but praise for the 'dear amiable young man, whom I really think (talking jokingly) I was a little in love with, and certainly attached to; he is so frank, so really young and merry, has such a nice open countenance with a sweet smile, and such a manly fine figure and appearance.'[6] But the Queen was obliged to abandon any thoughts of the young man. An alliance with the Grand Duke was, of course, out of the question. As eldest son of the Tsar, he was destined to rule Russia, not to play Prince Consort in England. A few days later she was commenting, 'after the . . . Grand Duke, no one is seen to advantage.'[7]

The Queen was certainly ready to bestow her affections on someone. She complained to Lord Melbourne that she seldom had young people of her own rank with her and stressed that excitement did her good. Sagely he told her, ' "But you may suffer afterwards . . . You must take care of your health, you complain of that langour increasing, and dislike for exertion; now it would be a dreadful thing for you if you were to take a dislike for business", which I assured him I never should. "You lead rather an unnatural life for a young person", he continued: "it's the life of a man." I did feel it sometimes, I said.'[8] The isolation of monarchy was beginning to weigh upon the young Queen.

A few days later the Queen again expressed her desire to see more of her contemporaries. 'Talked of my Relations having gone, and my liking to live with young people, for that then I felt that *I was young*, which I really often forgot, living so much, if not entirely, with people much older than myself.'[9] It is not surprising that when Uncle Leopold wrote and suggested a visit from her cousins Ernest and Albert, she welcomed the idea with enthusiasm.[10]

The King of the Belgians must have been relieved at her prompt acquiescence. Eighteen months earlier she had refused to take any heed of what the King had called a 'decisive arrangement for the years 1838–39' and told him so in no uncertain terms. It was, she declared, not her intention to change her present position until 1840 at the very earliest. Her reasons were that, first, she was 'not yet quite grown-up and . . . not strong enough in health', and moreover had a great deal to do 'which marrying now would render still more fatiguing.' In addition there was the question of age. Albert would need to be at least twenty before he married her, for 'it would not do, were I to marry a boy, for so

I rate a man of 18 or 19.' Her third reason was even more vexatious. Before she married him, Albert 'ought to be perfect in the English language; ought to write and speak it without fault, which is far from being the case now: his French too is not good enough yet in my opinion . . . Unfortunately.'[11]

Over a year later, when she told Lord Melbourne of her Uncle Leopold's project he was less than enthusiastic. 'Cousins are not very good things. Those Coburgs are not popular abroad; the Russians hate them.'[12] They then went through the list of eligible Princes together and Victoria declared 'not one . . . would do'. On the other hand she had no wish to marry a commoner for, as she put it, 'marrying a subject was making yourself so much their equal.'[13]

The Flora Hastings affair had undoubtedly weakened the monarchy, but the Bedchamber Question had been more important still. The Queen had not understood the deeper political issues involved. The crisis had been for her a personal crisis not a state crisis. Her correspondence with Lord Melbourne during the crisis was not usual constitutional conduct. If the monarchy were not to slip back into unpopularity the Queen needed to feel more secure. And what better way to stabilize a woman in nineteenth-century England than to give her a husband? The Tories undoubtedly felt that a husband's guidance and support would make the Queen see reason. Especially if he were one of them. Lord Melbourne also thought that the sooner she married the better, and indicated as much to her. For instance, when she and her mother were at loggerheads during the Flora Hastings episode, she told Melbourne how dreadful it was to have the prospect of torment for many years with her mother living in her house. But what, she asked, could be done? Her mother had declared 'she would never leave me as long as I was unmarried.' 'Well then, there's *that* way of settling it,' he said. But Victoria had found the alternative 'shocking'.[14]

In June she agreed to the visit of the Coburg cousins. But she was not at ease. She had no particular wish to see Albert, 'as the whole subject was an odious one, and one which I hated to decide about.'[15] The real problem for her was that the young man was aware of the possibility of a union between them, although there was no official engagement. She had no wish to keep him dangling and yet was incapable of making a firm decision. Lord Melbourne urged her not to allow herself to be pushed into marriage. She should make them understand that she could not do anything for a year, for marriage was a very serious question.[16] Was he thinking back over his marriage to 'Caro'; was he trying to reassure an anxious twenty-year-old; or did he confusedly realize that a future spouse might not view with too friendly an eye his influence over the Queen?

As the summer wore on, the Queen's doubts grew and with them her moodiness. On 15 July 1839 she wrote to Uncle Leopold, anxious to put several questions to him and to give him her feelings about her cousin's visit.

> First of all, I wish to know if Albert is aware of the wish of his Father and you relative to me? Secondly, if he knows that there is no engagement between us? I am anxious that you should acquaint Uncle Ernest, that if I should like Albert, that I can make no final promise this year, for, at the very earliest, any such event could not take place till two or three years hence.[17]

The Queen advanced arguments which must have dampened her uncle's spirits. Although all reports of Albert were favourable, she might not 'have the feeling for him which is requisite to ensure happiness'. She might 'like him as a friend, as a cousin and as a brother but not more'. She could, moreover, make no final promise as to marriage, as there was 'no anxiety evinced in this country for such an event'. If it were rushed it might produce discontent. She wished it to be remembered that she was 'not guilty of any breach of promise' for she never gave any.[18]

Victoria felt undoubtedly nervous about the visit, considering herself in a very painful position. For two full years she had enjoyed the freedom she had gained on coming to the throne and was not anxious to relinquish it. She was her own mistress and enjoyed a style of life which had long been denied her. And yet she was beginning to feel lonely, tired of having a man who was so much older as her aide. She became more demanding towards Lord Melbourne, counting on him for constant companionship. But the impatience of the young Queen full of youth and vitality with the ageing courtier was more and more evident. 'Lord Melbourne sat near me the whole evening and was very sleepy; he said it was "right to be so" after dinner. We did not meet for that I said and that I wondered he could sleep before so many.'[19] She went on to tell him that he had been snoring and ought to be in bed. On the following evening he made a great effort to keep his wits about him throughout the evening. The Queen was not satisfied. 'He took wine to keep himself awake,' she noted, 'which I feared might make him ill.'[20] The following day was Sunday and she upbraided her Prime Minister for 'he had behaved so ill at church, was so fidgety and slept during the sermon.'[21]

Lord Melbourne was sensitive to the Queen's change of heart towards him – and even made the Queen feel rather ashamed of her attitude. 'I was sadly cross to Lord Melbourne when he came in, which was shameful: I fear he felt it for he did not sit down of himself as he usually does, but waited until I told him to do so.'[22] She talked, too, of her 'growing disinclination to business' which Lord Melbourne told her she must conquer.[23] In fact the young Queen was really out of sorts. She was increasingly nervous about the Coburg visit. She realized that for her uncle the marriage was a foregone conclusion. But what changes would marriage bring? That was the problem.

Yet when, at the beginning of October, Albert wrote to tell his cousin that they could not set off before 6 October, Victoria rather paradoxically took umbrage and wrote to King Leopold: 'I think they [the cousins] don't exhibit much *empressement* to come here, which rather shocks me.'[24]

As Victoria wondered and waited, hesitated and dithered, what were the feelings of Albert? Who was this Prince who had been so carefully groomed by King Leopold to become Victoria's husband?

Albert of Saxe-Coburg – Albrecht Franz August Karl Emanuel, to give him his full name – was born in the ducal summer residence, the *Rosenau*, a modest hunting lodge on the southern edge of the forest of Thuringen, some four miles from Coburg, the former capital of the Duchy of Saxe-Coburg and Gotha. His father, Ernest I, Duke of Saxe-Coburg-Saarfeld, had married in 1817 the seventeen-year-old Princess Louise of Saxe-Gotha-Altenburg – sixteen years younger than himself. She bore him two sons – Ernest in 1818, Albert on 26 August 1819.

Ernest and Louise were by no means a perfect couple. The Duke was notoriously unfaithful to his wife almost from the outset. Her fidelity in the early years has been questioned. Several authors claim that Albert was in reality not his father's son. Max W.L. Voss, in 1921, gives him a Jewish father. 'Prince Albert of Coburg, the Prince Consort,' he wrote, 'is to be described without contradiction as a half Jew, so that since his time, Jewish blood has been circulating in the veins of the Hohenzollerns.'[25] This theory was taken up in less anti-semitic terms by Lytton Strachey in his biography of *Queen Victoria*, 'There were scandals', he informed his readers, 'one of the Court Chamberlains, a charming and cultivated man, of Jewish extraction, was talked of.'[26] Bolitho rightly contested Voss's theory and held that the Duchess's infidelity only started when Albert was four years old.[27] Kurt Jagow, writing in 1938, held that: 'All the stories about the Duchess's alleged

Kensington Palace: birthplace of Victoria.
(The Mansell Collection)

HRH The Duchess of Kent with the Princess Victoria, painted by Sir W.
Beechey, RA, etched by W. Skelton.
(The Mansell Collection)

The Princess Victoria, engraved by Dean.
(The Mansell Collection)

Princess Victoria at the age of seventeen by H. Collen.
(Reproduced by gracious permission of Her Majesty The Queen)

Princess Victoria by Count D'Orsay.
(The Mansell Collection)

Coronation of Queen Victoria, 1838, by Sir George Hayter.
(Reproduced by gracious permission of Her Majesty The Queen: Photograph: The Mansell Collection)

Leopold I of Belgium.
(The Mansell Collection)

Baroness Lehzen, sketched by Queen Victoria.
(Windsor Castle, Royal Library © 1990 Her Majesty The
Queen)

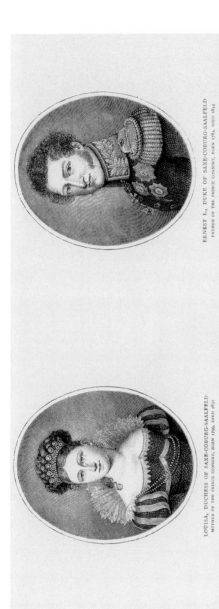

LOUISA, DUCHESS OF SAXE-COBURG-SAALFELD
MOTHER OF THE PRINCE CONSORT, BORN 1799, DIED 1831

ERNEST I., DUKE OF SAXE-COBURG-SAALFELD
FATHER OF THE PRINCE CONSORT, BORN 1784, DIED 1844

The mother and father of Prince Albert with views of his birthplace, The
Rosenau.
(The Mansell Collection)

The marriage of Queen Victoria and Prince Albert by Sir George Hayter.
(Reproduced by gracious permission of Her Majesty The Queen)

Albert, sketched by Victoria.
(Windsor Castle, Royal Library © 1990 Her Majesty The Queen)

unfaithfulness before Albert's birth and the conclusions from them are mere gossip.'[28] As Robert Rhodes James, Albert's biographer, notes, the letters of Louise's mother-in-law to her daughter, the Duchess of Kent, clearly show that the marriage was a happy one until Albert was at least two.[29]

Whatever the state of relations between the Duke and Duchess before Albert's birth, it declined shortly afterwards and culminated in a separation in 1824, when Albert was only five, and a divorce two years later. Technically the Duchess was the guilty party, but this simply reflects the double standard of morality of the day, for the Duke had been openly unfaithful to his wife almost from the outset. In 1823 Pauline Panam, alias Madame Alexandre, one of the Duke's old flames, grew tired of the Duke's broken promises and prevarications and published her memoirs, *Mémoires d'une Jeune Grecque*, in Paris.[30] This public statement was the last straw for the Duchess. The year before, she had met an army lieutenant, two years younger than she was – Baron Alexander von Hanstein. On 4 September 1824 she left Coburg for ever. She abandoned her two little boys, who were at the time ill in bed with whooping cough – and never saw them again. Six months after her divorce, in 1826, she married the Baron and lived happily with him until she died of cancer of the womb in August 1831.

Albert had been his mother's acknowledged favourite from birth and she had cared for and cosseted him. When he was only eight months old his mother wrote, 'Albert is superb, extraordinarily beautiful.'[31] He was indeed a pretty, rather feminine child. His grandmother, the Dowager Duchess of Coburg, spoke of him at two as 'very handsome, but too slight for a boy'.[32] She and his step-grandmother, the Duchess of Saxe-Gotha-Altenburg vied with one another 'which should show them [the two boys] the most love and kindness'.[33] Albert was also his uncle Leopold's favourite. And 'Albert', wrote his mother, 'adores his Uncle Leopold and does not leave him for a moment, he looks at him lovingly, kisses him all the time and is only happy when he is near him.'[34]

When Albert was four a tutor was engaged to superintend the education of Albert and his brother. The tutor was Herr Florschütz of Coburg, a young man of twenty-five. He, too, succumbed to Albert's charms. He described him as a most appealing child. 'Every grace had been showered by nature on this charming boy. Every eye rested on him with delight and his look won the heart of all.'[35] Florschütz, while obviously preferring Albert, saw the partiality the boy's mother showed towards her son as a fault. 'Duchess Louise was wanting in the essential qualifications of a mother. She made no attempt to conceal that Prince Albert was her favourite child. He was handsome and bore a strong resemblance to herself. He was in fact her pride and glory.'[36]

As one reads the memorandum on Albert penned by Florschütz, the tone makes one wonder whether his criticisms are not in reality an indication that the tutor was jealous of the mother's hold on the affections of this boy who undoubtedly attracted him. Much has been made of the fact that Albert preferred his male tutor to the women who had ruled over him earlier on. Theodore Martin, in the official biography written under Queen Victoria's supervision after her husband's death, noted that the Prince had 'even as a child shown a great dislike to be in the charge of women'.[37] David Duff believes Albert had 'strange and unnatural feelings towards his mentor, and these had to be sternly suppressed.'[38] If this were so, it would scarcely be abnormal, given the traumatic effect of his mother's departure and the fact that Florschütz was to supervise the boys' studies for some fifteen years. He was to be the only person permanently present in Albert's life, with the exception of his brother Ernest, during his childhood and adolescence.

Albert was a sensitive child and one can imagine the disastrous effect on him of his mother's sudden departure when he was only five. One wonders how he learnt, and from whom, that she was never to return. Was it his father and if so did the Duke blame his wife and condemn her in the eyes of his sons? Was the task given to Florschütz and if so did he take advantage of the fact and tell the boys how unworthy their mother was? Perhaps they were not told immediately and whispered their anxiety over their mother's non-return to one another. Victoria, in a memorandum to Colonel Grey in 1864 when he was writing *The Early Years of H.R.H. the Prince Consort*,[39] said that her husband 'spoke with much tenderness and sorrow of his poor mother, and was deeply affected in reading, after his marriage, the accounts of her sad and painful illness', but it is difficult to assess the value of this testimony.

In his journal and in his letters, Albert reveals nothing of the traumatic event. But in his childhood writings we can see traits which are often associated by psychologists with the loss of a parent. A tendency, for instance, to cry for no apparent reason other than that he had not lived up to the expectations of those around him. 'I cried at my lesson today', he wrote when he was six, 'because I could not find a verb.'[40] 'I wrote a letter at home. But because I had made so many mistakes in it the Rath tore it up and threw it into the fire. I cried about it.'[41] 'When I woke this morning I was ill. My cough was worse. I was so frightened that I cried.'[42] There is little doubt that the punitive attitude of his tutor can have done little to reassure the vulnerable child. Another trait which can be attributed to his emotional insecurity is his shyness. Albert in his early youth disliked visits from strangers, probably perceived as threats to his security: 'And at their approach would run to the furthest corner of the room, and cover his face with his hands, nor was it possible to make him look up, or speak a word. If his doing so was insisted upon, he resented it to the utmost, screaming violently.'[43] His gratitude towards all those who did him a kindness, albeit a trivial one, was touching and he had a tendency rare in children of his age to self-analysis and sadness.

Albert's desire to please his remaining parent was tinged with anguish and reflected his need for parental affection. When he went to stay with his grandmother he longed to be at home and wrote affectionate letters to his father. The Duke no doubt did his best to respond. But he was not a family man and Florschütz certainly did his best to become the pivot of the children's affection. He himself wrote, 'Thus deprived of a mother's love and care, the children necessarily depended more entirely on that shown by their tutor.'[44] Until Albert was eleven his tutor took his midday meal with the boys every day.

> Nor did the regard of Prince Albert for me cease with the termination of his studies. I was ever honoured with the proofs of his continued good will. The last mark of his affection was given to me but a short time before his death and I stand daily before the valued picture which he then sent me, to weep for my beloved pupil and friend.[45]

In 1863, after Albert's death, the Queen asked Count Arthur Mensdorff to write down all he could recollect of her husband's early years. The portrait, as one would expect, borders on the hagiographic. His main virtues were that he was 'of a mild, benevolent disposition', never 'noisy or wild', 'distinguished for perfect moral purity both in word and in deed' and 'feelingly alive to the sufferings of the poor'.[46] Florschütz commented on his less virtuous side. His mild disposition could give place to righteous anger, 'Surpassing his brother in thoughtful earnestness, in calm reflection and self-command, and evincing at the same time, more prudence in action, it was only natural that his will should prevail, and when compliance with it was not voluntarily yielded, he was sometimes disposed to have recourse to compulsion.'[47] This rather overweening attitude was to be applied to Victoria. Albert considered himself undoubtedly the superior partner and, as such, was to impose his will on her as he had on his brother.

If he was not 'noisy or wild' it was probably because he was not a very strong child. In the evening he would be overwhelmed by sleepiness and, says Florschütz, 'even his most cherished occupations or the liveliest games, were at such times ineffectual to keep him awake.'[48] If he were prevented from going to bed he would suddenly disappear and be found quietly sleeping somewhere. The first time his tutor was present at his supper, 'The young prince suddenly fell asleep and tumbled off his chair, but he was not hurt and continued to sleep quietly on the ground.'[49] Albert's notion of quiet play led him to collect anything and everything – encouraged by his tutor – and to spend hours labelling and categorizing, a habit he was to keep all his life.

Although his 'moral purity' made him something of a prig, he did have a rather heavy sense of fun not exempt from cruelty. His mimicry was appreciated when he was in his teens, for he could draw a fine, cruel portrait of his professors in gestures and in words. In later life it was slapstick comedy that he appreciated rather than wit. He was, in short, as normal a mixture of good and bad as most young men.

Was his childhood, as Robert Rhodes James says, 'happy and privileged'?[50] Albert himself gave two contradictory views. To Victoria he later declared his childhood the happiest years of his life. His eldest daughter Vicky was to note, however, 'Papa always said that he could not bear to think of his childhood he had been so unhappy and miserable, and had many a time wished himself out of this world.'[51] In fact he probably used his childhood as most of us do to reinforce his statements on the present – wanting to prove to his wife how much he had given up for her, or showing his daughter to what a great extent her childhood was more privileged than his own had been. Objectively there were good and bad points – surrounded by affection, but deprived of a mother; wanting for nothing yet ill-adapted to the Court life he was obliged to lead from the age of eleven. Clinging to a brother and a father who were far from sharing his own values, Albert must have had, as all children have, moments of deep happiness and of disappointment and grief.

By 1836 – when Albert was sixteen – it was obvious that the Princess Victoria of England would one day be Queen of England. For her Uncle Leopold no prince could be better suited to be his niece's spouse than his own Albert. But Leopold was a prudent man. He wanted to make quite sure that Albert was fit for the task. So Baron Stockmar was sent off to Coburg to give his opinion of Albert. He found him physically suitable: 'well grown for his age, with agreeable and valuable qualities; and who, if things go well, may in a few years turn out a strong, handsome man, . . . Externally therefore, he possesses all that pleases the sex, and at all times and in all countries must please. It may prove too, a lucky circumstance that even now he has something of an English look.'[52] With regard to his intellectual and psychological qualities, Stockmar was more cautious. Albert was certainly circumspect, discreet and cautious. 'But all this is not enough. He ought to have not merely great ability, but a *right* ambition and a greater force of will as well.'[53]

For Stockmar there was no doubt that affairs of state were of much greater importance than personal happiness or fulfilment. Albert would as Victoria's husband embark on a lifetime political career, and this demanded 'that earnest frame of mind which is ready of its own accord to sacrifice mere pleasure to real usefulness.'[54] For the moment Stockmar was not willing to assure Leopold that his nephew had the ambition necessary for such a task. The Prince's visit to England in 1836 had not been an unqualified success. The long hours, formal dinners, balls and celebrations had really proved too much for him. He had shown himself physically unfit for the pressures of English Court life and the vitality of the young Queen.

The solution of Leopold and Stockmar was not to abandon their plans but to set about seriously educating Prince Albert for his future role. Coburg was a Court which was at once too small, too conventional and too lax. Berlin was considered too formal and priggish. The solution was to begin the Prince's education in Belgium, where he would be under his uncle's eye and at the same time in a constitutional monarchy. So for ten months the two brothers stayed in Brussels under the care of Baron Wiechmann, a retired German officer. Albert studied history and modern languages and became a student of the eminent statistician and mathematician, M. Quetelet with whom he kept up a correspondence all through his life. He stayed in Brussels with his brother over Christmas, declining his father's invitation to return home. His excuse was that it would disturb his studies.

In April 1837 the two boys were sent to Bonn University – one of the most enlightened in Europe. There they stayed for eighteen months, studying Roman law, natural sciences, political economy, history and philosophy. As Fulford puts it: 'With his masculine character, his fondness for masculine society and his diffidence with women, he loved university life, which in those happy days was as sacred as the pulpit from the chatter of foolish and fashionable women.'[55] In the autumn of 1837 the brothers' holidays were taken in Switzerland and the north of Italy – after touring the Italian lakes on foot and visiting the treasures of Milan and Venice, Albert returned invigorated by his holiday and plunged himself once more into his studies.

In March 1838 Albert was summoned to Brussels so that his uncle could see for himself to what extent the past two years had prepared him for his future task. Having talked at length with Albert, Leopold wrote to Stockmar to give him his impressions. They were altogether favourable. Leopold had spoken to him about marriage to Victoria with honesty and kindness. 'He looks at the question from its most elevated and honourable point of view; he considers that troubles are inseparable from all human positions and that therefore if one must be subject to plagues and annoyances, it is better to be so for some great or worthy object than for trifles and miseries.'[56]

In January of the same year, Leopold had received a letter from Victoria in which she had declared that she wished 'to enjoy two or three years more of my present young girlish life before I enter upon the duties and cares of a wife.' But she added, 'You need not fear, dearest Uncle, that I should be faithless to my promise and change my mind, for if Albert remains what he is now it would be impossible. I think however that the end of this year or the beginning of the next would do to settle matters privately.'[57] This letter casts doubt on the young Queen's assertion that she had never in any sense pledged herself to Albert. It rather seems as if the idea had been so firmly planted in her head by Leopold that the fundamental question was not 'if' but 'when'.

As for Albert, talking the matter over with Leopold, and hearing him explain that his great youth would make it necessary to postpone the marriage for a few years, he, too, seemed to accept the union itself as something natural. 'But one thing', Leopold told Stockmar, 'he observed with truth. "I am ready", he said, "to submit to this delay if I have some certain assurance to go upon. But if after waiting, perhaps for three years, I should find that the Queen no longer desired the marriage, it would place me in a very ridiculous position and would to a certain extent ruin all the prospects of my future life." '[58]

This seems very far from eager love on both sides. Albert's attitude may at first seem priggish and one is tempted to retort that the English throne was certainly not without its compensations in terms of both lifestyle and interest. But in fact Albert might well have found happiness with a German princess of some lesser dukedom, who would not have obliged him to leave those he loved most. He would have been content with a less arduous life, with more time for matters of the intellect, in a country where he would not have been eternally qualified as 'a foreigner'. Victoria's attitude is not particularly attractive either. At this stage, when all possible suitors had been weighed, Albert was the only one who did not appear to be wanting ... but that was no reason for sacrificing the girlish pleasures of today for a marital tomorrow that could very well wait. But one must not be too hard on her either – she, too, was afraid of change.

The two young people did, however, have a pleasant running correspondence over the period between June 1836 and 1838. On the death of King William Prince Albert had written a rather formal letter in English to his cousin – whether of his own volition or encouraged by his entourage. He addressed to Victoria his 'sincerest felicitations on that great change which has taken place in your life'. She was now 'Queen of the mightiest land of Europe', and he wished her reign to be 'long, happy and glorious'. He also prayed her to think likewise sometimes of her cousins in Bonn, and 'to continue to them that kindness you favoured them with till now.'[59]

Rhodes James claimed that, 'In Queen Victoria's and Prince Albert's voluminous and meticulously maintained papers there is no record of any acknowledgement or reply to this letter.'[60] But there *was* a reply and it was warm and enthusiastic:

> My dearest Albert,
>   I cannot tell you how happy you have made me by your kind dear letter which I have just received. Many, many, thanks for it, my dear cousin, and for the good wishes contained in it.
>   . . .
>   My new situation is not an easy one, no doubt, but I trust that with good will, honesty and courage I shall not fail. I delight in the business which I have to do and which is not trifling either in matter or quantity. I must now conclude, begging you to believe, my dearest Albert, that you have no greater well-wisher and sincere friend than your ever devoted Cousin Victoria.[61]

Nor was this exchange of letters exceptional. In March 1837, when Albert told her of their imminent departure for Bonn, she wrote back to tell him 'how really and truly sorry I am to think that you are going further away from us', and to remind him that: 'The time is fast approaching when I had the great happiness of seeing you last year and I can assure you my dear cousin, I regret more than I can say, not to have this gratification repeated this year.' She thought of him often and 'amongst other places where we used to be together the Opera which is soon to begin will recall the delightful evenings we spent together vividly to my mind.'[62]

In August 1837 we find her again thanking Albert for his 'kind letter which gave me great pleasure' and asking him to send her 'a very little souvenir from each remarkable place you stop at'.[63] Albert did indeed keep a scrapbook of his journeys, which in due course he sent to the Queen. Rhodes James questions the Queen's remark in later life that this gift showed that Albert, 'in the midst of his travels, often thought of his young cousin'; he claims, 'There is little evidence of this, beyond the gift of the scrapbook.'[64] Albert did, however, write to Victoria twice in May: to tell her Ernest had been ill and that he had settled into Bonn; and for her birthday. The scrapbook itself takes on a different light when one realizes that it was made at the Queen's own request. When she received it she thanked her cousin warmly. She believed at this time that since she was Queen she would not be allowed to leave her kingdom. This was not in fact the case.

> Many many thanks for your kind letter and for the beautiful and interesting little Album which you have been so kind as to send me and which I received a few days ago. It has given me the greatest pleasure and the little views etc. are excessively pretty. It must have been a most delightful and interesting Tour and I cannot say how I envy your having seen Venice which of all other places, Naples and Paris excepted, I should like to see. Alas! the time when there was perhaps a possibility of my going abroad is passed and I fear now I shall never do so.[65]

Nor was the scrapbook the only gift he sent her. The preceding May he had announced that he would send her a painting, to which she replied, 'I shall be quite delighted to receive your painting whenever it is ready, and I can assure you my dear cousin, that no present could give me greater pleasure than a picture done by your own hand.'[66] That August, on his birthday, Victoria wrote again and stressed, 'You are, I am certain, dearest Albert, quite persuaded of my sincere attachment and affection for you.'[67]

It was probably the pressure from Uncle Leopold and Albert's father that caused the two young people to draw apart from one another. Writing to his tutor on the Coronation of Victoria, Albert noted that 'Papa had a little conversation himself with Victoria in which she told him, with some slight embarrassment, "My intentions are still the same but that could not happen before two or three years."' Albert thought this delay a 'great danger' but also noted that 'the Baroness [Lehzen] relieved Papa's anxiety by saying that she thought Victoria regarded herself as fully pledged.'[68]

In 1838 Albert wrote more than his cousin did and we find her in

August replying to his birthday greetings of the preceding May. Even then the reply was not very amiable. She hoped Ernest would not 'think it very wrong that I should write to the youngest *en préférence* and I must also ask forgiveness for that. Everybody who sees you both tells me how much you are improved *de toutes les manières*.' Her birthday wishes to him were simply put in a postscript: 'I seize this opportunity to wish you my dear Albert very many happy returns of your birthday.'[69]

Albert had, however, passed his uncle's tests and for Leopold the marriage was a foregone conclusion. He wrote to Stockmar:

> If I am not very much mistaken he possesses all the qualities required to fit him completely for the position he will occupy in England. His understanding is sound, his apprehension clear and rapid, and his feelings in all matters appertaining to personal appearance are quite right. He has got powers of observation and possesses much prudence, without anything about him that could be called cold or morose.[70]

The time before the expected marriage had to be filled in. What better way than to send Albert off to Italy again to become more polished and to have his mind formed by his new companion, who was none other than Stockmar himself. Theodore Martin held that it was the Queen who requested Stockmar to accompany the Prince, but this was a 'reconstruction' of the Queen twenty years later, for in a letter to Albert in May 1839 she wrote, 'I have not heard of Stockmar for an age. Where has he gone?'[71] For the first time in their lives, the two brothers were separated. Ernest went to Dresden to enter active military life. Up till then the brothers had shared their joys and sorrows, their sports and studies, and for both it was a severe wrench. Writing to his old university friend, Prince von Löwenstein, on 26 October 1838 Albert said, 'The separation will be frightfully painful to us. Until now we have never, as long as we can recollect, been a single day away from each other. I cannot bear to think of that moment.'[72]

Stockmar and Albert were in Florence from December to March 1839. Here he continued the well-regulated studious life he had lived in Bonn, 'rising at six and working till noon, dining simply at two o'clock, when his drink was water, and going to bed as a rule at nine.'[73] His only real distraction seems to have been music and he played both the piano and the organ. Stockmar insisted that he took some part in society life. Albert wrote an account of it to von Löwenstein – a description not unworthy of Molière's Alceste – 'I have thrown myself into the vortex of society. I have danced, dined, supped, paid compliments, been introduced to people and had people introduced to me, chattered French and English, exhausted every conceivable phrase about the weather, played the amiable – in short have made *bonne mine à mauvais jeu.*' He had, he declared, 'fairly drained the Carnival cup to the dregs and had hated it'.[74] A man with no small talk, who refused to show interest or admiration he did not feel, certainly required some training if he were to become the first gentleman of an English Court. As he wandered round Europe, several unpleasant but persistent traits of his character were revealed.

First his desire to win, to score off anyone. The best example is the manner in which he put the ageing Pope Gregory in his place: 'The Pope asserted that the Greeks had taken their models from the Etruscans. In spite of his infallibility, I ventured to assert that they had derived their lessons in art from the Egyptians.'[75] Perhaps this is what Stockmar, with undue kindliness, referred to as his '*espiègleries*', his way 'of treating things and men from the comical side'.[76]

Secondly his extremely peremptory judgements of what he saw. Rome he did not think much of: save for some beautiful palaces, it might just as well be any town in Germany. Italy was a most interesting country, and an inexhaustible source of knowledge, but, 'One contrives, however, to taste extraordinarily little of the enjoyment one promises oneself there. In many respects the country is far behind what one had expected. Climate, scenery, artistic feeling and skill, in all these one feels most disagreeably disappointed.'[77]

For Stockmar, Albert's overwhelming failing was that he had not during their time together 'shown the least possible interest in *political* matters'.[78] Even when important events were actually taking place this never induced him 'to read a newspaper'. He had, too, a 'perfect horror of all foreign newspapers' and declared the only readable and necessary paper was the *Augsburger Allgemeine,* and even that he did not read through.[79] The Baron, like Leopold, would so have liked him to show some interest in politics, especially in foreign affairs. Stockmar dreamt of seeing Germany united under Prussia, and a unity of purpose established between Germany and England. For him Albert was undoubtedly, above all, a means to an end. Over twenty years later, after Albert's death, he wrote, 'An edifice which for a great and noble purpose had been reared with a devout sense of duty by twenty years of laborious toil, has been shattered to its very foundations.'[80]

In 1839 Stockmar was far from sure that Albert would indeed be a useful element in the vast construction. At twenty he bore a striking physical and moral resemblance to his mother, who had been full of intellectual quickness and adroitness and cleverness – but he also had her 'way of not occupying himself long with the same subject'. In other words, a mind that was rather superficial. And he had – apart from his lack of interest in politics, which might be aroused – two major defects. To begin with, his constitution was not strong so that he tired quickly, appearing pale and exhausted after even a short exertion – though Dr Stockmar believed 'that by careful attention to diet, he could easily strengthen it and give it stamina.' As a result, no doubt, 'He dislikes violent exertion and both morally and physically tries to save himself. Full of the best intentions and noblest designs he often fails in carrying them into practice.'[81]

The other field in which there was much to be desired was '*les belles manières*'. 'This deficiency must', Stockmar explained, 'be principally laid to the account of his having in his earliest years been deprived of the intercourse and supervision of a mother, and of any cultivated woman. He will always have more success with men than with women. He is too little "*empressé*" with the latter, too indifferent and too reserved.'[82]

There is no doubt that Stockmar's diagnosis was extraordinarily perceptive, but the remedy suggested was hardly appropriate. He was determined to school the Prince to overcome his natural inclinations. Albert was to strive against his weak constitution and drive himself hard. A more regulated life would undoubtedly have given him greater satisfaction and might well have secured him a longer life.

While Stockmar was training Albert, Uncle Leopold's concern was with the young Queen. In August she was visited by Leopold's brother Ferdinand, his daughter Victoria and his sons. The Coburg atmosphere was established around her. To her relations she always spoke German, so that in their presence she was less able to converse with her Prime Minister, who did not know the language. In September King Leopold himself visited to make definitive plans for the arrival of Albert. The time was coming for the two cousins to meet again.

Already in May 1839 the Queen had written to tell Albert she looked 'forward with sincere pleasure to seeing you both at Windsor this autumn'. The tone was still not very cordial, 'I trust that neither of you will be ill. As you were both the last time you were in England.'[83] In June she acknowledged two letters from Albert, repeated her hope to have the pleasure of seeing the two brothers in England in the autumn and added, 'We have had the Grand Duke of Russia here for some time; ... He is a delightful amiable young man and I liked him extremely. I wish you could have made his acquaintance.'[84]

If the Queen was loath to pledge herself finally to Albert – not because of what he was but because of the satisfaction her freedom gave her – he was no more eager. His reluctance, however, was based on an unfortunate image he had of her. He wrote to Florschütz that Victoria was said to be 'incredibly stubborn', even if she was good-natured, and that she delighted 'in court ceremonies, etiquette and trivial formalities'. These were 'gloomy prospects', all the more gloomy as with time her defects would harden and it would 'become impossible to modify them'.[85]

When asked to recount Albert's early years from memory Arthur Mensdorff wrote to the Queen: 'Albert confided to me under the seal of the strictest secrecy that he was going to England in order to make your acquaintance and that, if you liked each other, you were to be engaged. He spoke very seriously about the difficulties of the position he would have to occupy in England but hoped that dear Uncle Leopold would assist him with advice.'[86]

On 10 October 1839 Victoria was full of expectation. It was the day on which she was to receive her cousins Albert and Ernest. At half-past seven that evening she greeted them at Windsor and found them 'grown and changed, and embellished'. She confided to her journal: 'It was with some emotion that I beheld Albert – who is *beautiful*.'[87]

The visit got off to a bad start. A grand reception had been organized in their honour – but their trunks had not arrived. They could thus not appear at eight o'clock when dinner was served. At table the Queen chatted as usual to Lord Melbourne: 'Talked of my cousin's bad passage; their not appearing on account of their *négligé*, which Lord Melbourne thought they ought to have done, *at* dinner and certainly after.'[88] After dinner they did indeed come in, despite their costume, and Victoria noted again, 'he is so handsome and pleasing.'[89] Her journal of the following day gave more details: 'so excessively handsome, such beautiful blue eyes, an exquisite nose, and such a pretty mouth with delicate moustachios and slight but very slight whiskers; a beautiful figure broad in the shoulders and a fine waist'.[90] That evening Albert was subjected to the late dancing he took such little pleasure in, but the Queen only noted that he 'dances so beautifully' and 'holds himself so well with that beautiful figure of his'.[91] On the Saturday, the afternoon was spent riding and Victoria had on either side of her Albert (with whom she talked a good deal) and Lord Melbourne.[92] Church on Sunday and 'Dearest Albert' sat near her and 'enjoyed the music excessively'.

On the Sunday afternoon, while the brothers went to Frogmore, a mile away in Windsor Great Park, the Queen told Melbourne that 'seeing them had a good deal changed my opinion (as to marrying), and that I must decide soon, which was a difficult thing.' Lord Melbourne praised Albert's looks and advised her to 'take another week'. Victoria confessed to him that she had now to admit the power of beauty.[93]

Beauty was indeed powerful and so, no doubt, was companionship. Four days after Albert's arrival her mind was made up. She told Melbourne of her decision. 'I said to Lord Melbourne, that I had made up my mind (about marrying dearest Albert) – "You have?" he said; "well then, about the time?" Not for a year, I thought; which he said was too long.'[94] He was, she noted, pleased, for he thought the news would be very well received, 'for I hear that there is an anxiety now that it should be, and I am very glad of it', and he added in an avuncular tone, 'You will be much more comfortable for a woman cannot stand alone for any time in whatever position she may be.'

Victoria must, however, have been nervous at actually broaching the question with Albert. 'Then I asked [Lord Melbourne] if I hadn't better tell Albert of my decision soon, in which Lord Melbourne agreed. How? I asked, for that in general such things were done the other way – which made Lord Melbourne laugh.[95] But the day passed and she said nothing. At dinner she was content to sit next to dearest Albert and to talk to him a great deal. Finally, after dinner, it was Melbourne who urged her to talk to Albert about it and settle it with him. She finally plucked up her courage on the following day.

> At half-past twelve I sent for Albert. He came to the closet where I was alone. After a few minutes I said to him that I thought he must be aware why I wished him to come, and that it would make me too happy if he would consent to what I wished (namely to marry me); we embraced each other over and over again, and he was so kind, so affectionate.[96]

Albert's description of the scene is equally romantic. 'Yesterday in a private audience Victoria declared her love for me, and offered me her hand, which I seized in both mine and pressed tenderly to my lips.'[97] One thing, however, is clear. Victoria was physically attracted to Albert. It was first and foremost his beauty that she admired. In a letter to her uncle on the second day of the cousins' arrival, she had already written, 'Albert's beauty is most striking, and he is most amiable and unaffected – in short, very fascinating.'[98]

Once all had been made clear between them, letters flew out announcing the news to a few very close friends and relatives. In their letters both show the same bemusement, the almost 'disbelief' that one can be loved so much. To King Leopold the Queen wrote, 'I love him more than I can say, and I shall do everything in my power to render this sacrifice as small as I can. . . . These last few days have passed like a dream to me, and I am so much bewildered by it all that I hardly know how to write. But I do feel very happy.'[99] Both Victoria and Albert wrote to Stockmar. Victoria, remembering that she had told him she would never marry, wrote: 'I *do* feel so guilty, I know not how to begin my letter – but I think the news it will contain will be sufficient to ensure your forgiveness. Albert has completely won my heart and all was settled between us this morning.'[100] Albert's letter to Stockmar was brimming over with happiness: 'Victoria is so good and kind to me that I am often at a loss to believe that such affection should be shown to me. I know the great interest you take in my happiness, and therefore pour out my heart to you.' At the end of his letter he quoted from Schiller:

> More or more seriously, I cannot write to you; for that, at this moment, I am too bewildered.
> 'Das Auge sieht den Himmel offen,
> Es schwimmt das Herz in Seligkeit.'
> [The eye sees Heaven open,
> The heart floats on a sea of blessedness.][101]

Each of them respected the division of roles of the period. Albert's aim was to be 'A personality of character which will win the respect, the love and the confidence of the Queen and of the Nation. . . . a "noble" Prince in the true sense of the word.'[102] Victoria's sensitivity was directed towards repaying Albert for the sacrifice he was making, tearing himself away from the Germany of his youth. Living in England was not going to be easy for him. As Rhodes James has put it: 'It was, after all, only his second visit to this cold, sea-tossed island with its peculiar food, uncongenial hours, chaotic politics, and deep suspicion of foreigners and particularly Germans.'[103]

10

The Royal Wedding

When Leopold received the news he was drinking the waters at Wiesbaden. No one could have been more delighted than he was. 'I had,' he wrote to his niece, 'when I saw your decision, almost the feeling of Old Zacharias, "Now lettest thou thy servant depart in peace."'[1] He had striven so hard for so long to bring about the match – at last a true Coburger would be, if not on the throne, at least near enough to influence the tide of events. 'Your choice', he wrote to his niece, 'has been for these last years my conviction of what might and would be best for your happiness.'[2]

In her letter to Leopold announcing her engagement Victoria had written: 'Mama herself must know nothing till then',[3] that is until the official declaration, and he in turn promised that until further orders he would say nothing to her mother, to Charles or Feodora. He wrote, however, to Stockmar: 'What grieves me is that my sister . . . is not to know of it. But as everyone says, she cannot keep her mouth shut and might even make bad use of the secret if it were entrusted to her, I quite see the necessity of it.' Victoria wanted to give herself time to consider how to persuade her mother to leave Buckingham Palace when she married. She talked the problem over with Lord Melbourne, who feared that she would have ' "great difficulty in getting her out of the house" '.[4] The Prime Minister had known of the decision even before the Prince himself, and had despatched a note to the Queen declaring that he had read 'with great satisfaction your Majesty's expression of feeling, as your Majesty's happiness must ever be one of Lord Melbourne's first objects and strongest interests.'[5] The Queen herself reported to King Leopold that Lehzen was very happy at the news.[6]

The reactions of Victoria's immediate entourage were all entirely favourable. For almost a month they alone knew of the engagement, a month during which the young couple walked and talked, rode and danced and generally got to know one another better. This was no doubt facilitated by the fact that Ernest, who was suffering from jaundice, was confined to his room. Albert was already helping the Queen in her work. He corrected some mistakes she had made when she was writing to the Duchess of Northumberland, and when she signed papers and warrants 'was so kind as to dry them with blotting paper for me'.[7] She learnt with satisfaction that he was not very impressed by beautiful women and hated 'those beauties who are so fêted' and even wished 'to spite them'. Lord Melbourne's opinion was that he 'ought to pay attention to the ladies'.[8] Victoria had the satisfaction of learning that Albert had never even befriended another woman. When he took her hands in his he told her they 'were so little he could hardly believe they were hands, as he had hitherto only been accustomed to handle hands like Ernest's'.[9] They exchanged gifts – Victoria gave him a ring engraved with the number fifteen – their engagement day – and a little seal she used to wear; he gave her a lock of his hair.

Physically they were undoubtedly attracted to one another and Victoria's journal is full of kisses and embraces. Inexorably the fourteenth of November, the day of Albert's departure for Coburg, drew nearer. The golden days of autumn at Windsor came to an end. That morning, 'We kissed each other so often, and I leant on that dear soft cheek, fresh and pink like a rose.' Then came the last kiss. Albert got into the carriage and she watched him drive off. 'I cried much,' she wrote that evening, 'wretched, yet happy to think that we should meet again so soon! Oh! how I love him, how intensely, how devotedly, how ardently!'[10]

Their first missives to one another were full of love. From Calais Albert wrote:

> I need not tell you that since we left all my thoughts have been with you at Windsor and your image fills my whole soul. Even in my dreams I never imagined that I should find so much love on earth. How that moment shines for me when I was close to you, with your hand in mine. Those days flew by so quickly, but our separation will fly equally so.[11]

Here is no bridegroom being reluctantly drawn to the altar, content, as Lytton Strachey pictured him, to be loved.[12] Albert, too, had discovered love. So far his life had been guided by Leopold and Stockmar, with little consideration for him as an individual with his own feelings. In some ways he was almost pathetic as he strove to do their bidding, to conform to the portrait of a prince they had painted for him. In one of his letters he sent greetings from Ernest, who was asleep but who 'will praise me, when he wakes for having done so. It is always nice to earn praise, to myself all the more, since I so seldom get it.'[13] No wonder that he told her over and over again, 'I cannot imagine how it is that I am the object of so much love and affection.'[14] As the days went by he found the separation more difficult, for Victoria had already become necessary to him – someone he could love, but also someone he could talk to without the fear of not living up to her expectations. 'Dearly Beloved Victoria, I long to talk to you; otherwise the separation is too painful. Your dear picture stands on my table in front of me and I can hardly take my eyes off it. I can sometimes imagine you are answering me, and this thought makes me most happy.'[15] His need to write to her was so great that 'I am like Don Basilio in the "Barbiere" and after each farewell begin all over again.'[16]

Meanwhile, now that they were apart, the news of the engagement could be announced. The Queen took up her pen to bring the news to her close relatives. She was, she told them, to marry Cousin Albert, 'the merits of whose character are so well-known by all who are acquainted with him that I need say no more than that I feel as assured on my own happiness as I can be of anything in this world.'[17] She had written to Feodora a few days before the others to tell her of her 'intense love for Albert, who is my Angel; quite perfection he is. I am only unworthy of him.'[18] All her relatives replied with cordial good wishes. Save the Duchess of Kent, who wrote to her daughter complaining bitterly that she had been kept in the dark and began once again plaguing her with letters complaining of her attitude.

On 23 November – over a month after the private engagement – came the official news of the intended marriage. The Queen held a Privy Council, 'all who were within call having attended'.[19] To Prince Albert, perhaps to impress him, she wrote that more than a hundred persons were present; to King Leopold she talked of eighty-two Privy Councillors present. Greville for his part noted that there were 'almost 80'.[20] 'A very full Council in any case which the great Duke Wellington himself attended.'[21]

When as many of the Councillors as could had taken their seats round a long table, the folding doors were thrown open and the Queen was handed in by the Lord Chamberlain. She wore a plain morning gown and at her wrist a bracelet containing Prince Albert's portrait.[22] She read the declaration in a 'clear, sonorous, sweet-toned voice', but her hands trembled so excessively that Greville wondered that she was able to read the paper she held.[23] Victoria herself wrote in her journal: 'I felt my hands shake but I did not make one mistake. I felt most happy and thankful when it was over.'[24] Croker, in any case, thought she did admirably. 'I cannot describe to you with what a mixture of self-possession and feminine delicacy she read the paper . . . her eye was bright and calm, neither bold nor downcast, but firm and soft.'[25]

The text of the declaration had been written by Lord Melbourne and as she read it she saw him 'looking kindly' at her with tears in his eyes. It was to be the last important event in her life during which she looked to Lord Melbourne for support. He seemed to Croker 'to look care-worn'.[26] The declaration informed the Councillors of a decision 'which deeply concerns the welfare of My people and the happiness of my future life', namely her intention to ally herself in marriage 'with the Prince Albert of Saxe-Coburg and Gotha'. Lord Lansdowne, in the name of the Privy Council, then asked that 'this most gracious and most welcome communication' might be printed.[27] The Queen's ordeal took no more than two to three minutes. Her uncle, the Duke of Cambridge, who had hoped she would marry his son, her cousin George, came into the small library where she had retired to wish her joy. The crowd, 'which was not great but very decent', cheered the Duke of Wellington and Peel, the Leader of the Opposition, and hooted at Lord John Russell and Lord Normanby – both of whom were Ministers. The Duchess of Gloucester asked her if addressing the Council 'was not a nervous thing to do'. Victoria replied, 'Yes but I did a much more nervous thing a little while ago.' 'What was that?' 'I proposed to Prince Albert.'[28]

Nearly two months later – on 16 January 1840 – Victoria had to meet Parliament and once again, this time in a speech from the throne, announce her betrothal. According to Greville she was 'well enough received – much better than usual – as she went to the House.'[29] Irritation against the Queen was still strong. She was, some Tories declared, becoming the centre of ambition and intrigue as the Bed-chamber Question had shown. Lord Wharncliffe told Greville, 'the real obstacle to the Tories coming into office was the Queen. . . . her antipathy to Peel rendered him exceedingly reluctant to take office. . . . If her political partisanship were to be limited she undoubtedly needed, in Tory eyes, a husband's guidance and support.'[30] There was, too, satisfaction with the union since if the Queen married and ensured her succession there would be no danger of seeing the King of Hanover on the British throne. The ultra-Tories were, however, filled with pre-judices against Prince Albert. According to Stockmar this was essentially due to 'the influence of Ernest Augustus of Hanover'.[31] Be that as it may, they certainly noised abroad that Prince Albert was a dangerous radical and an infidel and that George of Cambridge or a Prince of Orange would have made a better consort for the Queen.

The public, according to Stockmar, was 'tolerably indifferent as to the person of the bridegroom, but I hear it is generally complained that he is too young.'[32] He was indeed only twenty-one – the same age as Victoria. This opinion was to be echoed in *The Times* on the couple's wedding day: 'If the thing were not finally settled indeed, one might without being unreasonable, express a wish that the consort selected for a Princess so educated and hitherto so unfairly guided, as Queen Victoria – should have been a person of riper years, and likely to form more sound and circumspect opinions.'[33]

More severe criticism was to be found in the anonymous ballads that circulated.[34] For the pamphleteers, Albert had the double defect of being both the nephew of King Leopold, whom few held in high esteem, and a penniless German.

> He comes the bridegroom of Victoria's choice,
> The nominee of Lehzen's vulgar voice;
> He comes to take "for better or for worse"
> England's fat queen and England's fatter purse.

or again:

> Albert is victorious
> De Coburgs now are glorious,
> All so notorious
>   God serve the Queen.

No sooner was the announcement of the royal marriage made public than sinister rumours that the Prince was a Roman Catholic began to circulate. The charge was all the more damaging as the Queen had made no reference to the religion of her future husband in the declaration she had read to the Privy Council. This was not a careless omission. Melbourne had thought it wiser, he had explained to the Queen, not to mention religion since he could not employ the habitual formula of 'marrying into a Protestant family' since several branches of the Coburgs had become Catholic. Lord Melbourne had no desire to antagonize the Coburgs on the thrones of Spain and Belgium. King Leopold had, after all, married a French Catholic princess and their children would no doubt be brought up Catholics.[35]

Anti-Catholicism was particularly rife at this time because of a great

upheaval in the Established Church of England. The movement had
begun with a sermon preached from the university pulpit in Oxford by
John Keble, Regius Professor of Hebrew, at Christ Church on 14 July
1833, and with the publication of 'Tracts for the Times' written by
Newman, Pusey, Keble and others, advocating a revival of spiritual life
and restoring the patristic doctrines and practice in Church government and services.[36] The Queen, to put an end to the rumours
concerning Albert's religion, asked him to send her a short history of
the House of Coburg. It demonstrated, in the Prince's view, 'that to the
House of Saxony Protestantism, in a measure, owes its existence, for
this House [Coburg] and that of the Landgrave of Hesse stood quite
alone against Europe, and upheld Luther and his cause triumphantly.
This shows the folly of constantly assailing our House as Papistical.'
The Prince went on to add that not a single Catholic princess had been
introduced into the Coburg family since the appearance of Luther in
1521. He also sent the Queen a confession of faith which he had worked
out for himself in 1835 and then 'publicly avowed and swore to in our
High Church'.[37]

For the Queen the whole matter was ridiculous. As she told the
Prince, 'The Tories make a great disturbance that you are a Papist
because the words "a Protestant Prince" have not been put into the
Declaration – a thing which would be quite unnecessary, seeing that I
cannot marry a Papist.'[38] It was true, indeed, that under the Act of
Settlement the Sovereign's marriage with a Roman Catholic would
lead to an *ipso facto* forfeiture of the Crown, something the young
Victoria would never have envisaged.

The word Protestant was, however, not inserted into the declaration
read to the Houses of Parliament despite the cavil – probably because
Lord Melbourne knew he had little hope of quietening down the Tories
and every chance of angering the Irish Catholics, who supported his
Government. The matter thus led to discussion in both Houses of
Parliament. In the Lords the Duke of Wellington led the attack and
carried an amendment to the address censuring Ministers for having
failed to declare publicly that the Prince was a Protestant and able to
take Holy Communion in the form prescribed by the Church of
England. Wellington claimed that the public ought to know something
about Prince Albert other than his name, and also stated that his
amendment 'would give Her Majesty's subjects the satisfaction of
knowing that Prince Albert was a Protestant – thus showing the public
that this is still a Protestant State.'[39]

Greville thought the Duke had gone too far. 'I was grieved', he noted, 'to see him descend to such miserable humbug, and was in hopes he was superior to it, and would have put down the nonsense than have lent his sanction to it.'[40] Victoria wrote to her uncle: 'do what one will, nothing will please these most religious, most hypocritical Tories, whom I dislike (I use a very soft word) most heartily and warmly.'[41] Albert, though he could understand her being indignant with the Tories, 'for their grumbling and abuse is unbelievable', nevertheless thought it should not trouble her 'as Queen, except for your friendship for the good Lord Melbourne. Otherwise a constitutional Sovereign may be indifferent to what is said against his Ministry.'[42] A point of view which had never yet occurred to the young Queen.

Even the Bill for Albert's naturalization on 27 January 1840 did not pass smoothly through the Lords. In it was a clause giving the Prince precedence after the Queen. English constitutional law gave the highest rank after her husband to the wife of a King but had made no provision for the title and precedence of the husband of a Queen Regnant. It was obvious that the question could not remain unanswered; obvious, too, that the Queen had no desire to see her husband's status inferior to that of her uncles, or later to that of her children. As this meant that he would come before the Princes of the Royal Blood their consent was deemed necessary. Two of the Queen's uncles, the Duke of Sussex and the Duke of Cambridge, agreed to be put under the Queen's husband. Although a confidential note of Lord Montague showed that the Duke of Sussex 'was disposed to stand for what he called the rights of his family'.[43] Not so the Duke of Cumberland who had, under Salic law, become King of Hanover on Victoria's accession. To be perfectly honest, it seems that he was 'never applied to because they knew he would have refused.'[44] There is indeed no doubt that the Duke of Cumberland would have welcomed Salic law – preventing a woman from reigning – as an admirable thing in England as well, and he had always considered that his niece had taken a throne which should have been his as first male successor.

Melbourne was no doubt unwise to try to settle a fundamental question in a Bill purporting to be simply a Bill for the Naturalization of the Prince. It gave the Duke of Wellington the opportunity of adjourning the discussion of the Bill on the grounds that it proposed to give the Queen wide powers of which the House had had no previous notice. The Duke was supported by Lord Brougham, a Radical, on the grounds that such powers rested with Parliament not the Crown. In fact, according to Melbourne, it was Lord Lyndhurst and other friends of the King of Hanover who would not allow the clause to pass. The ministry was obliged to postpone the discussion. It was resumed four days later and passed the second reading with little further discussion. However, sensing that hostility had not subsided, the Government decided at the committee stage to confine the bill to the simple question of naturalization and dropped the question of precedence. Four days later, the third reading of the Naturalization Bill went through Parliament with no difficulty.

Greville begged Lord Fitzgerald to find some expedient for 'settling *à l'amiable* the question of Precedence, so as to pacify the Queen if possible, who was much excited about it.'[45] As an abstract question he considered the precedence unnecessary, but thought it would have been expedient to grant it: after all, 'it was useless to give the Prince so ungracious and uncordial a reception, and to render him as inimical to them [the Tories] as she already is.'[46] When he met the Duke of Wellington, who was his next-door neighbour, Greville asked him what he intended to do about the precedence. Wellington replied: 'Oh give him the same which Prince George of Denmark had: place him next before the Archbishop of Canterbury.' Greville replied, 'That will by no means satisfy the Queen', at which Wellington tossed up his head and said, 'What does that signify?'[47] Greville thereupon undertook some research, consulted the various constitutional authorities – Parke, Bosanquet and Erskine – and ancient practice, and finally came to the conclusion that by the laws of England the Sovereign was the fountain of honour and privilege; she might create new titles and had the prerogative of conferring privileges upon private persons such as granting place or precedence to any of her subjects save in Parliament or in the Council.[48]

As a result, by letters-patent issued on 5 March 1840, the Queen decided that the Prince should thenceforth, 'upon all occasions, and in all meetings, except when otherwise provided by Act of Parliament, have, hold, and enjoy, place, pre-eminence, and precedence next to her Majesty.'

This did not, however, solve the problem when the couple were abroad. At such times the Prince's position was often a subject of negotiation and vexation: 'the position accorded to him, the Queen always had to acknowledge as a grace and favour bestowed on her by the Sovereigns she visited.'[49]

While the Lords were questioning the Prince's religion and making difficulties as regards his precedency, the Commons were considering what his financial situation was to be. On 24 January 1840 Lord John Russell moved 'that Her Majesty be enabled to grant an annual income of £50,000 out of the Consolidated Fund for a provision to Prince Albert, to commence on the day of his marriage with Her Majesty, and to continue during his life.' This was the sum which had been granted Prince Leopold on his marriage with the Princess Charlotte. The days were gone when grants of this sort were easily accepted. 'Everybody,' noted Greville, 'except those who have an interest in defending it, think the allowance proposed for Prince Albert very exorbitant: £50,000 a year given for pocket money is quite monstrous and it would have been prudent to propose a more moderate grant for the sake of his popularity.'[50]

The amount was indeed thought needlessly extravagant by both Tories and Radicals. Joseph Hume, a Radical known for defending the public purse, moved an amendment that 21,000 pounds, the amount given to the royal dukes, instead of 50,000 pounds be voted annually to Prince Albert. He declared that he would really have preferred no annuity to be given to the Prince during the Queen's lifetime – but in this respect he had yielded to the wishes of his friends. He remarked that Lord John Russell must know the danger of setting a young man down in London with so much money in his pockets. He also insisted that the financial situation of the country was not good and indeed that people were starving.

The debate clearly showed the fragile position of the Palace. Discourteous and disloyal public speeches against the Queen were not rare, and since the beginning of Victoria's reign the discontent of the working classes had been rising. The root of their bitterness was not, of course, the young Queen's accession but the new Poor Law of 1834, which enabled only those prepared to enter a workhouse to obtain relief, the suffering and distress caused by the severe winter of 1837–8, the economic depression and the high price of bread which lasted into the 1840s. Those who refused to sacrifice their self-esteem and enter the workhouses endured even greater hardship than before. The condition of the poor had never been worse. Resistance met with repression. The situation was used by advocates of electoral reform – the Working Men's Associations and a few Radical Members of Parliament – to further their case for political change. A Charter was drawn up formulating the demands made on behalf of the working classes: universal male suffrage, annual Parliaments, vote by ballot, abolition of the property qualifications for parliamentary candidates, payment of Members of Parliament and equal electoral districts. In a word, political democracy.

It was not a very formidable programme, nor was it one that would in the first instance help the hungry masses, but it caught their imagination and channelled their discontent. At the time it was common to divide the Chartists into those who intended to rely on 'moral force', and those in favour of 'physical force'. Although this dichotomy is no doubt too simplistic, there is no doubt that the question of violence caused rifts in the movement. As K. H. Randell says, 'it is very possible that the majority of rank and file Chartists, meeting violence in their everyday lives, looked upon it as a natural weapon, to be used whenever the danger of retribution was not too immediate.'[51]

Such was the case at the end of 1839 when Chartists from the valleys marched on Newport. They were scattered by a small body of troops, but only after suffering casualties. Some were arrested and the new year – 1840 – opened with the Chartist trials. In the mood of nervousness, a report spread that the Chartists meant to set fire to London on the night of 14 or 15 January and as a result troops were kept under arms all night and the police and fire brigade ordered to be in readiness to act at a moment's warning.[52] On 18 January, a week before the debate on the Prince's allowance, John Frost, the organizer, and two of his henchmen, Zephaniah Williams and William Jones, were sentenced to death for leading the riots in Wales and Newport. Several others were given sentences of confinement and transportation. (In fact this sentence was later commuted to transportation for life; in 1856 they were granted an amnesty and returned to England on 3 May.) 'Parliament is about to meet,' noted Greville, 'Parties are violent, Government weak, everybody wondering what will happen. Nobody seeing their way clearly before them.'[53]

It was understandably feared by some that in this context too big a grant to Albert might seem a provocation. The Radical amendment aiming to reduce the grant from 50,000 pounds to 21,000 pounds was defeated by an overwhelming majority of 305 to 38. But on the very same evening Colonel Sibthorp, a Tory MP, moved that the annuity should be of 30,000 pounds, and this was supported by a majority of 262 to 158 – a majority composed of all the Radicals, most of the Conservatives and some of the Whigs. Among others Sir Robert Peel spoke in favour of the reduction. Melbourne told Stockmar: 'it is not the Tories only whom the Prince has to thank for cutting down his allowance. It is rather the Tories, the Radicals, and a great proportion of our own people.'[54]

Where the Government undoubtedly went wrong was in not gauging the extent of the opposition there would be. Not only was the problem not discussed beforehand with the Opposition, it also seems that proper soundings were not carried out among the Whigs. Even once the debate had started the Government might have retracted, but 'John Russell would go doggedly on and encounter this mortifying defeat, instead of giving way with the best grace he could. He lost his temper and flung dirt at Peel, like a sulky boy flinging rotten eggs.'[55] There certainly was good reason for reducing the sum. The country was in great distress and poverty was extreme. Moreover, the revenue of the country showed an ever-increasing deficit. The Prince of Denmark – the husband of Queen Anne – had indeed had 50,000 pounds a year but that was given him by the Queen and not the State.[56]

In committee Colonel Sibthorp tried to go further. He put forward a provision that if Albert survived the Queen and then remarried a Catholic, or failed to reside in the United Kingdom for at least six months a year, he should forfeit the annuity. The allusion to King Leopold was clear, for he had married a Catholic princess and no longer lived in England at all. Although this amendment was rejected, the ire of King Leopold was roused. 'I must confess', he wrote to his niece, 'that I never saw anything so disgraceful than the discussion and vote in the Commons. The whole mode and way in which those who opposed the grant treated the question was so extremely vulgar and disrespectful, that I cannot comprehend the Tories.'[57] In Leopold's opinion Albert's position was that 'of a male Queen Consort' and he should therefore have the same privileges and charges as George III's Queen Charlotte or William IV's Queen Adelaide. With regard to his own position Leopold noted: 'Another thing which made me think that Parliament would have acted with more decency, is that I return to the country now near £40,000 a year, not because I thought my income too large, as worthy Sir Robert Peel said, but from motives of political delicacy, which at least might be acknowledged on such occasion.'[58] One can only wonder that Leopold considered that his brief marriage to Charlotte should still so long afterwards bring him even 10,000 pounds a year – when he occupied another throne.

The Prince, contrary to what has generally been said, [59] was furious at the way he had been treated by the Tories. In his letter to Victoria he wrote:

> I am surprised that you have said no word of sympathy to me about the vote of the 28th, for those nice Tories have cut off half my income (that was to be expected), and it makes my position no very pleasant one. It is hardly conceivable that anyone could behave as meanly and disgracefully as they have to you and me. It cannot do them much good,

for it is hardly possible to maintain any respect for them any longer.
Everyone, even here, is indignant about it.[60]

Albert must have had the impression that the people of the cold, grey
island were not eager to make him welcome. Rank and fortune had
been refused him. His religion had been called into question. Victoria
herself seemed to have become more regal, more authoritarian since he
had left her shores. The young pair were indeed to go through a
difficult period of adjustment. Albert was pressed by Leopold to claim
now this, now that. Lord Melbourne urged Victoria to refuse or
temporize.

First came the question of an eventual peerage. Almost as soon as he
heard of the engagement, Leopold had started to urge Albert to seek
one, since he had himself declined a peerage – the Dukedom of Kendal
– in 1816 and later regretted it. On 21 November 1839 Victoria wrote
to inform Albert that Lord Melbourne and the whole Cabinet were
'strongly of the opinion that you should *not* be made a Peer'.[61] The
following day she in turn received a letter from Leopold pressing the
matter and explaining, 'the only reason why I do wish it is, that
Albert's foreignership should disappear as much as possible.'[62] It must
be noted that Queen Anne's husband, Prince George of Denmark had
been made a peer of the realm. Back flew Victoria's replies to both
uncle and fiancé. 'The whole Cabinet agrees with me in being strongly
of opinion that Albert should *not* be a Peer,' she told Uncle Leopold.
'Indeed, I see everything against it and nothing for it; the English are
very jealous at the idea of Albert's having any political power, or
meddling with affairs here – which I know from himself he will *not*
do.'[63] She wrote in the same terms to Albert, explaining that if he were
made a peer people would think he wanted to play some political role.
In true Melbournian fashion she continued, 'it is much better not to say
anything more about it now, and to let the whole matter rest.'[64] Albert
himself had at first not been in favour but when he was in Wiesbaden
Uncle Leopold set about convincing him: 'he suggested to me', Albert
wrote to Victoria, 'many reasons in favour of it, which we did not think
of at Windsor.' Albert's inclination was to put the question aside for the
moment. Rather naively he wrote, 'When I come to England life will
show what is necessary. It needs but the stroke of your pen to make me
a peer and to give me an English name.'[65]

On 27 November, immediately after the declaration of the
engagement to the Privy Council, Leopold wrote to Lord Melbourne
suggesting that Stockmar should act on behalf of Albert in the marriage

treaty. But that was not all. Declaring that his position in England from 1816 to 1831 gave him a special knowledge of the position of a husband of a queen, he launched into a long appreciation of Albert's virtues – 'steady . . . beyond his years', 'good sense', 'good judgement', 'pure-minded and well behaved', 'a natural gay, candid and amiable disposition' – all of which made him 'little inclined to forget himself and to meddle with affairs which are either not his own, or of which he understands nothing.' This might appear to make him an ideal consort. But 'the good sense and right feeling' of Albert must be shared by the Queen. If her husband were to become her 'safest and best friend' then the Queen herself would have to 'take from the very beginning a correct view of her married position'. Victoria should, in her uncle's opinion, 'be inspired with a strong and deep conviction that it is as well her own as the Prince's interest to make common cause and to live well together.' He writes, he says to Lord Melbourne, in whom his niece places unbounded confidence, so that he can speak to her and convince her of this. The end of the letter was more explicit: Leopold wanted to persuade the Prime Minister of the necessity of a peerage for Albert. Let him he says become 'as soon as possible and by all proper means as much an Englishman, as his nature will allow of . . . English to his very backbone', with an English name and an English title.[66]

Melbourne's reply, though delicately worded, made it clear that for him Victoria was the Queen, and Albert was not the King. He hoped Victoria would find the means of doing what is not easy, 'namely of reconciling the authority of a Sovereign with the duty of a wife'. The Prince should, of course, 'give advice in occasions of difficulty and crisis which in this country are sure to arise and in which it will be natural that the Queen should look to her husband for support and assistance.'[67]

Prince Albert was not an ambitious, self-seeking young man, as Leopold had been. He had been brought up by his uncle to believe that his destiny was to marry Victoria and become her guide. But in a sense he was very ill-adapted to the task. He was in no sense a courtier and palace life tired him. He was deeply attached to his native land and to his relatives. Britain was for him a foreign country. He genuinely wanted to remain a Coburger. Faced with Victoria's intransigence Albert capitulated.

As regards my peerage and the fears of my playing a political part, dear, beloved Victoria, I have only one anxious wish and one prayer: do not allow it to become a matter of worry to you. Let the papers and the

people, whoever they may be, be as angry with me as they like; only do
not let it cause you to mistrust my love, my honesty and my frankness to
you.[68]

Capitulation was all the easier as the idea of the peerage was Leopold's.
Albert himself had written to his grandmother over a month before.
'My position here will be very pleasant, in as much as I have refused all
the offered titles, I keep my own name and remain what I was.'[69]

The question of the Prince's household was to make their relationship become even more strained. Towards the end of November the
Queen wrote to tell him that 'young Mr Anson', Lord Melbourne's
private secretary, greatly wished to be with Albert. 'I am very much in
favour of it', Queen Victoria wrote, 'because he is an excellent young
man, and very modest, very honest, very steady, very well-informed,
and will be of *much use* to you.'[70] Albert was dismayed by the news. He
saw his establishment in a very different light – as an external image of
what he was. 'The maxim,' he wrote to Victoria, ' "Tell me whom he
associates with, and I will tell you who he is," must here especially not
be lost sight of.' The selection should therefore be made without regard
to politics since he wanted to keep himself free from all parties. Above
all, these appointments should not be mere 'party rewards', but they
should possess other recommendations besides those of party.

> Let them be either of very high rank, or very rich, or very clever, or who
> have performed important services for England. It is very necessary that
> they should be chosen from both sides – the same number of Whigs as of
> Tories; and above all I do wish that they should be well-educated men
> and of high character . . . [71]

Victoria's sharp retort was that he could rely entirely upon her to put
about him people who were pleasant and of high standing and good
character. 'You may', she added, 'rely upon my care that you shall
have proper people, and not idle and not too young. And Lord
Melbourne has already mentioned several to me who would be very
suitable.' She also informed him in the same missive that she had
received an ungracious letter from Uncle Leopold. 'He appears to me
to be nettled because I no longer ask for his advice, but dear Uncle is
given to believe that he must rule the roost everywhere.'[72]

Albert returned to the subject several times. He would have been
happy to have about him several highminded Germans who would
keep him company in a foreign land.

> Think of my position, dear Victoria; I am leaving my home with all its
> old associations, all my bosom friends . . . Except yourself I have no one

to confide in. And it is not even to be conceded to me that the two or three persons who are to have the charge of my private affairs should be persons who already command my confidence.[73]

But Melbourne was not in favour – and the Queen herself may well have seen this German element as a threat to her own intimacy with Albert. The Prince had grave doubts about Anson: not only was he Melbourne's secretary but he was also addicted to dancing! In any case, if he had to give way then at least Anson must leave Melbourne's service. This the Queen conceded. But that was all. On the rest she was adamant. His people had to be nominated immediately, in his absence – 'It will also not do to wait till you come'[74] – and they would be nominated by the Queen. 'I am distressed to tell you what I fear you do not like, but it is necessary, my dearest, most excellent Albert.'[75] Despite a renewed effort on Albert's part she remained inflexible. 'I am much grieved that you feel disappointed about my wish respecting your gentlemen, but very glad that you consent to it, and that you feel confidence in my choice.'[76]

To Uncle Leopold, whom she criticized when he intervened and upbraided when he was silent, the Queen wrote, 'Just two words (though you don't deserve half a one, as your silence is unpardonable) to say I have just heard from Albert, who, I am glad to say, consents to *my* choosing his people.'[77] In the event Anson was to prove a great success and to become a firm friend of the Prince's. The appointments of the Prince's establishment were in fact modelled on those of the Queen. The majority were permanent and played no role in politics. Two – the Groom of the Stole and one Lord in waiting were more closely connected with one or other party and changed with each ministry.

The wedding plans were yet another bone of contention. First there was the problem of the bridesmaids. Prince Albert wanted the Queen to exclude any young woman whose mother had a dubious past. Victoria, encouraged by Melbourne, decided to take no notice and the daughters of Lady Jersey and Lady Radnor were bridesmaids. Victoria was in fact extremely fair-minded – 'I always think', she wrote to the Prince, 'one ought always to be indulgent towards other people, as I always think, if we had not been well brought up and well taken care of, we might also have gone astray.'[78] Then came the problem of the honeymoon. Albert would have liked the pair of them to go away together alone for longer than the two days. It was usual in England, he claimed, for newly married people to stay for up to four or six weeks away from the town and society. 'It might perhaps be a good and delicate action not to depart from this custom altogether and to retire from the public eye for at least a fortnight – or a week.'[79] Back came the reply of the Queen of England. 'You forget, my dearest love, that I am the Sovereign, and that business can stop and wait for nothing. Parliament is sitting, and something occurs almost every day for which I may be required, and it is quite impossible for me to be absent from London.'[80]

Finally, on 28 January, the Prince left Coburg accompanied by his father and brother and by Lord Torrington and Colonel Grey, who had been sent to invest him with the insignia of the Garter. When he left, the people of Gotha turned out to wish him on his way. The streets were densely crowded. 'Every window was crammed with heads, every housetop covered with people, waving handkerchiefs and vying with each other in demonstrations of affection that could not be mistaken.'[81] When the carriages reached the house of the Dowager Duchess, Albert's grandmother, he got out to bid her a last farewell. The Duchess was desolate at the idea of losing her beloved grandson. 'She came to the window as the carriages drove off, and threw her arms out, calling out "Albert, Albert!" in tones that went to every one's heart, when she was carried away, almost in a fainting state, by her attendants.'[82] Albert's conflicting emotions as he left his homeland and his past are depicted by him in a letter written a month earlier to his aunt: 'Hope, love for dear Victoria, the pain of leaving home, the parting from very dear kindred, the entrance into a new circle of relations, all meeting me with the utmost kindness, prospects the most brilliant, the dread of being unequal to my position.'[83] Albert's party stopped to visit King Leopold in Brussels and then proceeded to Calais.

On 7 February the Prince arrived in Dover. It had taken him over five hours to cross the Channel from Calais. 'We had', Albert reports to the Queen, 'a terrible crossing . . . for the whole boat was crammed with sick people. I never remember having suffered so long or so violently . . . When we landed our faces were more the colour of wax candles than human visages.'[84] He was, however, most pleased with his reception – thousands were standing on the quay cheering their welcome.

He arrived at Buckingham Palace at half-past four on 8 February. Victoria was as nervous as he but she took him by the hand, embraced him and led him up to her room. "Seeing his *dear dear* face again put me at rest about everything,' she wrote in her journal.[85] That very afternoon the Lord Chancellor administered the oath of naturalization, and a banquet in honour of the Prince was held in the evening. On the evening before the wedding they read over the marriage service together and practised putting on the ring. That morning Victoria in her direct, concrete way had written in her journal: 'Monday, February 10 – the last time I shall sleep alone.'[86]

Before she saw him on the wedding morning – and she *did* see him, despite admonitions that it was against tradition – the Queen wrote a little note, which she had taken to her bridegroom's room. It read: 'Dearest – How are you today and have you slept well? I have rested very well and feel very comfortable today. What weather! I believe however the rain will cease. Send one word when you, my most dearly loved bridegroom, will be ready. Thy ever-faithful "Victoria R.".'[87] Victoria was serene and content, at ease in her country and her role. Prince Albert was tense and anxious in a foreign land. He sent a letter to his grandmother: 'In less than three hours I shall be standing before the altar with my dear bride! In that solemn moment I must once again ask your blessing, which I am well assured I shall receive and which shall be my protection and my joy! I must end. May God be my helper.'[88] Victoria did not feel the need to invoke God or to seek parental blessings.

The morning of the wedding was cold and wet. 'A dreadful day,' Greville noted, 'torrents of rain and violent gusts of wind'.[89] But this did not prevent a large crowd turning out to see the young couple as they passed. This was, after all, the first royal marriage that they had been able to see. For over a century royal marriages – those of the Prince Regent, of Princess Charlotte and of the Duke of Clarence (later William IV) – had all taken place in private and late at night. Victoria, too, would have preferred a private ceremony but Lord Melbourne would have none of it. 'It's of great importance that you should get over that dislike of going amongst everybody; mustn't let that be known; it would be very injurious.'[90] Victoria had already complained about the venue. She talked of her 'horror at being married in the Chapel Royal' and complained 'that everything was always made so uncomfortable for Kings and Queens.'[91] To no purpose.

The marriage took place in the Chapel Royal in St James's Palace. Great efforts had been made to accommodate as many seats for spectators as possible. Although in the chapel itself there was not a great abundance of seating, round the upper part a gallery had been erected; within the Palace seats had been put along the line of the procession wherever possible – in the tapestry room, in the armoury and on the staircase. The colonnade in the courtyard had been enclosed and was lighted by the lanterns above and the windows behind. The seats, rising in tiers, were covered with gold-coloured borders and fringes. The whole structure, although temporary, looked as if it had been constructed of solid masonry.[92]

The Chapel Royal itself was quietly elegant with its dark oak pews, seats covered in crimson velvet, and gilt columns and altar railing. The wall above the Communion table was hung with rich festoons of crimson velvet edged with gold lace. In front of the altar were two stools to be used by the royal pair during the ceremony. Behind those were four state chairs – two on the left for Victoria and her mother, two on the right for Albert and the Dowager Queen Adelaide. Behind were places for Albert's relatives and Victoria's uncles and close relatives, together with the elite of British nobility. Only two Conservative peers were present, the Duke of Wellington and Lord Liverpool.[93]

Albert's procession came first. It passed through Queen Anne's drawing room and the armoury room, down the grand staircase and along the colonnade, then into the chapel – to the rather ridiculous strains of 'See the Conquering Hero Come'. Albert wore the uniform of a British field marshal. Over his shoulders was hung the collar of the Order of the Garter, the greatest honour the Queen could bestow on him, surmounted by two white rosettes. He looked pale and pensive.

Once Albert was in his place the Lord Chamberlain left the chapel to fetch the Queen. Her procession was considerably longer. Victoria as she came down the aisle to the strains of the National Anthem was 'quite calm and composed', although she had 'trembled a little as she entered the chapel.'[94] She was paler even than usual. Her dress (which is now in the London Museum) was of rich white satin, trimmed with orange flower blossoms. On her head she wore a high wreath of the same flowers, over which a veil of Honiton lace was thrown, in the way of royal brides, so as not to conceal her face. In order to encourage British manufacture the Queen wore white satin manufactured in Spitalfields, with a broad flounce of lace made at Beer, near Honiton, in Devonshire – which had provided work for over two hundred people. The designs were destroyed after the lace had been made so that the pattern could not be reproduced and it remained unique.

Small but slight and well-proportioned, Victoria was not beautiful but she was vivacious, with a grace and simplicity of manner. She wore her Turkish diamond necklace and earrings and Albert's sapphire brooch. Her twelve bridesmaids were also simply dressed – in tulle and white roses. Lady Lyttelton thought they 'looked like village girls, among all the gorgeous colours and jewels that surrounded them.'[95]

The service itself took place at the altar and was performed by the

Archbishop of Canterbury, the Archbishop of York and the Bishop of London. Once again the royal protocol had not been thoroughly thought through. There had been no rehearsal and the bridesmaids were too numerous, or rather the train of white satin trimmed with orange flowers was 'rather too short for the number of young ladies who carried it. We were all huddled together, and scrambled rather than walked along, kicking each other's heels and treading in each other's gowns.'[96] Albert never seemed quite sure of what he should be doing, whether he should be sitting, standing or kneeling. 'Perhaps he appeared awkward from embarrassment but he was certainly a good deal perplexed and agitated in delivering his responses.'[97]

However, the ceremony itself was, according to the Queen, 'very imposing and fine and simple'.[98] One of the most touching moments was when Prince Albert was asked whether he would take this woman for his wife, and 'she turned full round and looked into his face as he replied "I will." '[99]

In contrast to the bridal pair, with only two-score years between them, were their aunts and uncles, the sons and daughters of George III. The Duke of Sussex gave away the bride and was 'greatly affected'.[100] The old Duke of Cambridge 'was decidedly gay, making very audible remarks from time to time' throughout the ceremony and, once it was over, handing the princesses down the steps 'with many audible civilities'.[101] The bride's mother, according to *The Times*, 'appeared somewhat disconsolate and distressed, and we fancied, but it might be fancy, that we saw the traces of tears upon her countenance.'[102] As for Melbourne, he carried the sword of state and was in the royal procession immediately before the Queen. He 'appeared proud of the dignity with which he was invested; but little attention was paid to him.'[103] The Dowager Queen Adelaide looked 'quite the *beau idéal* of a Queen Dowager – grave, dignified and very becoming',[104] dressed in purple velvet and ermine. The Queen turned and embraced her as she came back down the chapel after the ceremony.

Each of the twelve bridesmaids received from Her Majesty as a nuptial gift a brooch the Queen had designed herself. Each was formed of pure gold in the form of an eagle. The body was entirely covered with turquoises, the eyes were rubies, the beak a diamond. The claws of richly wrought gold rested on pearls of great size and value. A variety of portraits of Her Majesty and Prince Albert, superbly set in the lids of gold snuff boxes, were presented to all the foreign Ambassadors. There were also, for more general distribution, hundreds of gold rings bearing a medallion of Victoria, a striking likeness in profile.

Various confectioners in London had been called on to supply wedding cakes – one hundred in all, of various descriptions and sizes. They were distributed among the members of the royal family, the great officers of state, the Household and the foreign Ambassadors. Among the most prestigious were the fourteen made by Mr Gunter of Berkeley Square: they went to the two Princess Sophias, the Duchess of Kent, the Duke of Sussex, Viscount Melbourne, and members of the Cabinet. One of them was kept for the royal banquet to be held at St James's Palace in the evening – after the departure of the young couple – and attended by the couple's parents, Household and friends.

The return to Buckingham Palace was followed by a wedding breakfast. This brought together a small, select company – nine relatives, the Archbishop of Canterbury and the Bishop of London, Viscount Melbourne and six members of his administration including Palmerston, together with the Queen's Household and members of the suites of the royal family and of the Duke of Coburg. The Duke of Wellington was not invited. The Duchess of Gloucester was kept away by a severe cold.

The main wedding cake was more than nine foot in circumference and sixteen inches high. Two pedestals rose from the plateau of the cake, the upper one supporting another plateau, on which stood Britannia gazing upon the royal pair, who were in the act of pledging their vows. At their feet were two turtle doves, emblems of love and purity, and a dog representing the constancy of their attachment. Cupid could also be seen writing in his tablets with a stylus, 'February 10 1840', and the letters VA could also be seen. This masterpiece was designed by Mr Mawdett, chief confectioner to Her Majesty in Buckingham Palace, and constituted a remarkable piece of Victoriana, albeit a perishable one.

After the breakfast the young couple set off for Windsor – but not before the Queen had seen, alone, her Prime Minister.

> At twenty minutes to four Lord Melbourne came to me and stayed with me till ten minutes to four. I shook hands with him and he kissed my hand. Talked of how well everything went off. "Nothing could have gone off better", he said, and of the people being in such good humour. . . . I begged him not to go to the party; he was a little tired; I would let him know when we arrived; I pressed his hand once more, and he said "God bless you, Ma'am", most kindly, and with such a kind look.[105]

Albert, who had changed into a dark travelling outfit, went up to fetch the Queen down after her meeting. She, too, had changed and was wearing a white satin cloak trimmed with swan's down and a textured white velvet bonnet with plumes of feathers and a deep fall of Brussels point lace. According to Greville they 'went off in a very poor and shabby style. Instead of the new chariot in which most married people are accustomed to dash along, they were in one of the old travelling coaches, the postilions in undress liveries, and with a small escort.'[106]

Their reception in Windsor was nonetheless, according to the Queen, 'enthusiastic, hearty, and gratifying in every way, the people quite deafening us with their cheers, and horsemen, gigs, etc., going along with us.'[107] There were practically no security arrangements and the proximity of their well-wishers must have made them rather anxious. As they drove along, the houses 'glowed with crowns, stars and all the brilliant devices which gas and oil could supply.'[108] When they arrived at the Castle they looked round their rooms and, while Victoria changed her gown, Albert sat down and played at the piano. The nervous tension was, however, having its effect.

We had our dinner in our sitting room; but I had such a sick headache that I could eat nothing and was obliged to lie down in the middle blue room for the remainder of the evening, on the sofa, but, ill or not, I never, never spent such an evening . . . He called me names of tenderness, I have never yet heard used to me before . . . Oh! this was the happiest day of my life! May God help me to do my duty as I ought and be worthy of such blessings.[109]

11
Conflicts of Roles

When the couple returned to London after their brief three-day honeymoon a new era in the Queen's life began. Victoria was undoubtedly physically attracted to Albert. She admired his manly beauty, appreciated his tenderness and in her over-emphatic way declared him to be perfect. 'When day dawned (for we did not sleep much)', she wrote on the day after her bridal night, 'and I beheld that beautiful angelic face by my side, it was more than I can express! He does look so beautiful in his shirt only, with his beautiful throat seen.'[1] Their relationship was, from the beginning, based on affection. But their temperaments were very different and did not easily dovetail. In domestic affairs their tastes were different. The Queen enjoyed the pleasures of the table, the excitement of a ball, the delight of being entertained. She loved the town. Albert preferred the country, disliked small talk and Court society and liked to be in bed by eleven. Coming as he did from a life of comparative seclusion he found Court life a strain.

Guizot described a concert the royal couple attended in 1840:

> The Queen took a more lively interest in it than the greater part of her guests did. Prince Albert slept. She looked at him, half smiling, half vexed. She pushed him with her elbow. He woke up, and nodded approval of the piece of the moment. Then he went to sleep again still nodding approval, and the Queen began again.[2]

Nor was this a unique occasion. Lady Willoughby de Eresby, describing to a correspondent a musical party at Lady Normanby's London house in honour of the Queen and Prince Albert in June 1840, noted: 'Lady Williamson, Lady Barrington and Lady Hardwicke all sang divinely, supported by Lablache and Rubini. The Queen was charmed and

Cousin Albert looked beautiful, and slept as quietly as usual, sitting by Lady Normanby.'[3]

The Prince's boredom with Court life was obvious from the first. His marriage had rid him of the suspense that had marred his adolescence and his emotions were undoubtedly awakened by the enthusiastic love Victoria showered upon him. But he had been brought up to ponder and reflect, to worry and to look ahead. He perceived almost immediately the problems that were in store, for the Queen slipped easily back into the daily routine she had had before her marriage and the Prince had not expected to be so entirely locked out of the affairs of the State. The Queen dealt with them during long periods she spent alone with her Prime Minister. He was also excluded from her personal affairs, which were in the hands of Baroness Lehzen, who would brook no interference in her domain.

The Queen was in fact jealous of her prerogatives. She was strong-willed and autocratic. There was, as Lady Lyttelton noted, a 'vein of iron' running through her character[4] and she was determined to remain Queen of England in her own right. She did not want to share her power with anyone – as her treatment of the Prince of Wales in later years was to show.

Albert was not, however, simply 'a shy young man at first bewildered and then deeply moved by Victoria's passion'.[5] He, too, could be quite inflexible. He knew how to bide his time and choose his moment, for he had none of Victoria's impetuosity. He was, moreover, extremely lucid. He wrote to his friend, the Prince von Löwenstein, in the early days of his marriage. 'In my home life I am very happy and contented; but the difficulty in filling my place with the proper dignity is, that I am only the husband, and not the master in the house.'[6] Inevitably he was brought into conflict with the Queen's entourage and with the Queen herself.

The spirit of the age was certainly on Prince Albert's side. Mrs Stevenson, wife of the American Minister to the Court of St James's, noted with great satisfaction that Albert would not allow himself to be 'managed' by his wife, Queen though she were, but resisted her kindly but firmly.

> I think it is the best security for their future happiness. And I think it is always bad when a woman inverts the laws of Providence by taking the rein in her own hands. You know I never, even in my palmy days, asserted the equality of the sexes. Man is the head of woman, or rather in Scripture phrase, "The husband is the head of the wife, even as Christ is the head of the Church."[7]

Once she had married, Queen Victoria was subjected to this view of male superiority in a way that the celibate Queen Elizabeth I had never been. Almost a century later, Albert's biographer Hector Bolitho took a nineteenth-century stand when he wrote, 'When a woman is in love, her desire for public power becomes less and less.'[8] Whether it was cause or effect is another matter. Certainly Leopold, Stockmar and Melbourne, although their places in society were vastly different, were all convinced that Albert should fill Victoria's place in fact if not in form. King Leopold expressed this clearly: 'The Prince ought in business as in everything to be necessary to the Queen, he should be to her a walking dictionary for reference on any point which her own knowledge or education have not enabled her to answer. There should be no concealment from him on any subject.'[9] To fulfil this mission the Prince 'must not sleep, he must studiously imbibe that information on every subject, which may enable him to be ready and fit to render advice under all circumstances.'[10] Leopold was now in his intellectual prime. He had an intimate knowledge of politics and was a first-class linguist, speaking German, English, French, Italian and even Russian. How he must have chafed to see a slip of a girl on the throne he had intended to share with his late wife. Albert, at least, listened to him and took his advice. Victoria had already proved she could be only too independent.

In these first months of marriage Victoria clung to her role as Queen and the frictions between husband and wife were frequent. On one occasion an official box arrived from a Government department labelled 'sign immediately'. Albert thought the Queen was being treated as a glorified civil servant and urged her therefore to hold up her signature for a day or two. Victoria was so annoyed at his interference that she made a point of signing immediately.

Prince Albert complained of the Queen's want of confidence in him, evidenced by her refusal to share with him any discussion of political matters. Lord Melbourne, pressed by the Prince through his private secretary Anson, spoke to the Queen about it.[11] She told him that although she knew it was wrong, she preferred conversing with the Prince on other things. 'My impression', Lord Melbourne told Anson, 'is that the chief obstacle in Her Majesty's mind is the fear of difference of opinion and she thinks that domestic harmony is more likely to follow from avoiding subjects likely to create difference.'[12]

Stockmar thought that although the Queen had not started off on the right foot she should by degrees impart everything to him. But knowing the Queen's character he noted,' there is a danger in his [Albert's] wishing it all at once.'[13]

The Queen, however, continued not to show her husband the documents she received from State departments and she continued to receive Ministers alone, despite Lord Melbourne's intervention.[14] Albert thus found himself frustrated of what were considered at the time the normal rights of authority of husband over wife. For Albert there was no doubt that a Queen reigning in her own right was something of an anomaly. Much later, in 1850, he was to explain to the Duke of Wellington that he had considered it his job to 'fill up every gap, which, as a woman, the Queen would naturally leave in the exercise of her regal functions.'[15]

It was, however, a truly feminine function which was to facilitate Prince Albert's accession to the world of politics. Only a few weeks after her marriage Queen Victoria realized she was pregnant. The news did not fill her with joy. To the Dowager Duchess of Saxe-Coburg-Gotha she wrote:

> I must say that I could not be more unhappy; I am really upset about it and it is spoiling my happiness; I have always hated the idea and I prayed God night and day to be left free for at least six months, but my prayers have not been answered and I am really most unhappy. I cannot understand how any one can wish for such a thing, especially at the beginning of a marriage.[16]

To Leopold too she protested: 'about myself: really it is too dreadful. I cannot in any way see the good side of this sad business. Children seem literally raining down from Heaven this year.'[17] She confided to her cousin Maria II, Queen of Portugal, her loathing of big families. 'It is not only a disaster for oneself but also for the poor children, especially in royal families like this one, where if there are many children they are extremely poor, despite their very high rank which is also a disaster for the country. But no more of that.'[18]

But her real complaint was that childbearing restricted a woman's activity. When later, in 1858, the child she was now carrying, her eldest daughter, who had just married and gone to live in Berlin, declared that a married woman had much more liberty than an unmarried one, Victoria drew her a picture of the miseries of pregnancy:

> aches – and sufferings and miseries and plagues – which you must struggle against – and enjoyments etc. to give up – constant precautions to take, you will feel the yoke of a married woman . . . I own it tried me sorely; one feels so pinned down – one's wings clipped – in fact, at the best (and few were or are better than I was) only half oneself – particularly the first and second time. This I call the "shadow side" . . . And therefore I think our sex a most unenviable one.[19]

The early months of the pregnancy went well and Queen Victoria required no physician but Clark 'till the horrid thing takes place'. She saw Clark only once a week or so and 'nothing tires or hurts me. I sleep well and so in short I ought not to complain.'[20] She felt no affection for the body growing inside her own. It cramped her style, made her feel uncomfortable and generally reminded her that she was only a woman; '*the thing*', she wrote to King Leopold, 'is odious and if all one's plagues are rewarded only by a nasty girl, I shall drown it, I think. I *will* know nothing else but a boy. I never will have a girl!'[21]

The Queen's pregnancy was to transform Albert's position. Measures had to be taken to decide what would happen if the Queen were to die leaving an infant as heir to the throne. This meant passing a Regency Bill. Prince Leopold had been named Regent when Princess Charlotte was known to be pregnant and there seemed no reason to do otherwise than name the Queen's husband now. But the Prince – and Stockmar – feared Parliament would impose a council on the Regent. Stockmar advised Albert to discuss the affair not only with the Government but with the Opposition so that the most favourable solution might be adopted – that is, the one on which the Regency Bill of the Duchess of Kent was founded during Victoria's minority, a Regency without a council.[22] Stockmar began working to this end on both the Tories and the Opposition. He established contacts with Peel, who on 28 June told Lord Liverpool that there was an intrigue on foot among the Radicals for the purpose of setting up the Duke of Sussex as co-Regent. His advice to the Prince was to remain perfectly quiet and passive. He, Peel, would defend the Prince's interests.[23]

Stockmar also talked with Melbourne, who had come out against a Council of Regency on the grounds that the idea of dividing executive power was against the spirit of the English constitution.[24] A Regency Bill without a council went through both Houses without any opposition, save ironically that of the Duke of Sussex, who showed no gratitude to the Queen although she had bestowed the title of Duchess of Inverness on 10 April 1840 on his second morganatic wife.[25]

Prince Albert was grateful to Stockmar. Although there seems no reason to suppose that the Bill would not have passed without his intervention, Stockmar had convinced the Prince otherwise.[26] Albert was delighted with the Regency Bill. As he wrote to his brother: 'In case of Victoria's death and her successor being under eighteen years of age, I am to be Regent – *alone* – Regent without a Council. You will understand the importance of this matter and that it gives my position here in the country a fresh significance.'[27]

Having seen the Bill successfully passed, Baron Stockmar now returned to his home and family in Coburg. But not without a few last words of counsel to the Prince. His exhortations with regard to the Prince's relationship with his wife were singularly unhelpful. 'Keep watch over the moral and physical health of the Queen. Never lose self-possession or patience; but, above all, at no time and in no way, fail in princely worth and nobleness.'[28] Once Stockmar had left British shores the admonitions did not cease. Letters constantly exhorted the Prince to do his duty, to strive for nobility. Praise was measured out as if by some father confessor. In censorious tone he wrote in September: 'I am satisfied with the news you have sent me. Mistakes, misunderstandings, obstructions, which come in vexatious opposition to one's views, are always to be taken for what they are, – namely, natural phenomenon of life, which represent one of its sides, and that the shady one.'[29]

As Victoria's pregnancy advanced, her moments of revolt against the pressure being put on her to share her role with her husband became rarer. In August, when Parliament was prorogued, the Prince sat in an armchair next to the throne. In September his writing table was placed next to the Queen's, and in the same month Albert wrote to Baron Stockmar saying he was 'constantly provided with interesting papers' and underlining his satisfaction at the change in the Queen's attitude. 'I have come to be extremely pleased with Victoria during the past few months. She has only twice had the sulks . . . altogether she puts more confidence in me daily.'[30]

On the public front, too, Albert had strengthened his position. He organized and directed his first public concert on 29 April 1840, made his first public speech – to a meeting for the abolition of slavery – on 1 June, was given the freedom of the City of London on 28 August and was admitted to the Privy Council on 11 September.

'Now', he wrote to his brother, 'Victoria is also ready to give up something for my sake, I everything for her sake.'[31] On the political front, things were definitely looking up for Albert. On the purely domestic front, however, Lehzen still ruled supreme. She had, in particular, virtual control over the Queen's private expenditure. No bill for even minor expenses was paid until it had been signed by the Baroness. Seeking a role in his own household, Albert was frustrated by the place the Baroness held. From the beginning he saw her as his arch-enemy. He believed that it was she who hardened the Queen's resolve to keep her prerogatives and reign alone. In his letters to his brother we see constant references to petty victories won in his opinion against Lehzen – whom they both refer to as the old hag (*die Blaste*). When in

August 1840 the Queen decided that she, as Queen Anne had done, would take her husband in her carriage to Parliament and sit him beside her at the prorogation, Albert told his brother: 'In spite of Lehzen and the Master of the House, I shall drive *with* Victoria in a carriage to the House and sit beside her on a throne specially built for me.'[32]

Opinion concerning the Baroness was divided. Greville, for instance, considered her 'a clever agreeable woman'[33] and declared she was 'much beloved by the women and much esteemed and liked by all who frequent the Court' and had been 'a faithful and devoted servant of the Queen from birth'.[34] Lady Lyttelton, who worked for some time with her, found her 'very kind and helpful'.[35]

Anson, on the contrary, saw her as a 'danger to domestic happiness'. She tried to make it seem as if she interfered in nothing and yet, in a conversation with Baron Stockmar, 'she plainly showed she was active for mischief in every direction.'[36] Lord Ashley claimed that the Conservatives 'dreaded her violence and intemperance', politically speaking, and claimed that she had 'unfairly prejudiced the Queen's mind'.[37] It is true that Lehzen was a staunch Whig.

The real point at issue, however, concerns her relationship with Albert. Was she determined to drive a wedge between the couple, to refuse to admit that as the Queen's husband Albert had a right to a certain role? She appeared at least to begin with, well disposed towards the Prince. In April 1840, for instance, she told the American Minister's wife in her broken English that it was fortunate for 'de nation that the Queen had married such a good and humble-minded person'.[38] Stockmar, who at first had had nothing but praise for her, later came to believe that she did have a bad influence on the Queen and encouraged Victoria to withhold her confidence from Albert. When he told Melbourne that Victoria was more influenced by the Baroness than she was aware, Melbourne disagreed and stressed that the Queen never even mentioned the name of Lehzen to him[39]

In February 1841 Lord Melbourne ventured to say that in his opinion the Prince would be quite unjustified if he tried to force the Queen to send the Baroness away. Melbourne acknowledged that her constant interference must be irksome and annoying to him but considered he had 'no right to ask the Queen to make such a sacrifice of her own comfort'. Should the Prince put it as an alternative that either the Baroness must go or he would not stay in the house, the Queen, given her determination and obstinacy of character, might well reply, 'In this alternative you have contemplated the possibility of living without me, I will show you that I can contemplate the possibility of living without you.'[40] Not strong enough to attack Lehzen openly Albert whittled away her support within the Palace. The Prince had become so obsessed with the Baroness that he did not realise how disproportionate his resentment was. She was simply a rather narrow-minded, jealous woman who was entirely devoted to her mistress, whom she had served for seventeen years without ever taking a day off.

Victoria's pregnancy proceeded without incident. In her ninth month, on 10 November, she told Feodora: 'I am wonderfully well, really the Doctors say they never saw anybody so well . . . I take long walks, some in the highest wind, every day, and am so active, though of a *great* size I must unhappily admit.'[41] On 13 November the Queen and Court left Windsor Castle for Buckingham Palace in view of the approaching confinement. The birth came on Saturday 21 November 1840, three weeks earlier than expected. Nothing, declared the Queen in her journal, was ready.[42]

She felt the first twinges in the night, at half-past twelve. The real pains began at nine. Then: 'the last pains which are generally thought the worst I thought nothing of, they began at half past twelve [in the day] and lasted till ten minutes to two when the young lady appeared. I saw the time she was born like now. I never had any pain, nor any fever.'[43]

The Queen's first-born came into the world after over twelve hours' labour, nine months and eleven days after the wedding. Both Albert and the Duchess of Kent were in the room, as were the Queen's medical attendants. In an adjoining room, with the door open, were the Councillors, among them Melbourne, Palmerston and Lord John Russell. The infant Princess wrapped in flannel was brought into the room where the Ministers and great officers of state were assembled. She was laid upon the table for a moment for the observation of the authorities and then returned to her room to be dressed for the first time.

The Queen's dressing room was fitted up as a temporary nursery, 'until her little royal highness's apartments were got ready'. 'There was a marble and a silver bath for the young stranger, and her gorgeous cradle made in the form of a nautilus etc.'[44]

The Queen was sadly disappointed at not having had a boy. But she quickly softened. She spoke of her daughter as 'Our little Lady' and told cousin Ferdinand she was doing 'wonderfully. Growing and becoming more beautiful every day. She has big dark blue eyes and a beautiful complexion.'[45] She was in fact to bear a remarkable likeness to her mother.

Victoria remained in bed for over a fortnight, as was the custom of the time, sitting up for the first time on 6 December and getting out of bed for the first time on the following day.[46] King Leopold wrote to congratulate the Queen and to tell her that he hoped the Princess Victoria would be the first of a long line of children. The Queen was irate. She replied acidly:

> I think, dearest Uncle, you cannot really wish me to be the "Mamma of a large family" for I think you will see with me the great inconvenience a large family would be to us all, and particularly to the country, independent of the hardship and inconvenience to myself; men never think, at least seldom think what a hard task it is for us women to go through this very often.[47]

Stockmar had returned to London at the urgent request of Prince Albert in November. He had, however, as was his wont, been trying to direct the affairs of the royal couple from afar well before his arrival. On 1 October he had written sententiously to the Prince on the subject of a nurse for the child. 'Impress upon Anson the necessity for conducting this affair with the greatest conscientiousness and circumspection; for a man's education begins the first day of his life, and a lucky choice I regard as the greatest and finest gift we can bestow on the expected stranger.'[48] Although the birth had proceeded without difficulty, Stockmar – no doubt prompted by his memories of Charlotte's death and perhaps by the feeling that he might then have done more – sent a note to the Prince *after* the birth, once again instructing him as to what he must and must not do:

> sleep, stillness, rest, and the exclusion of many people from her room are just now the all in all for the Queen. You cannot be too guarded on these points. Be, therefore, a very Cerberus. You ought not yourself to be too much about the Queen just now, for your being near or talking with her may be too exciting.

The last sentence of the note no doubt disquieted Prince Albert quite unnecessarily:

> Although the Queen is now apparently so well, this ought not to lull us into careless security, for any agitation, but especially any excitement, too much speaking, etc., may bring on fever and dangerous consequences. Therefore, once again, the greatest prudence!![49]

Stockmar went unheeded at least in so far as Albert's presence by his wife's bedside was concerned. Throughout the last weeks of her pregnancy it was Albert who had sat by her bed and read to her as she wished. Albert it was who lifted her from bed to sofa. 'His care', the

Queen said, 'was like that of a mother, nor could there be a kinder, wiser or more judicious muse.'[50] In the evenings he dined with the Duchess of Kent and refused to go out. His constant presence before the birth had been soothing and not a source of increased excitement. His absence after it might well have had dire consequences. Fortunately Stockmar's counsel was not followed.

Albert, who had wanted a son above all, wrote to his brother Ernest, 'Albert, father of a daughter, you will laugh at me.'[51] But her coming was to change his status. He became father of the heiress to the throne (at least until he became father to an heir) and this was a much more prestigious position than that of Consort to the Queen. The Prince's daughter's name had to be introduced according to custom into the liturgy. The Queen insisted that the Prince's name be mentioned as well. So the Princess took her father with her as it were. On the very day of her birth, moreover, and because of it, the Prince had represented the Queen at a Privy Council for the very first time.

Immediately after her confinement the Queen directed that the despatch boxes from the Foreign Office, which had been withheld for a day or two after the birth until she could attend to affairs of state, should be sent to her husband.'[52] 'I have my hands very full,' Albert wrote proudly to his brother, 'as I also look after Victoria's political affairs.'[53]

The Princess Royal's christening took place on her parents' first wedding anniversary – 10 February 1841 – in Buckingham Palace. The infant was christened Victoria Adelaide Mary Louisa. The sponsors at the christening were the Duke of Saxe-Coburg-Gotha, Albert's father, represented in his absence by the Duke of Wellington; King Leopold, who was thus able to come to England without being accused of interfering by the British aristocracy, who begrudged him the 50,000 pounds a year allowance he was still receiving; the Queen Dowager; and the Queen's mother, the Duchess of Kent, her aunt, the Duchess of Gloucester and her uncle, the Duke of Sussex. Melbourne did not come to the christening on account of a bad attack of gout. 'It grieves me so much', the Queen wrote in her journal, 'as he has always been present at *every ceremony*, since I came to the Throne.'[54]

A new font was used. It was made of silver gilt in the form of a waterlily supporting a large shell. Inside the rim of the shell were small waterlilies floating on the edge. The water was brought from River Jordan. The christening went off extremely well in Albert's opinion. He already saw in his daughter of almost three months a being of exception. He told the Duchess Caroline: 'Your little grand-child behaved with great propriety and like a Christian. She was awake, but did not cry at all and seemed to crow with immense satisfaction at the lights and brilliant uniforms, for she is very intelligent and observing.'[55] After the christening there was a dinner in the picture gallery and then some instrumental music. 'The health of the little one was drunk with great enthusiasm.'[56] Victoria's enthusiasm was, however, marred by the fact that she was pregnant again. As Albert wrote to his brother 'Victoria is not very happy about it.'[57]

The Melbourne administration which had served Victoria since the beginning of her reign was, at the beginning of 1841, living on borrowed time. Indeed the Government had not been really secure since 1839 when, in the normal course of events, Sir Robert Peel should have formed a Conservative Government – but the Bedchamber dispute had brought back Lord Melbourne. As the months went by it became increasingly clear that the Whigs were unable to cope with the problems facing the country.

Britain was from 1837 to 1843 in the throes of the great industrial depression. The railway and shipbuilding booms broke in 1836 and, to make matters worse, 1838 was the year of the worst harvest since 1816, and 1839 was little better. This harsh economic climate played its part in the decline in Whig popularity. The social problems in the late thirties and early forties were all the more acute as the population in England and Wales had risen from 14 million in 1831 to 16 million in 1841 – an increase of 14.3 per cent. Bread and other necessities of life were beyond the means of many and poverty prevailed as never before. The fate of the poor was all the harder as, under the Corn Laws, heavy duties were put on all corn imported from abroad. Small wonder that agitation grew for their repeal.

Lord Melbourne was undoubtedly losing his hold on the House of Commons. His Government went from one defeat to the next. At the beginning of 1841 the Whigs lost four by-elections. The budget presented in May alarmed the agricultural interest by proposing a fixed duty on corn of eight shillings, and alarmed the commercial world by lowering the duties on foreign sugar and timber. On 18 May there was a division in the House on the part of the budget proposing to reduce the duties on foreign sugar, and the Government was defeated by 36 votes. During the debate, which had turned on the question of free trade (supported by the Whigs) versus protective measures (supported by the Tories), Palmerston made the premonitory statement:

> I will venture to predict that although our opponents may resist those measures [of free trade] tonight for the sake of obtaining a majority in the

division, yet if they should come into office these are the measures which a just regard for the finances and commerce of the country will compel themselves to propose.[58]

Defeated though it was, the Government did not resign. Melbourne was overruled on this issue by a majority of the Cabinet and reluctantly gave way. 'Under these circumstances', he told the Queen, 'of course I felt I could but go with them; so we shall go on, bring on the Sugar Duties, and then, if things are in a pretty good state, dissolve.'[59] Parliament, in these days of seven-year mandates, still had three years to run. The Government thus remained in office, wishing to make the chief issue for the general election their proposal to put a fixed duty on corn. They had every intention of bringing forward the question of the Corn Laws on 4 June. They were, however, foiled by Sir Robert Peel. As soon as the House met again, he gave notice of a vote of confidence. On 27 May Sir Robert brought forward his motion and, after a five-day long debate, Lord Melbourne's Government was defeated by one vote on 29 June. Parliament was accordingly dissolved on 29 June.

Prince Albert, well aware that the Government was tottering, had begun communicating with Melbourne – directly – and with Peel – through Anson – to ensure that this time there would be no Bedchamber Question and that the Queen would come out of this constitutional crisis with 'more *éclat* than she had done on a previous occasion'.[60] Melbourne prevaricated and the Prince thought he had fallen into his old lazy ways. Peel had four secret meetings with Anson. Peel was the very picture of moral rectitude. He would enforce nothing on the Queen. He would give no list of members he did not wish to see in the Royal Household, and should the Queen's personal feelings 'suffer less by forming an Administration to his exclusion, he should not be offended. Private life satisfied him and he had no ambition beyond it.'[61] In the end it was agreed that the simplest solution was for the most obviously Whig of the Ladies to resign their charge if there were to be a Tory Government.

Elizabeth Longford, in her biography of Victoria, seems to think that the Queen had not been informed of these dealings and goes so far as to claim, 'The Prince's courage as well as his kindness in by-passing the Queen were admirable, especially as she might well have expressed resentment when she found out.'[62] The Queen, however, was aware from the beginning of what was happening. Indeed on 11 May 1841 she herself drew up a memorandum clearly stating her position. 'The Queen considers it her right (and is aware that her predecessors were particularly tenacious of this right) to appoint her Household,'[63] she wrote unequivocally. But her position had in fact softened since 1839. She now conceded that although the Queen had always appointed her Ladies of the Bedchamber herself she had generally mentioned their names to the Prime Minister before appointing them, in order to leave him room for objection. Were he to believe any appointment injurious to his Government, 'the Queen would probably not appoint the lady.'[64] This was not a very strong commitment but it was clearly a change.

Melbourne for his part pressed the Queen not to create a new Bedchamber question. Writing to her on the eve of his departure he urged her not to make it an issue.

> If any difficulty should arise it may be asked to be stated in writing, and reserved for consideration. But it is of great importance that Sir Robert Peel should return to London with full power to form an Administration. Such must be the final result, and the more readily and graciously it is acquiesced in the better.[65]

The change in the Queen's attitude had, however, clearly been the result of pressure put on her and was far from internalized. When the Duchess of Bedford tendered her resignation in June, after Lady Normanby and the Duchess of Sutherland, a domestic scene was the immediate result – the Queen taxed the Prince, and Lord Melbourne, with compromising her. She had, she declared, never wished to give up three Ladies: 'The Queen said the Tories would say if she submitted to this that she had been vanquished and lowered before the world. The Prince said I fear the Ladies' gossip is again getting about you. The Queen on that burst into tears which could not be stopped for some time.'[66]

The Queen was being torn between the different conceptions of her role. One of the most powerful Whig factions was led by Lord John Russell and his brother the Duke of Bedford, whose wife was one of the Whig ladies involved. They led the Queen to believe that, as the Duke of Bedford put it, if his wife were to resign 'immediately on a change of government, an impression would be given to the public that we thought the Queen wrong in May 1839, that it would have the appearance of deserting her Majesty.'[67] Melbourne and the Prince, on the other hand, were convinced that she would harm her image and the monarchy itself if she persisted in keeping what she had thought of as her prerogative. Leopold, who was now himself a constitutional monarch in Belgium, put his influence on their side too. He insisted that Cromwell had shown that the country could exist and flourish without a monarchy, and 'the Sovereign should be reminded forcibly by this fact, that the Sovereign of a free people cannot be the Sovereign of a party.'[68] In the end, although the Queen railed and wept, although she was stubborn and hated being proved wrong, she adopted the views of Albert and both the outgoing and incoming Prime Ministers.

During the election the Queen paid a series of visits, arranged without consulting Albert, to the houses of members of the Whig nobility – the Duke of Devonshire at Chatsworth, the Duke of Bedford at Woburn Abbey, Earl Cowper, Melbourne's nephew, at Panshanger. She also lunched with Melbourne himself at his country residence, Brocket Hall. Albert accompanied her but did not enjoy these visits. He found the social programme that was put on extremely boring and repetitive. He was, too, rather jealous of the wealth and possessions that were paraded before him, and very conscious of the fact that he was not considered as more than a minor princeling by the English aristocracy.

The whole election rather got on his nerves. He had no respect whatsoever for the cut and thrust of adversarial politics. The election campaign, he wrote to his mother-in-law, 'empties purses, sets families by the ears, demoralises the lower classes, and perverts many of the upper, whose character wants strength to keep them straight. . . . All the world is rushing out of town to agitate the country for and against.'[69] The Prince believed it essential for the Crown to remain above party and not enter the political arena. 'I do not think it is necessary to belong to any party,' he wrote. 'Composed as party is here of two extremes both must be wrong. The exercise of an unbiased judgement may form a better and wiser creed by extracting the good from each.'[70]

Albert reproached the Queen with her partisan attitude to politics. Won over to the idea of constitutional monarchy, Albert believed the Crown must be prepared to work with whichever party or party combination was strongest in the House of Commons.

The 1841 election gave an overwhelming victory to the Conservatives. It was the only election between the first Reform Act, which had widened the franchise to include the middle class, and the second Reform Act of 1867, which gave the vote to the greater part of the working class, to give the Conservative party a majority. The Conservative party won 76 seats – 44 of them in the large towns. This urban Conservatism owed much to Peel himself. Alongside the traditional Conservative themes of law and order, and defence of the institutions (including the Church), he launched in the Tamworth Manifesto the quest for progressive improvement – a new ethic of Conservatism –

which was to flourish under Disraeli. Peel enlarged the party's social base; he also organized the party in the constituencies. It was in speaking of this election that the *Annual Register* replaced the term 'Whigs' by 'Liberals' for the first time.[71]

On 19 August 1841 a new Parliament, with a Conservative majority, assembled. For the first time in her reign the Queen was absent at the opening of the session – a clear indication that the results were not to her liking. There was a fortnight's debate on an amendment to the address which declared that Melbourne's Government no longer en-joyed the confidence of the country, and on 28 August the House divided at five o'clock in the morning. Confidence was refused by a majority of 91. Melbourne now had no choice but to resign. He had been Prime Minister continuously for seven years.

Lord Melbourne was thus removed both from power and from the daily intimacy he had enjoyed with the Queen since her accession. Gracefully he had told her in May, when she asked if he would mind leaving the premiership. 'Why nobody *likes* going out, but I'm not well, – I am a good deal tired, and it will be a great rest for me.'[72] On his last evening at Windsor he summed up his feelings in one simple sentence: 'I have seen you daily and I liked it better every day.'

For the Queen, Melbourne's fall from office was undoubtedly a blow. As she wrote to Leopold:

> after seeing him for four years with very few exceptions daily, you may imagine that I must feel the change – and the longer the time gets since we parted the more I feel it. Eleven days was the longest I was ever without seeing him and this time will be elapsed on Saturday, so you may imagine what this change must be.'[73]

> Victoria was convinced, however, as she said to Leopold, that it would 'not probably be for long'.[74]

Melbourne knew that there was little reason to believe that things would change rapidly. He encouraged her to rely more heavily on her husband. When he resigned his seals of office, he stressed that she was no longer alone. 'I have seen you every day,' he said, 'but it is so different now from what it would have been in 1839 – the Prince understands everything so well, and has a clever, able head.'[75] After taking leave of her he returned home and immediately wrote to her, asserting once again his confidence in Prince Albert's 'judgement, temper and discretion' and insisting that the Queen could do no better than to take advantage of Prince Albert's 'advice and assistance' and 'rely upon it with confidence'.[76]

Melbourne also tried, generously, to give Peel advice as to how to handle the Queen. As they were on opposite sides of the House this could not be done directly. So Melbourne used Greville as an intermediary. 'I think', Melbourne said when he met him at a dinner at Stafford House, 'there are one or two things Peel ought to be told and I wish you would tell him.' He went on to explain that the Queen must hear of everything from him, and

> whenever he does anything, or has anything to propose, let him explain
> to her clearly his reasons. The Queen is not conceited; she is aware there
> are many things she cannot understand, and she likes to have them
> explained to her elementarily, not at length and in detail, but shortly and
> clearly; neither does she like long audiences, and I never stayed with her
> a long time.[77]

The information was duly transmitted to Peel.

Sir Robert Peel's Government included the Duke of Wellington (who had a seat in the Cabinet without an office) and Gladstone (who was in the ministry as Vice President of the Board of Trade but was not given a seat in the Cabinet). The Council at which the new Ministers were appointed was held at Claremont on 4 September. The Queen conducted herself, Greville reported, 'in a manner which excited my greatest admiration and was really touching to see'.[78] The Queen took leave of her outgoing Ministers, with the exception of Melbourne, one by one after she had given audience to Peel. 'She looked very much flushed, and her heart evidently brim full, but she was composed, and throughout the whole of the proceedings, when her emotion might very well have overpowered her, she preserved complete self-possession, composure and dignity.'[79]

Although the Queen had behaved with great composure the departure of Melbourne affected her deeply. When he left she told him she hoped to hear from him frequently and he promised he would give her 'such information and advice as may be serviceable to Your Majesty with the sole view of promoting Your Majesty's public interests and private happiness.' A copious private correspondence thus began.

Albert was, however, determined that Melbourne should no longer be in any way the Queen's adviser. Had she not in the early months of their marriage trusted Melbourne more than she had trusted her husband? Besides, the two men were temperamentally incompatible, the antithesis of one another. The former Prime Minister was almost the caricature of an English aristocrat – gregarious, rather indolent, an epicure accomplished in the art of witty interchanges after dinner and

fond of the company of women. The Prince was very Germanic,
solitary, intolerant, finding social life timewasting and women of little
interest. In a word, Albert disapproved of Lord Melbourne and was
eager to sever the links between him and the Queen. On 3 September
1841 Anson wrote to Lord Melbourne:

> The Prince begs I will caution you (as this is the first letter written under
> the new Ministry), not to leave the Queen's letters where they could be
> seen or to repeat any satirical remark which may be made on any of the
> new people, which by repetition might get wind and do the Queen injury
> by making personal enemies.[80]

It was not Peel who was behind this desire for the correspondence to
cease, at least not at first. Greville told Melbourne on 4 September that
Peel, far from taking umbrage at the continuance of her former Prime
Minister's social relations with the Queen, hoped that they would not
be broken off. Peel had stressed to Greville that he was persuaded of the
Queen's fairness towards him and convinced that the idea of a Prime
Minister having anything to fear from Melbourne in his situation was
preposterous.[81]

Towards the end of September the Queen asked Lord Melbourne
whether he would soon visit her at Windsor. Melbourne wrote to
Prince Albert to ask his opinion. The Prince immediately sent for
Stockmar, who advised him not to reply but to leave the matter in the
Baron's own hands. Stockmar thereupon drew up a memorandum
which Anson was instructed to read aloud to Melbourne. Instead of
replying to Melbourne's question concerning a visit to Windsor, the
Baron launched into a veritable diatribe against the 'secret communication' between Her Majesty and Lord Melbourne. 'I hold therefore, this secret interchange an *essential injustice* to Sir Robert's present
situation. . . . I think it equally wrong to call upon the Prince to give an
opinion on the subject, as he has not the means to cause his opinion to
be either regarded or complied with.'[82]

Anson accompanied the reading of the memorandum with further
arguments. One of them concerned the speech Lord Melbourne had
made in Parliament on the previous day. Anson told him that his
speech had established him as the head of the Opposition party. This
particularly partisan argument shook Lord Melbourne, who really lost
his temper. 'God eternally d-n it! . . . Flesh and blood cannot stand
this. I only spoke upon the defensive which Ripon's speech at the
beginning of the session rendered quite unnecessary. I cannot be
expected to give up my position in the country, neither do I think that it
is in the Queen's interest that I should.'[83]

Melbourne's stupefaction was all the greater as he was convinced that communication of the sort he had with the Queen did not constitute a new precedent. Why then did Stockmar take up cudgels against this correspondence? Was he, as Lytton Strachey has portrayed him, an *éminence grise*, an invisible man behind the throne pulling the strings of the royal puppets?[84] Or was he merely the instrument Albert used to get rid of the fatherly figure he resented? The explanation is probably less dramatic and rather sadder. While the Baron had been away in Germany, the Prince's private secretary Anson had gradually taken his place, though no doubt without acquiring immediately the authority carried by the Baron. It was Anson the Prince now discussed things with, it was he who often took Lord Melbourne's former place next to the Queen at dinner. The Prince, too, had grown in stature, and was now serving the Queen directly as adviser. Stockmar needed to reassert his importance. He declared that so long as the Queen felt she could resort to Lord Melbourne for his advice she would not feel the necessity to place any real confidence in the advice she received from Peel.

His efforts were, however, thwarted and his influence even more compromised since, not surprisingly, Viscount Melbourne did not cease corresponding with the Queen. Less than three weeks later, on 25 October, Stockmar went to see Melbourne in person. Now his tactics had changed slightly. It was in the name of the English constitution that the correspondence was now declared irregular. The constitution, Stockmar told Lord Melbourne, meant to assign 'to the Sovereign in his functions a deliberative part'. He was not, however, sure that 'the Queen had the means within herself to execute this deliberative part properly', and in any case the only way for her 'to execute her functions at all was to be strictly honest to those men who at the time being were her Ministers'.[85]

Melbourne defended himself by declaring that there was really nothing dangerous in the correspondence and by quoting precedents. But Baron Stockmar would have none of it. These arguments 'might suffice to tranquillise the minds of the Prince and Anson'; he, Stockmar, was far from satisfied by them. Therefore Stockmar advised Lord Melbourne to wait until the Queen's confinement had passed and then 'state of your own accord to Her Majesty that this secret and confidential correspondence with her must cease.' He could explain to her that he had agreed to it against his better judgement in order not to agitate her at a time when her health needed to be watched carefully. Melbourne was, according to Stockmar, 'visibly nervous, perplexed and distressed'.[86] As a result Stockmar thought he had achieved his

aim and had persuaded Lord Melbourne to give up writing to the
Queen after the baby's birth.

Melbourne must have been fuming. Given the attitude of Stockmar
he did give up any idea of dining at the Palace and wrote to say so to
the Queen on 7 November 1841, stressing that it was in order not to
attract 'public notice, comment and observation'.[87] But the
correspondence continued, although not with its pristine vigour. He
had taken no notice of the Baron's remonstrances.[88]

What exactly was the content of this correspondence? Was it true
that it was dangerous? It certainly contained judgements on people.
Prince Metternich, for instance, Lord Melbourne 'takes . . . not to have
a very high opinion of the abilities of others in general' but he does have
'much of the French vivacity, and also much of their settled and regular
style of argument'[89] and on occasion judgements on foreign affairs.
'The King Leopold', wrote Lord Melbourne, 'still hankers after Greece;
but Crowns will not bear to be chopped and changed about in this
manner. These new kingdoms are not too firmly fixed as it is, and it will
not do to add to the uncertainty by alteration . . .'[90] But such comments
in no way contradicted Peel's view of foreign affairs nor in any way
harmed the incumbent Government. In any case they were few and far
between. The greater part of the correspondence concerned social and
personal matters, and the continuing instruction of the Queen in
matters constitutional. When the Queen asked him, for instance, how
the role of Prime Minister had developed, he explained that although
the political part of the English constitution was set down in Black-
stone, 'the work of conducting the executive government, has rested
so much on practice, on usage, on understanding, that there is no
publication to which reference can be made for the explanation and
description of it.' It can, however, he informed her, be found scattered
around in debates, protests, letters and memoirs. Who could take
objection to such helpful teaching?

Baron Stockmar, who did not give in easily, kept up his campaign.
On 23 November he wrote to Lord Melbourne recounting two incidents
to him. First that when he was in London a stranger had come up to
him and declared that Lord Melbourne and the Queen kept up a daily
correspondence, which showed that Melbourne was unduly influencing
the Queen. The second incident concerned Peel, who had, Baron
Stockmar wrote, told him that 'that moment I was to learn that the
Queen takes advice upon public matters in another place, I shall throw
up; for such a thing I conceive the country could not stand, and I would
not remain an hour, whatever the consequences of my resignation may

be.'[91] Despite all that Baron Stockmar did, however, the correspondence continued and did so until much later, when it declined and petered out naturally.

The Queen's confinement had been long and painful. 'My sufferings', she wrote in her journal, 'were really very severe and I don't know what I should have done but for the great comfort and support my beloved Albert was to me.'[92] Queen Victoria was 'taken unwell' at six o'clock on the morning of 9 November 1841. By seven, the three physicians – in addition to Dr Locock, who had taken up residence in Buckingham Palace a fortnight earlier – were in attendance. So were the Lord Chancellor, Sir Robert Peel, the Archbishop of Canterbury, the Bishop of London, the Duke of Wellington and the other great officers of state. The Duchess of Kent arrived at the Palace at nine. Prince Albert was in attendance throughout the birth and saw his son born at twelve minutes to eleven. The royal infant was carried into the adjoining room where the notables were assembled and they signed a declaration as to the birth of an heir to the British throne.

The joy at the Palace at the birth of a Prince was so great there was complete confusion as to who should do what. One of the results was that several messengers, 'each fancying that he alone had the honour of being the bearer of the gratifying intelligence, arrive in breathless haste at the same place, and almost at the same moment.'[93] The joy was all the greater as no Prince of Wales had been born since the birth of George IV in 1762. Victoria was alone among the Queens Regnant until then to have been blessed with direct heirs. Mary Tudor, Henry VIII's daughter, left no issue by her husband Philip of Spain; Elizabeth I died unmarried, and with her died the House of Tudor; Queen Anne had married George, Prince of Denmark, and the promise of direct heirs was frequent, but only one, William, Duke of Gloucester, lived long enough to make direct succession probable, and then at the age of ten he, too, sickened and died. No wonder *The Times* of 10 November spoke of Victoria as 'the model of a female sovereign'.

As 1841 drew to a close the Queen was in a state of depression – 'lowness' as Anson termed it.[94] Her second pregnancy went less well than her first – which is not to be wondered at, given how close together they came. Albert had steadily gained importance since her first pregnancy, and this was not really to Victoria's taste. She did not like being separated from him and positively disliked his taking part in the politics of the country. The men around her, on the contrary, saw with satisfaction that she was gradually being pushed out of her role of Queen into her role of childbearer, a far more womanly one. Stockmar wrote to Lord Melbourne, 'I expressed [to Peel] my delight at seeing the Queen so happy, and added a hope that more and more she would seek and find her real happiness in her domestic relations only.'[95] And Anson noted, 'I should say that her Majesty interests herself less and less about politics and that her dislike is less than it was to her present Ministers, though she would not be prepared to acknowledge it.'[96]

12

Albert's Search for Power

Victoria recovered slowly from her pregnancy. Three weeks after the birth she wrote to King Leopold: 'They think that I shall not get my appetite and my spirits back till I can get out of town.'[1] But despite the Queen's fatigue and low morale Albert pursued his vendetta against Lehzen. Anson had informed the Prime Minister almost on his appointment that everything at the Palace was working well, 'with the exception of our usual bane which still remained a constant source of uneasiness and which would always be a channel for intrigue and mischief.'[2] Anson, no doubt capturing his master's mood, noted on 26 December that the Baroness allowed no opportunity to escape her of creating mischief and difficulty. Her great aim was, he believed, to keep an influence over the nursery underlings. One wonders what was abnormal in this. It was customary at the time for governesses to remain after their first charges had grown to maturity to help with the babyhood of the next generation. No doubt such women were at times a bore. Their lives were restricted and unnatural. They lived vicariously, never marrying. Their maternal instincts fed on fussing around the 'children' they had cared for. Looked at objectively Baroness Lehzen was a rather pathetic figure.

But to the Prince she had become an obsession. He exaggerated her importance and her influence. He considered her 'a crazy, stupid intriguer, obsessed with the thirst of power, who regards herself as a demi-God, and anyone who refuses to recognize her as such is a criminal.'[3] The problem was, in Albert's eyes, that Victoria 'like every good pupil is accustomed to regard her governess as an oracle.'[4] He was moreover convinced 'that the Queen has more fear than love for the Baroness and that she would really be happier without her though she could not acknowledge it.'[5] With a singular pomposity for a man of twenty-two, he told Stockmar that Victoria had 'naturally a fine character, but warped in many respects by wrong upbringing', due of course to the influence of Lehzen.[6] He pitied his wife, for there could be 'no improvement' in her character until she saw Lehzen for what she was.

At the beginning of 1842 the royal couple were at Claremont. Albert had taken Victoria there for the change of air she badly needed. She had had two babies in quick succession and was suffering from what we would now call postnatal depression. On 15 January they were summoned back to Windsor for the Princess Royal's health was giving grounds for anxiety. 'Reached Windsor at one,' the Queen wrote in her diary. 'Went at once upstairs, and found poor dear "Pussy" looking thin and pulled down, but she was very pleased to see us, dear child.'[7]

Albert was appalled at the sight of his daughter and, convinced that she was suffering from consumption, over-reacted as any young father might. He blamed her ill-health on the incompetence of Dr Clark, whom he thought was starving her, and the nursery staff, behind whom he saw looming the meddlesome figure of Lehzen. This was manifestly unfair. The person in charge of the nursery was Mrs Southey, who had been recommended by the Archbishop of Canterbury and who had proved to be far from equal to her task. Victoria had realized this shortly after her son's birth and Mrs Southey, realising she had lost the royal confidence, wrote to Albert asking him, 'when Her Majesty and your Royal Highness can find a more efficient Superintendent of your Nursery dismiss me kindly.' No bird she declared could 'return more eagerly to her nest than I to my own home'.[8]

The Queen considered Albert's criticisms of Lehzen were unwarranted – and said so. Albert banged out of the room. He was furious – and must have avoided Victoria for the next few days, since their only contact seems to have been via Stockmar. On the eighteenth, two days later, he wrote to Stockmar, explaining that, 'All the disagreeableness I suffer comes from one and the same person, and that is precisely the person whom Victoria chooses for her friend and confidante.'[9] Victoria was, he claimed, too hasty and passionate for him to explain his difficulties to her. 'She will not hear me out but flies into a rage and overwhelms me with reproaches of suspiciousness, want of trust, ambition, envy etc. etc.'[10] He had then, he declared, only two alternatives. Either he did not reply and simply went away, which made him feel like 'a schoolboy who has had a dressing down from his mother and goes off snubbed', or he could become violent in his turn, and the result was terrible scenes. Those, he said patronizingly, 'I hate, because I am so sorry for Victoria in her misery.'

Enclosed in this letter to Stockmar was a note to Victoria, not penned off in anger on the sixteenth, which might make it excusable, but written two whole days later. It read: 'Dr Clark has mismanaged the child and poisoned her with calomel and you have starved her. I shall have nothing more to do with it; take the child away and do as you like and if she dies you will have it on your conscience.'[11] This is one of the few occasions on which the notes the couple wrote each other when they disagreed have survived. The picture given is far from the image usually projected of the royal couple: Vicky, Albert's dearly beloved eldest daughter, treated as an object, 'the child', that will prove how right he was and how wrong his wife was; no discussion but cold wounding notes to be read and reread, solving nothing. A note that Albert did not even send directly to his wife, but to Stockmar – who was to judge when the right moment had come to send it on. The right moment was no doubt that at which Victoria was most likely to give in and adopt her husband's point of view.

The Queen herself also had recourse to the Baron to ask him to intervene between herself and the Prince. 'I feel so forlorn and I have got *such* a sick headache!' she had written on the sixteenth when Albert had banged out of the nursery. 'I feel as if I had had a dreadful dream. I do hope you may be able to pacify Albert. He seems so very angry still. I am not.'[12] And also to ask him to see Lehzen and explain to her that there had been a little misunderstanding. On 19 January Victoria told Stockmar that she did not want to see the note Albert had given him for her.

> If Albert's note is full of hard words and other things that might make me angry and unhappy (as I know he *is* unjust) don't show it me but tell me what he wants, for I don't wish to be angry with him and really my feelings of justice would be too violent to keep in, did I read what was too severe.

In a postscript to her letter she added that she was not 'infatuated' with Baroness Lehzen as her husband believed.[13]

The Baron did not immediately send the Prince's note. Instead he sent the Queen a letter of his own containing the barely veiled threat that if such scenes recurred Albert would be obliged to leave England. 'A repetition of such distressing scenes would', he wrote, 'make his present position untenable.'[14] The Queen immediately, and generously, took all the blame on herself. 'Albert', she wrote to the Baron, 'must tell me what he dislikes and I will set about to remedy it. . . . When I am in a passion which I trust I am not very often in now, he must not believe the stupid things I say like being miserable I ever married and so forth.' She insisted that her only wish was that Lehzen should be given 'a quiet home in my house and see me sometimes'. She assured the Baron on her honour that she saw the Baroness very seldom and even then only for a few minutes and ended by reaffirming her love for her 'dearest angel' – Albert.[15]

The Baron must have judged that the Queen was now in a receptive frame of mind for he sent her the Prince's letter of the eighteenth and the note accompanying it. The Queen was understandably affected by it. Once again she justified herself as far as her relationship with Lehzen was concerned. 'I *never* speak to her or anybody about the Nursery,' she protested to Stockmar, 'I *never* go to *her* to complain which I fear Albert suspects I do; no, never.'[16] And then with a touching humility she tried to analyse her faults:

> There is often an irritability in me which (like Sunday last which began the whole misery) makes me say cross and odious things which I don't believe myself and which I fear hurt Albert but which he should not believe; but I will strive to conquer it though I knew *before* I married that this would be a trouble; I therefore wished *not* to marry, as the two years and a half, when I was completely my own mistress made it difficult for me to control myself and to bend to another's will, but I trust I shall be able to conquer it.[17]

The Queen was apologetic. Albert had won. The Queen gave way – nursery management was to be reformed and more important Baroness Lehzen's days with her were numbered, though she was not to leave England until September.

Stockmar told the Baroness in January that she would be universally condemned if she came between husband and wife. In July Albert interviewed her and suggested that on account of her health she should take six months' leave. It was obvious that this was to be a permanent arrangement. A pension of 800 pounds a year was offered and accepted. Albert told the Queen that he had seen Lehzen, who had expressed the wish to go to Germany in two months' time, and that he could only approve of this step. The Queen was, of course, upset but felt sure it was 'for our and her best'.[18] She spoke to Stockmar, who relieved her by assuring her that Lehzen herself felt she required rest and quiet for the sake of her health but would be ready to come and see the Queen whenever she sent for her. Then the Queen went off to see Lehzen. It says much for the Baroness's affection for the Queen that she did everything in her power to ease the separation. The Queen

> found her very cheerful, saying she felt it was necessary for her health to go away for of course I did not require her so much now and would find

others to help me, whilst she could still help me in doing little things for me abroad. She repeated she would be ready to come to me, whenever I wanted.[19]

Baroness Lehzen left the Palace on 23 September 1842. She did not take leave in person of the Queen but wrote her a letter, 'thinking it would be less painful'. The Queen's feelings were mixed: 'This naturally upset me and I so regret not being able to embrace her once more, though I am much relieved at being spared the painful parting.'[20] Victoria had presented her with a carriage as a farewell present but, ironically, it was Albert who escorted her to it. On the day after her departure the Queen told Lady Lyttelton, 'it was very painful to me waking this morning and recollecting she was really quite away. I had been dreaming she had come back to say goodbye to me, and it felt very uncomfortable at first. I had heard it mentioned before – that odd feeling on waking – but I had no experience of it. It is most unpleasant.'[21]

The Queen did not forget her governess, who had settled with a sister at Bückeburg in Hanover. For many years she wrote to her once a week – an interval subsequently lengthened to a month at the Baroness's own considerate request.[22] The correspondence was maintained for twenty-eight years, until the Baroness's death in 1870 at the ripe old age of eighty-five. The Queen saw her very rarely: once in 1845 in Gotha; then in 1858 when, on her way to see her daughter, she passed through Bückeburg. Since she had told her governess that the train would pass that way there was Lehzen, a pathetic figure, waving a handkerchief on the platform. She saw Lehzen one last time in 1866, after Albert's death, when the Baroness visited her at Reinhardtsbrunn. 'Saw my poor old Lehzen,' wrote the Queen in her journal, 'she is grown so old. We were both much moved.'[23]

When Theodore Martin was writing the biography of Prince Albert after his death, under the Queen's supervision, and stressed the Baroness's faults, Victoria once again showed her loyalty to her governess. She wrote to him to say that his treatment of Lehzen must be modified. She refused the term 'personal ambition' that Martin had used, and saw, with perception, that it was 'the idea that no one but herself was able to take care of the Queen' that had dominated Lehzen's way of thinking. 'Her devotion to the Queen was so great, her unselfishness and disinterestedness so great and the Queen owed her so much that she did *not* wish her faults to be brought forward.'[24] The Queen did, however, keep faith with her husband, too, for in the biography, at the express request of the Queen, no mention was made of the struggle between the Prince and the Baroness. Theodore Martin simply made a general allusion to his many difficulties in the household.[25]

Fidelity to old friends was one of the Queen's great qualities, as she was also to show with regard to Melbourne. He had remained Leader of the Opposition in the House of Lords until, in October 1842, he had had a paralytic stroke from which he never completely recovered. His hair turned white, he limped and became subject to fits of melancholia. He had hoped to be offered a place in the Liberal Government in 1846 but no offer came. From 1846 onwards his depression increased, and inactivity and isolation did little to help. In 1842 he had been at the hub of power and he had been surrounded by people; four years later he was treated with indifference.

As his health deteriorated so he worried more and more about his financial circumstances. On 30 December 1847 he wrote to the Queen telling her how he dreaded that before long he would 'be obliged to add another to the lists of failures and *banqueroutes* of which there have lately been so many'. He explained to her that it was his straitened circumstances that had led him to refuse the honour of the Garter – since the expense of accepting the blue ribbon amounted to some 1,000 pounds.[26] In 1848 he wrote to the Queen soliciting a pension and asking her to speak to Lord John Russell about it. Lord John Russell refused on the grounds that pensions were only given if the person concerned did not have 'a private fortune adequate to his station in life', which was assuredly not the case for Melbourne whose estate had a rent roll of some 18,000 pounds a year. Albert also insisted that a pension would be 'injurious to Lord Melbourne's reputation'.[27]

Melbourne's problem was that the bank had called on him to repay a loan of about 10,000 pounds, which they wished to lend at a higher rate. The Queen, typically, decided to lend Melbourne the money he needed herself. It was not to be for long. On 22 November the *Morning Chronicle* announced that he was dying. His family at Brocket did not expect that he would live through the day. But he lingered on for two more days, his mental activity already at an end. On 24 November he died, at just under seventy. His title passed to his brother, and became extinct on his brother's death in 1853.

The Queen had already been warned by Palmerston that Melbourne's end was imminent.

> Viscount Palmerston is here engaged on the melancholy occupation of watching the gradual extinction of the lamp of life of one who was not

more distinguished by his brilliant talents, his warm affections and his first-rate understanding than by those sentiments of attachment to Your Majesty which rendered him the most devoted subject who ever had the honour to serve a Sovereign.[28]

After the autumn of 1842, when the old Prime Minister's life was still ebbing out lonely at Brocket and Lehzen was settled in Germany, the Queen depended totally on Albert, as she was to do for the next nineteen years.

Albert's campaign to remove Lehzen was only one element in a deeper purpose. It was the beginning of his attempt to exercise a form of personal power such as no consort had ever had. He told Wellington that:

> His aim was to be the natural head of the family, superintendent of her household, manager of her private affairs, her sole confidential adviser in politics, and only assistance in her communication with the officers of the Government, her private secretary and permanent Minister.[29]

The relationship between Albert and Victoria was not one of equality. That he loved his wife is beyond doubt but he was a man of his time, irked by the superior position of his wife, determined to be, despite it, the dominant partner. Moreover, his nature was secretive. He kept his thoughts to himself and did not share his aspirations with her. He had no notion of compromise.

Albert sought, as he himself said, 'to sink his directing individuality in her, to put his will, his perceptions, his ability so much at her service as to be fused with his own.'[30] Convincing her of the futility of the years she had spent without him was part of this. He played on her desire to protect him, the stranger in a foreign land. Before he had come, had she not wasted her time and squandered her youth? Had he not, as it were, saved her from herself, sacrificing his happiness for hers?

Albert undoubtedly completely changed Victoria's perception of her past life. On 1 October 1842, seven days after Lehzen's departure, she wrote in her journal: 'Wrote and looked over and corrected one of my old journals which do not *now* awake very pleasant feelings. The life I led then was so artificial and superficial and yet I thought I was happy. Thank God! I know now what real happiness means.'[31] One evening in December she and Albert dined alone together and talked of former days and of her life before she married and came to the throne. She spoke of her 'unbounded affection for and admiration of Lord Melbourne which I said to Albert I hardly knew from what it arose, accepting the fact that I clung to someone and having very warm feelings. Albert thinks I worked myself up to what really became at last, quite foolish.'[32]

But if her affection for Melbourne was to be dismissed as simply foolish, her attachment to Lehzen was to appear more sinister. 'We talked of Lehzen's strange and unwise conduct, of which Albert gave me some remarkable instances. What has this Treasure of mine not had to put up with and how I blame myself for my blindness, which makes these retrospections very painful, yet it is such a relief to tell him everything.'[33]

One way of destroying Lehzen in Victoria's eyes was to see her as entirely responsible for the rift between Victoria and her mother. Instead of striving to create a better understanding between mother and daughter, she it was who had estranged them. The Duchess of Kent was not an easy woman and it took all Albert's diplomacy to improve Victoria's relationship with her after so many years. Soon, however, the Duchess was lunching and dining with her daughter. Victoria's reconstruction of her past life is admirably summed up by the Queen herself in an annotation, in 1869, to the letters she wrote between 1837 and 1840.

> The Queen's letters between 1837 and 1840 are not pleasing and indeed rather painful to herself. It was the least sensible and satisfactory time in her whole life and she must therefore destroy a great many. That life of mere amusement, flattery, excitement and mere politics, had a bad effect (as it must have on anyone) on her naturally simple and serious nature but all changed after 1840.[34]

Albert's capacity for reconstructing reality was not reserved for Victoria's past, he also embroidered on his own. When he came to England he had spoken of 'the pain of leaving home, the parting from dear kindred'. Yet he had left home for his travels two years earlier and had raged when his father called him to Carlsbad, thus interrupting his Italian tour. When his father returned to Coburg after his son's marriage, Albert gave way to grief, 'pale as a sheet and his eyes full of tears'.[35] Yet Duke Ernest plagued the Queen's ladies with his attentions and it is very probable that Albert was relieved to see his lecherous father leave Britain.

The reorganization of the care of the children decided in January 1842 was not an easy matter since the essential problem was that of finding a person capable of managing the royal nursery. The Queen asked Stockmar for advice. His first reply was a thirty-two page memorandum on the subject of education. 'Children', he declared, 'should be entrusted only to the guidance of good, of virtuous and intelligent persons.'[36] Since their royal positions inevitably prevented the Queen and the Prince from supervising their children as they would like to do, they must have complete confidence in the tutor they chose. The choice should be a joint one and the parents should act in 'harmony and union'. Referring obliquely to past disputes Stockmar claimed that greater responsibility for harmony lay with the Queen, who must be 'constantly on her guard against the temptation which the Constitutional Prerogative puts in her power'. The person at the head of the nursery must be of refined manners and experienced in dealing with children; she must also be a person of rank in order to have full authority over her staff.[37]

The Queen accepted Stockmar's point of view but she did not know where to find a person who would meet the requirements yet who would also consent to shut herself up in the nursery, far from society, as would be necessary if she were really to supervise everything.

Stockmar had already decided the ideal person would be Lady Lyttelton. Sarah Lyttelton had been a Lady of the Bedchamber since the Queen's accession in 1837. She had been doubtful about entering the Queen's service. She had accepted mainly because, recently widowed, she knew that the laws of the day would soon deprive her of her husband's estate, which would go to her eldest son. She did not find her tasks too heavy and soon settled into what she felt was 'a proper stiffness'. Her job was essentially to look after the Maids of Honour, which she did most successfully. She got on with everyone at Court, from Baroness Lehzen to the Duchess of Kent. Victoria liked her: she was very amenable and had the added advantage of being Melbourne's wife's first cousin.

Lady Lyttelton fell in love with Windsor: 'this most sublime of dwelling houses [which makes] one feel so well, so warm and so fresh, that I wonder our Kings and Queens don't live here for ever in earnest.'[38] She also fell half in love – in a matronly way, since she was now fifty-two – with Prince Albert, whom she described as 'handsome enough to be the hero of a fairy-tale – and very like one'. She became devoted to him, praising his prudence, his manliness and his depth of artistic feeling, demonstrated by the way he played the organ. She also admired the total truthfulness of the Queen: 'Not a shade of exaggeration in describing feelings or facts like very few other people I ever knew.' But she also commented, one feels not with entire approval, on the 'vein of iron' in the Queen's 'extraordinary character'. Perhaps this was too manly a virtue for her to appreciate in a woman.

When Stockmar suggested to her that she might be asked to fill the post she consulted her eldest brother, Lord Spencer, who was in favour. She then suggested two other candidates to the Baron and told him that if she herself were to accept the place it would only be if 'the Queen should heartily concur in it and make the offer her own'.[39] Two months later, at the beginning of April, the Queen noted in her journal that she and Albert had both come to the conclusion 'that none was so fit as Lady Lyttelton, only we feared she never would take the post'.[40] The Queen broached the question when out driving with her. 'She was very much flattered, much alarmed though, at the responsibility, and very diffident as to her own qualities.' The Queen told Albert 'of my great success, at which he was much pleased, and we both consider it as a great and kind sacrifice on Lady Lyttelton's part.'[41]

Stockmar in these early years really did play the role of power behind the throne. Putting ideas into the young couple's heads, but convincing them that the ideas were their own. Happy to see his solutions adopted, but not requiring that any credit for them be given him. Did he take Albert into his confidence? Or was he, too, duped? It is difficult to say.

In a long paper – which Stockmar had read and rephrased – Lady Lyttelton laid down her conditions. First of all she was to have complete authority in the nursery. Those under her were only to be allowed to address themselves to her 'in all their affairs, their wants, difficulties, contrarieties or disagreements'. Secondly she, for her part, would obey the royal parents but asked permission 'to ask questions, to discuss doubtful points, and even to maintain her own opinions by argument, without reserve'. Thirdly, should the Queen and Prince wish to rebuke her or find fault with her, it should be done in complete privacy and not in front of anyone else. Other points included her presence at any medical examination of the children (perhaps she was not entirely convinced of the capacity of Sir James Clark), her responsibility for choosing the children's clothes and the need to bring her daughters to live nearer the royal residence. From the first the Queen sang her praises. 'Nothing could go on better, than does the Nursery. Lady Lyttelton is of course perfection.'[42] She now enjoyed going to the nursery 'since Lady Lyttelton has charge and there are no frictions.'[43]

Albert had the German horror of mismanagement. With Lehzen gone in September, the domestic management of the Royal Household could be reformed. Stockmar began by preparing a remarkable memorandum exposing the incredible system then in operation.[44] Three officers of state – the Lord Steward, the Lord Chamberlain and the Master of the Horse – were responsible between them for the buildings, the staff, the service, the catering and the heating of the Queen's houses. Their responsibilities were not, however, distinct but overlapped. As the three highest Court officials were officers of state they changed with each change of ministry. 'Since the year 1830,' Stockmar noted, 'we find five changes in the office of the Lord Chamberlain, and six in that of the Lord Steward.'[45] The work was, according to Stockmar, parcelled out in the most ridiculous manner among them. Not without humour he noted: 'The Lord Steward, for example, finds the fuel and lays the fire, and the Lord Chamberlain lights it.'[46] The cleaning of the windows was the responsibility of the Woods and Forests on the outside, and that of the Lord Chamberlain on the inside. So it was rare for the Queen to look through perfectly clean glass. Mending or repairing anything was a complicated business. If a pane of glass or a scullery cupboard door needed mending the process was as follows: a requisition was prepared and signed by the chief cook, it was then countersigned by the clerk of the kitchen, then it was taken to be signed by the Master of the Household, then it was taken to the Lord Chamberlain's office, where it was authorized, and then laid before the Clerk of Works, under the office of Woods and Forests; the result, as might have been expected, was that the window or the cupboard remained broken for months.

The inefficiency of the royal residences was derided abroad. There was no one to attend to the comfort of the Queen's guests on their arrival at the royal residence, no one to show them to or from their apartments. 'It frequently happens at Windsor, that some of the visitors are at a loss to find the drawing-room, and at night, if they happen to forget the right entrance from the corridors, they wander for an hour helpless and unassisted.'[47] At home it was the corruption built into the system that was reviled. Its extent was legendary. Fresh candles, for instance, were placed in the living rooms each day and were removed on the following day, whether they had been lit or not. They thus became the perquisites of the footmen, who sold them. Food and stores were frequently stolen. The palaces were overstaffed – forty housemaids at Windsor and another forty at Buckingham Palace, each of them receiving full board and lodging and 45 pounds a year for six months' work. As for the footmen, they were employed in shifts, with one-third on duty, one-third on half duty and the final third resting. Two-thirds of the servants were not answerable to a head of department and could come on and off duty much as they pleased.[48]

It was an expensive Court but in no way a comfortable one. The kitchens were old and rat-infested, dinner was often late and cold, and the drains smelt. In addition, the Palace was far from safe. The lack of security at Buckingham Palace had been illustrated in December 1840 by the 'boy Jones'. Albert decided to introduce good management to ensure the security, hygiene and cleanliness that was so urgently needed. He determined to introduce some form of central control, as Stockmar had advised. But reform was, as can be imagined, unpopular. It was not in the interest of most of the staff, who benefited greatly from the chaotic system in force. Nor was the Prince helped by the politicians of the day. Sir Robert Peel, when he had been consulted in 1841, had deprecated any reform which might seem to lessen the authority of the great officers of state. Among Albert's virtues, however, were his tenacity and his attention to detail. He wrote to Peel on 2 November 1841:

> Much as I am inclined to treat the Household machine with a sort of reverence for its antiquity, I still remain convinced that it is clumsy in its original construction, and works so ill, that as long as its wheels are not mended there can neither be order, nor regularity, comfort, security nor outward dignity in the Queen's Palace.[49]

Albert continued to work away at the problem. But as he wrote to the Baron in December 1842, 'It always seems to me as if an infinity of small trivialities hang about me like an ever present weight. I mean by these the domestic and court arrangements to these I have chiefly applied myself, feeling that we never shall be in a position to occupy ourselves with higher and graver things, so long as we have to deal with these trifles.'[50] He persisted however and by the end of 1844 the Master of the Household had absolute authority over the whole internal economy of the Palace. The royal dwellings began to be properly managed, and substantial economies were realized.

If the security of the Queen was uncertain in Buckingham Palace, she was even more at risk when she went out. The first attempt on the Queen's life occurred on 10 June 1840, when she was expecting her first child. The couple were driving in a low carriage up Constitution Hill at about five in the afternoon when, Albert wrote:

> I saw a small disagreeable looking man leaning against the railing of Green Park only six paces from us, holding something towards us. Before I could see what it was, a shot cracked out. It was so dreadfully loud that we were both quite stunned. Victoria, who had been looking to the left, towards a rider, did not know the cause of the noise. My first thought was that, in her present state, the fright might harm her. I put both arms

around her and asked her how she felt, but she only laughed. Then I turned around to look at the man (the horses were frightened and the carriage stopped). The man stood there in a theatrical position, a pistol in each hand. It seemed ridiculous. Suddenly he stooped, put a pistol on his arm, aimed at us and fired, the bullet must have gone over our heads, judging by the hole made where it hit the garden wall.[51]

It was little short of a miracle that at such short range the man should have missed his aim. The Queen continued her drive amidst the enthusiasm of the immense crowd that gathered in carriages, on horseback, and on foot. 'All the equestrians', reported Greville, 'formed themselves into an escort, and attended her back to the Palace, cheering vehemently, while she acknowledged, with great appearance of feeling, these loyal manifestations.'[52] The culprit – Edward Oxford, an undersized, feeble youngster of eighteen – was declared insane and spent the next twenty-seven years in a lunatic asylum.

But no extra precautions were taken when the Queen drove or rode out, and two years later a second attempt was made on her life. On Sunday 29 May 1842 the Queen and Prince Albert were driving along the Mall towards Buckingham Palace when Albert, as he wrote to his father, 'saw a man step out from the crowd and present a pistol fully at me. He was some two paces from us.' Albert heard the trigger snap, but the shot must have misfired. Victoria, who had been bowing to the people on the other side of the carriage, noticed nothing. When the royal couple reached the Palace Albert asked the footmen who had been at the back of the carriage if they had seen anything, but they had noticed nothing. Albert reported the whole affair to the head of police and the Prime Minister. The Prince was beginning to think that he might have imagined the whole thing, when a boy of fourteen came to the Palace and said he had seen a man point a pistol at Victoria, but not fire, exclaiming afterwards, 'Fool that I was not to fire.'[53]

Meanwhile, as the doctor had insisted that Victoria go out in the open air as much as possible, the young couple decided to drive out as usual at four o'clock that afternoon. They drove off to Hampstead, simply giving orders to drive faster than usual. This foolhardy attempt to draw the fire of the would-be assassin was fully sanctioned by Peel. It was carried out with great secrecy. Colonel Arbuthnot, one of the equerries noted:

His Royal Highness directed me to ride close to Her Majesty, and to request Colonel Wylde to do the same, but His Royal Highness was so alive to the importance that the attempt on Sunday afternoon should be perfectly secret, that he desired me not to mention it even to him. Her Majesty appeared to be as fully alive as I was to the danger she was incurring, but was notwithstanding most calm, cheerful and composed, at the same time, I am sure, fully alive to the probability that from behind every tree she might be shot at.[54]

The Queen left her lady-in-waiting behind. 'I must expose the lives of my gentlemen but I will not those of my ladies.'[55] They went through the parks and it was on their return that another attempt on the Queen's life was made. Owing to the rapid pace the man was disconcerted and aimed too low. 'The shot', wrote Prince Albert, 'must have passed under the carriage, for he lowered his hand. We felt as if a load had been taken off our hearts, and we thanked the Almighty for having preserved us from so great a danger.' The assassin, a certain Francis, was standing near a policeman, who immediately seized him. It was exactly the same spot from which Oxford had fired at the couple two years previously. That evening when the Queen and Prince went to the Opera, 'the whole House rose, cheered and waved their hats and handkerchiefs. "God Save the Queen" was sung and there was immense applause at the end of each verse.'[56]

Francis was about twenty, the son of a machine-maker at Covent Garden Theatre and himself a cabinetmaker. He was condemned to death for high treason. Then on 1 July Sir Robert Peel wrote to Albert that, 'after careful consideration on the part of the judges and the Cabinet, they thought it best to commute the sentence of Francis, to Transportation for Life, with hard labour.'[57] He was sent off to Tasmania. The Queen was not vindictive – 'I, of course, am glad the poor wretch's life is spared,' she wrote, but although she was far from obsessive about her security she also noted, 'but Albert and I are of the same opinion that the law ought to be changed, and more security offered to me.'[58]

Two days after she wrote this a third attempt was made on her life, while she was driving in the Mall with King Leopold. The pistol misfired and a boy of sixteen tore the weapon out of the attacker's hands. The Queen in her journal noted, 'Odd enough to say, only two days ago I remarked to Albert, I felt sure an attempt on us would be shortly repeated.'[59] A remark which shows that she was not as carelessly indifferent to such actions as some biographers have assumed.

Peel was in Cambridge when he received the news of the new attempt on the Queen's life. He rushed back to Buckingham Palace. The boy Bean who had fired was, said Peel, 'the most miserable object he ever saw – only four foot and a few inches in height – very much deformed and sickly looking with a pitiable expression but certainly not a "simpleton".[60] Bean had eluded immediate capture and in the subsequent search for him all hunchbacked people in London were placed under arrest, until Bean was at last identified as the culprit. The time had obviously come for some precautions to be taken for the Queen's safety. Sir Robert Peel judged that these deranged individuals who had attacked the Queen had done so to seek publicity. The notoriety afforded by a trial for high treason flattered their morbid vanity. None of the attempts on the Queen's life had been political. The solution was, then, to change the law so that the would-be assassins were charged with misdemeanour rather than high treason. They could then be punished in a more degrading manner, which would, Peel believed, discourage the criminals. So a 'Bill for providing for the further protection and security of Her Majesty's person' was passed, making attempts on the Queen's life high misdemeanours punishable by transportation for seven years, or imprisonment, with or without hard labour, for a period not exceeding three years. The Court could also condemn the culprit to be publicly or privately whipped.

The new law did not prevent four more attempts on the Queen's life during her reign – in 1849, 1850, 1872 and 1882. Such dangers have always been one of the calculated risks of those who live in the public eye. Peel himself escaped assassination in January 1843 only because his secretary, Edward Drummond, was mistaken for him and killed in his place by a crazy twenty-seven-year-old Irish Protestant, Daniel McNaughten.

With his various reforms Albert gradually introduced into the Court what came to be termed Victorian values, though it would no doubt be more exact to speak of them as Albertian. Thrift was one of the values on which the reorganization of the royal residences rested. This may seem highly virtuous and necessary. Yet when one looks into things, thrift certainly had its darker side. At Windsor, for instance, the poor of the town were accustomed to come for scraps, a loaf of stale bread, or sometimes a hot meal. Charles Murray told a visitor that in a single year some 113,000 people had been given a meal.[61] The elimination of waste meant they had to be turned away. After Albert's reforms any surplus food had to be accounted for and transmitted to a recognized charity. Other economies meant that servants were no longer provided with toilet soap and no longer offered tea as an alternative to cocoa.[62]

That Albert was a good manager was evident at the home farm at

Windsor, which began making a profit once he had taken it over, and it was shown spectacularly by his administration of the estates of the Duchy of Cornwall, which he held in trust for his son, the Prince of Wales. The Duchy consisted of property in Cornwall, tin mines largely, and land in Lambeth and Kennington. In 1841 the estate brought in about 16,000 pounds a year; by the time the Prince of Wales came of age in 1859 the annual income was 60,000 pounds. This success story was undoubtedly due to the Prince's innate capacity for managing property and handling money. Peel, speaking of the royal visits from other European countries received by the Queen in 1844, noted in his Budget speech that they of necessity created a considerable increase of expenditure; but, 'through that wise system of economy which is the only true source of magnificence, Her Majesty was enabled to meet every charge, and to give a reception to the Sovereigns which struck every one by its magnificence, without adding one tittle to the burdens of the country.'

Hard work was perhaps the major Victorian value and Queen Victoria certainly was not idle; nor was she the workaholic that her husband had become before he was twenty-three. From the beginning Albert had worked too hard. Eight days after Vicky's birth, less than a year after his marriage, he wrote to his brother, 'I have a great deal to do and I hardly ever get out into the open air.'[63] Stockmar, returning to the Palace in the spring of 1843, saw how overworked the Prince was: 'The Queen is well, the Princess wonderfully improved, and round like a little barrel, the Prince of Wales, though suffering from his teeth, is strong on his legs, and has a steady, clear, and cheerful countenance. The Prince Father is well and contented, although he often looks pale, fatigued and exhausted.'[64]

The moral fervour that was to become a distinctive feature of the Victorian age also owed more to Albert than to Victoria. He wished from the beginning to raise the character of the Court.[65] Things were often, however, pushed to excessive lengths. He would not, for instance, allow any one to be seated in his presence. Lady John Russell, who was invited to the Palace shortly before her confinement, showed signs of fatigue. The Queen whispered to her to sit down, but put her behind Lady Douro so the Prince did not see this failure of etiquette. Victoria, unlike her husband, was quite unaffected and attentive to others. Her spontaneity and simplicity were endearing.[66] He modelled his own behaviour in such a way that, however much anyone wished to harm him, it could not be misconstrued. General Grey, in his work on the early life of the Prince, wrote, 'He imposed a degree of restraint and self-denial upon his own movements.... He denied himself the pleasure ... of walking at will about the town. Wherever he went, whether in a carriage or on horseback, he was accompanied by his equerry.'[67] Here indeed was no libertine, but a man almost obsessed with morality. Albert had the gaming tables removed from Windsor, there were no more bawdy stories, no more excessive drinking. The men were not allowed to stay in the dining room more than five minutes after the ladies left. Victoria was less quick to condemn than her husband. She did not appreciate those who were 'too strict and particular', she was not too severe towards others, conscious that circumstances in life could lead people astray. 'It is always right', she said, 'to show that one does not like what is obviously wrong but it is very dangerous to be too severe.'[68]

Albert's attitude towards religion was also much stricter than Victoria's. The Prince had a more doctrinal view of religion than the Queen, whose faith was more tied up with ethics, morality and the law of life than with the revelation. During their first Easter together they took Holy Communion together at Windsor, in St George's Chapel. The Queen had been struck by Albert's attitude towards Communion: 'The Prince had a very strong feeling about the solemnity of this act and did not like to appear in company either the evening before or on the day on which he took it, and he and the Queen almost always dined alone on these occasions.'[69]

Anson noted in a letter to Lord Melbourne that the Queen and Prince had been up to the Little Chapel in the Park and had luncheon afterwards at the cottage. He added, 'I think the Prince has more love of such sort of frolic than the Queen.'[70] The church or chapel could, however, have a deep effect on the Queen. When the Prince of Wales was christened at Windsor she said that St George's Chapel filled her 'with reverence and peaceful feelings'. 'The idea of it being the last resting place of those related to me, including my father, had nothing painful in it but on the contrary was calming for the spot is so fine, peaceful and hallowed.'[71]

Victoria disliked what she called 'a Sunday face' and was most adverse to the extreme wing of the Sabbatarian movement which was promoting the 'English Sunday'. She was against any idea of stopping the Sunday postal services, thinking it 'a very *false* notion of obeying God's will to do what will be a cause of much annoyance and possibly of great distress to private families.'[72] She also fought the idea of closing museums on Sunday. 'It is very well for those people who have no hard work during the week to go two or three times to church on Sunday and remain quiet for the rest of the day, but as regards the working class the practice is perfect cruelty.'[73]

The Queen was openminded, too, with regard to religions different from her own. She defended the Government's decision to increase the grant given to Maynooth, a training college for Catholic clergy in Ireland, which had come up against the opposition of the Protestants. 'I blush', wrote the Queen, 'for the form of religion we profess, that it should be so void of all right feeling and so wanting in Charity.'[74] She considered that the violent and bigoted passions displayed were not worthy of Protestantism. For the first but by no means the last time, she found herself on this issue opposed to Gladstone. Although Gladstone was not positively against the grant, he had once written a book against the subsidizing of the Roman Catholics and therefore felt obliged to resign from the Government.

Victoria did not like going against the wishes of others if it were possible to avoid doing so. That was why she respected the wish of her Uncle Sussex to be buried in the Harrow Road cemetery and not at Windsor, even though, as Greville noted, some thought 'the Queen should take on herself to have him buried with the rest of the Royal Family.' He was finally buried at Kensal Green, the Harrow Road cemetery, with royal honours.[75] Tolerance, if not a Victorian virtue, was certainly one of Victoria's.

One of the most attractive Victorian traits was a passion for knowledge. Both Victoria and Albert shared a desire to deepen their knowledge of the arts. Victoria was in some respects more accomplished than her spouse. She was, for instance, an excellent linguist. English was her mother tongue and she spoke it with no trace of a German accent – by contrast with Albert. She had had lessons in German and French and spoke them fluently, though she did not always write them correctly. She studied Italian, too. In other fields she and Albert were complementary. Both loved music, and they both played the piano and sang. Albert in addition played the organ and composed. He brought more musicians into the Court.

Among the visitors was Mendelssohn, who came frequently to the Palace in 1842–4. He described one of these visits to his mother:

> Prince Albert had asked me to go to him on Saturday at two o'clock, so that I might try his organ before I left England. . . . I begged that the Prince would first play me something, so that, as I said, I might boast about it in Germany; and he played a Chorale by heart. . . . Then it was my turn, and I began my chorus from 'St Paul' – 'How lovely are the messengers'. Before I got to the end of the first verse they both joined in the chorus.

Then at Albert's request the Queen herself sang one of Mendelssohn's songs. According to the composer, she 'sang it quite charmingly, in strict time and tune, and with very good execution. The last G I never heard better or purer, or more natural, from any amateur.' Then the Prince sang, and finally Mendelssohn improvised – 'and they followed me with so much intelligence and attention that I felt more at my ease than I ever did in improvising to an audience.'[76] The Queen loved Italian opera and she loved to sing. Her seriousness is demonstrated by her continuing lessons with Lablache, the famous opera singer from Naples who had become her singing master in 1836 and whose pupil she remained until the mid-1850s.

Another artistic bent the pair shared was that they both appreciated paintings and liked to paint. Landseer was in almost constant attendance at Court and other English artists, such as Maclise, Stanfield and Eastlake, were likewise honoured. Foreign artists were also welcomed and many are the portraits by Winterhalter, whose stiffness of movement and whose formalism were greatly appreciated by the Victorians. Some of the loveliest watercolours of the period are those of Charlotte Canning, lady-in-waiting to Queen Victoria, who excelled in drawing landscape and buildings. Queen Victoria asked her to accompany her on her travels to record 'views' at a time when photography was still in its infancy.[77] With the benefit of her teaching from the Academician Richard Westall and then from Edwin Landseer, Victoria herself found sketching in pencil or doing watercolours a lifelong amusement. After her marriage she also took up etching.

Victoria, however, never had the passion for knowledge that characterized Albert. Certainly she questioned Melbourne and sought to know more of English history – but this was in a sense utilitarian. Albert, on the other hand, had a genuinely inquiring mind. He visited everything – houses, factories, galleries, machines – always seeking to know how things worked, what they were used for. In Windsor he discovered priceless drawings carelessly thrown into drawers or cupboards, or in folders in the library – drawings by Holbein or Leonardo da Vinci for instance. He brought a scholarly mind to the problem and set about recording and classifying the unique treasures the Castle contained. Scientific matters also fascinated Albert. Lady Lyttelton noted in 1842, 'We have, I begin to notice, rather a raised tone of conversation of late – many bits of information, and naval matters and scientific subjects come up, and are talked of very pleasantly at dinner. The Prince, of course, encourages such subjects.'[78] One of Albert's favourite subjects of study was agriculture. He was interested in the yield of crops and the fattening of cattle and he set up a small model farm in Windsor Park in 1840. He took part in agricultural shows and his products often won prizes. In 1844, for instance, his pigs won first prize at Smithfield.

Both Victoria and Albert were committed to the idea of progress. In the early years of Victoria's reign the speed of life began to accelerate. The greatest innovations of these early years were the penny post, the railways and the telegraph. The Post Office had at the time a monopoly of conveying correspondence. Rowland Hill had proposed a scheme for reducing the rates paid for transporting a letter – more than sixpence on average – to a single fixed rate of one penny. There had been much opposition to this but the new rate was finally adopted and the Penny Post came into being in 1840. The Queen, who was a most prolific letter writer, approved of the scheme – and used it to a very considerable extent! In 1837, 80,000 letters and 441,000 newspapers had been delivered through the Post Office; by the end of Victoria's reign the deliveries had increased some 2,300 times to over two billion. The first telegraphic lines were built in Britain in 1845.

But the great revolution at the beginning of Victoria's reign was the coming of the train. The first railway line, the Stockton to Darlington, had been opened in 1825. In 1830 came the Manchester to Liverpool. When Victoria came to the throne 'the monsters', as the locomotives were called, still provoked almost as much hostility as approval. The upper classes, in particular, regarded the train with alarm. The locomotives ran through 'their' countryside, violated their peace, spoilt their landscapes and brought the *hoi polloi* out of the towns. The aristocracy, while often opposed to industrialization, were perfectly ready to accept some of its profits. Machines had plunged a part of the population into a state that the upper classes chose to ignore, although they did not shun the towns but set up elegant town houses in London. The social order had been disturbed. The revolution of 1830 on the continent and the Reform Bill riots of 1831–2 at home had spread the fear of the 'mob' and caused the aristocracy to regret the mythical time when the poor man at his gate was contented with his lot. The royal couple's attitude was very different. They made their first train journey from Slough to London in 1842 and the Queen had nothing but praise for the train. The journey lasted twenty-five minutes and Albert found it rather too fast, but the Queen revelled in it: 'I find the motion so very easy, far more so than a carriage and cannot understand how any one can suffer from it.'[79]

Patience and perseverance, we have already seen, were more Albertian than Victorian. So, too, was the sense of social duty. From the mid-1830s to the mid-1840s the harvests were consistently poor and prices of food rose in consequence. This in turn led to a stagnation of trade, an increase in unemployment and a lowering of wages. The result was destitution. The population of some manufacturing towns was fast decreasing, leaving in dire poverty the inhabitants who remained. 'Cobden stated that in the borough which he represented [Stockport] one house in every five was empty.'[80] In November 1842 the situation was described to Greville: 'There is an immense and continually increasing population, deep distress and privation, no adequate demand for labour, no demand for anything, no confidence, but a universal alarm, disquietude and discontent. Nobody can sell anything.'[81]

Sometimes the royal couple's attempts to play a social role misfired. Perhaps the best example is the fancy-dress ball held at the Palace on 12 May 1842. The idea was to help trade in London, which was greatly depressed. The guests were dressed in the costumes of the Plantagenet period, with Victoria as Queen Philippa and Albert as Edward III. The Queen's robe was magnificent – the stomacher was decorated with jewels worth more than 60,000 pounds. It was later put on view in the West End. Despite its worthy intentions such a display of wealth inevitably brought criticism. The splendour of entertainments like this in England was such that King Leopold wrote: 'There is hardly a country where such magnificence exists: Austria has some of the means but the Court is not elegant from its nature.'[82]

The Queen's social conscience was aroused whenever she met the individuals concerned or whenever a particular case came to her notice. When Peel's private secretary was assassinated in 1843, for instance, she gave 'poor Miss Drummond' an apartment at Hampton Court. But she was adamantly against any form of collective action on the part of the workers themselves. For the Chartists she had no sympathy whatever. Nor did she favour legislation that would ease the misery of the masses. An example was Lord Ashley's Bill to limit the hours of workers in mills and factories to ten hours a day. The Queen adopted the view of her Prime Minister Peel – shared not only by the Conservatives but also by some Liberal leaders like Bright and Cobden – that it would deprive industry of the equivalent of seven weeks' work a year and expose British manufactures to formidable competition from those other countries in which labour was not restricted. It was only thanks to Peel that the Queen was seen to be sensitive to her people's difficulties by agreeing to pay the new income tax, which she could have refused.

It was in 1843 that, faced with the financial deficit left by the Whigs, Peel created an income tax of seven old pence in the pound. He argued that no further indirect taxation could be imposed without harming trade. Until then there had never been such a tax in peacetime and it was understood that it would not last for more than three or at most five years. In fact it has remained to this day – though no longer at a flat rate of 3 per cent! The Queen heard from Peel that Brougham, a Radical leader, had prepared a resolution 'that none, not the highest (meaning *me*),' notes the Queen, 'would be exempt from this new Income Tax.'[83] Although he had no right to do this, there was a precedent – George IV had not wished to be exempt when a tax was levied in his reign. He had paid 10 per cent.

> Sir Robert thought I should also do so (but only three per cent, which however is rather hard) and wished to know whether he might announce this in the House this evening so that it might appear a gracious act on my part, without any legislation about it. This of course I at once consented to. It is very hard for my poor dear Albert who will have to pay £900.

The announcement made, as Peel had expected, 'a very great sensation' in the House.[84]

Sentimentality and demonstrations of excessive, even insincere grief are also associated with the Victorian era. Albert, for instance, in January 1844 indulged in such demonstrations on the death of his father, although he had not seen him for four years – when he could easily have either visited him or invited him to England – and although he did, in fact, find him extremely trying. Nonetheless he gave way to grief and wrote to his brother: 'We no longer have any home and this is a terrible thought. I shall never see him again, never see my home with him as I knew and loved it and as I grew up in it.'[85] This was to overlook the home he had with a family of his own – three children now, and a wife again pregnant. He also went immediately into deep mourning. He wrote to Ernest:

> Our little children do not know why we cry and they ask us why we are in black; Victoria weeps with me, for me and for all of you. This is a great comfort for me. And your dear Alexandrine will weep with you. Let us take care of these two jewels, let us love and protect them, as in them we shall find happiness again.[86]

He had Victoria send Ernest 'a pin with a curl of dear Father's hair' and thanked him on black-edged paper for 'the reliques', in particular a fruit knife. The Victorian fashion of mourning had begun. Bereavement took on a new importance. The deceased ceased to have anything but qualities. Duke Ernest's wife, the long-suffering Marie of Württemberg, made little pretence of mourning him. Six months after his death she cast off her widow's weeds and fled to Paris.

The great taboo of Victorian times was sex. Here Victoria was certainly more of a Hanoverian than a Victorian. She enjoyed her husband's embraces, took pleasure in seeing him shave or having him pull off her stockings. The birth of Victoria's children never made her more of a mother than a spouse. On the contrary. After the Prince of Wales's birth she wrote to King Leopold:

> I wonder very much whom our little boy will be like. You will understand how fervent are my prayers, and I am sure everybody's must be, to see him resemble his father in every respect, both in body and mind. Oh! my dearest uncle, I am sure if you know how happy, how blessed I feel, and how proud in possessing such a perfect being as my husband![87]

For Victoria the dark side of marriage was not sex, but the births that seemed so inevitably to follow!

Albert has often been spoken of as a prude. But this seems to owe more to his fidelity to his wife – far from the rule in aristocratic circles – than to any particular attitude he expressed. That he was determined not to give way to any temptation is certain. He had, after all, seen the result in his own family. His father's infidelities had led to those of his mother and had been imitated by his brother Ernest. Marriage was for Albert a means of constraint on man's sexual appetite. Speaking to Ernest of his future marriage, he said: 'Chains you will have to bear in any case and it will certainly be good for you. This is why the whole family wishes you to marry. The heavier and tighter they are, the better for you. A married couple must be chained to one another, be inseparable and they must live only for one another.' But marriage was not all negative: 'wedded life', he told his brother, 'is the only thing that can make up for the lost relationships of our youth.'[88]

The Victorian family was numerous – as was Victoria's – and it was headed by a paterfamilias. This was undoubtedly how Albert saw things. He summed it up in his portrait of the wife Ernest needed: someone 'who is young and good, not self-willed when you discuss things with her, but one who will influence you by her intelligence.'[89]

Victoria came to accept this point of view, although not without difficulty. With regard to the children, Albert was undoubtedly to be the head of the household. In her role as Sovereign she came to share her power with him, Albert's progress being facilitated by her repeated pregnancies – she had four children in the first five years of her marriage. Her third child, Princess Alice, known as Fatima because she was plump and flourishing, was born on 25 April 1843; her fourth, Prince Alfred, 'Affie', was born on 6 August 1844, less than eighteen months later.

From 1842 Albert was present when the Queen received Ministers. This seems to have been suggested by Peel. Before long the Queen was speaking of Albert as a monarch. 'Albert gave a long audience to Sir Robert Peel upon many topics,' she noted on 10 March 1843. It was at about this time that the Queen began announcing her decisions on public questions using the plural 'we' instead of the singular 'I' – indicating clearly that she was henceforth merging her own judgement with that of her husband. It was in the same year that, during her pregnancy, Albert held receptions on the Queen's behalf – an assumption of fresh power that was not well received by press and public. Once again the Queen had talked first to Peel, who had 'thought it would be quite right . . . Albert and I then concocted a note to Peel about the *levées* and that the presentation to *him* [the Prince] should be considered the same as to me.'[90]

In April 1843 the Queen wrote: 'held a council after which I saw the Duke of Wellington . . . Albert saw several of the other Ministers for me as I was rather tired.' Albert was indeed diligent and indefatigable. He wrote summaries of every interview in his own hand, penned memoranda, even gradually began to draft many of the Queen's official letters. From then on he was virtually a joint ruler. His ambition to be the tutor of the royal children, the private secretary of the Queen and her permanent Minister was now satisfied. He was, claimed Greville, King to all intents and purposes. Nonetheless he was still not accepted by the royal family as their equal and the Queen had constantly to protect and help him. When her first cousin, Augusta, the daughter of the Duke of Cambridge, was married at Buckingham Palace, for instance the Queen's uncle, the redoubted King of Hanover, had the intention of taking precedence over Albert and signing the register before him. He placed himself by the Queen and waited for the right moment. She knew very well what he was about, and just as the Archbishop was about to hand her the pen, she suddenly dodged round the table, placed herself next to the Prince, then quickly took the pen from the Archbishop, signed and gave it to Prince Albert, who signed next before the King of Hanover could do anything about it. On this particular occasion the King of Hanover had even created a disturbance at the church, as Albert told his brother:

He [Hanover] insisted on having the place at the altar, where he stood. He wanted to drive me away, and against all custom, he wanted to accompany Victoria and lead her. I was to go behind him. I was forced to give him a strong push and drive him down a few steps, where the First Master of Ceremonies took him and led him out of the chapel.[91]

King Leopold was highly amused by all this.

To the aristocracy Prince Albert remained all his life a foreigner, an outsider – a man who would show emotion openly by crying, a man full of sentimentality and censoriousness. His health was poor, he was a workaholic, never able to relax and take things easily – let alone indolently as was the aristocratic mode. He worked incessantly, one might almost say unnecessarily. Socially he was ill at ease – and perhaps because of this was a stickler for etiquette. He wooed the muses – singing, composing and drawing – effeminate occupations in the eyes of the English upper classes. He was decidedly not one of them. But to the rising middle classes the royal couple now served as a model of conduct, a means of differentiating themselves from their inferiors. Victorianism was above all a characteristic of the middle classes.

Queen Victoria, however, was never a typical Victorian. As we shall see there were some values the husband she adored never quite succeeded in inculcating.

13

Royal Travels

In 1842 Queen Victoria, still in her twenties, paid her first visit to Scotland. In June she had asked Sir Robert Peel to make arrangements for her to spend an early autumn there, but Peel and his advisers had objected. They doubted the advisability of travelling through the north of England, which was disrupted by the Chartists. The Home Secretary, Sir James Graham, finally agreed on condition they went by sea. For the royal couple it was, in a sense, their honeymoon, their first romantic journey.

Leaving their two children behind them, Victoria and Albert embarked from Woolwich on 29 August at seven in the morning in the *Royal George*. The journey was arduous and took three whole days and three nights. On Tuesday 30 August the Queen wrote in her journal: 'We heard to our great distress, that we had only gone 58 miles since eight o'clock last night. How annoying and provoking this is! We remained on deck all day lying on sofas; the sea was very rough towards evening, and I was very ill.'[1] The next night was no better. 'At five o'clock in the morning we heard, to our great vexation, that we had only been going three knots an hour in the night and were fifty miles from St Abb's Head.'[2] The evening was pleasanter. The Queen first saw Scotland from the deck and noted that the Scottish coast was 'very beautiful, so dark, rocky, bold and wild, totally unlike our coast'.[3]

The anchor was finally let down on 1 September at a quarter to one – 'a welcome sound' to the ears of the Queen.[4] The royal couple went first to Dalkeith Palace, where they were entertained for two days by the Duke of Buccleuch. The Palace was actually a large house constructed of reddish stone. The couple were 'very tired and both felt quite giddy when they were shown up a very handsome staircase' to their rooms which were 'very comfortable'.[5] They did not have much time to rest. In the afternoon they drove out and at eight they dined with a large party. The rest of their stay was no less occupied.

On 3 September they went to Edinburgh, where the Queen entered in state. A notice had been placed in the newspapers – the *Covenant* and the *Caledonian Mercury* published an official invitation from the Lord Chamberlain Lord de la Warr to the general public: 'The Queen will receive those Ladies and Gentlemen who may be desirous of paying their respect to Her Majesty at the Palace of Holyrood House on Friday the 2nd September at two o'clock. – Ladies may appear without trains and feathers – Gentlemen in Levée Dress.'[6]

The reception had, however, to be transferred to Dalkeith Palace as there were rumours of scarlet fever at Holyrood Palace. It was not held until Monday the fourth – the postponement was no doubt due to the fact that the poor Duke of Buccleuch had suddenly to provide for the descent on his home of several hundred of his royal guest's loyal Scottish subjects! Presentation to the Queen had normally to be made by someone who had previously been presented. As there were few such people in Scotland they were allowed to present several people on the same day. While they were in Dalkeith the royal couple also visited Lord Lothian's and Lord Dalhousie's homes. The latter was 'a real old Scotch castle of reddish stone' – Lady Dalhousie said there had been no British Sovereign there since Henry IV, four centuries earlier.[7]

Leaving Dalkeith they went to Dalmeny Park where they were entertained by the Earl of Rosebery. They then went to Scone Palace, visiting on the way Dupplin Castle and Perth, where the Queen received the keys of the city. The Scots were not used to receiving their Queen and the Lord Provost of Perth wrote to ask the authorities a multitude of questions – on which side of the carriage did the Queen sit (the right side); which knee is to be bent (the right); should the keys be presented kneeling (it is better – right knee); should the carriages precede or follow those of Her Majesty (follow); when they returned to their carriages should they put on their *chapeaux de bras* (cocked hats may be worn when the procession is moving).[8]

On leaving Scone the Queen paid brief visits to Dunkeld and Taymouth Castles, and rowed up to Auchmore sixteen miles away – the boatmen singing Gaelic songs all the way – landing at Lord Breadalbane's cottage, where they lunched. Then they went by road to Crieff. At Drummond Castle the royal party was received by Lord and Lady Willoughby d'Eresby. The Queen also visited Stirling Castle, where she was delighted to find that the Provost of Stirling had served for twenty-four years under her father, the Duke of Kent.

On 15 September – a Sunday – the Queen made her first visit to the Church of Scotland – worshipping in the small parish church of Blair Atholl, capable of holding only about five hundred persons. The fact that Queen Victoria had worshipped in the Church of Scotland occasioned a good deal of comment. The *Morning Post* criticized Her Majesty for having attended a service 'at the meeting-place of the Calvinists or Presbyterians, to whom Prelacy – the Prelacy Her Majesty has sworn to maintain – is the object of implacable hate and abhorrence, and the symbol of absolute damnation' (16 September 1844). The *Post*'s vigorous indictment of the Queen's conduct provoked a spirited rejoinder from the *Sun*. For the *Sun*, the *Post*'s article was bigoted and unworthy of the enlightened nineteenth century. By attending a Presbyterian place of worship the Queen had, declared the *Sun* on 17 September 1844, shown real religious feeling and 'set an example of toleration which is worthy of praise'.

Altogether the Queen spent a fortnight in her Scottish dominions. When she left she sent a message: 'The Queen cannot leave Scotland without a feeling of regret that her visit on the present occasion could not be further prolonged.' She had indeed fallen in love with Scotland. It was a country in which she relived English history: she saw the castle from which 'poor Queen Mary' escaped, she looked out of her window at a sycamore tree planted by James VI, and she signed her name in 'a curious old book' under the names of James I of England and Charles I.[9] She visited the room where James II murdered Douglas and saw the window out of which he was thrown. She already knew one version of Scotland's history, that recounted by Walter Scott in his novels, and those romantic pages came to life. She enjoyed the picturesqueness of Scottish customs. At Lord Breadalbane's, for instance, she was received by a number of his Highlanders drawn up in front of the house, with Lord Breadalbane himself in a Highland dress at their head, with pipers playing and a company of the 92nd Highlanders, also in kilts, standing by. It was, she declared, 'princely and romantic'.[10] She was fascinated by 'the young girls and children with flowing hair – and many of them pretty'.

Scottish food was new and agreeable, 'in particular breakfast with oatmeal porridge' and 'Finnan haddies' (smoked haddock).[11] Another aspect she particularly enjoyed was her meetings with ordinary people, who did not know who she was. The woman who gave her milk and a piece of bread when she was out walking, for instance, or the good-humoured little woman who cut bunches of flowers for the Duchess of Norfolk and herself. She tried to catch some of these homely people and their environment in watercolour: the little huts 'so low, so full of peat smoke'; the 'woman in the river with her dress tucked up almost to her knees, washing potatoes.'[12] The scenery pleased her, whether in Edinburgh, with 'everything built of massive stone there is not a brick to be seen anywhere',[13] or in the countryside, where she found the 'wildest and finest scenery' and Scottish streams 'clear as glass . . . the depth of the shadows, the mossy stones'.[14]

Albert, too, was full of enthusiasm, not least because the countryside resembled that of his beloved Thüringen. The quiet, the solitude, the remoteness held a great charm for him. Then there was the sport. He went deerstalking and returned from his sport 'dreadfully sunburnt, and a good deal tired'.[15]

The whole Scottish experience left so pleasant an impression that it was soon repeated. In August 1844 the royal couple spent another relaxing autumn on holiday in Scotland.

Meanwhile in 1843 the Queen was to go abroad for the first time at the invitation of Louis-Philippe, the King of the French. In 1843 Louis-Philippe thought a visit from the Queen of England would be both pleasant and useful to him. His father was Louis XVI's cousin, the Duke of Orléans, better known as Philippe Égalité because he renounced his title. Louis-Philippe was the eldest son, born in 1773. In 1792 he fought in the Revolution's army. He was expelled from France and wandered about Europe and America, earning his living. After the fall of Napoleon he returned to France and recovered his estates. This 'King of the Barricades' had been crowned by Parliament. He was seen by the French representatives as representing the middle way between the twin perils of reaction and anarchy. He was not King of France by the Grace of God but King of the French by the will of the people. He wanted to have public acclaim and aimed at having an ambitious and successful foreign policy. Should one of the most powerful sovereigns in Europe visit him, the shadow as to the legitimacy of his rule that had been over his family for the past thirteen years would be removed.

A visit would also put an end to the breach in the friendly relations of France and England that had occurred under the Melbourne Administration in 1840 as a result of the Eastern Question. Egypt had been seeking to cast off allegiance to the Sultan of Turkey, and its defiance was headed by Mehemet Ali, even though he was Viceroy. Louis-Philippe and his Minister of Foreign Affairs, Thiers, proceeded to implement a dynamic nationalistic foreign policy, encouraging Egyptian rebellion. By contrast, England and the other great powers had taken Turkey under their protection. The Four Powers – England, Russia,

Austria and Prussia – sent an ultimatum to Mehemet Ali, requiring him to evacuate North Syria. Guizot, the French Ambassador in London, had not been informed of the project, nor of course had the French Government. King Leopold wrote to the Queen, warning her of the risks of a policy of isolation of France.

> I cannot disguise from you that the consequences may be very serious, and the more so as the Thiers Ministry is supported by the Movement party and as reckless of consequence as your own Minister for Foreign Affairs, even much more so . . . He is strongly impregnated with all the notions of fame and glory which belonged to part of the Republican and Imperial times.[16]

English foreign policy was conducted at the time by Lord Palmerston. For Palmerston the French were once again entertaining Bonapartist dreams, seeking to control the expanding supply of raw cotton produced in the Middle East. Thiers rashly refused Palmerston's compromise suggestion whereby France's influence in southern Syria would be recognized. The British Government was divided. When they met to consider the Eastern Question, the Government was on the verge of dissolution. Lord John Russell was in favour of peace at all costs; Palmerston was determined to put an end to any hope of French predominance in Egypt and to crush Mehemet Ali at once. 'The Mistress of India', declared Palmerston, 'could not permit France to be mistress, directly or indirectly, of the road to her Indian dominions.'[17] Orders were issued to the British fleet to force Mehemet Ali to return to his allegiance to the Sultan. Beirut was bombarded. The French should logically have brought their support to Mehemet Ali. War seemed imminent. Louis-Philippe, however, did nothing. He was afraid that the war would upset the economy and give rise to social unrest. King Leopold, his son-in-law, vigorously encouraged him to avert catastrophe. Thiers resigned on 20 October 1840 and was succeeded by Guizot.

The royal couple were relieved. The Eastern Question had preoccupied them to such an extent that the pregnant Queen wrote humorously in a letter to King Leopold, 'I think our child ought to have, besides its other names, those of Turko-Egypt, as we think of nothing else.'[18]

On 13 July 1841 the Dardanelles Treaty was signed by England, Austria, Russia, Prussia and France. It closed the Bosphorus and the Dardanelles to all foreign battleships, conceded to Mehemet Ali the hereditary vice-royalty of Egypt and gave Syria back to the Ottoman Porte. Franco–British relations could now be more harmonious.

Queen Victoria was linked to the House of Orléans by a whole series of marriages. Louis-Philippe had two daughters, Princess Louise and Princess Clementine, and five sons: the Dukes of Orléans, of Nemours, of Aumale, of Montpensier and of Joinville. Both daughters had married into Victoria's family – Uncle Leopold had married Princess Louise, and Prince August of Saxe-Coburg-Kohary Princess Clementine. Prince August's sister, Princess Victoria, had married the Duke of Nemours. Queen Victoria felt herself drawn closer to the royal family of France in 1842 when, on 13 July, Louis-Philippe's eldest son, the Duke of Orléans, affectionately known as Chartres – his name before his father came to the throne – was killed. On his way from Neuilly to the Palais Royal, the horses drawing his carriage bolted at the toll-gate of the Étoile. The carriage had gone past the Porte Maillot at top speed and the Duke had been thrown out, smashing his head on the cobblestones. Had he been trying to jump? No one will ever know. In his will, found among his papers, he left the education of his children to his wife. But he also stated that she, being a woman, should never be Regent.

Victoria received letters from Leopold and Louise, who had gone to Paris immediately. She knew that Chartres was Louise's favourite brother. 'We can hardly think of anything', Victoria wrote to her uncle, 'but this terrible misfortune and of all of you.'[19] Louise, writing from France, described her parents as heartbroken, 'both grown old in looks, and their hair turned quite white'.[20] Thus it was that, when two of Louis-Philippe's sons – the Prince of Joinville and the Duke of Aumale – went to Windsor in August of the following year to convey an invitation to the Queen to visit the family in France, she was only too ready to go.

The Government, who was informed of the projected royal visit at the last moment, might have reacted unfavourably. Raikes in his diary wrote that the whole business 'was a wily intrigue managed by Louis-Philippe through the intervention of his daughter, the Queen of the Belgians, during her frequent visits to Windsor with King Leopold, and was hailed by him with extreme joy, as the first admission of the King of the Barricades within the pale of legitimate sovereigns.'[21]

The Queen's first visit abroad raised a constitutional question: could the Queen leave her British dominions without the sanction of an Act of Parliament? Did not the third clause in the Act of Settlement expressly state 'that no person who shall hereafter come to the possession of the Crown, shall go out of the dominions of England, Scotland or Ireland without the consent of Parliament'? In fact, said the Crown lawyers, the clause had been repealed in the first year of George I on account of his frequent journeys to Hanover. The Duke of Wellington, when consulted, had been in favour of appointing a Council of Regency on the grounds that George I, II and IV had all done so. But his advice was not followed.

Despite what Raikes wrote, neither the Prime Minister nor the Foreign Secretary offered any opposition to the project. They believed that the maintenance of good personal relations between the Queen and her continental colleagues could only increase peace and goodwill. There was no doubt that a friendly visit – which was the outcome of domestic sentiment rather than political design – might have a good effect in removing the lingering resentment occasioned in France by the action of the English Government on the Eastern Question.

The Queen and Prince Albert embarked at Plymouth on 25 August 1843 in the *Victoria and Albert*, a yacht especially constructed for the Queen that very year. The Captain was Lord Adolphus Fitzclarence, a natural son of William IV. The Queen, who was a good sailor, thoroughly enjoyed the cruise. Prince Albert was seasick at the first breeze.[22] After a few days cruising round the Isle of Wight and along the coast of Devonshire, the royal couple set off across the Channel for France. No English Sovereign had set foot on foreign soil since George III – except when George IV had been crowned in Hanover, of which he was also King. It was the first occasion on which an English Sovereign had visited a French Sovereign since Henry VIII – who had appeared on the Field of Cloth of Gold on the invitation of Francis I in 1520. Before leaving her shores the Queen had received addresses from the Mayors of Falmouth and Penrhyn and apologies from the Mayor of Truro, who was unable to give his address as he had accidentally fallen into the water in full municipal costume and both he and his address were too wet for presentation!

Navigation in the Channel was not as easy then as it is today. At half-past four on the morning of 2 September, 'we awoke', the Queen wrote, 'and being at a standstill, we asked where we were, the answer being "eight or ten miles from Cherbourg".'[23] The Queen was horrified as they had expected to be at Cherbourg at three.

Hardly had the couple began to dress when they heard a gun salute from a ship and saw the *Pluton* near them. Within a few minutes the Duke of Joinville was on board. The yacht proceeded along the French coast while they breakfasted with Joinville. 'He is', declared the Queen, 'such an amiable, agreeable companion, but his great deafness is a serious drawback to general conversation.'[24] As they approached Le

Tréport, 'situated in a small creek, with downs rising behind it, and a very picturesque old Church, very unlike anything English',[25] they saw the King's barge approaching.

'The good kind King was standing up in the boat, and so impatient to get out that it was very difficult to prevent his getting out of the boat before it was close enough. Then he came up as quickly as possible and warmly embraced me.'[26] The King was perhaps a little lacking in majesty, with his pear-shaped head, surmounted by a 'toupet', his thick whiskers and his big eyes. But his welcome was most cordial. Waiting for Victoria at the top of the steep flight of steps was the French King's Consort, Queen Marie Amélie. She was the daughter of Ferdinand, King of the Two Sicilies, and had married Louis-Philippe in 1809 when he was living in exile at Palermo. Waiting with her were Louise, Queen of the Belgians, Hélène, the Duchess of Orléans, Françoise, the Princess of Joinville.

Victoria admired the King's barge, was moved by the cheering of the people and the troops and was conscious of how different the houses and the people were from those in England. She was less impressed by the means of transport offered her. 'We then got into a curious old carriage, a sort of *char à bancs* with a top to it, in which we sat with the King and Queen and all the ladies of the family. There were eight horses, harnessed 'à la Française' (something like the way our state horses are harnessed).'[27] Lady Canning described the carriage as 'a mixture between one of Louis XIV's time and a marketing cart from Hampton Court. The body was like an enormous coach with a good deal of gilding and coats of arms and containing two or three rows of seats. The top was flat and supported with little pillars with draperies and curtains of flowery chinz.'[28]

The driver must have been unused to driving the coach, for the Queen 'met with what might have been an accident. As we were trying to go through a gate, only half of the horses would obey, the others refusing to do so, and the carriage was all on one side, the King in despair saying "cela me désole". After some trials we went on straight and came in at another gate.'[29] Lady Canning noted that when the horses refused to pass through the arch, 'we were taken for some miles along a very narrow field road, in deep dust, and over stones, and ruts and holes, till we expected to be overturned every moment, and did not at all approve of the Queen's running such risks.'[30]

The carriage finally arrived at the King's residence, the Château d'Eu. It was some three miles from the sea, sheltered from the western winds by high cliffs and overlooking a valley. The building itself went back to the sixteenth century and Louis-Philippe had extended it, respecting the style of the original. It had been confiscated during the Terror and under Napoleon had become an imperial palace. When the monarchy was restored the castle had been returned to the Orléans family. The Queen was charmed by Eu. 'The Château lit up, with a fine garden in front, had a charming effect.'[31] The first Roman Catholic chapel she had ever seen was, she declared, a jewel.[32]

As she had gone from Le Tréport, where she had landed, to Eu, the Queen looked eagerly around her, taking everything in. This part of France was, she thought, like Brighton, but prettier because there were more trees. She was surprised by the crucifixes at the corners of the roads. But it was the population that struck her above all as 'so extremely different from England, their faces, dress, manners, everything'.[33] The women wore pretty picturesque white caps or coloured handkerchiefs and aprons. She even saw a child in swaddling clothes.

On that first evening the whole party of the French royal family and the Court dined with the English visitors – some eighty people in all. Victoria sat between the King and Joinville. 'The "service"', Victoria noted, 'was very splendid but everything served differently than with us. The King and Queen carve themselves.'[34] Lady Canning considered the dinner was 'very handsomely done' but she wondered why Louis-Philippe had a pile of bread and rusks of all sorts at his side. 'Our Queen did not know what to do with her great French loaf. The table was not tidy and everybody's bread and crumbs and dirt stay all through the dessert.'[35]

The English royals retired at half-past ten and rose at half-past seven on the following day. The Queen 'felt as though it were a dream that I was at Eu, and that my favourite castle in the air of so many years, should at length be realised'.[36] Only the distant ringing of the church bells reminded her that it was Sunday, for the mill was going and the people sweeping and working in the garden.

The family atmosphere warmed the Queen's heart. 'I feel so at home with them all and as if I were one of them.'[37] 'The old King', Prince Albert wrote to Stockmar, 'was in the third heaven of rapture, and the whole family received us with a heartiness, I might say affection, which was quite touching.'[38] Victoria admired the pater familias side of Louis-Philippe, 'the good kind King'. Lady Canning was struck by the fact that 'The Queen of the French is always anxious to make people sit down and to put them at their ease; I am quite surprised', she added, 'to see how little form there is in comparison to what we are accustomed to.'[39] Queen Marie-Amélie told Victoria she had always had 'a maternal feeling for her and that since she had got to know her it had intensified'. She drove out with the Queen and noted, 'We were very merry and laughed a good deal.' Altogether, Victoria found the Queen delightful and very like her daughter Louise – who had always been, as King Leopold's wife, Victoria's favourite aunt. She was impressed by Hélène, Chartres's widow, whom she found 'very clever and sensible' and showing 'great fortitude and courage'. Joinville's wife Chica she described as 'sprightly', with a beautiful figure and 'fine large brown eyes'. The King and Joinville she found amusing and full of anecdotes.[40]

Lady Canning's impressions of Eu were much less favourable. The evenings were 'dullish, we dawdled on a long time in the downstairs gallery, and then went up.' The band of fifty men playing under the Queen's window 'almost deafened her', the Ladies of the Court were 'all rather tiresome'. They were lacking in elegance and, apart from the Princess of Joinville, were rather 'dowdy'. Lord Liverpool's 'incessant talking in disagreeable French' bored her to death.[41]

Worst of all were the picnics Louis-Philippe organized in the Forest of Eu on two of the five days' visit. The long drives into the forest were undertaken in vans with high seats without backs and bad springs, and were very tiring. 'For two and a half hours we drove about, after a good while longer we came to a long open tent with a great luncheon spread out.' The tent was ornamented with gilt minarets and lined with buff-coloured merino cloth. A dark-coloured drugget was placed on the grass so that the feeling to the foot was of softest velvet. Along the middle was placed the table, set for seventy-two persons. In the centre stood eighteen mahogany chairs for the royal party, while the other guests were placed on camp stools furnished with backs. 'Forty decanters of wine, alternated with carafes of water were set on the table in English style; whilst down the middle was placed the collation, composed of meats, pâtés, confectionery of the most recherché description, in fact everything that the most exquisite taste could suggest and wealth provide.'[42]

Dinner in the evenings was early – seven o'clock – and after dinner various entertainments were provided. On one evening the *Musique du Roi* gave a concert, with symphonies by Beethoven and Gluck, on another there was solo playing on violoncello and pianoforte and on the French horn. The latter instrument was played in a peculiar manner by a man who could sound chords, two or three notes at once. 'The Duke of Montpensier had the giggles and it caught from one person to another till all were in tears and the poor performer's sounds became stranger and stranger.'[43] But Lady Adélaide, the King's sister, went to compliment him afterwards and found that as his back was partly turned to the audience he had not realized what was happening.

Although presented as an informal family visit, political discussions had not been totally eliminated. The affair of the Spanish marriages had been discussed. Queen Isabella of Spain was thirteen and the choice of her husband was deemed of major importance by the great powers.

During her stay the Queen bought a number of 'very pretty things made at Dieppe in ivory' – little vases and statuettes. She received from Louis-Philippe a beautiful box of Sèvres china and 'two splendid pieces of Gobelins', tapestries which had been thirty years in the making and were to be hung in the oak dining room at Windsor, where the Queen usually dined when she was in residence. The tapestries represented 'The hunt of Meleager' and 'Atlanta weeping over the dead body of Meleager' and had been begun for Josephine's residence at Malmaison.[44] Lady Eleanor Stanley later noted that the panelling of the Oak Room 'is to be pulled to pieces for that and, as the two sides are not near long enough to admit the tapestry, it is to be turned back about two feet to make it fit . . . and the Prince after that flatters himself he is a man of taste, and talks of encouraging the arts!'[45]

Louis-Philippe was determined to immortalize the visit in pen and brush and had commissioned a series of paintings to fill a gallery of his castle with. The visit certainly seemed to have eased relationships between the French and the English. Guizot told the Queen of his great joy at their coming, and she noted, 'It seems to have done the greatest good, and to have caused the greatest satisfaction to the French. . . . The French naval officers give this evening a banquet on board the "Pluton" to our naval officers and I trust that the '*haine pour les perfides Anglais*" will cease.'[46] The King told her that the French officers had had a dinner at which her health had been drunk with great enthusiasm, 'which is not bad', he added, 'for French soldiers.'[47] He told her repeatedly how much he wanted to be closely allied with the English, for this was the surest means of preventing war in Europe. His love for the English was, he claimed, 'in his blood'.[48] Albert had no love for the French. In 1840 he had written, 'In quantities I detest them, in simple instances they amuse me.'[49] But even he was moved.

On arriving back in England the Queen spent four days with her children at the Pavilion in Brighton. She was 'quite unhappy to leave the yacht, and to have to live in a house again'.[50] But she was soon back on the sea again. On 12 September the *Victoria and Albert* sailed for

Ostend. The couple were to pay a visit to Uncle Leopold, who was impatient to know how they had got on with Louis-Philippe. There was a good deal of wind and a rough sea. As usual the Queen was not ill but Prince Albert succumbed. According to Lady Canning Victoria laughed heartily at the sight of first Prince Albert dreadfully overcome, then Lord Liverpool, and then Lord Aberdeen, 'all vanishing in haste'.[51]

The tour of Belgium lasted six days and the Queen visited Bruges, Ghent, Brussels and Antwerp. Prince Albert was pleased with the visit. He commented to Stockmar on the 'enthusiasm' the Belgians showed the royal couple, the manner in which the cities of Flanders 'had put on their fairest array' and the 'cordiality and friendliness' which met them everywhere and which 'could not fail to attract her [Victoria] towards the Belgian people'.[52] For Victoria the visit was more of a family visit – 'It was such a joy for me to be once again under the roof of one who has ever been a father to me!'[53] As for Lady Canning, the journey was not a success. 'Eu was twenty times better fun for me,' she noted. Only Brussels found favour in her eyes. It was 'one of the prettiest towns I ever saw. Every house so white and clean and gay like the best parts of Paris.'[54]

Stockmar was delighted by these visits to France and Belgium and wrote to congratulate the royal couple on their success. In his usual schoolmaster manner he went on to say, 'Let us pause to ask why it was a success,' and as usual he answered his own question, 'Because it was thought well over beforehand, because it was undertaken upon a definite plan, because the plan was adhered to to the letter. Let us make a vow to carry out like things in the like way.'[55]

The Queen's wardrobe for these foreign visits was not given much attention. Lady Canning 'was very much distressed, at Eu, to see our Queen appear in scarlet china crêpe the first night when it was so very hot.'[56] She wore the same dress some seven weeks later and Lady Eleanor Stanley noted, 'The Queen had on *the* cerise crêpe de chine, trimmed round the bottom with three rows of lace. It is a very handsome gown, and sets off her jewels and blue ribbon very well, but it looks very hot, being in fact, bright scarlet.'[57] The Queen's sense of colour was typically of the period and somewhat shocking to modern-day habits. She wore, for instance, for the big fête given by Louis-Philippe a puce satin dress, black mantilla, yellow bonnet and ribands, with a circle of wild roses in front. She lacked, it is true, any sense of fashion. Lady Canning described her wardrobe as she saw it on the ship going to Ostend:

I waited for her in her room with her collection of gowns hanging round
the walls: they are decidedly very badly chosen, and quite unlike what she
ought to have. Her dresser never ceased sighing and lifting up her hands
and eyes all the time I looked at them, and lamenting how little she cared
about her dress. Some gowns just come from Paris were less fitted for her
use than the rest.[58]

Three days later Lady Canning noted that she was very much distressed that the Queen had not been better dressed on this journey for
all the Belgians had noticed it. 'The Ghent day it was sad, her bonnets
would do for an old woman of seventy and her pink petticoat was
longer than her muslin gown.'[59] On the following day Charlotte
Brontë described the Queen as she drove through Brussels as a 'little,
stout, vivacious lady, very plainly dressed'.[60]

The Queen returned to Woolwich on 21 September. She spent the
autumn months visiting at home. In October she paid her first visit to
Cambridge. Dr Whewell, the Master of Trinity College, was at the time
Vice Chancellor of the university and invited the royal party to stay
at the Master's Lodge. He received her in the manner of the old,
ceremonial universities, meeting her outside the college gates and
delivering to her his Mace. As Master of Trinity, he handed her all his
keys of office, saying that the college was placed at her service. The
Queen was most impressed by the ceremonial aspects not least by the
fact that 'Both in going and returning the scholars threw down their
gowns for us to walk over, like Sir Walter Raleigh.'[61]

On the following day Albert received an honorary degree of Doctor
of Civil Law. Professor Sedgwick accompanied the royal party on a
visit to the Woodwardian Museum. 'The Queen seemed happy and
well pleased, and was mightily taken with one or two of my monsters,
especially with the Pelsiosaurus and gigantic stag.' Neither the Prince
nor the Queen were in a hurry 'and the Queen was quite happy to hear
her husband talk about a novel subject with so much knowledge and
spirit.'[62]

Before returning to Windsor they spent two nights at Wimpole, Lord
Hardwicke's seat – a large comfortable red brick house. Victoria was
godmother to Victor, the eighteen-month-old son of the Hardwickes,
one of their seven children.

At the end of November the Queen publicly acknowledged her
esteem for Peel by visiting him at Drayton Manor, where she stayed
from 28 November to 1 December. She and Albert travelled by rail, in a
comfortable carriage 'all lined and furnished in light blue satin'. The
Queen thought the journey pleasant: 'the train goes along very easily,

though not quite so fast as the Great Western.'[63] Peel's manor was two and a half miles from Tamworth, 'a fine simple house in the plain Elizabethan style'. With a touch of condescension the Queen repeatedly described the house and the various rooms as 'pretty' and 'simple'. The visit sparked off dissatisfaction among the Whigs. They were, Greville noted, 'provoked' and tried hard 'to persuade themselves and others that it is no mark of favour to him and that she is still very fond of them.' None of which signified, for in Greville's opinion, 'she cares really for nobody but her husband. The Tories have got fast hold of him, and through him of her.'[64]

From Drayton the couple went to Chatsworth – where they were received in a much grander manner. Although the Duke of Devonshire would have willingly dispensed with the visit, he treated the Queen royally. He met her at the station and conducted her back in his own coach and six, with a coach and four following and eight outriders. Not only was the house beautiful, with its marble hall and grand staircase, it was also magnificently placed – the wild woods with their waterfalls, the terraces with their fountains, surrounded by fine mountain scenery, enchanted Victoria. As did the cascades and fountains illuminated in the evening.[65] It was as they walked through a rockery in the course of being made that they came upon 'a large conservatory, the most stupendous and extraordinary creation imaginable. Its height is 64 feet and its length 275 and its width 154 feet. The whole is entirely of glass.'[66] The conservatory had been planned by the Duke's gardener Joseph Paxton and was to serve as a model for the Crystal Palace some seven years later.

After three days they left Chatsworth with real regret. The Queen would have liked to stay a day or two longer. But they were expected at Belvoir Castle, where the Duke of Rutland received them. A fox hunt had been organized. 'Albert and Lord Wilton were the whole time with the Hounds,' Victoria wrote proudly, 'though many were unable to keep up.'[67] The pace was tremendous and there had been many falls. Even Greville acknowledged that the Prince 'acquitted himself in the field very creditably'. He was, Greville noted, 'supposed to be a very poor performer in this line, and, as Englishmen love manliness and dexterity in field sports, it will have raised him considerably in public estimation to have rode well after the hounds in Leicestershire.'[68] The Queen herself was conscious of this and wrote:

> One can hardly credit the absurdity of people here, but Albert's riding so boldly and hard has made such a sensation that it has been written all over the country, and they make much more of it than if he had done

some great act! It rather disgusts one, but still it had done, and does, good, for it has put an end to all impertinent sneering for the future about Albert's riding.[69]

These visits to her subjects greatly pleased the Queen and she constantly encouraged invitations from the nobility. Perhaps she wanted to relive the Royal Progresses she had undertaken as Princess under her mother's control, perhaps she simply wanted to share with Albert her knowledge of the great houses of England. She always asked for the list of guests invited to meet her to be submitted beforehand but rarely suggested any changes. Her preference was for meeting new people rather than seeing in each place the same old friends.

In 1844 her journeying was restricted during the first part of the year by mourning. On 29 January Prince Albert's father died and his brother Ernest became Duke of Saxe-Coburg-Gotha. Albert wrote to Stockmar in February to explain that a new epoch had begun in his emotional life. 'My youth, with all the recollections linked with it, has been buried with him around whom they centred.'[70] He prepared to return to his homeland for the first time in four years. Not so much to mourn his father or comfort his grandmother but to sever his links as it were. 'I will, therefore, at once,' he told Stockmar, 'close accounts there, and set about putting the machine into a state in which it may go working on for the future.'[71] His brother he deemed quite incapable of ruling the duchy wisely.

Lady Lyttelton considered the Queen's attitude with regard to his going to Coburg quite exemplary: 'so feeling and so wretched, and yet so unselfish, encouraging him to go and putting the best face upon it to the last moment.'[72]

It was the first time that the couple had been parted since their marriage. Albert wrote to his wife from Dover: 'I have been here about an hour and regret the lost time which I might have spent with you. Poor child! You will, while I write, be getting ready for luncheon and you will find a place vacant where I sat yesterday. . . . thirteen more [days] and I am again within your arms.'[73] Albert's letters have been rather unfairly characterized as cold and distant. There was no lyrical strain in Albert but he thought of his wife continually. 'I cannot go to bed', he wrote from Ostend on 28 March, 'without writing two words more' – despite an unpleasant passage, despite arriving stiff with cold. 'It is now close on eleven, I am sleepy and must therefore conclude. My prayers are with you.'[74] He wrote to tell the Queen when he arrived in Cologne, and again when he crossed the Rhine: 'Six a.m. Just up. . . . The day is fine and about seven I shall cross the Rhine by the bridge of boats. Every step takes me further from you – not a cheerful thought.'[75]

On the thirty-first he reached his destination – immediately he told her: 'I arrived in Gotha safely about two hours since.' He bid her 'Farewell, my darling' and begged her to fortify herself 'with the thought of my speedy return'.[76] From Reinhardsbrunn he sent her flowers – an auricula and a pansy – together with a chronicle of his time there. His letters seem more those of a father than a lover – but that was his way. He could tell her he was 'delighted by your dear letter', or that her 'dear words have done me good, and you need never be afraid that you write too much or too long', but he no doubt considered it more normal to express concern at the fact that she missed him than to say how much he missed her. Only once did he note – when he went to his home at the Rosenau, the visit which undoubtedly touched him most – 'how glad I should be to have my little wife beside me, that I might share my pleasure with her.'

On his return to England he noted in his diary, 'Crossed on the 11th. I arrived at six o'clock in the evening at Windsor. Great joy.' In those two words was a wealth of pent-up emotion.[77]

During the summer travelling was out of the question because the Queen was advanced in her fourth pregnancy. But this did not prevent visitors from elsewhere coming to see her. Rulers came from Russia, Saxony, France and Prussia to do homage to the Queen and, when possible, to obtain political advantage.

On 1 June the King of Saxony and the Tsar Nicholas I of Russia both arrived in England to pay their respects. The former was a family friend and an ideal guest because he went out sightseeing all day, and was enchanted with everything he saw. The latter had suddenly announced his arrival on 30 May – only two days before he arrived! It was his habit to make sudden visits like this. He was a fine-looking man, over six feet tall with regular features, a keen eye and bushy mustachios. He came enveloped in an ample cloth cloak, trimmed with fur, and on his head he wore a turban. The Emperor went to the Russian Embassy, where he took up his abode. On the following day Prince Albert went to collect him and bring him to Buckingham Palace. The Queen gave a great reception at Windsor in honour of her two guests, and also took them to the opera and to the races. She was impressed by the personality and the physique of the Emperor.

He is certainly a very striking man, still very handsome. His profile is beautiful, and his manners most dignified and graceful; extremely civil. The expression of the eyes is severe, and unlike anything I ever saw before. He gives Albert and myself the impression of a man who is not happy, and on whom the burden of his immense power and position weighs heavily and painfully. He seldom smiles, and when he does, the expression is not a happy one. He is very easy to get on with.[78]

Victoria was pleased with the Emperor for he paid compliments to Albert, saying that it was 'impossible to see a better-looking man' and that he had a 'noble' air.[79]

Every evening they held large dinners in the Waterloo Chamber at Windsor. On the last two evenings uniform was worn as the Tsar disliked being in evening dress and was indeed quite embarrassed in it. He told Victoria that without military uniform, 'he felt as if one had skinned him.' His habits had surprised the English Court – he slept on a sack made of leather, stuffed with hay or straw, stretched on a camp-bed. And he persisted in this custom even when he was abroad. He was clearly from a different culture. 'Very clever I do not think him', Victoria told Leopold, 'and his mind is not a cultivated one. His educa-tion has been neglected; politics and military concerns are the only things he takes great interest in. The arts, and all the softer occupa-tions, he does not care for.' She had also found him 'stern and severe with strict principles of duty which nothing on earth will make him change.' She did not doubt his sincerity when he claimed that despot-ism was the only possible mode of government and when he accused his entourage of hiding things from him and changing his policies when they applied them. In fact the Emperor Nicholas, who had succeeded Alexander I in 1825, was noted for the reactionary character of his policy. He repressed all liberal tendencies in Russia and during his reign Warsaw was taken and Poland entirely subdued.

Victoria had feared the constraint and bustle of the visit: 'But by living in the same house together quietly and unrestrainedly (and this Albert, and with great truth, says, is the great advantage of these visits, that I not only *see* these great people, but *know* them), I got to know the Emperor and he to know me.'[80] In the event she had enjoyed it. When the time came to leave, Nicholas I told her with emotion how touched he had been by her kindness to him and added that she could count upon him at all times.

There was, not unexpectedly, a political object in the Tsar's visit to England. He wanted to maintain Russia's traditional policy as it had been formulated in the days of Peter the Great. Turkey was in an impoverished and weakened state and Russia wanted Britain to agree as to who should inherit the Sultan's lands. Emperor Nicholas dis-trusted the cordial relations established between England and France, which might well lead to a restraint on his ambition in the East. France might wish to establish herself in Syria and Egypt for instance. The conversations with Sir Robert Peel and Lord Aberdeen were put in a memorandum drawn up by Count Nesselrode and transmitted to England. The document was put in the secret archives of the Foreign Office but published some ten years later at the time of the Crimean War. The memorandum ran:

> Russia and England are mutually penetrated with the conviction that the Ottoman Porte should maintain itself in the state of independence and of territorial possession which at present constitutes that Empire, as that political combination is the one which is most compatible with the general interest of the maintenance of peace.[81]

Nevertheless the tone of the text gives the clear impression that Russia had the firm intention of attacking Turkey as soon as possible.

On 6 August 1844 – between royal visits – Victoria's fourth child, Prince Alfred, was born.

On the last day of August the Prince of Prussia, later to be the Emperor of Germany, arrived. 'I like him very much. He is extremely amiable, agreeable and sensible; cheerful and easy to get on with.'[82] A friendship began which was to be cemented by four subsequent visits of the Prince to England, in 1848, 1851, 1853, and 1856, and finally by a marriage between the Prince's eldest son and the Queen's eldest daughter.

The Queen had intended to visit Ireland in the autumn of 1844 but the country was in a volatile state because of the agitation for the Repeal of the Union which had been launched by Daniel O'Connell. O'Connell had been drawn into politics through the demand for Roman Catholic emancipation; when emancipation was granted by the Act of 1829 he became a national hero. A Member of Parliament since 1829, he was a great, if somewhat demagogic, orator. A Celt, he referred to the English people as the base, brute and bloody Saxon. In 1843 he declared the year was to be 'the Repeal Year'. Meetings were held and the movement gathered momentum. The Government decided to forbid further meetings and to arrest O'Connell even though he had shown himself against any form of violence or illegality. The movement then broke into two camps. One clung to O'Connell and passive resistance, the other was more militant and determined to rebel at the earliest opportunity. This second group became known as 'Young Ireland'.

O'Connell's trial before a wholly Protestant jury began on 16

January 1844. On 30 May of the same year he was found guilty and condemned to one year's imprisonment, to pay a fine of 2,000 pounds and to give a security of 5,000 pounds for his good behaviour during a term of seven years. O'Connell issued a proclamation to the Irish people commanding them to keep quiet, and sent an appeal to the Lords. They referred the appeal to twelve judges – who could not agree on a series of technical points so that the question went back to the Lords. The decision now rested with four Law Lords. On 4 September 1843, three of them voted that the judgement should be reversed; only Lord Brougham was against. It was undoubtedly wise of the Government to consider that this was no time for a royal visit to Ireland.

In September, therefore, the royal couple set off to Scotland again, where Lord Genlyon had put his house in Perthshire, Blair Athol, at the Queen's disposal. The Court was delighted – at last the mourning for the Duke of Coburg was over and the black ribbons and fans could be discarded before the departure. The Queen was still recovering from Prince Alfred's birth. She would go out in her wheeling chair. 'She is not strong enough yet to see much,' Lady Canning wrote, 'for all the walks here are long and most of them very steep.'[83] The charm of Scotland worked again. The Queen appreciated the quiet life they spent in the Highlands. In her diary she noted that 'independently of the beautiful scenery, there was a quiet, a retirement, a wildness, a liberty and a solitude' about their surroundings.[84] The Prince shared her feelings. On 22 September 1844 he wrote to the Dowager Duchess of Coburg: 'We are all well, and live a somewhat primitive, yet romantic, mountain life, that acts as a tonic to the nerves, and gladdens the heart of a lover, like myself, of field-sports and of Nature.'[85]

No sooner had the royal couple left Blair at the beginning of October than another royal visit began. On 6 October the King of the French landed at Portsmouth. Many French newspapers were against this return visit because of the Tahiti affair. An indigenous princess, Queen Pomaré, reigned at the time over Tahiti, where missionary Protestants had established a certain English influence. They included the British Consul, Pritchard. This influence was counterbalanced by advantages which had been given to the interests of France, in particular the freedom to practise Catholicism. In 1843 Queen Pomaré, pressed by Admiral Dupetit-Thomas, agreed that Tahiti would become a French protectorate. This had been done on the Admiral's initiative but had later been backed by the French Government. The Admiral had then simply annexed Tahiti and removed Queen Pomaré from the throne. The French Government in February 1844 disavowed the Admiral's actions. Meanwhile the British Consul, Pritchard, had been imprisoned on the island for having tried to stir up opposition to the annexation. He was quickly freed and returned immediately to England, complaining of the way he had been treated by the French. In July 1844 the two countries were bordering on war. It took all the coolness of Lord Aberdeen and Guizot to resist the bellicose propaganda of the press on both sides of the Channel. France expressed her regret and offered an indemnity of 25,000 francs to Pritchard, which was in fact never paid.

In October, Louis-Philippe came with the Duke of Montpensier and the Foreign Minister Guizot. They were welcomed at Portsmouth by Prince Albert and the Duke of Wellington. This was the first time a reigning French Sovereign had ever come to Britain on a visit to the monarch. The last time a King of France had set foot on British soil was in 1356, after the Battle of Poitiers, when the Black Prince had brought Jean II back to Windsor as a captive. Louis-Philippe himself, who had lived in England as Duke of Orléans from 1800 to 1807, had last been in England in 1815. When Louis XVIII went to Ghent, he took refuge in England where he remained until the battle of Waterloo enabled him to return to the Palais Royal. He was much moved at his reception by the Queen.

The King's arrival was awaited with all the more curiosity since his daughter Louise, Queen of the Belgians, had sent Victoria a wealth of instructions contained in two long letters. Her father had, for instance, expressed his intention of taking an English breakfast but was unaware of the copious nature of the meal. He must therefore not be given breakfast, and indeed should have no more than two meals a day, one of which should include a bowl of chicken broth. Queen Victoria should not only prevent the King from eating too much, she should also prevent him from riding on horseback 'for my father is naturally so imprudent and so little accustomed to caution and care.' Comfort was not to be a problem. All he required was a hard bed – he generally slept on a horsehair mattress with a plank of wood under it, 'but any kind of bed will do, if it is not too soft' – and a large table on which he could spread his papers.[86] No wonder Lady Canning wrote: 'At two o'clock he arrived, this curious King. Worth seeing if ever body was!' She noted his emotion and his affection for the Queen. 'The old man was much moved, I think, and his hand rather shook as he alighted; his hat quite off, and grey hair seen. His countenance is striking, much better than the portraits, and his embrace of the Queen was very parental and nice.'[87]

At dinner that first evening he 'talked much of England – of having lived here so long, and liked it so much'.[88] He recalled the old revolutionary days when he had been obliged to take refuge under the name of Chabot in Graubunden, in Switzerland, where he taught in a school for twenty pence a day and cleaned his own shoes.[89] 'He is', wrote the Queen, 'an extraordinary man.' He said the French nation did not wish for war even if at times they seemed bellicose. He also told her the French did not understand commerce as the English did, nor the necessity of good faith, which gave Britain such stability. France could never in his opinion declare war on England for she was the Triton of the seas and had the greatest Empire in the world.[90]

During his stay in England Louis-Philippe visited Claremont, Hampton Court and Twickenham, where he had formerly lived. He was invested at Windsor with the Order of the Garter at an unusually magnificent ceremony, followed by a splendid banquet in St George's Hall. He, too, endeared himself to the Queen by praising Albert and showing full appreciation of his qualities and talents. What gratified her most was that he treated Albert completely as his equal, calling him 'My brother!' It did not occur to Victoria that Louis-Philippe, as an heir to the revolution, desperately needed to be seen as their equal.

Louis-Philippe left England on the thirteenth. He had intended to go back by Portsmouth but when he arrived there with Queen Victoria and Albert the sea was too rough and a violent gale was blowing. So he travelled up to London and crossed from Dover to Calais on the following day. He was enchanted by his visit.

The year 1844 was one of the grandest in Queen Victoria's reign. In August 1845 the Queen set off on what was to be for her probably the most moving of all her foreign trips. The couple had been married for five and a half years and she was at last to see the Thüringen valley of her husband's youth. They planned to go to Coburg by way of Belgium and Prussia. She was to be absent for a month. This time the question of providing a regency in her absence was not raised. The party consisted of Lord Aberdeen, Lord Liverpool, Lady Canning and Lady Gainsborough, who had the advantage in Albert's eyes that they had already travelled with the royal couple and lived with them in Scotland. The only aim of the visit was to have an opportunity of seeing the neighbourhood and the family. 'If strangers wish to come,' Albert insisted, 'don't encourage them to remain. They would only wish to watch us.'[91]

As Victoria prepared to leave on 8 August, both Vicky and Alice were with her while she dressed. 'Why am I not going to Germany?' asked the eldest. 'Most willingly would I have taken her,' noted the

Queen in her journal, 'and wished much to have taken one of dearest Albert's children to Coburg; but the journey is a serious undertaking particularly the first time, and she is very young too; but what chiefly decides us is a visit to the King of Prussia, where I could not have looked after her.'[92]

The royal yacht had been especially prepared. The inside woodwork was painted like a sort of satin wood, a very pale oak; the bridges and the galleries between the paddleboxes had been widened and the cabins ventilated. The King and Queen of the Belgians met them at Malines and escorted them to Vervier. At the Prussian frontier they were met by the Chevalier Bunsen. Then at Aix la Chapelle they found the King of Prussia and his brother Prince William. The Queen found it very 'singular' to hear German spoken and was amused to hear people say she looked 'very English'.[93] From there they went to Cologne, then to the station at Bruhl. They went by rail to Bonn and there Albert took Victoria to the little house where he had lived as a student.

But there were official visits, too. A grand banquet was given at the Palace and the King of Prussia made a remarkable speech in which he said:

> Gentlemen, fill your glasses! There is a word of inexpressible sweetness to British as well as to German hearts. Thirty years ago it echoed on the heights of Waterloo from British and German tongues, after days of hot and desperate fighting, to mark the glorious triumph of our brotherhood in arms. Now it resounds on the banks of our fair Rhine, amid the blessings of that peace which was the hallowed fruit of the great conflict. That word is *Victoria!*[94]

His Majesty then drank to the health of the Queen and Prince Albert. The Queen was greatly affected. She turned towards the King and kissed his cheek. Albert, too, was deeply affected. The speech brought, as he told Stockmar, a lump to his throat and from that time forward he believed that Prussia should take the lead in German unity.

Although the Queen was well received the question of German treatment of the Prince rankled. To Victoria's annoyance, Archduke Frederick of Austria, the uncle of the Emperor of Austria, claimed and was given precedence over the Prince in the King of Prussia's palace. For a long time she was reluctant to accept further offers of hospitality from the Prussian Court. Her opinion of her royal hosts was ambivalent: 'The Queen is an amiable natural person, but a little ultra in her politics. The King, amiable and amusing in the highest degree, acts chiefly from impulse but is not so ultra.'[95]

The final destination was Coburg. On 18 August they arrived.

Ernest, Duke of Coburg, was there in full uniform to welcome them. Indeed the whole population turned out to meet her. There were dense masses all along the road between the frontiers and the town. The people poured in in crowds from the surrounding countryside into the town. The journey was a veritable pilgrimage. 'I cannot say how much I felt moved on entering this dear old place,' the Queen noted, 'and with difficulty I restrained my emotion.'[96] On the following day they went to the country house of the Rosenau, Albert's birthplace. 'If I were not who I am,' wrote the Queen, '*this* would have been my real home, but I shall always consider it my second one.' Before breakfast they went upstairs, 'where he and Ernest used to live, which is quite in the roof, with a tiny bedroom on each side, in one of which they both used to sleep. The view is beautiful. The paper of the room is still full of holes from their fencing, and the same table is there on which they were dressed when little.'[97]

After spending the Prince's birthday – 26 August – at the Rosenau the royal pair returned to Reinhardsbrunn then on to Gotha. Here she saw 'my dear good Lehzen, who arrived this afternoon and whom we both received in our room. She remained only a little while with me. I found her unchanged only grown much quieter, and it made me very happy to see her again.' Lehzen came again on the following day 'for a little while before dressing'.[98] On 30 August there was an excursion to the Thüringen Forest. Here a great *battue* of game was organized. It was not at all to the English taste. Although it was called a 'deer hunt', it accorded little with an Englishman's idea of sport.

> Three hundred men besides had been employed beating the woods for ten days to drive the deer to this spot and to enclose them in about a quarter of a mile of wood walled round with canvas; this was divided into two parts. We walked across part of it to a little temple built of fir and heather; the poor stags were still in the other division of the enclosure and the shooters were stationed in different little turf foots, four or five guns together. Then a signal was given and an army of *chasseurs* instantly threw down the canvas wall between the two halves and about fifty stags and hinds rushed in. . . . Then everybody fired at the poor things who were driven in and out of the wood and up and down the hill till all were killed – it was a piteous sight, much the worse from the bad shooting, for most of the poor beasts were dreadfully wounded long before they were killed.[99]

The slaughter was carried on for two hours without a break. By the end, fifty-five animals, thirty-one of them stags, were stretched dead or wounded on the turf. Even the Queen was critical: 'I cannot say that this sort of sport is to my liking and it seems to me that it is hardly *real* sport. . . . even the Gentlemen, none of them a sportsman's point of view, care for what really amounts to a kind of slaughter.'[100] In England the *battue* did little for Prince Albert's image. Anson complained to Melbourne that *Punch* was at the head of a campaign to denigrate the Prince, followed by the *Chronicle* and even *The Times*, and that the aristocracy called him a haughty foreigner despite his efforts to do good in his adopted country.[101]

On 3 September 1845 the Queen and the Prince set off homewards. The journey to Antwerp took four days. Instead of returning immediately to England, the royal party paid Louis-Philippe a flying visit at Le Tréport. The King spent a day showing the couple the new additions to his house – his new Victoria gallery, containing pictures illustrating both Victoria's former visit to France and the King's own visit to Windsor, his park and his fish ponds. The King of the French and Queen Victoria also talked politics, while Prince Albert was out with the Duke of Joinville visiting a yacht. 'The King', Queen Victoria recorded in her journal, 'told Lord Aberdeen as well as me, he never would hear of Montpensier's marriage with the Infanta of Spain (which they are in a great fright about in England) until it was no longer a political question, which would be when the Queen is married and has children. This is very satisfactory.'[102] Lord Aberdeen was greatly satisfied, the Prince was less enthusiastic. No one imagined that within a year Montpensier and the Infanta would be wed.

14

A Neutral Crown?

The summer of 1845 had been cold and wet and the grain harvest was poor. The autumn in Britain had been wetter than any in living memory. More disturbing still, a potato disease which had originated in America in 1844 had spread to the British Isles. In Ireland, where the potato was the staple food, it was a social calamity. Experts sent reports that at least half the Irish potato crop was ruined by the new blight. A commission set up in Dublin to collect accurate information on the extent of the deficiency declared 'that in 4 electoral divisions nine-tenths of the crop had been destroyed; in 93 between seven- and eight-tenths; in 125, seven-tenths; in 16, six-tenths; in 596, practically one-half of the crop; and in 582 divisions, four-tenths . . . '[1] They also said that the harvest would probably be affected in the following year as well. Three to four million Irish peasants could not survive unless something was done. The British Government was well aware of the political implications, as Albert told his brother: 'It is impossible to argue with famished people.'[2]

The Anti-Corn Law League in England demanded the opening of the ports for the free entry of grain. The first five years of Victoria's reign had been years of economic depression, with bad harvests and widespread unemployment. The depression had fostered not only an increasing demand for all to be able to play a part in the democratic process – Chartism – but also agitation against the Corn Laws. Since 1815 the Corn Laws had graduated the tariff on the importation of foreign grain. To maintain the price of domestic grain, high tariffs were applied to foreign grain – which would have been cheaper – so that it was sold at the same price as domestic corn.

Until the 1840s British farmers still produced enough to feed the workers in the new towns and factories. But as the population increased and became more and more concentrated in the towns, it became necessary to develop international trade to compensate for the loss of agriculture. The system gave the landed interest a monopoly of the home market and landlords undoubtedly profited greatly. But the landlords' interest was contrary both to that of the consumer and to that of the industrial class generally. The Anti-Corn Law Association was set up in Manchester in 1838 by seven men determined to use every legal means possible to bring about the repeal of the Corn Laws. It was an exemplary pressure group. First it succeeded at an early stage in recruiting to its ranks Richard Cobden and John Bright – both of whom were well known. Then it campaigned by sending out addresses and other publications to the people at large. Lectures were given throughout the major manufacturing towns to show how unjust the Corn Laws were. Its leaders were complementary. Richard Cobden, the son of a yeoman farmer and a partner in a Manchester cotton factory, was a man of the people; Charles Villiers, the head of the movement in Parliament, was an aristocrat by birth and connections; John Bright was an orator of remarkable gifts. All three were radicals with no party tie. All three were totally disinterested. Their aim was to eliminate hunger, to provide cheap food for the masses. There was no talk of class warfare.

The movement rapidly gained strength in the early 1840s. Greville noted in his journal in 1843 that the Corn Laws and the question of the condition of England were in everybody's minds. 'Newspapers', he wrote, 'are full of letters and complaints on these subjects.'[3] It was, however, the Irish famine that was to give urgency to the Anti-Corn Law League's demands.

By October 1845 Peel was already disquieted and on 13 October he wrote to Sir James Graham, the Home Secretary. He explained that accounts of the state of the potato crop in Ireland were becoming very alarming; reports from Ireland were, however, often exaggerated and inaccurate so it was best to delay acting upon them immediately; if, however, the accounts were verified then some means of relief must be found. 'The removal of impediments to import', wrote Peel, 'is the only effectual remedy.'[4] On 31 October the Cabinet met at Robert Peel's house. Peel advised that Parliament should be assembled before Christmas and said that he believed that before Parliament was summoned the Cabinet should 'make its choices between determined maintenance, modification, and suspension of the existing Corn Laws'.[5] He himself came down clearly in favour of suspension but the Cabinet was deeply divided.

The Cabinet was therefore adjourned until 6 November without a decision being taken. On that day Peel proposed to give notice of a Bill after Christmas to modify the Corn Laws. Only three of his colleagues – Aberdeen, Graham and Sidney Herbert – supported him. This time Peel was determined either to see his point of view prevail or to resign, thus abdicating power at a moment when he was at the height of a very prosperous career. The Queen had, of course, been informed by her Prime Minister of his difficulties. Writing from Windsor on 5 November she invited Peel to spend the night at Windsor if the Cabinet was over in time, and if not to come on the following morning.

No firm conclusion was reached at this meeting and on the eve of the next Cabinet meeting Peel told the Queen that before they asked her to convene Parliament it was necessary to be sure that the Cabinet was completely agreed as to the emergency measures required. He added that, 'to such measures, if adopted, there ought to be a reference in Your Majesty's speech from the Throne.'[6] However, Peel warned the Queen that he feared there might be serious differences of opinion on the repeal of the Corn Laws. The Queen's reply, on 28 November, was even more supportive:

> The Queen is very sorry to hear that Sir Robert apprehends further differences of opinion in the Cabinet. . . . The Queen thinks the time is come when a removal of the restrictions upon the importation of food cannot be successfully resisted. Should this be Sir Robert's own opinion, the Queen very much hopes that none of his colleagues will prevent him from doing what it is right to do.[7]

But again the Cabinet separated without reaching a decision. Meanwhile on 22 November Lord John Russell, the Whig leader, issued a 'letter to the Electors of the City of London' announcing that he had been converted to the advocacy of total repeal. *The Times* published the letter on 27 November. The newspaper also contained an attack on the Government for failing in its duties to Queen and country, and declared the paper in favour of total repeal of the Corn Laws.

On 4 December, just before the crucial Cabinet meeting, *The Times* published a leading article beginning: 'The doom of the Corn Laws is sealed.' It disclosed that Peel had decided on the repeal of the Corn Laws. There were those, however, who didn't believe it was possible for a Cabinet secret to be leaked. The *Standard*, for instance, published an emphatic contradiction of the story on 5 December under the head-line: 'Atrocious fabrication by *The Times*: The Cabinet has come to no decision whatever upon the subject of the Corn Laws.' On the same day, after yet another inconclusive meeting, Sir Robert Peel decided he could serve the Queen better in a private rather than in a public capacity and went to see her at Osborne on the Isle of Wight to tender his resignation. Prince Albert wrote of Peel's arrival at Osborne: 'he was visibly much moved and said to me that it was one of the most painful moments of his life, to separate himself from us.'[8] In his letter of resignation Peel expressed belief that the only solution to the economic crisis was the total repeal of the Corn Laws.[9] He expressed his regret at having to leave the Queen's service and went on to say that one of the greatest pleasures he had had in official life was the frequent opportunity afforded him of witnessing Her Majesty's 'domestic happiness' and rejoicing in the influence of her 'virtuous example'. He also thanked the Queen for the generous support he had received from the Prince and herself.[10]

In fact, although the Queen had become attached to Peel, his real admirer was Albert. After having berated the Queen for being a partisan of Melbourne's he had formed a much stronger and no less partisan attachment to Peel. Having tried to force the Queen to stop writing to Melbourne, Albert was to entertain his own, more political, correspondence with Peel at a time of crisis. The Queen had accepted Peel's resignation and called on Lord John Russell to form a Whig Government. Albert kept Peel informed of every step of the Queen's negotiations with the Whig leader – Peel's prime political opponent. He told Peel that Lord John was consulting with his colleagues and that everything depended on the line taken by Lord Lansdowne, the veteran Whig leader. He noted that Lord John was afraid of not having a majority in the House of Commons and equally afraid of the House of Lords, and that he had asked 'whether the Protection party, which had the majority, could not form a Government: but agreed with us that the experiment would be highly dangerous.'[11]

There was between Peel and the Prince Consort an affinity of temperament. Albert had from the first appreciated in Peel what his party reproached him with – his independence. Anson wrote: 'Sir Robert Peel was determined to adopt his own line, and not to be turned aside by the fear of making political enemies, or losing support. He was determined either to stand or fall by his own opinion; and the Prince felt that in such a man's hands the interests of the Crown were most secure.'[12] Peel's administration had exercised less patronage than his predecessors and had brought lasting reforms in many areas. It was this reforming zeal which pleased Prince Albert. Despite the principle of political neutrality which the Prince held necessary for a constitu-

tional monarch, he favoured and supported Peel openly. Albert, as
Peel, underestimated the importance of parties for the healthy development of political life.

The Prince was for Peel the intermediary with whose help he had
gained the confidence and support of the Queen, and Peel was to be
the intermediary who gave Albert further entry into the counsels of
the Queen. Greville noted how much things had changed: when Lord
Lansdowne and Lord John Russell went to Windsor on 16 December
1845 the first novelty that struck them was the manner of their
reception.

> Formerly the Queen received her Ministers alone; with her alone they
> communicated, though of course Prince Albert knew everything; but
> now the Queen and Prince were together, received Lord Lansdowne and
> John Russell together, and both of them always said *We* – "We think,
> or wish, to do so and so; what had *we* better do etc.". The Prince is
> become so identified with the Queen that they are one person, and as
> he likes business, it is obvious that while she has the title he is really
> discharging the functions of the Sovereign. He is King to all intents and
> purposes.[13]

At times the Queen still hankered after the advice of Melbourne.
When she had first sent for Russell he was in Edinburgh and only
arrived in Windsor on the eleventh. In the meantime Victoria asked
Melbourne to come and give her advice, but he pleaded failing health
and in fact wisely refused to interfere. On 13 December the Queen
saw Lord John Russell again at Windsor, this time accompanied by
Lord Lansdowne. He asked the Queen whether, if he undertook to
repeal the Corn Laws, she would secure for him the full support of
Peel and his followers. Peel had already told the Queen that he would
support 'in a private capacity' any Whig proposal for gradual repeal of
the Corn Laws.[14]

The long suspense that had prevailed since Peel had resigned came
to an end on 18 December, when the Queen informed Sir Robert that
Lord John Russell had finally, after his consultations, accepted office.
In a sense Peel was not sorry to lay down what he considered the
burden of government. He wrote to a friend – Sir Thomas Freemantle –
on the day after Lord John's acceptance, declaring: 'on every personal
and private ground I rejoice at being released from the thankless and
dangerous post of having the responsibility of public affairs.' He was
referring no doubt to the continual criticism of the press, and above all
to the death of his secretary, Edward Drummond, who had been shot in

the back while walking in Whitehall and died four days later. The murderer was Daniel McNaughten, a mechanic from Glasgow, and his target had been Peel himself – McNaughten believed he had been persecuted by the Conservatives in Glasgow. Peel, and the Queen, thought McNaughten should be hanged but he was acquitted of murder on the grounds of insanity, on the basis of what became the 'McNaughten rules'.

Where his public role was concerned, Peel declared he had had enough of being expected to 'conform not to [his] sense of the public necessities, but to certain party doctrines, to be blindly followed, whatever new circumstances may arise, or whatever be the information which a Government may receive.'[15] Peel had originally been a party man and had played a considerable role in welding the Conservatives into a party – united on certain issues. He it was who had first had the idea of a mandate, when in 1834 he produced the first programme to be given to electors before they voted – the Tamworth Manifesto. Age and responsibility had made him more autocratic. He now believed that he should be allowed to lead as he wished and that his party should follow in his footsteps.

Peel had in fact used the Irish famine as a pretext for his pressure for the repeal of the Corn Laws. Repeal could do little for the Irish. Ireland was not equipped to deal with corn – there were few mills and few millers – since the staple food was potatoes. Peel's desire for repeal was more deeply rooted. After the 1845 tariff changes, corn was the only primary product having a high degree of protection. By maintaining the Corn Laws the Government was lending credibility to the arguments of the League that they were continued only because the class which benefited from them had a monopoly power over government and legislation. Peel believed that the prosperity of British agriculture depended not on high tariffs – which were an artificial prop – but on the introduction of more modern methods and scientific farming. Even before the ministerial crisis, he had told Prince Albert that he had intended to announce his conversion to Parliament and seek support for it before the general election of 1847. He told Sir Thomas Freemantle: 'Whatever country squires may think, it is not safe to guarantee the continuance of the present Corn Laws.'[16] Walter Bagehot, writing on the character of Sir Robert Peel, said that Peel was as 'afraid of catching revolution as old women are of catching cold'.[17] It may well be that Peel's decision was timely and may have contributed to the peaceful state of Britain in 1848 when revolution spread through Europe.

When Lord John Russell tried to form his Government, he found that the Whigs were doubtful as to whether it was in their interests to form a Government committed to an alteration in the Corn Laws in the face of such powerful opposition in Parliament and in the country. After eleven days of fruitless negotiation, Lord John announced on 19 December that he was obliged to abandon any idea of forming a Government because one of his prominent followers had refused to support him. It was later discovered that the follower in question was Lord Grey, and the reason had nothing to do with the Corn Laws. He simply refused to join any Cabinet in which Lord Palmerston was again to be Foreign Secretary. He also demanded a place in the Cabinet for Richard Cobden, one of the leaders of the Corn League. Russell, who had never been over-eager to be Prime Minister in such circumstances, declared he could not carry the repeal through Parliament with a weak Cabinet. His decision was probably sensible, though it is difficult to see why he took such a long time reaching it. The Whigs were, after all, in a minority in the Commons, where they could only count on ninety to a hundred votes, and they had a strong majority against them in the Lords.

On the morning of 20 December the Queen summoned Sir Robert Peel to Windsor and asked him to withdraw his resignation. Forgetting his reservations about the trials of office, Peel accepted with alacrity. He told the Queen he needed no time for reflection and would of course stand by the Queen in her difficulty. Queen Victoria was full of 'extreme admiration in our worthy Peel, who shows himself a man of unbounded loyalty, courage, patriotism and high-mindedness'; his conduct towards her was 'chivalrous almost'; never had she seen him 'so excited and determined'.[18]

The ministerial crisis of 1845–6 had shown that the personal influence of the Queen in domestic politics might be beneficial to her subjects. Such was the view of the *Examiner*, one of the most radical newspapers in the country – a journal not noted for its support of the Crown. On 27 December 1845 the paper published an article praising the role played by the constitutional monarch.

> In the pages of history the directness, the sincerity, the scrupulous observance of Constitutional rule, which have marked Her Majesty's conduct in circumstances the most trying, will have their place of honour. However unused as we are to deal in homage to Royalty, we must add that never, we believe, was the heart of a monarch so warmly devoted to the interests of a people, and with so enlightened a sense of their interests.[19]

The behaviour of the Queen thus did a great deal to restore the influence of the Crown by showing she was above the struggles between factions. Albert was delighted with the outcome. He wrote to his stepmother: 'We are glad in soul that we have survived the ministerial crisis and are now standing exactly where we stood before – upon our feet – whereas during the crisis, we were very nearly standing on our heads.'[20] He told Stockmar more explicitly that the crisis had been a source of real advantage to the Crown.[21]

Peel returned to Downing Street. 'I resume power', he wrote to Princess Lieven, 'with greater means of rendering public service than I should have had if I had not relinquished it. But it is a strange dream. I feel like a man restored to life after his funeral service had been preached.'[22] He summoned his late Cabinet colleagues to tell them he had resumed office and to ask for their help in abolishing the duties on foreign corn. Only Lord Stanley refused – he believed it was in the interest of Britain to have a strong rural population under a landed aristocracy. He was replaced at the Colonial Office by William Gladstone. The Duke of Buccleuch decided, on the contrary, that in the new circumstances he could return to the Cabinet. 'Recent events', he told the Prime Minister, 'have rendered the measure proposed by you one of necessity, and no longer one of expediency.'[23]

On 19 January 1846 the Queen opened what was to be one of the most crucial Parliaments of her reign. Prince Albert accompanied her in his uniform of Field Marshal, wearing the Orders of the Garter and the Golden Fleece. The atmosphere was one of expectation. Since 1841 the speech from the throne had been acknowledged to be the words of the Prime Minister delivered by the Sovereign, and everyone wondered how far Peel would go. They were not disappointed. The Queen laid down, in scarcely veiled terms, a startling project of legislation. She declared that in the past she had given her assent to measures calculated to extend commerce and stimulate domestic skill and industry by the repeal and relaxation of duties. Prosperity had resulted from these measures and was a strong testimony in favour of the policy pursued. She went on to say: 'I recommend you to take into your early consideration, whether the principles on which you have acted may not with advantage be more extensively applied.'[24]

Although she had not pronounced the word 'corn', in the debate that followed both Houses acrimoniously debated the repeal of the Corn Laws. In the best tradition of the English constitution, the carefully guarded words of the Prime Minister were read by the Queen and gave rise to a fundamental debate on an issue which was to revolutionize the commercial policy of the country and to cause the rise of the commercial classes at the expense of the landed. Peel had not asked for a general election to secure a majority for repeal and there were many who felt that he should have consulted the electorate before recommending the repeal of the Corn Laws he had himself promised to uphold. But he was determined to create a majority within the House of Commons, even if more members of the Opposition than of the Conservatives voted in favour. Peel's argument was simple. It was the responsibility of the two Houses to decide matters of policy and not that of the electorate. A general election dominated by the question of repeal would, in Peel's opinion, have produced a House of Commons lacking in independence, because it was tied by pledges.

But Peel had not only not sought an election, he had not even sought to inform his party of his intentions. When the debate began there was still a question on everyone's lips: how far would Peel go? Would he simply reduce duties in line with the eight-year timetable for gradual repeal he had originally envisaged; or would he go for a much quicker repeal in order to settle the question? It was only when Peel stood up and addressed the House that his followers knew his decision: he proposed a rapid lowering of duties over the next three years, 1846–9, after which a nominal duty of one shilling per quarter would be levied. In compensation he offered various forms of relief for country rates and loans to agriculture. His plan concerned many foodstuffs, including sugar, cheese, butter and dried fish. But the only subject discussed was corn.

Peel explained his point of view, his change of heart, in one of the greatest speeches of his life. He took an almost unprecedented course, rising immediately after the speeches of the mover and seconder of the Address. He did not enter into details of the measure foreshadowed in the Queen's speech but removed all shadow of doubt as to his determination to repeal the Corn Laws totally. When he sat down there was an absence of cheering from those behind him. But the Queen wrote: 'the Queen must congratulate Sir Robert Peel on his beautiful and indeed unanswerable speech of last night which we have been reading with the greatest attention.'

Over the years leading up to the repeal of the Corn Laws, the Conservative party had become seriously split and the activities of Bentinck and Disraeli have been blamed. But they merely articulated within it the complaints and resentment against Peel. In 1841 he had formed an administration which was one of the strongest of the century, with a comfortable majority of eighty seats. The year 1843 saw the creation of the Young England group by four romantic Tories. The group was informally led by Disraeli. Although it presented no numerical threat, it was a good example of the increased questioning of the leadership among Conservative backbenchers. In 1844 Peel had to face two major revolts in his own party. First over the Government's Factory Bill, which proposed to limit the hours of work of children in textile mills to no more than six hours a day. Some Members of Parliament wanted to take advantage of the Bill to reduce the working hours of women and young persons to ten hours a day. An amendment was moved by Ashley and carried, with ninety-five Conservatives voting in favour. Peel was against the amendment and withdrew the Bill.

The second revolt was over the Government's proposed revision of the tariff on imported sugar. The problem was complicated by the desire to tax foreign sugar grown by slave labour more heavily than foreign sugar produced by free labour. On 14 June Philip Miles, Member for Bristol and a representative of the West Indian interest, proposed an amendment aimed at destroying the Bill. It was carried by twenty votes, with support from sixty-two Conservatives. Three days later Peel risked the life of his Government by insisting on a reversal of this vote. Everyone thought that the Government would be defeated and the Queen therefore rejoiced when Peel won the day.

Peel's attitudes inevitably meant that there was a certain bitterness about his leadership. *The Times* on 17 June 1844, the morning after the reversal of the sugar vote, underlined Peel's remoteness from his party. Towards the end of 1845 the enemies of the repeal of the Corn Laws stepped up their activity. In December the Central Protection Society met in London and decided to drop its rule of non-intervention in parliamentary elections and called on its members to bring pressure to bear on their local Members. Protectionist meetings were held all over the country to promote petitions to Parliament and exact pledges from constituency Members of Parliament against repeal. Members who said they were willing to support Peel were in many cases told by constituents or patrons they should resign.[25]

Finally came the Queen's Speech and Peel's oration on repeal. On 27 January 1846 Peel's resolutions embodying his financial policy came before the House. Prince Albert was in the gallery. Lord George Bentinck publicly accused the Prince during the debate of being

> seduced by the First Minister of the Crown to come down to this House to usher in, to give éclat, and, as it were, by reflection from the Queen, to give the semblance of a personal sanction of Her Majesty to a measure

which, be it for good or evil, a great majority at least of the landed aristocracy of England, of Scotland and of Ireland, imagine fraught with deep injury, if not ruin to them.

Albert's presence in the gallery led to a questioning of the Crown's constitutional impartiality. It contradicted the conventional wisdom that grew up later and states that the fact that today 'the Crown is dissociated from party and above party is Prince Albert's contribution to British politics.'[26] The Queen thought it scandalous for her husband to be criticized by 'gentlemen who did nothing but hunt all day, drink Claret or Port Wine in the evening and never studied or read about any of these questions.'[27] But the Queen may well have told her husband how unwise he had been – for he never went to the House of Commons again.

Peel underestimated the hostility he would meet from his own back-benchers. Over a hundred backbenchers spoke against their leader during the debate on the second reading (9–27 February). The extent and vigour of the attacks launched against him took him by surprise. The effect on Peel was to make him rise above party and make a direct appeal for repeal and free trade. At the end of his speech on the second reading he said: 'When I do fall, I shall have the satisfaction of reflect-ing that I do not fall because I have shown subservience to a party. I shall not fall because I preferred the interests of party to the general interests of the community.'[28] Disraeli denounced Peel's speech as a 'glorious example of egotistical rhetoric' and a 'gross betrayal of party principles'.

On 27 February, 231 voted for repeal. The second reading of the Bill passed with a majority of ninety-seven, thanks to the Opposition. The vigour of Peel's opponents caused the battle between protectionists and free traders to drag on for five months. The arguments against Peel ranged from contestation of the economic principle, to the increased charges on the Treasury from the inadequacy of the compensation offered to agriculture, to the charge of capitulation to the Anti-Corn Law League. The Bill finally passed the Commons in the early hours of 16 May by a majority of ninety-eight. It was not until 28 June that the Bill passed its third reading in the Lords. Only the Queen's assent was now necessary for it to become law.

That same night, in the Commons, Peel was defeated on a Bill con-ferring extraordinary powers on the executive in Ireland. Bills such as this had been introduced by successive Governments and were known as Coercion Bills for short. Peel was defeated by an amalgamation of the regular Opposition plus the Irish Catholics plus the protectionists.

The Duke of Wellington was in favour of dissolution. Cobden expressed the same idea and claimed that the confidence the middle classes had in Peel's policy would ensure him a working majority. Peel, however, once again refused to envisage an election. He thought that to dissolve on a Coercion Bill for Ireland would 'shake the foundations of the legal union' and ensure 'a worse return of Irish members, rendered more desperate, more determined to obstruct by every artifice, the passing of a Coercion Bill in the new Parliament.'[29] In a memorandum to the Duke of Wellington, Peel declared: 'The hope of getting a stronger majority is no justification for a dissolution.'[30]

That Peel did not wish to dissolve on the Coercion Bill can be easily understood. He had worked during his term of office to maintain the union with Ireland by conciliating the Roman Catholic majority. He now believed it was necessary to act 'in a spirit of kindliness, forbearance and generosity'.[31] He had elaborated plans for offering better education at university level for Irish Catholics and for endowing the Maynooth training college for priests. The provision of this higher education for the Roman Catholic majority, laity and priests, led to the resignation from the Cabinet of Gladstone – who had once written a book attacking the principle of subsidizing Papists – and to a veritable anti-Peel campaign from the Anglican ultras. Peel's proposals took effect, but the uproar against them revealed the depth of anti-Catholic feeling in Britain. The Queen had been entirely on Peel's side and had encouraged him to persist despite the opposition from within his own party. 'It is not honourable to Protestantism', she wrote, 'to see the bad and violent and bigoted passions displayed at this moment.' The measures were, in her opinion, wise and tolerant and she did not understand Gladstone. In any case his speech of resignation she found 'very unintelligible'. No wonder that Peel did not want the central issue of an election campaign to be not solving the Irish problem but repressing revolt in Ireland.

From the Treasury Bench he watched the protectionists go into the Opposition lobby. There was no doubt that the issue was the Corn Laws and not coercion in Ireland. At the very last meeting of the Cabinet, Peel said he was convinced that 'the formation of a Conservative Party was impossible while he continued in office.' He had made up his mind to resign and strongly advised the resignation of the entire Government. Some declared their assent. None objected and 'when he asked whether it was unanimous, there was no voice in the negative'.[32]

Three days later Peel tendered his resignation to the Queen. She had, Gladstone said, put a good face on it for she had more experience and judgement now. In his resignation speech Peel generously said that the name which ought to be, and would be associated with the repeal of the Corn Laws was that of Richard Cobden and he praised Cobden for his pure and disinterested motives. Lord Stanley and Gladstone thought Peel had gone too far. Cobden had, after all, held up 'the landholders of England to the people as plunderers.'[33] Aberdeen, too, regretted the tone of that part of the speech. Even Prince Albert thought it would have been better if Peel had not praised Cobden.[34]

On leaving office Sir Robert Peel retired to his country seat at Drayton. One of the first to write to him there was Queen Victoria, 'expressing her deep concern at losing his services, which she regrets as much for the country as for herself and the Prince.' She added that, 'In whatever position Sir Robert Peel may be, we shall ever look on him as a kind and true friend.'[35] Writing from Drayton on 24 July Peel thanked the Queen for her support and confidence. He reminded the Queen of her promise to give him a portrait of herself and the Prince. He hoped they would be 'in that simple attire in which when he has had the frequent happiness of being admitted to your private society' he had seen them.[36] He also asked for the Prince of Wales – 'born very shortly after Sir Robert Peel entered into Your Majesty's service' – to be included in the portrait.

Aberdeen told Gladstone that Peel had made up his mind never again to lead the Conservative party, never again to accept an office. He had, he said, made up his mind to quit Parliament, but that 'probably on the Queen's account and in deference to her wishes he had abandoned this part of his intentions.'[37] Gladstone thought this position untenable. 'The country will demand that they who are the ablest shall not stand by inactive,' he told James Graham on 10 July.[38]

Peel himself was not sad. He told Gladstone he had been twice Prime Minister and nothing could induce him again to take part in the formation of a Government: 'the labour and anxiety were too great.' He detailed the immense accumulation of duties: correspondence with the Queen, several times a day 'and all requiring to be in my own hand and to be carefully done'; correspondence with peers and Members of Parliament, also necessarily in his own hand; seven or eight hours in the House of Commons 'to listen to such trash'; 'seeing what the various departments are doing and all the questions connected with them.'[39]

The paradox of Peel was put in a nutshell by Greville.

Successful to the uttermost of general expectation; personally he vanquished the dislike of the Queen and ingratiated himself entirely with her. He terminated dangerous contests and embarrassing disputes, he restored peace, he put the finances in good order. It would be difficult to point out any failure he suffered, and easy to show that no Minister ever had to boast of four more prosperous years or more replete with public advantage and improvement.... At the end of all this triumph, popularity, prosperity, and power is a voluntary fall, a resignation of office in the midst of such a storm of rage, abuse and hatred as no other Minister was ever exposed to.[40]

Peel was undoubtedly a pragmatist, changing his political position as the circumstances changed. This led, as always in politics, to the charge of inconsistency, even of betrayal. His one great error, no doubt, was to believe that political parties were not of great importance and that a Prime Minister could act from what can only be described as an extra-party position. But the nineteenth century was not the eighteenth and the widening of the suffrage had already begun to solidify the party structure. Disraeli attacked Peel from another point of view. He claimed that Peel 'traded on the ideas and intelligence of others. His life has been one great appropriation clause. He is a burglar of others' intellect.... there is no statesman who had committed political petty larceny on so great a scale.'[41]

Walter Bagehot, on the other hand, chose Sir Robert Peel as the prototype of a constitutional statesman, defined as 'in general a man of common opinions and uncommon abilities'. He had, claimed Bagehot, 'the powers of a first-rate man and the creed of a second-rate man'. He was never in advance of his times and showed no originality. 'Of almost all the great measures with which his name is associated, he attained great eminence as an opponent before he attained even greater eminence as their advocate.... He was converted at the conversion of the average man.' For Bagehot, Peel's genius lay in his capacity as an administrator not as a creator. He condemned him as 'a business gentleman' as opposed to the 'profound thinker'.[42]

This has the tone of a class judgement and class judgements abounded where Peel was concerned. But with hindsight it remains, as G. Kitson Clark has shown, Peel's inability to take his party along with him which was his real defect. Had he had a warmer, less righteous personality he might have communicated his convictions. As it was, he never even tried. He believed that he was perfectly free to act as he thought good: 'it was a belief which sprang from the old orthodox view of the senatorial function of a statesman and was echoed in the objection which many Conservatives still entertained to men giving specific pledges to constituents.'[43] But this was no longer the orthodoxy even of the Conservative party; and economic Conservatism was even more centred on party than political Conservatism. In rejecting the political party, Peel rejected the most important channel for change, and because of this his brilliant political career came to an end.

After some hesitation he did, however, remain in Parliament until his death. In July 1850, he was thrown from his horse as he was riding up Constitution Hill and died after three days of agony. As Aberdeen noted, grief was universal. The rich and the poor, the high and the low, the Queen and the common labourer, in England and abroad, all mourned him. 'The death of Robert Peel', Guizot wrote to Aberdeen, 'makes me grieve deeply for you and for myself. We three have for five years carried out sensible honest policies.'[44]

The Queen wrote to King Leopold that Peel was a great loss to her and that her husband 'felt and feels Sir Robert's loss dreadfully. He feels he has lost a second father.'[45] The Queen had proposed to confer a distinction on Lady Peel but Lady Peel refused, saying she wished to bear no other name than that by which her late husband had been known and honoured, and that in addition he had left behind a record of his wish that no member of his family should receive any public award for any public service he had rendered to his country. It was therefore decided by the House of Commons to follow the precedent set on the death of the Earl of Chatham and to erect a monument to his memory in the collegiate church of Westminster.

The consequences of the repeal of the Corn Laws dominated British politics for the next five years. On Sir Robert Peel's resignation the Queen had no alternative but to call on Lord John Russell, the leader of the Opposition, to take his place. Her relations with Lord John's ministry were to suffer on account of the Foreign Secretary, Lord Palmerston – whom Lord John had insisted on returning to the Foreign Office.

The major problem facing the Russell administration was the condition of Ireland. The havoc caused by the potato blight reduced the wealth of the country. The worst privations were among the poorer classes. For many emigration was the only viable solution. Between 1846 and 1851 the population of Ireland fell from over 8 million to 6 and a half. Poverty led to famine and disease. The Queen, in her speech from the throne on 19 January 1847, spoke of the 'greatly increased mortality among the poorer classes'.[46] As a result the Government suspended every restriction on the import of food. The Navigation Laws were immediately suspended, and they were to be wiped out in 1849, throwing open British trade to the shipping of all nations (except for British and colonial coastal trade). By 1850 a system of virtually total free trade had been adopted in Britain. A new Irish Poor Law was introduced, based on the English principle that the propertied classes must support the poor. By June 1847 destitution was so severe that over three million persons were given daily survival rations by the Government.

The blight ruined many small landowners. A new court (the Encumbered Estates Court) was set up, giving landlords who were obliged to sell their land a simple, short, inexpensive method of selling and transferring it. This brought new proprietors to Ireland – about 7,500 between 1849 and 1857 – many of whom were speculators. They bought for profit, treated their tenants poorly and increased the tension in the country. Serious crime spread as the landlords became enemies to be shot, and the assassins were supported by mass opinion. Finally, after an election in 1847, when Russell was at the head of 325 Liberals – with 226 Protectionists and 105 Conservative Free Traders in opposition – he passed a stringent Coercion Act. It was generously supported by Peel, even though Liberal opposition to such an Act a year earlier had forced him out of power.

What achievements there were under the Whigs between 1846 and 1852 were haphazard. The ten-hours Bill got through in 1847 only because traditional party alignments had broken down. The Public Health Act of 1848 owed more to the energy of Chadwick than it did to governmental concern. The Government spent much of its time concentrating on ways of surviving, counting on temporary, ad hoc alliances with Peelites or Protectionists, Radicals or Irish.

15

Domestic Life

After the appointment of Lady Lyttelton in 1842 the nursery became for the young couple a haven of relaxation. Lady Lyttelton was good-humoured and humorous, patient and intelligent. She looked after the children for eight years, giving the Queen regular reports on the children's diet, on their behaviour and on their mental and physical progress. Diet was very different from today, with little protein. The staple Victorian family dishes of boiled beef and carrots, semolina or rice pudding were common food as the children grew. Baroness Bunsen, the wife of the Prussian Ambassador, observed, 'The wife of a rich man of business would think the meals served up to the Queen's children not good enough for her own nursery.'[1] When they were ill they received the same panaceas as the other children of the day – castor oil and Gray's powder for upset stomachs. The children were, however, on the whole healthy – good teeth, no rickets or bandy legs – and even rarer, Victoria lost no child at birth or in infancy and, indeed, her offspring lived to be married. This was not merely because they were royal and had better conditions than other children – the Queen's eldest daughters, Vicky and Alice, both lost two children in infancy.

Life in the nursery was spartan, with cold baths and open windows. There were only small fires in the children's rooms – and indeed elsewhere, for the Queen hated heat. There was, too, almost a neurosis with regard to the children's security. Prince Albert was undoubtedly over-anxious. 'The last thing we did before bedtime', Lady Lyttelton noted, 'was to visit the access to the children's apartments, to satisfy ourselves that all was safe. And the intricate turns and locks and guardrooms and the various intense precautions, suggesting the most hideous dangers which I fear are not altogether imaginary made one shudder.' The most important key was 'never out of Prince Albert's own keeping'.[2] According to Lady Lyttelton, threatening letters of the most horrid kind (probably written by mad people) and aimed directly at the children were frequently received. The Queen never mentioned them in her journal, nor did Prince Albert in his numerous memos on bringing up his children. Were they just nursery gossip and exaggeration?

There was plenty of warmth in the relationship between the couple and their children. Victoria and Albert were young parents – indeed in the early 1840s they were still joyous youngsters themselves, 'making with the help of the gardener and five men, a snow man nearly 12 foot high'.[3] Or amusing themselves with 'card tricks and other tricks', Albert as usual being the life and soul of this kind of party.[4] Small wonder that they were capable of romping round Windsor with their children on a sledge, with Albert acting as coachman,[5] or a few years later, entering with zest into games of hide and seek with them.

The Queen was full of naturalness and spontaneity during this period, as her relations with Lady Lyttelton showed. One morning Victoria rushed into the governess's room in her dressing gown to ask her to come and see a magnificent rainbow.[6] Another time, when Lady Lyttelton was anxious about Lady Exeter's health and was told by the Queen that she had taken a turn for the worse, the news affected Lady Lyttelton greatly – whereupon the Queen said directly: ' "Oh, but perhaps I am overstating what is in the letter! You must see the letter! Where is it? Oh in the Prince's room. I'll go for it." '[7] Taking her feet out of her footbath, the Queen slipped, all wet, into a pair of shoes and ran all along her private corridor to the Prince's room to fetch the letter! Mendelssohn remembered how the Queen and Prince Albert knelt down and picked up the leaves of music that the wind had blown out of a large portfolio while he was talking to the Prince.[8]

Although she was Queen, Victoria was perfectly willing to take her part in looking after her youngsters, even when they were turbulent.[9] Victoria's relationship to her children was complex. She resented having them – especially so soon and in such quick succession. At twenty-five she already had four babies. At thirty-one she had seven – and there were still two more to come. The first two births brought depression in their wake, but the next three births were uneventful. However, as the pregnancies followed one another, she came to fear that she would eventually die in childbirth. Sir James Clark warned Prince Albert after the birth of their ninth child, a daughter Beatrice in 1857, when the Queen was thirty-eight, that the Queen's mental stability would be threatened were she to have a tenth addition to her family. The Queen had an extraordinarily strong constitution and when her eighth child, Leopold, was born, she had discovered the advantages of chloroform – introduced into Great Britain by Dr James Young Simpson in 1847. There was much criticism of this means of producing unconsciousness and the medical journal *The Lancet* expressed intense astonishment at the Queen's use of it. But the Queen was delighted. 'The effect was soothing, quieting and delightful beyond measure.'[10]

The Queen had no desire to breastfeed her children. She was in other senses 'modern'. Her third child, Alice, was the first to be vaccinated; it was thanks to this royal patronage that Dr Jenner's invention of some years earlier at last became popular. Contrary to a widely held belief that Victoria was not interested in her children, she was in fact very preoccupied with them. Lady Eleanor Stanley complained to her friend, Lady Haddo, that the Queen talked only of her children.[11] Lady Lyttelton was glad that the coming of a second child had caused the Queen to be a little less attentive to her eldest. Like all very young mothers the Queen was too demanding. The baby was never good enough, had never made enough progress. The Queen took the baby with her all the time and when she was not with her she thought of her.[12] Lady Canning confirmed that the Princess was too much the object of her mother's attention.[13]

At two, Vicky was a precocious child and often naughty, as intelligent children can be. In Lady Lyttelton's wise opinion she was '*over* sensitive and affectionate, and rather irritable in temper at present; but it looks like a pretty mind, only very unfit for roughing it through a hard life, which hers may be.'[14] There is no doubt that too much was expected of her. 'Poor little body! She is always expected to be good, civil and sensible.'[15] At times she was tender and touching, sweet and charming, at others a regular handful. On the whole she kept her tantrums for her governess and the nursery, clever enough to realize that she must be on her best behaviour with her parents. So her mother's diary was always full of praise. 'Pussy was with us for some time, so dear and good, playing with us very happily. What a pleasure it is to see her so improved in health and developing so rapidly in mind.'[16] Or again, six months later: 'Pussy came down to me; she is such a dear affectionate child and so engaging. Showed pictures to her which she particularly likes.'[17]

From the first, however, the strongest bond was clearly between the baby girl and her father. 'Had Pussy with us for nearly an hour, and she was so funny and amusing. She is so fond of her dear Papa, running up to him and looking for him, calling to him in such an endearing little way. My dearest Albert is so fond of her too.'[18] Or again: 'Pussy came down to our luncheon and remained with us afterwards. She was excessively funny and dear, teasing her dear Papa a good deal, by continually calling "Papa, Papa" and asking to be taken up on his knee, which he good-naturedly did whilst he was writing and she was quiet and good.'[19]

Every clever remark she made, and there were many, was noted down and commented on by her doting parents. When Vicky was three the Grand Duke of Russia came and smoked continuously so that the smell of tobacco pervaded his rooms, much to the Queen's disgust. Vicky walked about sniffing the air near his door, saying: 'Princess smell the Grand Duke.'[20] At four she was taught some poems by Lamartine, which included the line, 'Voilà le tableau qui se déroule à mes pieds.' Shortly afterwards, during a ride, the young Princess gazed down from a hilltop on the fields below and repeated the line.[21] She had, noted Lady Canning, 'quite a royal memory and knew me and my name after four months' absence';[22] 'Yesterday Princess Mary of Cambridge [who was ten] went out walking with her and talked French to the *Bonne* but made two mistakes of gender. The little Princess heard them and said nothing at the time and mentioned them both after they came home – in private.'[23]

Vicky was brought up, as many eldest children are, almost as a young adult. In October 1843, for example, when she was only three, she spent the evening with her parents and the Court when they were singing and playing music. They sang a whole requiem of Mozart's. The Princess was 'so quiet and good', contenting herself with occasional comments such as 'I like the music' or 'Look at my pretty frock' – it was white muslin, worked with blue between the tucks – and 'playing at bo-peep with the Queen's scarf, nobody paying her the least attention, and she not seeming to expect any but to be really quite amused with the music.'[24]

Vicky was a strong-willed, often difficult child and very often Victoria did not always know how to handle her, nor indeed did her governess. When she was almost four, Lady Lyttelton finally obtained an addition to the nursery staff – a clergyman's daughter Sarah Anne Hildyard, known to the children as Tilla, came as governess to the Princess. Lady Lyttelton was convinced that the Princess's rages and general insubordination were partly due to the fact that she was bored. She was proved right by the enthusiasm with which Vicky took to work – at a desk with a blackboard, maps and all the general school paraphernalia.

Miss Hildyard quickly realized Vicky's potential and initiated her into the world of history, literature and science. She learnt Latin, read Gibbon's *Decline and Fall of the Roman Empire* and, for relaxation, Dickens, the Brontës, George Eliot and Shakespeare.

Vicky no doubt sensed her father's support, that she was as a child his pride and joy, and treated her mother badly. Writing to Vicky after her marriage, the Queen told her daughter: 'a more insubordinate and unequal tempered child and girl I think I never saw! I must say so honestly, now, dear. The tone you used to me, you know, shocked all who heard you.'[25] Indeed it was not until Vicky was married that she and her mother managed to bridge the communication gap that arose between them. In her letters Victoria expressed the love she felt and always had for her first-born, giving her advice, asking innumerable questions, showing genuine solicitude and affection. So much so that Vicky writes, 'Dear Mama, I did not think you would miss me as you do, I was often such a plague to you.'[26]

The Prince of Wales, Albert (or Bertie), was born less than a year after his sister. That his role was to be different from that of his sister and his future siblings was already apparent at his christening on 25 January 1842, which was marked with exceptional pomp. The Queen woke on the morning to the sound of bells ringing and guns firing. There was a lunch for all royal guests in the white breakfast room of the Castle, a lunch for visitors and Ladies of the Household in the Oak Room, a collation for Ambassadors, Foreign Ministers, Knights of the Garter, Cabinet Ministers and others in the Van Dyke Gallery and adjoining rooms. In the evening a grand banquet was held at half-past seven in St George's Hall.

The choice of godparents had been a highly political issue. King Frederick William of Prussia had let it be known that he would be willing to be godfather. Stockmar was against, since the High Church party in England had not appreciated the setting up of an Anglo-Prussian Protestant bishopric in Jerusalem by the two Governments and had held Prince Albert partly responsible. King Leopold, on the other hand, was eager to have Prussia brought into the western European circle so that it would not support Russia. King Leopold had his way, but his schemes were to be upset by the instability and eccentricity of King Frederick William – who was, indeed, to go insane.

The whole affair caused discontent in Russia, Paris and Vienna and also led to mutterings in England. Was the Court not leaning too much towards Germany? Evidence of this, it was claimed, could be found in the preponderance of German guests and the fact that there were three

German godparents – in addition to King Frederick William, Prince Ferdinand of Saxe-Coburg and the Duchess of Saxe-Coburg-Gotha. On the English side there were also three: the Duke of Cambridge, Princess Sophia and Grandmama. Further proof that the suspicion of 'Germans' was not unfounded came in the form of a battle over the baby's heraldic arms. Albert had the right to the arms of a Duke of Saxony and considered it therefore legitimate that they be quartered for his son with the arms of England. The Herald's College, when consulted as was customary, strongly objected to the Royal Arms of England being quartered with those of an insignificant dukedom. The Queen overrode their objections and ill-feeling and unpleasant comments against Albert grew.

Bertie was a fine, chubby baby. The Queen noted his progress less assiduously in her journal, as is usual for a second child. The Boy or the Baby, as she called him in his first months, progressed perfectly normally. At nine months old 'the Baby now stands up at a sofa or chair and crawls extremely well and quickly.'[27] When he was a year old it seemed to his mother that he was 'so much thinner and smaller than Vicky'[28] and this worried her. 'Both children at breakfast and the little boy sitting up very nicely. He has such a nice face, and good eyes – if he only were not so thin.'[29] Lady Lyttelton said of him at this age, 'He is very intelligent and looks through his large clear blue eyes, full at one, with a frequent very sweet smile.'[30] Certainly he was on occasion 'passionate and determined enough for an autocrat, but he still has his lovely mildness of expression and calm temper in the intervals.'

By the age of two it was clearly accepted in the household that Bertie was not as precocious – or as intelligent – as his elder sister. He was, however, Lady Lyttelton's favourite and she alone seems really to have appreciated his qualities. Her opinion never varied in the eight years she spent with the children. He inherited, she claimed, his mother's passion for truth. At three he was, according to Lady Lyttelton, 'not articulate like his sister, but rather babyish in accent. He understands a little French and says a few words, but is altogether backward in language, very intelligent and generous and good-tempered with a few passions and stampings occasionally.' She appreciated his politeness and his manner; he bowed and offered his hand beautifully, 'besides saluting *à la militaire* all unbidden'. He was very handsome, 'but still very small in every way'.[31] He remained a small child. At four he was not as tall as his sister Alice, though he was almost two years older. Teaching him was, even his governess admitted, difficult. He was wilfully inattentive: getting under the table, upsetting the books and sundry other anti-studious practices. For the Queen all this could be put down to the fact that he had been born too close to Vicky. 'Bertie and I both suffered (and the former will ever suffer) from coming so soon after you,' she wrote to her eldest daughter in 1858, recommending her not to have a second child too soon.[32] His parents saw Bertie as a retarded child.

With the eyes of today we may interpret things very differently. From his earliest days Bertie was compared to his elder sister, who was considered by his father in particular to be a paragon of all the virtues – her only fault was that she was not a boy. Throughout the Prince's life, Vicky held a very special place in his affections. He spent long hours with her in the nursery and his son must soon have been made to feel how inferior he was to his exceptional sister. He began to display all the symptoms of a second, less-loved child. Stammering, flying into fits of rage to be noticed, refusing to leave babyhood. Albert has often been praised for the part he played in stretching his daughter's mind; he must also bear a large part of the responsibility for the slow development of his son.

Alice, Victoria's third child and second daughter, was, according to her father, 'the beauty of the family and "an extraordinarily good and merry child."'[33] From the beginning she was a reasonable child – but not as interesting as Vicky was. When Lady Lyttelton gave lessons to Princess Alice and Prince Alfred, who followed her, she found them 'soothing' compared to the turbulent elder children. For Victoria, her third daughter was 'good, amiable Alice' – praise that, in context, seems almost derogatory.

Alice had many accomplishments; she loved music, played the piano well and had a veritable gift for acting which she showed in the plays the children put on for their parents' pleasure. A good skater, a good horsewoman and a good dancer, Alice was into the bargain pretty, with finer, more delicate features than her sisters, and she had a flair for clothes, which her sisters lacked. Yet she was totally unsure of herself – never really fully able to fend for herself. She was devoted to her father but he spent more time with his clever eldest daughter, and with the son he did not appreciate but felt he had to train to be king. Alice, who felt things with intensity, must have had the sensation of being eclipsed.

Prince Alfred, Queen Victoria's fourth child and second son, was known to the family as Affie. When he was born on 6 August 1844 it was obvious that Ernest, the reigning Duke of Coburg, would have no children. Thus, after Ernest's death, Albert's children would succeed. Bertie, as heir to the English Crown could not inherit – nor could the girls – so the new baby was the immediate heir. 'The little one', Albert wrote to his brother, 'shall from his youth be taught to love the small dear country to which he belongs in every respect as does his Papa.'[34] Victoria found him, when she gave him his religious lesson, 'so attentive and intelligent that it is easier and pleasanter to teach him, than any of the others.'[35]

The relationship of the children was on the whole harmonious. There was a certain antagonism between Vicky and Bertie, although on the whole in his early years he was her willing slave. One story illustrates their relationship particularly well. In 1846 the Princess Victoria and the Prince of Wales were on the royal yacht. They were heard in a heated argument one day about which of them was the owner of the Scilly Isles: 'Vicky said they were hers, and the Prince of Wales was equally sure they belonged to him; and another day the Princess was heard telling her brother all the things she meant to do when she was Queen, and he quite acquiesced in it, and it never seemed to strike either of them that it would be otherwise.'[36] This was, of course, quite a natural conclusion for them to come to. After all, Vicky was the eldest and in their family Mama was Queen and Papa was not King – one wonders when Vicky learnt the hard truth and how it affected her.

All through her life Vicky protected her younger sister Alice. Although Alice probably suffered from living in the shadow of her brilliant sister, the two girls got on well. Throughout their childhood they shared a room and had each other to confide in. The strongest relationship among the elder children, however, was that between Alice and Bertie. 'Bertie and Alice are the greatest friends and always playing together,' wrote the Queen at the end of 1844.[37] His younger sister watched over him and felt responsibility for him. Bertie could, however, also show great affection for his elder sister. Lady Lyttelton noted when Bertie was six and Vicky seven:

> His sister has been lately often in disgrace and though she is not 'Alee' [Princess Alice] his little attentions and feeling on the sad occasions have been very nice – never losing sight of her, through a longish imprisonment in her room; and stealing to the door to give a kind message, or tell a morsel of pleasant news – his own toys quite neglected, and his lovely face quite pale, till the disgrace was over.[38]

When Lady Lyttelton left the Queen's service in November 1850 the picture she drew of the four eldest children's farewells is almost a thumbnail portrait of each of them. The Prince of Wales, 'who has seen so little of me lately, cried and seemed to feel most'. Vicky said 'many striking, feeling and clever things. Princess Alice's look of soft tenderness I never shall forget; nor Prince Alfred with his manly face in tears, looking so pretty.'[39]

Despite the disapproval of both Lady Lyttelton and Baron Stockmar, the royal children were often snatched away from lessons by their parents for what were called 'treats'. They were taken to the zoo or to the circus or to the theatre. Trips to the theatre developed in Bertie a lifelong love for the stage. It was encouraged no doubt by the dramatic performances organized each year at Christmas at Windsor after 1848 – in that year *The Merchant of Venice* was presented with the well-known actors Mr and Mrs Kean in the cast.

The children were also gradually initiated into their social role as members of the royal family. Bertie attended his first review in Windsor Great Park, in honour of Tsar Nicholas I, when he was not quite three. He wore a broad military sash over his shoulders, sat in the Queen's carriage and clapped with delight when the troops marched past. When Vicky was only two she had asked to be lifted up in the royal carriage 'to look at the people' – 'to whom she bowed very actively whether in sight of her or not.'[40] Their first official public appearance took place in 1849 – Vicky was eight and her brother seven. The Queen had promised to open the new Coal Exchange in London on 30 October but she went down with chicken-pox two days before. The Lord Mayor of London was most upset at the idea of wasting the 5,000 pounds they had spent on their preparations. The Prince agreed to replace her and took the two eldest children with him. 'The poor little Queen', noted Lady Eleanor Stanley, 'was sadly vexed . . . at her two children making their first appearance at any public thing in State without her.'[41]

When the Queen toured without her children she missed them and very early on they were taken on her journeys whenever possible. In November 1842, when Bertie was one, and Vicky two, they were thus the guests of the Duke of Wellington at Walmer. Along the route, crowds turned out to see the Queen – and Lady Lyttelton observed acidly, 'The children will grow up under the strangest delusions as to what travelling means and the usual condition of people in England! They must suppose one always finds them shouting and grinning and squeezing, surrounded by banners and garlands.'[42]

In 1849 the four eldest children accompanied their parents on an official visit to Ireland. Despite the unrest there had been earlier, the family received a tremendous welcome – 'the enthusiasm and excitement shown by the Irish people was extreme,' the Queen noted when they were in Cork.[43] At Dublin – where she wore a 'soft coloured green poplin with a design of gold shamrocks in it' – the reception was extraordinary; in Belfast 'not quite as enthusiastic'.[44] Everywhere they were greeted with arches bearing the words 'a hundred thousand welcomes' (*Cead mille faille*). As a tribute to Ireland the Queen created Bertie Earl of Dublin, noting, 'He has *no* Irish title though he is born with several Scottish ones which he inherited from James 1st.'[45] The whole journey went off well. The only incident occurred on the way back to Scotland. An enormous storm caused the waves to break over the deck: 'The first great wave that broke over the ship, threw everyone down in every direction. . . . Poor little Affie was thrown down and sent rolling over the deck which was swimming with water, getting quite drenched.'[46]

At a time when the children of the affluent lived in nurseries and knew only governesses, the royal children were very close to their parents and surprisingly free and easy with them. The retreats the couple were to build themselves were to reinforce this family spirit.

Staying in other people's houses had made the Queen feel the time had come to have a country residence of her own. True, there was the Pavilion at Brighton but it had only a few bedrooms, no private gardens and, while its situation might once have been ideal, the town had grown up around it and it was no longer private. Although it was, as Lady Canning noted, 'impossible not to admire the perfect finish of the decorations and how well everything is made to suit,'[47] it was not to the Queen's taste. After their visit in 1845, when the royal couple had been upset by the crowds, they never returned. It was eventually sold to the town – the Brighton Corporation – in 1850. The Queen had never thought of it as a seaside resort, remarking that one could only see a little morsel of sea from one of her sitting-room windows. It was indeed: 'a strange Chinese thing, haunted by ghosts best forgotten.'

So it was that during one of their morning walks, the royal couple talked of buying a place of their own, perhaps in the Isle of Wight. Victoria had first visited the island in 1831 and had stayed in Norris Castle. She had visited it again in 1833. Now, ten years later, the Queen remembered how pleasant the island was. It was not large – twenty-three miles by thirteen – and yet was very varied, with cliffs and coves, rivers and brooks. They talked the idea over with Peel and he recommended two properties on the island.

Of the two, Osborne seemed the more suitable. In addition to the house there was a park of 2,000 acres, a farm and a wood. The asking price of 30,000 pounds was high, So the couple decided to rent the property for a year to see how they liked it. The owner, the daughter of the third Duke of Grafton, agreed. Finally it was bought for 26,000 pounds the following year. Prince Albert was a hard bargainer. He pretended to Lady Isabella that he was not really interested but he wrote to his brother announcing that he would buy it – and make the purchase out of the Queen's own funds so that it would belong to them 'and not to the inquisitive and impudent people'. The advantage would be that when the Prince was designing, planning, gardening or farming, he would no longer need the approval of the Office of Woods and Forests.

The Queen was delighted at the purchase. How nice it was 'to have a place of one's own, quiet and retired'.[48] She wrote to Melbourne:

> It is impossible to see a prettier place, with woods and valleys, and *points de vue*, which would be beautiful anywhere; but all this near the sea (the woods grow into the sea) is quite perfection; We have a charming beach quite to ourselves. The sea was so blue and calm that the Prince said it was like Naples. And then we can walk about anywhere by ourselves without fear of being followed and mobbed, which Lord Melbourne will easily understand is delightful.[49]

The Prince was enthusiastic. Here at last was a place far from Court where he could come into his own. The family spent a week in the old Osborne House in October 1844. It was a charming Georgian house. The first and second floors contained sixteen bedrooms and sitting rooms – which was hardly adequate accommodation, in Albert's opinion, for a royal suite. Victoria was quite happy with the smallness but Albert's view prevailed. And rightly so since the house was also to be used for meetings of the Privy Council and official business. Greville, attending a Council in the original house on 14 September 1845, found it

> a miserable place and such a vile house that the Lords of the Council had no place to remain in but the entrance hall, before the Council. Fortunately the weather was fine, so we walked about, looking at the new house the Queen is building; it is very ugly, and the whole concern wretched enough. They will spend first and last a great deal of money there, but it is her own money and not the nation's.[50]

The clearing of the land for the new building began in the middle of May and the first cornerstone was laid on 23 June 1845. The royal family spent a good part of the summer at Osborne and the islanders founded the Royal Victoria Yacht Club on her birthday, 24 May, to welcome her. Prince Albert was determined the house should be well and truly his down to its very design. Not a modest man he even decided to be his own architect, despite the fact that the profession was already well established. The Royal Institute of British Architects had conferred diplomas on associates and fellows since its foundation in 1834. The Prince used as technical counsellor a 'master-builder', Thomas Cubitt from Norfolk. In London he had planned much of what is known as Belgravia. He thought of the island as a sort of Riviera in the Channel and he chose an Italianate style for the new Osborne. The building was meant to be a sort of grand composition, in which the landscape and the magnificent view of the river Solent played a part.

The outside of Osborne is as strange to our eyes today as the Brighton Pavilion looked to Albert and Victoria. It is a curious mixture, with a flat roof, a first floor loggia and two non-symmetrical campaniles – the flag tower and the clock tower – which differ both in weight and pattern. It undoubtedly inspired in suburban villas the love of the tower, not always well proportioned to the whole. The house is interesting for its use of new techniques, many of them very economical. Cast iron girders replaced wooden beams, and pillars of cast iron were plastered and painted to look like marble; brick and cement were stuccoed so as to give the appearance of stone; fountains were made in metal and terracotta; plate glass was used in the principal rooms; and most of the wood was deal, with oak and mahogany reserved for the state rooms. A form of central heating was installed to supplement the fires, hot air rising up flues to warm the floors. Albert also had water closets installed for the first time in a royal residence.

In February 1846 Victoria and Albert went to see how the work was progressing. 'We shall go', the Prince wrote to the Dowager Duchess of Coburg, 'on the 27th to the Isle of Wight for a week, where the fine air will be of service to Victoria and the children; and I, partly forester, partly builder, partly farmer and partly gardener, expect to be a good deal upon my legs and in the open air.'[51] Victoria was delighted to see Albert happy and relaxed. 'It is so good for him,' she wrote. 'It is a relief to be away from all the bitterness which people create for themselves in London.'[52]

It was good, too, for Bertie, who was treated more and more as if he were sick. A memorandum from Dr A. Combe in June 1846 insisted that the strictest attention should continue to be paid to everything which can in any way impart 'that tone to his nervous system which it still wants'. The Prince, he said, needed: 'Much exposure to the open air ... long drives in an open carriage – one of the most valuable sedative tonics we possess.' Flat places must be avoided. Buckingham Palace was therefore 'objectionable' and even Windsor was not 'a suitable locality', at least during 'three parts of the year, when the soil is moist or absolutely wet'. Change of air was recommended, hot weather and exposure to the sun to be avoided. The boy should have cold bathing and light plain nourishment. Soft pillows or beds were harmful. Above all, 'bracing air is of first importance.'[53] Osborne was thus ideal for him.

On 15 September 1846 the royal family spent their first night in the new house at Osborne. 'Nobody smelt paint or caught cold', Lady Lyttelton wrote, 'and the worst is over. It was a most amusing event coming here. Everything in the house is quite new, and the drawing-room looked very handsome.'[54] As the Queen entered the house for the first time, Lucy Kerr, one of her Maids of Honour, threw an old shoe into the house after her – this was an old Scottish custom. On the first evening in the house the young couple – still under thirty – held a 'house-warming' ceremony at which, with some emotion, the Prince recited in German the first lines of a prayer to 'bless our going out and coming in.' Lady Lyttelton made the sobering remark: 'And truly, entering a new house, a new palace, is a solemn thing to do, to those whose probable space of life in it is long, and in spite of rank, and health, and youth, downhill now.'[55]

The furniture and decorations at Osborne reflected Albert's taste – and were to be seen later as eminently Victorian. The interior decoration was on the whole more Germanic than Italian. Among the best-known pieces are a painted billiard table, and the furniture of the Horn Room made in Frankfurt. Everywhere there were marble statues, most of them of the royal family: Albert and Victoria, as Edward III and Philippa; Albert in Roman armour; marble models of the hands and feet of the children; busts and statues of the family and statuettes of their favourite dogs and ponies. Pictures by Winterhalter and Landseer adorned the walls – of Albert showing a hunting trophy to Victoria, of the entire family group, and so on.

In Osborne, Prince Albert had found a never-ending occupation. He staked out new growing areas, he traced the lines of roads and paths, he began a tree nursery in March 1846 and was forever planting and replanting. Osborne also had a farm and Prince Albert made of it a profitable concern, with fruit-producing orchards, piggeries, hay fields and a dairy.

It was at Osborne that the Queen bathed in the sea for the first time:

Drove down to the beach with my maid and went into the bathing machine, where I undressed and bathed in the sea (for the first time in my life), and a very nice bathing woman attending me. I thought it delightful till I put my head under the water, when I thought I should be stifled.[56]

What she appreciated most, however, was the intimacy she enjoyed at Osborne with her family – and above all with Prince Albert. 'Never do I enjoy myself more', she wrote, 'or more peacefully than when I can be so much with my beloved Albert – follow him everywhere.'[57]

In these years of the late 1840s Albert was not yet totally obsessed with work and found time for his wife and children. He taught his children to swim and to fly kites, and also had them taught more manual tasks during their long stays at Osborne. The young Princes were taught to build and to farm. They worked side by side with ordinary labourers for two or three hours every day, under a foreman who criticized their work and filled in a time sheet. It was sent every week to the Prince, who then paid them the standard rate for their work. Each child was also given a vegetable garden, flower garden, greenhouse, hothouse, forcing frames and tool sheds, and there was even a carpenter's shop. Once again the children were paid the going rate for any produce they grew. This was one aspect of the Prince's educational system that even Bertie responded to. His first biographer, writing under his supervision, says:

> This was undoubtedly a wise way of teaching them to sympathise with the lot of the working classes, and though it may have been carried somewhat too far, it was possibly the means of giving the King [Bertie, Edward VII] that interest in farming which afterwards made him a famous stock-breeder and a kind and thoughtful country landlord.[58]

For the boys Albert also had a model fort erected with real brass firing cannons so that they could practise military tactics.

Meanwhile the girls were receiving a domestic education. A Swiss cottage was installed in the grounds of Osborne House. It was a small wooden chalet with a sitting room and kitchen, where the children were taught to scrub and wash and cook. 'The Queen rightly held that a domestic training was the chief part of the education of girls at any rank, and for many years she always had served at her table a dish that had been made by one of her daughters.'[59]

Despite the pleasures of Osborne, Scotland was not forgotten. In August 1847 the royal couple set off from Osborne and sailed along the Welsh coast and past the Isle of Man to Scotland. This time they were accompanied by Vicky and Bertie, and took their governess, Miss Hildyard, to look after them. The Queen's half-brother, Prince Charles of Leiningen, also went with them. They had been lent Ardverikie, a house by Loch Laggan which was leased by Lord Abercorn from Lord Henry Bentinck. The Queen was once again delighted with the remoteness and wildness of Scotland. Of Ardverikie she wrote, 'It is quite close to the lake, and the view from the windows, as I now write, though obscured by rain, is very beautiful and extremely wild.'[60] There was not a village, house or cottage within four or five miles. A persistent Scotch mist enveloped Loch Laggan and the surrounding country; when it lifted it was to give way to a veil of steady rain. The Queen did not mind getting wet but Prince Albert hated it. Prince Albert nevertheless took long walks or went out shooting, coming home frozen and wet to the skin.

While she was at Ardverikie the Queen received letters from her doctor, Sir James Clark, who was also in Scotland – the guest of Lord Aberdeen's brother and sister, Sir Robert and Lady Alicia Gordon, at their newly built castle of Balmoral. It was only forty-five miles away as the crow flies but he reported that he had sunny days and fine air. The royal couple decided that it would be better next time to abandon the wet west coast and to investigate the Deeside in the east, near Aberdeen, reputed to be the driest district in Scotland. All the same, Ardverikie did have one great advantage. It was a real retreat. Reporters called it an 'un-come-at-able place' because they were quartered on the other side of Loch Laggan, which could only be crossed on a flying bridge that belonged to the royal party.[61] Such solitude was rare and the Queen appreciated the quiet and simple life they led there.

The aim therefore was to find a place similarly isolated on the eastern side of the Highlands. The opportunity soon occurred: to acquire the castle of Balmoral itself. On 24 August 1848 Albert wrote exultantly to his brother: 'Balmoral is a castle which I have bought in Scotland. It has 10,000 acres of forest. I bought the lease from Lord Aberdeen for 27 years, for £2,000. It belonged to his brother, Sir Robert Gordon, who had just built the castle and entered it shortly before he died. It is said to be situated in the healthiest place in the Highlands.'[62] A fortnight later he and Victoria went to visit it for the first time. The main railway systems of Scotland and England were now virtually completed and, as the weather was bad, the Queen decided to go to Perth by train. She found this so agreeable that it became her usual way of going to Scotland.

The Queen wrote of the castle:

It is a pretty little castle in the old Scottish style. There is a picturesque tower and garden in front, with a high wooded hill; at the back there is a wood down to the Dee; and the hills rise all around. There is a nice little hall with a billiard-room; next to it is the dining-room. Upstairs (ascending by a good broad staircase) immediately to the right and above the dining room is our sitting-room, a fine large room – next to which is our bedroom, opening into it a little dressing-room which is Albert's. Opposite, down a few steps, are the children's and Miss Hildyard's three rooms. The ladies live below, and the gentlemen upstairs.'[63]

It was in fact a building no bigger than the original Osborne had been. But it was pretty, with mullioned windows and flamboyant tracery, turrets projecting at angles and round towers with cone-shaped roofs. The Queen was charmed by it, for it was small and cosy.

There was no luxury in the house and little room. For those attending the Queen it was rather like going on a camping holiday. The most disgruntled of Balmoral's first inhabitants was undoubtedly Lord Malmesbury, who was living there as Minister in attendance.

The rooms were so small that I was obliged to write my despatches on my bed and to keep the window constantly open to admit the necessary quantity of air ... and my private secretary lodged three miles off. We played at billiards every evening, the Queen and the Duchess being constantly obliged to get up from their chairs to be out of the way of the cues.[64]

But he had to recognize that the atmosphere was pleasant and cheerful and the royal couple evidently perfectly happy and very kind to everyone.

Even Greville, who was no lover of Courts, was impressed when he stayed in the original Balmoral. The royal couple certainly appeared to him in a good light in their Highland retreat: 'They live there without any state whatever; they live not merely like private gentlefolks, but like very small gentlefolks, small rooms, small establishment. There are no soldiers and the whole guard of the Sovereign and the whole Royal Family is a single policeman, who walks about the grounds to keep off impertinent intruders or improper characters.'[65]

What the Queen appreciated above all else at Balmoral was the sense of freedom. Here was a real retreat, far away from the madding crowds. 'It was so calm, and so solitary,' she noted, 'it did one good as one gazed around; the pure mountain air was most refreshing. All seemed to breathe freedom and peace, and to make one forget the world and its sad turmoils.'[66] Here she could roam about at will – and she did just that. 'The Queen', Greville noted, 'is running in and out of the house all day long, and often goes about alone, walks into the cottages and sits down and chats with the old women.'[67]

When the children were in Balmoral they often accompanied Victoria on these impromptu visits. She noted in September 1849:

> Met the children and after seeing Albert go off, walked with them to the village, where we went to see old Mrs Grant (John's mother) a fine, hale old woman who was very friendly, showing us her little cottage and saying I had brought peace and happiness as well as fine weather and that she hoped the Lord would bless me. Next went to Mrs Frazer's and I gave her stuff for a dress as I did to old Mrs McDougal, who would not believe it and said 'For me? The Lord Bless ye.'[68]

The Highlands also provided relaxation for Albert. Even when he brought with him his cares and anxieties, and despite the numerous memorandums he wrote and the letters he penned, Albert was more relaxed here than elsewhere. Greville, meeting Prince Albert at Balmoral for the first time, thought, 'He seemed very much at his ease, very gay, pleasant and without the least stiffness or air of dignity.'[69]

The scenery was wild but not desolate. Here the Queen could spend much of her time out of doors and ride and walk to her heart's content. They ascended Loch-na-Gar – the mountain whose 'steep frowning glories' were praised by Byron – 'the view getting finer and finer' and 'no road, but not bad ground – moss, heather and stones.' Up she went on her pony, with the ghillies moving some of the stones from time to time to make it easier. Occasionally she would get off her pony and walk a bit. Albert, meanwhile, had shot some ptarmigan and then rejoined her near the peak. 'We got off and walked, and climbed up some steep stones, to a place where we found a seat in a little nook, and had some luncheon. It was just two o'clock, so we had taken four hours going up.'[70]

Another occupation was accompanying Albert on his stag-hunting expeditions, sometimes with Bertie. In the Balloch Buidh they scrambled up an almost perpendicular place to where there was a little box made of hurdles and interwoven with branches of fir and heather. There they waited,

> watching and quite concealed; some had gone round to beat, and others again were at a little distance. We sat quite still, and sketched a little; I doing the landscape and some trees, Albert drawing Macdonald as he lay there. This lasted for nearly an hour, when Albert fancied he heard a distant sound, and, in a few minutes, Macdonald whispered that he saw stags, and that Albert should wait and take a steady aim.

On that particular day Albert shot a magnificent stag and the keepers claimed that Victoria had 'brought the good luck'.[71]

About five miles from the castle at Alt-na-Giubhsaich were two shiels, or stone huts, used by the ghillies. Victoria and Albert had them transformed into a retreat which would house a small party. 'To the one in which we live,' the Queen wrote, 'a wooden addition has been made. We have a charming little dining-room, sitting-room, bed-room and dressing-room all *en suite*.'[72] There was also a little room for the Maid of Honour and one for her maid and the Queen's, and a little pantry. In the other house, only a few yards away, joined by a corridor, was the kitchen, the store room and a loft where the male servants slept. From this secluded base the couple would go walking to the loch, known as 'Muich' – meaning darkness or sorrow – which was some twenty minutes away. Sometimes they rowed up to the head of the loch and fished for trout. The small company would dine early and after dinner they played whist or some other game. The silence and solitude were only interrupted by the waving of the fir trees.

Conditions could be severe. On occasion the wind blew so hard on the lake that the rowing boat would not go forward. Once the Queen and Lady Douro were forced to leave the boat and ride home, 'along a sort of sheep-path on the side of the lake . . . It was very rough and very narrow, for the hill rises abruptly from the lake; we had seven hundred feet above us, and I suppose one hundred feet below.' They arrived home safely, having had one of those adventures 'which are always very pleasant to look back upon'.[73] Some of the expeditions were long. From Invercauld to the top of Ben-na-Bhourd 'we must have been at least 18 miles riding and walking.'[74]

The Queen and the Prince took an active part in local activities. They often went to the Highland Gathering at the Castle of Braemar or on some other estate nearby, where they watched 'putting the stone', 'throwing the hammer' and 'caber', and the race up the hill of Craig Cheunnich. After the games there would be Highland dances. They took part in a salmon leistering in September 1850 – 'all our tenants were assembled with poles and spears or rather "leisters" for catching salmon.' One salmon was speared, 'after which we walked to the ford, or quarry, where we were very successful, seven salmons being caught, some in the net, and some speared. Though Albert stood in the water some time he caught nothing.'[75] They were invited by the local nobility to such typical Scottish festivities as torchlight balls in the open air.

This primitive, romantic, mountain life was what Prince Albert loved.[76] Small wonder that Victoria was full of praise for this part of her kingdom. Lady Lyttelton complained that the Queen was convinced that 'Scotch air, Scotch people, Scotch hills, Scotch rivers, Scotch woods are all far preferable to those of any other nation'; adding waspishly, 'The chief support to my spirits is that I shall never see, hear or witness these various charms.'[77]

Lady Lyttelton was not the only one to be irritated by the Queen's love for Scotland. When the Prime Minister of the day, Lord John Russell, was informed of the Queen's determination to spend a part of each year over six hundred miles away from the capital, he realized that this meant that, for Government to continue, a Minister would always need to be in attendance. The expense would moreover have to be borne by the Privy Purse. But he was in no position to dissuade her. The castle was not purchased with any public money and the Queen had, after all, the right to live in whatever part of her kingdom she wished. He probably hoped that the Queen's love of the Highlands would not last; that she would tire of the solitude and the discomfort, not to mention the journeying and the weather – which even in the driest part of Scotland was cold and often damp. But the Queen did not tire of it and over the years a ceaseless procession of Ministers attended the Queen in the inaccessible part of the Highlands that she loved.

In 1843, within two years of the birth of the heir to the throne, an anonymous pamphlet appeared: 'Who should educate the Prince of Wales.' The pamphlet gave expression to a widespread feeling of anxiety. Memories of the social and political mischief wrought by former Princes of Wales were still alive in popular memory. Stockmar had begun badgering the royal parents as early as 6 March 1842 on the same subject. In his missive he wrote:

> George III either did not understand his duties as a parent or he neglected them. The errors of his sons were of the most glaring kind, and we can find their explanation only in the supposition that their tutors were either incapable of engrafting on their minds during their youth the principles of truth or morality, or that they most culpably neglected their duties, or were not supported in them by the royal parents. There can be no doubt that the conduct of these Princes contributed more than any other circumstance to weaken the respect and influence of Royalty in this country, and to impair the strong sentiments of loyalty among the English people, for which they have been for centuries distinguished. That George IV by his iniquities did not accomplish his own exclusion from the throne was owing to the strength of the English constitution and the great political tolerance and reflection of this practical people.[78]

The parental responsibility of Victoria and Albert was thus tremendous. They could not model themselves on George III, even if he was seen as a great upholder of the domestic virtues, for he had not succeeded in educating his own sons properly. The young couple must therefore come to grips with the problem early on. 'Good education', underlined the Baron, 'cannot begin too soon.' The first necessity was the regulation of the child's natural instincts – a matter of even greater importance when it was a question of the heir to the throne.[79]

This memorandum disturbed the Queen greatly and she turned to Lord Melbourne for advice. What, she asked, should be the character and position of the Prince of Wales in England? Lord Melbourne replied:

> George IV was so conscious of having mixed himself unrestrainedly in politics, and of having taken a very general part in opposition to his father's government and wishes, that he was naturally anxious to exonerate himself from blame, and to blame it upon the necessity of his position rather than upon his own restless and inter-meddling disposition.

His excuse was in Melbourne's eyes neither valid nor justifiable. The task of the Queen and Prince Albert must be to make the Prince of Wales 'understand correctly his real position and its duties, and to enable him to withstand the temptations and seductions with which he will find himself beset when he approaches the age of twenty-one.'[80]

Queen Victoria had her own views on several aspects of education. She believed that the greatest maxim of all was that 'the children should be brought up as simply, and in as domestic a way as possible; that (not interfering with their lessons) they should be as much as possible with their parents and learn to place their greatest confidence in them in all things.'[81] Something which neither she or her husband had been able to do.

The Queen's views on religious education are evident in her concern for her eldest daughter. She believed that it was at its mother's knee that the child should learn religion, but by 1844 the Queen was clearly aware that the pressure of public duties and pregnancies was making it impossible to keep this part of Vicky's education wholly within her own hands. 'It is already a hard case for me', she wrote, 'that my occupations prevent me being with her when she says her prayers.'[82] She set down very clearly therefore the principles which were to guide the child's instructors. 'I am *quite* clear that she should be taught to have great reverence for God and for religion, but that she should have the feeling of devotion and love which our Heavenly Father encourages His earthly children to have for him and not one of fear and trembling.'[83]

After hours of discussion and a plethora of ponderous memorandums from Stockmar, the royal couple themselves wrote a memorandum in January 1847 laying down the system to be applied in educating their children. The children so far, and any future children, were to pass through a number of classes. The first class was the nursery and from the child's first month to its fifth or sixth year this would be the centre of its life. 'The chief objects here are their physical development, the actual rearing up, the training to obedience.' They were to be taught their language and the two principal foreign languages – French and German, both spoken and written – and they were also to be taught figures and counting. Religious instruction began from their fourth year.

The second class would last one or two years. 'Here elementary instruction is the main object' and also the supervision by one person 'for the development of character'.[84] Vicky and Bertie were to be promoted to Class II in February 1847. The Queen continued the religious instruction of Vicky while Lady Lyttelton instructed the Prince of Wales. Vicky was given her own maid. She would remain with her governess until her ninth or tenth year, when she would begin to be trained to go into society by a Lady, who should remain with her until she married. The third class was to be entered by the Prince of Wales in his sixth or seventh year, when he would be given a tutor and a personal valet. In his twelfth or thirteenth year he would pass into a fourth class, when he would be introduced into life and the world.

Thus were the years mapped out. Victoria and Albert went about this business of education very seriously. Curiously, the Queen did not envisage instructing Bertie in religious affairs – although she was to give lessons to her other sons. She had grown up in a very feminine world with her mother and her governess. Her friend in her earliest years had been her half-sister Feodora. She was probably bowing to the narrow views of Prince Albert when she wrote, 'At six years at the latest I think he should be given entirely over to the tutor and be taken entirely away from the women. A very respectable man should be found to act as his valet. Further I do not say anything as I wish that he should grow as truly under his father's eye and be guided by him so that when he has reached the age of sixteen or seventeen he may be a real companion to his father.'[85]

Before the time came for the Prince of Wales to be transferred to Class III with his own tutor, the year 1848 had brought much trouble on the continent – confirming Baron Stockmar in his opinion that the higher the rank an individual occupied, the more he was exposed to the vicissitudes of fortune.[86] Since positions of royalty were more and more insecure, and the art of government more and more difficult, it was of great importance to reinforce constitutional democracy against republicanism; one way of achieving this end was, in Baron Stockmar's opinion, to give the future monarch a good education in accordance with the spirit of the age.

From April 1849 the Prince of Wales's education was entrusted to Reverend Henry Mildred Birch, a thirty-three-year-old master at Eton. He was given 800 pounds a year. At Eton he had been responsible for forty to fifty boys, their ages ranging from ten to nineteen. 'He seems to be nice and kind and fond of children and judicious in his views on education,' noted the Queen.[87] Bertie was to be taught 'religion, English-reading, dictating, learning by heart, writing, calculating, the four species, geography, French, German, music, drawing.' French and German were to be taught by a governess but in the presence of the tutor. Writing was to be pursued daily, 'as the Prince's hand is very feeble and unsteady'. Lessons were to last half an hour. With regard to religion, 'The Prince will not go to Church till he has passed his eighth birthday' and 'Sunday is to be kept as a day of recreation and amusement in which the Prince will be glad to see a little more of his brother and sisters than the occupations of the week will allow.'[88]

This last point irked Mr Birch who wrote to inform Baron Stockmar that he did not know of any family where cricket or games would be allowed on the day of rest.[89] The Queen retorted immediately: 'The Sunday has always been treated as a holiday and the child has either had playfellows or played with his brother and sisters, painted or had treats on that day.'[90] She later insisted in a letter to Baron Stockmar that Birch must be prepared to join in or at least be present at those 'innocent amusements' that Bertie would engage in – theatricals, dances, shooting, etc. She wanted no 'priestly domination' but 'moderate attitudes'.[91] She was not in favour of 'the extreme severity of the Sunday in this country when carried to excess'.[92] This preservation of Sunday as a day of fun was something the Queen was clearly seriously attached to.

Birch spoke to Baron Stockmar of his new charge, Bertie, after three months in the royal employ. He complained that he got painfully tired of his occupation and felt the want of a little time to himself and the need of a little conversation with adults. Furthermore, he did not want to teach the boy maths and science and was totally against one and the same man trying to teach everything. Six months later he was again complaining – that his salary was smaller than that he had received at Eton and that he had no holidays.

During the first year Birch spent with Bertie, lessons were a disaster. The Prince of Wales refused to pay attention, flew into rages if pressed and was then too exhausted to do anything. On 31 July 1850 Birch had written to the Prince telling him, 'the conduct of the Prince of Wales begins to frighten me. I begin to search myself and see if my ingenuity can devise any other mode of dealing with him but I seem to have tried every expedient.' What was the problem? Whenever Birch tried to teach him anything difficult, Bertie showed 'an unwillingness to give himself the slightest trouble or exertion'.[93]

For his part, Prince Albert did not, on principle, interfere in the details of the children's upbringing but only superintended 'the principles, which are difficult to uphold in the face of so many women', and gave 'the final judgement. From my verdict there is no appeal. Unfortunately, also I am the executive power and have to carry out the sentence.'[94] With Bertie, his solution was simple: apply greater rigour. According to the first biographer of Edward VII: 'Everything thus concurred to make the beginning of the path in life of the most genial and charming of British Sovereigns rough and hard and difficult. In the matter of his education his parents seem to have carried conscientiousness to that extreme point at which it is almost impossible to distinguish it from harshness.'[95]

The Prince continued both to be severe and to treat his son as abnormal. He had called in a phrenologist in 1847 and did so again in 1850. Sir George Combe, on his second visit, reported to Sir James Clark on the 'natural dispositions' of the Prince of Wales. He said he had improved very considerably over the past three years. He was in better health, had grown and his excitability had diminished. The phrenologist noted 'that a hard ringing voice and an imperious manner, excite self-esteem and combativeness into activity and provoke them to opposition; whereas kind, soft, tender tones, accompanied by benevolent looks, directly address themselves to benevolence.'[96] The Prince should thus be treated with gentle firmness and kindness. This would bring out all his good qualities. Albert took no notice at all of this advice.

With time Birch's relationship with Bertie improved. 'I seem to have got at his heart,' he reported to the Prince in November 1850, 'and he seems to have given up the struggle against authority.'[97] On Christmas Eve of the same year he told the Prince that Bertie was now more amiable and teachable, more anxious to please. The Prince was now

... almost nine. From that time onwards Birch began to find excuses for his pupil and to defend him in the regular reports the Prince required. In April 1851, for instance, he wrote: 'I am vexed at the slow progress in writing and spelling but we must not forget that there are few English boys who know so much French and German or who know so much general information and with time, care and patience I do not despair of the writing and spelling.'[98] What the Prince of Wales could not bear, explained his tutor, was 'a certain drudgery'. So pleased was he with his pupil's progress that he was ready to stay on if the royal couple thought it would be good for the child.

Prince Albert in a memorandum summed up the advantages and disadvantages of Mr Birch. He was full of 'zeal and assiduity' and a 'strong sense of morality and religion' but he also had 'great wants' the principal of which were 'want of range in the field of knowledge' and 'a certain harshness of manner connected with the tone of voice'. Nothing, esteemed Prince Albert, had occurred to make him wish to deviate from the agreement that Birch should leave after two years.[99] Perhaps he even distrusted Bertie's attachment to his tutor.

Thus it was that the Prince of Wales was brutally cut off by his father from the tutor who had managed finally to earn the child's affection. Lady Canning noted: 'It has been a terrible sorrow to the Prince of Wales who has done no end of touching things since he heard that he was to lose him. He is such an affectionate, dear little boy; his little notes and presents which Mr Birch used to find on his pillow were really too moving.'[100] Prince Albert offered the place of tutor in June 1851 to Frederick Waymouth Gibbs. But his power was to be severely restricted. Prince Albert himself was to indicate the manner in which the education of the young Prince should be conducted and was to superintend the carrying out of his directives. Bertie's troubles were far from over.

Lord Melbourne had advised the Queen: 'Be not over-solicitous about education. It may be able to do much, but it does not do so much as is expected from it. It may mould and direct the character, but it rarely alters it.'[101] But Baron Stockmar and the Prince believed in leaving nothing to chance. A system of education was devised for Bertie which denied him any freedom or independence and which sought to repress any originality.

The Prince of Wales continued to dislike academic study. His memory was retentive but he had a strong distaste for reading. Prince Albert's system was certainly not designed to bring out his natural gifts. Now he had a tutor whose main task seems to have been the noting down of all

the boy's shortcomings. It was difficult to fix his attention on arithmetic, he was excited and disobedient, 'he quarrelled with Prince
Alfred'. The Prince made faces. He spat, he swore, he threw things on
the floor in anger. Even when he amused himself play-acting he gave
himself the principal role and gave his six-year-old brother the sub-
ordinate role. The diaries of his tutor show how every small incident
was built up, scrutinized and used to reinforce the prisonlike existence
the boy, still only eleven, was subjected to. Story books were banished;
even Sir Walter Scott's novels were outlawed as frivolous.

The Prince was starved of company. His father considered it unwise
for him to mix with boys of his own age. The Prince pushed conscientiousness in the education of his son to the point of harshness. The
tutor Gibbs was humourless and unimaginative, the ideal man to put
Coburg ideals into practice. Law not love was to rule the schoolroom.
He tried with great difficulty to make the system work. Stockmar had
warned him – in the strictest confidence – that the young Prince was
in fact 'an exaggerated copy of his mother' and that it would probably
be difficult to achieve what the Prince Consort wished but that he must
make it the business of his life to do the best he could. And if he could
not make anything of the eldest boy he must try with the younger one.

Much later, when he was King, Bertie looked back with pain on
these years of stress and strain. It is much to his credit that he did not
express any deep resentment against his father in later life. Albert had
tried to make his son in his own image but there was little of the father
in the boy. Albert was deeply German; Bertie was to give his heart
to France. Albert found communication difficult, as his love of memorandums shows; Bertie was born with a natural social ease. Albert was a
man of learning; Bertie was intuitive. Whereas his father was a man of
duty, Bertie had a love of life.

16
Foreign Affairs

During the earliest years of her reign the Queen, knowing little of foreign affairs, was content to agree to all her Foreign Minister did. She was eager from the outset, however, for things to be explained to her. Lord Palmerston thus became quite naturally her instructor. In the first letter he wrote to her, three days after her accession, he explained to her that letters varied in form and style according to the rank and character of the people to whom they were addressed. The conclusion of letters addressed by one Sovereign to another, for instance, had to be written in the hand of the Sovereign. He sent her with these explanations some letters to sign with the appropriate ending in pencil at the end of each. The pencil marks would, he assured her, be carefully rubbed out when she sent the letters back.[1]

The Queen often wrote asking precise questions and Palmerston dutifully replied. Could she write any day to Paris by the usual post or could she only send her letters by the diplomatic courier? Back came the reply – the diplomatic courier left the Foreign Office on Tuesday and Fridays, the ordinary post went to Paris every day but Sunday; the Queen could use either but in the latter case her letters might be examined at the French post offices.[2] Should she send back all the formal letters Lord Palmerston sent her from other Sovereigns? Indeed she should: all public documents of this sort were sent to the archives of the Foreign Office.[3] So the correspondence went backwards and forwards and the young Queen, who had no experience and no knowledge of such matters, gradually learnt how the system worked. With great patience Palmerston pointed out reference books, such as the Almanach de Gotha, where the Queen might look up the details of her foreign visitors, and had atlases prepared with maps 'which may be useful to Your Majesty when reading the foreign despatches'.[4]

Viscount Palmerston was fifty-three at the time. He was, like Lord Melbourne, a quizzical, cynical man of the world. He had entered the House of Commons as a Tory at twenty-three, had become an under-secretary at twenty-five and Minister of Foreign Affairs at forty-six. That was in 1830. By then he had transferred his allegiance to the Whigs. He had a strong personality and little respect for hierarchy. He married Lord Melbourne's sister, the beautiful Emily Lamb, on 11 December 1839, two years after the death of her husband, the fifth Earl Cowper. Palmerston was a fine shot and a fearless rider. When Victoria, at the beginning of her reign, went riding with Palmerston and Melbourne, Peel is said to have thought this hardly fitting for a young single girl, and Haydon prayed for her protection 'from the poison of Melbourne and Palmerston – too dangerous, too fascinating for her purity of principles.'[5]

Palmerston certainly charmed the Queen in these early years. He explained things to her in both letters and meetings. By established constitutional practice, all important draft instructions were submitted for the royal approval. Under William IV, Palmerston had got into the habit of having them copied and sent on their way in urgent cases before word came back that they had been approved. If the King's comments were unfavourable – and they almost never were – a correction could always be sent. All incoming despatches were sent to Windsor only after they had been seen by Palmerston.

When the Queen married, a subtle change came over the Queen's letters to her Foreign Minister. They became more authoritative, though still conciliatory. This was due to the influence of Prince Albert and to the ideas of the Prince and Baron Stockmar. The Queen began to require more detailed explanations and even justifications. She had not been married a year when the first real disagreement occurred. The Queen criticized Palmerston's reluctance to move towards a rapprochement with France after the Mehemet Ali crisis. The royal couple had been against Palmerston's policy of ordering the British fleet to use force to compel Mehemet Ali to return to his allegiance to the Sultan in November 1840. But despite a split within the Cabinet, despite disagreement with Lord John Russell, who was in favour of peace at any price, Palmerston had stood firm. War with France had seemed inevitable. In the event, however, although the French had encouraged Mehemet Ali to abandon his allegiance to the Sultan of Turkey, Louis-Philippe took no action and Palmerston's coercion succeeded.

Palmerston was not willing to submit to the Queen's wishes on major policy issues – nor on the day-to-day running of the Foreign Office. In 1841, for instance, the Queen sought – on behalf of her mother – the promotion of a young man called Kuper to the post of Secretary of the Legation. Kuper had originally been appointed to the Foreign Office because his father had been chaplain to Queen Adelaide, and he was already there when Palmerston first entered it. The difficulty was that he was thought to be a foreigner, although he was probably born in Great Britain.

Although nepotism was habitual in the Foreign Office, Palmerston's response to the Queen's request was a flat 'no'. 'It is', he explained, 'for many reasons desirable that all your Majesty's diplomatic agents should be entirely and unquestionably British subjects, both by birth and by blood.' There were so many reputable candidates for office who were good British subjects, he insisted, 'it would tend to give well-founded dissatisfaction if foreigners were on those occasions to be preferred; and then, in the next place, no diplomatic agent who is not purely and entirely British can represent with full advantage and the necessary weight British interests in foreign countries.'[6]

The Queen hoped that the strain between monarch and the Ministry of Foreign Affairs would disappear when Palmerston left it when Melbourne's Government fell. Peel appointed Lord Aberdeen. His policy was clearly more to the taste of the royal couple since it involved improving relations with France and the United States. For Palmerston, France had been the natural enemy, the natural rival, with interests contrary to those of Britain in the Levant, in Greece, Spain, Belgium, North Africa and the Pacific. Aberdeen, on the contrary, struck up a friendship with François Guizot, the leading French politician – both were devout Protestants and convinced monarchists. However, Aberdeen found that there was still hostility to France among his fellow ministers. In 1840–1 the French had at last achieved victory in Algeria, and in August 1844, despite promises and reassurances to the contrary, the French attacked Morocco. The commander of the naval expedition to Tangiers was, moreover, the Duke of Joinville, Louis-Philippe's third son, who had recently published an alarming pamphlet about the possibility of challenging British naval power. In the late summer of 1844 it seemed to many that war with France was inevitable. Aberdeen found himself isolated in the Cabinet and a few months later the Government fell.

In the budget of 1845, the naval estimates were increased and the Duke of Wellington busied himself with plans for the defence of the British Isles. Relations with the United States were in an even worse

state than relations with France – the boundaries with Britain's provinces were unsettled and had defied negotiation. The Ashburton Treaty
of August 1842 was to settle the question, giving the United States just
over half of the disputed land on the American–Canadian frontier.

While Aberdeen was Foreign Secretary he did not achieve the same
freedom in the conduct of affairs that Palmerston had enjoyed under
Melbourne. The Prime Minister scrutinized all levels of diplomatic
activity, read and amended draft despatches and even suggested new
points of view. Aberdeen was thus controlled as Palmerston never had
been. But this did not mean that Aberdeen treated Victoria any better
than Palmerston had done. He had already been Foreign Minister
some eleven years earlier; he was a fine scholar – he had had a new
chair in Modern History created for him at the University of Paris
when he was only twenty-five; and moreover his youngest daughter
Frances, if she had lived, would have been Victoria's age. He treated
the Queen as an inexperienced youngster just as Palmerston had.

He did, however, have the skills of a courtier and his paternalism was
less offensive than Palmerston's aggressiveness. He took great care to
consult the Queen on diplomatic appointments, but rarely acted on
her suggestions. He promised, for instance, to remove Sir Edward
Disbrowe from The Hague – in Victoria's opinion he was hostile to
King Leopold – but somehow the time was never ripe. In January 1844
Victoria complained that despatches were sent off before she could
approve them. Aberdeen apologized – it was, he claimed, all due to 'the
press of business in the office'.[7] Nonetheless, he continued to behave as
he had before and the following year the Queen was again obliged to
remonstrate. Aberdeen replied suavely that there had been no change,
that things continued as they had under George IV and William IV:

> This practice has usually been to submit to Your Majesty the drafts of
> despatches at the same time that they are sent from this office. Should
> Your Majesty then be pleased to make any remark or objection, it would
> be immediately attended to by Lord Aberdeen, who would forthwith
> either make any necessary alterations, by additional instructions, or he
> would humbly represent to Your Majesty the reasons which induce him
> to think that the interest of Your Majesty's service require an adherence
> to what had already been done.[8]

The Queen was increasingly anxious to bring foreign affairs under
the influence of the Crown – partly, no doubt, because of Albert's
interest in the field. It would be wrong, however, to see her simply as a
pawn in Albert's scheme of things. As Rhodes James has said: 'It is

because they worked together as a team that it is dangerous – except in certain clear, specific cases – to give the credit or otherwise to either of them individually.'[9] Be that as it may, there is no doubt that the royal couple came to regard the supervision of foreign affairs as within the Sovereign's province. Yet this was in contradiction with the constitutional principle which gave Parliament sole supremacy in the control of all departments of government. The Crown had to be consulted on foreign policy, and its approval was necessary for sending instructions from the Foreign Office to diplomatic representatives abroad. In case of disagreement between the Crown and the Foreign Secretary, the matter had to be referred to the Prime Minister. Should the Queen consider the Prime Minister's decision unsatisfactory, she could appeal to the Cabinet by asking the Prime Minister to put her views to it. Were the Cabinet to uphold the Prime Minister and a point of view that the Crown didn't like, the Sovereign was helpless. The Crown could insist on consultation, but its views could not be enforced if they were rejected. The influence of the Crown was dependent on its powers of persuasion.

The Queen's relations with her successive Governments in the 1840s and 1850s were to be marred by a struggle over her right to supervise foreign affairs. As the Queen travelled abroad, she came to know her foreign relatives better and to consider that they had certain inalienable rights: she was to find that there could be a conflict of feeling between her private obligations and her public obligations to her country. It was with difficulty that she conceded to successive Governments their freedom of action.

Peel left office in 1846 and with him Lord Aberdeen. Lord Palmerston returned to the Foreign Office as a member of Lord John Russell's Government, determined to strengthen Britain militarily and diplomatically. He had been a vigorous critic of Lord Aberdeen's policy, particularly with regard to the Ashburton Treaty – on 21 March 1843 he had spoken for three and a half hours against a motion congratulating Ashburton on it. This was the culmination of the campaign he had launched against it in a newspaper he could always count on to uphold his point of view, the *Morning Chronicle*. The treaty was, he claimed, both disgraceful and disadvantageous – not surprising, he said, since a half-Yankee had led the negotiations. This was a reference to Lord Ashburton's interests in America.

Where France was concerned, Palmerston had not openly criticized Aberdeen's attempts to improve relations, nor the Queen's visits to Eu. He had, however, damned them with faint words of praise in the House of Commons: 'I do not depreciate the visits of sovereigns but however gratifying they may be, they do not impress me with such entire confidence with regard to the maintenance of our mutual peaceful relations as to justify any reduction in British armaments.'[10] Influence abroad, he claimed, could only be maintained by the operation of one or other of two principles: hope and fear.

It was not surprising, therefore, that Victoria and Albert saw Palmerston reinstated in the Foreign Office with some apprehension. They feared he would destroy the friendly relations Peel's Government had established with France and the United States. They were not wrong. On Palmerston's return, Anglo–French relations immediately deteriorated. The Foreign Secretary had not forgotten his distrust of Louis-Philippe and the French.[11] The occasion of the Franco–British rupture was to be the Spanish marriages. Lord Aberdeen had sent Sir Robert Peel in 1845 a summary of what had been agreed at Eu. Among the suitors for the hand of Queen Isabella of Spain were the Count of Trapain, son of Francis, King of the Two Sicilies, Don Enrique, Duke of Seville, her first cousin, and his brother Don Francisco, Duke of Cadiz, the sons of the Infante Don Francisco de Paula. The persistent efforts of the French Government to promote the candidature of Count Trapain failed completely. Louis-Philippe had, however, agreed that his son, the Duke of Montpensier, would not marry the Infanta Fernanda until Queen Isabella was married and had ensured her succession. Lord Aberdeen, for his part, agreed to withdraw Prince Leopold of Saxe-Coburg from the list of suitors.

On 19 December 1846, three weeks after his return to the Foreign Office, Palmerston wrote a despatch to Henry Lytton Bulwer, the British representative at Madrid, discussing the marriage of Queen Isabella. The injudicious despatch stated clearly that the British Government did not actively support any of the princes who were candidates for the Queen of Spain's hand, but neither did it make any objection to any of them. It went on to say that there were three candidates. By including the name of Prince Leopold of Saxe-Coburg among the candidates, it in effect reinstated him as a suitor alongside Francisco and Enrique. The despatch was shown to Count Jarnac, the French Ambassador in London, who sent a copy of it to Louis-Philippe and to Guizot. The French then sent the despatch to the Spanish Government. Since it also contained caustic criticisms of the Spanish Government and its absolutism, the Queen of Spain considered that it indicated that there was an alliance between the English Government and the party of her enemies within.

The French Government, for its part, claimed that the English had reneged on the deal made at Eu and had thus released France from its agreement with Aberdeen. Louis-Philippe was thus given a pretext for following the course he was clearly eager to take. It is impossible to know whether the French would have acted differently if Aberdeen had remained in power. With Palmerston in command, both sides were visibly eager to pick a quarrel. Palmerston provoked the French, but their reaction was to say the least radical: they proposed the immediate double marriage of Isabella with Don Francisco, a man believed to be impotent, and the Infanta with the Duke of Montpensier.

As these networks of royal alliances were being renegotiated, Queen Victoria received a memorandum from Palmerston explaining that the British Government had no objection to the first of these marriages – though they regretted that a young Queen should have been forced to 'accept for husband a person whom she can neither like nor respect and with whom her future life will certainly be unhappy at home' – but that the marriage of the Duke of Montpensier was a different matter, for it had political implications that must exercise a most unfortunate effect upon the relations between England and France.[12]

The King of the French persuaded his wife Queen Marie Amélie to announce the double event to Queen Victoria. The Queen sent a curt reply. She said that the news of the marriages had caused her surprise and very keen regret and stressed that she had always been 'sincere' with them. If the Queen and the Prince deplored the breakdown of the Eu agreement, Palmerston for his part was content. He did not disguise the fact that he felt himself in no way bound by any agreement made by Aberdeen, and that, as he saw it, a marriage between a French prince and the Infanta was bound to evoke Great Britain's strongest and most justifiable objections. Such a marriage would bear evidence to a revival of the ambitions of France.[13] The British Minister of Foreign Affairs urged Count Jarnac to indicate to M. Guizot that if the French were to proceed with the marriage they would forfeit the friendship and confidence of England. Victoria was for once entirely in agreement with Palmerston.

She did, however, sound a note of restraint. She was not in agreement with Palmerston's proposal to raise Mr Bulwer, the Minister in Madrid, to the rank of Ambassador, and she cautioned Palmerston against encouraging any sort of insurrection in France.

The marriages took place on 10 October, three weeks before the date announced in the Royal Palace of Madrid. Isabella was sixteen, the Infanta fourteen. For weeks the watchword in the British press was 'French perfidy'. A month later the Queen thought all this had gone too far. 'The Queen thinks', came a note to Palmerston on 7 November, 'it would be well to check now, if possible, the violent tirades in *The Times* on the French Government. It is not dignified and will end in enraging the French nation, which fortunately till now is not ill-disposed towards us.' Palmerston replied that he had already, on his own initiative, let it be known to *The Times* that it would be better to allow the subject of the Montpensier marriage to drop.[14]

The loss of the English alliance harmed Louis-Philippe in the eyes of Europe and encouraged resistance within France. Austria took advantage of the estrangement between England and France to absorb the Republic of Cracow, the last remnant of free Poland – in defiance of the Treaty of Vienna. Isabella soon consoled herself for her miserable marriage. Within a few years she was said to be having love affairs with many of the officers and sergeants of her guard. She frustrated the French dynastic ambitions that rested on the Duke of Montpensier and the Infanta by having four children, and no one inquired as to who had engendered them. In April 1847 Albert told his brother:

> The marriage in Spain has turned out as it was to be expected. The couple have separated, the King follows the inspirations of a miraculous nun who is paid from Paris, the Queen had her lovers and at present she is kept a prisoner in the castle by the King . . . What will Louis Philippe have to answer for in heaven![15]

The Queen had hoped that Palmerston would not be long at the Foreign Office. A general election was scheduled for 1847 and Russell's Government was, she believed, a transition government. The Whigs were kept in power by divisions among the Tories, however, even though the polls did not give them an overall majority – Whigs 325; Peelites 105; Conservative Protectionists 226. The Queen marked her indifference to the welfare of the new Government by not being present at the opening of the newly elected Parliament.

It was not long before the differing views of the royal couple and Palmerston became apparent. The case in point was Portugal, where a revolutionary junta had risen in revolt against Queen Maria, whose husband Ferdinand was a Coburger and a first cousin of both the Queen and the Prince. The root of Portugal's problems lay in the contradictory settlements made in 1822, when a liberal constitution had been introduced, and in 1826, when a more conservative charter had given back certain powers to the Crown and the aristocracy. Since Maria had come to the throne, some fifteen revolutions of varying intensity had put Constitutionalists and Carlists in power alternately.

When Ferdinand married Maria he brought with him Herr Dietz, another Coburger and his former tutor, who became his adviser, occupying in Portugal a situation similar to that of Stockmar in Britain. Dietz was an absolutist and an ardent ally of the Carlists. In 1847 the Queen of Portugal, in danger of losing her throne, appealed to Queen Victoria for protection. Palmerston dictated the reply: the Queen of Portugal should reform the constitution and dismiss her reactionary counsellor Dietz.[16] At Maria's request the British Government agreed to mediate. The Queen of Portugal was to offer the rioters amnesty, the constitution was to be adopted again and a new, reformed ministry was to be promised. If the rebels did not agree to give themselves up, English, Spanish and French power was to force them.[17] It was the first time that a foreign power had intervened in internal affairs in Portugal in favour of the Crown.

The royal families abroad were not at all aware of Queen Victoria's constitutional situation. Seeing that she was Queen of a prosperous, powerful country, they attributed to her more power than she actually had and continually sent her personal appeals. The Queen was, however, obliged to lay these appeals before her Foreign Secretary and in many cases had to send back tepid, non-committal answers very different from those she would have liked to pen. In 1847, for instance, the King of Prussia sent a letter directly to the Queen asking for encouragement of Prussian efforts to dominate the German federation (Germany had since 1815 been composed of thirty-nine states). Palmerston protested to the Prussian Ambassador that it was irregular practice for the Queen of England to correspond directly with foreign monarchs unless they were her relatives. All correspondence, he insisted, must pass through the hands of her Ministers.[18]

Albert tried to influence the Foreign Office by sending long ponderous memorandums explaining his point of view. Palmerston took no notice of them for he had no wish to be advised by anyone. In any case, his views differed fundamentally from those of the Sovereign and her spouse. He was a champion of the growing liberal movements throughout Europe, whereas Queen Victoria and Prince Albert favoured the very reigning monarchies that these movements were trying to destabilize or overthrow.

There is difference of opinion as to the immediate cause of the conflagration which was to make 1848 the year of revolutions. Lord Malmesbury traced the origins of the outbreak to the popular disturbances in Munich in early February. There the King had dismissed his

Prime Minister, Prince Wallenstein, for advising him to expel his mistress, Lola Montes, from Bavaria. The Prime Minister was objecting to the powerful political influence she had acquired over the King. Lola Montes had first become known in society when she appeared in London, at Lord Malmesbury's house, where she sang ballads. It was said that her husband had been shot by the Carlists. In fact she was a complete imposter. She was from Cork and had married an Irish officer in the service of the East India Company in India. Lord Malmesbury had made her acquaintance in a railway carriage between Southampton and London and had later allowed her to sell trinkets and laces to his guests. She went on the stage at the opera house and was a failure, but she subsequently captivated the King of Bavaria. She amused him by stinging the faces of his generals with her whip if they were not turned out well enough. When the disturbances started in Munich the troops refused to fire on the people, and Lola Montes was driven out.

There were others who saw the starting point as the agitation for reform in Sicily. In January 1848 the royal troops were beaten and the insurgents insisted on a return to the constitution of 1812 and the assembly of a Parliament at Palermo. It has, however, been more customary to say that the epicentre was Paris, and that it was the opposition of Louis-Philippe and M. Guizot to the reform banquets – fixed for 22 February – that started a process that was to shake so many thrones to their foundations.

At its inception the movement in France, both inside and outside Parliament, sought simply to drive Guizot from office and force on the King a Cabinet which would put through electoral reform.[19] The opposition hoped to be able to bring about reform by peaceful agitation. On 21 February Guizot prohibited the reform banquet in Paris and drafted 60,000 soldiers into the capital. At first it looked as if the Government was in command, but a hard core of activists had taken up the Government's challenge and organized a grand procession up the Champs Elysées to the banqueting hall. The crowd got out of hand, breaking street lamps, overturning omnibuses and building barricades. All the same, the police seemed capable of dealing with what were sporadic, unorganized disturbances.[20]

The following day, however, larger gatherings were organized in the narrow streets of the centre of the town, where barricades could be set up more easily. The National Guard was called in to restore order, but went over to the side of the demonstrators. From then on the insurrection made rapid headway. On 24 February, Louis-Philippe abdicated in favour of his grandson, the Comte de Paris, and fled from the capital. Escorted by some two hundred men, Louis-Philippe and his Queen set off with their entourage to Versailles. There they hired an ordinary carriage to take them to Dreux, where they spent the night in a private house. Here they procured disguises and set off on their journey to the coast as Mr and Mrs Smith, travelling mostly by night. They reached Honfleur on Saturday, 26 February, in the morning. Bad weather prevented them from boarding a boat at Trouville and they stayed in Honfleur until the following Thursday, when they left in a French fishing boat for Le Havre. There they boarded the *Express* which took them to Newhaven, on the Sussex coast. This last phase of their journey was organized by Mr Featherstonehaugh, the British Consul at Le Havre.[21]

Meanwhile, in London, the Queen and Prince Albert were following events closely – Albert with great anxiety. 'European war is at our doors,' he wrote on 27 February 1848, 'France is ablaze in every quarter, Louis-Philippe is wandering about in disguise, so is the Queen; ... Guizot is a prisoner, the Republic declared, the army ordered to the frontier, the incorporation of Belgium and the Rhenish provinces proclaimed.'[22] Two days later he wrote to the Dowager Duchess of Coburg, because he had just learnt of the death of his grandmother, the Dowager Duchess of Gotha: he explained that he could not give way to his own private grief, harassed as he was by the terrible present. 'Augustus, Clémentine, Nemours, and the Duchess of Montpensier, have come to us one by one like people shipwrecked; Victoire, Alexander, the King, the Queen, are still tossing upon the waves, or have drifted to other shores: we know nothing of them.'[23] Queen Victoria was at the time in the last days of her pregnancy with her daughter Louise, who was born on 18 March 1848. Albert wrote to Stockmar: 'though it be a daughter, still my joy and gratitude are very great, as I was often full of misgiving, because of the many moral shocks which have crowded upon Victoria of late.'[24]

Nevertheless, Victoria's journal does not show her in any great state. 'My only thoughts and talk were politics, and I never was calmer or quieter or more earnest. Great events make me calm. It is only trifles that irritate my nerves,' she wrote to her uncle.[25] Louis-Philippe, she thought, had brought much of this on himself, 'by that ill-fated return to a Bourbon policy'.[26] She also thought the King had not really behaved very royally. 'Certainly at the very last if they had not gone they would all have been massacred ... but there is an impression they fled too quickly.'[27]

As soon as he landed, Louis-Philippe wrote to Queen Victoria asking her for refuge.[28] Lord John Russell agreed that the Queen should

assent.[29] Others appealed for sanctuary, too. When the news of the
revolution reached Algiers, the Duke of Aumale immediately prepared
to leave. He and all the rest of the French royal family, with the
exception of the Duchess of Orléans and her two sons, took refuge in
England: the Duchess of Montpensier, after a narrow escape from a
mob at Abbeville, was brought over from Boulogne by her husband's
aide-de-camp General Thierry; the Duchess of Nemours travelled with
her three children, accompanied by the Duke of Montpensier, to
Granville – then Jersey – where they remained until 9 March, when
they journeyed on incognito to Portsmouth; the Prince and Princess of
Joinville and the Duke and Duchess of Aumale arrived on 22 March at
Dartmouth, having embarked at Gibraltar.

The Duchess of Orléans went to Germany, where she remained for
the rest of the year. She must have been affected by her memories of the
fearful scenes enacted before her eyes in Paris. On Louis-Philippe's
abdication she had gone alone to the Chamber of Deputies with her two
sons to have the Count of Paris proclaimed King; a mob had broken in,
armed with swords and pikes and muskets, and had prevented the
reading of the proclamation.

The ex-King and Queen of the French, who had assumed the title of
the Count and Countess of Neuilly, were installed at Claremont, where
Prince Albert went to pay his respects on 5 March. Guizot, too, was
among this cohort of French exiles who sought refuge in London. Two
days later they came, with Palmerston's agreement, to visit Victoria at
Buckingham Palace. The poverty of the family deeply shocked the
Queen. She wrote to Lord Palmerston:

> The Queen fears (indeed knows) that the poor Duke and Duchess of
> Nemours are in sad want of all means; and she knows the poor Duchesse
> of Orleans is equally so. It is very lamentable and the Queen feels much
> for them, for it is a position which, if one reflects on it, requires great
> courage and resignation to submit to. It would be infamous if the Re-
> public gave them nothing. The Queen fears Lord Normanby is inclined
> to be on too friendly and confidential terms with M. Lamartine. Did
> Lord Palmerston caution him? We should do all that is right but not
> show any *empressement* towards what is after all a great calamity.[30]

Palmerston's reply came back on the same day.

> He also deeply lamented the pecuniary difficulties in which some
> members of the French royal family were for the moment placed. He had
> twice told Count Jarnac that whenever the Count thought it desirable he

would pay over a thousand pounds out of secret service money for the use of the royal family to any banker whom Count Jarnac might name. He would do this on condition that the royal family should not know where the money came from and would not therefore feel under any sense of obligation to the British Government.[31]

Palmerston, too, could make noble gestures.

As the months went by, the Queen found that the misfortune of some can be the good fortune of others. There was no end to the jewellers and artists arriving from Paris, half ruined and with beautiful and tempting things, some of which she could not resist buying. On occasion she even profited from the royal family's impecuniousness. 'Their situation is sadder than ever, which I can realise only too well from the fact that I have just bought something she [Victoire] was obliged to part with. It shows how pinched they must be.'[32]

Things were finally settled with the new French regime in October 1848, when the French National Assembly voted to restore to the Orléans family 'the enjoyment of their incomes', and this 'almost without discussion and with hardly a dissentient voice'.[33] Lord John Russell informed the Queen at the end of November that King Louis-Philippe should have more than a million pounds sterling.[34]

In addition to their misfortunes the French royal family had suffered attacks of illness throughout November. The Duke of Nemours, the Duke of Joinville and the exiled Queen were particularly badly affected. When the water of Claremont was analysed, it was found that they had been poisoned by lead, which had been dissolved in it from the new cistern. Lady Canning wrote: 'The poor man [Nemours] looks quite like death just as you would imagine of a slow poison to look, quite blacked and blue and yellow.'[35]

The French royal family remained at Claremont – although at times the Queen wished it were otherwise. On July 1848, for instance, she accompanied Albert to Claremont, 'which was in its greatest beauty, and which it always makes me a little sad to have lost for the present.'[36] She nevertheless entertained the Nemours, the Joinvilles and the King and Queen regularly. Victoire, the wife of the Duke of Nemours, was in fact to become a close friend of the Queen's. This was not always to the taste of the Court. 'We have the Nemours here still,' Lady Canning wrote, 'and I cannot say they are much improved but rather the reverse for they are both so very dull. She is very pretty and nice to look at, but besides having a tiresome voice she has nothing to say and everybody's mouth is shut by the number of topics we are all scrupulous of broaching in their presence.'[37]

On 26 August 1850 Louis-Philippe died; the sad news greeted Victoria and Albert almost immediately on their return from a brief visit to the King of the Belgians at Ostend. On the following day Victoria went to Claremont. Nemours told her that the hospitality she had shown his father had been the means of softening his last moments, for it had enabled him to be 'among his own family'. He hoped she would continue to extend her hospitality to his family, and she readily did so.[38]

Less than two months later, Queen Louise of the Belgians, Louis-Philippe's daughter and King Leopold's wife, died. Her husband was not overcome – he had in 1849 embarked on his last liaison, with Mademoiselle Arcadie Claret de Viscourt, the daughter of a lieutenant-colonel of infantry attached to the war ministry.[39] He was to have two sons by her and the liaison was to last until his death. That Louise had known of his infidelity and suffered from it is obvious from a pathetic letter she wrote him early in 1849:

> What more could I ask on earth than to be your friend, to be your old friend? All my happiness I owe to you; all that is lacking from my happiness is my fault, alone, and I blame only myself for all that troubles me. If I am no longer young, if I have none of the gifts or graces that might have made your home a happy one, if I have been unable to bring any pleasure to your life, I must attribute it to my ill fortune. And so, if I cannot but regret, I only regret what I cannot do for you.[40]

Victoria on the other hand sincerely mourned Louise. In her diary on 13 October 1850 she gave vent to her grief.

> I think no one understood her perfect, beautiful, unselfish and self-denying character better than I did. United with all this there was an elevation of mind, of feelings – a courage, a clear sightedness, a cheerfulness and a rectitude of judgement rarely seen in conjunction with so wonderfully humble, meek and gentle a character.... With her acute feelings she must have suffered, as she *did* severely at the disasters that befell her family and particularly from the manner in which their fall had taken place.[41]

Prince Albert wrote to Stockmar: 'Victoria is greatly distressed. Her aunt was her only confidante and friend. Sex, age, culture, feeling, rank – in all these they were so much on a par, that a relation of unconstrained friendship naturally grew up between them.'

The events in France fanned the smouldering discontent in Germany, in Austria, in Italy. In Germany it expressed itself in a desire for unity

Lord Melbourne, sketched by Queen Victoria.
(Windsor Castle, Royal Library © 1990 Her Majesty The Queen)

Lady Flora Hastings.

Lady Flora Hastings.
(Windsor Castle, Royal Library © 1990 Her Majesty The Queen)

Windsor Castle in Modern Times by Sir Edwin Landseer.
(Reproduced by gracious permission of Her Majesty The Queen)

Sir John Conroy.
(Windsor Castle, Royal Library © 1990 Her Majesty The Queen)

The Duchess of Kent by Sir George Hayter.
(Windsor Castle, Royal Library © 1990 Her Majesty The Queen)

Windsor Castle, engraved by A. Willmore after Birket Foster.
(The Mansell Collection)

The Royal Family, 1846, by Winterhalter.
(Reproduced by gracious permission of Her Majesty The Queen)

State procession to the opening ceremony of the Crystal Palace, 1851, Lithograph by Butler.
(The Mansell Collection)

Funeral of the Duke of Wellington, by Haghe.
(Windsor Castle, Royal Library © 1990 Her Majesty The Queen)

Group on the lower terrace, Osborne, August 1853. Left to right: Victoria, Princess Royal; Albert Edward, Prince of Wales; Princess Alice; Prince Alfred. Photographer: Dr E. Becker.

Queen Victoria and Prince Albert, 30 June 1854. Photographer: Roger Fenton.
(Copyright reserved. Reproduced by gracious permission of Her Majesty The Queen)

Entry of Queen Victoria into Paris, by Bajot and Daurats.
The visit to Emperor Napoleon III, 1855.
(Windsor Castle, Royal Library © 1990 Her Majesty The Queen)

Arrival of the Queen at Eu, by Charlotte Canning.
(Windsor Castle, Royal Library © 1990 Her Majesty The Queen)

Drawing room in the private appartments at Eu, by Eugène Lami.
(Windsor Castle, Royal Library © 1990 Her Majesty The Queen)

The Emperor Napoleon III and Empress Eugénie, Queen Victoria and Prince Albert visit the Hall of Mirrors at the Palace of Versailles, 20 August 1855, by Victor Chavet. (Windsor Castle, Royal Library © 1990 Her Majesty The Queen)

Queen Victoria and Prince Albert inspecting the sick and wounded Grenadier guardsmen from the Crimea War, 20 February, 1855, by G. H. Thomas.
(Windsor Castle, Royal Library © 1990 Her Majesty The Queen)

The Royal Family at Osborne, 26 May, 1857. Left to right: Prince Alfred, Prince Albert, Princess Helena, Princess Alice, Prince Arthur, Queen Victoria with Princess Beatrice, Victoria, Princess Royal, Princess Louise, Prince Leopold, Albert Edward, Prince of Wales. Photographer: Caldesi. (Copyright reserved. Reproduced by gracious permission of Her Majesty The Queen)

The Royal residence at Balmoral by Fripp.
(Windsor Castle, Royal Library © 1990 Her Majesty The Queen)

Victoria, The Princess Royal, on her wedding day, 25 January, 1858, with
her parents Queen Victoria and the Prince Consort, from a daguerreotype
of T. R. Williams.
(Copyright reserved. Reproduced by gracious permission of Her Majesty
The Queen)

Queen Victoria and the Prince Consort, Osborne, July 1859. Photographer: Miss Day.

The Mausoleum, Frogmore.
(The Mansell Collection)

Queen Victoria with Victoria, Princess Royal, 25 June, 1857.
(Copyright reserved. Reproduced by gracious permission of Her Majesty
The Queen)

among the smaller states. At Mannheim and Karlsruhe, crowds assembled and clamoured for a German Parliament, the freedom of the press and the arming of the people. Riots caused the authorities to yield. In Baden, Darmstadt, Nassau and the electorate of Hesse, in Oldenburg and Brunswick and in the other smaller states, concessions were made hastily. The larger states – Bavaria, Saxony, Hanover – resisted popular pressure until forced into action by the triumph of the revolutionaries in Austria and Prussia. The Queen's closest relations – her half-brother Charles of Leiningen, her half-sister Princess of Hohenlohe-Langenburg, Prince Albert's brother the Duke of Saxe-Coburg-Gotha – all suffered severely in these revolutionary days, but their thrones survived.

The country which most preoccupied the royal couple during this period was undoubtedly Prussia. On the day Princess Louise was born, barricades were put up in Berlin and the King of Prussia's authority questioned. The riots were serious and King Frederick William IV tried to suppress the movement by force. He was finally obliged to make concessions: the freedom of the press; the assembly of a Diet for 2 April; and the incorporation of East and West Prussia and Posen in the Bund, which was to take the place of the old Confederation of States. The Crown Prince of Prussia (afterwards Emperor William I), who was supposed – wrongly – to have ordered the troops to fire on the people, fled from his palace in Berlin and arrived in London on 27 March. He took up residence in the house of the Prussian Ambassador, the Chevalier Bunsen.[42] Victoria had originally intended that the Prince should be one of Princess Louise's godfathers, but this was seen as inopportune both by Albert[43] and by the Prime Minister.[44] The Prince remained in England till the end of May, when he returned to Berlin. On leaving he told Bunsen's wife that he could not have spent this period of distress and anxiety in a better place or country.[45]

Meanwhile, at the instigation of his Ministers, Frederick William IV placed himself at the head of the movement for German unity in defiance of Austria. This was all the easier to do as Prince Metternich had fled. This energetic, unscrupulous *eminence grise* of Ferdinand I, Emperor of Austria, had escaped from Vienna in disguise after the mob had sacked his palace. Austrian domination over far-flung territories collapsed. Lombardy and Venetia declared themselves independent. The King of Sardinia put himself at the head of the agitation for Italian unity.

With Europe in turmoil, it was over events in Spain that Palmerston and the royal couple were once again to clash. Revolt was smouldering and the Spanish Government foolishly prorogued the Cortes. This was immediately followed by a popular rising in Madrid on 26 March. Lord Palmerston had been watching events and had sent the British Ambassador in Madrid, Sir Henry Bulwer, a letter asking him to advise the Spanish Queen that she should change her Ministers. Sir Henry Bulwer sent a copy of the despatch to the Duke of Sotomayor, the head of the Spanish Government, and arranged for it to be published in the opposition newspapers. The Spanish Government was angered by this interference in their domestic affairs and returned the despatch to the Foreign Office declaring that it was 'offensive to the dignity of a free and independent nation'.[46] Sir Henry Bulwer was asked to leave Spain within forty-eight hours.

Lord John Russell, the Prime Minister, had seen Lord Palmerston's despatch in advance and had intimated to his Foreign Secretary that he objected to it. Shortly after, he was with the Queen and told her what he had said to Palmerston: ' "No! *did* you say that," said the Queen. He said, "Yes". "Well then," she replied, "It produced no effect for the despatch *is* gone. Lord Palmerston sent it to me. I know it is gone." '[47]

Palmerston was attacked in Parliament by the Opposition in both houses. Lord John himself declared he was shocked. It was without precedent that 'a despatch of a British Secretary of State should be returned by the Minister of a Foreign Government as unfit to be retained or received.'[48] But Palmerston survived the storm and continued to play a personal role in the difficult events of the time. And it continued to be a role often diametrically opposed to the desires of the Sovereign and her spouse.

With regard to Italy, for instance, Palmerston was in favour of the country's ridding itself of the Austrian yoke, whereas the sympathies of the Prince and Queen were largely with the Austrian Emperor. Were Italy to become a single united country, thrones would need to be sacrificed. The Italian Risorgimento had Palmerston's blessing. 'I cannot regret the expulsion of the Austrians from Italy . . .' he wrote to King Leopold in June 1848, 'her rule was hateful to the Italians and has long been maintained only by an expenditure of money and an exertion of military effort which left Austria less able to maintain her interests elsewhere.'[49] The Queen, on the other hand, was quite against Italian independence. On 1 July she told the Minister of Foreign Affairs that she could not conceal from him that she was 'ashamed of the policy which we are pursuing in this Italian controversy'.[50]

In June, it was over Portugal that dissension arose. The Queen had wanted the British representative at Lisbon, Sir Hamilton Seymour, to keep out of local party intrigues. Whereupon Palmerston drafted a despatch to Seymour couched in the following words.

> As it is evident that the Queen and Government of Portugal will listen to no advice except such that agrees with their own wishes, I have to instruct you to abstain in future from giving any longer any advice to them on political matters. ... You will however at the same time positively declare to the Portuguese Government that if by the course of the policy they are pursuing they should run into any difficulty, they must clearly understand that they will not have to expect any assistance from England.[51]

The Queen was appalled by the tone and referred the matter to the Prime Minister, saying she thought it 'almost a mockery of Lord John, the Cabinet, the Country and herself which can really not go on so'.[52] Lord John hesitated between his monarch and his Minister, writing many letters in which he took alternately Palmerston's and the Queen's side and seeing himself as an umpire rather than the effective leader of the Government. Finally he declared that the despatch ought to be toned down and that it should adopt a tone of commendation rather than reproach.[53] He also rejected Palmerston's view that British Ministers abroad might communicate unofficially with parties whose aim was to overthrow existing Governments. 'Such conduct would be unfriendly and unfair to the foreign sovereign, impolitic and perilous as regards ourselves.'[54] The Queen exulted. Palmerston agreed to draft a despatch in accordance with the wishes of the Queen and the Prime Minister – but he managed to delay the sending of it for another two weeks ...

It must not be assumed from the Portuguese affair that the Queen was always able to make her mark on British foreign policy. When the Prime Minister and the Foreign Secretary agreed on the substance of a policy, the Queen's remonstrations were disregarded. This was the case, for instance, when the Queen tried to force the Foreign Secretary to give up his policy of cooperation with the new government in France. When she realized that her protests were of no avail, she retreated from her position.[55] The Queen nonetheless found it difficult to accept that the Crown was obliged to accept a foreign policy it thought wrong when its means of persuasion were exhausted. Her dislike of her Foreign Secretary intensified. 'The Queen', she wrote to Lord John Russell in August 1848, 'must say she is afraid that she will have no peace of mind and there will be no end of troubles as long as Lord Palmerston is at the head of the Foreign Office.'[56]

During the tumultuous year of 1848, 28,000 despatches were received or sent out at the Foreign Office.[57] Revolution put great pressure of work on Government and Head of State alike. But the real anxiety lay elsewhere: would revolution spread to Britain?

The difference between the social structure in France, Britain's near neighbour, and Britain was at the time very great. France was a country of small proprietors, with over six million landowners, the vast majority having small holdings of less than five acres. In England and Wales some 500 members of the peerage owned almost half of the total acreage. Some 1,300 members of the gentry and landed commoners possessed most of the remainder. The nobility in England was thus wealthy, with palatial town houses and estates which were often self-sufficient. The nobility also had political power. In British Cabinets between 1832 and 1866, sixty-four Ministers were aristocrats, twelve were lawyers and five were primarily businessmen.[58] The gap between business interests and aristocracy was not as great as might have been thought. One-third of the aristocratic Members of the House had business interests.

This social structure might be thought to facilitate revolution. Inequality was more flagrantly visible, and far fewer people than in France had anything to lose. The landless British peasants who made up one-fifth of the population were not slaves, but they were not free. Their hands were not chained but their spirits were.[59] Hired out by the week or the day, they were usually without work all through the winter. As for the workers in the towns, their situation had been minutely described, in particular by Engels, and they seemed even more ready for revolution.

The Queen and her Consort were fully aware of the deprived state in which the working classes lived. As far back as 1844 Albert had become president of a Society for the Improvement of the Working Classes. He was in favour of stimulating the upper and middle classes into action by bringing them into voluntary movements aimed at improving the lot of the working classes.

The events of 1848 in France caused renewed activity among the Chartists in Britain. The movement was at the time split between the constitutional radicals and those in favour of the use of physical violence. The leader of the movement, Feargus O'Connor, was in the first group, completely hostile to any unconstitutional proceedings. The Chartists decided, therefore, to show their strength. The pretext was the presentation to Parliament of a great national petition, with signatures which were said to number nearly five million. A general assembly of all the Chartists in the land was to take place on Kennington Common on 10 April. It was thought that some 150,000 demonstrators would gather. The Government was determined to prevent any events similar to those which had occurred in France in February 1848. On 6 April a notice was placarded throughout London:

> Whereas the assemblage of large numbers of persons, accompanied with circumstances tending to excite terror and alarm in the minds of her Majesty's subjects, is criminal and unlawful ... and whereas a meeting has been called to assemble on Monday next, the 10th instant, at Kennington Common ... All persons are hereby cautioned and strictly enjoined not to attend or take part in or be present at any such assemblage or procession ...

It was signed by the Commissioners of the Metropolitan Police.

It had been decided that no opposition would be made to the constitutional right of meeting to petition, nor to the proper presentation of the petition, but should there be any attempt to form an organized procession, the Chartists would be stopped by force of arms if necessary. The Queen departed for Osborne with the Prince and her family on 8 April and it is difficult to believe that the date was pure coincidence. Alarm was universal. Prince Albert was convinced that the situation was fraught with danger since the organization of the Chartists was extraordinarily good. The defensive measures were organized and supervised by the Duke of Wellington himself. The bridges over the Thames were the main points of concentration – bodies of foot and horse police were posted at their approaches on either side. Twelve hundred infantrymen waited at the dockyards and thirty pieces of heavy field ordnance were kept ready at the Tower for transport by steamer to any spot which might be threatened. At other places, troops were carefully placed out of sight but within command. No troops were visible on the streets, only the police. In addition to the regular civil and military force, some 170,000 special constables were enrolled.[60] People living in the roads converging on Kennington Common kept their doors and windows shut and in many cases barricaded.

The crowd that assembled was diversely estimated at between 15,000 and 150,000 – but is calculated by the *Annual Register* to have been around 40,000. The petition was then consigned to three cabs, which were to take it to Parliament. When the meeting broke up, the return of the Chartist crowd towards town was stopped at the bridges – they were closed for a considerable time and there was some struggling to force a crossing. However, the crowd was manoeuvred into small groups, and finally small parties of not more than ten each were allowed to cross. By three o'clock the great mass had disbanded.

The Chartists claimed that the national petition in favour of the six points of the Charter was signed by 5,706,000 people. On 13 April, however, it was reported from the Select Committee on Petitions that the petition contained only 1,975,496 signatures – many of them false. Among them appeared, for instance, Victoria Rex, the Duke of Wellington, Sir Robert Peel, and names that were not names, such as 'No Cheese', 'Pugnose', etc. The ridicule occasioned by these false signatures was very damaging to the credibility of the Chartists.

Social unrest was, however, still strong enough in the north of England for the movement to make itself felt violently six weeks later. *The Times* reported on 31 May:

> The evil counsels of the worst of the Chartist leaders appear to have taken root amongst large classes of the operatives of the West Riding of Yorkshire ... Owing to the depression of the worsted manufacture, and the introduction of machinery that has superseded the use of manual labour in the process of woolcombing, much distress and suffering have for a considerable time been experienced by the manufacturing operatives ... Hence they have – more perhaps in a spirit of desperation than by any well-grounded belief in the principles of Chartism – followed the advice of advocates of physical force.

Angry meetings had continued in London in May and on 6 May five of the most conspicuous leaders were arrested on a charge of sedition. They were tried at the Old Bailey in July and sentenced to two years imprisonment. But it was not until August that the movement was finally quelled. The partisans of violence had planned a general rising in London and other major towns for 16 August. However, the movement had been infiltrated and as each arrangement was made it was reported to the Government. The authorities therefore knew exactly how and when to act: 'on the very night that a general rising of the Chartists was to have taken place,' Prince Albert reported to Baron Stockmar, 'the leaders of the conspiracy, to a man, were seized and imprisoned neatly and simultaneously.'[61] Large quantities of weapons, ammunition and tow-balls, for use in setting fire to public buildings, were found in the houses where the men were arrested. Chartism was totally discredited.

On 5 September 1848 the Queen prorogued Parliament in person. The ceremony took place for the first time in the Peers' Chamber in the new Houses of Parliament, rebuilt after the fire of 1834. The Duke of Nemours and the Prince of Joinville were present with her and popular enthusiasm ran high. In her speech from the throne the Queen declared:

> The strength of our institutions has been tried, and has not been found wanting. I have studied to preserve the people committed to my charge in the enjoyment of that temperate freedom which they so justly value. My people, on their side, feel too sensibly the advantages of order and security to allow the promoters of pillage and confusion any chance of success in their wicked designs.[62]

Many writers, including Karl Marx, attributed the outbreak of revolution in 1848 to the misery and desperation of the masses. That this explanation alone is unsatisfactory can be seen from events in Ireland. The potato famine had led to one of the greatest tragedies of the century. Apart from those who died of actual starvation, there were deaths from typhus, cholera and dysentery – even among those who sought to flee to America and elsewhere and died on the 'plague ships'. All this should have given force and direction to the revolutionary spirit. There had indeed been an outbreak of agrarian crime in response to the 'Young Ireland' movement. The Habeas Corpus Act was suspended, troops were installed in the towns and warships sent to the Irish harbours. An Act was passed making written incitement to insurrection a felony punishable by transportation. Yet when the young radicals known as 'Young Ireland' called on the people to rise it was a badly organized, poorly led affair. Agitation culminated in what came to be known as the 'Cabbage-garden insurrection'. The police, who had taken refuge in a cottage, were attacked by rebels in the cabbage garden outside. A volley from the police dispersed the insurgents and the ringleaders were caught and sentenced to death. Their sentence was later commuted to one of transportation.

By the beginning of 1850 the counter-revolution had taken place virtually everywhere. The advent of Prince Charles Louis Bonaparte came at the right psychological moment and was welcomed by all parties in France. He was elected President of the Republic on 10 December 1848 by five and a half million out of seven and a half million votes. He had sworn to preserve the Republic, but by 1850 was charting its destruction. Elsewhere, Joseph Mazzini and his followers had been crushed by the Austrians. The Republican Government had been suppressed in Rome, Pope Pius IX restored to the Vatican and the Duke of Tuscany restored to power. King Ferdinand ruled again over the Two Sicilies. The revolution in Hungary had been suppressed. In Austria, reaction surpassed anything Metternich had attempted;

and the Tsar's regime in Russia reached the pinnacle of repression. Everywhere on the continent, force had vanquished opinion.

It was at this point that the most dramatic episode in the saga opposing the Queen to Palmerston occurred: the Don Pacifico controversy. Some British subjects had had their property destroyed during the disturbances in Athens in 1847. The main sufferer was a Portuguese Jew, Don Pacifico. He was a British subject by virtue of having been born, like his father, in Gibraltar, but he lived in Athens, where he was the Portuguese Consul General. His house had been attacked by an anti-Semitic mob. His wife's jewellery had been stolen and the house had been set on fire. Pacifico sent for the police but they made no effort to control the mob, which included the fourteen-year-old son of General Zavellos, the Minister of War. Don Pacifico claimed 31,534 pounds from the Greek Government, with interest at twelve per cent to run from 1847. The claim was refused and he turned to the British Government to help him, citing his British citizenship.

Palmerston was not sorry to have a pretext to intervene in Greek affairs. He was hostile to Prince Otto, the Bavarian who was on the Greek throne, regarding him as an unintelligent despot. After negotiating with the Greek Government for twenty months, the Foreign Secretary decided to act. The pressure he exerted was out of all proportion to the offence. The British Mediterranean fleet was ordered to enter the Port of Piraeus, the Greek vessels in the harbour were seized and Athens was blockaded. The Greeks appealed to France and Russia. Russia remonstrated with Great Britain but was told to mind its own business. France had more success with conciliation and a convention was arranged in London. It offered Britain certain terms. Palmerston delayed sending an account of the terms to Mr Wyse, the British representative in Athens, while he obtained better terms in Athens: the Greek Government delivered to him the full amount claimed. The French accused Palmerston of doublecrossing them and recalled the French Ambassador from London. France and Britain were in open diplomatic conflict. Queen Victoria, who vigorously condemned Palmerston's part in the whole affair, found that this time her Prime Minister Lord John Russell shared her views. According to Greville he was quite ready to remove Palmerston from the Foreign Office at the Queen's request, without himself resigning.[63] The Opposition, however, decided to use the Don Pacifico affair to launch a severe attack on the foreign policy of the Government and Lord John was thus obliged to stand by his Foreign Secretary.

On 17 June the Conservative leader, Lord Stanley, moved a vote of censure on the Government in the House of Lords. It was carried by 169 to 132. Two days later Palmerston informed the French Government that Britain would stand by certain clauses of the London agreement, and not insist on the better terms obtained from Athens. He also offered Lord John his resignation. Lord John was obliged to refuse it, for it was the whole Government that was under attack and not simply the Foreign Secretary. If there were to be a resignation it would have to be of the entire Government. The only course now open to the Prime Minister was to persuade the House of Commons to reverse the condemnation of the Lords. To appeal to the people, as it were, against the Establishment.

On 20 June Lord Roebuck moved a resolution declaring that the Government's foreign policy had preserved Britain's honour and dignity, and had been 'the best calculated to maintain peace between England and the various nations of the world'.[64] The debate lasted four days. Palmerston's policy was challenged by Gladstone, Cobden and Bright. He made a brilliant speech, nearly five hours long, defending his actions and challenging the verdict of the Lords. In a powerful peroration, he claimed that 'as the Roman in days of old, held himself free from indignity when he could say "Civis Romanus sum", so also a British subject, in whatever land he may be, shall feel confident that the watchful eye and the strong arm of England will protect him against injustice and wrong.'

The speech was acclaimed. It was a personal triumph and vindicated Palmerston's actions. The debate continued for two days, at the end of which the House of Commons reversed the sentence passed in the House of Lords by 310 votes to 264 – a majority of 46. The middle classes were solidly behind Palmerston. His admirers commissioned a portrait of him to be painted and presented to Lady Palmerston; he was invited to a celebration dinner by 250 members of the Reform Club – with nine courses and eighty-one different dishes.

The rhetoric had no effect on the judgement of the Queen, however. On 12 August she drafted a formal memorandum to the Prime Minister explaining what she expected from her Foreign Secretary.

> She requires (1) That he will distinctly state what he proposes in a given case, in order that the Queen may know as distinctly to *what* she has given her royal sanction; (2) Having once given her sanction to a measure that it be not arbitrarily altered or modified by the Minister; such an act she must consider as failing in sincerity towards the Crown, and justly to be visited by the exercise of her constitutional right of dismissing that Minister. She expects to be kept informed of what passes

between him and the Foreign Ministers before important decisions are taken, based upon that intercourse, to receive the foreign despatches in good time, and to have the drafts for her approval sent to her in sufficient time to make herself acquainted with their contents before they must be sent off.[65]

The memorandum contained an explicit condemnation of Lord Palmerston. 'His modes of proceedings were often too violent and abrupt, the language of his despatches was often less calculated to conciliate than to mortify and offend, and his general demeanour towards other Governments was very frequently such as to inspire them with undefined alarm.' She recognized that he was 'able, sagacious, patriotic and courageous', but at the same time he was 'wilful and passionate'.[66] Lord John Russell sent the memorandum to Palmerston and on the following day Palmerston asked to see the Prince. 'He was very much agitated, shook, and had tears in his eyes, so as to quite move me.' What affected Lord Palmerston most was the 'accusation that he had been wanting in his respect to the Queen'.[67] Palmerston's protestations that he would not fail to follow the Queen's instructions were hollow, however, and he immediately reverted to his old ways. In September came the Haynau incident.

The Austrian, General Haynau, had come on a visit to England. The Radicals stirred up public feeling against him because of the brutality with which he had crushed the Hungarian insurrection. In London, workers assaulted and insulted the man they called 'the Austrian butcher'. He had to be smuggled away by the police. Lord Palmerston sent a note of apology to the Austrian Ambassador, in which he expressed the opinion that Haynau had shown ' a want of propriety' in visiting England 'at the present moment'. The Queen wanted to amend the despatch – only to find that, once again, it had already been sent. Lord John Russell advised her to recall it and insist on its being replaced by a new note without the paragraph she thought injurious to the Austrians. This was eventually done. But friction continued.

In 1851 the arrival in England of Kossuth, the Hungarian revolutionary, was to constitute a new chapter in the struggle between Palmerston and the Crown. Kossuth had taken refuge in the Turkish dominions in 1849 and Russia and Austria had demanded his extradition. Turkey refused. Under pressure – in particular from the English Government – the Russian and Austrian Governments withdrew their demands. Two years later Kossuth was finally given permission to leave the country for the United States. The American Government placed a steam frigate at his disposal to convey him to New York. The

French authorities refused to allow him to pass through France, but the sympathy for Hungarian independence was strong among English liberals and he was allowed, indeed invited, to speak in Britain. He spoke with passionate eloquence in excellent English and the crowds thronged to see him. The doctrine he put forward was that no Government had the right to interfere in the internal dissensions of a foreign state.

Palmerston had made up his mind to receive Kossuth. The Queen wrote to Lord John Russell, the Prime Minister, in an attempt to prevent this. She claimed that any official reception would be seen as an approval of Kossuth's language and doctrines. Lord John went further than the Queen and intimated to Palmerston that any private reception, even in Palmerston's own home, would be equally objectionable. Palmerston threatened resignation: 'I do not choose to be dictated to as to whom I may or may not receive in my private home.' Russell summoned the Cabinet to consider the situation. Palmerston yielded to their unanimous opinion and promised he would not receive Kossuth. The Queen, however, told Lord John that she had every reason to believe that Palmerston had seen him after all.[68]

Hardly had Kossuth left England than a more dramatic confrontation arose. On 4 December 1851 came news of the *coup d'état* carried out by Louis Napoleon in Paris on 2 December. The Queen immediately wrote to Lord John Russell to ask him to instruct the British Ambassador in Paris, Lord Normanby, not to take any part in what was happening. Lord John immediately replied that her directions would be followed. Lord Normanby had, he told her, asked whether he should suspend his diplomatic functions; but the Cabinet were unanimously of the opinion that he should not do so.[69] Lord Palmerston accordingly wrote to Lord Normanby, transmitting the Queen's instructions that 'nothing should be done by Her Ambassador at Paris, which could wear the appearance of an interference of any kind in the internal affairs of France.'[70] For once the Queen seemed to have obtained exactly what she wanted.

A day later, however, she received the reply of Lord Normanby to a despatch from Lord Palmerston dated 6 December. Lord Normanby mentioned that he had called on M. Turgot, the Minister of Foreign Affairs, to transmit the Queen's message and apologize for any delay. Turgot had replied that the delay was of no importance since he had heard from M. Walewski that Palmerston had expressed to him the British Government's entire approbation of the act of Louis Napoleon, and the conviction that he could not have acted otherwise than he had done. The Queen immediately sent the despatch to Lord John Russell, asking for an explanation. When it became clear that Palmerston had acted in complete contradiction to the line of neutrality desired by the Queen, the information was immediately conveyed to the Cabinet by Lord John. Palmerston's resignation was demanded by the Prime Minister with the unanimous approval of the Cabinet. He resigned on 20 December 1851. He was offered the post of Lord Lieutenant of Ireland and a peerage of the United Kingdom. He refused both and withdrew to Broadlands. The Prince and the Queen were triumphant. The Radicals declared it was all a foreign plot to get rid of the people's Minister.

It was surprising in a sense that Lord John had at last been goaded into action. Over and over again his authority as Prime Minister had been flouted by Palmerston and he had done nothing. The Duke of Bedford told Greville that Lord John was 'in fact fascinated and enthralled' by his Foreign Minister.[71] It was true, too, that he never had a real majority in the House and that he feared that if he sacked Palmerston he would lose the support of the Radicals.

Exactly two months after Lord Palmerston's dismissal, Lord John Russell's Government was defeated in the House of Commons. 'I have had my tit for tat with John Russell,' Palmerston wrote, 'and I turned him out on Friday last.'[72] The triumph of the royal couple had been shortlived.

17

Mid-century Grandeur

The reality was that Palmerston's 'tit for tat' owed less to the Queen's problems with her Foreign Minister than to a surprising move by the Pope and the intolerance it inspired. At the close of 1850 the serenity of the internal political atmosphere was shattered by a Papal Bull of 24 September from the Vatican. It announced the reestablishment by the Pope of the Roman Catholic hierarchy in England and the appointment of Dr Wiseman as Cardinal Archbishop of Westminster. Religious feeling and religious antagonism had grown in Britain during the 1840s, beginning with the birth of the Oxford Movement headed by Newman, Keble, Pusey and Ward, the 'Tractarians' who had tried to reform and revitalize the Church of England from within. Members of the Oxford Movement used practices such as confession, alien to the Protestant conscience, and were accused of Romanism. Newman did, in fact, leave the Church of England in 1845 to embrace the Catholic faith – and was to become a Cardinal of the Church of Rome. In his wake there were numerous other conversions from Anglicanism to Catholicism, especially in the upper classes of society.

The Pope had misinterpreted the Oxford Movement to mean that the English as a people wanted to be brought back into the fold of the Catholic Church. The Papal Bull, which was seen as the reversal of the Reformation, revived strong Protestant feeling and hundreds of protests were addressed to the Queen in person. In her journal, the Queen herself spoke of 'an extraordinary proceeding of the Pope', which had divided 'this country publicly and openly into an Archbishopric and Bishoprics', as if England were again restored to 'the number of Catholic Powers'.[1]

Bigotry was, however, alien to the Queen and she had little sympathy with the 'Papal Aggression Movement' in whose name effigies of the Pope and Cardinal Wiseman replaced those of Guy Fawkes and were burnt in bonfires on 5 November. She wrote to the Duchess of Gloucester:

> I would never have consented to say anything which breathed a spirit of intolerance. Sincerely Protestant as I always have been and always shall be, and indignant as I am at those who call themselves Protestants, while they are in fact quite the contrary, I much regret the unchristian and intolerant spirit exhibited by many people at the public meetings. I cannot bear to hear the violent abuse of the Catholic religion, which is so painful and so cruel towards the many good and innocent Roman Catholics.[2]

The Queen criticized more strongly the Puseyite party, whom she referred to as 'snakes in the grass', than she did the Catholic priests.[3]

The Queen's Prime Minister, Lord John Russell, was more virulent and decidedly anti-Catholic. On 4 November he addressed a letter to the Bishop of Durham, declaring that the Pope's action showed 'a pretension of supremacy over the realm of England and a claim to sole and undivided sway which is inconsistent with the Queen's supremacy, with the rights of our bishops and clergy, and with the spiritual independence of the nation as asserted even in Roman Catholic times.' In his letter, the Prime Minister listed all the things the Protestants took objection to – honouring the saints, claiming infallibility for the Church, using the sign of the cross, muttering the liturgy, recommending confession, distributing penance and absolution – things advocated and practised by the High Church Anglicans, whom he referred to as 'the unworthy sons of the Church of England herself'.[4]

When the Queen opened Parliament in person on 4 February 1851, the continuing controversy meant that, both going and returning, she was greeted with cries of 'No Popery' intermingled with the cheers, Papal aggression formed a prominent topic in the speech Russell had written for her. She declared that she had resolutely decided to maintain the rights of her Crown against encroachment, while at the same time respecting the religious liberty so justly prized in Britain. She announced that legislation would be laid before Parliament.

Russell introduced his Bill – known as the Ecclesiastical Titles Bill – almost immediately. Its aim was to prevent the assumption by Roman Catholics of titles taken from any place within the United Kingdom. After a discussion lasting through four nights, the introduction of the Bill was supported by 395 votes to 63 – a majority of 332. The size of this majority conceals, however, the acrimony and hatred that the Bill aroused. As the Queen noted, '*all* the distinguished followers of Sir

Robert Peel', including Mr Gladstone and all the Roman Catholic members etc., voted against it.[5] Roebuck, in the name of the Radicals, claimed it was 'one of the meanest, pettiest and most futile measures that ever disgraced even bigotry itself.' The Irish resisted it fiercely, nor were they appeased by the Government's agreeing to exclude Ireland from the Bill. Russell had stirred up so much animosity that, within a week of the vote on the Ecclesiastical Titles Bill, he met defeat in resisting a motion to extend the franchise, just as Peel had fallen on the morrow of the Corn Laws. He resigned on 22 February.

The Queen immediately sent for Lord Stanley, the head of the biggest party in opposition, to ask him to form a Government. Lord Stanley told her that he could not undertake to form a new Government. The reason was that there was serious division of opinion among his followers on the one question of vital importance to their existence as a party – Protection. Some of the ablest party men objected to any proposal to tax foreign corn and yet if the protectionists did not do that then they would lose all credibility. He suggested to the Queen that she call on a coalition of Whigs and Peelites, but should this fail he was, he declared, ready to try again. Victoria and Albert were ready to try this solution. Lord Aberdeen was called but refused to attempt to form a ministry on the grounds that no ministry could stand which would not undertake to deal with Papal aggression, which he personally would not do. On 26 February the Queen sent again for Lord Stanley.

Stanley's second attempt at forming a ministry proved no better than his first. The Queen received a letter from him asking when he could come 'to explain to me the reasons why with deepest regret he must resign into my hands the trust of forming a government!!'[6] Victoria was, in a sense, relieved. So no doubt was Lord Stanley. Albert noted, 'Lord Stanley arrived at half past five. We were struck by the change in his countenance, which had lost the expression of care and anxiety, so marked on the previous interviews.'[7] In the House of Lords, Lord Stanley publicly declared that there was in his party a lack of experience. The Queen turned to the Duke of Wellington, now eighty-two, for advice. He urged her to call back Lord John Russell. This she did. 'The last act of the drama', Greville wrote on 4 March, 'fell out last night as everybody foresaw it would and must.'[8] Russell returned with his government unchanged.

The reinstatement of the Whigs was in fact to nobody's liking – but was tolerated because nobody wanted a dissolution. On their return to office, the Government produced a new edition of the Ecclesiastical Titles Bill, simplified and less dramatic. It simply declared illegal the assumption of such titles. No one was satisfied. It was too lenient for some, resented even in its weakened form by others. It was passed by both Houses – and then remained a dead letter. It was never put into operation and, after remaining on the statute book for twenty years, was quietly repealed.

In mid-century, fourteen years after Victoria's accession, the people of Great Britain discovered how their country was changing. As the year drew to a close the results of the census became known. The population of Great Britain had topped twenty million (20,793,000), an increase of just over two million (10 per cent) in a single decade. In 1801 no provincial city had contained 100,000 inhabitants; fifty years later there were seven. The Midland cities had expanded rapidly over the past decade, Manchester going from 300,000 to 400,000, Liverpool from 290,000 to 390,000, Birmingham from 180,000 to 230,000. As for London, it had increased by 415,000 (21 per cent) and now had a population of 2,363,000. From about 1845 onwards, more people in England were living in an urban environment than in a rural one. And the population was young. Over 50 per cent of the people in England and Wales were under twenty in 1850.

The middle of the nineteenth century – which was also, curiously, to be the mid-point of the Queen's married life – was marked by two events which symbolize the first half of the century and leave their mark on it: the Great Exhibition of 1851 and the death of Wellington in 1852.

Throughout 1850 Prince Albert was already engaged on the project which was to emerge as the Great Exhibition of 1851. He had made his proposal to the Society of Arts, of which he was president, in July 1849 and had been ardently supported by Sir Robert Peel, who was Prime Minister at the time. The French had been the first to adopt the idea of bringing together great public collections of works of art and industry, but Prince Albert's plan was on a grander scale and was international in scope. The idea was to obliterate the memory of the 1848 disturbances and show that the world's progress depended on working together, since the prosperity of one country depended on the prosperity of others. 'The Exhibition of 1851', he was later to say, 'is to give us a true test and a living picture of the point of development at which the whole of mankind has arrived in this great task of applied science and a new starting point from which all nations will be able to direct their further exertions.'[9]

On 30 July 1849 the Prince held a conference at Buckingham Palace with three of the most active members of the Society of Arts, Henry

Cole, Francis Fuller and John Scott Russell. They came to the decision to hold the exhibition, not in the quadrangle of Somerset House, which had been offered by the Government, but in Hyde Park. Application was made to the proper authorities and the plan was approved. Prince Albert is seen as the father of the Exhibition, but much of the work and many of the ideas stemmed from Henry Cole. He was an assistant keeper at the Record Office who had also reorganized the Post Office and edited numerous periodicals, not to mention writing children's books, painting watercolours and designing tea services. With regard to exhibitions he was no novice – at the Society of Arts, he had helped in the conception of exhibitions of arts and manufactures in 1847, 1848 and 1849. His great ambition was to improve industrial design in Britain.

In September, Prince Albert wrote of his plans for a 'world industrial exhibition' to Stockmar and rejoiced that: 'Agents report from the manufacturing districts that the manufacturers hail the project with delight and will cooperate heartily; and the East India Company promises to contribute a complete collection of all the products of India.' He realized, however, that 'to win over the Continent will be no easy matter.'[10] What he had not reckoned with was the outcry there was to be in Britain.

At first all went well. A Royal Commission was appointed to carry out the preparations for this pacific demonstration of friendly rivalry. The scheme was inaugurated on 21 March 1850 at a banquet given by the Lord Mayor to the chief magistrates of all the towns in the United Kingdom, to which the foreign Ambassadors were also invited. The speech Prince Albert made on this occasion gave a clear idea of what progress meant to him. 'Nobody', declared the Prince, 'who has paid any attention to the peculiar features of our present era, will doubt for a moment that we are living at a period of most wonderful transition, which tends rapidly to accomplish that great end, to which, indeed, all history points – the realisation of the unity of Mankind.'[11] It is a picture in which progress is seen as linear: 'The distances which separated the different nations and parts of the globe are rapidly vanishing before the achievements of modern invention' while 'the great principle of division of labour, which may be called the moving power of Civilization, is being extended to all branches of science, industry, and art.'[12] In former times the gifted had sought universal knowledge; now knowledge was becoming the property of the community. Man's mission was to discover Natural Laws and conquer Nature by compliance with them.

The speech brought the Prince congratulations. 'Albert', Victoria wrote to her uncle, 'is indeed looked up to and beloved as I could wish he should be. . . . People are much struck by his great power and energy; by the great self-denial and constant wish to work for others, which are so striking in his character.'[13] Prince Albert was indeed working hard – too hard to look after his health. The Prince was sleeping badly and began to look very ill. His doctor had prescribed a complete change of air and activity. Victoria was so concerned for his health that, although she was over four months' pregnant, she was willing to go to Brussels, where he could rest.[14] But the Prince was too busy and too stubborn to entertain the idea. It was still not clear how large the building was to be, or how space should be allotted between the different countries. More important still, money had to be found and this meant canvassing support.

Although the idea of an exhibition had at first seemed popular, opposition grew up in the press and in Parliament. First as to where the exhibition should actually be held. 'The Exhibition', Prince Albert wrote to Baron Stockmar, 'is now attacked furiously by *The Times* and the House of Commons is going to drive us out of the Park. There is immense excitement on the subject. If we are driven out of the Park, the work is ruined. Never was anything so foolish.'[15] *The Times* wrote of the exhibition as the cause of a veritable desecration of Hyde Park through the introduction of commerce and the hoi polloi. Residents of Kensington protested that the building would destroy their view of the Serpentine. When the subject was debated in the House of Commons on 4 July, opposition to the project was defeated by a very large majority, not least because of an unexpected factor – Prime Minister Peel had met his death the day before and it was common knowledge that his voice would have been among those in support of holding the exhibition in Hyde Park.

Hardly had this problem been solved than another arose – the subscriptions that had been collected were far short of the projected cost. This obstacle was met in turn, by the suggestion that a guarantee fund be created to meet any contingent deficiency. In July the Prince wrote to Baron Stockmar from Osborne.

> In town it became at last quite impossible to go on longer, and I am sorry to say I was again suffering from sleeplessness and exhaustion. Nevertheless, in all the matters which I had in hand, I had triumphant success. *The Times* has had to back out of the position it took up about the Park, and we have managed to get together a guarantee fund of £200,000, which enables us to erect our building, for the subscriptions are very backward.[16]

The design of the building was another issue that had to be decided. The Commissioners examined some 245 designs sent in by architects from all over the world. At first, a design by a French architect seemed to have been chosen. Then Joseph Paxton, the superintendent of the Duke of Devonshire's gardens at Chatsworth, who was not a professional architect, produced a scheme which was both original and simple: an enormous conservatory modelled on those at Chatsworth. Paxton published an engraving of his plans in the *Illustrated London News* five days before the final decision was due. They were greeted with such enthusiastic approval that the committee had no option but to accept Paxton's submission.

Materials used for the new building were iron and glass – an unusual combination at the time. The columns and girders were of cast iron, each set of four columns and four girders forming a square of twenty-four feet, which could be raised to any height or expanded sideways by joining other columns and girders to them. The simplicity of the construction meant that the building could be constructed very rapidly. It could also be taken to pieces with great ease and put up somewhere else in exactly the same way. It was an enormous structure which was to cover eighteen acres of ground. The order for the work was accepted by the contractors on 26 July 1850. At that time not a pane of glass nor a bar of iron had been prepared. The first column was raised two months later, on 26 September, and by 31 December the construction was finished. It had been made from prefabricated parts put together by unskilled labour, and nothing so vast had ever been built so quickly.

The building was baptised the 'Crystal Palace' by *Punch*. It was 300 feet long and 64 feet high – roughly four times as long as St Paul's Cathedral and twice as wide. It was so high that it was unnecessary to clear the trees on the site, since the long arched roof of ribbed glass simply enclosed them. As they were elms now in full leaf, they conveyed a feeling of freshness and repose. The framework of iron was painted a cobalt blue. The hangings were mostly scarlet. The floor was of pine. There were two fountains, and much statuary and coloured porcelain.

The Queen went to look at it completed for the first time on 18 February 1851 with the Prince and their five children. She proclaimed it 'one of the wonders of the world, which we English may indeed be proud of.'[17] It was a really beautiful building, light, airy and gay. From the outside it was in the form of a parallelogram; inside was a cruciform structure with naves and transepts of equal width. The transept rose tier upon tier of slender columns carrying arches of cobweb-like fineness.

Although goods were now pouring in from all quarters, the exhibition was still the object of violent attacks. Insular prejudice against foreigners was voiced in the House of Commons by Colonel Sibthorp, who considered that free trade had enabled foreigners to rob Britain of her markets, and now the exhibition was to deprive her of her honour. Fortunately for Albert, Colonel Sibthorp was so reactionary that he was not to be taken seriously – he even went so far as to pray in the House of Commons that hail or lightning would be sent from Heaven to destroy the exhibition. But he was not alone in showing jealousy and dislike of anything coming from abroad. Cardinal Manning declared that the exhibition would endanger faith and morals and concentrate in one space all the corrupting moral elements of Europe. The Prince wrote to the Dowager Duchess of Coburg in April:

> I am more dead than alive from over-work. The opponents of the Exhibition work with might and main to throw all the old women into a panic, and to drive myself crazy. The strangers, they give out, are certain to commence a thorough Revolution here, to murder Victoria and myself, to proclaim the Red Republic in England. The plague is certain to ensue from the confluence of such vast multitudes, and to swallow up those whom the increased prices of everything has not already swept away. For all this I am to be responsible, and against all this I have to make efficient provision.[18]

Opposition from abroad was strong, too. At first, the King of Prussia was against the Prince of Prussia and his son accepting Victoria and Albert's invitation to attend. He had been told that London was the centre for all types of revolutionaries to gather. They saw, it was said, the exhibition as an occasion to destroy the existing order of affairs by assassination. In the end, thanks to Albert's entreaties, the Prince did come with his wife and son.

Victoria followed these debates and discussions with anxiety. She totally espoused her husband's cause. As opposition to his project mounted, she became more and more eager to support him in private and in public. Another private inspection of the Crystal Palace took place on 29 April. 'We remained two hours and a half', said the Queen, 'and I came back quite beaten and my head bewildered from the myriads of beautiful and wonderful things which now quite dazzle one's eyes. Such efforts have been made, and our people have shown such taste in their manufactures.' So much was going on, with some 20,000 people engaged in arranging the exhibits, that the Queen found the noise 'overpowering'. Albert was 'terribly fagged' but: 'Great as is his triumph, he never says a word about it, but labours to the last, feeling quietly satisfied in the country's glory, and in having gone on steadily in spite of the immense difficulties and opposition.'[19] There were 13,937 exhibitors of which 7,381 were British and colonial, and 6,556 foreign, coming from forty different countries.

The distribution of the exhibits was geographical. The whole of the building west of the great transept was given over to the United Kingdom and its colonies. To the east were foreign countries and their colonies in order of their latitude. This was true in general, but all working machinery was placed at the north-western end, where power was supplied from eight large boilers placed in a separate building. There were four separate classes of exhibits: raw materials, machinery, manufactures and fine arts. So splendid was the array of British goods that Victoria rejoiced that the exhibition was there, 'as it goes to prove that we are capable of doing almost anything.'[20] The Queen also singled out on this preliminary visit some of the foreign goods: the French exhibits, 'in which there are most exquisite things from Sèvres, Aubusson and the Gobelins Manufactures'; the 'splendid exhibits in porcelain and iron from Berlin'; and 'lovely embroideries from Switzerland'.[21] Another visit to the exhibition was paid by the royal couple on the following day, this time with the Prince and Princess of Prussia, together with their son and daughter. Now the fountains were playing and the flowers and palms increased the charm of the place.

The Great Exhibition was a veritable microcosm of the period. There, there could be seen the locomotive and the textile machine, Applegarth's extraordinary printing machine, capable of turning out 10,000 sheets an hour, Krupp's steel cannon, Bakewell's copying telegraph, which could deliver facsimile copies at the end of the line, and steam mills for crushing sugar cane. Alongside these technical achievements came the Sèvres porcelain, Beauvais tapestries, Bohemian engraved glass and furniture intricately carved or elaborately sculpted. If the British contribution to the first category was immense, the tastelessness of much of the British part of the Fine Arts section was undeniable. The *Spectator* on 8 November 1851 was to speak of 'the prodigious amount of ugliness' contained in the English part of the exhibition, and William Morris, then seventeen, took objection to the rococo banality of the British fine arts objects.

On 1 May 1851 the exhibition opened. 'The great event', the Queen recorded in her diary, 'has taken place. A complete and beautiful triumph and a glorious and touching sight.'[22] The day was 'bright, and all bustle and excitement'. Green Park and Hyde Park seemed to be one densely crowded mass of human beings, all of them in the highest good humour. 'I never saw Hyde Park look as it did – people as far as the eye could reach.'[23] It was estimated that some 700,000 people lined the route taken by the royal couple when they went to take part in the opening ceremony.[24] As they drew near the Crystal Palace the Queen and her retinue could see the flags of all the nations floating on the roof of the gigantic edifice. 'The glimpse of the transept through the iron gates, the waving palms, the flowers, statues, myriads of people filling the galleries and seats around, and the flourish of trumpets as we entered, gave us a sensation which I can never forget', the Queen wrote, 'and I felt much moved.'[25]

The royal couple entered the palace, Albert leading the Queen, with Vicky holding her father's hand and Bertie in full Highland dress holding his mother's. The Queen was dressed in pink and silver, wearing the Koh-i-noor diamond. 'The sight as we came to the middle, where the steps and chair ... were placed, and the beautiful crystal fountain just in front of it, was magical – so vast, so glorious, so touching.'[26] The whole event, down to the fear that something might go wrong, reminded her of her Coronation, 'but this day's festival was a thousand times superior.' Once the national anthem had been sung, Albert left the Queen's side and at the head of the Commissioners, 'a curious assemblage of political and distinguished men', read her a long report, to which she replied briefly. Then came the procession down the nave, then back up again. Once the royal couple had returned to their places, the exhibition was declared open.

The Queen's admiration for her husband was accompanied by a strong sense of satisfaction at having got the better of the protectionists. 'Albert's name is immortalised, and the wicked and absurd reports of dangers of every kind, which a set of people, viz. the *soi-disant* fashionables and the most violent Protectionists spread, are silenced. It is therefore doubly satisfactory that all should have gone off so well and without the slightest accident or mishap.'[27]

Sir George Grey was indeed able to report to the Queen on 2 May that there had not been one accident, one police case due to the crowds. The perfect order of the people was commented on by Jules Janin in the *Journal des Débats*, and reflected no doubt the opinion of many foreigners.

> What a strange people the English are! Always calm, never in a hurry . . . patient even when transported with enthusiasm. As the English do not want to be governed, they govern themselves and should someone behave in a disorderly fashion the passer-by will immediately help the policeman . . . This crowd came in an orderly fashion and has disappeared in the same way! Noone would have said at three o'clock that

30,000 people eager to see and hear everything could have been contained in this building.[28]

The Great Exhibition captured the imagination of the people. From the day it opened until the day it finally closed it was one seething mass of enchanted visitors. Some six million people visited it between 1 May and 15 October 1851, over a million a month. The entrance fee varied. There were admission days for one pound, days for five shillings, days for two and six, days for a shilling and even sixpenny days; on two occasions, admission was free. There were also season tickets at three guineas for a man and two for a woman. The aged Duke of Wellington was also a frequent visitor, arriving very early and invariably being recognized and cheered. The Queen visited the exhibition almost daily, arriving before ten in the morning and making her way through each section in turn. For once the Queen was not eager to leave London in July: 'under ordinary circumstances it is a pleasure . . . but the thought grieves me that this bright time, this great epoch in our lives and in the annals of the country – this season which was looked forward to all last year with such anxiety and hope by so many, by others with trembling – is now past.'[29]

Victoria paid her final visit to the exhibition on 14 October. 'It looked so beautiful,' she wrote in her diary. 'I could not believe it was the last time I was to see it.' With her habitual realism she went on, 'The canvas is very dirty, the red curtains are faded, and many things are very much soiled.' Yet despite everything 'the effect is fresh and new as ever, and most beautiful.'[30] The glass fountain had already been removed to make room for the platform for the closing ceremony on 15 October. The Queen wanted to attend and Albert had had much difficulty in persuading her that she could hardly be a spectator of that melancholy event. 'A very wet day, appropriate to the really mournful ceremony of the closing of the Exhibition,' she wrote in her diary.[31]

The London season of the year of the Great Exhibition had been exceptionally brilliant. On 13 June the Queen had given a fancy-dress ball at which all guests had to wear costumes of the Restoration period. The Queen wore a dress of grey watered silk, trimmed with gold and silver lace, with bows of rose-coloured ribbons fastened by bunches of diamonds. The front of the dress, decorated with large pear-shaped emeralds, was opened so the underskirt of cloth of gold with a silver fringe could be clearly seen. Her shoes and gloves were embroidered with roses and fleurs-de-lys in gold. As a headdress she wore a diamond and emerald crown and her hair was plaited with pearls. The Prince was decked out in a more garish costume: a rich orange coat, with sleeves which turned up to reveal crimson velvet, and pink epaulettes on the shoulders. With it he wore breeches of crimson velvet with pink satin bows and gold lace. His stockings were of lavender silk. He wore a hat with white ostrich feathers. Among the other guests, Gladstone stood out, masquerading as a judge of the High Court of Admiralty, and the Duke of Wellington wore the garb of a general of the Restoration period, in frock coat of scarlet cloth with double rows of gold lace and slashed sleeves of white satin.

Perhaps the most notable event of the season, however, came later, on 9 July, when the Lord Mayor and the Corporation of the City of London gave a ball at the Guildhall to celebrate the success of the Great Exhibition. The Queen and the Prince accepted invitations. They were cheered all the way to the Guildhall; and they found, more touchingly, that when they left the ball in the early hours, loyal crowds had waited all night to cheer them again. 'A million of people', the Prince wrote to Baron Stockmar, 'remained till three in the morning in the streets and were full of enthusiasm towards us.'[32]

The exhibition had undoubtedly increased the popularity of the monarchy. It had had other positive effects as well, as Lord John Russell told the Queen.

> The grandeur of the conception, the zeal, invention and talent displayed in the execution and the perfect order maintained from the first day to the last, have contributed together to give imperishable fame to Prince Albert. . . . it is to his energy and judgement that the world owes both the original design and the harmonious and rapid execution.[33]

In the immediate term, the exhibition improved Anglo–French relations. The President of the French Republic, Louis Napoleon, had from the first given cordial support to the project. Much of the attractiveness of the exhibition was undoubtedly due to the French contribution. The English acknowledged the superiority of French artistic feeling and skill, the French paid tribute to English machinery and workmanship. This led to commercial advantages on both sides.

The real significance of the exhibition was that it marked in a particularly striking way the triumph of the industrial revolution, for it was a glorification of industry. The *Observer* realized this when it wrote, at the time the exhibition opened, that it would 'form an era at once in the national and in the industrial annals of the world'; for it would attract 'the greatest human assemblage ever collected together upon one small spot of the earth's surface,' and 'determine the exact degree up to which, in the middle of the nineteenth century, the skill and ingenuity of man have arrived.'[34]

This was the age of machinery, and Britain had a head start among the nations of the world in mechanical engineering, which had first been applied to Britain's textile manufactures. Until 1825 the export of machinery had been prohibited by law so that Britain might maintain her advantage. However, it was finally realized that producing more machinery would mean that it could be produced more cheaply; and that in any case it was futile to attempt to keep British inventions secret. As a result the restriction was removed. This gave considerable stimulus to the production of iron and steel – and this, in its turn, was to lead to the development of transport in the form of iron ships and steel railway lines.

It was between 1830 and 1850 that British industry made its biggest advances compared with industry in other countries. By the time of the Great Exhibition the cotton industry was completely modernized and the numbers employed in the engineering and metallurgical industries had increased considerably. Capital was not raised, as it was to be in both France and Germany, by the Government. It was private individuals and companies that raised capital for and administered the growth of the mines and the factories, the canals and the railways. In Victoria's reign, people got into the habit of depositing their savings in banks rather than keeping them at home. As the deposits were used to finance productive enterprises, so the banking system expanded. In 1837, when the first Limited Liability Act was passed, the organization of joint-stock companies was regulated and the personal liability of each shareholder was limited to the amount of his share. Previously, if the company went bankrupt, the entire property of each individual shareholder could be used to pay the company's creditors. The new Act caused a flood of wealth to pour into limited liability companies, which provided much of the capital for new industries, and London became the financial capital of the world.

Mass production made goods cheaper so that, although wages remained low, the standard of living of the poorer classes gradually increased. But all was not rosy. This new large-scale production was characterized by the alternation of booms and slumps in trade, producing alternate waves of prosperity and depression – the famous economic cycles that were a direct result of the industrial system.

The most significant development during the period between 1830 and 1880 was the transport revolution, brought about by the introduction of the railway. It was to alter completely the intensity and the character of industrial life. Although the first line in Britain, from Stockton to Darlington, had been built between 1821 and 1825, it was not until the 1830s that railway building really got under way. Here again it was private investment that financed the railways – whereas in Belgium all railways were state railways and in France a mixed system was adopted. In the railway mania of 1843–7, many Englishmen speculated frantically on the building of railways and were ruined when the great railway slump came in 1846–7. With no state control, unnecessary, competing lines were built and it has been estimated that the railways cost about twice as much to construct as they need have done. By the date of the Great Exhibition, there were 6,000 miles of railway line in Great Britain.

Other kinds of communication were developing fast. The first ocean-going steamship, the *Great Eastern*, was launched in 1838; the electric telegraph had come into being in 1837, the year in which Victoria ascended the throne. By 1851 Britain was prosperous, dominant and full of self-confidence. The middle classes lived comfortably, thanks to Britain's industrialists – and to the economic wisdom of Peel's free trade policy, implemented despite all the resistance he had faced.

At the time of the Great Exhibition the grave social unrest of the 1830s and early 1840s was forgotten. The prosperity of Britain engendered a period of social harmony. 'Liberal' became a term of praise as production, wages and profits continued to rise. Not until the 1870s, with the exception of a short slump in 1866, did prosperity come to a halt and agriculture fall into its long depression.

Because this was an era of prosperity the Great Exhibition raised questions about design, style and taste. It encouraged the use of new materials. Into the houses of England came beds with fretwork panels and papier mâché decorations. The hip-bath, in sheet iron, zinc or copper, became popular and was removed from the kitchen to a room of its own. Some of the hip-baths were really beautiful, with the outside japanned and the inside marbled. Some had a high, curved, sloping back and a large, deep, oval basin and were put in front of the open fire in the bedroom. They were filled and emptied by hand. Then there was the Sitz bath, with a little seat, the lounge bath, with mahogany railings, the slipper bath, and even a portable metal hip-bath for travelling.

Eating, too, was to be influenced by the Great Exhibition. There were three refreshment rooms of different classes within the Crystal Palace and, according to the *Observer*, 'the country visitors by whom it is now inundated, divide their time pretty fairly between the sightseeing and the eating and drinking.'[35] A bountiful supply of bread and cold meat could be had for seven (old) pence. No cooking was allowed and no alcoholic beverages. Visitors consumed over a million bottles of soft drinks – one of Messrs Schweppes' first mass contracts – and almost two million buns. Two new refreshments formerly reserved for the upper classes were tried out: ice cream and jelly. Ice cream was not a success – in this day of rudimentary dentistry it simply gave the public toothache. Jelly, on the other hand, became extremely popular.

Above all, the exhibition was a financial success. A profit of 186,000 pounds was made. But Albert paid a personal price. The work, together with the attacks and calumnies he had endured, had not helped him to remain fit. He lived on his nervous energy and the strain was apparent. Baron Stockmar, who had been in the Palace during the winter of 1850 and the spring of 1851, had extracted a promise from him to slow down. But Albert was not really capable of this – in August 1851 we find him writing to the Baron:

> I promised you, no doubt, not to embark in anything new after the close of the Exhibition, and I have, moreover, made up my mind to retreat into my shell as quickly as possible; but I am not free to choose as regards the considerable surplus with which we shall wind up. For its application I have devised a plan of which I send you a copy.[36]

A further scheme was to grow out of the success of the Great Exhibition. The Prince, as his memorandum showed, was very much against any idea of making Crystal Palace as it stood into a winter garden – as Paxton himself had suggested – or a public promenade or even a museum of antiquities. The building should, he thought, be removed as had been promised. The idea promoted by the Prince was to purchase thirty acres of ground nearly opposite the Crystal Palace, surrounding the present Exhibition Road in Kensington, and to construct on it four institutions, 'corresponding to the four great sections of the Exhibition – Raw Materials, Machinery, Manufactures and Plastic Art.'[37] Each of these institutions was, in the Prince's original plan, to contain a library, rooms for study, lecture rooms, exhibition space and rooms for discussions and commercial meetings.

The Commissioners decided that the palace would be removed as the Prince wished, and the Government concurred. Nevertheless, in April 1852, there was a 'demonstration' of society people in favour of the rescue of the Crystal Palace from impending destruction. The committee of noblemen and gentlemen who wished to preserve the palace had advertised the demonstration, calling on the public to show how concerned they were by the idea of its demolition. No fewer than 80,000 people took part in what the *Annual Register* called the 'promenade'. The

Government was not to be intimidated; the committee was threatened with action from the Lord Chancellor if they attempted 'a repetition of the promenade'.[38] On 30 April the Queen heard from Disraeli that the motion for the retention of the Crystal Palace had been negotiated. 'This is no doubt a good thing,' she wrote. 'Now it will be sold and put up anew in some other place, as a winter garden.'[39]

The palace was bought by the London Brighton and South Coast Railway for 70,000 pounds.[40] It was to be dismantled, taken to Sydenham and re-erected there. A new railway line was laid from London Bridge to the palace grounds. In March, Victoria and Albert took Vicky and Alice to visit the new Crystal Palace under construction. In November they returned to see it again. 'It was a most interesting visit. This stupendous and beautiful undertaking has progressed immensely and we went through every part of the building. The works of art consisting entirely of sculpture are really beautiful.'[41] The palace was a success once again and continued to attract visitors until it was destroyed by fire in 1936.

Meanwhile, on Prince Albert's recommendation and with the help of Disraeli, now Chancellor of the Exchequer, the Commission bought a vast piece of land adjoining Hyde Park. It cost some 342,000 pounds, of which 165,000 pounds came from the Great Exhibition's surplus funds. The Prince's scheme was carried out though with considerable modification. The buildings that were eventually built include the Victoria and Albert Museum – originally opened as the South Kensington Museum.

In 1851 the Great Exhibition had united the people in happiness and celebration; the death of the Duke of Wellington on 14 September 1852, although it had been long expected, united the nation in grief. He died peacefully in his armchair at Walmer Castle. In her journal the Queen noted:

> One cannot think of this country without "the Duke", our immortal hero. The Crown never possessed – and I fear never will – so devoted, loyal and faithful a subject, so staunch a supporter! To us (who alas! have lost now so many of our valued and experienced friends) his loss is irreparable, for his readiness to aid and advise, if it could be of use to us, and to overcome any and every difficulty, was unequalled.[42]

The Duke had been born on 1 May 1769, the descendant of two Anglo-Irish families. For the nation, he was the hero of Waterloo, the Iron Duke, saviour of the nation – the general who, according to legend, had never lost a single English gun. For Victoria, he was much more. He had been present at her birth, godfather by proxy at her baptism. He was a necessary part of every great ceremony concerning the Sovereign. He had been present at the christenings of all the royal children and godfather to one of them – Prince Arthur. One of his last services to the royal family had been to offer Prince Albert the post of Commander-in-Chief before his own retirement in 1850. The Duke's idea had been to appoint Prince Albert as a figurehead and put under him, as Chief of Staff, the general who had most experience in the army. This was to misread the Prince. Had he accepted the position he would undoubtedly have been more active and omnipresent than the Duke realized. But Albert refused – on the grounds of inexperience and, more important, that his task as private secretary to the Queen was increasingly absorbing. The Duke had led a very active life even in his final years. During the ten years preceding his death he had attended the House of Lords regularly and was always one of the earliest to arrive.[43] When there he spoke plainly and to the point.

The Queen put her household into mourning, a mark of regard rarely granted by a Sovereign to a subject. In her general order to the army, she wrote: 'In him Her Majesty has to deplore [the loss of] a firm supporter of her throne; a faithful, wise and devoted councillor; a valued and honoured friend.'[44] Ten thousand people saw the coffin at Walmer before it was taken to Chelsea, almost two months after the Duke's death. The funeral was to be a state funeral and therefore was the responsibility of the Lord Chancellor's department. It cost 27,968 pounds, of which nearly 23,000 pounds went to the undertakers – the body was enclosed in four coffins of lead, oak, pine and mahogany.

The first stage of the ceremony, the removal of the coffin from Walmer to the station at Deal, a two-mile journey, was accompanied by torches and took an hour and a half. In London, the coffin was taken to Chelsea Hospital for the lying-in-state. There it was met by the Lord Chamberlain and a hundred Grenadier Guards. It lay in state for three days. The Queen and the Prince went on 11 November. The light was kept dim at the entrance to the hall where the coffin had been put, so that the blaze of the hall itself could be better appreciated. There the walls and ceiling were draped in black, trellised with silver cords, as were the niches in which pairs of soldiers from the Duke's regiments, arms reversed, stood like statues. Eighty-three enormous candelabra, representing the number of the Duke's years, illuminated the scene. The coffin was on a dais, covered with cloth of gold, under a canopy of black velvet which was scattered with silver stars and lined with silver tissue decorated with black spangles. At the foot of the coffin were the medals and orders of the Duke. On it were the Duke's cocked hat and sword. 'The whole effect was theatrical, eccentric, powerful and imperially pagan; it compelled admiration.'[45]

On the third day, the lying-in-state was opened to the public. There were scenes of the utmost confusion. Three people were actually crushed to death. The notion of queueing, now seen as essentially British, had not yet been imported from the continent. 'The multitude actually smoked like a heated haystack from the pressure and strain upon individuals.'[46] The *Observer* painted a graphic picture of the scene.

> The screams of females, and the shrieks of young children were heard in all directions – still the crowd accumulated – still the vast mass of human beings progressed – and still the police held aloft their batons, threatening the dense moving, swaying mass. A cry was heard amidst the crowd – a body was seen to fall and on the shoulders of four men the lifeless form of a female was borne out. There was no life in that body, yet the crowd, notwithstanding the solemn scene, pressed onwards. Another and another body was carried away, and yet the eagerness of the multitude was not restrained. The onward progress of the crowd still pursued its course. A melancholy scene – the dead being borne over the shoulders of the living.[47]

The funeral of the Duke of Wellington was 'the last tribute of a great nation to its greatest man'.[48] The funeral car was designed as a national heirloom. The hearse can still be seen today in the crypt of St Paul's. It had a soldier-like simplicity and grandeur. It was of immense size and of great weight – being entirely of bronze. It was drawn by twelve black horses, harnessed three abreast and covered with velvet hangings on which the Duke's arms were embroidered. All along the route taken by the funeral procession, endless rows of seats covered with black cloth had been erected – some 300,000 in all. People watched from these seats, from the windows and the roofs. But the great majority of the crowd, estimated at one and a half million, were standing. Many had waited through a night of wind and heavy rain. Many wore black. The soldiers marched with slow step and reversed arms. Not a regiment was missing from this grand military spectacle. It was the first time in the history of the British army that men of every arm and every regiment in the service marched together. The vast, silent, respectful crowd, as it saw the Duke's horse go by without its rider, led by an aged groom to the roll of muffled drums, realized that this was the passing of an epoch. The Queen watched the funeral procession go by from the new balcony of Buckingham Palace. 'It was the first funeral', she wrote, 'of any one I had known and who was dear to me that I had ever seen! To realise that this great Hero, the most loyal and devoted subject that ever lived, is really gone, makes me truly sad.'[49] The Duke was laid to rest in St Paul's by the side of Nelson.

No sooner was the Duke buried than the sparring between rival political parties resumed. The Free Traders were determined to force the Government to declare without ambiguity against Protection. On 17 December Lord Derby's Government was defeated by nineteen votes. Lord Derby resigned. This time the Duke of Wellington was not there to give the Queen his advice. She asked Lord Aberdeen to form a coalition government of Whigs and Peelites and offered Palmerston the post of First Lord of the Admiralty. Palmerston declined. He wanted to return to the Foreign Office – but the royal couple were against. Aberdeen finally persuaded him to take the Home Office. On 23 December 1852 the new Government was installed.

After the end of the Great Exhibition, Prince Albert turned his energies to creating a new family home in Scotland. The estate was nominally his but his personal means were slender. For a long time it was thought that Albert had been able to use the 500,000 pounds the Queen had received as a legacy from a certain John Camden Nield. The old man had no known relatives so the Queen accepted the gift – but she increased the legacies given to the executors from a hundred pounds to a thousand pounds, restored the chancel of the church where her benefactor was buried and put up a memorial window in his memory. The money was used not for Balmoral but for the mausoleum of Frogmore.[50]

Albert found the original castle much too small and was eager to pull it down and create a baronial Scottish home. Victoria dipped into her purse. Albert was delighted. On 8 September 1852 he spent the entire morning with William Smith, an architect from Aberdeen, choosing a site for his new edifice. The general plan is difficult to see from the ground but can be clearly seen from the air – two rectangular blocks, each with its own courtyard, are connected corner to corner. At the point where they meet is a square tower, five floors high, typical of the castles of Scottish barons.

The first stone was laid on 28 September 1853. The stone was prepared and suspended over the place where it was to rest – there was below it a cavity for a bottle containing a parchment and some coins. The Reverend Mr Anderson prayed for a blessing on the work and then the Queen signed the parchment recording the day on which the stone was laid. Victoria's signature was followed by that of the Prince, the royal children and the Duchess of Kent. One of each of the coins then current were also placed in the bottle, which was sealed up and placed in the cavity. The Queen then spread the mortar with a trowel and the stone was lowered. Once she had struck the stone into place with a mallet, she poured oil and wine over it and declared the stone duly laid.[51]

Two years later the new house was habitable. Arriving in September 1855 the Queen noted: 'At a quarter-past seven o'clock we arrived at dear Balmoral. Strange, very strange, it seemed to me to drive past, indeed through, the old house; the connecting part between it and the offices being broken through. The new house looks beautiful.'[52] For the time being, the gentlemen were still obliged to live in the old house, as were most of the servants. As the royal couple entered their new home an old shoe was thrown after them for good luck. Albert had positioned the house well. 'The view from the windows of our rooms, and from the library, drawing-room, etc. below them, of the valley of the Dee, with the mountains in the background, – which one never could see from the old house, is quite beautiful.'[53]

The house was extremely comfortable. In the house-block and the tower there were some 180 windows designed to let a maximum of sunlight into the stone building. A heating system, with hot air rising up wall-flues and beneath floors, was supplemented by fireplaces in the sixty-eight public rooms and private apartments. There were four baths for the royal couple and their children. Everyone else continued the custom of washing in hip-baths before the fire. There were, on the other hand, fourteen water closets, which could not all have been reserved for the royal family.

Both Queen Victoria and the Prince developed a strong attachment to Balmoral. Despite its size, it was the most private of their residences. They admired the local people and their direct homespun ways. The countryside, with its heather and its dark green pines, its russet leaves and its mountain snows, was a feast for the eye in any season. The mountain air was clean and fresh, the sport to Albert's taste. Here the royal family lived in simplicity. There were now eight children. Osborne had been the childhood delight of the four eldest children; for the other five, Balmoral was in their childhood to rival the southern seaside resort. When the Scottish castle was built, Princess Helena was nine, Princess Louise, the artistic Princess, was seven, Prince Alfred was five and Prince Leopold two. Two years later Princess Beatrice, Queen Victoria's ninth and last child, was born. For all of them Balmoral was to offer a refuge from the curious and a chance of leading a happy family life.

18

The Crimean War and the Indian Mutiny

The dispute that broke the peace in Europe in 1853 had as its immediate cause the question of who was responsible for the custody and protection of the holy places significant to Christians in the Turkish empire. As head of the Orthodox Church, Tsar Nicholas of Russia supported the claims of the Greek Church. Louis Napoleon, the new French head of state, saw himself as the hereditary protector of the Roman Catholics. The French claim went back to 1740, when Turkey had given France the custody of several of these places near Jerusalem – the Great Church of Bethlehem, the Sanctuary of the Nativity, the Tomb of the Virgin, the Stone of the Anointing, the Seven Arches of the Virgin in the tomb of the Holy Sepulchre. France had, however, let her guardianship slide and it was monks of the Greek Church who were effectively in charge. In 1850 Louis Napoleon, in an attempt to win support from the clerics in France, declared that he had the right to replace the Greek monks by Latin monks. This demand was immediately supported by Austria and Spain – both Roman Catholic powers. The Sultan gave way, causing bitter resentment in Russia. The Tsar invoked the Kutchuk Kainardji Treaty, signed with Turkey in 1774, recognizing Russia as the guardian of the holy places.

The underlying causes of the conflict were complex and far-reaching. Russia had no outlet to the sea except through the Baltic, which was frozen in winter, and through the Bosporus, which was open all year but controlled by the Turks. Turkey was weak, so this was no bad time for Russia to try and help the Turkish empire disintegrate more rapidly. The Tsar also identified the French Emperor with revolution. A. J. P. Taylor, in his *Struggle for the Mastery of Europe*, puts forward the idea that the struggle between France and Russia was a cover for the far greater struggle between revolution and conservatism.[1] Austria was not against coercing the Turks either, as she wished to obtain the Danubian provinces of the Porte. For the French Emperor external war would help things at home and, even more important, would break up the coalition which had destroyed Napoleon I. As for England, her aim was to prevent Russia from advancing towards the British possessions in India – the integrity of the Ottoman empire was thus a touchstone of British diplomacy. Called on to adjudicate on the rival claims of France and Russia with regard to the holy places, the Porte attempted to please both parties – and satisfied neither.

Towards the end of 1852 Russia sent soldiers to the Moldavian frontier. France at once threatened to send her fleet to Syria. In February 1853, the Tsar sent Prince Menshikoff to Constantinople to enforce the Russian demands. Russia was at this time under the illusion that Britain would never support France, whose interests were too clearly contrary to her own. This conviction was reinforced by the memory of the Tsar's visit to England nine years earlier, in 1844. Lord Malmesbury claimed that at that time the Tsar, Sir Robert Peel (then Prime Minister), the Duke of Wellington and Lord Aberdeen (then Foreign Secretary) had drawn up and signed a memorandum, 'the spirit and scope of which was to support Russia in her legitimate protectorship of the Greek religion and the Holy Shrines and to do so without consulting France.'[2] In 1853, with Lord Aberdeen Prime Minister in Britain, and Turkey in a worse state than ever, this was for Tsar Nicholas an ideal moment to attack.

Britain urged Turkey to agree to accept any solution which both France and Russia would consider satisfactory, and at the same time remonstrated with France for having opened up the whole question. Napoleon III sent a more conciliatory negotiator to Constantinople and Russia ceased her warlike preparations in Moldavia. War might have been averted had not Lord Aberdeen sent Lord Stratford de Redcliffe as Ambassador to Constantinople. Lord Stratford hated the Tsar, who had refused in 1832 to accept him as Ambassador at St Petersburg. He now did all he could to disrupt the negotiations and openly boasted that this was his personal revenge against the Tsar. Prince Albert told Baron Stockmar: 'The prospects of a peaceful settlement in the East do not improve. Lord Stratford fulfils his instructions to the letter, but he so contrives that we are getting constantly deeper and deeper into a war policy.'

The Tsar demanded that the Turks conclude a convention with Russia which would give Russia a protectorate over all Greek Christians in Turkey. This implied a political as well as a religious protection.

The Turks refused and the Tsar threatened to occupy Moldavia and Wallachia, dependencies of Turkey, until Turkey gave way. In response to this threat, both Britain and France sent fleets to the Dardanelles. Russian troops under Prince Gorchakov crossed into Moldavia on 2 July. The war had virtually begun.

Meanwhile a conference of the ambassadors of Britain, France and Prussia, together with the Austrian Foreign Minister, assembled in Vienna on 24 June, aiming to reach a peaceful solution to the difficulty. On 31 June they adopted the Vienna Note. It was sent to Russia and Turkey as a proposal for a settlement which was honourable and fair to both parties. The Turks, the Note declared, should observe the spirit of previous treaties with Russia and make no alteration in the position of their Christian subjects without first consulting both the Russian and French Governments. Russia was, of course, to withdraw her army from the provinces. The Tsar accepted the Note promptly on 10 August. The British Ambassador, although he urged Turkey to accept it in his official capacity, privately persuaded Turkey to reject the Note and promised British help if there were a war with Russia. Turkey finally declared war on Russia on 4 October 1853.

For Queen Victoria there was no doubt that the real cause of the war was 'the selfishness and ambition of one man'[3] – Tsar Nicholas of Russia. Prince Albert sent a pressing request to Baron Stockmar:

> Come soon, if you can. Your counsel and support will be of extraordinary value to us! The Turks have declared war; what will the four Powers do? By this our mediation policy is knocked on the head. We cannot look on and see the Porte destroyed by Russia; . . . To leave the Porte in the lurch is death to the Ministry, to declare war is not much else.[4]

The Cabinet was divided. Aberdeen still hoped to settle by negotiation; Palmerston thought that only war could resolve the situation. Aberdeen wanted to put pressure on Turkey; Palmerston insisted that it was Russia who was the real menace. Then, on 30 November 1853, a Russian fleet destroyed the Turkish fleet at Sinope, a Turkish port on the Black Sea, killing some 4,000 men. Only 400 of the crews of the sunken vessels survived – and they were wounded. Known as the massacre of Sinope, it seems to have been almost an accident. A Russian squadron came across the fleet when it was searching for ships conveying guns to rebels in the Caucasus. Shots were fired, battle became general and the Turkish fleet was destroyed. The news reached London on 12 December.

When the Cabinet met to discuss the consequences of Sinope, Lord

Palmerston was absent. He had resigned from the Government on 15 December over the Reform Bill. He resigned solely because he was against the extension of the franchise proposed by Aberdeen, but he probably expected that a threat of resignation would bully his colleagues into accepting his point of view and he was surprised at being taken at his word. On 23 December Palmerston wrote to Aberdeen suggesting that there had been a misunderstanding. He had resigned only because he believed no more amendments could be made to the Reform Bill. He now knew this was not so. Although Palmerston's special pleading was obvious, Aberdeen accepted the withdrawal of his resignation.

It had not, however, been without effect for the Queen and the Prince. Russophobia had been growing rapidly in Britain even before the Russian occupation of Moldavia and Wallachia. The Tsar was unpopular. The Russian interventions in Poland and more recently in Hungary had done nothing to dispel fear and hostility towards him. Russophobia was brought to a climax by the 'massacre of Sinope'. The defeat of the Turks at Sinope at sea, where Britons believed they ruled supreme, made the people furious. Aberdeen was blamed and he was said to have been bought by Russia; Palmerston was seen as the one Minister whom the people could trust.[5] His resignation therefore stirred the imagination of the people into an even greater fury. It was known that Palmerston had been forced to resign by the Crown in 1851 – this time, too, it was rumoured that it was Prince Albert who was behind the whole affair. 'It is pretended', the Prince wrote to his brother, 'that I whisper in Victoria's ear, she gets round old Aberdeen, and the voice of the only *English* Minister, Palmerston, is not listened to – ay, he is always intrigued against, at the Court and by the Court.'[6]

Scurrilous attacks on the Prince flourished. The Queen was his puppet, they said, he received his orders from Moscow. The radical press attacked the Prince by name on 7 January 1854. The *Daily News* said: 'Above all the nation distrusts the politics, however they may admire the taste, of a Prince who has breathed from childhood the air of courts tainted by the imaginative servility of Goethe.'[7] The Conservative press was equally xenophobic – but its arguments were different. According to the *Morning Herald*, for instance, the Prince was playing a totally unconstitutional role – and the paper let it be known that the Prince was present at the interviews Ministers had with the Queen, not as a silent onlooker but as a vigorous participant in discussion. It was also said that the Prince kept up an active correspondence with foreign

Courts, 'with the view of defeating the policy of Her Majesty's responsible advisers'.[8]

Albert was bitter, but lucid. He wrote to his brother on 7 January 1854:

> You are right to look into the near future with fear. It looks very black for the whole world. Here the hue and cry for war has grown to a degree that I should never have thought possible. The people have generously made me their scapegoat. Because war has not yet broken out, they logically say the interest of the Coburg family, which is Russian, Belgian etc., is preferred to the alliance with Louis Napoleon.[9]

Albert believed that one of the principal elements behind these attacks was the hostility and bitterness of the old High Tory or Protectionist party against him on account of his friendship with Peel, and his success with the Great Exhibition. There was also a faction against the Prince in the army, including Lord Raglan, who had never forgiven the Crown for not having made him Commander-in-Chief. After the death of the Duke of Wellington it was Lord Hardinge, an intimate friend of Peel's and a former Governor General of India, who had been appointed and who conferred regularly with the Prince on military questions.[10]

These attacks made Albert reflect on all the wrong England and the English had done him. When he first came over to Britain he had been met by a lack of knowledge and an unwillingness to consider the position of the husband of a Queen Regnant. 'Peel cut down my income, Wellington refused me my rank, the royal family cried out against the Foreign interloper, the Whigs in office were only inclined to concede to me just as much space as I could stand upon.'[11] He had therefore kept quiet and acted tactfully. Now the journalistic controversies had brought to light the fact that he had taken an active interest in politics for years and the public, instead of appreciating his reserve and tact, fancied itself betrayed. Albert complained: 'the whole press has for the last week made "a dead set at the Prince".... My unconstitutional position, correspondence with Foreign Courts, dislike to Palmerston, relationship to the Orleans family, interference with the army, etc., are depicted as the causes of the decline of the State, the Constitution, and the nation.'[12]

The *Daily News* announced that it was J. A. Roebuck's intention to demand categorical explanations from the Ministers on the rumours concerning the improper interference of the Prince in government business.[13] The *Spectator* traced the progress of the rumours:

a whisper, which was first insinuated for party purposes, has grown into a roar, and a constructive hint has swelled into a positive and monstrous fiction. . . . The story, not only told in all parts of England a day or two ago, but by some believed, was, that Prince Albert was a traitor to his Queen, that he had been impeached for high treason, and, finally, that on a charge of high treason he had been arrested and committed to the Tower.[14]

It was almost as if Britain, having remained so calm and unrevolutionary in 1848, was making up for lost time.

The Queen naturally came to the defence of her husband. She also realized that the very institution of monarchy was under attack. 'In attacking the Prince,' she wrote to Aberdeen, 'who is one and the same with the Queen herself, the throne is assailed, and she must say she little expected that any portion of her subjects would thus requite the unceasing labours of the Prince.'[15]

On 31 January 1854 Lord John Russell and Lord Aberdeen, as soon as Parliament reassembled, reaffirmed their complete confidence in the Prince's unimpeachable loyalty to the Crown. Lord Derby spoke in the Lords to the same effect. The Prince's right to be the Sovereign's adviser was completely vindicated. The Queen wrote to Baron Stockmar of the 'triumphant refutation of all the calumnies in the two Houses of Parliament.' She noted that, 'The position of my beloved lord and master has been defined for once and all.'[16] Gone was the time when the young, newly married Victoria allowed Albert no part in the affairs of state. The opposition press reacted diversely to the announcement that the Government supported the Court. The *Daily News* declared itself discontented with the debate. The radical *Morning Advertiser* left the debate on the Prince out of its parliamentary report on 31 January. The conservative *Morning Herald*, which had bitterly attacked the Prince, now declared him constitutionally removed from discussion and gave its opinion that the affair ought never to have been brought before Parliament. Later in the same year, after sounding out the British Ambassador, Napoleon III was to ask the Prince to come and inspect the summer camp of 100,000 troops along the Normandy coast. Here at last was recognition of Prince Albert. The royal couple accepted, and the visit took place from 3 to 8 September.

Meanwhile the Queen, in her Speech from the Throne on 30 January, had spoken of the efforts that were still being made to restore peace between Russia and Turkey. However, few believed that war could be averted. War was, in any case, 'popular beyond belief' – as Victoria wrote to Uncle Leopold[17] – and active preparations for it were being made. The Sinope massacre and the pressure of public opinion made war seem inevitable even to the most strenuous advocates of peace with Russia, such as the Member of Parliament Mr Graham.[18] The Queen herself began to be affected by the warlike spirit of her people. She told her uncle in a letter:

> The last battalion of the Guards (Scottish Fusiliers) embarked today. They passed through the court-yard here at seven o'clock this morning. We stood at the balcony to see them. The morning fine, the sun shining over the towers of Westminster Abbey, and an immense crowd collected to see the fine men, and cheering them immensely as with difficulty they marched along. They formed line, presented arms, and then cheered us very heartily, and went off cheering. It was a touching and beautiful sight. Many sorrowing friends were there, and one saw the shake of many a hand. My best wishes and prayers will be with them all.[19]

On 28 March 1854 Britain declared war on Russia. France had done so on the preceding day. The Crimean War had begun.

By this time the royal couple knew that Prussia would not join Britain. In mid-March the Queen had received a letter from the King of Prussia exhorting her not to go to war. He asked if the war was commensurate with the sacrifices in human lives it would demand and declared: 'I am resolved to maintain a position of complete neutrality; and to this I add, with proud elation, My people and myself are of one mind. They require absolute neutrality from me.'[20] The Queen's reply was to remind Prussia that it was one of the five Great Powers – 'the guarantors of treaties, the guardians of civilisation, the champions of right, and ultimate arbitrators of the nations.'[21] Were those obligations to be renounced then Prussia would be renouncing the status it had held since 1815. The draft was in Prince Albert's hand and was sent to Lord Clarendon for approval. He declared that he had read it with pleasure and admiration, for it gave a faithful picture of the conduct and position of the King of Prussia. The truth was that Bismarck, a new force in Prussian politics, was determined to safeguard the possibility of an alliance with Russia. He had no difficulty in convincing the King not to go to war with Russia since the King's sister was the wife of the Tsar.

It was not until September that the Crimean War proper began. On the fourteenth the allied armies reached the Bay of Eupatoria, to the north of Sebastopol. The armies were badly equipped – tents were abandoned for lack of transport, ambulances for lack of drivers. The march towards Sebastopol began on the nineteenth – the French on the wing near the sea, with the Turks under Selim Pasha, the British on the inland side. The Russian army tried to stop the advance of the allies on the Alma, a river to the north of Sebastopol, on 20 September. The battle lasted three hours and the Russians were routed. Losses were, however, heavy – 2,002 British dead, including twenty-five officers. Despite the fact that the men were tired and there was a lack of transport, Lord Raglan wanted to attack Sebastopol immediately. If this had been done Sebastopol would probably have fallen, for it was unprepared. But both General Canrobert and Sir John Burgoyne were against and the advance was not made. The allies thus gave General Todleben an extra three weeks in which to prepare the Russian defences. Sebastopol was by then almost impregnable.

After the decisive victory of the Alma, the British were convinced the war was almost over. The allied forces marched to Balaklava and the bombardment of Sebastopol began. But the Russians had decided to adopt offensive tactics. They marched round to the rear of the British position. On 25 October they attacked Balaklava, the source of the British supplies. Even though the Turks fled before the enemy, the Russians were again routed.

It was at this moment that Lord Raglan, who was waiting for infantry reinforcements, saw that the Russians were preparing to carry off the guns which the Turks had abandoned in the redoubts. He sent an order to Lord Lucan to stop them. Lord Lucan instructed Lord Cardigan and his Light Brigade to deal with the problem. Six hundred and seventy-three men rode down that valley of death straight for the guns, on a venture that was entirely hopeless. Only one hundred and ninety-five returned. They had achieved nothing, nor had there been the slightest hope that they might. 'It was magnificent, but it was not war,' was the comment of the French General Bosquet on this terrible sacrifice. Lord Cardigan told the Duke of Newcastle plainly that Lord Lucan was entirely to blame, 'by misconceiving Lord Raglan's orders, not obeying them and not exposing himself'. The Queen noted of Lord Cardigan that 'not one of the officers who went into that action, he believed, ever thought they would return of it alive!' 'Alas!' she continued, 'the Second Charge of the Light Cavalry was, to use Lord Raglan's own words "a fatal mistake" . . .' She 'trembled with emotion, as well as pride, in reading the recital of the heroism of these devoted men'.[22]

The charge of the Light Brigade appalled the British public and in Parliament an inquiry was demanded. It was widely assumed that the Duke of Newcastle – the Secretary for War – was responsible. On 13 December Lord John Russell raised the matter in Cabinet and demanded Newcastle's resignation. He thought that Palmerston should succeed him. Palmerston opposed Lord John Russell's suggestion and won admiration for his loyalty to his colleague.

The Russians had claimed Balaklava as a victory – and in the field it was. But the attack on the British base, which had been the major aim, had not succeeded. After Balaklava the Russians planned an attack on the allied position at Inkerman. The Russian sortie from Sebastopol on 5 November was, however, mismanaged. The commander lost his way in the mist and a confused mêlée resulted in which officers lost their men and men their officers. At the end of the day, the Russians lost 12,000 men, the British 2,600 and the French 1,800. Another victory for the allies.

Throughout this period the Queen's journal is filled with news of the battles. 'The victory is no doubt a very brilliant one, but I fear dearly bought,' she wrote on 16 November.[23] On the following day, a letter from the front 'shows what sufferings from cold, and what privations are already being endured.'[24] On 22 November she counted the losses: 'the Russians had lost in killed, wounded and prisoners, 15,000!! 4,000 had been counted dead on the ground. The Guards had however lost fearfully! The anxiety and uncertainty increased sadly.'[25] She added that George, the Duke of Cambridge, was quite overcome, and so worn out by the fatigue and excitement of that great day that he had been obliged to go to Constantinople to rest for a few days. The Queen herself was in a fever of excitement. 'I felt so grand and thankful and could hardly contain myself.'[26] Then on 24 November came Ernest Leiningen – straight from Constantinople – and she relived the battles all over again.

The Queen became more and more nationalistic as the war went on. 'You will understand it', she wrote to Augusta, 'when I assure you that I regret exceedingly not to be a man and to be able to fight in the war. My heart bleeds for the many fallen, but I consider that there is no finer death for a man than on the battlefield!'[27] When, in November, Lord Raglan declared that he needed reinforcements and it was found that transport was a problem, the Queen immediately offered to lend the royal yacht. In the event this was not necessary as Cunard offered to put its merchant ships at the Government's disposal.

Russia was the enemy and Victoria was irritated by her husband's attempts at impartiality. This was not the time for such things. When Lord Aberdeen made a statement in the House of Lords that a Day of Humiliation and Prayer should be celebrated for the success of British arms, she rejected the idea, objecting to the term 'humiliation' – she refused to talk of the great sinfulness of the nation when British conduct had been honest and unselfish and the war had been brought about by the selfishness, ambition and want of honesty of one man and his servants. The Queen believed all that she was told of the disgraceful conduct of the enemy. 'The Russians', she wrote, 'have not buried their dead and have abandoned their wounded; both these things are shameful. Several wounded Russians shot at our soldiers and officers as they were tending them, and there was great confusion in our ranks.'[28] In her journal on 30 November she noted General Bentinck's testimony as to: 'The nature of the warfare which he described "as most unpleasant from being so uncivilised – the Russians being so cruel and savage and fighting in a stupid, dogged way".'[29]

Until the beginning of November the troops had not suffered greatly, though cholera had taken a certain toll. But winter was on its way. On 4 November a terrific storm and driving snow overturned their tents and destroyed twenty-one vessels laden with supplies in Balaklava Bay. Two-thirds of the transport horses died. The nine miles between the camp and Balaklava had become virtually impassable. Cholera raged once more and with it scurvy and dysentery. The allied armies were only half as strong as those they were besieging, now General Winter had come to attack them, too. It would have been sensible to withdraw the troops and attack again in the spring. But the armies remained where they were. At the end of February 1855, 8,898 British troops had died in hospital since the beginning of November 1854, and there were still 13,608 men there to be cared for.[30]

The terrible tale of the suffering of the soldiers in the Crimea was told to the British public by the first war correspondent, W. H. Russell of *The Times*. He told of the soldiers' valour and of the excellent relations between the British and French troops. But he told, too, of mismanagement, of the winter waiting and of the state of the British hospitals at Scutari. He contrasted them to the French military hospitals, which were admirably run by the French Sisters of Mercy. A fund had been opened to support those British hospitals in the autumn and one of the first 'appeals' went out. More than 25,000 pounds was collected. Lady Charlotte Canning told her mother that the Government was to send out:

> a band of nurses to Scutari and Miss Nightingale is to head them. Her family have consented and there can be no one so well fitted as she is to do such work. She has such nerves and skill and is so gentle and wise and quiet, even now she is no bustle or hurry tho' so much is in her hands.[31]

Charlotte knew how effective Florence Nightingale was. As chairman of the committee for the Institution for the Care of Sick Gentlewomen in Distressed Circumstances, Charlotte had engaged the young girl as superintendent to reorganize their new premises at Harley Street – and had been severely criticized for engaging a gentlewoman without the permission of her parents. Florence Nightingale was to challenge the army's attitude towards the sick and wounded. She set up the first efficient British military hospital and thus reduced deaths from infected wounds and lack of sanitation. The Queen envied her 'being able to do so much good and look after the noble brave heroes, whose behaviour is admirable. Dreadfully wounded as many are, there is never a murmur or a complaint.'[32] For these 'brave men' she, her daughter and her household began knitting woollen comforters, socks and mittens. Their example was speedily followed.

The bad news from the front continued. 'The sickness has alas! increased, particularly cholera,' and there was 'the greatest confusion about the clothing – the officers having still no change and being in a dreadful state of dirt – quite covered with vermin!' 'The French, however,' noted the Queen, 'also suffer dreadfully only they have no "Times" reporter to trumpet it out.'[33] On Christmas Eve the Queen found the time distressing. 'How many, many a home is sad and mourning dear ones and how cold and dreary are our beloved and noble heroes in the Crimea.'[34] On Boxing Day she read General Codrington's diary, which gave 'a most deplorable account of the sufferings caused by the terrible weather. The poor young recruits die very fast after arriving. All this is heartbreaking.'[35]

The Queen had found 1854 a year of worry, sorrow and anxiety but also a year of glory and success. Prince Albert had found it more trying – and he was quite immune to the glamour of war. He had been scandalously attacked, he had written long memorandums on military improvements and he had been criticized for doing so. He could not understand why his idea of a German Foreign Legion had been considered an insult by the troops.

When Parliament reassembled on 23 January 1855, the public out-cry against the incompetence of the Government was expressed in the demand, directed by Roebuck, for a committee to be appointed to inquire into the mismanagement of the war. On 31 January the House voted against the Government by 305 votes to 148 and the ministry resigned. After trying other solutions in vain, the Queen was obliged to appoint Palmerston as Prime Minister.

While the soldiers were living out the winter in the mud of the trenches by day and the mud of their tents by night, and Britain was in the throes of Cabinet crises, peace negotiations started in Austria. A four-point plan had been drawn up and was under discussion. The four points the allies considered necessary for the signing of a peace treaty were: the establishment of a European protectorate over Moldavia and Wallachia; freedom of navigation on the Danube; the end of Russia's domination in the Black Sea; Russia's renunciation of any idea of extending a protectorate over the Christian subjects of the Turkish empire, leaving their liberties and privileges to be guaranteed to the Great Powers by the Sultan. Agreement was quickly reached on points one, two and four. The problem remained the curbing of Russian power in the Black Sea. The conference in Vienna closed without an agreement being reached. Then, on 2 March, came the death of Tsar Nicholas: 'the Emperor of Russia died at twelve today of pulmonary apoplexy, brought on by influenza!' noted the Queen, 'he has alas! the blood of many thousands on his conscience.'[36] His successor, Alexander II, was convinced that Russia could not bear the strain of war much longer. Negotiations were resumed in Vienna on 15 March but collapsed again in June. Peace now depended on success in the field rather than on diplomacy.

Fighting had started again round Sebastopol in February. In March a Russian sortie managed to seize and fortify a knoll in front of the town. In May, Count Cavour, the Prime Minister of Piedmont, had sent a contingent of soldiers to fight alongside the allies in the hope that this would give him a seat at the peacemaking conference which would follow the end of the war. The entente between the allies deteriorated as the war dragged on. One issue was the idea of the Emperor of the French that he might himself go to fight in the Crimea. When he had first put the idea, back in February, the notion alarmed everyone. 'Lord Palmerston', the Queen noted, 'is greatly against the Emperor's going, on account of the immense risk and the great inconvenience of his absence from France.'[37] His own entourage, well aware of his ignorance of the art of war, and that his defeat would mean ruin for them, were also hostile. Fleury, the Emperor's most confidential officer, told Lord Clarendon that the Emperor was entirely mistaken in believing that his going to Sebastopol was popular with the army generally, or that he would be well received by the troops in the Crimea. As Queen Victoria noted 'They adhered to him, as Emperor, but did not like being under the command of any one, but a professional man, looking upon the Emperor as a civilian. His plans might be ever so good, they would not carry with them the confidence of the Army.'[38]

When Lord Clarendon saw the Emperor in March he told him of 'the danger threatening the Alliance, from a want of consideration for the feelings of the British Army'. His taking supreme command would be accepted but not popular. However, 'should it be intended that the English should act merely as carriers or, at the most, be considered only fit to go on rotting in the trenches, whilst the glory of the new campaign fell solely to the lot of the French, then a feeling would be aroused which would wreck the Alliance.' The Emperor replied that he was anxious for bold steps to be taken in the Crimea in order to put an end to the siege, which threatened to ruin his whole army. He was losing some 3,000 men a month. But he thought it of the greatest importance that, 'wherever the field of glory lay, the two flags should be seen waving together.'[39]

The French and British Governments now both suggested privately to the Queen that she should invite the Emperor and Empress to visit England and try to convince him that his idea of going to fight in the Crimea was unwise.[40] The invitation was accepted and preparations for the visit began. The rooms they were to use in Windsor had been occupied not so long before by Tsar Nicholas and King Louis-Philippe. They were, however, redecorated. The Rubens Room, which was to be the Empress's drawing room, was refurbished with crimson brocade furniture. Next to it, her bedroom was hung with red satin, with fine old pictures, handsome furniture and a really beautiful bed, with feathers at the top of the canopy. It was just as it had been in George IV's state bedroom but renovated and enlarged, with the addition of the Emperor and Empress's monogram. On the toilet table in the Empress's dressing room, the Queen put out her own gold set. The Emperor's bedroom was furnished in green velvet, and the Emperor also had a sitting room and a reception room. 'A good deal of new furniture has had to be got, though there was much fine old furniture in store, which has been carefully renovated.'[41]

Prince Albert went to Dover to meet the guests, who had been delayed in the Channel by a thick fog. They were taken by carriage to Paddington station, through streets crowded with Londoners, and 'were enthusiastically cheered the whole way'.[42] At Windsor the excitement was intense – the Queen and her children had been for a drive through the decorated streets, and by five o'clock were ready waiting. The guests did not arrive until seven. 'I cannot say what indescribable emotion filled me,' wrote the Queen, 'how much all seemed like a wonderful dream. These great meetings of sovereigns, surrounded by very exciting accompaniments, are always very agitating.'[43] When her guests arrived, her two eldest children were waiting with her. She embraced first the Emperor and then 'the very gentle, graceful and evidently very nervous Empress'. She presented her two eldest children to them. 'Vicky with very alarmed eyes, making low curtsies. The Emperor embraced Bertie.'[44]

Of all royal visits to Windsor, this was to be on the personal level the most successful. Napoleon III brought a touch of French panache to a well-ordered Court. His entourage fascinated the Queen; so did his wife and so did the Emperor himself. Among his entourage was the Countess of Montebello, whose grandmother, one of Marie Antoinette's ladies, had been guillotined; the Baroness of Mallaret, whose mother was the daughter of Rostopshin, the man who set fire to Moscow; and the Count Charles Tascher de la Pagerie, whose father was first cousin to the Empress Josephine.[45]

Victoria, who was quite incapable of jealousy, wrote of Eugénie: 'the profile and line of the throat and shoulder are quite beautiful, the expression charming and gentle – quite delightful. Winterhalter's pictures of her are very like. She is very lively and talkative, when at her ease, which she soon was with me.'[46] The Queen's journal is studded with descriptions of the way Eugénie dressed, which the Queen consistently admired. Even Albert was appreciative. 'The Empress looked lovely in a pale green dress, trimmed with Brussels lace, a shawl to match and a white bonnet, no ornaments whatever. Albert admired her toilette extremely.'[47] This did not disturb the Queen in any way. It was almost as if she were pleased to see that he was behaving in a normal way and not with the misogyny that usually characterized him: 'altogether I am delighted', she wrote, 'to see how much he likes and admires her, as it is so seldom I see him do so with *any* woman.'[48] Two days later she noted with satisfaction: 'Albert feels, as I do, much pleased with everything and likes the Emperor and Empress, the latter particularly.'

Victoria was full of praise for Eugénie's manner: 'the most perfect thing I ever saw, so gentle, graceful and kind and so modest and retiring.'[49] But it was her 'Spanish liveliness and vivacity', her 'spirit and courage' that impressed her most. Eugénie took the keenest interest in the war and was all in favour of the Emperor's going. She explained her husband's strategy: 'the French need to be taken by surprise, they must never have the last word.'[50] Victoria would have been afraid to allow Albert to go to the front but Eugénie saw no greater danger for Napoleon III 'there than anywhere else – in fact than in Paris'.[51] Ironically, hardly had Napoleon and the Empress returned to Paris than he was indeed shot at when out riding in the Bois de Boulogne – he was not, however, hurt. Victoria was horrified. 'Thank God! he escaped,' she noted, and then added, 'and that it did not happen here.'[52]

The Emperor had totally charmed the Queen. Victoria, as Lord Clarendon told Greville, 'never had conversed with a man of the world on a footing of equality' and his flirtatious manner 'was of a character to flatter her vanity without alarming her virtue and modesty, she enjoyed the novelty of it without scruple or fear.'[53] Napoleon III set out to please her. He told her of the first time he had seen her, when he was a simple spectator in Green Park, when she set out to prorogue Parliament on her accession. He was very friendly with the children, 'especially Arthur whom he envied us for possessing'.[54] Vicky was totally under the charm of the Emperor and the Empress.[55] When the Empress gave her a ruby and diamond watch, she 'was in ecstasies'.[56] The Emperor praised Albert. He deferred to the couple before he read his address to the City. It had been translated for him and he begged them to correct his pronunciation and asked their advice about one or two expressions.[57]

During the visit the Queen reflected that at first she had been nervous, but that the Emperor's manner was soothing. He was 'so very quiet, his voice low and soft' and so easy to talk to.[58] He was not at all the upstart she had been led to expect. 'Nothing could be more civil, amiable, or well bred than the Emperor's manner – so full of tact.'[59] He was not a handsome man for he was 'extremely short, but with a head and bust which ought to belong to a much taller man.'[60] But he rode well 'and looks well on horseback, as he sits high.'[61] Above all, 'One would imagine that he had been educated as a Crown Prince. His manners have something which in English we call "fascinating".'[62]

Three things made him even more fascinating. First his rapid rise in fortune: six years before he had been 'an exile, poor and unthought of'. Then his relationship to Napoleon I; there was something thrilling in thinking 'of a granddaughter of George III dancing with the nephew of our great enemy the Emperor Napoleon, now my most firm ally, in the Waterloo Gallery.'[63] And lastly he was a target for assassins, which made her feel protective. 'I own,' she said of their visit to the Crystal Palace, now at Sydenham, 'I felt rather anxious as we passed along through the multitude of people, who, after all were very close to us, and walking, on the Emperor's arm, I hoped I might possibly be a protection for him.'[64] Napoleon III had thus made an excellent impression on his hosts. 'I believe him capable of kindness, affection, friendship and gratitude,' wrote Victoria. She was 'very glad to know this wonderful and remarkable man'[65] with whom she got on as 'famously' as Albert did with the Empress.

The visit was a triumph and the Emperor had been welcomed with great popular enthusiasm. Greville corroborated this. He wrote on 20 April 1855:

> The fineness of the weather brought out the whole population of London, as usual kept in excellent order by a few policemen. . . . I am glad that the success of the visit has been so great, and the contentment of all the parties concerned so complete, but it is well that all will be over tomorrow, for such excitement and enthusiasm could not last much longer, and the inconvenience of being beset by crowds and the streets obstructed, is getting tiresome.[66]

The Queen had in fact done her guests proud: a great banquet in St George's Hall, Windsor; a review of the household troops in Windsor Park; a state ball; and, the highlight of the four days in Windsor, the investing of the Emperor with the Order of the Garter. Then in London: a visit to the opera house in Covent Garden, where *Fidelio* was being sung, and a visit to the Crystal Palace. The leavetaking was tender: 'All the children began to cry and the Empress said she hoped she would see me soon again in Paris.'[67] Once they had gone everything seemed dull. But the visit could still be mulled over and talked about. Two days later the Queen noted: 'Saw Stockmar and talked together of the Emperor, his wonderful character and his talent, his attractiveness and their difference to those of Louis-Philippe. Albert is as much interested as I.'[68]

Palmerston had taken advantage of the visit to have political discussions with the French Emperor. He was convinced that Napoleon III was ready to make peace on terms which he, Palmerston, considered too soft. The British Prime Minister would like to have taken a more extreme position. He wanted, for instance, to give the Crimea back to Turkey, from whom Catherine the Great had wrested it in 1774, and to force Russia to evacuate the territories she had conquered in the Caucasus over the past twenty-five years. Palmerston believed that if the allies captured Sebastopol then Austria could be persuaded to declare war on Russia. Napoleon III agreed with one point – that the time was not ripe for peace.

Palmerston also managed to dissuade Napoleon III from helping the Poles, who had always been popular in France. Prince Adam Czartoryski had offered to send regiments of Polish refugees to help in the war against Russia, in the hope that the allies would include the liberation of Poland in their war aims. Palmerston was against, for this would have antagonized Austria. Reluctantly, Napoleon III agreed to adopt the same position as the English. But Palmerston was not able to persuade the Emperor to abandon his idea of going to the Crimea. He went back to France as determined as ever to lead his troops into battle. Less than a week later, however, he abandoned the idea of leaving France for so long for fear of 'what his uncle and Prince Napoleon might be up to'.[69]

The war in the Crimea continued and the Queen followed carefully the heroic actions and the sufferings and privations of her troops. In February she had visited the men in hospital and was deeply touched. 'It makes one's heart bleed to see [the soldiers] so mutilated ... I spoke to each man, questioning them as to their wounds ... I had meant to make some kind of general speech, but I was so agitated that it all stuck in my throat.'[70] She also gave some thought to their return to civilian life. 'I cannot say how touched and impressed I have been by the sight of these noble, brave, and so sadly wounded men, and *how* anxious I feel to be of use to them and to try and get some employment for those who are ruined for life. Those who are discharged will receive very small pensions but not sufficient to live upon.'[71] Nor was this a vain promise. Sir Thomas Ironbridge, who had at Inkerman 'one leg and the foot of the other carried away by a round shot', was, for instance, made one of the Queen's aides-de-camp.[72] After her visit to Chatham military hospital on 3 March she noted:

> The sight of such fine, powerful frames laid low and prostrate with wounds and sickness on beds of suffering or maimed in the prime of life is indescribably touching to us *women* who are born to suffer and can bear pain more easily, so different to men and soldiers accustomed to activity and hardship, whom it is particularly sad and pitiable to see in such a condition.[73]

On 18 May and for the first time, the Queen herself distributed war medals to the officers and men who were back in England or on leave. The ceremony took place at Horse Guards Parade, where a royal dais was put up. Victoria wrote:

> At first I felt so agitated I could hardly hold the medal as I handed it with its blue and yellow edged ribbon ... Many of the Privates smiled, others hardly dared look up, – and many said "Thank Your Majesty" and all touched my hand, the first time that a simple Private has touched the hand of his Sovereign and that, – a Queen! – I am proud of this tie which links the lowly brave to his Sovereign. Nothing could exceed the good manner of the men.[74]

Throughout July, reinforcements were poured into Sebastopol from Russia and on 16 August Prince Gorchakov made an attempt to raise the siege. He crossed the Chernaya river and attacked the French and Sardinians, but he was obliged to retreat with heavy losses. The French were beginning to protest against the war and to claim, not without reason, that it was the British Prime Minister who was responsible for its continuation and that France was just a tool in English hands. The victory of the Chernaya and the Queen's visit to Paris were for a time to silence these murmurs.

It was on 18 August that the Queen and Prince Albert, accompanied by the Prince of Wales and the Princess Victoria, set off for France. They arrived at Boulogne, where the Emperor met them, and then went to Paris by train. From there they went to St Cloud, where the palace had been placed entirely at their disposal for the nine days of their visit. It was the first time since the reign of Edward II that a reigning English Sovereign had paid a state visit to Paris.

Victoria was again under the spell of the French imperial charm, and this time not only her host but also the surroundings enthralled her. Napoleon III flattered her and this short over-plump woman with no sense of dress revelled in his compliments. Albert was incapable of the exaggerated courtesies the Emperor showered on her. 'I know few people', the Queen wrote at the end of her visit, 'whom I have felt involuntarily more inclined to confide in and speak unreservedly to – I should not fear saying anything to him. I felt – I do not know how to express it – safe with him.'[75] Here in Paris the Queen was as gay and cheerful as she had been in her youth. Once again she admired Eugénie who, even though she was pregnant, still showed her eye for beautiful clothes. Under Eugénie the great French dress designers flourished and she it was who made Worth's fortune. The English Queen was still wearing the poke bonnets of Louis-Philippe's day and carried everywhere an enormous white satin bag which made her look even shorter. It had, moreover, been embroidered with a large fat poodle in gold.

To welcome the royal couple Paris had decked herself out with banners, flags, arches, flowers, inscriptions, illuminations. 'This beautiful city . . .' wrote the Queen, 'full of people, lined with troops, beautifully kept and most enthusiastic.'[76] Prince Albert was greatly impressed by the new Paris created by Napoleon III with the aid of Baron Haussmann. He told King Leopold:

Paris is signally beautified by the Rue de Rivoli, the Boulevard de Strasbourg, the completion of the Louvre, the great open square in front of the Hôtel de Ville, the clearing away of all the small houses which surrounded Notre Dame, by the fine Napoleon barracks, the completion of the Palais de Justice, and restoration of the Sainte Chapelle, and especially by the laying out of the ornamental grounds in the Bois de Boulogne, which really may be said to vie with the finest English parks. How all this could have been done in so short a time no one comprehends.[77]

Their time in Paris was packed with activities. To the surprise of the French Court, the thirty-six-year-old Queen of England openly showed her enjoyment without putting on airs. She participated in everything, from a tour of the Louvre in baking heat to a ball at the Hôtel de Ville, with boundless energy. Paris enchanted her. 'I am delighted, enchanted, amused and interested, and think I never saw anything more beautiful and gay than Paris – or more splendid than all the Palaces.'[78]

She was shown all the major sights: the Sainte Chapelle, Notre Dame and the Palace of the Tuileries, which was now Louis Napoleon's principal palace. The Palais de l'Elysée she found 'very pretty, but the decorations excepting in one or two rooms are not nearly finished and it is a small building.'[79] The Conciergerie, she learnt, had been Louis Napoleon's prison fifteen years earlier – that was before he was sent to the fortress of Ham, escaped dressed as a workman and made his way to London. Versailles was the scene of a grand picnic. She went to see the tomb of Napoleon – whose ashes Louis-Philippe had brought back from St Helena in 1840. The tomb was not yet completed and the Emperor's coffin lay in a side chapel. It was covered with black velvet. Above it stood a great bronze eagle, and at the foot was the hat worn at Eylau and the sword of Austerlitz. Purple velvet hung on the walls. Marshal Canrobert reports:

> There was not a word. Everyone contemplated the coffin in silence . . . After a moment of meditation, of absolute silence, the Queen with a respectful, calm and severe expression, turned to the Prince of Wales and putting her hand on his shoulder said, "Kneel down before the tomb of the great Napoleon". At that moment a terrible storm, to which the torrid heat of the last few days had been working up, burst forth. Great peals of thunder shook all the windows of the chapel, and their sound went echoing round the vaults.[80]

The Queen noted in her journal:

> The organ of the church was playing "God Save the Queen" at the time, and this solemn scene took place by torchlight, and during a thunder-

storm. Strange and wonderful indeed. It seems, as if in this tribute of respect to a departed foe, old enmities and rivalries were wiped out, and the seal of Heaven placed upon that bond of unity, which is now happily established between two great and powerful nations.[81]

The Palais of Saint Germain gave her the opportunity to see the rooms that James II had occupied, now sad and neglected. Malmaison gave Napoleon III an excuse to talk about his memories of the Empress Josephine. At Versailles, Empress Eugénie, who was fascinated by Marie Antoinette, received them in one of the 'cottages'. They also visited the castle itself, and the Trianon and the fountains, which were especially turned on for them, excited great admiration.

The climax of the visit was an evening celebration at Versailles. For an evening it recovered its past splendour. The grand courtyard of the chateau was as light as day on that Saturday night. Flower-filled boudoirs hung with blue damask had been prepared for Victoria and Albert in the apartments once occupied by Marie Antoinette. From there they passed through the state apartments of Louis XIV, magnificently lighted – with the immense fireplaces turned into gardens of flowers and plants – to the gallery of mirrors. At each corner an orchestra of two hundred musicians had been set up, with flowers and shrubs concealing the music stands. Garlands hung from the ceiling and interlaced with each other, while thousands of torches and chandeliers were reflected in the mirrors throwing light on the scene. From the windows the scene outside was even more spectacular. The great sheet of water was enclosed by a series of Renaissance porches joined together by trelliswork. In the centre was a triumphal arch, surmounted with a double shield with the arms of France and England. At the two nearest corners were two other porticos with the initials of their Majesties. Under the arches the fountains played.

At ten o'clock came a firework display. Its grand finale was a picture of the towers and battlements of Windsor Castle. At half-past ten the Emperor opened the ball with the Queen of England. There had not been a ball at Versailles since the time of Louis XVI and it had been modelled on a print of a fête given by Louis XV. At eleven o'clock the Court proceeded to supper in the theatre. Their Majesties ate in the state box, which commanded a view of all the others. 'The whole stage was covered in,' wrote the Queen, 'and four hundred people sat down to supper at forty small tables of ten each, each presided over by a lady, and nicely selected, and all by the Empress's own desire and arrangement.'

Victoria and Albert's two eldest children also responded eagerly to the welcome of their hosts. Vicky never tired of praising the beauty, kindness and goodness of the Empress. For Bertie, France was a whole new world – and he gave his heart to the country. He liked its beauty, the liveliness of the people, the comprehension and warmth of the Emperor. 'You have a nice country,' he told him, 'I would like to be your son.'[82] When the visit was drawing to a close, reluctant to leave Paris, he asked the Empress if she could not get permission for him and his sister to stay a little longer. She replied that that was impossible because his parents could not do without them. 'Not do without us!' the boy replied, 'don't fancy that, for there are six more of us at home and they don't want us.'[83] From this time on, Bertie preferred France to Germany, his father's country, and he was to prove it some fifty years later when, as King Edward VII, he established with France the *Entente Cordiale*.

For the Emperor the visit was an outstanding personal and political success. As he smiled at his royal guest, 'one might plainly see,' noted the *Manchester Guardian*, 'mixed with an unfeigned deference and respect ... a sentiment of intense self-satisfaction at having gained a great political point at which he had been aiming.'[84]

In the next month, September 1855, the assault on Sebastopol was resumed. The British again attacked the Redan, while the French attacked the neighbouring Malakov fortress. The allied forces attacked at twelve o'clock. By the end of the day the assault on the Malakov had been successful and it was in the possession of the French. The English attack against the Redan did not succeed. The Queen commented: 'This last is very vexatious and I fear we must have lost heavily.' She nonetheless telegraphed to the Emperor, congratulating him on the news of the taking of the Malakov.[85] The French victory cost them 7,500 casualties, killed and wounded, including fifteen generals, but it was a prelude to the fall of Sebastopol. A few hours later the Russians exploded their ammunition, set fire to the whole of the town, sank their vessels and executed a swift evacuation across a floating bridge. On 9 September, after a siege of 349 days, the allies occupied the ruins. Sebastopol had not fallen – it had been erased.

The fall of Sebastopol was celebrated by the royal couple at Balmoral. A great bonfire was lit by Albert at the top of Craig Gowan. The gentlemen from the surrounding area immediately came up, followed by all the servants, and gradually the whole of the small population of the valley.[86]

For some in authority in Britain, however, British honour had been dimmed by the blaze of glory surrounding the French army. In London the civic authorities suggested that there should be no general illumination of the city. The Prime Minister rejected the idea of a special thanksgiving day on a weekday – the victory was not, he claimed, a decisive one which would end the war. Indeed there was none of the organized rejoicing that usually follows victory. The defeat at the Redan soured the victory which ended the siege. It came as a shock to a nation which, since Waterloo, had been convinced of its military superiority over the French.

For Napoleon III the end of the siege was a triumph. On 29 December the Imperial Guard returned from Sebastopol to Paris. The Emperor met them at the Place de la Bastille and led them through the streets to the Place Vendôme, cheered all the way by enthusiastic crowds.

Napoleon III was now ready for peace. Palmerston was not. But although he had hoped to force the Russians to cede the Crimea to Turkey, he was obliged to agree to negotiate. After the preliminary terms had been agreed in Vienna, the final treaty was to be settled at a peace conference. Palmerston suggested that it be held in Brussels but Napoleon III insisted on it being held in Paris – thus effacing the French humiliation at the Congress of Vienna. It opened on 25 February 1856, under the presidency of the French Foreign Minister, Walewski. When Palmerston pressed for harsh terms, Napoleon III told Lord Clarendon, the British Minister of Foreign Affairs who was there to negotiate, that although the French were tired of war, they would be in favour of a war to liberate the Poles. This would transform the war against Russia into a revolutionary war against Russia and Austria. Palmerston was thoroughly alarmed and abandoned his opposition to the proposed peace terms.

After a month of hard bargaining the treaty was signed on 30 March. The Russians were not forced to make the territorial concessions Britain had hoped for. They retained both the Crimea and Circassia. They did not even cede the whole of Bessarabia, only a small area in the south which they had taken in 1828. They did have to agree, however, to the neutralization of the Black Sea; Russia was not to rebuild Sebastopol as a fortress, nor to have any naval bases. The Danube, too, was to be brought under international control. The Sublime Porte was formally admitted to participation in the public law and concert of Europe, and the independence and territorial integrity of the Ottoman empire was guaranteed. As for the original cause of the dispute, the Sultan agreed to treat his subjects better, without distinction of creed or race, and the Powers renounced their right to interfere collectively or separately in the internal affairs of Turkey. Both France and Russia thus abandoned their rival claims to protect the Christians.

The terms of the treaty were highly advantageous to Turkey. For Britain the neutralization of the Black Sea was a clear, if temporary, gain. France gained little materially but Napoleon III established his position in Europe; until the rise of Bismarck, his was the major influence on the continent. The other great gainer was Italy. Despite Austrian resistance, Cavour took his place at the Council in Paris.

The Crimean War had led to a complete stagnation of domestic policy, virtually limited to producing budgets which would enable the country to bear the cost of the war. It also introduced a new period of Palmerstonian government. Apart from a short period in 1858–9, when Derby was Prime Minister, Palmerston held office from February 1855 until his death in October 1865. An unexpected assessment of Palmerston was written by the Queen in 1856. 'Albert and I agreed that of all the Prime Ministers we have had, Lord Palmerston is the one who gives the least trouble, and is most amenable to reason and most ready to adopt suggestions. The great danger was foreign affairs, but now that these are conducted by an able, sensible and impartial man [Lord Clarendon], and that he [Lord Palmerston] is responsible for the *whole*, everything is quite different.'[87]

Hardly a year had passed since the conclusion of the Crimean War when Great Britain suddenly found herself facing an utterly unexpected explosion of violence in India. Although it is still referred to as the Indian Mutiny, because it began in a native regiment in the British service and was to include the violent revolt of many other native regiments, it was in reality far more than a mutiny. It was a rising of the Indians against the British, of the Hindu and the Muhammadan against the Christian. It was a war of independence.

The English had made their first official appearance in India in the seventeenth century. On the last day of the sixteenth century, Queen Elizabeth I had incorporated the East India Company by charter and it had come to govern the greater part of the peninsula in qualified partnership with the British Government. In 1763, by the Treaty of Paris, French power on the subcontinent was limited to two trading settlements with no military establishment – Pondicherry and Chandernagore. Victorious over the French, the English East India Company had also embarked on a struggle for power with the various native powers and princes. Its territories expanded with astonishing speed as a result of almost continuous war and annexation. In 1833 an important change took place in the East India Company's constitutional position. Its charter was renewed by Parliament on condition that it abandoned its commercial monopoly and, indeed, ceased to carry on trade at all. At the same time the Governor-General of Bengal was transformed into the Governor-General of India, with power to legislate in council for the whole of British India.

In 1848 India was made up of two parts: one was under the government of the English East India Company, the other was made up of the Feudatory States over which the British exercised greater or lesser control, but no direct responsibility. In this second part the British often kept native princes on their thrones who were tyrannical sovereigns – in many cases they were protected by the British from what would otherwise have been the natural consequences of misrule. Lord Dalhousie became Governor-General of India in 1848 and over the next eight years brought a new India into being. He extended the frontiers of British India, consolidated and unified British territory within and developed India's national resources. In 1849, after a successful war against the Sikhs in the Punjab, he annexed the whole of this vast region to British India. His next annexation was of a much smaller area – Kikkim in the Himalayas, to the north of Bengal. This gave Britain an important tea-growing district. Then, in 1853, as a result of the second Burmese War, Pegu in lower Burma was annexed.

In central India, other annexations were carried out as the result of the doctrine of 'lapse'. When a Hindu had no legal heirs it had long been the custom for him to adopt an heir and bequeath the principality to him. However, no adoption was valid unless it received the assent of the suzerain power. If such assent was not given, the principality lapsed to that power. In one case after another, Dalhousie refused to recognize adoptions and absorbed the territories concerned into the British dominions: the Maratha principality of Satara was annexed in 1849, Jhansi and Magpur in 1853. Less important were the annexations of Jaipur, Baghat, Udaipur and Budawal. Although Dalhousie's action was entirely legal, it was a departure from the custom of the times and was viewed with alarm in several states.

Britain had thus annexed states as a result of victory in war and as a result of lapse of heirs. A third ground was persistent misgovernment by native rulers despite repeated remonstrances. This was to be the fate of the kingdom of Oudh. For almost a century the Oudh dynasty had been an ally of the British – and its rule had been notoriously oppressive for half a century. There had been repeated British warnings about the misgovernment of the country and in 1856 Dalhousie decided to act. On 13 February the formal annexation of Oudh to the dominions of the East India Company was proclaimed, while the King's private property was confiscated and sold. The kings of Oudh had been noted all over India for their staunch loyalty to the English in India. At every native court it was whispered that to be loyal to England was to invite ruin. The seeds of suspicion and distrust were sown.

By 1856, after eight years as Governor-General, Dalhousie had increased British India by between a third and a half. Together with this went administrative reform and modernization. Anxious to bind together the old British India with the new, Dalhousie devised a comprehensive scheme of railways. He covered India with roads and canals. He set up a telegraph system and a cheap postal system. He reformed the civil service, improved education and passed social laws – Hindu widows were allowed to remarry, for instance, and persons who changed their religion were relieved from forfeiture. When Dalhousie left India in March 1856 – a dying man – it was believed in Britain that he had handed over to Lord Canning a country that was in a state of lasting tranquillity. Suddenly, on 10 May 1857, came news of the outbreak of the Indian Mutiny at Meerut.

The causes of the Indian Mutiny have long been debated. Of course, they were multiple. In a sense, Lord Dalhousie's policy had prepared the Indians for revolution because it had brought rapid change which had not been assimilated. The new system of progressive education was hated by Hindu and Muslim alike because it undermined the teachings of their faiths. The missionary seminaries were likewise considered wicked. The material progress Dalhousie ushered in was intelligible to very few – the natural conservatism of the uneducated was disturbed not reassured by the railways and roads, arousing suspicions of a new assault on their national faith. Social reforms had broken the policy of neutrality with regard to issues touching on religious beliefs. There were, too, plots and intrigues against the British Raj fostered by those at Oudh and elsewhere who had lost their power.

Another element which made the Mutiny significant was the spread of the feeling that Britain was no longer strong. The end of the war against Russia had shown that the British were no longer pre-eminent either in the field or at the negotiating table. Palmerston's policy of greatness had collapsed. The period was therefore propitious for a revolt against English rule. The army in India was, after all, essentially an army of Indian soldiers, the sepoys, especially since the Crimean War had diminished the number of Europeans serving in India: when Lord Canning arrived there were some 233,000 Indians to 45,000

Britons, a ratio of five to one. Moreover, the sepoys had two new grievances against the British. In the first place, with the annexation of new provinces, they no longer got increased pay and allowances when they went there – since these territories were now British, only home service pay was paid. Secondly, Lord Canning, almost on arrival in 1856, issued the General Service Enlistment Act, which made all future recruits enlisting in the Bengal army liable for foreign service. Most of these troops were of high caste and belonged to families who expected their sons and the sons of their sons to join the army in their turn. But to serve in Burma – which was the particular motive of the Act – they would have to cross the sea, 'the black water', as they termed it. By doing so they would lose their caste. Conditions were thus created in which it would be extremely difficult for them to maintain their rules.

All these grievances meant that India was in an inflammable condition. It only needed a spark to set it alight. That spark was the introduction into India of the Enfield rifle. This rifle replaced the smooth-bore musket after the Crimean War. It had the characteristic that the cartridge could not be rammed home unless it had been previously greased. The sepoys were told by those hoping to stir up resistance to the British that the lubricant used was a mixture of pig fat and cow fat. The troops were made up partly of Muslims, who could not touch pig fat, and partly of Hindus, who regarded the cow as a sacred animal and who could not touch ox or cow fat without loss of caste. The issue of these cartridges was stopped in January 1857 but the rumour continued that the fats had been mixed to offend both Muslim and Hindu.

The story was later traced to a curious source. At Dumdum near Calcutta, a man of low caste asked a sepoy to give him some water from his cup. The sepoy was a Brahman and refused, saying that if he did so his cup would be polluted, since the other man was low caste. The first man replied sneeringly that the Brahman was about to lose his caste in any case since the Government were making cartridges greased with defiling fats and he would have to bite them in loading his rifle. The Brahman was devastated. The story spread like wildfire, causing a veritable panic. This was the version given the parliamentary commission which later examined the Mutinies in the East Indies. Lord Roberts, in his account of the Mutiny,[88] considers that despite the causes of discontent there would have been no Mutiny had the British officers been younger and more alert. 'Brigadiers of seventy, Colonels of sixty and Captains of fifty. It is curious to note how nearly every military officer, who held a command or a high position on the staff in Bengal when the Mutiny broke out, disappeared from the scene in the first few weeks and was never heard of officially again.'[89]

On Saturday, 9 May 1857, eighty-five men of the Bengal Native Cavalry were tried by a court martial and sentenced to long periods of imprisonment for refusing to use what they still considered to be contaminated cartridges. On the following day the entire native garrison at Meerut, which was the largest military station in India, mutinied. They killed several officers, released the soldiers from prison, set fire to their huts and shot every European they met. The European troops managed to drive them out of the encampments but did not pursue them and allowed them to march on to Delhi forty miles away. General Hewitt, one of Lord Roberts's 'generals of seventy', was in command at Meerut, and neither he nor Archdale Wilson, the brigadier, made any effort to warn the garrison at Delhi.

The living representative of the old dynasty still lived with his family in Delhi. The mutineers proclaimed him Emperor of the restored Mogul Empire. The native regiments in Delhi joined the mutineers one after the other. The British arsenal was held for a time by European soldiers and then had to be blown up to prevent it falling into the hands of the mutineers. In Delhi the native cavalry and the sepoy infantry went on the rampage – murdering Europeans, burning down their houses, committing atrocities on European women and children. The date was 10 May. Victoria only learnt of the outbreak from Lord Palmerston on 26 June.

On 1 July the Queen wrote in her journal about the 'mutiny among the native troops and the murders of Europeans at Meerut, and at Delhi'. But far worse was to come. At Lucknow, Cawnpore, Benares, Bareilly, Allahabad, the sepoys rebelled – in many cases murdering any whites they could find. Most of the rebels went to Delhi. Fortunately for the British, four thousand sepoy troops stationed at Mecan Meer, five miles from Lahore, were disarmed by the Judicial Commissioner, who had been left in command. With the local European military, he ordered a parade for daybreak. Twelve guns loaded with grape-shot were placed along one side of the parade ground. The troops were formed up in a line of columns facing the guns and ordered to pile arms. Sullenly they obeyed, for to hesitate was death. The rifles were carried off in carts.

As the Mutiny spread it became obvious that the Bengal army was the centre of rebellion. There were insurgents in central India, too, but it soon appeared that the risings in Bombay and Madras would not be serious. The blackest story of the rebellion is that of Cawnpore, on the great trunk road between Delhi and Calcutta, 270 miles from the former, 684 miles from the latter. In May 1857 there were some 3,000 native troops and some 300 Europeans there, under the command of Sir Hugh Wheeler, an old man of seventy-five. He appealed to Nana Sahib, a neighbouring Prince, to help him keep order. The Prince agreed and came with two cannons and 300 men. When the garrison revolted, however, the Prince put himself at the head of the rebels.

Meanwhile Wheeler had taken refuge with some thousand Europeans, over half of them women and children, in an old hospital. For nineteen days they held out against continuous assaults from the rebels. Nana Sahib, whose prestige was beginning to crumble in the face of their resistance, offered to allow them a safe passage down the river to Allahabad if they would lay down their arms. They agreed. Boats were prepared on the Ganges. The women and children were all aboard and the men were following when a bugle sounded: the awnings of their boats burst into flames, the native boatmen dived into the sea and a hail of fire poured into the boats. A hundred and twenty-two women and children were unlucky enough to survive, many of them badly wounded. They were taken back to the town and imprisoned in a house, in dreadful conditions, for nearly four weeks. On 15 July a company of sepoys was ordered to the house and told to fire through the windows. This they did, firing too high – whether from inefficiency or a sense of mercy. Nana sent five men that same evening with swords to finish the job. On the following morning their bloody remains were thrown into a dry well.

When the British army arrived on 17 July, they discovered what had happened and saw the floor strewn with hair, clothing and other articles, and everything soaked in blood. There was a blazing desire for revenge. 'The horrors committed on the poor ladies – women and children – are unknown in these ages,' Queen Victoria wrote to King Leopold, 'and make one's blood run cold.'[90] From then on the rebels were treated with great severity and few taken in arms were spared.

Four days after the surrender at Cawnpore and the treacherous conduct of Nana, the British garrison of Lucknow was shut up in the Lucknow residency and the famous siege began. Within the lines there were some 2,000 people – nearly half of them non-combatants, including 130 women and children. There were plenty of guns and ammunition and no lack of food, but the enclosure to be defended was about a mile in circumference and outside the enemy was only a few yards away. This meant that vigilance had to be constant – and was consequently exhausting. There were, too, incessant casualties as attacks were repelled. The defenders were cut off from outside communication and the moral strain was also very great. Cholera, smallpox and fever took their toll.

Within six months the empire which it had taken a century to create was shattered. However, the English were determined to reconquer what they had lost. This was no easy task, given the magnitude of the rebellion. That they were able to do so was in part due to John Lawrence, who raised the Sikhs to replace the sepoys. His act not only reinforced the British army, it also meant that the warlike Sikhs would not swell the forces of the enemy. Delhi fell before the attacks of the reinforced army on 20 September, after six days' fighting. The Mogul Emperor was captured. It was not the end of the rebellion but it was the beginning of the end.

In November, England's aid for her sorely pressed Indian Army reached Calcutta – 30,000 men with Sir Colin Campbell at their head. He it was who effected the relief of the imprisoned garrison of the residency at Lucknow on 17 November. Yet, with the back of the revolt broken by the capture of Delhi and the rescue of the residency garrison, the insurgents became more rather than less active. Not until March was the city of Lucknow in the hands of the British once more.

The history of the Indian Mutiny is full of thrilling events, deeds of valour and endurance. The protagonists assume heroic proportions, from the telegraph clerk in Delhi who kept on flashing his warning to the Punjab until the mutineers broke in and hacked him to pieces, to General Havelock or John Nicholson, who died in combat. The unsung hero of the crisis was Lord Canning, who was criticized throughout both in India and in England. He insisted on justice and not vengeance. He refused absolutely to give in to a blanket condemnation of all those connected in any way with the revolt, insisting that there were different degrees of guilt, and he persisted in giving his trust and confidence to the loyal Muslim and the loyal Hindu. He showed a wisdom rare in such circumstances.

While the suppression of the Mutiny followed its course, India was at the heart of the Government's discussions in London. Parliament decided to abolish the East India Company. The time had come for the Crown to assume direct responsibility for the empire built up by the commercial company. A Bill was passed by both Houses and received the Royal Assent on 2 August 1858. It transferred to the Crown the powers and territories of the East India Company. The administration of India was entrusted to a Secretary of State assisted by the Council of India. The council was composed of fifteen paid members appointed by the Secretary of State, and nine of the fifteen had to have recently served in India and have resided there for at least ten years.

This transfer of authority was formally announced to the peoples of India on 1 November 1858. The terms of the proclamation were revised by Victoria personally. She was far from satisfied with the original draft of Lord Stanley and wrote to Lord Derby asking him to:

> write it himself in his excellent language, bearing in mind that it is a female Sovereign who speaks to more than one hundred million of Eastern people assuming the direct government over them after a bloody civil war, giving them pledges which her future reign is to redeem, and the principles of her government. Such a document should breathe feelings of generosity, benevolence, and religious feeling, pointing out the privileges which the Indians will receive in being placed on an equality with the subjects of the British Crown and the prosperity following in the train of civilisation.[91]

Lord Derby accepted the Queen's criticisms with a good grace and the second draft was warmly approved by the Queen. In it her views were made particularly clear with regard to the respect of the religion of her new subjects.

> Firmly relying on the truth of Christianity, and acknowledging with gratitude the solace of religion, we disclaim alike the right and the desire to impose our convictions on any of our subjects. It is our Royal will and pleasure that no one shall in any wise suffer for his opinions or be disquieted by reason of his religious faith or observance. We will show to all alike the equal and impartial protection of the law, and we do strictly charge and enjoin those who may be in authority under us that they abstain from all interference with the religious belief or worship of any of our subjects under pain of our highest displeasure. It is our further will that, so far as may be, our subjects, of whatever class or creed, be fully and freely admitted to any offices the duties of which they may be qualified by their education, abilities, and integrity duly to discharge.[92]

The Queen's pleasure in her new territory, which added nearly two hundred million human beings to those who already owed her direct allegiance, and more than 800,000 square miles to the British dominions, was immense. She wrote to the Viceroy in 1858: 'It is a source of great satisfaction and pride to her to feel herself in direct communication with that enormous Empire which is so bright a jewel of her Crown, and which she would wish to see happy, contented and peaceful.'[93]

The new administration set about its task of pacification and restoration of confidence. The old practices with regard to the adoption of heirs for principalities were reinstated; a rule was instituted that there should be at least half as many white troops in India as there were sepoy forces; a complete revision of the system of taxation was undertaken. The Queen's first Viceroy of India was Lord Canning – and he was fully to justify the trust she put in him.

19
Family Affairs

In the letter Prince Albert wrote to Stockmar on 10 September telling him of the bonfire that had been lit to celebrate the fall of Sebastopol, he also told him that Prince Frederick William was coming on the following evening. Fritz was the young and handsome heir of the Prince of Prussia and this announcement delighted the Baron. One of his grand designs was to see the young Prince married to Vicky – such a match would strengthen the links between Britain and Germany, which he hoped would soon be unified and liberal. For Albert, here was a way of reorientating British politics towards Germany and away from France. He put no trust in Napoleon III and, indeed, showed throughout his life a keen aversion for things French.

Queen Victoria was reticent. She was not in favour of political marriages and was not prepared to sanction any engagement unless it was the wish of Vicky herself. But she was a romantic. When she saw the young Prince again – he had already visited them in 1851 – she found him 'the same unaffected amiable young man he always was, only much less shy – and with a great deal of conversation'; she could not help her heart beating at the visit, 'as it may and probably will decide the fate of our dear eldest child.'[1] Prince Frederick William seemed to her to have a lot of interesting things to say about his journeys to Russia, Italy and Sicily and seemed 'to have travelled with great use and advantage'.[2] After six days with them at Balmoral, the Prince laid his proposal of marriage before them. When he asked whether he 'might touch on a subject very near to his heart – his great wish to belong to our family', the Queen could only squeeze his hand and say how happy she and her husband would be. He said he had already thought of the possibility of marriage in 1851. He hoped they would not think he was hurrying on matters too much, but said that he thought

Vicky 'so sweet and charming, so clever and natural, that he could not any longer delay this explanation.' Albert also expressed his great pleasure, 'adding with what joy and complete confidence we should give our child to him.'[3] Prince Frederick William was indeed straightforward, frank and extremely well-intentioned, if not very quick-witted. The Queen was amused by his inability to understand the rules of a parlour game which Prince Albert tried to teach him.

The total spontaneity of Fritz's interest in Vicky must be questioned. When he first met her in 1851 she was only ten and the Prince himself twenty. She was now fourteen and he twenty-four. The Prince did also tell the royal pair that the King of Prussia had always been in favour of this union and that he had given his consent to the Prince's journey for him to ask for her hand. The Queen's desire to leave the choice to her daughter seems to have evaporated suddenly for it was decided that she should know nothing of the proposal until after her confirmation – which was to take place six months later – and that the marriage itself could not take place until she was seventeen. The matter was meanwhile to be kept a secret, except from 'his parents and the King and Queen, also Mama and a few others. We have since', noted the Queen, 'decided on Uncle Leopold, Lord Clarendon and Lord Palmerston.' The justification was that, 'Though Vicky knew nothing, we said we had no doubt about what her answer would be.'[4]

The night brought the Queen doubts, however. 'Slept very little all night,' she wrote, 'being so excited and agitated. Of course now we are agitated about what Vicky herself may feel and think and so anxious she should love Fritz as he deserves, and as I do not doubt she will.'[5] Albert seems to have been entirely free of doubts, busily writing to Lord Clarendon to tell him how things stood. Lord Clarendon and Lord Palmerston both sent congratulatory letters and were 'delighted at the prospect of such a union which they think politically of great importance'.[6]

Keeping the secret from Vicky must have been well-nigh impossible. The Queen spent her time 'telling him [the Prince] every kind of little incident, which he liked to hear about Vicky'. Frederick William was given every opportunity of 'getting to know her well'.[7] Vicky must at least have suspected something . . .

Fritz kept his would-be mother-in-law acquainted with all 'the little things that occur, which indicate her affection in such a childlike, charming way'.[8] She expressed her sorrow at his going in a very feeling way, giving him a drawing she had done for him and some poems on the Highlands she had specially written out for him. He consulted the

Queen on his wish to give Vicky a simple gold bracelet before he left. The air was full of such expectation that finally the Queen said that 'something would have to be told her and that he had better tell her himself.'[9] It took him all of four days to summon up courage. On 29 September, the young people and Victoria and Albert went for a ride up Craig-na-Ban. Fritz picked a piece of white heather, an emblem of good luck which he gave to Vicky – and this enabled him to make an allusion to his hopes and wishes. Victoria wrote: 'When we got off our ponies Fritz gave me a wink, implying that he had said something to Vicky and she was extremely agitated and nervous.'[10] When they returned to the Castle, Victoria and Albert saw Vicky alone. She told them she had suspected nothing until the last two days – 'when various little things put it into her head.'[11]

The Queen asked Vicky whether she felt the same about Fritz as he did about her: 'she said eagerly "Oh! yes", with an indescribably happy look.' Vicky was not quite fifteen. She found Fritz handsome and attentive. Above all he was her father's choice and she followed his advice in everything. Albert had told her that 'Fritz was very excellent and very good and that we should give her to him with perfect confidence'; he also told her that 'if she had not liked him, we should never have forced her to this step, for which she expressed great gratitude.'[12] Albert had been in favour of finding out her feelings before Fritz left so that he should not have to wait in uncertainty for some six or seven months. Perhaps he was remembering how Victoria had kept him waiting for an answer . . .

The Queen welcomed her first prospective son-in-law into the family – she embraced him tenderly, 'as I quite feel to love him as my own child.'[13] To the Prince's father she wrote: 'I already regard Fritz as my own child for he has shown such child-like faith and affection towards me.'[14] To his mother she wrote of her delight in 'the pure, ardent love of these two innocent young creatures'.[15] But she insisted that, although it was a long time, Fritz would have to wait for two years. 'She is still half a child and has to develop herself both physically and morally before their marriage takes place.'[16]

The British press leaked the news – which it did not welcome. *Punch*, as soon as it learnt that Prince Frederick William had come to Balmoral, had reported: 'A very suspicious-looking eagle has been observed hovering about the Royal palace of Balmoral. It is supposed that the bird of ill-omen has an eye towards HER MAJESTY'S dovecote.'[17] *The Times* referred to Prussia as a second-rate, paltry power and questioned, 'Is it, then, or is it not expedient, that a daughter of

England should take her place upon the throne of Prussia.' Prussia was linked to Russia and the Princess might well be 'in a situation in which devotion to her husband must be treason to her country'.[18]

Six months later, in April 1856, Vicky was confirmed and King Leopold came over for the ceremony. Now the great news could become public and Princess Victoria could make her debut. Vicky's sisters and brothers learnt the news – Alice cried, Bertie was pleased and wrote to Fritz immediately to congratulate him.[19] Vicky made her first appearance at a drawing room on 10 April 1856, 'wearing feathers and train', dressed 'quite simply in white, with a train of white antique moiré, both this and her gown ... trimmed with cornflowers', and a circlet of the same flowers – Fritz's favourites – on her head.[20] On 9 May a ball was given at Buckingham Palace for the young Princess, in the new ballroom and concert room devised by Prince Albert. The Queen, who was still considered one of the most graceful dancers of the day – both in minuets and country dances – took a lively part in the celebrations.

Albert began to take in hand Vicky's preparation for the role she would play as future Queen of Prussia. He allotted an hour every evening to his personal instruction of her, teaching her history and setting her subjects for essays. He explained to her that her mission was the liberalization of Germany. He also wrote long letters about the state of Prussia to his future son-in-law.

Victoria was anxious for her daughter – 'her extreme youth', she wrote to Augusta, 'fills me with anxiety and misgivings.' A totally inexperienced seventeen-year-old child, used to parental care, was to be sent 'into a strange country to live among complete strangers', wrote the Queen; 'she herself somewhat fears the separation.'[21] The Queen wanted the young pair to spend as little time as possible in Berlin – to be there in the first years of their marriage would be 'physically and morally harmful'.[22]

In November, Fritz was staying at Windsor when the Queen's half-brother, the Prince of Leiningen, died. 'I am in such poor spirits,' she wrote to Princess Augusta, 'and my heart and soul have but the one sad thought! I have lost my only and dearly beloved brother and nothing can compensate this loss. ... Dear Fritz is so good and sympathetic but I am so sorry for his sake that he should visit us at such a moment.'[23] This was all the more true as Vicky grieved so much that she made herself quite ill. It was her first real sorrow.

While Vicky was making her debut into society, things were also changing for Bertie. In the autumn of 1856 he was allowed out of the schoolroom and away from its daily grind for the first time when it was not holiday time. He went incognito, as Baron Renfrew, on a walking tour in Devon with his tutor Mr Gibbs and Colonel Cavendish. The secret of the Prince's identity leaked out, however, and there were demonstrations of loyalty to him by the public, which did not please his parents. The tour was brought to an abrupt end.

Prince Albert was beginning to realize that the education Bertie was undergoing – and the choice of word is deliberate – was not adapted to his intelligence and his temperament. He sought advice, curiously, from Lord Granville, President of the Council in Lord Palmerston's Government. Lord Granville suggested that the Prince should mix more with boys of his own age and insisted on the fact that education need not necessarily be bookish. He recommended travel as a source of education well fitted to the boy's temperament.[24]

The result was a second tour of England, this time in the Lake District. In addition to Gibbs and Cavendish, four boys from Eton accompanied him. They were handpicked by the headmaster: three aristocrats – Charles Wood, George Cadogan and Frederick Stanley – and William Henry Gladstone, eldest son of the future Prime Minister, William Ewart Gladstone. Once again Prince Albert was dissatisfied with the experiment. Bertie's diary pained him – it was so inadequate.

The method was nevertheless given a further trial. In 1857 Bertie was sent on his first prolonged excursion on the continent. First he went to Königswinter, near Bonn, to study German language and literature. Albert was perhaps trying to combat his son's attraction to France. Afterwards Bertie and the four boys of the former expedition were to go walking in Switzerland. Among the Prince's companions, in addition to Gibbs and the Eton boys, were his private secretary General Charles Grey and his equerry Colonel Henry Ponsonby. Ponsonby described the Prince as 'one of the nicest boys I ever saw, and very lively and pleasant.'[25] Yet Albert was not impressed. A month after his departure he was entreating his son to send longer letters 'and give us your impression of things and not the mere bare facts.'[26]

On 24 October 1857 the Prince of Wales landed at Dover. He had been away from England, and his family, for almost four months. He was to be once again submitted to his father's surveillance – and not unnaturally to find it even more difficult to bear. There was, however, some indication that his parents realized he was growing up. He was given an annual allowance of one hundred pounds and was allowed to choose his own clothes, which his parents would pay for. This privilege was accompanied by a ponderous minute from the Queen as to the exact place to be filled by clothes in his life. 'We do not wish', she wrote, 'to control your own tastes and fancies, which, on the contrary, we wish you to indulge and develop.' Unfortunately she added: 'but we do expect that you will never wear anything extravagant or slang, not because we don't like it, but because it would prove a want of self-respect and be an offence against decency, leading – as it has often done in others – to an indifference to what is morally wrong.'[27]

Meanwhile, on 16 May 1857, Vicky's betrothal had been officially announced in Berlin. Immediately afterwards, on the twenty-fifth, the Queen sent a message to Parliament asking for a provision for the Princess. This was the first time she had asked for support for any of her children and she was far from sure of how it would be received. The Government proposed a dowry of 40,000 pounds. Despite vociferous opposition from Roebuck, the Radical critic of the Crimean War, the Government's proposal went through easily, with 328 in favour and only 18 against.

One of the first duties of the betrothed couple was to stand as sponsors to the Queen's new baby – Beatrice – born on 14 April and christened on 16 June in the private chapel of Buckingham Palace. Prince Frederick William stayed in England for two months and was involved in a veritable social whirl – state visits to the theatre, the annual ceremonies at Ascot, the first Handel festival at the Crystal Palace. During the summer of 1857 there were many royal visitors to England, including in August a visit to Osborne of the Emperor and Empress of the French. This visit was at the express desire of Napoleon III, who wanted to strengthen the Anglo-French alliance. Political discussions centred chiefly on the Eastern Question.

The constant exchanges the Queen and the Prince had during this period with the royal families of Europe led her to define her husband's rank. On 25 June 1857, by royal letters-patent, she conferred on him the title of Prince Consort. It achieved the desired result when they were abroad – when the Prince went to Belgium to be present at the marriage of Archduke Maximilian to Princess Charlotte of Belgium in July, he was given precedence immediately after the King of the Belgians and before the Austrian archdukes. For the English, it changed nothing, according to a sneering editorial in *The Times*. Albert's own feelings were conveyed to his brother in a letter written from Balmoral.

> This ought to have been done, as you thought yourself, at our wedding, but you also know in what state affairs were here at the time. The Tories cut off my apanage in the House of Commons and my Parliamentary rank in the House of Lords, the Royal Family were against the newcomer.[28]

The bitterness is obvious. The rank had been given him – but too late. The memorandum of 1856 in which the arguments for giving Albert the title are set out is a curious document. The Queen noted that she would 'have preferred it being done by Act of Parliament' but 'it was thought better upon the whole to do it *now* in this simple way.' She was sure that by this method there could be no obstruction from her Ministers. The decision was based on two very different arguments. The first was the humiliation and embarrassment Albert had suffered because of his lack of title. Here the amazing scenes back in 1843 at the wedding of the Grand Duke and Duchess of Mecklenburg-Strelitz were quoted, when the King of Hanover tried to supersede the Prince. The second was the fear that Prince Albert's own children – Bertie in particular – would deny their father the position their mother had given him, considering it a 'usurpation over them, having the law on their side'.[29]

Certainly there had been a tradition in Britain of opposition of royal sons to their parents but it was most unlikely, given his character, and despite their temperamental antipathy, that Bertie would try to harm his father. This sombre vision of their son had probably originated in his father's mind for Albert wrote to his brother Ernest:

> What pressed the question is the fact that our children, who are all princes of the country and of the house, are growing up. If their father is not a prince of the country, wicked people might later on succeed in bringing up the Prince of Wales against his father, and tell him that he should not allow a *foreign* prince to take a place before him.[30]

As the date of Vicky's marriage drew nearer, the thought of leaving England and her family and going off to the Prussian Court increasingly distressed the Princess. The date had been fixed for the last week in January 1858 and throughout 1857 she found herself continually doing things for the last time – her last happy summer as a child in the happy group of brothers and sisters at Osborne, her last holiday free of ties at Balmoral. The Queen understood these feelings, as she wrote to Augusta:

> Even when one has every reason to be a quite happy wife, yet, all the same, the severance from childhood is grave and sad, especially when one has to leave one's home. The poor child feels this very deeply and the slow tearing of oneself away from the best loved places and loveliest memories is a hard trial, which must naturally have some effect upon her health.[31]

Vicky had indeed not been very well at the beginning of the month. There was a suggestion at about this time that, as was the usual practice of Prussian princes, the pair should be married in Berlin. The Queen would not hear of it. 'Whatever may be the usual practice of Prussian Princes,' she wrote, 'it is not every day that one marries the eldest daughter of the Queen of England. The question therefore must be considered as settled and closed.'[32]

Thus it was that the future Court of the Princess came for a three-week visit to England. Seventeen German royalties were also Victoria's guests for the festivities preceding the wedding. The day of 24 January – 'Poor dear Vicky's last unmarried day' – was an occasion of present-giving and affection. After breakfast the family gifts for Vicky were laid out on two tables in the large drawing room. 'Fritz's pearls', noted the Queen, 'are the largest I ever saw, one row.'[33] On a third table were three fine candelabra, the royal couple's gift to Fritz. Both Vicky and Fritz were, not unnaturally, delighted with their gifts. After lunch the party returned to the present-room, where many more gifts had been set out, including those from the ladies and gentlemen of the Household. Earlier, before going to church, Vicky had given her mother a brooch containing her hair and had clasped her in her arms saying, 'I hope to be worthy to be your child.'[34] At the end of the day, her parents accompanied Vicky to her room, kissed her and gave her their blessing. 'She was much overcome,' her mother wrote, 'I pressed her in my arms, and she clung to her truly adored papa with much tenderness.'[35]

The wedding took place at St James's Palace on 25 January 1858. 'It was', noted the Queen, 'the second most eventful day of my life as regards feelings. I felt as if I were being married over again myself, only much more nervous.'[36] The marriage procession formed at Buckingham Palace was composed of more than twenty carriages. Just before they left, the Queen and Crown Princess posed for a daguerreotype together with the Prince, but the Queen trembled so much that her image came out indistinct. Then it was time to go. In the first carriage travelled Prince Albert and Uncle Leopold, in the uniforms and with the batons of field marshals, together with the two eldest boys. The three sisters, Alice, Louise and Helena, followed. They wore pink satin trimmed with Newport lace, with cornflowers and marguerites in their hair. Next came the younger boys in Highland dress. Vicky, in a gown of white moiré silk trimmed with Honiton lace, was in a carriage with her mother sitting opposite her. Victoria wore the lilac and silver so popular with brides' mothers at the time.

When they reached St James's, the bride was taken by her mother to a dressing room, where her father and uncle and her eight bridesmaids were waiting for her. The bridesmaids wore white tulle with circlets and bouquets of pink roses and white heather. The procession that entered the chapel was headed by Bertie and Alfred, followed by Lord Palmerston with the Sword of State, followed in turn by the Duchess of Kent looking handsome in violet velvet trimmed with ermine and white silk; then came the Queen with her two little boys on either side and the three girls behind. As the royal procession entered, the Queen was struck by the pallor and nervousness of Fritz as he waited at the altar. He bowed to them as they entered.[37] Once the Queen and those accompanying her had taken their places, the bride's procession entered; 'our darling flower looked very touching and lovely with such an innocent, confident and serious expression, her veil hanging back over her shoulders, walking between her beloved father and dearest Uncle Leopold.' Vicky knelt beside her fiancé and they joined hands. Victoria was reminded 'vividly of having in the same way proudly, tenderly, confidently, most lovingly' knelt by Albert on that very spot.

Victoria seemed surprised that when her parents embraced her tenderly after the ceremony, Vicky 'shed not one tear'. Then the bride and bridegroom left the chapel hand in hand. For the first time at a wedding, Mendelssohn's Wedding March was played as the party went up to the Throne Room to sign the register. 'I felt so moved, so overjoyed and relieved,' the Queen recorded, 'that I could have embraced everybody.'[38]

Through cheering crowds the new couple and their relatives and guests proceeded to Buckingham Palace, where the newly married pair inaugurated a royal wedding custom by appearing on the balcony to greet the crowds who had been waiting for them so eagerly. Then came the wedding breakfast and the departure. The married couple set off for Windsor Castle. 'We dined', Victoria wrote, '*en famille*, but I felt so lost without Vicky.'[39] In the evening a messenger came from Windsor with a letter from the bride – the Eton boys had met them in the town and dragged their carriage from the railway station to the Castle to show their joy. Before going to bed, Victoria penned a reply to her daughter's 'dear little note', the first of the multitude of letters she was to write to her married daughter. She told her that they missed her at dinner but knew her to be 'in other but truly safe and loving hands'. She congratulated her daughter: 'You behaved excessively well so that you have only added to the love and affection so many bear to you.' The double standards of Victorian times towards women and men were echoed as Victoria talked to her daughter of the significance of marriage. It was 'a very solemn act, the most important and solemn in everyone's life, but much more so in a woman's than in a man's' and the wife's task was 'to make his life and his home a peaceful and happy one and to be of use to him and be a comfort to him in every possible way.'[40]

On 27 January the whole Court went to Windsor – the couple having enjoyed a brief honeymoon of two days. Prince Frederick William was invested with the Garter in the Castle, and on the following day the whole family returned to London. The days passed swiftly and on Monday, 1 February, came 'The last day of our dear child being with us, which is incredible, and makes me at times feel sick at heart.'[41] Vicky's emotion was even greater; she confided in her mother, 'I think it will kill me to take leave of dear Papa.'[42] The weather on the day of departure was in tune with their feelings – 'a dull, still, thick morning.'[43] Victoria, struggling against her sad feelings, went to her daughter's room to wake her. Both mother and daughter broke down and wept in each other's arms. When the time came for them to get into their carriage, the Queen clasped Vicky in her arms and blessed her. She kissed 'good Fritz' and pressed his hand again and again. He was unable to speak, and there were tears in his eyes. She embraced them both again at the carriage door. It was, for the Queen, 'A dreadful moment, and a dreadful day. Such sickness came over me, real heartache when I thought of our dearest child being gone, and for so long.'[44] It began to snow just before Vicky left and continued to do so all day.

The Prince Consort, together with Bertie and Alfred, accompanied Vicky and her husband to Gravesend, from where they were to sail for Germany. The first thing Victoria did once her daughter had left was to write to her. 'An hour is already past since you left – and I trust that you are recovering a little.' The Queen expressed the feelings so common to mothers when their children leave home:

> Yes it is cruel, very cruel – very trying for parents to give up their beloved children, and to see them go away from the happy peaceful home – where you used all to be around us! That is broken, and you, though always our own dear child, and always able to be at home in your parents' house, are no longer one of the many, merry children who used to gather so fondly round us.[45]

For Vicky it was, as the Queen well knew, her parting from the father she idolized that upset her most. Her letter to him is the cry of a seventeen-year-old, so touching that it must be quoted in full.[46]

> My Beloved Papa,
> The pain of parting from you yesterday was greater than I can describe;
> I thought my heart was going to break when you shut the cabin door and

were gone – that cruel moment which I had been dreading even to think of for two years and a half was past, – it was more painful than I had ever pictured it to myself.

Yesterday evening I felt weighed down by grief, today though very melancholy I am able to think with more composure of all that has passed – and of all that is to come.

I miss you so dreadfully dear Papa, more than I can say; your dear picture stood near me all night, it was a comfort to me to think that I had even that near me. I meant to have said so much yesterday, but my heart was too full for words. I should have liked to have thanked you for all that you have done for me, for all your kindness. All your love etc. I shall most earnestly endeavour to deserve. To you, dear Papa, I owe most in this world. I shall never forget the advice it has been my privilege to hear from you at different times, I treasure your words up in my heart, they will have with God's help an influence on the whole of my life. You know dear Papa, how entirely you possess the deep confidence, reverence and affection of your child, who is proud to call herself such; and I may say of my husband too; and we feel secure and happy in the thought that you will never refuse us your precious advice, in anxious moments.

I feel that writing to you does me good, dear Papa, I feel that I am speaking to you, and though the feeling that I cannot see you or hear your dear voice in return makes the tears rise to my eyes, yet I am thankful that this is left to me. Goodbye, dearest Papa – I must end. Your most dutiful and affectionate daughter, Victoria.

The parting had affected Albert no less. On the day after her departure, before receiving her letter, he had written:

My heart was very full when yesterday you leaned your forehead on my breast to give free vent to your tears. I am not of a demonstrative nature, and therefore you can hardly know how dear you have always been to me, and what a void you have left behind in my heart: yet not in my heart, for there assuredly you will abide henceforth, as till now you have done, but in my daily life, which is evermore reminding my heart of your absence.[47]

Vicky had been deeply influenced by her father. He had communicated to her not only his outlook on life but also his political liberalism. This was not to ease her integration into the Prussian Court. Count von Bismarck, asked his opinion of the 'English marriage', said:

I must separate the two words to give you my opinion. The "English" in it does not please me. The "marriage" may be quite good, for the Princess has the reputation of a lady of brain and heart. If the Princess can leave the English woman at home and become a Prussian then she may be a blessing to the country. If our future Queen on the Prussian throne remains the least bit English then I see our Court surrounded by English influence.[48]

Vicky's vision of her task in Prussia was simple. 'I feel', she wrote to her parents, 'that I am serving you both and proving my deep gratitude to you, in doing my duty here and in imitating your great and glorious example, I may I hope be of real use to you.'[49] It was undoubtedly 'the English influence' she was to favour.

The Queen was still reconciling herself to the idea of Vicky's absence when she became involved in an embarrassing ministerial crisis. Early in 1858 – on the evening of 14 January to be precise – an attempt was made in Paris on the life of the French Emperor. At half-past eight he was driving with the Empress to a gala performance at the Opera. The Opera House was then in the rue Lepelletier; alongside it was a narrow alley leading to the boulevard des Italiens. It was there that Felice Orsini, an Italian refugee well-known in England, was lurking with his three accomplices. As the imperial carriage drew up, they threw three bombs at it. The effect was devastating: the canopy over the door of the Opera House crashed down and a fragment broke the gas pipes in front of the building. All the street lights and theatre lights went out, glass was everywhere, horses bolted, people screamed in agony. Ten bystanders were blown to death, two of the Emperor's horses were killed. Miraculously, the Emperor and his wife were not seriously hurt. The Emperor's nose was cut by a piece of broken glass, Eugénie's cheek was grazed and she had a splinter of glass near her left eye. Orsini himself was among the 156 people wounded.

This attempt at assassination rocked Anglo–French relations because it was found that Count Orsini had, as a man of good birth, been well received in Britain, and his appeals in favour of the Italian provinces of Austria had been met with much sympathy. London was a sanctuary for political refugees and, on his visit to Windsor in 1855, Napoleon III had urged Queen Victoria to expel refugees of this type. A strongly worded despatch from Count Walewski, the French Foreign Minister, now reiterated the request. Palmerston sent no reply. Nevertheless, he did recognize that the Government had some responsibility in allowing fugitives refuge without exercising any control over their behaviour. He therefore prepared and introduced a Bill to strengthen the law dealing with conspiracy to murder. Before the Bill reached its second reading, however, the anti-British outcry in the French press – reinforced by the revelation that the bombs had been made in

Birmingham – caused domestic opposition to the Bill to build up and the Government lost the second reading, 234 to 215. Palmerston resigned at once. Victoria was for once in full sympathy with her Prime Minister and had no desire to see him go. But go he did, and Lord Derby began his second administration, with Disraeli leading the House of Commons as Chancellor of the Exchequer and Lord Malmesbury at the Foreign Office. Derby's Government was to remain in power for over a year, even though it was a minority Government.

The Prince of Wales had returned from his travels to find himself put back into the Coburg system. He spoke to his mother early in 1858 of his impatience to travel and see other countries, and 'his wish NOT to enter the Navy, which I had told him had never been intended, and of his equally great wish to serve in the Army, which, as a profession, I said he could not, though he might learn in it'.[50] His parents eventually promised that he would be allowed at least to have some military experience later. Meanwhile the time had come to test his religious education.

On 1 April 1858 the heir apparent was confirmed in the private chapel at Windsor. To his parents' surprise, the sixteen-year-old boy had acquitted himself well on the previous day when his examination took place before the Archbishop. 'Wellesley [Dean of Windsor] prolonged it a full hour and Bertie acquitted himself extremely well,' Prince Albert wrote to Baron Stockmar.[51] 'Bertie was examined for an hour by the Dean before the Archbishop ...' the Queen told her daughter, 'and he answered very well, going through the first part of the catechism, bringing him all through the Belief, which he had to explain – to the sacraments and confirmation.'[52] Albert hoped that the ceremony had made 'an abiding impression on his mind'.[53] Victoria noted that on the following morning he was 'quiet and gentle and seemed properly impressed'.[54]

As a reward for his pains, Bertie was allowed a holiday tour with his tutor – this time for a fortnight in Ireland. On his return he was established at White Lodge in Richmond Park, in order, as his father wrote to Baron Stockmar, 'to be away from the world, and devote himself exclusively to study, and prepare for a military examination'.[55] Once again Albert had devised a plan for the further education of his son. Three equerries, serving in a monthly rotation, were to polish the Prince's manners. Two of them, Major Christopher Teesdale and Major Lloyd-Lindsay, had each won the Victoria Cross in the Crimea; the third, Lord Valletort, had spent his youth attending his invalid father.[56] Prince Albert addressed a confidential memorandum to the three men, telling them exactly what the Prince should be taught with regard to 'appearance, deportment and dress', 'manners and conduct towards others', and 'the power to acquit himself creditably in conversation, or whatever may be the occupation of society'. As an example of his advice, the Prince was not to loll or slouch or put his hands in his pockets; he was to be punctual and he was not to indulge in practical jokes; gossip, cards and billiards were to be regarded as useless.[57] The Prince, not surprisingly, found this new life boring, with its monastic seclusion only relieved now and then by a dinner for some famous man or other.

In November 1858, on Bertie's seventeenth birthday, he received a document signed by both his parents. It declared to him his emancipation from parental authority and control. It acknowledged that he may have thought his education severe, but his welfare was their only object; knowing what seductions of flattery he would be exposed to, they wished to prepare and strengthen his mind against them. He was now his own master. The letter, according to Greville, made a profound impression on the Prince and touched him to the quick.[58] The young man was also given some advantages – rooms for his sole use and an increased personal allowance. More important to him on his seventeenth birthday was the fact that at last Mr Gibbs, the tutor he had resisted for years, was to be replaced by a Grenadier Guardsman, Colonel the Hon. Robert Bruce. 'Poor Mr Gibbs', the Queen told Vicky, 'leaves tomorrow. He has failed completely the last year and a half with Bertie – and Bertie did what he liked.'[59] The latter remark was probably inspired by Gibbs's version of events.

In the same month the Prince of Wales was allowed to pay a three-week visit to Berlin, where his sister was awaiting the birth of her first child. The Prince Consort despaired of his son. He entreated his daughter:

> Do not miss any opportunity of urging him to hard work. Our united efforts must be directed to this end. Unfortunately he takes no interest in anything but clothes, and again clothes. Even when out shooting he is more occupied with his trousers than with the game! I am particularly anxious that he should have mental occupation in Berlin. Perhaps you could let him share in some of yours, lectures etc.[60]

But Albert's counsels were of no avail. The Queen complained to her daughter that when Bertie returned from Berlin he spoke of nothing but parties and theatres. Of the finer works of art he had seen he said nothing unless explicitly asked.[61]

Almost as soon as he had returned from Berlin, the Prince was sent off to Rome to study art, archaeology and current affairs – still longing for an active career in the army. While in Rome he kept a diary, as his father had bid him. It was totally uninspired. When the Prince Consort asked his son for his comments and reflections, he simply replied disarmingly, 'I am very sorry that you were not pleased with my Journal as I took great pains with it, but I see the justice of your remarks and will try to profit by them.'[62]

The Prince's tour continued via Gibraltar, North Italy and Switzerland. Returning home in June he was despatched immediately to Edinburgh to undergo three months' cramming before going up to Oxford in the autumn. There the unhappy youngster, still dreaming of the army, specialized in history, law and natural science – in particular its practical applications. He joined Christ Church College in the grade of 'nobleman', which has now disappeared. At the time, the social hierarchy in Oxford was marked and noblemen were distinguished from common scholars by the gold tassels on their caps. At Christ Church there was a special table where the more lordly undergraduates dined. The Prince of Wales was matriculated and became an undergraduate. He went to debates at the Oxford Union and became a member of the Bullingdon Club, an association of wealthy, leisurely young men who enjoyed hunting. In the view of the Prince Consort, 'The only use of Oxford is that it is a place for study, a refuge from the world and its claims,'[63] and he considered that Bertie wasted too much time in recreational and society pursuits. But it was here that, despite the fact that his father had not allowed him to live in college, Bertie mixed freely for the first time with men of his own age. He developed an ease of manner and an affability which added to his natural charm.

Training Bertie's younger brother Alfred for his future life was also to prove complicated. He wanted to be a sailor. But at the same time it was virtually certain that he would assume the Coburg Crown, for his uncle, Albert's brother, did not seem able to provide an heir. Preparing to rule a small German people in a traditional state was no easy matter; it was all the more complicated because, if by misfortune his elder brother died, he would be the heir to the English throne. Duke Ernest, his uncle, was not happy; if this young lad was going to succeed him, was it wise to prepare him for the navy? Would he not be better employed learning the history of Coburg? Albert replied that Alfred's wish to enter the navy might indeed make him reluctant to become Sovereign in Coburg-Gotha. The danger was there. But as regards his wish to enter the navy, it was a passion which his parents believed they did not have the right to subdue. Alfred was a strong-willed child. He was also extremely persistent. He had, for instance, secretly learned to play the violin. In any case, he would probably not succeed for twenty to twenty-five years at the earliest. 'What is he to do in all that time?' Albert enquired of his brother, 'if he enters the navy he will have enjoyed all he can in the time.'[64]

However, to allay Ernest's fears, Prince Albert sent Alfred to visit Coburg-Gotha in May 1857. After several changes in plan, Alfred arrived safely and his uncle had the task of introducing him to what had been his father's home. Albert was sad: 'It seems so strange', he wrote to Ernest, 'that he is to see all those dear places and that I am not with him.'[65] Alfred was delighted with Coburg: 'the place which he liked best of all that he visited on his journey.'[66] He was delighted, too, with the kindness of Ernest and Alexandrine and the love and friendship they showed him. Alfred's journey woke Albert's memories of the 'paradise of our childhood'[67] and he found it difficult to return to reality. Not without bitterness he noted, 'Sentimentality is a plant which cannot grow in England, and an Englishman, when he finds that he is being sentimental, becomes frightened at the idea, as of having a dangerous illness, and he shoots himself.'[68]

It was Albert's search for sentimentality that took him to Coburg in the following May. He wanted to visit his daughter in Berlin, but he could not resist revisiting the scenes of his childhood. It was a mistake. On the evening of his arrival he went to the theatre, where he 'struggled manfully to keep drowsiness at bay'.[69] The afternoon he had spent in the Hofgarten, walking about and reflecting, 'Ah me! On the whole, the impression on my mind is one of profound sadness! I have become an utter stranger here and know scarcely any one, while those I used to know have aged so much that I find it hard to puzzle out the old faces again.'[70] On the following day he visited the new burial ground and the mausoleum, the museum, a magnificent new brewery, the new railway station and the new barracks, but his heart was not in it. 'I got up with a headache and a general malaise', he wrote to Victoria, 'and have kept these two uninvited guests with me till now. I have eaten nothing all the day, to rob my stomach of the shadow of a pretext for behaving ill. I will now take "a draught" and go to bed, but not without first wishing you "Goodnight".'[71]

Victoria, for her part, had found the absence of her husband less difficult to bear than it had been before. She wrote to her eldest daughter: 'I feel of course the absence of my life and light – very much – but I am so determined not to give way – hear so constantly by telegraph and am so busy – that I feel it less than in '54 even, and decidedly less than in '44; at least I can keep up.'[72]

The reason was that Albert had become more and more involved with business and had gradually turned into a workaholic. 'Man is a beast of burden', he had written to his brother in 1856, 'and he is only happy if he has to drag his burden and if he has little free will. My experience teaches me every day to understand the truth of this more and more.'[73] The Queen all through her married life had put her husband resolutely first. Her children came far behind in her preoccupations. During her final pregnancy in 1856, she had felt abandoned. Albert could not understand how, with eight children, she could lack companionship. Yet Victoria's relationship with her two eldest children was difficult. Vicky's intelligence was so obviously considered by Prince Albert as superior to that of his wife that Victoria felt somewhat daunted by her. Bertie, because of the way he was treated, was full of rebellion, and he must also have resented the fact that his mother so clearly considered that everything Albert did was right and just. In a letter to Augusta in October 1856, Victoria wrote, with the honesty which always characterized her: 'even here [in Balmoral] where Albert is often away all day long, I find no especial pleasure or compensation in the company of the elder children.'[74] Certainly she went out with them – driving or riding or walking – but, as she had admitted before to Augusta, 'only very exceptionally do I find the rather intimate intercourse with them either agreeable or easy.'[75] She tried herself to understand why this was so and detected three reasons: first and foremost, 'I only feel properly *à mon aise* and quite happy when Albert is with me'; secondly, she had never been used to being with young people for she had grown up alone; thirdly, children 'had to be kept in order and therefore must not become too intimate'.

It has often been suggested that Victoria did not in fact like her children – especially her eldest. That this was not so can be seen by the very close links she was to establish with Vicky once she was engaged. 'I find her very good company and this important event in her life has now brought us even closer together,' she wrote. 'I experience everything she feels and since I myself still feel so young our relationship is more like that of two sisters.' Nor was this a passing sentiment – there are 3,777 letters still in existence from Victoria to her daughter bearing witness to her affection for her.[76]

Victoria felt all the more ill at ease with her children since Prince Albert did not hesitate to scold her in front of them, which did little for her authority. She was also embarrassed to be pregnant again at a time when her eldest children were themselves of childbearing age. Pregnancy, as she described it to her first-born, was full of 'sufferings and miseries and plagues', and she had '8 times for 9 months to bear with those above-named enemies and real misery . . . and I own it tried me sorely.'[77] After the birth of Prince Leopold, her second to last child, she had had a sort of nervous hysterical crisis. Prince Albert, instead of calming her, made her worse, treating her like a child. He had a most unpleasant habit of refusing to talk things out and of drawing up his recriminations in written form. This example from one such occasion gives us some insight into them.

> The whole offence which led to a continuance of hysterics for more than an hour, and the traces of which have remained for more than 24 hours, was: that I complained of your turning several times from inattention the wrong leaves in a Book which was to be marked by us as a Register and test the completeness of a collection of Prints.[78]

It did not occur to the Prince that chastising her as a child was no way to calm her. Nor was his decision that: 'If you are violent I have no other choice but to leave you . . . I leave the room and retire to my room in order to give you time to recover yourself, then you follow me to renew the dispute and to have it all out.'[79] The Prince's Olympian calm and superior attitude jangled the Queen's nerves still further. The Prince's reaction then was to 'sincerely and deeply pity' her for the sufferings she underwent.

These scenes were usually an expression of some deep apprehension on the part of the Queen, a sign that she needed comfort and reassurance. The Prince had no understanding at all of her needs and his righteous attitude usually made things worse. In February 1855, for instance, when another such scene was being enacted, he unfeelingly asked: 'What are you really afraid of in me? What can I do to you, save, at the most, not listen to you long enough when I have business elsewhere.'[80] In 1856 he complained that she did not find consolation in her children as she should when she was distressed. This, he noted, was because she scolded them too much: 'It is not possible to be on happy friendly terms with people you have just been scolding.'[81] Did he not realize that this might well apply to his treatment of the Queen?

During these arguments Albert occasionally, with great calm and reflection, said unforgivable things to his wife – and, by contrast with her, he never apologized. On one occasion, when the Queen had obviously made some remark concerning their future son-in-law, he wrote:

Fritz is prepared to devote his whole life to your child whom you are
thankful to be rid of – and because of that you turn against him . . . This
is not a question of bickering, but of attitudes of mind which will agree as
little as oil and water and it is no wonder that our conversations on the
subject cannot end harmoniously and I am trying to keep out of your
way until your better feelings have returned and you have gained control
of yourself.[82]

His attack was unjust. The Queen was not eager to see Vicky go. She
was, on the contrary, living through the difficult period of readjustment
which occurs in every close-knit family when the first children leave. At
the same time Victoria was once again pregnant. Albert was not willing
to forgive what he considered her tantrums but he was willing to ignore
them, an attitude that was hardly likely to help her retain her equi-
librium. On the subject of her pregnancy, he explained that he made
'the most ample allowance for your state', as did everyone else in the
house. 'We cannot, unhappily,' he went on, 'bear your bodily sufferings
for you – you must struggle with them alone – the moral ones are
probably caused by them, but if you were rather less occupied with
yourself and your feelings . . . and took more interest in the outside
world, you would find that the greatest help of all.'[83]

Once the pregnancy was over, the storms died down for a time. But
every now and again conflict would break out again. The couple were
deeply attached to one another but their relationship was based on the
subservience of the Queen to the Prince. Things were all the more
complicated as he continually insisted that 'wishes . . . in the case of a
Queen, are commands, to whomever they may be given.'[84] So that
Victoria had to agree with him in order not to seem to be using her
queenly prerogative. After their marriage, his letters to her, though
they certainly use the language of a lover and show his need of her
physical presence, usually begin with phrases such as 'Dear, Good
Little One', 'Dear Child', and only very rarely, as during the engagement period, 'Dear, beloved Victoria'.

In the autumn of 1858 the Queen and the Prince went to Cherbourg
on a visit aimed to boost the French alliance. The Queen's royal yacht
was accompanied by a strong escort of men-of-war, practically the
whole French navy was sent out to meet her and there was no doubt
that the two countries were out to impress one another. But, 'The
evening was splendid. The sea like oil, and the sun throwing over
everything a beautiful golden light.'[85] The Queen witnessed the opening of the new arsenal and surveyed the French fortifications. Para-

doxically, the Emperor had used the military defences facing the English shore as a new link between them.

After France the Queen went to Germany on a visit to her married daughter. It was a long journey by way of Antwerp and Malines – where they met King Leopold – to Aix la Chapelle, where they were joined by her daughter's father-in-law, the Prince of Prussia. From there they went to Hanover and visited the blind King George, before arriving at the castle of Babelsberg, some three miles from Potsdam, their daughter's residence.

Fritz had told Vicky's father in May that she was pregnant. Victoria's comment testified to her firm belief that pregnancy early in marriage was a mistake: 'The horrid news contained in Fritz's letter to Papa upset us dreadfully,' Victoria told her daughter.[86] Three days later she wrote: 'I am so unhappy about you! It is well Fritz is not in sight just now or he would not have been graciously received.'[87] When her daughter spoke of her pride in being able to give birth to an immortal soul, her mother replied prosaically, 'I own I cannot enter into that; I think much more of our being like a cow or a dog at such moments; when our poor nature becomes so very animal and unecstatic.'[88]

Victoria was eager to see her daughter and had hoped to take two of Vicky's younger sisters, Alice and Lenchen (Helena), with her, as 'a surprise for you and them'. But she found 'opposition and resistance' where she had expected 'to find joy and light'. She speaks of Miss Hildyard's opposition, but behind that there was undoubtedly Prince Albert's. 'Papa says that I should be fidgeting myself about your sisters all the time which would be very unpleasant as it would take my mind from you.'[89] And moreover it would be no better if they came again in the winter, 'for Papa, who is very hard-hearted and a great tyrant on all such occasions – won't hear of any one then, so that if you want to see them you have nothing for it but to come to your own loved home.'[90] Vicky was disappointed, as she wrote to her mother, but for her – 'Papa is an oracle and what he decides must be right.'[91]

Albert continually sought to suppress the Queen's impulses towards her children. He even told his wife that she was writing to Vicky far too much and that it would be much better if she wrote only once a week. 'When you do write to Papa again,' she instructed her daughter, 'just tell him what you feel and wish on that subject for I assure you – Papa has snubbed me several times very sharply on the subject and when one writes in spite of fatigues and troubles to be told it bores the person to whom you write, it is rather too much.'[92]

Victoria's new closeness with her daughter was certainly not to her husband's taste. 'Papa', Victoria told Vicky, 'says you write too much – he is sure you make yourself ill by it, and constantly declares (which I own offends me much) that your writing to me at such length is the cause of your often not writing fully to him.'[93]

In the autumn of 1858 it was the subject of Alfred which caused new dissensions. The Queen was deeply hurt by her husband's decision to send Affie away. Alfred was then only thirteen and the Queen thought him much too young to go to sea. She poured out her heart to Vicky.

> I have been shamefully deceived about Affie, it was promised me that the last year before he went to sea, he should be with us, instead of which he was taken away and I saw but very little of him, and now he is to go away for many months and I shall not see him God knows! when, and Papa is most cruel upon the subject. I assure you, it is much better to have no children than to have them only to give them up! It is too wretched.[94]

In October she wrote with some pathos of Affie's imminent departure. 'Alas I look forward with horror to the separation from him this day week. Two children in one year. It is horrible.'[95] On 27 October came the parting. 'Dearest Affie is gone; and it will be ten months probably before we shall see his dear face which shed sunshine over the whole house, from his amiable, happy, merry temper.'[96]

On 27 January 1859, Victoria, then thirty-nine, became a grand-mother with the birth of Prince William, Vicky's son, the future Kaiser William II. The Queen delighted in the idea of being a grandmama: 'to be that at thirty-nine,' she told her daughter, 'and to look and feel young is great fun, only I wish I could go through it for you, dear, and save you all the annoyance.'[97] As she could not be with her daughter, she sent her own doctor, Doctor Martin, to be present at the delivery. She was very upset not to be 'where every other mother is – and I ought to be and can't at her daughter's bedside.'[98] It was probably just as well that the Queen was not there, for the baby that came into the world seemed lifeless and his mother was unconscious. It was over an hour before slapping and swinging brought the child to life. Not until three days later did anyone realize that the baby's left arm was paralysed, the shoulder socket torn away and the surrounding muscles grievously injured. The damage was permanent.

Queen Victoria was not able to be at the infant's christening either. In Prussia babies had to be christened as soon as possible after their birth. She wrote to King Leopold, 'it almost breaks my heart not to witness our first grandchild christened! I don't think I ever felt so bitterly disappointed about anything as about this!'[99] The child was named Frederick William Victor Albert.

When the Queen's first grandson was born, she already knew that the peace of Europe was to be challenged by her French ally. The Emperor wanted to promote the unification of Italy, by war if necessary, under a king from the royal house of Sardinia. In her Speech from the Throne at the opening of Parliament on 3 February 1859, Victoria stated clearly that she would not be a party to the Emperor's plans. In April, Austria unexpectedly declared war on Sardinia and Napoleon III rallied to the help of his Italian ally. The royal couple feared a spread of the conflict. The English public supported Sardinia and its courageous resistance to Austrian tyranny. Italian unity had found a directing force in Count Cavour, who had promised that Savoy and Nice would be ceded to France if the French would help the Italians to expel the Austrians from Italy and support the building of a kingdom around Sardinia. The alliance was cemented by the marriage of the Emperor's cousin Napoleon, son of Napoleon I's youngest brother, King Jerome, with Clotilda, daughter of the King of Sardinia.

In June 1859, Derby's Government resigned. It had been defeated on a Reform Bill introduced by Disraeli and had failed to win a majority in the election which followed. After some toing and froing Palmerston became Prime Minister again. The Queen was far from delighted – Palmerston was, after all, known for his pro-Italian, anti-Austrian policy. But she soon had cause for satisfaction. On 12 July 1859 – after battles at Magenta and Solferino – an armistice was signed between France and Austria at Villafranca. Palmerston and his Foreign Minister Russell considered that Napoleon III had thrown away full Italian unity at Villafranca by concluding an armistice without consulting his allies. French losses had in fact been enormous – at Solferino alone they had lost over 11,000 men – but all the same the Emperor's decision was unwise. Speculation remains as to why Napoleon III made peace. Jasper Ridley has advanced four factors: the shock of the butchery of Solferino; dissatisfaction with the Piedmontese, who allowed the French to do most of the fighting and then reaped most of the advantages; fear that a great European war might break out; alarm at the spread of revolution in Italy.[100] The peace was not popular in France, especially within the army. For Britain, the end of the war did not improve relations with France because there was great resentment at the annexation of Savoy and Nice (to the mystification of the French Emperor, who could not understand what the two provinces had to do with England) and more generally with the Emperor's conduct.

Events on the continent had severely shaken Prince Albert. In his opinion Austria had behaved badly. 'The Austrian management of the war', he wrote to his brother in June 1859, 'has been bad beyond all belief, and is only to be compared with their management of their policy. They violated all the rules of diplomacy and law for the sake of gaining great military advantages, only to renounce the latter for no reason at all.'[101]

In 1859 Fritz and Vicky paid two visits to England, one in early summer, the other in November – each time without their baby. He was too frail, it was feared, to stand the Channel crossing. Vicky, although she now had more poise, was still a child in many ways. She slipped back into a father–daughter relationship with Albert without any problem. They discussed politics and she continued to imbibe her father's wisdom again. With her mother she spoke of the problems she had with her in-laws. Augusta, whom the Queen had thought so pleasant, was an embittered woman who sought to dominate her husband, who did not love her. She was restless, exhausting to be with, always finding fault.

In the long vacation of 1860 there was to be a striking expansion of Bertie's foreign travels. During the Crimean War, the Dominion of Canada had sent a regiment to help Britain; as a gesture of gratitude, Queen Victoria had promised that the Prince of Wales should pay a visit when he was old enough. The moment came in 1860. It was the first time that an heir to the throne of England crossed the Atlantic. He visited the oldest of England's overseas settlements, and also the American republic. At the time, the notion of imperial consciousness had not yet come into being. Whether on the political left or on the right, it was believed that the colonies were certain to break away from England as their population and wealth increased. The United States of America were still viewed with distrust. Not only was America a republic, a form of government the English did not appreciate, it was also a place to which thousands of anti-English Irishmen had fled in the 1840s, stimulating the century-old animosity between America and what had been the mother country. The Prince's visit was not, therefore, viewed with enthusiasm. There were those who thought that it was a mistake to tighten ties that might better be slackened. Prince Albert, on the contrary, believed firmly 'in the progress and expansion of the British race and [in the] . . . useful cooperation of the royal family in the civilisation which England has developed and advanced.'[102]

The Prince went to Canada as the Queen's deputy. He was to open the tubular bridge spanning the St Lawrence, a major engineering triumph of the age – given the name Victoria – and to lay the foundation stone of the new parliamentary buildings in Ottawa. He disembarked in Newfoundland on 24 July, ten days after leaving Plymouth. It would be hard to exaggerate the success of his journey. The young Prince was received everywhere with exceptional pomp and for the first time his social talents were exercised to the full. The Duke of Newcastle, who was part of the Prince's entourage, informed the Queen that this 'practical school' was definitely improving the Prince and that 'the development of mind and habit of thought' was very perceptible.[103] He would, said the Duke, be much disappointed if the Queen and the Prince were not pleased with the change.

For the first time in his life the Prince was not badgered and harassed. His programme was strenuous but he accomplished it with exuberance, shooting the rapids on a timber raft at Ottawa, dancing every one of the twenty-two dances at the Mayor's ball in Quebec, even accepting the offer of the French acrobat, Blondin, to wheel him across the Niagara Falls in a barrow on a tightrope – until his entourage intervened and forbade it.[104]

In the United States, the Prince was no longer an official visitor; he went incognito as a student, under the title of Baron Renfrew. Except in Washington, where he was a private guest of the President, he stayed in hotels and not in private houses. His progress through the country from his starting place in Detroit was nonetheless triumphal. The Prince had an ease and a charm which pleased the Americans, whose style of reception was less deferential – as no doubt befitted a republic. The Prince was genial and he was accessible. His inexhaustible vitality was perfectly in tune with the New World, and his personal popularity increased as he travelled. General Bruce wrote of his reception in New York that it had 'thrown all its predecessors into the shade'; he even conceded that, although the primary cause of the success of the tour had been the veneration in which the Queen was held, it was true that

> the Prince of Wales has so comported himself as to turn it to the fullest account and to gain for himself no small share of interest and attraction. He has undergone no slight trial, and his patience, temper and good breeding have been severely taxed. There is no doubt that he has created everywhere a most favourable impression.[105]

Queen Victoria was delighted. 'He was immensely popular everywhere,' she wrote to her daughter in Prussia, 'and really deserves the highest praise, which should be given him all the more as he was never spared any reproof.'[106]

The Prince's return was delayed by transatlantic storms. He left

Portland, Maine, on 20 October but it was not until 15 November that he docked in Plymouth. He had spent his nineteenth birthday, on 9 November, on board ship.

Bertie had tasted popularity, he had basked in the Queen's approval, he had known a relative freedom. But within a few days of his return all that was to change. Back he was sent by the Prince Consort to Oxford, with the same rules and regulations as those he had known before his departure. Even General Bruce thought the continuation of the strict discipline was no longer appropriate to the situation.[107] But Albert was adamant. Neither was the strict supervision relaxed in January 1861, when the Prince was transferred to Cambridge. He joined Trinity College, but was still not allowed to live in college – although the Master, Dr Whewell, allotted him rooms for occasional use. He was lodged in a spacious mansion, Madingley Hall, together with General and Mrs Bruce, Captain Grey, and his Oxford tutor, Mr Herbert Fisher. The dwelling was pleasant, the stables excellent – but it was four miles out of town.

In 1860, it was the turn of Princess Alice to become the centre of parental attention. Alice had played a key role in family life, mediating between the younger children and her mother, coaxing Bertie into better ways. 'Good, amiable Alice', as her mother often called her, was on the surface gentle and caring. She did not have her elder sister's quick mind and ready reception of parental gospel. She had an interest in music and the arts, and above all a strong desire to be helpful – not only to her family but also to ordinary people. She had not travelled with her parents as her two elder siblings had. It was only when she was fourteen, on 27 July 1857, that she dined with her parents and their guests for the first time. By her next birthday she was turning into a young woman. 'She is such a dear sweet child,' wrote her mother, 'and will I think be very pretty; she has such a slight graceful figure.'[108] Alice was now the eldest daughter at home, with for the first time a bedroom to herself.

The Queen was in no hurry to see her second daughter depart as her first daughter had. 'I am glad to say,' she wrote to Vicky in April 1859, 'Alice has arrived at her sixteenth birthday (in three weeks) without any engagement, or even thought of one, and the longer we can keep this off – the better.'[109] To King Leopold the Queen wrote, 'I shall not let her marry for as long as I can.'[110] The Queen genuinely believed that 'Alice is not at all anxious to marry; only the day before yesterday she said to me she could not dream or think of going away from us – or from here!'[111]

Others, however, thought differently and saw Princess Alice, as did Lord Clarendon, as 'full of lark' and eager to get away from the parental home. The first idea that was seriously mooted was that Alice should wed 'the Orange Boy', as Prince William, heir to the throne of Holland, was called. Vicky made enquiries as to his character and was not hostile.

> He is shy but no more so than any other young man and it is not his fault that he is plain. Besides he has got nice blue eyes and white teeth, good hair and complexion and I think something frank about him. I cannot help thinking that his bad, loose habits come from bad company and from never having associated with people of his own rank and then when one has such a father and is left to get on alone in the world at eighteen I think it must want a very rare character and unusual qualities to keep in the straight path of duty and virtue.[112]

The Queen was sceptical and caustic – 'He is', she told Vicky, 'twenty and not eighteen – and the "white teeth" I fear cannot be his own, as he had bad ones when we saw him three years ago.'[113] Lord Clarendon was much in favour of the match and Prince Albert saw its political advantages.

By the time Prince William announced his intention to visit England in January, Vicky had changed her opinion and told her mother she was 'as little delighted as you seem'.[114] Princess Alice was all aquiver. The Queen found him less unpleasant than the reputation which had preceded him. 'He is very shy and does not talk readily of his own accord but he pays great attention to what is said (I mean when Papa talks at breakfast etc. about politics and military matters etc.).'[115] This, she felt, was in clear contrast to Bertie's behaviour.

Was Prince Albert really willing to see his second daughter marry a man who was clearly dissolute – on the grounds that Holland was liberally inclined and the heir to the throne likely to listen to his counsels? We shall never know, for Alice herself took things in hand. She found the Dutch Prince not at all to her liking. He spoke little and virtually turned his back on her. All desire to be Queen of Holland disappeared. Alice would have none of him.

Meanwhile, Vicky had been vetting other suitors and had reported favourably on the two young German Princes – Louis of Hesse-Darmstadt and Heinrich, his brother. They came to London in June 1860. Prince Albert told Stockmar there was no doubt that the elder Prince of Hesse-Darmstadt, Louis, and Alice had formed a mutual liking, and that although the visit happily passed without any declaration being made, 'we had no doubt it would be followed by further advances from the young gentleman's family.'[116] The match was looked on favourably by Victoria.[117] The Prince was Protestant, he was handsome and he was pure; in addition a quiet dukedom like Hesse-Darmstadt did not require its prince to be continually there, so Alice and her future husband could come to England regularly.

In the summer of 1860, Vicky's second child, a girl, Charlotte, was born in Berlin. In the autumn of 1860, the royal family went to see their daughter in Germany again. They were eager to see their first grandson, as well as the new baby, and to visit Stockmar, who had lived in Coburg since his retirement in 1857. They reached Coburg, accompanied by Princess Alice, on 25 September. The day was over-shadowed by the death of Prince Albert's stepmother, Marie, the Dowager Duchess of Saxe-Coburg and Gotha, the day before. 'We knew', noted Victoria in her diary, 'that she could live but a short time, but for the moment she had been much better. Albert had had a letter on Saturday dictated by herself, rejoicing to see us. What a sad arrival for us!'[118]

Vicky and Fritz came to meet them with Ernest, the Duke of Coburg. Because they were in mourning, they were received at the station quietly, with no demonstrations of joy. As they drove up to the door of the palace, under the archway, it seemed to the Queen a painful contrast to fifteen years ago, when everything was bright and happy. They were received at the door by Alexandrine (Duke Ernest's wife) and Vicky, in the deepest German mourning. The Queen was greatly affected. 'Could hardly speak, I felt so moved, and quite trembled.' The family remained together for some time and then

> our darling grandchild was brought. Such a little love! He came walking in . . . in a little white dress with black bows, and was so good. He is a fine, fat child, with a beautiful white soft skin, very fine shoulders and limbs, and a very dear face, like Vicky and Fritz and also Louise of Baden. He has Fritz's eyes and Vicky's mouth and very curly hair. We felt so happy to see him at last.[119]

Every morning for the remainder of the Queen's stay in Germany, her grandson came to her. 'He is such a darling, so intelligent,' she wrote on 27 September.[120]

The visit was not to be without its emotions. On 1 October, driving back from Coburg, the Prince met with an alarming accident. The horses of his carriage bolted and ran straight into a closed level-crossing. One of the horses was killed and the coachman badly injured. Prince Albert had had the good sense to jump out of the carriage before the collision so was only bruised and cut. When Victoria was informed she went to him at once. He was on his valet's bed, with lint compresses on his nose, mouth and chin. 'He was quite cheerful, had not been in the least stunned, there had not been any injury and the features would not suffer.'[121]

On the fourth Victoria and Albert went to Stockmar's house. The couple had already seen the old gentleman several times during their visit, but this time they went to his house in the Weberstrasse. Here a remarkable meeting occurred. 'Saw Madame de Stockmar for the first time. She is very clever, and was *zuvorkommend* [affable] and pleasant, and much pleased to see us' – as well she might be after all this time. This, then, was the long-suffering woman whose husband had deserted her for months at a time to take up residence at the English Court. 'She is', noted the Queen, 'like Stockmar, rather plain in her style of dress, nothing on her head and no grey heir.'[122]

Alice's engagement was not announced until December 1860, but the royal family knew of it before. On 3 November the Queen, now back in England, wrote to Princess Augusta:

> I cannot tell you how overjoyed we are at this event, for dear Louis is an excellent person; he has such an upright, sincere nature, so much kindness, he is so alert and cheerful and at the same time so modest. . . . The good, exquisite Alice is radiant, and everyone is infected by her ill-concealed joy.[123]

The official proposal was made on 30 November. The Queen reported: 'After dinner, while talking to the gentlemen, I perceived Alice and Louis talking before the fireplace more earnestly than usual, and, when I passed to go to the other room, both came up to me, and Alice in much agitation said he had proposed to her, and he begged for my blessing.' That evening Albert sent for Louis to come to his room and then called in the Queen and Alice. For the Queen it was 'a most touching, and to me most sacred moment'.[124]

A few days later, on 4 December, the Queen received an incognito visit at Windsor from Empress Eugénie, who had lost her beloved sister Paca three months earlier. She had come to England in search of health. 'She looked thin and pale,' wrote the Queen, 'and she was as kind and amiable and natural as she had always been.' The Queen was struck by the contrast between this visit and that of 1855. 'Then all state and excitement. Thousands on thousands out, and the brightest sunshine. Now all in private, and a dismal, foggy wet December day!'[125]

The Prince Consort was eager to see Bertie engaged as well. His tour of North America had not endeared him to his father. It was, in essence, too Hanoverian. The *New York Herald* had reported that 'he whispered soft nothings to the ladies as he passed them in a dance',[126] the *New York Times* spoke of a young lady who had 'chatted, danced and flirted with the Prince in the most bewitching manner'.[127] There was no doubt in his father's eyes that such conduct must be stopped – and the Prince Consort believed, unwisely, that a wife would be the end of it.

Prince Albert therefore drew up a list of suitable candidates. Vicky was asked to help her parents and she duly sent photographs for her brother's appraisal. The problem was that there were few Protestant princesses. The Prince of Wales proved difficult to please. Photographs of the beautiful Princess Elizabeth of Wied, later to be Queen of Rumania, did not inspire him. Finally, and with reluctance, Princess Alexandra, the Danish Princess, was presented to the Prince as a possibility. She was undeniably beautiful but there were political complications. German nationalists wanted to take the duchies of Schleswig and Holstein away from Denmark. That would give Germany control of the Baltic straits and, by building a canal through the two duchies, an outlet to the North Sea. If Britain were to create an alliance with the Danish Court it would thus confound Prussian interests. The Prince Consort and Victoria supported Prussia and Germany on the Schleswig-Holstein question. But the Prince of Wales must marry. The Prince Consort told his son that if he were interested in Princess Alexandra, all objections would be overcome. Vicky and her husband, the Crown Prince of Prussia, supported the match, even though it was contrary to their country's interests. Only the Prince Consort's brother Ernest raised objections. Vicky suggested that she should invite Bertie and allow him, by chance, to meet the Danish Princess. The meeting was scheduled for 1861.

On 5 December 1860, Prince Albert felt unwell. He shivered and was violently sick. The Queen described him as 'very weak'.[128] On the following day he felt slightly better and penned his weekly letter to Vicky.

> I was too miserable yesterday to be able to hold my pen. As, however, I have not written to you since the great Alician event, you would regard me as not merely unwell and stupid, but devoid of feeling as well, if I were to be quite silent. Alice and Louis are as happy as mortals can be, and I need scarcely say that this makes my heart as a father glad.[129]

The Prince's attack of illness was severe. On 11 December he told his daughter that he was beginning to feel like himself again. He added:

'My attack was the real English cholera, a personage with whom I had not the smallest curiosity to make acquaintance, and I hope not to renew it.'[130] According to his future father-in-law, Louis was already complaining that the marriage was being unnecessarily postponed. 'Such a man!' commented the Prince, 'He desires to see the fairest moments of his life curtailed, because he knows the issue and longs to leap towards it at once. How wisely is it ordained that in general we do not know our destiny and end.'[131] An ironic remark: only a few months later, the Prince would be dead.

20

Death in the Family

When 1861 was barely a day old, news came that King William IV of Prussia was dead. He had been incurably insane and had been seriously ill for some time. Vicky was in Berlin on New Year's Eve. Her heart was heavy because she had that very evening put her brother Affie back on the train for England. It was half-past one in the morning when her wardrobe maid brought in a telegram saying the King was in his dying throes and that the Prince Regent was going to Sans Souci immediately.

'We got up', she wrote later to her mother, 'in the greatest hurry and dressed – I hardly know how; I put on just what I found, and had no time to do my hair or anything.'[1] It was a very cold, crisp night, minus twelve degrees centigrade. At two o'clock in the morning Vicky and her husband went on foot in the snow to the Prince Regent's, and from there with the Prince and his wife to the railway station. The four of them were the sole passengers in the train from Berlin to Potsdam. When they arrived at Sans Souci, they went straight to where the King lay. The stillness of death was in the room. The only light came from the fire and a dim lamp. They approached the bed and stood there at the foot of it, not daring to look at one another or say a word. 'You might have heard a pin drop – no sound was heard but the crackling of the fire and the death rattle – that dreadful sound which goes to one's heart and which tells plainly that life is ebbing.'

For an hour they stood, watching and listening, not even daring to sit down. The Queen of Prussia was sitting in an armchair at the head of the bed. Her arm was under the King's head and her head was on the pillow on which he lay. With her other hand she wiped the perspiration from his forehead over and over again. 'I never spent such an awful time,' Vicky recounted, 'and to see the poor Queen sitting there quite rent my heart – three, four, five, six, seven struck and we were still standing there – one member of the royal family came in after the other and remained motionless in the room, sobs only breaking the stillness.' By five o'clock on the afternoon of the following day, Vicky felt so sick and faint and unwell that Fritz sent her to bed. She rose at one o'clock in the morning, and dressed, and returned to the King's bedside, but the King breathed his last while she was on her way.

> I went into the room where the King lay, and I could hardly bring myself to go away again. There was so much of comfort in looking there at that quiet peaceful form at rest at last after all he had suffered – gone home at last from this world of suffering – so peaceful and quiet, he looked like a sleeping child – every moment I expected to see him move or breathe – his mouth and eyes closed and such a sweet and happy expression – both his hands were on the coverlid.

But in fact Vicky was deeply affected. 'I have seen death for the first time!' she told her mother. 'It has made an impression upon me that I shall never, never forget as long as I live – and I feel so ill, so confused and upset by all that I have gone through in the last forty-eight hours.'[2] The Queen's thoughts were constantly with her daughter. As Vicky penned the lines above, the Queen was writing: 'I trust, dearest child, this sad and to you so novel scene, (I have never even yet witnessed a death bed) will not be too much for your warm and feeling heart.'[3] The King's funeral was arranged, and close on its heels the Coronation of the new King. The Crown of Prussia passed to Prince William, now sixty, and his wife Princess Augusta. Little did either Victoria or her daughter imagine that the new King would rule for thirty years and that, under the guidance of Bismarck, he would follow a policy often directly counter to the wishes of the English throne.

In February came the twenty-first anniversary of the marriage of Queen Victoria and Prince Albert. Six of their nine children were with them. Vicky was, of course, in Prussia, the Prince of Wales was established at Madingley Hall, near Cambridge, and Alfred was back at sea again. Prince Albert's diary began at this time to show that he was under great strain. He worked hard, rising at seven and beginning immediately to read and answer letters and prepare speeches or drafts of despatches. He read the morning papers after breakfast. Spreading a newspaper over one of the tables, he would bend over it and refuse to listen to any questions, saying in German, *Störe mich nicht, ich lese das fertig* (Don't disturb me, I am busy reading).[4] His papers show that he took note of articles of importance in all the leading journals.

At about half-past ten in the morning, he would either go out with the Queen or go shooting. 'Not for a good many years did he go out with me on the days he shot,' noted the Queen, 'that was only quite in the earliest years, when he had not so much to do.' In the shooting season he usually went out three or four times a week. But even his sport was no real relaxation; he treated it rather as a task to be done. 'He always walked very fast, when out shooting, and got very quickly through with it. He would say, "I don't understand people making a business of shooting and going out for the whole day. I like it as an amusement for a few hours." '

Work built up steadily, and his frequent attacks of illness showed that his body was growing weaker under the strain. In February, for instance, he had an attack of toothache which caused an inflammation of the nerves – it was probably an abscess. 'My sufferings', he recorded in his diary on 17 February, 'are frightful and the swelling will not come to a proper head.'[5] The Queen, though acknowledging that he had been suffering badly with toothache, wrote to her daughter:

> I hope, however, it is a little better today, but dear Papa never allows he is any better or will try to get over it, but makes such a miserable face that people always think he's very ill. It is quite the contrary with me always; I can do anything before others and never show it, so people never believe I am ill or ever suffer. His nervous system is easily excited and irritated and he's so completely overpowered by everything.[6]

As the illness became protracted, however, the Queen began to have more sympathy for her husband. 'It has been a most trying, wearing and distressing time,' she told her daughter, 'for I could not bear to see him suffer so much and to be so despondent and weak and miserable – I would so willingly have borne it all for him; we women are born to suffer and bear it so much more easily, our nerves don't seem so racked, tortured as men's are!'[7] On 26 February the Queen and Prince went to Osborne for ten days, partly to allow the Prince to recuperate.

At the same time, the Duchess of Kent, who had been staying with them at Buckingham Palace, returned to Frogmore. She had been in poor health for some time. She also suffered a blow from the death two days later of Sir George Couper, her secretary and the comptroller of her household for many years. A painful infection of her right arm prevented her from writing and playing the piano. She could not read much nor bear being read to.[8] When Queen Victoria returned from Osborne, she and the Prince visited her mother at Frogmore. They found that, although she was in great pain, there were no alarming symptoms. Three days later, however, Sir James Clark informed them that the Duchess had suddenly been seized with a shivering fit, which he regarded as a very serious sign. The couple rushed to her bedside.

> The way seemed so long but by eight we were at her bedside. . . . Albert went up, and when he returned with tears in his eyes, I saw what awaited me . . . with a trembling heart I went up the staircase and entered the bedroom, and here, on a sofa, supported by cushions, the room much darkened, sat, leaning back, my beloved Mama, breathing rather heavily in her silk dressing-gown with her cap on, looking quite herself.[9]

The Queen knelt down and kissed her mother's hand and placed it next to her cheek. But although the Duchess opened her eyes she did not recognize her daughter. She brushed her hand off. Victoria went out sobbing into the corridor.

The doctors told the Queen there was no hope, for consciousness had left her mother. The hours passed – partly watching the unconscious figure, partly seeking to forget in sleep. 'I heard each hour strike, the cock crow, the dogs barking at a distance. Every sound seemed to strike into one's inmost soul. What would dearest Mama have thought of our passing a night under her roof, and she not to know it!' At four in the morning, she crept down again to her mother's room. All was still. The silence was broken only by her mother's heavy breathing and the striking of a large watch in a tortoiseshell case, which had belonged to her father – and which she had not heard for twenty-three years. At half-past four she returned to bed. At seven-thirty she was back at her mother's bedside. The end was near. 'I sat on a footstool holding her dear hand . . . the dear face grew paler . . . the features longer, sharper. The breathing became easier . . . Fainter and fainter grew the breathing. At last it ceased.' The clock struck half-past nine at that very moment. 'Albert lifted me up and took me into the next room, himself entirely melted into tears, which is unusual for him, deep as his feelings are, and clasped me in his arms.'[10]

The Queen poured a flood of emotion into her diary and into long letters to King Leopold, her mother's brother.

> What a blessed end! Her gentle spirit at rest, her sufferings over. But I, – I, wretched child! who had lost the mother I so tenderly loved, from whom for these forty-one years I had never been parted except for a few weeks, what was my case? My childhood – everything seemed to crowd upon me at once. I seemed to have lived through a life, to have become old! What I had dreaded, and fought off the idea of for years, had come, and must be borne. The blessed future meeting and *her* peace and rest, must henceforward be my comfort.[11]

In her will, the Duchess bequeathed all her property to the Queen and appointed the Prince Consort her sole executor. It was an additional burden for him, made heavier by the death of Sir George Couper. Vicky, on hearing of her grandmother's death, set out for England, arriving on 18 March. Both Houses of Parliament voted addresses of condolence to the Queen – Lord Palmerston in the House of Commons, Lord Granville in the Lords were eloquent and sympathetic. They insisted on the care and attention with which the Duchess of Kent had so admirably prepared her daughter for the throne. Benjamin Disraeli, who seconded the debate in the Commons, was more intuitive.

> It is generally supposed that the anguish of affection is scarcely compatible with the pomp of power, but that is not so in the present instance. She who reigns over us has elected, amid all the splendour of empire, to establish her life on the principle of domestic love. It is this, it is the remembrance and consciousness of this, which now sincerely saddens the public spirit, and permits a nation to bear its heart-felt sympathy to the foot of a bereaved throne, and to whisper solace to a royal heart.[12]

For the Queen it was a great sorrow, as she told King Leopold, not to have Feodora, her half-sister, with her at this time. Feodora was more deeply religious than Victoria, and more serene in the face of death. 'If I could but once have looked on dear Mama's face again!' she wrote, 'I am sure it looks peaceful and happy even now. My heart is full of gratitude for all her love – alas! lost to me in this life for ever! but to live again hereafter with her, never to be separated.'[13]

The Duchess of Kent died at seventy-five. The Queen's grief may seem today overly tinged with self-pity. But there is no doubt that Albert did little to convince her it was necessary to take up the threads of her life again. On the contrary, in a letter to Stockmar, he explained that for the last two years Victoria's constant care and attention had been to keep watch over her mother's comfort, and that the influence of this upon her own character had been 'most salutary'. He added: 'You may conceive it was and is no easy task for me to comfort and support her and to keep others at a distance, and yet at the same time not to throw away the opportunity which a time like the present affords, of binding the family together in a closer bond of unity.'[14]

The Queen gave way to what may seem excessive grief, undoubtedly encouraged by her husband. The couple retired to Osborne. Although Vicky tried by letter to draw her mother out of her grief, it was not until 9 April that Victoria went down for the first time to luncheon with her family – still taking breakfast and dinner upstairs in her room. She wrote to Vicky:

You are right, dear child, I do not wish to feel better. My head has been tiresome and troublesome and I can still bear little or no noise. The relief of tears is great – and though since last Wednesday night I have had no very violent outburst, they come again and again every day, and are soothing to the bruised heart and soul.[15]

Albert, whether purposely or not, maintained her grief by dragging out the work of sorting out her possessions. 'Every evening,' she wrote, almost a month after her mother's death, 'we are occupied with the dear papers. The preliminary sorting is finished – and now remains the arranging of those that are sorted.'[16] So every evening her mother's presence was revived. The Queen sorted out all the letters she had ever written to her mother, all the cuttings of her hair which her mother had preserved, her mother's notes on her child's babyhood – each a reminder of her mother's attachment to her. She found, too, relics of her father she had never seen – his writing desk, his Garter purse, a drawing of the room in which he died. Dwelling on all this must have intensified – and prolonged – her overwhelming grief. To Queen Augusta of Prussia she wrote, 'I am not actually ill, but my nerves are terribly upset and I can only bear the most complete quiet. To lose a beloved mother is always terrible and the blank can never be filled.'[17]

Prince Albert, who had been the instrument of reconciliation between mother and daughter after the estrangement that had marked the first years of her reign, must have reminded her of those sad times, for she wrote to King Leopold:

Oh! I am so wretched to think how, for a time two people most wickedly estranged us! . . . But thank God! that is all passed long, long ago, and she had forgotten it, and only thought of the last very happy years. And all that was brought about by my good angel dearest Albert, whom she adored, and in whom she had such unbounded confidence.[18]

The Duchess's body was laid to rest on 25 March, in St George's Chapel, Windsor. But the royal couple had agreed to make Frogmore her permanent burial place. Her remains were removed there on 17 August – the vault was 'so airy, so grand, and simple, that affecting as it was,' noted the Queen, 'there was no anguish or bitterness of grief, but a feeling of calm and repose.'[19] It was the Duchess of Kent herself who had, in a formal request written to the Prince in March 1859,[20] asked not to be buried among the Hanoverians at Windsor. The place she had chosen was a mound, at Frogmore: it had been created from the earth excavated to make an artificial lake in Queen Charlotte's day. Work had begun well before the Duchess died. A shaft was dug into the mound, with a sarcophagus to be placed at the bottom and a circular temple to be constructed on top. The work was almost completed by the time of her death and it was consecrated on 29 July.

The Queen pensioned off her mother's servants and took Lady Augusta Bruce, the Duchess's Lady-in-Waiting, as one of her own bedchamber women. She also decided to continue the allowances that her mother had made to Feodora and her son Victor of Hohenlohe-Langenburg, and to Charles of Leiningen's son, Edward. Victoria took a certain pleasure – as was the custom of the day – in the approval shown to her grief. Had she realized that rumours concerning her sanity were being spread as a result of her seclusion, she might well have modified her conduct. It would have helped if she had been encouraged to do so by Prince Albert. The Prince, writing to his brother in June, told him: 'Victoria is very well and I cannot understand how these horrid, vile rumours about her mental state could arise. People here and on the continent are much occupied with these rumours. They have annoyed me tremendously as I know what the consequences may be. She herself is perfectly unaware of all this scandal.'[21]

Gradually, however, the Queen was returning to a more normal existence, though not without difficulty. On the last day of April she had held a Council for the declaration of Alice's marriage, 'and though I did not break down it agitated me dreadfully – and I finally knocked completely up and had to leave the dinner.'[22] The announcement of the marriage was received with general approval by the Council and four days later by Parliament. When the question of Alice's dowry was raised, a dowry of 30,000 pounds, with an annuity of 6,000 pounds, was voted without a single dissenting voice. A fortnight later the royal couple returned to Osborne for the Whitsun holidays. Prince Louis of Hesse, Alice's fiancé, came to join them for a second visit – and had an attack of measles. He recovered rapidly but young Prince Leopold caught it from him and suffered much more, making his mother very anxious. Albert insisted that, in spite of Leopold's illness, Victoria should leave Osborne and go with him to 'that tiresome horticultural garden – which I curse for more reasons than one – and have to leave poor little, sick Leopold behind here – in his bed which makes me sadly anxious, and adds to my low spirits!' As she explained to Vicky, she thought it was 'both cruel and wrong' to leave a sick child behind, 'when I have nothing earthly to do till the 19th.' She was distressed and annoyed and concluded, 'men have not the sympathy and anxiety of women. Oh! no!'[23]

The month of June was a busy one for the Prince and he suffered from aches and pains. 'Am ill, feverish, with pains in my limbs and feel very miserable,' he wrote in his diary on the sixteenth.[24] For the Queen, 19 June marked her first public engagement since her mother's death – a drawing room. It was a summer of cloudless skies and great heat and she complained that she felt half melted by the fearful heat of the drawing room, which lasted two hours. King Leopold and his second son had been staying since May and they left, after five weeks, on 25 June. On the following day the Crown Prince and Princess of Prussia – Vicky and Fritz – came with their two children. Throughout July there was no lack of additional visitors. Max and Charlotte of Austria came, then Louis's mother, the Princess Charles of Hesse; later came Fritz of Baden, then the Duke of Oporto and, finally, the King of Sweden. The Court was still in deep mourning and Baron Stockmar wrote to the Prince questioning the wisdom of such mourning. The Prince's reply shows that he had supported and probably encouraged the Queen to withdraw from public life. 'The people', he tells the Baron, 'were surprised at the time that the Queen was ready to do so much; I cannot therefore admit that the mourning has been carried to excess.'[25]

The Crown Prince and Princess stayed for seven weeks, starting off on their return journey to Germany on 16 August. Five days later the Queen embarked on her third visit to Ireland, together with Prince Albert, the Princesses Alice and Helena and Prince Alfred, who had only just returned from the West Indies. The visit was inspired in part by a desire to see the Prince of Wales, who was learning how to be a soldier at the Curragh camp. Bertie had been sent for ten weeks to the camp attached to the second battalion of the Grenadier Guards. He was kept hard at work on a course of infantry training, but he found opportunities for relaxation far from the supervision of his guardians. In one of his copious memorandums, the Prince Consort had laid down that camp life should be a school of social as well as military instruction for the Prince of Wales. He was to be given a brigadier's quarters and was to give dinner parties twice a week to senior officers; he was to dine twice in his Regimental Mess; once a week he was to be the guest of honour of other regiments in strict rotation. The other two evenings were to be spent quietly in his own quarters.[26] The social plan was executed to the letter; the military instruction, which provided for a promotion every fortnight from the grade of ensign upwards, was too rapid for Bertie and he slipped behind Prince Albert's schedule. Colonel Bruce reported to the Prince Consort on 15 August that there was no hope that his son would be able to command a battalion by the end of the month.[27]

The Queen travelled by rail from Southampton to Holyhead and then crossed to Kingstown. She took up her residence in Viceregal Lodge in Phoenix Park. Great numbers of people lined the streets and greeted her with enthusiasm. On Saturday, 24 August, she went to the Curragh to review the 10,000 soldiers there – among them Bertie. Affie stayed with his brother until the following day. On the morning of the twenty-sixth, the royal family celebrated Prince Albert's forty-second birthday. 'Alas! there is so much so different this year,' noted the Queen, 'nothing festive, and we on a journey and separated from many of our children, and my spirits bad. But I wished him joy, warmly, tenderly.'[28] The gifts from the Queen and from his children had been brought with them and were ready waiting for him when he came downstairs in the morning. Among the presents from the Queen were a picture by Portaels and a pair of Lancaster breechloading rifles. The Crown Princess and Princess Alice had both done drawings for him. For Victoria, the day was tinged with melancholy. 'I missed the little ones – above all, baby – and sadly I thought of poor dear Vicky.'[29]

In the afternoon Victoria and her family went south by train.

> It was very hot. The country for some distance was very unattractive, except for the outline of distant hills which were visible from time to time. It is astonishing how wanting in population this part of the country is – large plains, a good deal cultivated, here and there a small house, with a few cabins, but no villages, and hardly any towns, except the few close upon the railway.[30]

The Queen enjoyed her two-day visit to Killarney. She was sketching again and writing long descriptions of all she saw in her journal. She was now really on the mend.

From Ireland the royal party went across England to Balmoral, where they were joined by Louis of Hesse and Princess Feodora. 'The Queen herself', wrote Prince Albert, 'is well. I regret to say I have a cold, but am in other respects well.'[31] The autumn of 1861 was dry and the weather most agreeable. The highlights of the Scottish holiday were described in what the Queen called her *Leaves from the Journal of Our Life in the Highlands*.[32] They were the Great Expeditions – expeditions into the Highlands by carriage, on horseback and on foot. The landscape was particularly beautiful, with its native firs and its lochs against backgrounds of blue hills. The royal party was small and in principle voyaged incognito. Walker, the police inspector, was sent on in advance – 'to order everything in a quiet way without letting people suspect who we were: in this he entirely succeeded,' the Queen had written on the first expedition the year before.[33]

On this occasion, in September 1861, the second expedition took them to Invermark and Fettercairn. Crossing a burn, they came across 'a picturesque group of shearers . . . chiefly women, the older ones smoking.'[34] They were on their way home from the south to the north. The royal party took lunch in a Highland cabin, visited Lord Dalhousie's shooting lodge and stayed the night at a quiet little inn in Fettercairn called the Ramsay Arms.

> We dined at eight, a very nice, clean, good dinner. Grant and Brown waited. They were rather nervous but General Grey and Lady Churchill carved, and they had only to change the plates, which Brown soon got into the way of doing. A little girl of the house came in to help – but Grant turned her round to prevent her looking at us! The landlord and landlady knew who we were, but no one else except the coachman, and they kept the secret admirably.[35]

They travelled forty-two miles the first day, forty the second and came home well satisfied: 'being out a great deal here – and seeing new and fine scenery,' said the Queen, 'does me good.'

The third expedition took place about a fortnight later.[36] Once again there was the fine, wild scenery, high hills, and no one living there. This time they went even further – sixty-nine miles on the first day, sixty on the second. 'This was the pleasantest and most enjoyable expedition I ever made,' the Queen noted, 'and the recollection of it will always be most agreeable to me, and increase my wish to make more . . . Have enjoyed nothing as much, or indeed felt so much cheered by anything, since my great sorrow.'

Meanwhile Bertie, on leaving Ireland, had gone to visit his sister in Berlin. Officially he went to acquire further military education because he was to take part in the autumn manoeuvres of the German army. The real reason was to allow him to meet the young lady his sister had singled out as a possible bride – Princess Alexandra, eldest daughter of Prince Christian of Schleswig-Holstein-Sonderburg-Glucksburg. Through his wife, Prince Christian was heir to the throne of Denmark, and on 15 November 1863 he ascended as King Christian IX. The Princess had been brought up in Copenhagen. Eligible, attractive Protestant princesses were rare so, although the problem still remained that such a match would anger Prussia – still firmly attached to the idea of annexing Schleswig-Holstein – it had been agreed that the Prince and Alix should meet and see if they suited one another.

When he saw the Princess, the Prince was not struck with her beauty but found her charming.[37] Vicky wrote to her parents:

I see that Alix has made an impression on Bertie, though in his own funny, undemonstrative way, he said to me that he had never seen a young lady who pleased him so much. At first I think he was disappointed about her beauty and did not think her as pretty as he expected, ... her beauty consists more in the sweetness of expression, grace of manner, and extreme refinement of appearance, she grows upon one the more one sees her, and in a quarter of an hour he thought her lovely, but said her nose was too long and her forehead too low.[38]

When Bertie returned to Scotland, where the royal family were, the Queen's impression was that 'Bertie is certainly much pleased with her – but as for being in love I don't think he can be, or that he is capable of enthusiasm about anything in the world.'[39] Back in Berlin, Vicky was very disappointed. 'I own it gives me a feeling of great sadness when I think of that sweet lovely flower – young and beautiful – that even makes my heart beat when I look at her – which would make most men fire and flames – not even producing impression enough to last from Baden to England.' And she concluded, 'I love him with all my heart and soul but I do not envy his future wife!'[40]

The Prince had found the young woman agreeable and had then come back home and refused to commit himself one way or the other. On the other hand, if the Princess and her parents were invited to Windsor, it seemed to Prince Albert that Bertie would have to propose to the Princess – so long as she pleased him as much as she had when they had first met.[41] Meanwhile, Queen Victoria asked Vicky to find out from Prince Christian what his daughter had thought of Bertie. At this stage, Bertie suddenly got cold feet. 'A sudden fear of marrying and above all of having children (which for so young a man is so strange a fear) seems to have got hold of him.'[42]

The royal couple's minds were torn away from Bertie's problems by the tragedy affecting the Coburg family in Portugal. Ferdinand, cousin to both Albert and Victoria, had married Maria da Gloria, Queen of Portugal. When she died in 1853, the eldest of their five sons, Pedro, had succeeded his mother and become King of Portugal. In November 1861 two of Pedro's brothers came to stay at Windsor. On their way home they learned that one of their brothers, Ferdinand, had died of typhoid fever. Five days later, on 11 November, King Pedro died of the disease.[43] Prince Albert was deeply affected. The King was only twenty-five and Prince Albert had treated him like a son, believing that through him real democracy would come to Portugal. Victoria and Albert did not need this fresh loss in a winter that was already so depressing and sad. The Queen recalled what John Brown had said when they had left Balmoral at the beginning of November. She was so struck by his remarks that she reported them to her daughter: 'he hoped we should all be well through the winter and return all safe' . . . 'and above all, that you may have no deaths in the family.'[44] He had added that twelve years earlier he had lost three brothers and one sister within six weeks. The irony of Brown's pronouncements was to be even more acutely felt a month later . . .

Another event was to upset the Prince Consort even more than the death of his relatives. It concerned Bertie. Three days after his son's twentieth birthday, the Prince Consort received a letter from Baron Stockmar reporting that all Europe was agog with the rumour that the Prince of Wales was having an affair with an actress. Albert was devastated. He over-reacted. As Woodham-Smith has noted, 'on the subject of sex, the Prince Consort was unbalanced.'[45] Woodham-Smith rightly points out that in most aristocratic families of the day some sexual experience before marriage – the sowing of wild oats – was considered perfectly normal. The reaction of the Prince Consort was curious. Instead of speaking to his son about it, he first conducted a searching inquiry. Then, on 16 November 1861, he wrote him a long letter. It began:

> I write to you with a heavy heart on a subject which has caused me the deepest pain I have yet felt in this life, having to address my son, in whom we had during twenty years fondly hoped to rear a Prince, and an ornament to a great and powerful and religious nation, as one who has sunk into vice and debauchery.

Lord Torrington, said Albert, had confirmed that the story was going round the London clubs of how some young officers had procured for the Prince at Curragh a 'woman of the town'. It was said that the Prince had sexual intercourse with her at another officer's hut, 'a course you kept up till you left the camp'. The Prince had been unwilling to believe this but the inquiry had shown 'a course of deception and profligacy' on the part of the Prince which had filled his father's heart with shame. The affair had even defiled the royal palace, for 'Nelly Clifden boasts even of having been down here at Windsor to meet you when you last stayed here with us for your birthday.'

The Prince went on to explain that he had always known his son was thoughtless and weak, ignorant and easily led – but he had not thought him 'depraved'. The letter continued by telling Bertie that Nelly Clifden was now given the nickname 'Princess of Wales', and by painting a ferocious picture of what would happen next. The young woman in question 'will probably get a child and attribute it to you'. If the Prince denied the charge she would drag him before the courts – 'she will be able to give before a greedy multitude disgusting details of your profligacy.' The Prince would be 'hooted and yelled at by a lawless mob!!'[46]

Why was the Prince so distraught? He feared, no doubt, that his son might return to the libertine customs of Victoria's forebears, customs he knew only too well himself from the behaviour of his father and his brother. Then there was the fear that the Princess who had been so carefully chosen might want to have nothing to do with his profligate son. The Prince was, in any case, in poor health and his low state may have caused him to exaggerate the affair out of all proportion.

At a time when he was literally worrying himself sick, the Prince Consort still went about his usual business. On 22 November he went to Sandhurst to inspect the new buildings. It poured with rain and he returned to Windsor wet and shivering. He was sleeping badly and complained of rheumatism. On 24 November he wrote in his diary: 'Am full of rheumatic pains, and feel thoroughly unwell. Have scarcely closed my eyes at night for the last fortnight.'[47] Still greatly out of sorts, he decided to go and see the Prince of Wales at Madingley on the twenty-fifth. Although it was a cold, stormy day, he took a long walk with his son – overlong because the Prince of Wales lost the way – and he came back reassured, but even more unwell. That day he could not join Victoria in her walk as he usually did because of pains in his back and legs. The following day saw no improvement. The Prince was weary and weak. Victoria wrote to her daughter on the twenty-seventh:

> Dearest Papa ... is not well ... with a cold with neuralgia – a great depression which has been worse these last five days – but I hope will be much better tomorrow. The sad part is – that this loss of rest at night (worse than he has ever had before) was caused by a great sorrow and worry, which upset us both greatly – but him especially – and it broke him quite down I never saw him so low.[48]

Albert himself put his illness down to Bertie's escapade. 'I am at a very low ebb,' he wrote to his daughter. 'Much worry and great sorrow (about which I beg you not to ask questions) have robbed me of sleep during the past fortnight and for the past four days am suffering from headache and pains in my limbs which may develop into rheumatism.'[49]

To begin with, the Queen was rather irritated with her husband, who was continually complaining about his aches and pains. 'Dr

Jenner', she told her daughter on the thirtieth, 'said yesterday evening Papa was so much better, he would be quite well in two or three days – but he is not inclined himself ever to admit he is better!'[50] He was sleeping badly, felt chilly and uncomfortable and had lost his appetite.

On 1 December, however, Albert was aroused from his sickness by the Trent affair. Civil War had broken out in America in the preceding April and the Queen's Government had issued a proclamation of neutrality. A wise move, since public opinion in England was divided – but on the whole public opinion favoured the South. This was particularly true of the Prime Minister, Palmerston, and the Chancellor of the Exchequer, William Gladstone. The Queen and the Prince were inclined to favour the North.

As the crisis unfolded, the President of the Confederate States, Jefferson Davis, was eager to obtain recognition by the Courts of Europe and to this end he sent two envoys – Mr Mason to the Court of St James and Mr Slidell to the Court of the Tuileries. They embarked at Havana, in the English mail steamer *Trent*. The *Trent* was intercepted by a Federal Union warship on the high seas, a couple of shots were fired across her bow, she was boarded and the emissaries from the South were taken off. This was a flagrant violation of international law. On 30 November, three days after the *Trent* arrived at Southampton, Palmerston sent the Queen a draft of the despatch to be forwarded to Washington. Its terms were peremptory and uncompromising, demanding immediate reparation and redress.

The Prince Consort read the draft at seven in the morning, on 1 December. He recognized that the British Government could not allow the Union Jack to be insulted, but they must, he thought, assume that this had been done without the assent of President Lincoln. Otherwise Great Britain might find herself at war with the United States. In a note to Palmerston, Prince Albert explained his position: let the British Prime Minister assume that an over-zealous officer of the Federal Union fleet had acted on his own initiative. By eight o'clock the Prince had drafted a memorandum and he brought it to the Queen. He told her that he had scarcely been able to hold his pen while writing it. With minor changes it was written out by the Queen and despatched to Lord Palmerston and Lord Russell. The suggestions of the Prince were accepted and a moderated version of the despatch was sent to Washington. There the Government assented to the British Government's demands and freed the four people taken from the *Trent*. Any risk of war between Britain and America was averted.

After writing the memorandum Albert insisted on going to the chapel in the Castle. He looked 'very wretched and ill, but insisted on going through all the kneeling. He came to luncheon but could eat nothing.'[51] In the evening he came to dinner with his family but was still unable to eat anything. He talked, however, and even told stories. After dinner he sat very quietly, listening to Alice and Maria playing on the piano, and went to bed early.[52]

Sir James Clark and Dr Jenner seemed unable to do anything. On that day and on the next they simply expressed their regret that there was no improvement. The Prince was now shivering with cold and still unable to eat. On 3 December the Queen noted, 'My anxiety is great, and I feel utterly lost when he, to whom I confide all, is in such a listless state and hardly smiles.'[53] Lord Palmerston was convinced that Prince Albert ought to have another doctor called in and suggested this to the Queen. She replied tartly:

> The Queen is very much obliged to you for the kind interest displayed in your letter received this day. The Prince has had a feverish cold the last few days, which disturbed his rest at night, but Her Majesty has seen His Royal Highness before similarly affected and hopes that in a few days it will pass off. In addition to Sir James Clark, the Queen has had the advantage of the constant advice of Dr Jenner, a most skilful physician, and Her Majesty would be very unwilling to cause unnecessary alarm, where no cause exists for it, by calling in a medical man who does not upon ordinary occasions attend at the Palace.[54]

The Queen's lack of any real apprehension was due to the reports she received from her doctors. 'Good kind Sir James Clark has been here since yesterday and reassured me, saying there was no cause for alarm, either present or future. It looked as if it were likely to turn into a low fever, but he felt sure Albert would soon be better.'[55]

Albert himself was far from optimistic and this has been taken as a sort of death-wish. But there is no doubt that Albert in no way welcomed death. He was, on the contrary, extremely apprehensive of having 'the low fever' from which his Portuguese relatives had died. The chronicle of these December days shows Albert still padding around the apartments in his blue quilted dressing gown, going from room to room, his looks and manner 'very disheartening and sad'.[56] He was in a state of great discomfort. 'His manner all along was so unlike himself and he had sometimes such a strange, wild look.'[57] He was sleepless and unable to eat. On 3 December he had some orange jelly, on the fourth no nourishment at all except for a little raspberry vinegar in Seltzer water. The doctors administered ether and Hoffman's drops. The Queen was constantly by his bedside, and so was Alice. She seemed more mature than her eighteen years, ministering to him in a way the Queen was incapable of. A contemporary wrote:

> The Princess Alice's fortitude has amazed us all. She saw from the first that both her father's and mother's firmness depended on her firmness and she set herself to the duty. He loved to speak openly of his condition and had many wishes to express . . . He could not speak to the Queen of himself, for she could not bear to listen, and shut her eyes to the danger. His daughter saw that she must act differently, and she never let her voice falter, or shed a single tear in his presence. She sat by him, listened to all he said, repeated hymns, and then when she could bear it no longer, would walk calmly to the door and rush away to her room, returning with the same calm and pale face, without any appearance of the agitation she had gone through.[58]

Although he was in a 'very uncomfortable, panting state,'[59] which frightened the Queen and her daughter, the Prince Consort still had his wits about him. He asked for the latest news and on 5 December learnt with great sorrow of the death of Lady Canning at Calcutta. At times during the next week the Prince Consort seemed more like himself, holding little Beatrice's hand or smiling affectionately at his wife. On 6 December he asked to be brought the plans of Alice and Louis's future home: the Queen noted, 'Found dearest Albert quite himself, so dear and affectionate when I went in with little Baby, whom he kissed and he quite laughed at some of her new French verses, which I made her repeat.'[60]

Sir Charles Phipps, the Prince's Equerry, took it upon himself to keep Lord Palmerston informed of the Prince's health. He considered that 'everything connected with the subject requires much management. The Prince himself, when ill, is extremely depressed and low, and the Queen becomes so nervous and so easily alarmed, that the greatest caution is necessary.'[61] That was why Sir James Clark and Dr Jenner had not sent for another medical man.

It has been suggested that to spare the Queen anxiety the truly critical state of his illness was kept from her. But it seems more likely that the doctors themselves were not immediately aware of the nature of the disease. On 7 December Dr Jenner went to see the Queen and told her as gently as possible that they had all along been watching Albert's state, suspecting fever but unable to judge what it might be and how exactly to treat him. However, that morning they had found a slight eruption on the lower part of the stomach, which left them in no doubt as to what it was – 'viz. gastric and bowel fever.'[62]

So Dr Jenner had not realized until then that the Prince had the dreaded typhoid fever. Yet it was Dr Jenner who, in 1849–51, working in the London fever hospital, had made the first clinical, pathological observations which had allowed him to distinguish typhoid fever from typhus. Daphne Bennett, in her biography of Prince Albert, has cast doubt on the diagnosis of typhoid, claiming that it does not fit all the facts. She suggests that he may have died of a chronic wasting disease.[63] Three facts are used to support this thesis: first, at no time in the Queen's journal or in other accounts of the Prince's illness is a consistently high temperature mentioned as one of the symptoms; secondly, there is no evidence of a source of infection from which the Prince might have contracted the disease, either at Sandhurst, in Cambridge or at Windsor; lastly, although several people were in very close, daily contact with the Prince, no one else was infected.

Against this it must be argued that, during the last few days of his life, the Prince did have a high temperature. Typhoid is, moreover, a disease which sets in insidiously and all the early symptoms were present in the Prince's case – headache, lassitude, discomfort, sleeplessness, feverishness; as they may be found at the onset of most infectious diseases, and in the terminal phases of not a few chronic diseases, the doctors were not at first sure that the Prince had typhoid. From 7 December onwards Dr Jenner was perfectly clear in his own mind that Prince Albert had typhoid and it is difficult to believe that he had misinterpreted his patient's rash. He even wrote to Dr Edmund Parkes, a pioneer in sanitation, on 19 December – 'The Prince of course had typhoid fever.'[64]

The diagnosis of typhoid fever curiously reassured the Queen. Although she was still extremely anxious, she was now writing in terms simply of a long illness – of 'the dreadful loss this long illness would be – publicly as well as privately.'[65] The doctors told her the illness was caused by too much hard work and worry – and that, she decided, must be stopped. On 8 December things took a turn for the better. The sun was shining, the Blue Room where the Prince was lying looked bright and cheerful and for the first time since his illness the Prince asked for some music – 'a fine chorale played at a distance.'[66] A piano was brought into the next room and Alice played *Ein Feste Burg ist Unser Gott*. Tears came to the Prince's eyes. 'When I went to him, after dinner,' wrote the Queen, 'he was so pleased to see me, stroked my face and smiled, and called me *Weibchen* (dear little wife).'[67]

On that day Sir James Clark and Dr Jenner called in further advice, a sure sign that they were now convinced of the gravity of the situation. Sir Henry Holland, one of the physicians-in-ordinary of the Prince since 1840, and Dr Watson, one of the physicians extraordinary to the Queen, examined the Prince. Colonel Phipps told Palmerston that Dr Watson considered the Prince very ill; 'the malady is very grave and serious in itself – and that even the Prince's present weakness is very great – in short he says it is impossible not to be very anxious.'[68]

By 9 December it was no longer possible to conceal the Prince's illness from the public. Guests who had been invited had had to be put off and the newspapers on 9 December reported that the Prince's illness was 'likely to continue for some time'.[69] Alarm spread to the Cabinet. Lord Palmerston pressed Phipps to tell Sir James Clark and Dr Watson that they might share responsibility 'with some other eminent medical man not yet called in'. He insisted that this was 'a matter of the most momentous national importance, and all considerations of personal feeling and susceptibilities must absolutely give way to the public interest.'[70]

The Prince Consort was not an easy patient. He was restless and irritable. When the Princess or the Queen was reading to him he would change his mind about what he wanted read, or express dissatisfaction. On the tenth and eleventh, however, the Prince was less querulous and in fact seemed much better. His nights were much better and he was taking beef tea. On the morning of the eleventh the Queen went to his room at eight o'clock, she found him sitting up, 'and he laid his dear head (his beautiful face, more beautiful than ever has grown so thin) on my shoulder and remained a little while, saying, "it is very comfortable so, dear child." '[71] As he was being assisted by the Queen from his bed to the sofa, he paused to look at his favourite picture, saying, 'It helps me through half the day.'

The Prince was now reluctant for the Queen to leave him and she spent the greater part of the day in his room. The fever increased on the twelfth and his breathing was shorter. His listlessness and impatience were more marked and his mind wandered at times. Sir Charles Phipps was sufficiently anxious to communicate his fears to Palmerston who replied:

> Your telegram and letter have come upon me like a thunderbolt. I know that the disorder is one liable to sudden and unfavourable turns, but I had hoped that it was going on without cause for special apprehension. The result which your accounts compel me to look forward to as at least possible, is in all its bearings too awful to contemplate. One can only hope that Providence may yet spare us so overwhelming a calamity.[72]

On the following day the Prince's breathing was faster and more difficult. Dr Jenner told the Queen this might be a serious symptom and lead to congestion of the lungs. The Queen saw that Albert was losing his strength. However, towards evening, he rallied – the pulse improved and he was more like his former self. There did seem to be a gleam of hope. On the Saturday morning the Prince of Wales arrived, summoned by a telegram from Alice. Reports were now more cheerful and at about six in the morning Her Majesty was told that 'there was ground to hope the crisis was over.'[73] When the Queen went in, however, she had a different impression. 'The room had the sad look of night-watching, the candles burnt down to their sockets, the doctors looking anxious.' Albert looked beautiful, with his face lit up by the rising sun, but his eyes were 'unusually bright, gazing as it were on unseen objects and not taking notice of me'.[74]

By twelve o'clock the doctors confirmed the Queen's impressions: 'We are very much frightened,' 'but don't and won't give up hope.' Sir James Clark continued to reassure the Queen – every hour and every minute was a gain, he told her, and he had seen much worse cases than that of the Prince. The breathing was, however, still very rapid. The Queen noted:

> There was what they call a dusky hue about his face and hands, which I knew was not good. . . . Albert folded his arms, and began arranging his hair, just as he used to do when well and he was dressing. These were said to be bad signs. Strange! as though he were preparing for another and greater journey.[75]

At about half-past five the Queen, who had been in the adjoining room, went back into the Prince's room. His bed had been wheeled towards the middle of the room and she sat down beside it. ' "*Gutes Frauchen*", he said, and kissed me, and then gave a piteous moan, or rather sigh, not of pain, but as if he felt that he was leaving me, and laid his head upon my shoulders, and I put my arm under his.' A moment later, 'he seemed to wander and to doze.'

Alice, Bertie, Helena, Louise and Arthur came in one after the other and took his hand – but he was dozing and did not respond to them. Four of his children were absent. Vicky, now twenty-one, was in Berlin expecting her third child and too weak to travel. Affie was on military manoeuvres in Mexico. Leopold was in the South of France, convalescing after a particularly hard winter. Beatrice was kept away – she was judged too young and too impressionable. The Prince suddenly opened his eyes and asked for Sir Charles Phipps, who came in and kissed his hands, as did General Grey and Sir Thomas Biddulph.

The Prince's breathing became worse and he was bathed in perspiration. The doctors said it might be an effort of nature to throw off the fever. Some time later, the Queen left the room but had to be recalled when a rapid change set in. She knelt by the side of the bed. On the other side was Princess Alice. At the foot knelt the Prince of Wales and Princess Helena. General Bruce, the Dean of Windsor, Sir Charles Phipps and General Grey were also present. Surrounded by his family, the members of his Household and his servants, the Prince Consort died at a quarter to eleven on the night of 14 December. 'Two or three long but perfectly gentle breaths were drawn, the hand clasping mine, and (oh it turns me sick to write it) all, all was over. The heavenly spirit fled to the world it was fit for.'[76] Queen Victoria collapsed, unable to utter a word or shed a tear. Phipps lifted her up and she was carried into the Red Room. Then the words came from the depths of her heart: 'There is no one to call me Victoria now.'

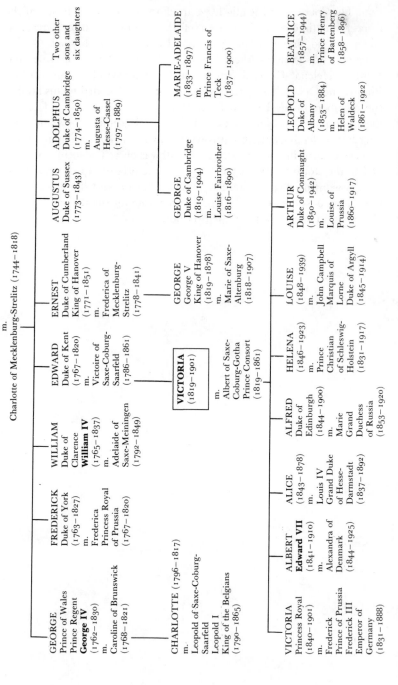

GEORGE III (1738–1820)
m.
Charlotte of Mecklenburg-Strelitz (1744–1818)

GEORGE
Prince of Wales
Prince Regent
George IV
(1762–1830)
m.
Caroline of Brunswick
(1768–1821)

FREDERICK
Duke of York
(1763–1827)
m.
Frederica
Princess Royal
of Prussia
(1767–1820)

WILLIAM
Duke of
Clarence
William IV
(1765–1837)
m.
Adelaide of
Saxe-Meiningen
(1792–1849)

EDWARD
Duke of Kent
(1767–1820)
m.
Victoire of
Saxe-Coburg-
Saarfeld
(1786–1861)

ERNEST
Duke of Cumberland
King of Hanover
(1771–1851)
m.
Frederica of
Mecklenburg-
Strelitz
(1778–1841)

AUGUSTUS
Duke of Sussex
(1773–1843)

ADOLPHUS
Duke of Cambridge
(1774–1850)
m.
Augusta of
Hesse-Cassel
(1797–1889)

Two other
sons and
six daughters

CHARLOTTE (1796–1817)
m.
Leopold of Saxe-Coburg-
Saarfeld
Leopold I
King of the Belgians
(1790–1865)

VICTORIA
(1819–1901)

m.

Albert of Saxe-
Coburg-Gotha
Prince Consort
(1819–1861)

GEORGE
George V
King of Hanover
(1819–1878)
m.
Marie of Saxe-
Altenburg
(1818–1907)

GEORGE
Duke of Cambridge
(1819–1904)
m.
Louise Fairbrother
(1816–1890)

MARIE-ADELAIDE
(1833–1897)
m.
Prince Francis of
Teck
(1837–1900)

VICTORIA
Princess Royal
(1840–1901)
m.
Frederick
Prince of Prussia
Frederick III
Emperor of
Germany
(1831–1888)

ALBERT
Edward VII
(1841–1910)
m.
Alexandra of
Denmark
(1844–1925)

ALICE
(1843–1878)
m.
Louis IV
Grand Duke
of Hesse-
Darmstadt
(1837–1892)

ALFRED
Duke of
Edinburgh
(1844–1900)
m.
Marie
Grand
Duchess
of Russia
(1853–1920)

HELENA
(1846–1923)
m.
Prince
Christian
of Schleswig-
Holstein
(1831–1917)

LOUISE
(1848–1939)
m.
John Campbell
Marquis of
Lorne
Duke of Argyll
(1845–1914)

ARTHUR
Duke of Connaught
(1850–1942)
m.
Louise of
Prussia
(1860–1917)

LEOPOLD
Duke of
Albany
(1853–1884)
m.
Helen of
Waldeck
(1861–1922)

BEATRICE
(1857–1944)
m.
Prince Henry
of Battenberg
(1858–1896)

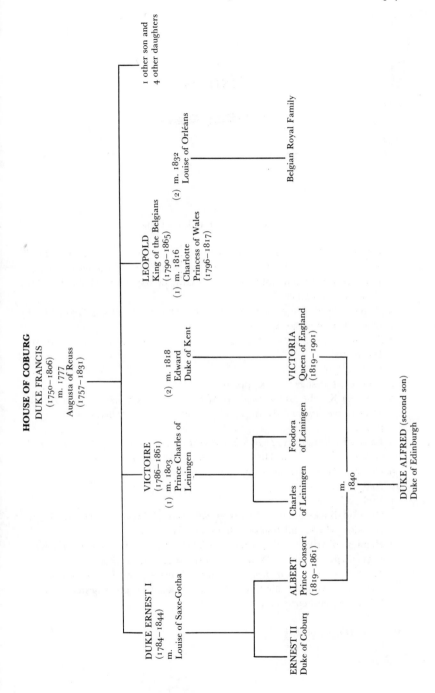

Notes

Chapter 1   The Lost Heir

1 RA 50030, Robert Gardiner to Benjamin Blomfield, 3 November 1817.
2 Thomas Creevey, *A Selection of the Letters and Papers of Thomas Creevey*, ed. John Gore (London, John Murray, 1948), p. 266. Lady Holland to Mrs Creevey, September 1817.
3 Roger Fulford, *George the Fourth* (London, Duckworth, 1935). George IV to Queen Caroline, 30 April 1796.
4 A. Aspinall, ed., *Letters of George IV* (3 vols, Cambridge, CUP, 1938), vol. III, p. 508.
5 Ibid., p. 519.
6 Creevey, *Letters and Papers*, pp. 181–2.
7 Cornelia Knight, *Autobiography of Miss Cornelia Knight with Extracts from her Journals and Anecdote Books* (2 vols, London, W. H. Allen, 1861), vol. I, p. 240.
8 Lady Charlotte Bury, *Diary Illustrative of the Times of George the Fourth*, ed. J. Galt (2 vols, London, Henry Colburn, 1838), vol. II, p. 203.
9 Creevey, *Letters and Papers*, p. 197. 21 June 1814.
10 Ibid., pp. 197–8.
11 Ibid., p. 198.
12 Duke of Buckingham, *Memoirs of the Court of England during the Regency* (London, Hurst and Blacket, 1856), vol. II, p. 156.
13 Hemlow d'Arblay, *The Journals and Letters of Fanny Burney (Mrs d'Arblay)*, 1791–1840, ed. Joyce Hemlow (Oxford, 1972), pp. 103–4.
14 Mary Frampton, *The Journal of Mary Frampton*, ed. Harriet Georgiana (London, Mundy, 1885), p. 267. The Countess of Ilchester to Lady Frampton, 26 February 1816.
15 Ibid.
16 Bury, *Diary*, vol. I, p. 65.
17 Ibid.

18 d'Arblay, *Journals and Letters*, p. 136. 16 May 1816.

19 *La Belle Assemblée*, June 1816.

20 *Observer*, 5 May 1816.

21 Hansard, 20 June 1816.

22 A. Aspinall, ed., *Letters of the Princess Charlotte* (London, Home and Van Thal, 1949), p. 245.

23 Baron Stockmar, *Memoirs of Baron Stockmar*, ed. Baron E. von Stockmar (2 vols, London, 1872), vol. I, p. 43. 25 October 1816.

24 Aspinall, *Letters of the Princess Charlotte*, p. 262. Princess Charlotte to Sophie Mensdorff, 7 February 1817.

25 Stockmar, *Memoirs*, vol. I, p. 61.

26 Aspinall, *Letters of George IV*, vol. II, p. 210. Charlotte to her mother, 10 October 1817.

27 Frampton, *Journal*, p. 299. The Countess of Ilchester to the Marchioness of Lansdowne, 11 November 1817.

28 RA 50032, Robert Gardiner to Benjamin Blomfield, 4 November 1817.

29 RA 50030, Robert Gardiner to the Regent, 4 November 1817.

30 RA 50037, 5 November 1817.

31 Ibid.

32 RA 50067, 9 November 1817.

33 RA 50040, 5 November 1817.

34 Frampton, *Journal*, p. 299. The Countess of Ilchester to the Marchioness of Lansdowne, 11 November 1817.

35 Ibid.

36 RA 50067, 9 November 1817.

37 RA 50045. The Prince in fact was mistaken. The Princess's labour lasted forty-six hours.

38 RA 50045.

39 Stockmar, *Memoirs*, vol. I, p. 60.

40 Ibid., p. 64.

41 Ibid., pp. 64–5.

42 Knight, *Autobiography*, vol. II, pp. 349–50.

43 RA Y54/81, Memorandum by Anson, 4 October 1841.

44 Stockmar, *Memoirs*, vol. I, p. 66.

45 Ibid.

46 Ibid., pp. 66–7.

47 RA 50090.

48 RA 50088, Prince Leopold to the Prince Regent, 1 January 1818.

49 RA M45/13, Baron Hardenbrock to Ernest, Duke of Saxe-Coburg-Saarfeld.

50 Bury, *Diary*, vol. I, p. 8.

51 Creevey, *Letters and Papers*, p. 272. Lord Folkestone to Creevey, 23 February 1818.

52 Stockmar, *Memoirs*, vol. I, p. 2.

53 d'Arblay, *Journals and Letters*, vol. X, p. 747.

54 Stockmar, *Memoirs*, vol. I, p. 55.

55 d'Arblay, *Journals and Letters*, vol. X, p. 747.

56 RA 50058, Queen Charlotte to the Regent, 9 November 1817.

57 RA Y79/14, King Leopold to Queen Victoria, 9 December 1853.

58 RA Y154, Dr Croft to Baron Stockmar, 16 November 1817.

59 Carola Oman, *The Gascoyne Heiress: The Life and Diaries of Frances Mary Gascoyne* (London, Cecil, Hodder and Stoughton, 1968).

CHAPTER 2   THE LINE OF SUCCESSION

1 Baron Stockmar, *Memoirs of Baron Stockmar*, ed. Baron E. von Stockmar, vol. I, p. 50.

2 Charles Greville, *The Greville Memoirs, 1817–1860*, ed. H. Reeve (3 vols, London, Longmans, Green, 1875), vol. I, p. 7.

3 Stockmar, *Memoirs*, vol. I, p. 50.

4 Greville, *Memoirs*, vol. I, p. 5.

5 John Wilson Croker, *Correspondence and Diaries*, ed. L. J. Jennings (London, John Murray, 1885), p. 42.

6 Greville, *Memoirs*, vol. I, p. 6.

7 William Hazlitt, *Dramatic Essays* (London, 1895), p. 69.

8 A. Aspinall ed., *Letters of the Princess Charlotte*, p. 189.

9 Stockmar, *Memoirs*, vol. I, pp. 51–2.

10 Thomas Creevey, *A Selection of the Letters and Papers of Thomas Creevey*, ed. John Gore, p. 148.

11 Aspinall, *Letters of the Princess Charlotte*, p. 31. Princess Charlotte to Miss Mercer Elphinstone, 26 October 1812.

12 Creevey, *Letters and Papers*, p. 289. Mr Creevey to Miss Ord, 24 August 1822.

13 Percy Bysshe Shelley, 'Sonnet: England in 1819', in *Poetical Works* (Oxford, OUP, 1970), pp. 574–5.

14 A. Aspinall ed., *Letters of George IV*, vol. II, p. 223. William, Duke of Clarence to Queen Charlotte, 16 December 1817.

15 Creevey, *Letters and Papers*, p. 269. Notes of a conversation with the Duke of Kent in Brussels, 11 December 1817.

16 Ibid., p. 271.

17 *Annual Register 1818*, p. 84.

18 Ibid., p. 87.

19 Creevey, *Letters and Papers*, pp. 276–7. The Duke of Wellington to Mr Creevey, 16 July 1818.

20 Ibid., p. 269.

21 Augusta, Dowager Duchess of Coburg, *In Napoleonic Days, Extracts from her Diary*, ed. H.R.H. Princess Beatrice (London, John Murray, 1941), p. 189.

22 Creevey, *Letters and Papers*, p. 269.

23 Ibid., p. 270.

24 RA 45340, the Duke of Kent to Baron Mallet, 26 January 1819.

25 RA M2/25, the Princess of Leiningen to the Duke of Kent, 25 January 1818.

26 *The Times*, 27 April 1818.

27 Croker, *Correspondence and Diaries*, p. 39. Mr Croker to Sir Robert Peel, 26 November 1817.

28 Frances Williams Wynn, *Diaries of a Lady of Quality from 1797 to 1844*, ed. A. Hayward (London, 1864), p. 211.

29 RA Add7/1327, the Duke of Kent to the Regent's Private Secretary, 18 November 1818.

30 Stockmar, *Memoirs*, vol. I, p. 78.

31 Lieut-General the Hon. C. Grey, *The Early Years of H.R.H. the Prince Consort* (London, Smith, Elder, 1867), p. 12.

32 Creevey, *Letters and Papers*, p. 308. Mr Creevey to Miss Ord, 17 August 1820.

33 Ibid., p. 317.

34 Ibid., p. 308. Mr Creevey to Miss Ord, 17 August 1820.

35 Ibid., p. 316.

36 Mary Frampton, *The Journal of Mary Frampton*, ed. Harriet Georgiana, pp. 317–18.

37 Creevey, *Letters and Papers*, pp. 359–60.

38 Ibid., p. 363. Mr Creevey to Miss Ord, 8 August 1821.

39 Ibid., p. 363. Viscount Hood to Henry Brougham, 8 August 1821.

40 Croker, *Correspondence and Diaries*, p. 60.

41 Ibid.

42 Creevey, *Letters and Papers*, p. 370. Mr Creevey to Miss Ord, 27 August 1821. Contrary to what Creevey wrote, George IV in fact stopped at Hanover and did not go as he originally intended to Berlin and Vienna.

43 Princess Lieven, *The Private Letters of Princess Lieven to Prince Metternich. 1820–1826*, ed. Peter Quennell (London, John Murray, 1937), p. 200. Princess Lieven to Prince Metternich, 23 December 1821.

44 Ibid., p. 224. Princess Lieven to Prince Metternich, 13 January 1823.

45 Creevey, *Letters and Papers*, p. 431. Mr Creevey to Miss Ord, 25 June 1825.

46 Ibid., p. 438. Countess Grey to Mrs Taylor, February 1826.

47 Lieven, *Private Letters*, p. 151. Princess Lieven to Prince Metternich, 31 January 1822.

48 Creevey, *Letters and Papers*, p. 370. Mr Creevey to Miss Ord, 3 September 1822.

49 Ibid., pp. 369–70. Mr Creevey to Miss Ord, 27 August 1821.

50 RA Y69/26, King Leopold to Queen Victoria, 16 December 1842.

51 RA M4/26, the Duchess of Kent to Lord Grey, 28 January 1831.

52 Cecil Woodham-Smith, *Queen Victoria, 1819–1861* (London, Hamish Hamilton, 1972), p. 42.

53 RA Z/286, the Duchess of Kent to Polyxene von Tubeuf, 19 January 1820.
54 Croker, *Correspondence and Diaries*, vol. I, p. 155.
55 Lieven, *Private Letters*, p. 6. Princess Lieven to Prince Metternich, 25 January 1820.

CHAPTER 3   A SOLITARY CHILDHOOD

1 cf. Norman Gash, *Aristocracy and the People* (London, Edward Arnold, 1979), ch. 1; Asa Briggs, *Victorian Cities* (London, Odhams, 1963), ch. 8.
2 Thomas Creevey, *A Selection of the Letters and Papers of Thomas Creevey*, ed. John Gore, p. 538. Mr Creevey to Miss Ord, 14 February 1829.
3 Mary Frampton, *The Journal of Mary Frampton*, ed. Harriet Georgiana, pp. 315–16. Mrs Campbell to the Countess of Ilchester, 27 June 1819.
4 Creevey, *Letters and Papers*, p. 349. Mr Creevey to Miss Ord, 29 January 1821.
5 Princess Lieven, *The Private Letters of Princess Lieven to Prince Metternich, 1820–1826*, ed. Peter Quennell, p. 111.
6 Creevey, *Letters and Papers*, p. 425. Mr Creevey to Miss Ord, 10 November 1824.
7 *The Letters of Queen Victoria, 1837–1861*, ed. A. C. Benson and Lord Esher (3 vols, London, John Murray, 1907), vol. I, p. 19. Despite the dates given in the title, the first volume contains two chapters with letters from 1821 to 1836.
8 Creevey, *Letters and Papers*, p. 282.
9 Hansard, 3 July 1820. Vol. 2, pp. 143ff.
10 cf. F.M.L. Thompson, *English Landed Society in the Nineteenth Century* (London, Routledge and Kegan Paul, 1963).
11 Conroy Papers, ZC, Balliol College Library, Oxford.
12 cf. Caroline Bauer, *Posthumous Papers* (4 vols, London, Remington, 1884–5), vol. I, p. 44.
13 Ibid., vol. II, p. 106.
14 Ibid., vol. II, p. 121.
15 Ibid., vol. II, p. 135.
16 Ibid., vol. II, p. 137.
17 Ibid., vol. II, p. 312.
18 RA *Queen Victoria's Journal*.
19 *Letters of Queen Victoria*, vol. I, p. 41. Princess Victoria to King Leopold, 25 November 1828.
20 Ibid., vol. I, pp. 14–19.
21 Charles Greville, *The Greville Memoirs, 1817–1860*, ed. H. Reeve, vol. II:i, p. 195.
22 Margaret Oliphant, 'The domestic life of the Queen', in Robert Wilson, *The Life and Times of Queen Victoria* (2 vols, London, Cassel, 1900), vol. I, p. 18.
23 Cecil Woodham-Smith, *Queen Victoria, 1819–1861*, p. 61.
24 *Letters of Queen Victoria*, vol. I, p. 42. Princess Feodora to Princess Victoria,

May 1829.

25 Ibid., vol. I, p. 18.

26 Elizabeth Longford, *Victoria R.I.* (London, Weidenfeld and Nicolson, 1964), p. 30.

27 *Letters of Queen Victoria*, vol. I, p. 15.

28 Woodham-Smith, *Queen Victoria*, p. 73.

29 Rev. G. Davys, 'Diary', in Marquis of Lorne, *V.R.I. Her Life and Empire* (London, Harmsworth Books, n.d.), pp. 56–62.

30 Ibid., p. 57. 21 April 1823.

31 Ibid., p. 58, 28 May 1823.

32 Ibid., p. 59, 30 June 1823; p. 60, 12 January 1824.

33 RA *Queen Victoria's Journal*, 24 February 1837.

34 Hansard, 27 May 1825. Vol. 13, pp. 909–27.

35 Davys, 'Diary', p. 62. 6 April 1825.

36 Ibid.

37 Ibid., p. 57. 17 April 1823.

38 RA MP 116/6.

39 RA MP 116/5.

40 RA MP 116/2, 1 March 1830.

41 Ibid.

42 RA MP 116/7, 2 March 1830.

43 RA MP 116/8, 2 March 1830.

44 RA MP 116/9, 3 March 1830.

45 RA MP 116/10, 2 March 1830.

46 RA MP 116/11, 23 March 1830.

47 Greville, *Memoirs*, vol. I:i, p. 214. 29 May 1829.

48 RA Y203/81, Baroness Lehzen to Queen Victoria, 2 December 1867, with the Queen's annotations in the margin.

49 Sir Walter Scott, *Journal* (2 vols, Edinburgh, 1891), vol. I. 19 May 1828.

50 George Thomas, Comte d'Albemarle, *Fifty Years of my Life* (2 vols, London, Macmillan, 1874), vol. II, p. 227.

51 Charles Knight, *Passages of a Working Life during Half a Century* (3 vols, London, 1864).

52 RA Y36/128, Princess Feodora to Queen Victoria, 17 March 1843.

53 *Annual Register 1830*, p. 132.

54 Greville, *Memoirs*, vol. I:ii, p. 170.

55 Ibid.

56 *Letters of Queen Victoria*, vol. I, pp. 44–5. The King of the Belgians to Princess Victoria, 31 August 1832.

CHAPTER 4   THE KENSINGTON SYSTEM

1 RA M7/67; Add V2. Memorandum by the Prince of Leiningen, 1841.

2 Charles Greville, *The Greville Memoirs, 1817–1860*, ed. H. Reeve, vol. I:ii, p. 199.

3 Cecil Woodham-Smith, *Queen Victoria, 1819–1861*, p. 70.

4 RA M4/16, the Duchess of Clarence to the Duchess of Kent, 12 January 1830.

5 RA M7/42, Baron Stockmar to the Duchess of Kent.

6 Princess Lieven, *The Unpublished Diary and Political Sketches*, ed. Harold Temperley (London, Cape, 1925), pp. 34–7.

7 *The Letters of Queen Victoria, 1837–1861*, ed. A.C. Benson and Lord Esher, vol. I, p. 40. The Duchess of Clarence to Princess Victoria, May 1821.

8 RA M4/20, the Duchess of Kent to the Duke of Wellington, 27 June 1830.

9 RA M4/21, the Duke of Wellington.

10 Greville, *Memoirs*, vol. I:ii, p. 196.

11 Hansard, 6 July 1830. Vol. I, pp. 500ff.

12 Hansard, 15 November 1830.

13 *Fraser's Magazine*, March 1831.

14 Dormer Creston, *The Youthful Queen Victoria* (London, Macmillan, 1952), p. 150.

15 cf. Woodham-Smith, *Queen Victoria*, p. 85.

16 Greville, *Memoirs*, vol. I:iii, p. 3. 4 July 1833.

17 Ibid.

18 RA MP 115/1, the Duchess of Kent to Lord Melbourne, 11 July 1835.

19 RA MP 115/4, Lord Melbourne to the Duchess of Kent, 3 July 1835.

20 RA MP 115/7, Lord Melbourne to the Duchess of Kent, 8 July 1835.

21 RA MP 115/71, King William IV to Lord Melbourne, 8 July 1836.

22 RA MP 115/73, the Duchess of Kent to Lord Melbourne, 12 July 1836.

23 RA MP 115/75, Lord Melbourne to the Duchess of Kent, 13 July 1836.

24 RA MP 115/9, Lord Melbourne to King William IV, 12 July 1835.

25 RA MP 115/28, King William IV to Lord Melbourne, 12 July 1835.

26 RA MP 115/37, King William IV to Lord Melbourne, 17 July 1835.

27 RA MP 115/41, the Duchess of Kent to Lord Melbourne, 27 July 1835.

28 RA MP 115/47, King William IV to the Duchess of Kent, 28 July 1835.

29 RA M5/78, the Duchess of Kent to Princess Victoria, 30 July 1835.

30 RA MP 115/52, King William IV to Lord Melbourne, 5 August 1835.

31 RA MP 115/56, the Duchess of Kent to Lord Melbourne, 9 August 1835.

32 RA MP 115/58, King William IV to Princess Victoria, 22 August 1835.

33 RA M5/84, the Duchess of Kent to Princess Victoria, 2 September 1835.

34 Greville, *Memoirs* vol. I:iii, p. 315.

35 RA *Queen Victoria's Journal*, 3 September 1835.

36 Ibid., 26 February 1838.

37 Greville, *Memoirs*, vol. I:iii, p. 321.

38 Ibid., p. 371.

39 Ibid., p. 375.

40 Ibid., pp. 375–6.

41 *Letters of Queen Victoria* vol. I, p. 63. King Leopold to Princess Victoria, 17 June 1836.

42 Ibid., p. 83. King Leopold to Princess Victoria, 11 April 1837.

43 RA M7/12, King William IV to Princess Victoria, 18 May 1837.

44 RA *Queen Victoria's Journal*, 19 May 1837.

45 RA M7/15, 28 May 1837.

46 RA M7/13, Memorandum by Baroness Lehzen, undated. Written at Princess Victoria's request.

47 RA MP 115/99.

48 RA MP 116/47, the Duchess of Kent to Lord Melbourne, 28 May 1837.

49 RA *Queen Victoria's Journal*, 24 May 1837.

50 RA LP, Princess Victoria to Princess Feodora, 5 October 1834.

51 RA Y34/11, Princess Feodora to Princess Victoria, 5 November 1834.

52 RA *Queen Victoria's Journal*, 25 July 1834.

53 RA LP, Princess Victoria to Princess Feodora, 15 January 1837.

54 RA LP, Princess Victoria to Princess Feodora, 5 February 1837.

55 *Letters of Queen Victoria*, vol. I, p. 43. King Leopold to Princess Victoria, 22 May 1832.

56 Ibid., p. 45. King Leopold to Princess Victoria, 21 May 1833.

57 Ibid.

58 Ibid., p. 48. King Leopold to Princess Victoria, 18 October 1834.

59 Ibid.

60 Ibid.

61 Ibid., p. 49. Princess Victoria to King Leopold, 22 October 1834.

62 Ibid., p. 50. Princess Victoria to King Leopold, 19 November 1834.

63 Ibid., p. 64. Princess Victoria to King Leopold, 2 September 1836.

64 Ibid., p. 69. Princess Victoria to King Leopold, 21 November 1836.

65 Ibid., p. 74. Princess Victoria to King Leopold, 16 January 1837.

66 Ibid., p. 75. Princess Victoria to King Leopold, 23 January 1837.

67 Ibid., p. 92. Princess Victoria to King Leopold, 16 June 1837.

68 Ibid., p. 66. King Leopold to Princess Victoria, 11 November 1836.

69 Ibid., p. 78. King Leopold to Princess Victoria, 3 February 1837.

70 Ibid., p. 91. King Leopold to Princess Victoria, 15 June 1837.

71 Ibid., p. 75. Princess Victoria to King Leopold, 23 January 1837.

72 Ibid., p. 78. Princess Victoria to King Leopold, 6 February 1837.

73 Lord Esher, ed., *The Girlhood of Queen Victoria* (2 vols, London, John Murray, 1912), vol. I, p. 93.

74 Ibid., p. 121.

75 RA LP, Princess Victoria to Feodora, 27 September 1834.

76 RA LP, Princess Victoria to Prince Leiningen, 27 July 1834.

77 *Watchman*, 4 May 1828.

78 *The Times*, 30 April 1828.

79 *Morning Journal*, 6 May 1829.

80 *Morning Herald*, 12 June 1830.

81 Ibid., 20 April 1833.

82 *Court Journal*, 25 May 1833.

83 *Bell's Weekly Messenger*, 2 June 1833.
84 *Letters of Queen Victoria*, vol. I, p. 60.
85 Robert Rhodes James, *Albert Prince Consort* (London, Hamish Hamilton, 1983), p. 36.
86 *Letters of Queen Victoria*, vol. I, pp. 60–1. King Leopold to Princess Victoria, 13 May 1836.
87 RA Y88/11, Princess Victoria to King Leopold, 17 May 1836.
88 RA LP, Princess Victoria to Louise, 20 May 1836.
89 RA *Queen Victoria's Journal*, 24 May 1836.
90 RA LP, Princess Victoria to King Leopold, 24 May 1836.
91 RA LP, Princess Victoria to Princess Feodora, 31 May 1836.
92 Kurt Jagow, ed., *Letters of the Prince Consort 1831–61* (London, John Murray, 1938), p. 13. Prince Albert to Duchess Marie of Saxe-Coburg and Gotha, 1 June 1836.
93 RA 88/15, Princess Victoria to King Leopold, 7 June 1836.
94 RA *Queen Victoria's Journal*, 13 September 1836.
95 RA MP 115/79, Lord William Russell to the Duchess of Kent, 3 May 1837.
96 RA MP 115/80, the Duchess of Kent to Lord William Russell, 8 May 1837.
97 RA MP 115/81, Sir Herbert Taylor to Lord Melbourne, 11 May 1837.
98 *The Times*, 21 June 1837.
99 *Letters of Queen Victoria*, vol. I, p. 95. Princess Victoria to King Leopold, 19 June 1837.

Chapter 5 Victoria Regina

1 RA *Queen Victoria's Journal*, 20 June 1837.
2 *Letters of Queen Victoria, 1837–1861*, ed. A. C. Benson and Lord Esher, vol. I, p. 93. King Leopold to Princess Victoria, 17 June 1837.
3 RA MP 115/107, 20 June 1837.
4 RA *Queen Victoria's Journal*, 20 June 1837.
5 *Letters of Queen Victoria*, vol. I, p. 93. King Leopold to Princess Victoria, 17 June 1837.
6 Charles Greville, *The Greville Memoirs, 1817–1860*, ed. H. Reeve, vol. I:iii, p. 415.
7 Ibid.
8 Ibid.
9 RA *Queen Victoria's Journal*, 20 June 1837.
10 RA MP 115/111, 30 June 1837.
11 Ibid.
12 Greville, *Memoirs*, vol. I:iii, p. 415.
13 RA LP, Princess Victoria to King Leopold, 19 June 1837.
14 Greville, *Memoirs*, vol. I:iii, p. 416.
15 Ibid.

16 John Wilson Croker, *Correspondence and Diaries*, ed. L. J. Jennings, vol. II, p. 359.

17 Thomas Creevey, *A Selection of the Letters and Papers of Thomas Creevey*, ed. John Gore, p. 664. Mr Creevey to Miss Ord, 20 June 1837.

18 Greville, *Memoirs*, vol. I:iii, p. 417.

19 1 Vict. cap. 77.

20 *Annual Register 1837*, p. 35.

21 *Letters of Queen Victoria*, vol. I, p. 68. Princess Victoria to King Leopold, 21 November 1836.

22 RA Y88/46, Queen Victoria to King Leopold, 20 June 1837.

23 RA LP, Queen Victoria to Princess Feodora, 20 June 1837.

24 Greville, *Memoirs*, vol. I:iii, p. 418.

25 RA *Queen Victoria's Journal*, 20 June 1837.

26 Ibid.

27 Ibid.

28 Ibid.

29 RA *Queen Victoria's Journal*, 4 February 1838.

30 Ibid., 20 June 1837.

31 RA M7/46, the Duchess of Kent of Princess Victoria, 12 June 1837.

32 Ibid.

33 RA M7/50, Queen Victoria to the Duchess of Kent, 14 June 1837.

34 *Letters of Queen Victoria*, vol. I, p. 87. King Leopold to Princess Victoria, 25 May 1837.

35 Ibid.

36 RA M7/44, Prince Leiningen to Princess Victoria, 10 June 1837.

37 RA M7/45, Princess Victoria to Prince Leiningen, 10 June 1837.

38 RA M7/44, Prince Leiningen to Princess Victoria, 10 June 1837.

39 RA Add A11/12, Baron Stockmar to King Leopold, 8 June 1837.

40 RA M7/55, Princess Victoria to Lord Liverpool, 15 June 1837.

41 RA M7/56, Memorandum by Princess Victoria, 15 June 1837.

42 RA MP 116/50, Lord Duncannon to Lord Melbourne, 13 June 1837.

43 RA M7/67, Memorandum by Prince Leiningen.

44 RA M7/60, Memorandum by Queen Victoria, 20 June 1837.

45 RA Z482, John Conroy to the Duchess of Kent, 15 July 1837.

46 Ibid.

47 RA M7/60, Memorandum by Queen Victoria, 20 June 1837.

48 RA document added to Z482, John Conroy to the Duchess of Kent, 5 July 1837.

49 RA MP 116/82, 26 June 1837.

50 RA MP 116/83, Lord Melbourne to John Conroy.

51 Greville, *Memoirs*, vol. II:i, pp. 14–15.

52 RA M7/65, the Duchess of Kent to Queen Victoria, undated.

53 RA Z482/4, the Duchess of Kent to Queen Victoria, 26 July 1837.

54 Ibid.

55 Greville, *Memoirs*, vol. II:i, p. 7.
56 Ibid., p. 16.
57 RA Z482/6, the Duchess of Kent to Queen Victoria, 20 July 1837.
58 RA Z482/12, Queen Victoria to the Duchess of Kent, 17 August 1837.
59 Ibid.
60 RA LP, Queen Victoria to King Leopold, 1 August 1837.
61 RA *Queen Victoria's Journal*, 16 November 1837.
62 Ibid., 15 January 1838.
63 Ibid., 27 February 1838.
64 Ibid.
65 Ibid., 1 March 1838.
66 Creevey, *Letters and Papers*, p. 576. Mr Creevey to Miss Ord, 22 August 1831.
67 Greville, *Memoirs*, vol. II:i, p. 22.
68 RA *Queen Victoria's Journal*, 14 January 1838.
69 Greville, *Memoirs*, vol. I:iii, p. 129. 'This anecdote', Greville added, 'seems to me very plausible.'
70 RA *Queen Victoria's Journal*, 21 September 1838.
71 Elie Halévy, *Histoire du Peuple Anglais au 19ᵉ siècle*. vol. II: *Du Lendemain de Waterloo à l'avènement de Sir Robert Peel, 1815–1841* (Paris, Hachette, 1923), p. 469.
72 *Lord Melbourne's Papers*, ed. Lloyd C. Sanders (London, 1889), p. 257.
73 Bulwer Lytton, *St Stephen's*, a poem (London, 1865).
74 RA *Queen Victoria's Journal*, 1 November 1837.
75 Ibid., 26 February 1838.
76 Ibid., 17 November 1837.
77 Greville, *Memoirs*, vol. II:i, pp. 130–1.
78 RA *Queen Victoria's Journal*, 27 December 1837.
79 Ibid., 20 February 1838.
80 George Thomas Keppel, Comte d'Albemarle, *Fifty Years of my Life*, p. 378.
81 RA *Queen Victoria's Journal*, 17 July 1837.
82 RA LP, Queen Victoria to Princess Feodora, 13 November 1837.
83 RA *Queen Victoria's Journal*, 2 January 1838.

Chapter 6   The First Six Months

1 RA LP, Queen Victoria to Princess Feodora, 23 October 1837.
2 RA LP, Queen Victoria to Princess Feodora, 5 November 1837.
3 6 George IV, c.77.
4 Thomas Creevey, *A Selection of the Letters and Papers of Thomas Creevey*, ed. John Gore, p. 650. Mr Creevey to Miss Ord, 20 May 1835.
5 *Quarterly Review*, June 1826.
6 RA *Queen Victoria's Journal*, 13 July 1837.

7 Ibid.

8 LC 1/46, Department of the Lord Chamberlain.

9 RA LP, Queen Victoria to Princess Feodora, 8 January 1838.

10 RA LP, Queen Victoria to Princess Feodora, 12 May 1838.

11 Mary Frampton, *The Journal of Mary Frampton*, ed. Harriet Georgiana, p. 401. Mary to her mother, 31 May 1838.

12 RA *Queen Victoria's Journal*, 10 May 1838.

13 Charles Greville, *The Greville Memoirs, 1817–1860*, ed. H. Reeve, vol. II:i, p. 91.

14 Frampton, *Journal*, p. 403. Mrs Mundy to her aunt Mary Frampton, 31 May 1838.

15 RA *Queen Victoria's Journal*, 22 August 1837.

16 Ibid., 29 August 1837.

17 RA LP, Queen Victoria to Louise, Queen of the Belgians, 7 October 1837.

18 RA LP, Queen Victoria to King Leopold, 7 October 1837.

19 RA *Queen Victoria's Journal*, 28 September 1837.

20 Ibid.

21 RA LP, Queen Victoria to Princess Feodora, 8 October 1837.

22 RA LP, Queen Victoria to Louise, Queen of the Belgians, 7 October 1837.

23 A letter from Princess Lieven quoted in Dormer Creston, *The Youthful Queen Victoria*, p. 113.

24 House of Lords, 20 December 1837.

25 RA *Queen Victoria's Journal*, 23 December 1837.

26 *Annual Register 1838*, p. 73.

27 RA Z482/39, the Duchess of Kent to Baron Stockmar, 11 November 1837.

28 Ibid.

29 RA *Queen Victoria's Journal*, 20 February 1838.

30 RA Z484/36 Memorandum by Couper, 15 February 1850.

31 Creevey, *Letters and Papers*, p. 677. Mr Creevey to Miss Ord, 27 January 1838.

32 Greville, *Memoirs*, vol. II:i, p. 15.

33 RA LP, Queen Victoria to Princess Feodora, 8 October and 13 November 1837.

34 Vera Watson, *A Queen at Home* (London, W. H. Allen, 1952), p. 18.

35 *The Letters of Queen Victoria, 1837–1861*, ed. A. C. Benson and Lord Esher, vol. I, p. 104. King Leopold to Queen Victoria, 27 June 1837.

36 Greville, *Memoirs*, vol. II:i, p. 16.

37 *Letters of Queen Victoria*, vol. I, p. 104. King Leopold to Queen Victoria, 27 June 1837.

38 RA LP, Queen Victoria to King Leopold, 25 June 1837.

39 RA LP, Queen Victoria to Princess Feodora, 29 June 1837.

40 RA LP, Queen Victoria to King Leopold, 25 June 1837.

41 RA LP, Queen Victoria to Princess Feodora, 2 July 1837.

42 Charles Murray, 'Three weeks at Court: a diary kept at Windsor by the late

Sir Charles Murray', *Cornhill Magazine*, January 1897.
43 *Letters of Queen Victoria*, vol. I, pp. 102–3. Queen Victoria to King Leopold, 25 June 1837.
44 Ibid., p. 105. King Leopold to Queen Victoria, 30 June 1837.
45 Ibid., p. 148. King Leopold to Queen Victoria, 2 June 1838.
46 Ibid., pp. 149–50. Queen Victoria to King Leopold, 10 June 1838.

CHAPTER 7   THE CORONATION

1 RA *Queen Victoria's Journal*, 28 June 1838.
2 Ibid.
3 Christopher Morris, *The Tudors* (London, Fontana, 1955), p. 132.
4 Ibid., p. 118.
5 House of Lords, *Debates*, 28 May 1838.
6 Mary Frampton, *The Journal of Mary Frampton*, ed. Harriet Georgiana, pp. 404–5. Mrs Mundy to Lady Frampton.
7 Charles Greville, *The Greville Memoirs, 1817–1860*, ed. H. Reeve, vol. II:i, p. 105.
8 RA *Queen Victoria's Journal*, 28 June 1838.
9 *The Letters of Queen Victoria, 1837–1861*, ed. A. C. Benson and Lord Esher, vol. I, p. 144. King Leopold to Queen Victoria.
10 Ibid., p. 144. Queen Victoria to King Leopold, 25 April 1838.
11 Greville, *Memoirs*, vol. II:i, p. 105.
12 Ibid., pp. 106–7.
13 Thomas Raikes, *A Portion of the Journal Kept by Thomas Raikes from 1831 to 1847* (4 vols, London, 1856–7), vol. II, p. 107. In French in the book: 'c'est le plus beau jour de ma vie. Il prouve que les Anglais pensent que j'ai toujours fait la guerre en loyal homme . . . Ah vraiment, c'est un brave peuple.'
14 RA *Queen Victoria's Journal*, 28 June 1838.
15 Greville, *Memoirs*, vol. II:i, p. 106.
16 Frampton, *Journal*, p. 407. Mrs Mundy to Lady Frampton, 29 June 1838.
17 *Letters of Queen Victoria*, vol. I, p. 145. Queen Victoria to Lord Melbourne, 5 May 1838.
18 Recollections of Lady Wilhelmina Stanhope, in Marquis of Lorne, *V.R.I. Her Life and Empire*, p. 89.
19 They were the Duke of Grafton, the Earls of Westmorland, Essex, Limerick and Leicester, Lord Dufferin and Lord Rolle.
20 RA *Queen Victoria's Journal*, 28 June 1838.
21 cf. Harriet Martineau, *Autobiography* (3 vols, London, 1877).
22 Greville, *Memoirs*, vol. II:i, p. 107.
23 Stanhope, in Lorne, *V.R.I.*
24 cf. Lady Clementine Davies, *Recollections of Society in France and England* (London, 1872), p. 90.

25 RA *Queen Victoria's Journal*, 28 June 1838.
26 Ibid.
27 Ibid.
28 Ibid.
29 Greville, *Memoirs*, vol. II:i, p. 107.
30 Lord Beaconsfield, *Correspondence with his Sister*, ed. R. Disraeli (London, 1886), p. 139. 29 June 1838.
31 Greville, *Memoirs*, vol. II:i, p. 107.
32 RA *Queen Victoria's Journal*, 28 June 1838.
33 Ibid.
34 Ibid.
35 Stanhope, in Lorne, *V.R.I.*
36 Greville, *Memoirs*, vol. II:i, p. 108.
37 Ibid.
38 RA *Queen Victoria's Journal*, 28 June 1838.
39 Ibid.
40 Ibid.
41 Greville, *Memoirs*, vol. II:i, p. 109.
42 Ibid.

CHAPTER 8   SCANDALS AND POLITICAL CRISES

1 RA *Queen Victoria's Journal*, 28 April 1838.
2 *Morning Post*, 14 September 1839. Written Statement by Lady Flora Hastings, March 1839. This issue of the *Morning Post* published a collection of documents relating to this scandal, see below.
3 Sir James Clark's Statement, *The Times*, 6 October 1839.
4 RA *Queen Victoria's Journal*, 2 February 1839.
5 Cecil Woodham-Smith, *Queen Victoria, 1819–1861*, p. 165.
6 RA MP 115/23, Lady Portman's Statement, 17 March 1839.
7 Conroy Papers, ZC, Balliol College Library, Oxford.
8 Lady Portman's Statement, 17 March 1839.
9 Sir James Clark's Statement.
10 Charles Greville, *The Greville Memoirs, 1817–1860*, ed. H. Reeve, vol. II:i, p. 172.
11 Ibid.
12 Lady Flora Hastings's Statement.
13 Ibid.
14 Sir James Clark's Statement.
15 RA Z486/2, Lady Portman's Statement, 17 February 1839.
16 Lady Flora Hastings's Statement.
17 RA Z486/1, Certificate of Dr Clarke and Dr Clark, 17 February 1839.
18 Lady Flora Hastings's Statement.

19 Ibid.

20 RA *Queen Victoria's Journal*, 23 February 1839.

21 Lady Flora Hastings's Statement.

22 Woodham-Smith, *Queen Victoria*, p. 168.

23 *Morning Post*, 14 September 1839, Letter from Lady Flora Hastings to her uncle Mr Hamilton Fitzgerald, 8 March 1839.

24 Ibid. Lord Hastings to Lord Melbourne.

25 Ibid.

26 Ibid.

27 Ibid. Lord Hastings to Lord Tavistock, 1 March 1839.

28 Ibid. Lord Hastings to Lord Portman, 1 March 1839.

29 Greville, *Memoirs*, vol. II:i, p. 172.

30 Lady Flora Hastings's Statement.

31 RA MP 115/123, Lady Hastings to Queen Victoria.

32 *Morning Post*, 14 September 1839. Lord Melbourne to Lady Hastings, 7 March 1839.

33 Ibid. Correspondence between Lady Hastings and Lord Melbourne.

34 RA *Queen Victoria's Journal*, 16 April 1839.

35 Greville, *Memoirs*, vol. II:i, p. 177.

36 *The Holland House Diaries, 1831–1840*, ed. Abraham D. Kriegel (London, Routledge and Kegan Paul, 1977), p. 395.

37 RA *Queen Victoria's Journal*, 16 June 1839.

38 Ibid., 27 June 1839.

39 Ibid., 1 July 1839.

40 Greville, *Memoirs*, vol. II:i, p. 172.

41 RA MP 115/141, Mr Doyle to Lord Melbourne, 29 April 1839.

42 *Morning Post*, 22 July 1839.

43 Ibid., 14 September 1839.

44 Conroy Papers, ZC, *The Dangers of Evil Counsel*, by a Voice from the Grave of Lady Flora Hastings to her most Gracious Majesty the Queen, 1839.

45 Ibid., *Warning Letter to Baroness Lehzen*, by a Voice from the Grave, 1839.

46 Ibid., *The Palace Martyr!*, by the Honourable **, 1839.

47 *The Letters of Queen Victoria, 1837–1861*, ed. A. C. Benson and Lord Esher, vol. I, p. 194. Lord Melbourne to Queen Victoria, 7 May 1839.

48 RA *Queen Victoria's Journal*, 7 May 1839.

49 Ibid.

50 *Letters of Queen Victoria*, vol. I, p. 195.

51 Ibid.

52 RA *Queen Victoria's Journal*, 7 May 1839.

53 *Letters of Queen Victoria*, vol. I, p. 198. Lord Melbourne to Queen Victoria, 8 May 1839.

54 RA *Queen Victoria's Journal*, 8 May 1839.

55 Lord Esher, ed., *The Girlhood of Queen Victoria*, vol. II, p. 163n.

56 *Letters of Queen Victoria*, vol. I, p. 198. Queen Victoria to Lord Melbourne, 8 May 1839.

57 Ibid., pp. 198–9.

58 Ibid., p. 199.

59 Ibid., p. 200.

60 Ibid.

61 Ibid.

62 Robert Rhodes James, *Albert Prince Consort*, p. 73.

63 Cf. William Flavelle Monypenny, *The Life of Benjamin Disraeli* (6 vols, London, John Murray, 1912), vol. II, pp. 305; 312ff.; 350; 358ff.; 382.

64 *Letters of Queen Victoria*, vol. I, p. 200. Queen Victoria to Lord Melbourne, 8 May 1839.

65 Ibid.

66 Ibid., p. 202. Lord Melbourne to Queen Victoria, 9 May 1839.

67 Ibid. Melbourne was alluding to the unsuccessful attempts of Soult, Thiers and Broglie in France.

68 Ibid.

69 Esher, *Girlhood of Queen Victoria*, vol. II, p. 168. Note to Lord Melbourne, 9 May 1839.

70 Ibid., pp. 168–9.

71 Greville, *Memoirs*, vol. II:i, pp. 165–6.

72 RA *Queen Victoria's Journal*, 9 May 1839.

73 Esher, *Girlhood of Queen Victoria*, vol. II, pp. 169–70.

74 RA *Queen Victoria's Journal*, 9 May 1839.

75 Esher, *Girlhood of Queen Victoria*, vol. II, pp. 173–5.

76 Greville, *Memoirs*, vol. II:i, pp. 209–10. 12 May 1839.

77 *Holland House Diaries*, p. 400.

78 *Letters of Queen Victoria*, vol. I, pp. 219–20. Queen Victoria to King Leopold, 14 May 1839.

79 *Diary of Royal Movements*, by a London Correspondent, p. 117.

CHAPTER 9   COURTSHIP

1 RA *Queen Victoria's Journal*, 24 May 1839.

2 Ibid., 27 May 1839.

3 Ibid.

4 Ibid.

5 Ibid., 29 May 1839.

6 Ibid.

7 Ibid., 3 June 1839.

8 Ibid., 29 May 1839.

9 Ibid., 10 June 1839.

10 Ibid., 17 June 1839.

11 RA LP, Queen Victoria to King Leopold, 24 January 1838.

12 RA *Queen Victoria's Journal*, 18 April 1839.

13 Ibid.

14 Ibid., 17 April 1839.

15 Ibid., 12 July 1839.

16 Ibid.

17 RA Y89/41, Queen Victoria to King Leopold, 15 July 1839.

18 Ibid.

19 RA *Queen Victoria's Journal*, 13 September 1839.

20 Ibid., 14 September 1839.

21 Ibid., 15 September 1839.

22 Ibid., 23 September 1839.

23 Ibid., 30 September 1839.

24 *The Letters of Queen Victoria, 1837–1861*, ed. A. C. Benson and Lord Esher, vol. I, p. 235. Queen Victoria to King Leopold, 1 October 1839.

25 Max W.L. Voss, *England als Erziehe*, translated in Hector Bolitho, *Albert the Good, and the Victorian Reign* (New York, D. Appleton, 1932), pp. 21–2.

26 Lytton Giles Strachey, *Queen Victoria* (London, Chatto and Windus, 1921), p. 78.

27 Bolitho, *Albert the Good*, p. 22.

28 Kurt Jagow, *Letters of the Prince Consort 1831–61*, p. 4.

29 Robert Rhodes James, *Albert Prince Consort*, p. 21.

30 cf. Pauline Panam, *Memoirs of a Young Greek Lady or Mme Pauline Adelaïde Alexandre Panam, versus the Reigning Prince of Saxe-Coburg*, ed. V.E.P. Chasles (London, 1823).

31 Theodore Martin, *The Life of H.R.H. The Prince Consort* (5 vols, London, Smith, Elder, 1877), vol. I, p. 2.

32 Ibid., p. 3. The Dowager Duchess of Coburg, 11 August 1821.

33 Lieut-General the Hon C. Grey, *The Early Years of H.R.H. The Prince Consort*, p. 32.

34 Martin, *Life of the Prince Consort*, vol. I, p. 3.

35 Ibid., p. 5.

36 Grey, *Early Years*, p. 75.

37 Martin, *Life of the Prince Consort*, vol. I, p. 5.

38 David Duff, *Albert and Victoria* (London, Frederick Muller, 1972), p. 60.

39 Grey, *Early Years*, p. 8.

40 Ibid., p. 34. Extract from the Prince's diary, 28 February 1825.

41 Ibid., 26 March 1825.

42 Ibid., 23 January 1825.

43 Grey, *Early Years*, p. 81.

44 RA Z276/6, Memorandum by Florschütz, undated.

45 Ibid.

46 Grey, *Early Years*, p. 57.

47 Ibid., p. 82.

48 RA Z276/6, Memorandum by Florschütz, undated.

49 Ibid.

50 Rhodes James, *Albert Prince Consort*, p. 30.

51 *Dearest Mama – Private Correspondence of Queen Victoria and the Crown Princess of Prussia, 1861–1864,* ed. Roger Fulford (London, Evans, 1968), pp. 24–6. Vicky to the Queen, 21 December 1861.

52 Baron Stockmar, *Memoirs of Baron Stockmar,* ed. Baron E. von Stockmar, vol. I, pp. 365–7. Baron Stockmar to King Leopold.

53 Ibid.

54 Ibid.

55 Roger Fulford, *The Prince Consort* (London, Macmillan, 1966), p. 31.

56 Stockmar, *Memoirs,* vol. II, p. 2.

57 RA LP, Queen Victoria to King Leopold, 24 January 1838.

58 Stockmar, *Memoirs,* vol. II, p. 2. King Leopold to Baron Stockmar, March 1838.

59 Jagow, *Letters of the Prince Consort,* p. 14. Prince Albert to Queen Victoria, 26 June 1837.

60 Rhodes James, *Albert Prince Consort,* p. 52.

61 RA LP, Queen Victoria to Prince Albert, 30 June 1837.

62 RA LP, Queen Victoria to Prince Albert, March 1837.

63 RA LP, Queen Victoria to Prince Albert, 14 August 1837.

64 Rhodes James, *Albert Prince Consort,* p. 93.

65 RA LP, Queen Victoria to Prince Albert, 3 December 1837.

66 RA LP, Queen Victoria to Prince Albert, 26 May 1837.

67 RA LP, Queen Victoria to Prince Albert, 25 August 1837.

68 Hector Bolitho, *The Reign of Queen Victoria* (London, Collins, 1949), p. 52.

69 RA LP, Queen Victoria to Prince Albert, 14 August 1838.

70 Stockmar, *Memoirs,* vol. II, p. 2. King Leopold to Baron Stockmar.

71 RA LP, Queen Victoria to Prince Albert, 15 May 1839.

72 Grey, *Early Years,* p. 184.

73 Martin, *Life of the Prince Consort,* vol. I, p. 29.

74 Ibid., p. 30.

75 Grey, *Early Years,* p. 200.

76 Stockmar, *Memoirs,* vol. II:i, p. 6.

77 Martin, *Life of the Prince Consort,* vol. I, p. 32.

78 Stockmar, *Memoirs,* vol. II, p. 7.

79 Ibid.

80 Théodore Juste, *Le Baron Stockmar* (Brussels, Muquardt, 1873). 14 December 1861.

81 Stockmar, *Memoirs,* vol. II, p. 6.

82 Ibid., p. 7.

83 RA LP, Queen Victoria to Prince Albert, 15 May 1839.

84 RA LP, Queen Victoria to Prince Albert, 10 June 1839.

85 Bolitho, *Reign,* p. 53.

86 RA Z272/7, 16 March 1863.

87 RA *Queen Victoria's Journal,* 10 October 1839.

88 Ibid.

89 Ibid.
90 Ibid. 11 October 1839.
91 Ibid.
92 Ibid., 12 October 1839.
93 Ibid., 13 October 1839.
94 Ibid., 14 October 1839.
95 Ibid.
96 Ibid., 15 October 1839.
97 Grey, *Early Years*, p. 226. Prince Albert to Baron Stockmar, 16 October 1839.
98 *Letters of Queen Victoria*, vol. I, p. 237. Queen Victoria to King Leopold, 12 October 1839.
99 Ibid., p. 238. Queen Victoria to King Leopold, 15 October 1839.
100 Martin, *Life of the Prince Consort*, vol. I, p. 40. Queen Victoria to Baron Stockmar, 15 October 1839.
101 Grey, *Early Years*, p. 226. Prince Albert to Baron Stockmar, 16 October 1839.
102 Ibid.
103 Rhodes James, *Albert Prince Consort*, p. 83.

CHAPTER 10   THE ROYAL WEDDING

1 C. Grey, *The Early Years of H.R.H. the Prince Consort*, p. 161. King Leopold to Queen Victoria, 24 October 1839.
2 Ibid.
3 RA Y89/52, Queen Victoria to King Leopold, 15 October 1839.
4 RA *Queen Victoria's Journal*, 17 October 1839 and 16 November 1839.
5 *The Letters of Queen Victoria, 1837–1861*, ed. A. C. Benson and Lord Esher, vol. I, p. 239. Lord Melbourne to Queen Victoria, 16 October 1839.
6 RA Y89/52, Queen Victoria to King Leopold, 15 October 1839.
7 RA *Queen Victoria's Journal*, 19 and 27 October 1839.
8 Ibid., 22 October 1839.
9 Ibid., 1 November 1839.
10 Ibid., 14 November 1839.
11 Kurt Jagow, ed., *Letters of the Prince Consort 1831–61*, p. 26. Prince Albert to Queen Victoria, 15 November 1839.
12 cf. Lytton Strachey, *Queen Victoria*.
13 Jagow, *Letters of the Prince Consort*, p. 27. Prince Albert to Queen Victoria, 17 November 1839.
14 Ibid., p. 28. Prince Albert to Queen Victoria, 21 November 1839.
15 Ibid., p. 30. Prince Albert to Queen Victoria, 30 November 1839.
16 Ibid., p. 31. Prince Albert to Queen Victoria, 1 December 1839.
17 *Letters of Queen Victoria*, vol. I. p. 245. Queen Victoria to the Duke of Sussex, 14 November 1839.

18 RA LP, Queen Victoria to Feodora, 10 November 1839.

19 Charles Greville, *The Greville Memoirs, 1817–1860*, ed. H. Reeve, vol. II:i, p. 247.

20 Ibid.; *Letters of Queen Victoria*, vol. I, p. 248. Queen Victoria to Prince Albert, 23 November 1839; *Letters of Queen Victoria*, vol. I, p. 250. Queen Victoria to King Leopold, 26 November 1839.

21 John Wilson Croker, *Correspondence and Diaries*, ed. L. J. Jennings, vol. II, p. 359.

22 *Letters of Queen Victoria*, vol. I, p. 248. Queen Victoria to Prince Albert, 23 November 1839.

23 Greville, *Memoirs*, vol. II:i, p. 247.

24 RA *Queen Victoria's Journal*, 23 November 1839.

25 Croker, *Correspondence and Diaries*, vol. II, p. 359.

26 Ibid.

27 Ibid.

28 Greville, *Memoirs*, vol. II:i, p. 247.

29 Ibid., p. 253.

30 Ibid., pp. 253–4.

31 Baron Stockmar, *Memoirs of Baron Stockmar*, ed. Baron E. von Stockmar, vol. II, p. 22.

32 Ibid.

33 *The Times*, 10 February 1840.

34 David Duff, *Albert and Victoria*, p. 155.

35 *Letters of Queen Victoria*, vol. I, p. 251. Lord Melbourne to Queen Victoria, 27 November 1839.

36 The movement culminated in 1841 with the publication by Newman of the Tract no. 90.

37 Jagow, *Letters of the Prince Consort*, p. 34. Prince Albert to Queen Victoria, 7 December 1839.

38 *Letters of Queen Victoria*, vol. I, p. 252. Queen Victoria to Prince Albert, 27 November 1839.

39 Theodore Martin, *The Life of H.R.H. The Prince Consort*, vol. I, p. 58.

40 Greville, *Memoirs*, vol. II:i, p. 253.

41 RA Y89/60, Queen Victoria to King Leopold, 9 December 1839.

42 Jagow, *Letters of the Prince Consort*, p. 36. Prince Albert to Queen Victoria, 10 December 1839.

43 *Lord Melbourne's Papers*, ed. Lloyd C. Sanders, p. 494.

44 Greville, *Memoirs*, vol. II:i, p. 266.

45 Ibid., p. 263.

46 Ibid., p. 266.

47 Ibid., p. 263.

48 cf. Appendix in Greville, *Memoirs*, vol. II:i, pp. 396–406.

49 Martin, *Life of the Prince Consort*, vol. I, p. 62. Memorandum by the Queen, May 1856.

50 Greville, *Memoirs*, vol. II:i, p. 258.

51 Keith Henry Randell, *Politics and the People 1835–50* (London, Collins, 1972), p. 23.

52 Lord Malmesbury, *Memoirs of an Ex-Minister* (2 vols, London, Longmans, Green, 1884), p. 80.

53 Greville, *Memoirs*, vol. II:i, p. 250.

54 Stockmar, *Memoirs*, vol. I, p. 346.

55 Greville, *Memoirs*, vol. II:i, p. 258.

56 Ibid.

57 *Letters of Queen Victoria*, vol. I, p. 270. King Leopold to Queen Victoria, 31 January 1840.

58 Ibid.

59 Martin, *Life of the Prince Consort*, vol. I, p. 60.

60 Jagow, *Letters of the Prince Consort*, p. 58. Prince Albert to Queen Victoria, 4 February 1840.

61 *Letters of Queen Victoria*, vol. I, p. 248. Queen Victoria to Prince Albert, 21 November 1839.

62 Ibid., p. 250. King Leopold to Queen Victoria, 22 November 1839.

63 Ibid., p. 251. Queen Victoria to King Leopold, 26 November 1839.

64 Ibid., p. 252. Queen Victoria to Prince Albert, 27 November 1839.

65 Jagow, *Letters of the Prince Consort*, p. 28. Prince Albert to Queen Victoria.

66 RA MP 117/6, King Leopold to Lord Melbourne, 27 November 1839.

67 RA MP 117/12, Lord Melbourne to King Leopold, 8 December 1839.

68 Jagow, *Letters of the Prince Consort*, p. 37. Prince Albert to Queen Victoria, 10 December 1839.

69 Ibid., p. 25. Prince Albert to Duchess Caroline of Saxe-Gotha-Altenburg, 11 November 1839.

70 *Letters of Queen Victoria*, vol. I, p. 253. Queen Victoria to Prince Albert, 29 November 1839.

71 Jagow, *Letters of the Prince Consort*, p. 37. Prince Albert to Queen Victoria, 10 December 1839.

72 *Letters of Queen Victoria*, vol. I, p. 254. Queen Victoria to Prince Albert, 8 December 1839.

73 Jagow, *Letters of the Prince Consort*, p. 41. Prince Albert to Queen Victoria, 18 December 1839.

74 *Letters of Queen Victoria*, vol. I, p. 261. Queen Victoria to Prince Albert, 23 November 1839.

75 Ibid.

76 *Letters of Queen Victoria*, vol. I, p. 262. Queen Victoria to Prince Albert, 26 December 1839.

77 Ibid. Queen Victoria to King Leopold, 27 December 1839.

78 Ibid., p. 257. Queen Victoria to Prince Albert, 11 November 1839.

79 Jagow, *Letters of the Prince Consort*, p. 55. Prince Albert to Queen Victoria.

80 *Letters of Queen Victoria*, vol. I, p. 269. Queen Victoria to Prince Albert, 31 January 1840.

81 Grey, *Early Years*, p. 297.
82 Ibid.
83 Jagow, *Letters of the Prince Consort*, p. 45. Prince Albert to the Duchess of Kent, 6 December 1839.
84 Ibid., p. 60. Prince Albert to Queen Victoria, 7 February 1840.
85 RA *Queen Victoria's Journal*, 8 February 1840.
86 Ibid., 9 February 1840.
87 *Letters of Queen Victoria*, vol. I, p. 217.
88 Jagow, *Letters of the Prince Consort*, p. 61. Prince Albert to Duchess Caroline of Saxe-Gotha-Altenburg, 10 February 1840.
89 Greville, *Memoirs*, vol. II:i, p. 267.
90 RA *Queen Victoria's Journal*, 1 February 1840.
91 Ibid., 5 December 1839.
92 *The Times*, 11 February 1840.
93 Malmesbury, *Memoirs*, p. 83.
94 Lady Wilhelmina Stanhope, in Marquis of Lorne, *V.R.I. Her Life and Empire*, p. 120.
95 Lady Lyttelton, *The Correspondence of Sarah Spencer Lady Lyttelton, 1787–1870*, ed. The Hon. Mrs Hugh Wyndham (London, John Murray, 1912), p. 297.
96 Stanhope, in Lorne, *V.R.I.*, p. 120.
97 Ibid.
98 RA *Queen Victoria's Journal*, 10 February 1840.
99 Stanhope, in Lorne, *V.R.I.*, p. 120.
100 Ibid.
101 Ibid.
102 *The Times*, 11 February 1840.
103 Ibid.
104 Stanhope, in Lorne, *V.R.I.*, p. 122.
105 RA *Queen Victoria's Journal*, 10 February 1840.
106 Greville, *Memoirs*, vol. II:i, p. 267.
107 RA *Queen Victoria's Journal*, 10 February 1840.
108 *The Times*, 11 February 1840.
109 RA *Queen Victoria's Journal*, 10 February 1840.

CHAPTER 11   CONFLICTS OF ROLES

1 RA *Queen Victoria's Journal*, 11 February 1840.
2 Princess Lieven, *Une Vie d'ambassadrice au siècle dernier*, (London, Ernest Daudet, 1903), p. 285.
3 Charles Kirkpatrick Sharpe, *Letters from and to E. K. Sharpe*, ed. A. Allardyce (Edinburgh, 1888), p. 524.
4 Hector Bolitho, *Albert the Good, and the Victorian Reign*, p. 164.
5 Robert Rhodes James, *Albert Prince Consort*, p. 82.

6 C. Grey, *The Early Years of H.R.H. the Prince Consort*, p. 319.
7 Edward Boykin, ed., *Victoria, Albert and Mrs Stevenson*, (London, Frederick Muller, 1957), pp. 252–3.
8 Bolitho, *Albert the Good*, p. 86.
9 RA Y54/8, Memorandum by Anson, 15 August 1840.
10 Ibid.
11 RA Y54/4, Memorandum by Anson, 28 May 1840.
12 Ibid.
13 Ibid.
14 cf. Grey, *Early Years*, p. 319.
15 Theodore Martin, *The Life of H.R.H. The Prince Consort*, vol. II, p. 260. Prince Albert to the Duke of Wellington, 6 April 1850.
16 RA LP, Queen Victoria to Marie of Würtemberg, 4 June 1840.
17 RA LP, Queen Victoria to King Leopold, 26 June 1840.
18 RA LP, Queen Victoria to Maria II, Queen of Portugal, 26 June 1840 – written in French.
19 *Dearest Child – Private Correspondence of Queen Victoria and the Crown Princess of Prussia. 1858–1861*, ed. Roger Fulford (London, Evans, 1964), p. 78. Queen Victoria to Vicky, 24 March 1858.
20 RA LP, Queen Victoria to King Leopold, 15 June 1840.
21 Ibid.
22 Baron Stockmar, *Memoirs of Baron Stockmar*, ed. Baron E. von Stockmar, vol. I, p. 38. 18 June 1840.
23 Ibid., p. 41. 28 June 1840.
24 Ibid. 29 June 1840.
25 Daughter of Arthur, second Earl of Arran, and widow of George Buggin.
26 Grey, *Early Years*, p. 352.
27 Hector Bolitho, ed., *The Prince Consort and his Brother* (London, Cobden-Sanderson, 1933), p. 21. Prince Albert to his brother, 17 July 1840.
28 Martin, *Life of the Prince Consort*, vol. I, p. 90. Baron Stockmar to Prince Albert, 4 August 1840.
29 Ibid., pp. 90–1. Baron Stockmar to Prince Albert, 2 September 1840.
30 Bolitho, *Prince Consort and his Brother*, p. 30. Prince Albert to his brother, undated (September 1840).
31 Ibid.
32 Ibid., p. 22. 1 August 1840.
33 Charles Greville, *The Greville Memoirs, 1817–1860*, ed. H. Reeve, vol. II:i, p. 246.
34 Ibid., p. 110.
35 Lady Lyttelton, *The Correspondence of Sarah Spencer Lady Lyttelton, 1787–1870*, ed. The Hon. Mrs Hugh Wyndham, p. 279.
36 RA Y54/12, Memorandum by Anson, 2 January 1841.
37 RA Y54/59.
38 Boykin, *Victoria Albert and Mrs Stevenson*, p. 251.

39 *The Letters of Queen Victoria, 1837–1861*, ed. A. C. Benson and Lord Esher, vol. I, p. 283. Memorandum by Anson, Minutes of Conversation with Lord Melbourne and Baron Stockmar 28 May 1840.

40 RA Y54/16, Memorandum by Anson, 17 February 1841.

41 RA LP, Queen Victoria to Feodora, 10 November 1840.

42 RA *Queen Victoria's Journal*, 21 November 1840.

43 RA LP, Queen Victoria to Feodora, 14 December 1840.

44 Boykin, *Victoria, Albert and Mrs Stevenson*, p. 276.

45 RA LP, Queen Victoria to Ferdinand, 25 December 1840, in French.

46 RA LP, Queen Victoria to Feodora, 14 December 1840.

47 RA Y90/11, Queen Victoria to King Leopold, 5 January 1841.

48 Martin, *Life of the Prince Consort*, vol. I, p. 97. Baron Stockmar to Prince Albert, 1 October 1840.

49 Ibid., p. 98. Baron Stockmar to Prince Albert, 21 November 1840.

50 Grey, *Early Years*, p. 246. Memorandum by the Queen.

51 Bolitho, *Prince Consort and his Brother*, p. 33. The Duchess of Kent to Ernest, Albert's postscript, 12 November 1840.

52 Greville, *Memoirs*, vol. II:ii, p. 52.

53 Bolitho, *The Prince Consort and his Brother*, p. 34. Prince Albert to his brother, 24 November 1840.

54 RA *Queen Victoria's Journal*, 24 January 1842.

55 Kurt Jagow, ed., *Letters of the Prince Consort 1831–61*, p. 72. Prince Albert to Duchess Caroline.

56 Ibid.

57 Hector Bolitho, *The Reign of Queen Victoria*, p. 74.

58 Martin, *Life of the Prince Consort*, vol. I, p. 108.

59 Ibid., p. 107.

60 RA Y54/16, Memorandum by Anson, 17 February 1841.

61 RA Y54/17, Memorandum by Anson, 19 February 1841.

62 Elizabeth Longford, *Victoria R. I.*, p. 156.

63 RA M12/35, Memorandum by the Queen, 10 May 1841.

64 Ibid.

65 *Letters of Queen Victoria*, vol. I, p. 385. Memorandum by Lord Melbourne to Queen Victoria, 30 August 1841.

66 RA Y54/47, Memorandum by Anson, 11 June 1841.

67 RA C21/53, the Duke to the Duchess of Bedford, 11 June 1841.

68 RA Y54/55, Memorandum by Anson, 14 July 1841.

69 Martin, *Life of the Prince Consort*, vol. I, p. 113. Prince Albert to the Duchess of Kent, 18 June 1841.

70 RA Y54/3, Memorandum by Prince Albert, 15 April 1840.

71 The *Annual Register* for the first time applies the term Liberals to the Whigs during the 1841 elections.

72 RA *Queen Victoria's Journal*, 9 May 1841.

73 RA LP, Queen Victoria to King Leopold, 8 September 1841.

74 Ibid.
75 RA *Queen Victoria's Journal*, 28 August 1841.
76 RA LP, Lord Melbourne to Queen Victoria.
77 Greville, *Memoirs*, vol. II:ii, p. 39.
78 Ibid., pp. 36–7.
79 Ibid.
80 RA MP 117/102, Anson to Lord Melbourne, 3 September 1841.
81 Greville, *Memoirs*, vol. II:ii, p. 40.
82 RA Y54/86, Memorandum by Baron Stockmar, 5 October 1841.
83 RA Y54/85, Memorandum by Anson, 6 October 1841.
84 Lytton Strachey, *Queen Victoria*, pp. 105–6.
85 *Letters of Queen Victoria*, vol. I, pp. 442–3. Memorandum by Baron Stockmar, 25 October 1841.
86 Ibid.
87 Ibid., p. 451. Lord Melbourne to Queen Victoria, 7 November 1841.
88 RA Y54/100, Memorandum by Anson, 26 December 1841.
89 *Letters of Queen Victoria*, vol. I, p. 451. Lord Melbourne to Queen Victoria, 7 November 1841.
90 Ibid., p. 445. Lord Melbourne to Queen Victoria, 26 October 1841.
91 RA MP 117/98, Baron Stockmar to Lord Melbourne, 23 November 1841.
92 RA *Queen Victoria's Journal*, 2 December 1841.
93 *Diary of Royal Movements*, by a London Correspondent, p. 152.
94 RA Y54/100, Memorandum by Anson, 26 December 1841.
95 RA MP 117/98, Baron Stockmar to Lord Melbourne, 23 November 1841.
96 RA Y54/100, Memorandum by Anson, 26 December 1841.

CHAPTER 12   ALBERT'S SEARCH FOR POWER

1 *The Letters of Queen Victoria*, 1837–1861, ed. A. C. Benson and Lord Esher, vol. I, pp. 456–7. Queen Victoria to King Leopold, 29 November 1841.
2 RA Y54/87, Memorandum by Anson, 8 October 1841.
3 RA Add U2/2, Prince Albert to Baron Stockmar, 16 January 1842.
4 Ibid.
5 RA Y54/16, Memorandum by Anson, 17 February 1841.
6 RA Add U2/2, Prince Albert to Baron Stockmar, 15 January 1842.
7 RA *Queen Victoria's Journal*, 15 January 1842.
8 Betty Askwith, *The Lytteltons* (London, Chatto and Windus, 1975), p. 70.
9 RA Add U2/4, Prince Albert to Baron Stockmar, 18 January 1842.
10 Ibid.
11 RA Add U2/4, Prince Albert to Baron Stockmar, 18 January 1842.
12 RA Add U2/1, Queen Victoria to Baron Stockmar, 16 January 1842.
13 RA Add U2/5, Queen Victoria to Baron Stockmar, 19 January 1842.
14 RA Add U2/6, Baron Stockmar to Queen Victoria, 19 January 1842.

15 RA Add U2/7, Queen Victoria to Baron Stockmar, 19 January 1842.
16 RA Add U2/8, Queen Victoria to Baron Stockmar, 20 January 1842.
17 Ibid.
18 RA *Queen Victoria's Journal*, 25 July 1842.
19 Ibid.
20 Ibid., 24 September 1842.
21 Lady Lyttelton, *The Correspondence of Sarah Spencer Lady Lyttelton, 1787–1870*, ed. The Hon. Mrs Hugh Wyndham, p. 331. October 1842.
22 Sidney Lee, *Queen Victoria* (London, John Murray, 1904), p. 123.
23 Elizabeth Longford, *Victoria R. I.*, p. 163.
24 RA 169/57, Queen Victoria to Mr Martin, November 1893. Cf. also RA 169/59 and 169/60.
25 Theodore Martin, *The Life of H.R.H. The Prince Consort*, vol. I, p. 297.
26 RA A4/172.
27 RA A4/174–7.
28 *Letters of Queen Victoria* vol. II, p. 242.
29 Martin, *Life of the Prince Consort*, vol. II, p. 260. Prince Albert to the Duke of Wellington, 6 April 1850.
30 Ibid.
31 RA *Queen Victoria's Journal*, 1 October 1842.
32 Ibid., 17 December 1842.
33 Ibid.
34 Y167/16, Queen Victoria to Sir Theodore Martin, 18 February 1869.
35 RA *Queen Victoria's Journal*, 28 February 1840.
36 RA M12/14, Memorandum by Baron Stockmar, February 1842.
37 Ibid.
38 Askwith, *Lytteltons*, p. 64.
39 RA M12/13, 16 February 1842.
40 RA *Queen Victoria's Journal*, 6 April 1842.
41 Ibid.
42 Ibid., 3 June 1842.
43 Ibid., 12 June 1842.
44 Baron Stockmar, *Memoirs of Baron Stockmar*, ed. Baron E. von Stockmar, vol. II, pp. 118–26.
45 Ibid., p. 119.
46 Ibid., p. 121.
47 Ibid., p. 124.
48 Vera Watson, *A Queen at Home*, p. 66.
49 Martin, *Life of the Prince Consort*, vol. I, p. 139. Prince Albert to Sir Robert Peel, 2 November 1841.
50 Kurt Jagow, ed., *Letters of the Prince Consort 1831–61*, p. 82. Prince Albert to Baron Stockmar, 27 December 1842.
51 Hector Bolitho, ed., *The Prince Consort and his Brother*, p. 19. Prince Albert to his brother, 12 June 1840.

52 Charles Greville, *The Greville Memoirs, 1817–1860*, ed. H. Reeve, vol. I:iii, p. 288.

53 Jagow, *Letters of the Prince Consort*, pp. 76–8. Prince Albert to Duke Ernest I of Saxe-Coburg and Gotha, 1 June 1842.

54 Colonel Arbuthnot's Statement, 29 May 1842.

55 Frances, Baroness Bunsen, ed., *Memoirs of Baron Bunsen* (2 vols, London, Longman, 1868), vol. II, p. 16.

56 RA *Queen Victoria's Journal*, 31 May 1842.

57 Ibid., 1 July 1842.

58 Ibid.

59 Ibid., 3 July 1842.

60 Ibid.

61 David Duff, *Albert and Victoria*, p. 214.

62 Ibid.

63 Bolitho, *Prince Consort and his Brother*. Prince Albert to his brother, December 1840.

64 Stockmar, *Memoirs*, vol. II, p. 100.

65 C. Grey, *The Early Years of H. R. H. The Prince Consort*, p. 353.

66 Lyttelton, *Correspondence*, p. 328. 7 May 1842.

67 Grey, *Early Years*, p. 354.

68 *Letters of Queen Victoria* vol. I, p. 257. Queen Victoria to Prince Albert, 11 December 1839.

69 Grey, *Early Years*, p. 331.

70 MP 117/127, 7 August 1841.

71 RA *Queen Victoria's Journal*, 25 January 1842.

72 Hardy, p. 48.

73 Ibid.

74 RA *Queen Victoria's Journal*, 15 April 1845.

75 Ibid., 21 April 1843; Greville, *Memoirs*, vol. II:ii, p. 156.

76 Marquis of Lorne, *V.R.I. Her Life and Empire*, pp. 140–2; quotation of a letter of Felix Mendelssohn-Bartholdy to his mother.

77 Cf. Virginia Surtees, *Charlotte Canning: Lady-in-Waiting to Queen Victoria and Wife of the First Viceroy of India, 1817–1861* (London, John Murray, 1975).

78 Lyttelton, *Correspondence*.

79 RA *Queen Victoria's Journal*, 17 February 1843.

80 James Edwin Thorold Rogers, *Cobden and his Modern Political Opinion: Essays* (London, 1841), p. 20.

81 Greville, *Memoirs*, vol. II:ii. 2 November 1842.

82 *Letters of Queen Victoria*, vol. I, p. 497. King Leopold to Queen Victoria, 20 May 1842.

83 RA *Queen Victoria's Journal*, 16 March 1842.

84 Ibid.

85 Bolitho, *Prince Consort and his Brother*, p. 69. 4 February 1844.

86 Ibid.

87 *Letters of Queen Victoria* vol. I, p. 460. Queen Victoria to King Leopold, 7 December 1841.

88 Bolitho, *Prince Consort and his Brother*, p. 25. 22 August 1840.

89 Ibid., pp. 25–6.

90 RA *Queen Victoria's Journal*, 17 March 1843.

91 Ibid.

CHAPTER 13 ROYAL TRAVELS

1 RA *Queen Victoria's Journal*, 30 August 1842.

2 Ibid., 31 August 1842.

3 Ibid.

4 Ibid., 1 September 1842.

5 Ibid.

6 Vera Watson, *A Queen at Home*, p. 72.

7 RA *Queen Victoria's Journal*, 4–5 September 1842.

8 Watson, *Queen at Home*, pp. 75–6. Lord Provost of Perth to Sir Williams, 1 September 1842.

9 RA *Queen Victoria's Journal*, 6 September 1842.

10 Ibid., 6–9 September 1842.

11 Ibid., 2 September 1842.

12 Ibid., 9 September 1842.

13 Ibid., 2 September 1842.

14 Ibid., 12 September 1842.

15 Ibid.

16 *The Letters of Queen Victoria, 1837–1861*, ed. A. C. Benson and Lord Esher, vol. I, p. 286. King Leopold to Queen Victoria, 26 July 1840.

17 Evelyn Ashley, ed., *Life of Lord Palmerston*, (London, Richard Bentley, 1871), vol. II, p. 293.

18 *Letters of Queen Victoria*, vol. I, p. 306. Queen Victoria to King Leopold, 16 October 1840.

19 Theodore Martin, *The Life of H.R.H. The Prince Consort*, vol. I, p. 144.

20 Ibid.

21 Thomas Raikes, *A Portion of the Journal Kept by Thomas Raikes from 1831 to 1847*.

22 *Diary of Royal Movements*, by a London Correspondent, p. 236.

23 RA *Queen Victoria's Journal*, 2 September 1843.

24 Ibid.

25 Ibid.

26 Ibid.

27 Ibid.

28 Virginia Surtees, *Charlotte Canning*, p. 95. September 1843.

29 RA *Queen Victoria's Journal*, 2 September 1843.

30 Surtees, *Charlotte Canning*, p. 98. 3 September 1843.
31 RA *Queen Victoria's Journal*, 2 September 1843.
32 Ibid., 3 September 1843.
33 Ibid., 2 September 1843.
34 Ibid.
35 Surtees, *Charlotte Canning*, p. 96. 2 September 1843.
36 RA *Queen Victoria's Journal*, 3 September 1843.
37 Ibid.
38 Martin, *Life of the Prince Consort*, vol. I, p. 181.
39 Surtees, *Charlotte Canning*, p. 100.
40 RA *Queen Victoria's Journal*, 5 September 1843.
41 Surtees, *Charlotte Canning*, p. 88.
42 *Illustrated London News*, 16 September 1843.
43 Surtees, *Charlotte Canning*, p. 101.
44 Martin, *Life of the Prince Consort*, vol. I, p. 178.
45 The Hon. Eleanor Stanley, *Twenty Years at Court*, ed. Mrs Steuart Erskine (London, Nisbet, 1916), p. 45.
46 RA *Queen Victoria's Journal*, 4 September 1843.
47 Ibid.
48 Ibid.
49 RA Y54/18, Prince Albert, 15 August 1840.
50 Surtees, *Charlotte Canning*, p. 106.
51 Ibid., p. 109.
52 Martin, *Life of the Prince Consort*, vol. I, pp. 184–5.
53 *Letters of Queen Victoria*, vol. I, p. 616.
54 Surtees, *Charlotte Canning*, pp. 113, 115.
55 Martin, *Life of the Prince Consort*, vol. I, pp. 191–2.
56 Surtees, *Charlotte Canning*, p. 99.
57 Stanley, *Twenty Years at Court*, p. 39.
58 Surtees, *Charlotte Canning*, p. 110.
59 Ibid., p. 115.
60 Elizabeth Cleghorn Gaskell, *Life of Charlotte Brontë* (2 vols, London, 1857), vol. 2, p. 240.
61 RA *Queen Victoria's Journal*, 25 October 1843.
62 Anon, *The Life and Times of Queen Victoria* (London, Cassell, 1950), p. 146.
63 RA *Queen Victoria's Journal*, 28 November 1843.
64 Charles Greville, *The Greville Memoirs, 1817–1860*, ed. H. Reeve, vol. II:i, p. 211.
65 RA *Queen Victoria's Journal*, 1 December 1843.
66 Ibid.
67 Ibid., 5 December 1843.
68 Greville, *Memoirs*, vol. II:i, p. 216.
69 RA *Queen Victoria's Journal*, 12 December 1843.
70 Martin, *Life of the Prince Consort*, vol. I, pp. 204–5.
71 Ibid.

72 Ibid., p. 206.

73 Kurt Jagow, ed., *Letters of the Prince Consort 1831–61*, p. 91.

74 Ibid.

75 Ibid., p. 92.

76 Ibid., p. 93.

77 Martin, *Life of the Prince Consort*, vol. I, p. 211.

78 *Letters of Queen Victoria*, vol. II, p. 14. Queen Victoria to King Leopold, 4 June 1844.

79 Ibid.

80 Martin, *Life of the Prince Consort*, vol. I, p. 222. Queen Victoria to King Leopold, 11 June 1844.

81 Wilson, *Life and Times*, p. 162.

82 RA *Queen Victoria's Journal*, 31 August 1844.

83 Surtees, *Charlotte Canning*, p. 133.

84 RA *Queen Victoria's Journal*, 11 September 1844.

85 Jagow, *Letters of the Prince Consort*, p. 93. Prince Albert to the Dowager Duchess of Coburg, 22 September 1844.

86 *Letters of Queen Victoria*, vol. II, p. 23. Queen Louise to Queen Victoria.

87 Lady Lyttelton, *The Correspondence of Sarah Spencer Lady Lyttelton, 1787–1870*, ed. The Hon. Mrs Hugh Wyndham p. 349. Lady Lyttelton to Mrs Henry Glynne, 8 October 1844.

88 Martin, *Life of the Prince Consort*, vol. I, p. 237.

89 RA *Queen Victoria's Journal*, 10 October 1844.

90 Ibid., 9 October 1844. Passages in French, underlined in Queen Victoria's Journal.

91 Hector Bolitho, ed., *The Prince Consort and his Brother*, p. 79. Prince Albert to his brother, 23 May 1845.

92 RA *Queen Victoria's Journal*, 8 August 1845.

93 Ibid., 11 August 1845.

94 Wilson, *Life and Times*.

95 RA *Queen Victoria's Journal*, 16 August 1845.

96 Ibid., 18 August 1845.

97 Ibid., 20 August 1845.

98 Ibid., 30 August 1845.

99 Surtees, *Charlotte Canning*, p. 163.

100 RA *Queen Victoria's Journal*, 30 August 1845.

101 MP 117/132, 29 September 1845.

102 RA *Queen Victoria's Journal*, 9 September 1845.

CHAPTER 14   A NEUTRAL CROWN?

1 Quoted by Peel in his speech on the repeal of the Corn Laws.

2 Hector Bolitho, *Albert the Good, and the Victorian Reign*, p. 232n.

3 Charles Greville, *The Greville Memoirs, 1817–1860*, ed. H. Reeve, vol. II:ii,

p. 136. 16 January 1843.

4 C.S. Parker, *Sir Robert Peel* (3 vols, London, 1891–9), vol. III, p. 223.

5 Ibid.

6 Ibid., p. 237. Sir Robert Peel to the Queen, 27 November 1845.

7 Ibid., p. 238. Queen Victoria to Robert Peel, 28 November 1845.

8 Bolitho, *Albert the Good*, p. 234n.

9 Ibid., p. 233; Parker, *Sir Robert Peel*, vol. III, p. 239.

10 Bolitho, *Albert the Good*, p. 235.

11 Parker, *Sir Robert Peel*, vol. III, p. 242.

12 RA Y55/10, Memorandum by Anson, 30 April 1843.

13 Greville, *Memoirs*, vol. II:ii, p. 323.

14 *The Letters of Queen Victoria, 1837–61*, ed, A. C. Benson and Lord Esher, vol. II, pp. 62–3.

15 Parker, *Sir Robert Peel*, vol. III, p. 254.

16 Ibid.

17 Cf. Norman St John Stevas, *Walter Bagehot* (London, Bloomington, 1959).

18 *Letters of Queen Victoria*, vol. II, p. 75. Queen Victoria to King Leopold, 23 December 1845.

19 *Examiner*, 27 December 1845.

20 Hector Bolitho, *The Reign of Queen Victoria*, p. 92n.

21 Kurt Jagow, ed., *Letters of the Prince Consort 1831–61*, p. 99. Prince Albert to Baron Stockmar, 6 January 1846.

22 Theodore Martin, *The Life of H.R.H. The Prince Consort*, vol. I, p. 318.

23 RA C44/89, Buccleuch to Robert Peel, 22 December 1845.

24 *Annual Register 1846*, Queen's Speech, 19 January 1846.

25 Norman Gash, *Aristocracy and the People*, p. 240.

26 Cecil Woodham-Smith, *Queen Victoria, 1819–1861*, p. 199.

27 Cf. Elizabeth Longford, *Victoria R. I.*, p. 183.

28 Robert Peel, *The Speeches of Sir Robert Peel Delivered in the House of Commons* (4 vols, London, 1853), vol. IV, p. 654.

29 Lord Cardwell Edward Stanhope, ed., *Memoirs of Sir Robert Peel* (London, Murray, 1875), vol. II, p. 298.

30 Ibid.

31 Peel, *Speeches*, vol. IV, p. 497.

32 William Ewart Gladstone, *Diaries*, ed. M. R. D. Foot and H. C. G. Matthew (Oxford, Clarendon Press, 1974). vol. III, p. 552.

33 Ibid., p. 553.

34 RA C25/35, Memorandum by Prince Albert, 4 July 1846.

35 Parker, *Sir Robert Peel*, vol. III, p. 451. 1 July 1846.

36 Ibid., p. 500. Sir Robert Peel to Queen Victoria, 24 July 1846.

37 Gladstone, *Diaries*, p. 553.

38 Ibid., p. 556.

39 Ibid., p. 559.

40 Greville, *Memoirs*, vol. II:ii, p. 325.

41 Hansard, speech by Disraeli, 15 May 1846.

42 Walter Bagehot, 'The Character of Sir Robert Peel', in *Biographical Studies*, ed. R.H. Hutton (London, 1881).

43 G. Kitson Clark, *Peel* (London, Duckworth, 1936), p. 70.

44 Parker, *Sir Robert Peel*, vol. III, p. 553.

45 RA Y95/20, Queen Victoria to King Leopold, 9 July 1850.

46 *Annual Register 1847*, p. 2.

CHAPTER 15   DOMESTIC LIFE

1 Frances, Baroness Bunsen, ed, *Memoirs of Baron Bunsen*.

2 Lady Lyttelton, *The Correspondence of Sarah Spencer Lady Lyttelton, 1787–1870*, ed. The Hon. Mrs Hugh Wyndham, p. 326. 3 February 1842.

3 RA *Queen Victoria's Journal*, 14 January 1842.

4 Ibid., 11 July 1842.

5 Lyttelton, *Correspondence*, p. 326. 12 February 1842.

6 Ibid., p. 328. 7 May 1842.

7 Ibid., p. 330. 23 September 1842.

8 Felix Mendelssohn-Bartholdy, Marquis of Lorne, *V.R.I. Her Life and Empire*, pp. 140–2.

9 Lyttelton, *Correspondence*, p. 335. 4 December 1842.

10 RA *Queen Victoria's Journal*, 22 April 1853.

11 Lady Eleanor Stanley, *Twenty Years at Court*, ed. Mrs Steuart Erskine, p. 29. 5 February 1843.

12 Virginia Surtees, *Charlotte Canning*, p. 319. 6 October 1841.

13 Ibid., p. 332. 23 October 1841.

14 Lyttelton, *Correspondence*, p. 329. 7 May.

15 Ibid.

16 RA *Queen Victoria's Journal*, 5 June 1842.

17 Ibid., 27 December 1842.

18 RA *Queen Victoria's Journal*, 8 January 1842.

19 Ibid., 18 August 1842.

20 Stanley, *Twenty Years at Court*, p. 41.

21 Stanley, *Twenty Years at Court*.

22 Surtees, *Charlotte Canning*, p. 124. 13 January 1844.

23 Ibid.

24 Stanley, *Twenty Years at Court*, p. 53.

25 *Dearest Child – Private Correspondence of Queen Victoria and the Crown Princess of Prussia, 1858–1861*, ed. Roger Fulford, pp. 124–5.

26 *Dearest Mama – Private Correspondence of Queen Victoria and the Crown Princess of Prussia. 1861–1864*, ed. Roger Fulford, p. 45.

27 RA *Queen Victoria's Journal*, 11 August 1842.

28 Ibid., 22 January 1843.

29 Ibid., 25 January 1843.
30 Lyttelton, *Correspondence*, p. 329.
31 Ibid., p. 340. 16 February 1844.
32 *Dearest Child*, p. 147. Queen Victoria to Vicky, 27 November 1858.
33 Martin, *Life of the Prince Consort*, vol. II, p. 195. Prince Albert to Baron Stockmar, 17 December 1843.
34 Hector Bolitho, *Albert the Good and the Victorian Reign*, p. 137.
35 RA *Queen Victoria's Journal*, 11 November 1849.
36 Stanley, *Twenty Years at Court*, p. 122. Lady Eleanor Stanley to her father, 27 September 1846.
37 RA *Queen Victoria's Journal*, 3 November 1844.
38 Lyttelton, *Correspondence*, p. 372. October 1847.
39 Ibid., pp. 409–10.
40 Ibid., p. 334. 22 November 1842.
41 Stanley, *Twenty Years at Court*, p. 178. Lady Stanley to her mother, 28 October 1849.
42 Lyttelton, *Correspondence*, p. 333. 22 November 1842.
43 RA *Queen Victoria's Journal*, 5 August 1849.
44 Ibid., 11 August 1849.
45 Ibid., 12 August 1849.
46 Ibid.
47 Surtees, *Charlotte Canning*, pp. 105–6.
48 Martin, *Life of the Prince Consort*, vol. I, p. 248. Queen Victoria to King Leopold, 25 April 1845.
49 *The Letters of Queen Victoria, 1837–1861*, ed. A. C. Benson and Lord Esher, vol. II, p. 41. Queen Victoria to Lord Melbourne, 3 April 1845.
50 Charles Greville, *The Greville Memoirs, 1817–1860*, ed. H. Reeve, vol. V, p. 229.
51 Martin, *Life of the Prince Consort*, vol. I, pp. 322–3.
52 RA *Queen Victoria's Journal*, 3 March 1846.
53 RA M12/41, Memorandum by Dr A. Combe, June 1846.
54 Lyttelton, *Correspondence*, p. 364. 16 September 1846.
55 Ibid.
56 RA *Queen Victoria's Journal*, 30 July 1847.
57 Ibid., 6 July 1849.
58 Richard R. Holmes, ed., *Edward VII: His Life and Times* (undated), p. 63.
59 Ibid.
60 RA *Queen Victoria's Journal*, 21 August 1847.
61 Martin, *Life of the Prince Consort*, vol. I, p. 425. Prince Albert to the Duchess of Kent, 27 August 1847.
62 Hector Bolitho, ed., *The Prince Consort and his Brother*, p. 105. 24 August 1848.
63 RA *Queen Victoria's Journal*, 8 September 1848.
64 Lord Malmesbury, *Memoirs of an Ex-Minister*.
65 Greville, *Memoirs*, vol. II:iii, p. 296. 15 September 1849.

66 RA *Queen Victoria's Journal*, 8 September 1848.
67 Greville, *Memoirs*, vol. II:iii, p. 296. 15 September 1849.
68 RA *Queen Victoria's Journal*, 7 September 1849.
69 Greville, *Memoirs*, vol. II:iii, p. 296. 15 September 1849.
70 RA *Queen Victoria's Journal*, 16 September 1848.
71 Ibid., 18 September 1848.
72 Ibid., 30 August 1849.
73 Ibid., 11 September 1849.
74 Ibid., 6 September 1850.
75 Ibid., 13 September 1850.
76 Kurt Jagow, ed., *Letters of the Prince Consort 1831–61*, p. 95. Prince Albert to the Dowager Duchess of Coburg, 22 September 1844.
77 Lyttelton, *Correspondence*, p. 393. 5 October 1849.
78 Martin, *Life of the Prince Consort*, vol. II, p. 175. Memorandum by Baron Stockmar, 6 March 1842.
79 Ibid.
80 *Letters of Queen Victoria*, vol. I, p. 365. Lord Melbourne to Queen Victoria.
81 RA M12/35, Memorandum, 4 March 1844.
82 RA M12/39, Memorandum, 13 November 1844.
83 Ibid.
84 RA M12/55, Memorandum, 3 January 1847.
85 RA M12/35, Memorandum by the Queen, 4 March 1844.
86 RA M14/36, Memorandum by Baron Stockmar, undated.
87 RA *Queen Victoria's Journal*, 22 April 1849.
88 RA M14/37, Memorandum by Prince Albert, 12 April 1849.
89 RA M14/41, Mr Birch to Baron Stockmar.
90 RA M14/38.
91 RA M14/45, Queen Victoria to Baron Stockmar, 26 November 1849.
92 RA M/58, Memorandum by the Queen, 15 December 1849.
93 RA M14/116, Mr Birch to Baron Stockmar, 31 July 1850.
94 Holmes, *Edward VII*, pp. 61–2.
95 Ibid.
96 RA M14/107, Dr George Combe to Sir James Clark, 22 June 1850.
97 RA M15/8, Mr Birch to Baron Stockmar, 8 November 1850.
98 RA M14/52, Mr Birch to Prince Albert, 17 April 1851.
99 RA M15/17, Memorandum by Prince Albert, November 1850.
100 Surtees, *Charlotte Canning*.
101 *Letters of Queen Victoria*, vol. I, p. 365.

CHAPTER 16   FOREIGN AFFAIRS

1 Brian Connell, *Regina vs. Palmerston: The Correspondence between Queen Victoria and her Foreign and Prime Minister* (London, Evans, 1962), p. 23.
2 Ibid., p. 26.

3 Ibid., p. 27.

4 Ibid.

5 B. R. Haydon, *Autobiography and Memoirs*, ed. A. P. D. Penrose (London, 1927), vol. IV, p. 448.

6 Connell, *Regina vs. Palmerston* pp. 29–30.

7 RA B5/39, Queen Victoria to Lord Aberdeen, 13 January 1844; RA B8/13, Lord Aberdeen to Queen Victoria, 15 January 1844.

8 RA B9/150, Lord Aberdeen to Queen Victoria.

9 Robert Rhodes James, *Albert Prince Consort*, p. 134.

10 Palmerston in the House of Commons, 4 February 1845.

11 Evelyn Ashley, ed., *The Life of Palmerston*, p. 368.

12 Connell, *Regina vs. Palmerston*, p. 62.

13 Ibid., pp. 63–4.

14 Ibid., p. 65.

15 Hector Bolitho, ed., *The Prince Consort and his Brother*, p. 96. Prince Albert to his brother, 2 April 1847.

16 *Letters of Queen Victoria, 1837–1861*, ed. A. C. Benson and Lord Esher, vol. I: ii, p. 137.

17 Bolitho, *Prince Consort and his Brother*, p. 95. Prince Albert to his brother, 2 April 1847.

18 Frances, Baroness Bunsen, ed., *Memoirs of Baron Bunsen*, vol. II, p. 149.

19 Cf. Stanislas Mitard, *Les Origines du radicalisme démocratique* (Paris, 1952), ch. 3; Léo R., Loubère, *Louis Blanc* (Evanston, 1960), pp. 56ff.

20 Cf. Georges Duveau, *1848: The Making of a Revolution* (New York, 1948); Jean Bruhat, *Les Journées de février* (Paris, 1948); Jean Tulard, *La Préfecture de police sous la Monarchie de juillet* (Paris, 1964), pp. 168ff., police reports for 22 February.

21 Cf. Palmerston Papers, Broadlands. Report from Featherstonehaugh to Lord Palmerston, 3 March 1848.

22 Theodore Martin, *The Life of H.R.H. The Prince Consort*, vol. I, p. 480. Prince Albert to Baron Stockmar, 27 February 1848.

23 Ibid., p. 479. Prince Albert to the Dowager Duchess of Coburg, 29 February 1848.

24 Martin, *Life of the Prince Consort*, vol. I, pp. 480–1. Prince Albert to Baron Stockmar, 18 March 1848.

25 *Letters of Queen Victoria*, vol. II, p. 197. Queen Victoria to King Leopold, 4 April 1848.

26 RA Y93/28, Queen Victoria to King Leopold, 18 April 1848.

27 RA Y93/23, Queen Victoria to King Leopold, 11 April 1848.

28 RA Y48/75, King Louis-Philippe to Queen Victoria, 3 March 1848.

29 RA J67/82, Lord John Russell to Queen Victoria, 3 March 1848

30 RA J49, Queen Victoria to Lord Palmerston, 10 March 1848.

31 RA J50, Lord Palmerston to Queen Victoria, 10 March 1848.

32 RA *Queen Victoria's Journal*, 16 August 1848.

33 Constantine Henry Phipps, First Marquis of Normanby, *A Year of Revolution from a Journal Kept in Paris in 1848* (2 vols, London, 1857).

34 RA J69/171, Lord John Russell to Queen Victoria, 26 November 1848.

35 Virginia Surtees, *Charlotte Canning*, p. 177.

36 RA *Queen Victoria's Journal*, 17 July 1848.

37 Surtees, *Charlotte Canning*, p. 177.

38 RA *Queen Victoria's Journal*, 27 August 1850.

39 Joanna Richardson, *Dearest Uncle* (London, Jonathan Cape, 1961), p. 182.

40 Ibid., p. 181.

41 RA *Queen Victoria's Journal*, 13 October 1850.

42 Martin, *Life of the Prince Consort*, vol. II, p. 57.

43 Ibid. Prince Albert to Baron Stockmar, 30 March 1848.

44 RA C56/29, Lord John Russell to Queen Victoria, 11 April 1848.

45 Bunsen, *Memoirs of Baron Bunsen*, vol. II, p. 182.

46 Martin, *Life of the Prince Consort*, vol. II, p. 66.

47 Charles Greville, *The Greville Memoirs, 1817–1860*, ed. H. Reeve, vol. II:iii, pp. 169–70.

48 Martin, *Life of the Prince Consort*, vol. II, p. 66.

49 Ashley, *Life of Palmerston*, vol. I, p. 98.

50 *Letters of Queen Victoria*, vol. II, p. 215.

51 Ibid., p. 212. 16 June 1848.

52 RA C8/22, Queen Victoria to Lord John Russell, 16 June 1848.

53 RA A79/4, Lord John Russell to Queen Victoria, 17 June 1848; RA A79/8, Lord John Russell to Lord Palmerston, 18 June 1848.

54 RA A79/8, Lord John Russell to Lord Palmerston, 18 June 1848.

55 RA J4/16 and J4/17.

56 RA J4/84, Queen Victoria to Lord John Russell, 11 August 1848.

57 Martin, *Life of the Prince Consort*, vol. II, p. 64. Lord John Russell to Prince Albert, 18 June 1849.

58 Harold Laski, 'Le Personnel du Cabinet en Angleterre 1801–1924', *Revue de Droit Public*, 1933, pp. 94–116.

59 Cf. Henry Colman, *The Agriculture and Rural Economy of France, Belgium. Holland and Switzerland* (London, 1848).

60 *Annual Register 1848*, p. 52.

61 Martin, *Life of the Prince Consort*, vol. II, p. 105. Prince Albert to Baron Stockmar, 20 August 1848.

62 Ibid., p. 106.

63 Greville, *Memoirs*, vol. II:iii, p. 335.

64 *Annual Register 1850*, p. 74.

65 RA C9/46, Queen Victoria to Lord John Russell, 12 August 1850.

66 Ibid.

67 Martin, *Life of the Prince Consort*, vol. II, p. 307.

68 *Letters of Queen Victoria*, vol. II, pp. 392–400.

69 Martin, *Life of the Prince Consort*, vol. II, p. 411.

70 Ibid., p. 412.
71 Greville, *Memoirs*, vol. II: iii, p. 166.
72 Ashley, *Life of Palmerston*, vol. I, p. 334.

CHAPTER 17   MID-CENTURY GRANDEUR

1 RA *Queen Victoria's Journal*, 29 October 1850.
2 Theodore Martin, *The Life of H.R.H. The Prince Consort*, vol. II, pp. 339–40. Queen Victoria to the Duchess of Gloucester, December 1850.
3 RA Y95/49, Queen Victoria to King Leopold, 24 December 1850.
4 Sir Spencer Walpole, *The Life of Lord John Russell* (London, 1889), vol. II, p. 121. Letter from Lord John Russell to the Bishop of Durham.
5 RA *Queen Victoria's Journal*, 26 March 1851.
6 Ibid., 27 February 1851.
7 C46/79, Memorandum by Prince Albert, 27 February 1851.
8 Charles Greville, *The Greville Memoirs, 1817–1860*, ed. H. Reeve, vol. II:iii, 4 March 1851.
9 H.R.H. The Prince Consort, *Principal Speeches and Addresses* (London, John Murray, 1862), p. 112.
10 Kurt Jagow, ed., *Letters of the Prince Consort, 1831–61*, p. 153. Prince Albert to Baron Stockmar, 10 September 1849.
11 Martin, *Life of the Prince Consort*, vol. II, p. 247.
12 Ibid., p. 248.
13 Martin, *Life of the Prince Consort*, vol. II, p. 149. Queen Victoria to King Leopold.
14 Ibid., p. 243.
15 Jagow, *Letters of the Prince Consort*, p. 162. Prince Albert to Baron Stockmar, 28 June 1850.
16 Martin, *Life of the Prince Consort*, vol. II, p. 299. Prince Albert to Baron Stockmar, 20 July 1850.
17 RA *Queen Victoria's Journal*, 18 February 1851.
18 Martin, *Life of the Prince Consort*, vol. II, p. 359. Prince Albert to the Dowager Duchess of Coburg, 15 April 1851.
19 RA *Queen Victoria's Journal*, 29 April 1851.
20 Ibid.
21 Ibid.
22 Ibid., 1 May 1851.
23 Ibid.
24 Martin, *Life of the Prince Consort*, vol. II, p. 369.
25 RA *Queen Victoria's Journal*, 1 May 1851.
26 Ibid.
27 Ibid.
28 *Journal des Débats*, 2 May 1851.

29 RA *Queen Victoria's Journal*, 18 July 1851.

30 Ibid., 14 October 1851.

31 Ibid., 15 October 1851.

32 Martin, *Life of the Prince Consort*, vol. II, p. 383. Prince Albert to Baron Stockmar, 14 July 1851.

33 RA *Queen Victoria's Journal*, 19 October 1851.

34 *Observer*, 4 May 1851.

35 Ibid., 20 July 1851.

36 Martin, *Life of the Prince Consort*, vol. II, p. 391.

37 RA F25/1, Memorandum by Prince Albert, 10 August 1851.

38 *Annual Register 1852*, p. 55.

39 RA *Queen Victoria's Journal*, 30 April 1852.

40 RA F25/97, 10 May 1852.

41 RA *Queen Victoria's Journal*, 12 March 1852.

42 Ibid., 14 September 1852.

43 Cf. *Annual Register 1853*, p. 508.

44 Ibid.

45 John Morley, *Death, Heaven and the Victorians* (University of Pittsburgh Press, 1971), p. 83.

46 *Annual Register 1852*, p. 189.

47 *Observer*, 14 November 1852.

48 *Annual Register 1852*, p. 191.

49 RA *Queen Victoria's Journal*, 19 November 1852.

50 Cf. *Annual Register 1852*, p. 130. Cecil Woodham-Smith (*Queen Victoria, 1819–1861*, p. 278) believed that, as was customarily stated, the legacy went towards the transformation of Balmoral. An examination of the accounts of the Nield succession shows this to be untrue.

51 RA *Queen Victoria's Journal*, 28 September 1853.

52 Ibid., 7 September 1855.

53 Ibid.

CHAPTER 18 THE CRIMEAN WAR AND THE INDIAN MUTINY

1 Cf. A.J.P. Taylor, *Struggle for Mastery in Europe 1848–1918* (Oxford, 1954).

2 Lord Malmesbury, *Memoirs of an Ex-Minister*, vol. I, p. 402.

3 *The Letters of Queen Victoria, 1837–1861*, ed. H. C. Benson and Lord Esher, vol. III, p. 25. Queen Victoria to Lord Aberdeen, 1 April 1854.

4 Theodore Martin, *The Life of H.R.H. The Prince Consort*, vol. II, p. 519. Prince Albert to Baron Stockmar, 5 October 1853.

5 Cf. Prince Albert, in Martin, *Life of the Prince Consort*, vol. II, p. 534.

6 Ernest II, Duke of Saxe-Coburg-Gotha, *Memoirs* (London, Remington, 1890), vol. II, p. 46.

7 *Daily News*, 7 January 1854.

8 Martin, *Life of the Prince Consort*, vol. II, p. 539.

9 Hector Bolitho, ed., *The Prince Consort and his Brother*, p. 141. Prince Albert to his brother, 7 January 1854.

10 Martin, *Life of the Prince Consort*, vol. II, p. 558. Prince Albert to Baron Stockmar, 24 January 1854.

11 Ibid., pp. 559–60. Prince Albert to Baron Stockmar, 24 January 1854.

12 Ibid., p. 533. Prince Albert to Baron Stockmar, 27 December 1853.

13 *Daily News*, 11 January 1854.

14 Martin, *Life of the Prince Consort*, vol. II, p. 562. Prince Albert to Baron Stockmar, 24 January 1854.

15 Ibid., p. 541. Queen Victoria to Lord Aberdeen, 4 January 1854.

16 Ibid., p. 564. Queen Victoria to Baron Stockmar, 1 February 1854.

17 Ibid., vol. III, p. 31. Queen Victoria to King Leopold, 14 February 1854.

18 C. S. Parker, *Sir Robert Peel*, vol. II, p. 226.

19 Martin, *Life of the Prince Consort*, vol. II, pp. 32–3. Queen Victoria to King Leopold, 28 February 1854.

20 Cf. Martin, *Life of the Prince Consort*, vol. III, pp. 40–3.

21 Ibid., vol. II, p. 44. Queen Victoria to the King of Prussia, 17 March 1854.

22 RA *Queen Victoria's Journal*, 12 November 1854.

23 Ibid., 16 November 1854.

24 Ibid., 17 November 1854.

25 Ibid., 22 November 1854.

26 Ibid.

27 *Further Letters of Queen Victoria*, ed. Hector Bolitho (London, Thornton Butterworth, 1938), p. 51. Queen Victoria to Princess Augusta, 23 October 1854.

28 Ibid.

29 RA *Queen Victoria's Journal*, 30 November 1854.

30 Sir Spencer Walpole, *A History of England, from the Conclusion of the Great War in 1815* (London, Longmans, Green, 1890–), vol. V, p. 125.

31 Virginia Surtees, *Charlotte Canning*, p. 189.

32 RA *Queen Victoria's Journal*, 8 December 1854.

33 Ibid., 17 December 1854.

34 Ibid., 24 December 1854.

35 Ibid., 26 December 1854.

36 Ibid., 2 March 1855.

37 Ibid., 28 February 1855.

38 Ibid., 5 March 1855.

39 Ibid.

40 Malmesbury, *Memoirs*, vol. II, p. 12.

41 RA *Queen Victoria's Journal*, 15 March 1855.

42 Malmesbury, *Memoirs*, vol. II, p. 18.

43 Cf. Martin, *Life of the Prince Consort*, vol. III, ch. 62.

44 RA *Queen Victoria's Journal*, 16 April 1855.

45 Ibid., 18 April 1855.
46 Ibid., 16 April 1855.
47 Ibid., 19 April 1855.
48 Ibid.
49 Ibid., 17 April 1855.
50 Ibid.
51 Ibid.
52 Ibid., 28 April 1855.
53 David Duff, *Albert and Victoria*, p. 114.
54 *Further Letters of Queen Victoria*, p. 55. Queen Victoria to Princess Augusta, 23 April 1855.
55 RA *Queen Victoria's Journal*, 17 April 1855.
56 Ibid., 19 April 1855.
57 Ibid., 18 April 1855.
58 Ibid., 16 April 1855.
59 Ibid., 17 April 1855.
60 Ibid., 16 April 1855.
61 Ibid., 17 April 1855.
62 *Further Letters of Queen Victoria*, p. 55. Queen Victoria to Princess Augusta, 23 April 1855.
63 RA *Queen Victoria's Journal*, 17 April 1855.
64 Ibid., 20 April 1855.
65 Ibid., 21 April 1855.
66 Charles Greville, *The Greville Memoirs, 1817–1860*, ed. H. Reeve, vol. III:i, p. 129.
67 RA *Queen Victoria's Journal*, 21 April 1855.
68 Ibid., 23 April 1855.
69 Ibid., 28 April 1855.
70 Ibid., 20 February 1855.
71 Ibid., 22 February 1855.
72 Ibid., 18 May 1855.
73 Ibid., 3 March 1855.
74 Ibid., 18 May 1855.
75 RA J76/92, Queen Victoria to Baron Stockmar, 1 September 1855.
76 RA *Queen Victoria's Journal*, 18 August 1855.
77 Kurt Jagow, ed., *Letters of the Prince Consort, 1831–61*, p. 232. Prince Albert to King Leopold, 29 August 1855.
78 *Letters of Queen Victoria*, vol. III, p. 172. Queen Victoria to King Leopold, 23 August 1855.
79 RA *Queen Victoria's Journal*, 20 August 1855.
80 'Journal of Marshal Canrobert', *Revue hebdomadaire*, November 1901.
81 RA *Queen Victoria's Journal*, 24 August 1855.
82 Greville, *Memoirs*, vol. III:i, pp. 283–6.
83 Ibid.

84 *Manchester Guardian*, 22 August 1855.

85 RA *Queen Victoria's Journal*, 10 September 1855.

86 Ibid.

87 Ibid., 21 August 1856.

88 Frederick Sleigh Roberts, Lord Roberts, *Forty-One Years in India* (2 vols, London, 1897), see vol. I.

89 Ibid., pp. 456–7.

90 *Letters of Queen Victoria*, vol. III, p. 313. Queen Victoria to King Leopold, 2 September 1857.

91 Ibid., p. 379.

92 Martin, *Life of the Prince Consort*, vol. IV, pp. 335–6.

93 *Letters of Queen Victoria*, vol. III, p. 389. Queen Victoria to Viscount Canning, 2 December 1858.

CHAPTER 19   FAMILY AFFAIRS

1 RA *Queen Victoria's Journal*, 14 September 1855.

2 Ibid., 17 September 1855.

3 Ibid., 20 September 1855.

4 Ibid.

5 Ibid., 21 September 1855.

6 Ibid., 24 September 1855.

7 Ibid., 22 September 1855.

8 Ibid., 24 September 1855.

9 Ibid., 25 September 1855.

10 Ibid., 29 September 1855.

11 Ibid.

12 Ibid.

13 Ibid.

14 *Further Letters of Queen Victoria*, ed. Hector Bolitho, p. 60. Queen Victoria to Prince William, 23 October 1855.

15 Ibid., p. 58. Queen Victoria to Princess Augusta, 22 October 1855.

16 Ibid., p. 59.

17 *Punch*, September 1855.

18 *The Times*, 3 October 1855.

19 *Further Letters of Queen Victoria*, p. 64. 8 April 1856.

20 Ibid.

21 Ibid., p. 66. Queen Victoria to Princess Augusta, 15 April 1856.

22 Ibid.

23 Ibid., pp. 79–80. Queen Victoria to Princess Augusta, 14 October 1856.

24 E. Fitzmaurice, *The Life of Granville George Leveson Gower, Second Earl Granville, 1815–1891* (2 vols, London, Longman, 1905), vol. I, p. 224.

25 Arthur Ponsonby, *Henry Ponsonby* (London, Macmillan, 1942), p. 26.

26 RA Z141/19, Prince Albert to Bertie.

27 Lord Esher, *The Influence of King Edward and Essays on Other Subjects* (London, 1915), p. 10. Queen Victoria to Bertie, 26 October 1857.

28 Hector Bolitho, ed., *The Prince Consort and his Brother*, p. 177. Prince Albert to his brother, 29 September 1857.

29 *The Letters of Queen Victoria, 1837–1861*, ed. A. C. Benson and Lord Esher, vol. III, pp. 244–7.

30 Bolitho, *Prince Consort and his Brother*, p. 177. Prince Albert to his brother, 29 September 1857.

31 *Further Letters of Queen Victoria*, p. 89. Queen Victoria to Princess Augusta, 5 September 1857.

32 *Letters of Queen Victoria*, vol. III, p. 321. Queen Victoria to Lord Clarendon, 25 October 1857.

33 RA *Queen Victoria's Journal*, 24 January 1858.

34 Ibid.

35 Ibid.

36 Ibid., 25 January 1858.

37 Ibid.

38 Ibid.

39 Ibid.

40 *Dearest Child – Private Correspondence of Queen Victoria and the Crown Princess of Prussia, 1858–1861*, ed. Roger Fulford, p. 27. Queen Victoria to Vicky, 25 January 1858.

41 RA *Queen Victoria's Journal*, 1 February 1858.

42 Ibid.

43 Ibid, 2 February 1858.

44 Ibid.

45 *Dearest Child*, p. 28. Queen Victoria to Vicky.

46 Ibid., pp. 31–2. Vicky to Prince Albert, 5 February 1858.

47 Theodore Martin, *The Life of H.R.H. The Prince Consort*, vol. IV, p. 169. Prince Albert to Vicky, 3 February 1858.

48 *Letters of the Empress Frederick*, ed. Sir Frederick Ponsonby (London, Macmillan, 1929), p. 10. Bismarck to General Von Gerlach, 8 April 1858.

49 *Dearest Mama – Private Correspondence of Queen Victoria and the Crown Princess of Prussia, 1861–1864*, ed. Roger Fulford, p. 45. Vicky to Queen Victoria, 15 February 1858.

50 RA *Queen Victoria's Journal*, 7 January 1858.

51 Martin, *Life of the Prince Consort*, vol. IV, p. 206. Prince Albert to Baron Stockmar, 2 April 1858.

52 *Dearest Child*, p. 83. Queen Victoria to Vicky, 1 April 1858.

53 Martin, *Life of the Prince Consort*, vol. IV, p. 206. Prince Albert to Baron Stockmar, 2 April 1858.

54 *Dearest Child*, p. 83. Queen Victoria to Vicky, 1 April 1858.

55 Martin, *Life of the Prince Consort*, vol. IV, p. 206. Prince Albert to Baron Stockmar, 2 April 1858.
56 Ibid.
57 Lord Esher, 'The character of King Edward', *Quarterly Review*, July 1910.
58 Charles Greville, *The Greville Memoirs, 1817–1860*, ed. H. Reeve, vol. III:ii, p. 213. 4 November 1858.
59 *Dearest Child*, p. 142. Queen Victoria to Vicky, 10 November 1858.
60 Egon Caesar, Count Corti, *The English Empress: A Study in the Relations between Queen Victoria and her Eldest Daughter*, trans. E. M. Hodgson (London, Cassell, 1957). Prince Albert to Vicky, 17 November 1858, p. 50.
61 RA Add U/32.
62 RA Z461/92, Bertie to Prince Albert, 10 March 1858.
63 Esher, *Influence*, p. 28. Prince Albert to Bertie, 27 November 1859.
64 Bolitho, *Prince Consort and his Brother*, p. 169. Prince Albert to his brother, undated.
65 Ibid., p. 172. Prince Albert to his brother, 13 April 1857.
66 Ibid., p. 173. Prince Albert to his brother, 23 April 1857.
67 Ibid.
68 Ibid.
69 Martin, *Life of the Prince Consort*, vol. IV, p. 236. Prince Albert to Queen Victoria, 29 May 1858.
70 Ibid.
71 Ibid., p. 238. Prince Albert to Queen Victoria, 30 May 1858.
72 *Dearest Child*, p. 109. Queen Victoria to Vicky, 29 May 1858.
73 Bolitho, *Prince Consort and his Brother*, p. 166. Prince Albert to his brother, 14 November 1856.
74 *Further Letters of Queen Victoria*, p. 75. Queen Victoria to Princess Augusta, 6 October 1856.
75 Ibid., p. 59. Queen Victoria to Princess Augusta, 22 October 1855.
76 Counted by Count Corti, author of *The English Empress*.
77 *Dearest Child*, p. 77. Queen Victoria to Vicky, 24 March 1858.
78 RA Z140/9–18, Prince Albert to Queen Victoria, 9 May 1853.
79 Ibid.
80 RA Z140/22–4, Prince Albert to Queen Victoria, 9 February 1855.
81 RA Z140, Prince Albert to Queen Victoria, 1 October 1856.
82 RA Z140/32–7, Prince Albert to Queen Victoria, 5 November 1856, translated.
83 RA Z140/40–1, Prince Albert to Queen Victoria, undated.
84 RA Z140/60–3, undated.
85 RA *Queen Victoria's Journal*, 19 August 1858.
86 *Dearest Child*, p. 108. Queen Victoria to Vicky, 26 May 1858.
87 Ibid., p. 109. Queen Victoria to Vicky, 29 May 1858.
88 Ibid., p. 115. Queen Victoria to Vicky, 15 June 1858.
89 Ibid., p. 123. Queen Victoria to Vicky, 21 July 1858.

90 Ibid.

91 Ibid., p. 124. Vicky to Queen Victoria, 24 July 1858.

92 Ibid., p. 131. Queen Victoria to Vicky, 21 September 1858.

93 Ibid., p. 135. Queen Victoria to Vicky, 1 October 1858.

94 Ibid., p. 134. Queen Victoria to Vicky, 27 September 1858.

95 Ibid., p. 139. Queen Victoria to Vicky, 18 October 1858.

96 Ibid., p. 140. Queen Victoria to Vicky, 27 October 1858.

97 Ibid., p. 120. Queen Victoria to Vicky, 30 June 1858.

98 Ibid., p. 144. Queen Victoria to Vicky, 17 November 1858.

99 *Letters of Queen Victoria*, vol. III, p. 414. Queen Victoria to King Leopold, 1 March 1859.

100 Jasper Ridley, *Napoleon III and Eugenie* (London, Constable, 1979), p. 453.

101 Kurt Jagow, ed., *Letters of the Prince Consort, 1831–61*, p. 336. Prince Albert to the Prince Regent of Prussia, 15 June 1859.

102 Martin, *Life of the Prince Consort*, vol. V, pp. 15–16.

103 RA Z467/42, the Duke of Newcastle to Queen Victoria, 23 September 1860.

104 Lord Sandwich, *Memoirs*, ed. Mrs Stewart Erskine (London, 1919), p. 44.

105 Z172/17, General Bruce to Sir Charles Phipps, 14 October 1860.

106 Philip Magnus, *King Edward the Seventh* (London, John Murray, 1964), p. 41. Queen Victoria to Vicky, 31 October 1860.

107 Sidney Lee, *Queen Victoria*, p. 112. General Bruce to Prince Albert, 14 August 1860.

108 RA Y103/14, 27 April 1858.

109 *Dearest Child*, p. 171. Queen Victoria to Vicky, 2 April 1859.

110 RA Y104/13, Queen Victoria to King Leopold, 19 April 1859.

111 *Dearest Child*, p. 212. Queen Victoria to Vicky, 11 October 1859.

112 RA Z28/71, Vicky to Queen Victoria, 2 November 1859.

113 *Dearest Child*, p. 220. Queen Victoria to Vicky, 6 November 1859.

114 RA Z29/11, Vicky to Queen Victoria, 30 December 1859.

115 *Dearest Child*, p. 231. Queen Victoria to Vicky, 1 February 1860.

116 Jagow, *Letters of the Prince Consort*, p. 348. Prince Albert to Baron Stockmar, 9 June 1860.

117 RA Y100/22, Queen Victoria to King Leopold, 31 July 1860.

118 RA *Queen Victoria's Journal*, 24 September 1860.

119 Ibid., 25 September 1860.

120 Ibid., 27 September 1860.

121 Ibid., 1 October 1860.

122 Ibid., 4 October 1860.

123 *Further Letters of Queen Victoria*, p. 113. Queen Victoria to Princess Augusta, 3 November 1860.

124 RA *Queen Victoria's Journal*, 30 November 1860.

125 Ibid., 4 December 1860.

126 *New York Herald*, 19 September 1860.

127 *New York Times*, 29 September 1860.
128 RA *Queen Victoria's Journal*, 5 December 1860.
129 Martin, *Life of the Prince Consort*, vol. IV, p. 255. Prince Albert to Vicky, 6 December 1860.
130 Ibid., p. 259. Prince Albert to Vicky, 11 December 1860.
131 Ibid.

CHAPTER 20   DEATH IN THE FAMILY

1 *Dearest Child – Private Correspondence of Queen Victoria and the Crown Princess of Prussia, 1858–1861*, ed. Roger Fulford, p. 297. Vicky to Queen Victoria, 2 January 1861.
2 Ibid.
3 Ibid., p. 306. Queen Victoria to Vicky, 2 February 1861.
4 Theodore Martin, *The Life of H.R.H. The Prince Consort*, vol. V, pp. 274–5. Memorandum by Queen Victoria to Theodore Martin, January 1862.
5 Ibid., p. 295.
6 *Dearest Child*, p. 308. Queen Victoria to Vicky, 16 February 1861.
7 Ibid., p. 310. Queen Victoria to Vicky, 21 February 1861.
8 Martin, *Life of the Prince Consort*, vol. V, p. 308. Prince Albert to Baron Stockmar, 4 March 1861.
9 RA *Queen Victoria's Journal*, 15 March 1861.
10 Ibid., 16 March 1861.
11 Ibid.
12 Martin, *Life of the Prince Consort*, vol. V, p. 325.
13 Ibid., p. 326. Feodora to Queen Victoria, 19 March 1861.
14 Ibid., p. 335. Prince Albert to Baron Stockmar, 5 April 1861.
15 *Dearest Child*, p. 319. Queen Victoria to Vicky, 10 April 1861.
16 Ibid.
17 *Further Letters of Queen Victoria*, ed. Hector Bolitho, p. 117. Queen Victoria to Princess Augusta, 27 March 1861.
18 *The Letters of Queen Victoria, 1837–1861*, ed. A. C. Benson and Lord Esher, vol. III, p. 560. Queen Victoria to King Leopold, 9 April 1861.
19 RA *Queen Victoria's Journal*, 16 August 1861.
20 RA M10/72.
21 Hector Bolitho, ed., *The Prince Consort and his Brother*, p. 213. Prince Albert to his brother, 18 June 1861.
22 *Dearest Child*, p. 327. Queen Victoria to Vicky, 1 May 1861.
23 Ibid., p. 336. Queen Victoria to Vicky, 31 May 1881.
24 Martin, *Life of the Prince Consort*, vol. V, p. 364.
25 Ibid., p. 369. Prince Albert to Baron Stockmar, 7 July 1861.
26 RA Z446/15, 13 March 1861.
27 RA Z446/38.

28 RA *Queen Victoria's Journal*, 26 August 1861.

29 Ibid.

30 Ibid.

31 Martin, *Life of the Prince Consort*, vol. V, p. 368. Prince Albert to Baron Stockmar, 6 September 1861.

32 Cf. *Leaves from the Journal of Our Life in the Highlands, 1848–1861*, ed. A. Helps (London, Smith, Elder, 1868).

33 RA *Queen Victoria's Journal*, 4 September 1860.

34 Ibid., 20 September 1861.

35 Ibid.

36 Ibid., 9 October 1861.

37 Philip Magnus, *King Edward the Seventh*, p. 48. The Prince of Wales to his parents, 25 September 1861.

38 RA Z461/92, Vicky to her parents, 26 September 1861.

39 *Dearest Child*, p. 353. Queen Victoria to Vicky, 1 October 1861.

40 Ibid., p. 356. Vicky to Queen Victoria, 12 October 1861.

41 RA Z141/91, Prince Albert to Bertie, 7 October 1861.

42 *Dearest Child*, p. 357. Queen Victoria to Vicky, 10 October 1861.

43 Ibid., p. 365. Queen Victoria to Vicky, 9 November 1861.

44 Ibid.

45 Cecil Woodham-Smith, *Queen Victoria, 1819–1861*, p. 416.

46 Z141/94, Prince Albert to Bertie, 16 November 1861.

47 Martin, *Life of the Prince Consort*, vol. V, p. 417.

48 *Dearest Child*, pp. 369–70. Queen Victoria to Vicky, 27 November 1861.

49 Prince Albert to Vicky, 30 November 1861

50 *Dearest Child*, p. 70. Queen Victoria to Vicky, 30 November 1861.

51 RA *Queen Victoria's Journal*, 1 December 1861.

52 Ibid.

53 Ibid., 3 December 1861.

54 RA Z140/62, undated.

55 RA *Queen Victoria's Journal*, 3 December 1861.

56 Ibid., 4 December 1861.

57 Ibid., 5 December 1861.

58 G. Barnett-Smith, *Queen Victoria* (London, Routledge and Kegan Paul, 1887), p. 351.

59 RA *Queen Victoria's Journal*, 4 December 1861.

60 Ibid., 6 December 1861.

61 Palmerston Papers, Broadlands. Colonel Phipps to Lord Palmerston, 6 December 1861.

62 RA *Queen Victoria's Journal*, 7 December 1861.

63 Daphne Bennett, *King without a Crown* (London, William Heinemann, 1977), appendix II, p. 381.

64 RA Add. 17/142, Dr Jenner to Dr Parkes, 19 December 1861.

65 RA Z142; RA *Queen Victoria's Journal*, 7 December 1861.

66 RA *Queen Victoria's Journal*, 8 December 1861.

67 RA Z142; RA *Queen Victoria's Journal*, 8 December 1861.

68 Palmerston Papers. Colonel Phipps to Lord Palmerston, 9 December 1861.

69 Martin, *Life of the Prince Consort*, vol. V, p. 433.

70 Ibid., p. 435. Lord Palmerston to Colonel Phipps, 10 December 1861.

71 RA Z142; RA *Queen Victoria's Journal*, 11 December 1861.

72 Martin, *Life of the Prince Consort*, vol. V, p. 437.

73 Ibid., p. 438.

74 RA Z142, 14 December 1861.

75 Ibid.

76 Ibid.

Index

Note: V = Victoria and A = Prince
Albert

Abercorn, James Hamilton, 2nd
Marquess and 1st Duke of, 288
Abercromby, James (later Lord
Dunfermline), 90
Aberdeen, George Hamilton Gordon,
4th Earl of, 143, 245, 251, 254, 288;
and Spanish marriages, 257, 304;
supports Corn Law Repeal, 260,
270, 272; as Foreign Secretary, 301;
declines to form ministry, 327;
forms coalition government, 343;
and Crimean War, 346, 347, 348,
350, 353
Addington, Henry, later 1st Viscount
Sidmouth, 99
Adelaide, Queen, 22, 56, 57–8, 59,
102, 177, 301; marriage, 24, 25;
death of daughters, 31, 40;
coronation, 60; becomes Queen
Dowager, 86; at V's marriage, 184,
185; as godmother to Princess
Royal, 197
Adelaide of France, 244
Adelbert of Prussia, Prince, 79
Albemarle, Augustus Frederick
Keppel, 5th Earl of, 52, 119
Albert of Saxe-Coburg and Gotha,
Prince Consort, 10, 56, 151, 341,
351, 358, 360, 376, 378; visits
England, 77, 157; first meeting with
V, 78; sees Lehzen as schemer, 87,
193–5, 209–12; proposed visit to
England, 149–50; birth,
upbringing and character, 152–6,
162–3, 204, 233; appearance and
qualities, 156–7; education, 157–8;
correspondence with V, 159–61,
163, 168–9, 248–9; second visit to
England, 164; proposed to by V,
165; question of religion, 171–2;
precedence, 173–4; difficulties over
annuity, 174–8; peerage sought for,
178–80; household, 180–1;
wedding plans, 181–2; leaves
Coburg, 182; marriage, 183; dislike
of court life, 188–9; 'only the
husband, not the master', 189; 'be
necessary to the Queen', 190;
domestic friction, 190–1, 210–12,
392–4; Regency Bill, 192; at birth
of Princess Royal, 195, 197; care of
V in pregnancy, 196–7, 207;
conviction that Crown should be
non-party, 201; at birth of Prince of
Wales, 207; anxiety over children,
210–11, 274–5; influence on V,
215–16, 300; domestic reforms,
218–20, 223–4; and assassination
attempts on V's life, 220–3;
attitude to etiquette, morals and
religion, 224–5; artistic
accomplishments and thirst for
knowledge, 226–7; and agriculture,
227–8; and industrial progress and
social conscience, 228–9, 316;
death of father, 230, 248; as
paterfamilias, 231, 287, 395;

sharing of power with V, 231–2; unpopularity as foreigner, 233, 251, 348; first visit to Scotland, 235–7; as sportsman, 237, 247–8, 256–7, 290–1, 408; visit to French Royal Family, 240–4; visits Coburg, 248–9, 391; relationship with Peel, 261–2; attacked for visit to House of Commons, 267–8; devotion to Vicky, 276–7, 280, 385, 398; buys Osborne, 283–5; buys Balmoral, 288–92; education of children, 294, 296–8, 380, 388–9; and revolutions of 1848, 317; and Great Exhibition, 328–40; poor health, 330, 339, 404, 408–12, 414; rebuilds Balmoral, 343–4; visit to France, 362–5; created Prince Consort, 381–2; Vicky's marriage, 382–4; workaholic, 392, 407; visits Cherbourg and Vicky, 394–5; on Austrian affairs, 398; on Princess Alice's marriage and engagement, 401, 403; accident at Coburg, 402–3; and candidates as bride for Prince of Wales, 403–4, 416; and death of Duchess of Kent, 409–11; visit to Ireland, 413–14; and 'affair' of Prince of Wales, 417–18; and *Trent* affair, 419; illness and death, 418–25

Alexander of Orange, Prince, 77

Alexander I of Russia, Tsar, 18, 32

Alexander II of Russia, Tsar, 148–9, 163, 356

Alexandra of Denmark, 404, 415, 416

Alexandre, Madame *see* Panam, Pauline

Alexandrine of Saxe-Coburg and Gotha, 391, 402

Alfred, Prince, Duke of Edinburgh, 280, 283, 298, 344; birth, 232, 251; at Vicky's wedding, 384, 385;

wish to join Navy, 390; and Saxe-Coburg succession, 390–1; leaves home, 396, 406, 407; visit to Ireland, 413

Alice, Princess, 254, 274, 279, 280, 340, 379, 395; birth, 232; vaccinated, 276; at Vicky's wedding, 383; prospective marriage, 400–3; dowry approved by Parliament, 412; visit to Ireland, 413–14; and death of A, 420, 421, 422, 424, 425

Alma, battle of the, 352

Almanach de Gotha, 299

Althorp, Lord, later 3rd Earl Spencer, 95

Amorbach, 18, 25, 35, 39

Anderson, Revd Mr, 343

Anne, Queen, 72, 116, 177, 194, 207

Annual Register, The, 317, 339

Anson, George, 180, 181, 194, 196, 204–5, 207, 208, 225, 257; meetings with Peel, 199; on Sir Robert Peel, 260

Anti-Corn Law League, 258, 259, 268

Arbuthnot, Colonel, 221

Arran, Arthur/Gore, 2nd Earl of, 19

Arthur, Prince, Duke of Connaught, 341, 359, 424

Ashburton, Alexander, Baring, 1st Baron, 303

Ashburton Treaty, 302, 303

Ashley, Anthony, later 7th Earl of Shaftesbury, 194, 229, 267

Augsburger Allgemeine, 162

August of Saxe-Coburg-Kohary, Prince, 239

Augusta, Princess, 32, 40

Augusta, Princess of Prussia (later German Empress), 379, 382, 392, 398; as Queen, 407, 411

Augusta of Cambridge, Princess (Grand Duchess of Mecklenburg-

Strelitz), 232, 381
Augusta of Saxe-Coburg-Saalfeld, 32, 153
Augustus of Saxe-Coburg, Prince, 309
Aumale, Duke of, 239, 310

Baden, Grand Duke of, 23
Bagehot, Walter, 263, 270
Baillie, Dr Mathew, 6, 9
Balaklava, battle of, 352, 353, 354
Balmoral, 288, 343, 365, 376, 382, 392
Barham, Lady (later Countess of Gainsborough), 111
Barrington, Lady, 188
Bathurst, Henry, 3rd Earl, 7
Bauer, Caroline, 41–3
Bauer, Karl, 43
Bavaria, Ludwig I, King of, 308
Bean (assassin), 223
Beatrice, Princess, 421, 424; treatment of V's diaries, 62; birth, 275, 344; christening, 381
Beauchamp, John, 3rd Earl, 61
Bedford, Duchess of, 200
Bedford, Francis Russell, 7th Duke of, 200, 201, 324
Belgian National Congress, 53
Belgium, 53, 76, 171, 254, 309, 381; invasion of, 113–14; A's education in, 157–8; V and A visit, 245–6
Belvoir Castle, 64, 247
Bennett, Daphne, 422
Bentinck, Lord George, 267
Bentinck, Lord Henry, 288
Bergami, Bartolomeo, 12, 27, 28
Berkeley, Mary, Countess of, 22
Bessborough, Frederick Ponsonby, 3rd Earl of, 94
Biddulph, Sir Thomas, 424
Birch, Revd Henry, 295–7
Bismarck, Otto von, 351, 367, 386, 407
Blatchford, Lady Isabella, 284

Blondin, Charles, 399
Blore, Edward, 102
Bolitho, Hector, 152, 190
Bonn University, 157, 159, 180
Bosquet, General, 352
Bourdin, Mademoiselle, 50
Brazil, Emperor of *see* Pedro IV of Portugal
Breadalbane, John Campbell, 2nd Marquess of, 235, 236
Bright, John, 229, 259, 321
Brighton Pavilion, 4, 11, 30, 102, 106, 244, 283; sale of, 107
Brock, Mrs (nurse), 47
Brocket Hall, 94, 99, 201, 215
Brontë, Charlotte, 246
Brougham, Henry, Lord, 2, 3, 26, 28–9, 97, 108, 173, 230, 252
Brown, John, 416–17
Browning, Elizabeth Barrett, 99
Bruce, Colonel the Hon. Robert, 389, 399, 400, 413, 425
Bruce, Lady Augusta, 412
Brunswick, Charles Frederick, Duke of, 76
Buccleuch, Walter, 5th Duke of, 234, 235, 265
Buckingham, Richard Temple, 1st Duke of, 4
Buckingham House *see* Buckingham Palace
Buckingham Palace, 99, 111, 138, 167, 182, 219, 221, 222, 232, 328, 379; V. moves to, 101–4; lack of security at, 147, 220; wedding breakfast at, 186; birth of Vicky at, 195; birth of Prince of Wales at, 207
Buggin, Lady Cecilia: marriage to Duke of Sussex, 19; recognized and created Duchess of Inverness, 192
Bulwer, Sir Henry Lytton, 304, 305, 314
Bunsen, Chevalier, 255, 313
Burdett Coutts, Miss, 120

Burgoyne, Sir John, 352
Byng, George, 121
Byron, Lord, 95, 290

Cadogan, George, 380
Cambridge, Adolphus Frederick,
  Duke of, 18, 19, 84, 85, 170, 173,
  232; marriage grant, 21; marriage,
  22; refuses to testify against
  Caroline, 27; at V's marriage, 185;
  godfather to Prince of Wales, 279
Cambridge, Princess Augusta of
  Hesse-Cassel, Duchess of, 22
Cambridge University, 97, 246
Campbell, Lady, 5
Campbell, Sir Colin, 373
Canning, Charles John, Earl, 369,
  370, 373, 375
Canning, Charlotte, Lady, 227, 253,
  354–5; visits Belgium and France
  with V, 241, 242, 243, 245; visits
  Coburg with V, 276, 278; on Prince
  of Wales and Mr Birch, 297; on
  dullness of Nemours, 311; death of,
  421
Canning, George, 94
Canrobert, General, 352, 363
Cardigan, James, 7th Earl of, 352
Carlists, 72
Carlos of Spain, Don, 72
Carlton House, 4, 11, 44, 102
Caroline, Queen, 1, 12, 13; returns to
  England, 26; faces prosecution, 27,
  37; refused access to Coronation
  ceremony, 28; death of, 29
Castlereagh, Lord, 21, 39
Cavendish, Colonel, 380
Cawnpore, 371
Charlemont, Countess of, 111, 128
Charles X of France, King, 118
Charles of Hesse, Princess, 413
Charles of Leiningen, Prince, 23, 33,
  167, 412; supports 'Kensington
  system', 55–6; tries to intervene

between V and Duchess of Kent,
  88–9; pleads for V, 90; at V's
  Coronation, 118; goes to Scotland
  with V, 288; and revolution of
  1848, 313; death of, 379
Charles Emich of Leiningen, Prince,
  38, 46, 56
Charles Louis Bonaparte, Prince, 319
Charlotte, Princess: birth, 1;
  entanglement with Charles Hesse,
  1–2, 13; engagement to Prince of
  Orange, 2–4, 76; marriage to
  Leopold, 5–6, 59, 175, 183; in
  childbirth, 1, 7–9; death, 10–15,
  16, 17, 18, 19, 20, 22, 23, 26, 39, 61,
  69, 192
Charlotte, Queen, 1, 13–14, 34, 101,
  177, 411
Charlotte of Belgium, Princess, 381,
  413
Charlotte of Württemburg, Queen, 32
Charlotte Augusta of Clarence,
  Princess, 31
Chartists, 175–6, 229, 234, 258,
  316–18
Chatsworth, 201, 247, 331
Chernaya River, 362
Christian IX of Denmark, 415, 416
Christinos, 72
Claremont, 14, 43, 112, 203, 254;
  home of Leopold and Charlotte, 6;
  and Duke and Duchess of Kent, 24,
  67; V's memories of, 44, 74; Louis
  Philippe in exile at, 310; poisoned
  water at, 311
Clarence, William, Duke of *see*
  William IV
Clarendon, Edward Hyde, 1st Earl of,
  72
Clarendon, George William Villiers,
  5th Earl of, 351, 356–7, 359, 366,
  377, 401
Claret de Viscourt, Mlle Arcadie, 312
Clark, Dr (later Sir) James, 63, 192,

218, 288, 296, 409; and Flora
Hastings affair, 128–31, 136–8,
140; and Vicky's health, 210–11;
warns A on future pregnancies for
V, 275; and fatal illness of A, 420–4
Clarke, Sir Charles, 131
Clementine of Orleans, Princess, 239,
309
Cleveland, Wilhelmina, Duchess of
(as Lady Wilhelmina Stanhope),
121, 123, 126
Clifden, Nelly, 417
Clotilda of Sardinia, Princess, 397
Cobden, Richard, 229, 259, 264, 269,
270, 321
Coburg, 9, 10, 24, 152, 153, 156, 157,
168, 216, 248–9, 254–7, 390–1,
402
Coburg, Dowager Duchess of, 182,
183, 191, 197, 309, 332
Codrington, General Sir William, 355
Cole, Henry, 329
Combe, Dr, 285
Combe, Sir George, 296
Conroy, Sir John, 33, 37, 40, 47;
marriage, 38, 44; influence over
Duchess of Kent, 53, 54, 55–7, 62,
63; ordered out of V's confirmation,
64; puts pressure on V, 66, 69, 79,
87–9; exhorbitant terms for
retirement, 90–3; attacked by
Times, 110; and Flora Hastings
affair, 128–9; resigns from service,
136–7
Constitution, the (newspaper), 140
Conyngham, Henry, 1st Marquess,
29, 81
Conyngham, Lady, 28, 29, 45
Corn Laws, 198–9, 258–60, 262, 263,
265–6, 269–70, 272
Cornwall, Duchy of, 107–8, 224
Costa, Signor, 104
Couper, Sir George, 90, 110, 408, 410
Coutts and Co., 107

Cowper, 5th Earl, 300
Cowper, 6th Earl, 201
Cowper, Lady (later Lady
Palmerston), 300
Cracow, Republic of, 306
Cranborne Lodge, 4
Creevey, Thomas, 3, 19, 23, 27, 28,
29, 37, 39, 43, 93, 102, 110
Crimean War, 347, 351–7, 361–2,
365–7, 369, 370, 381, 398
Croft, Sir Richard, 6–9, 14
Croker, John Wilson, 25, 29, 34, 170
Crystal Palace, 247, 331, 332, 334,
338–40, 359, 360, 381
Cubitt, Thomas, 284
Cumberland, Ernest, Duke of (later
King of Hanover), 1819: marriage
grant, 21, 37, 75, 82, 83, 84;
becomes King of Hanover, 85, 107,
170–1; tries to refuse A precedence,
232–3, 382
Cumberland, Frederica, Duchess of,
1819, 25
Cumberland Lodge, 45
Cunard, 353
Czartoryski, Adam, Prince, 360

Daily News, 348, 349, 350
Dalhousie, Lord, 235, 368, 415
D'Arblay, Alexander, 13
D'Arblay, Fanny, 4, 5
Davis, Jefferson, 419
Davys, Revd George, 47, 50, 64
De La Warr, George, 5th Earl, 235
Delhi, 371, 372, 373
Demidoff, Anatole, Prince, 118
Derby, Edward Stanley, 14th Earl of,
343, 350, 367, 374; as Lord Stanley,
143, 265, 270, 327; second
administration, 388; resigns, 397
Devonshire, William Cavendish, 6th
Duke of, 2, 40, 201, 247, 331
Dietz, Herr, 307
Disbrowe, Sir Edward, 302

Disraeli, Benjamin, 125, 143, 203,
    266–7, 268, 271, 340; Chancellor of
    the Exchequer, 388, 397, 410
Douro, Marchioness of, 224, 291
Downshire, Dowager Marchioness of,
    22
Doyle, Mr, 138
Drummond, Edward, 223, 229, 263
Duff, David, 154
Duncannon, John Ponsonby, 1st
    Baron, 90
Dundas, Sir David, 34
Dundas, Thomas, 1st Baron, 109
Durham, Countess of, 111

*Early Years of HRH the Prince Consort,
    The*, 154
East India Company, 367, 368, 373
Eastern Question, 237–8, 381
Eastlake, Sir Charles, 227
Edward VII (as Prince of Wales),
    189, 224, 290; birth, 207, 225, 231,
    270, 278–9; christening, 225;
    character as child, 279; lifelong love
    of stage, 282; created Earl of
    Dublin, 283; Osborne
    recommended for health, 285–6;
    education of, 294–8; attends Great
    Exhibition, 331, 334; meets
    Emperor of France, 358;
    accompanies parents to France,
    362, 365; on Vicky's engagement,
    379; at Vicky's wedding, 384, 385;
    confirmed, 388; visits Berlin,
    389–90; at Oxford, 390, 400; North
    American tour, 398–400; at
    Cambridge, 400, 407; question of
    marriage, 404; Princess Alexandra
    chosen for, 404, 415, 416; at the
    Curragh, 413, 417; visits Vicky,
    415; illness and death of father,
    424, 425
Edward of Leiningen, Prince, 412
Eliza of Hohenlohe-Langenburg,

    Princess, 70
Elizabeth I, Queen, 116, 190, 207,
    367
Elizabeth of Wied, Princess, 404
Elizabeth Georgina Adelaide of
    Clarence, Princess, 31, 40
Ellenborough, Lady, 41
Enrique, Don, Duke of Seville, 304
Entente Cordiale, 365
Ernest I of Saxe-Coburg-Gotha,
    Duke, 77, 151, 152–4, 160, 182,
    186, 187, 216, 221; death of, 230,
    248
Ernest II of Saxe-Coburg-Gotha,
    Prince, 160, 161, 168, 169, 197, 230,
    231, 381, 404; visits England, 77,
    78; birth and childhood, 152–4;
    education, 157; succeeds as Duke,
    248; V and A visit, 256–7, 402; and
    succession in Coburg, 280, 390–1
Ernest of Leiningen, Prince, 353
Ernest Augustus of Hanover *see*
    Cumberland, Ernest, Duke of
Ernest Christian Charles of
    Hohenlohe-Langenburg, Prince,
    46, 70
Esterhazy, Prince, 127
Eugenie, Empress, 255, 362, 364;
    attempt on life, 387; at Windsor,
    403
Examiner, The, 264
Exeter, Marchioness of, 275
Exeter, Marquess of, 66
Express (steam packet), 309

Featherstonehaugh, G. W., 309
Feodora of Leiningen, Princess, 23,
    33, 39, 48, 56, 167, 294; George
    IV's interest in, 46; marriage to
    Ernest of Hohenlohe-Langenburg,
    46; correspondence with V, 52, 75,
    78, 86, 100, 101, 103, 106, 110–11,
    112–13, 195; visits England (1834),
    70; at V's Coronation, 118; told of

V's engagement, 169; and
revolutions of 1848, 313; on
mother's death, 410; at Balmoral,
414
Ferdinand II of Portugal (Ferdinand
of Saxe-Coburg), 72, 171, 195, 306,
416
Ferdinand II of Two Sicilies, 241, 319
Ferdinand of Portugal, Prince, 416
Ferdinand of Saxe-Coburg, Prince,
163, 279
Fernanda, Infanta (Duchess of
Montpensier), 304, 305, 309
Fisher, Dr John, Bishop of Salisbury,
38, 44
Fisher, Elizabeth (wife of Sir John
Conroy), 38
Fisher, Herbert, 400
Fisher, Major-General, 38
FitzClarence, Lady Augusta, 67
FitzClarence, Lord Adolphus, 240
Fitzgerald, Hamilton, 132, 134–5,
139
Fitzgerald, Lord, 174
Fitzherbert, Mrs Maria, 1, 30
Fitzwilliam, Charles Wentworth, 5th
Earl, 109, 117, 121
Fitzwilliam, Lady Anne, 121
Fitzwilliam, William Wentworth, 4th
Earl, 109
Florschutz, Herr, 153–5, 156
Frampton, Mary, 104–5, 117, 120
Francis, John, 222
Francis of Two Sicilies, 304
Francisco de Paula, Infante Don, 304
Frederick III of Prussia ('Fritz') visits
Balmoral and betrothal to Vicky,
376–9, 381; wedding, 384–5; and
Vicky's pregnancy, 394, 395; visits
to England, 398, 413; becomes
Crown Prince at death of Frederick
William IV, 407
Frederick William IV of Prussia, 307,
332, 350; V's visit to, 255;

godfather to Prince of Wales, 278,
279; and revolutions of 1848, 313;
death of, 406, 407
Freemantle, Sir Thomas, 262, 263
Frogmore, 343, 408, 411
Fuller, Francis, 329

Gainsborough, Lady, 254
Garth, Colonel Thomas, 37
George I, 85, 240
George II, 121, 240
George III, 36, 93, 101, 107, 119, 177,
185, 240, 359; insanity, 12, 13, 16;
death of, 26, 34; as parent, 292, 293
George IV, 16, 37, 39, 40, 56, 60, 76,
79, 90, 207, 230, 240, 292;
disastrous marriage, 1, 12, 183;
relations with Charlotte, 2–4; her
marriage, 5; her death, 11, 14;
brothers' marriages, 20–1, 24, 25;
becomes King, 26; collects evidence
for divorce, 26–8; Coronation, 28,
115, 117, 125; deteriorating health,
30–1, 52; hatred of Duke of Kent,
31, 41; at V's christening, 32–3;
shows more interest in V, 45–6;
death, 52–3, 61; improvements at
Windsor, 105; at Brighton, 107;
politics, 293
George of Cambridge, Prince, 170,
171, 353
George of Cumberland, Prince, 75,
395
George of Denmark, Prince, 174, 177,
207
Gibbs, Frederick Waymouth, 297–8,
380, 389
Gladstone, William Ewart, 203, 226,
265, 269, 270, 321, 327, 336, 380,
419
Gladstone, William Henry, 380
Gloucester, Princess Mary, Duchess
of, 32, 35, 45, 170, 186, 197, 326

Gorchakov, Prince, 347, 362
Gordon, Lady Alicia, 288
Gordon, Sir Robert, 288
Graham, Sir James, 143, 234, 259, 260, 270
Grandineau, M. (French tutor), 49
Granville, George Leveson-Gore, 2nd Earl of, 380, 410
Great Eastern (steamship), 338
Great Exhibition (1851), 328, 331, 333–5, 336, 343
Gregory XVI, Pope, 162
Greville, Charles, 45, 91–2, 112, 118, 120, 122, 125, 126, 130, 134, 169, 170, 172, 176, 221, 229, 324, 389; on Duke and Duchess of York, 16, 17; V 'short, plain-looking child', 51; on Leopold becoming King of the Belgians, 54; opinion of Conroy, 62; on V's journeys, 62, 66; her accession, 83, 84–5; and Melbourne, 94, 95, 98; V's 'peremptory disposition', 112; on V's Coronation, 118, 120, 122, 125, 126; on Flora Hastings affair, 130, 134; on Bedchamber affair, 145; on A's precedence, 174–5; on wedding, 183, 187; on Lehzen, 194; used as intermediary by Melbourne, 203–4; A 'King to all intents and purposes', 232, 262; on V's visit to Peel, 247; on Corn Laws, 259; 'paradox' of Peel, 270–1; Osborne an 'ugly house', 284; at Balmoral, 289; on Russell's recall, 327; on Napoleon's effect on V, 359, 360
Greville, Lady Charlotte, 30
Grey, Charles, 2nd Earl, 58, 62, 95, 122
Grey, General Sir Charles, 154, 182, 224, 334, 380, 424
Griffiths, Mrs (nurse), 6, 8
Grisi, Giulia, 74, 104

Guizot, F. P. F., 189, 238, 244, 253, 272, 300, 304, 305, 308–9, 310

Hanstein, Baron Alexander von, 153
Hardinge, Sir Henry, 1st Viscount, 349
Hastings, Lady, 135–6
Hastings, Lady Flora, 63, 91; part of Conroy faction, 128; suspected pregnancy, 129–32; gossip concerning, 133–5; illness and death, 137–8
Hastings, Lord, 132–4, 139
Havelock, Sir Henry, 373
Haynau, General, 322
Helena, Princess, 344, 383, 395; visits Ireland, 413; at A's deathbed, 424, 425
Herbert, Sidney, 260
Hesse, Captain Charles, 1, 13
Hildyard, Sarah Anne, 277, 288, 289, 395
Hill, Sir Rowland, 228
History of the Rebellion, 72
Holland, Lady, 1
Holland, Lord, 136, 145
Holland, Sir Henry, 422
Hume, Joseph, 175

Indian Mutiny, 367, 368, 371–3
Inkerman, battle of, 353
Inverness, Duchess of *see* Buggin, Lady Cecilia
Ireland, Dr John, 125
Ironbridge, Sir Thomas, 361
Isabella II of Spain, 72, 82, 118, 244, 257; marriage, 304–6

Jarnac, Count, 304, 305, 310, 311
Jenkinson, Lady Catherine, 89
Jenner, Dr Edward, 276
Jenner, Dr (later Sir) William, 419; at A's fatal illness, 420, 421, 422
Jersey, Lady, 181

John VI of Portugal, 72
Joinville, François d'Orleans, Prince of, 239, 240, 241, 242, 257; his alarming pamphlet, 301; in exile, 310, 311, 319
Joinville, Françoise, Duchess of, 241, 243, 310
Jones, Edmund ('the Boy'), 147, 220
Jordan, Mrs, 17–18, 24

Katherine Amelia of Baden, Princess, 18
Keble, John, 172, 325
Kensington Palace, 37, 38, 39, 40, 53, 67, 101; Kent apartments in, 25; V's birth at, 26; her christening, 32–3; her early years at, 41, 44, 46–7, 52, 98; told of accession in, 81; her first Council at, 82–4; leaves for Buckingham Palace, 103
'Kensington System', 54–5, 56, 57, 66, 68, 69, 79
Kent, Edward, Duke of, 76, 90, 235; exile in Brussels with Mme St Laurent, 18; search for wife, 18, 20; marriage grant, 20–2; appearance and character, 23; marriage, 24–5; returns to England for V's birth, 26; her christening, 32–3; illness and death at Sidmouth, 33–5, 38; debts, 39; repaid by V, 109
Kent, Victoire of Saxe-Coburg, Duchess of, 18, 41, 43, 47, 52, 53, 153, 192, 217, 343, 377; courtship of, 22; first marriage and children, 23; marriage, 24–5; pregnancy and return to England, 25–6; birth of V, 26; her christening, 32–3; at Sidmouth, 33–4; death of Duke, 34; return to Kensington, 35, 36; poverty of, 39–40; and V's education, 48–50; relations with Conroy, 55–6; campaigns for recognition for self and V, 58–9;

refuses to attend William IV's Coronation, 60–1; takes V on series of tours, 61–2, 65–6; request for permanent residence, 62–3; publicly insulted by King, 67–8; supports German marriage for V, 77; and V's accession, 81; earlier dissension with William over V's name, 85; growing rift with V, 87–9, 91, 92; pleads for Conroy, 90–3; debts, 109–10; at V's Coronation, 126; Flora Hastings affair, 128, 131, 135, 136–7, 138; not told of V's engagement, 167, 169; at V's marriage, 184, 185; at birth of Princess Royal, 195, 197; at birth of Prince of Wales, 207; improved relations with V, 216; godmother to Prince of Wales, 279; told of Vicky's secret betrothal, 377; at her wedding, 384; ill-health and death, 408–9, 410; her attachment to V revealed, 411; burial at Frogmore, 411–12
Kew Palace, 24, 62–3
Knight, Charles, 52
Knight, Cornelia, 2, 10
Kossuth, Ferencz, 322–3

Lablache, Luigi, 74–5, 104, 188, 227
Lamb, Lady Caroline, 94–5, 150
Landseer, Sir Edwin, 133, 227, 286
Lansdowne, Henry, 3rd Marquess of, 82, 99, 261, 262
Lauderdale, James Maitland, 8th Earl of, 29, 30, 31
Lawrence, John, 373
Lawrence, Sir Thomas, 105
Leaves From Our Life in the Highlands, 414
Lehzen, Baroness Louise, 51, 52, 57, 66, 69, 79, 103, 113, 160, 167, 171, 217, 218; governess to Princess Feodora, 39, 56; and V, 47, 48, 55,

56, 63, 64; V's attachment to, 87, 88, 90, 125, 149, 213, 256; at V's Coronation, 125; role in Hastings affair, 128, 129, 134–5, 139–40; conflict with A, 189, 193–5, 209–12; leaves England, 213; death, 213; visited by V, 213, 256

Leopold, Prince, 276, 344, 393, 412, 424

Leopold of Saxe-Coburg (later Leopold I of the Belgians), 4, 7, 8, 9, 12, 14, 18, 56, 93, 129, 171, 182, 222, 233, 255, 278, 302, 314, 362; marriage, 5–6; sorrow at Charlotte's death, 10–11; granted annuity, 11, 175; lends Claremont to the Kents, 24–5; correspondence with V, 31, 44, 71–4, 80, 86, 92, 112, 146, 153, 191–2, 202, 206, 208, 229, 231, 239, 250, 272, 309, 328, 350, 372, 396, 409, 411; at V's christening, 32; Duke of Kent's death, 34; advises Duchess to stay in England, 35; regular visits to Kensington, 37–8; finances Duchess, 39, 110; as father figure, 41; affair with Caroline Bauer, 41–3; offered thrones of Greece and Belgium, 53; leaves for Belgium, 54; at Ramsgate, 66; warns V against King and Court, 68–9; rumours of marriage with V, 75–6; in favour of German marriage for V, 77; intends V to marry A, 78–9; envisages opposition on V's accession, 81–2; acknowledges V's difficulties with mother, 88; stays at Windsor, 105, 106; instructs V on business of government, 112; sees growing influence of Melbourne, 113–14; declines to attend V's Coronation, 118; suggests visit of Ernest and A, 149; education of A, 156–8; impressions of A, 158, 161,

179; visits V, 163; pleasure at engagement of V and A, 167; anger over A's annuity, 177; seeks peerage for A, 178–80; strained relations with V, 180–1; intellectual prime, 190; advice to V on new Household crisis, 200–1; V and A visit, 245; death of Queen Louise, 312; at Vicky's confirmation, 379; wedding of daughter, 381; at Vicky's marriage, 383; death of Duchess of Kent, 409–10; in England, 413

Leopold of Saxe-Coburg, Prince, 304

Leuchtenberg, Duc de, 72

Lieven, Princess, 30, 34, 38, 57, 92, 107, 265

Lincoln, Abraham, 419

Lindsay, Lady Charlotte, 22

Liverpool, Charles Jenkinson, 3rd Earl, 192, 243, 245, 254; advice to V over Conroy, 89–90; at V's marriage, 184

Liverpool, Robert Jenkinson, 2nd Earl, 27

Lloyd-Lindsay, Major, 388

Locock, Dr (later Sir) Charles, 207

Londonderry, Marquess of, 117

Longford, Elizabeth, Lady, 199

Louis XVIII, 24, 118, 253

Louis of Hesse-Darmstadt, Prince, 401, 405, 412, 414, 421

Louis Napoleon, Prince *see* Napoleon III

Louis Philippe, 118, 119, 245, 257, 300, 306, 357, 360, 362; becomes King of the French, 53; daughter's marriage to Leopold, 54, 114; invites V to France, 239; visit of V and A, 240–4; visits England, 253–4; and Spanish marriages, 304–5; abdicates, 308–9; asks V for asylum, 310; at Claremont, 310–11; death, 312

Louise, Princess, 344; birth of, 309, 313; at Vicky's wedding, 383; at A's deathbed, 424

Louise, Queen of the Belgians, 54, 253, 255; at Windsor, 105–6; marriage, 114, 239; death, 312

Louise of Saxe-Gotha-Altenburg, Duchess of Saxe-Coburg-Gotha, 152–4

Lucan, Earl of, 352

Lucknow, 371, 372, 373

Lyndhurst, John Copley, 1st Baron, 143, 173

Lyttelton, Sarah, Lady, 111, 184, 189, 213, 248, 275; appointed to care for royal children, 217–18, 294; on Princess Victoria, 276–7; on Prince of Wales, 279; leaves Royal service, 281–2; on Osborne, 286; V's attitude to Scotland, 292

Lytton, Edward, 97

McNaugton, Daniel, 223, 262

Magenta, battle of, 397

Mallet, Baron de, 24

Malmesbury, James Harris, 1st Earl of, 13

Malmesbury, James Harris, 3rd Earl of, 289, 307, 308, 346, 388

Manchester Guardian, The, 365

Manning, Cardinal, 332

Maria da Gloria, Queen of Portugal, 51, 72–3, 82, 118, 191, 315, 416; revolt against, 306–7

Marie of Württemburg, Duchess of Saxe-Coburg, 231, 402

Marie Amelie, Queen of France, 241, 242–3, 305, 309, 311

Martin, Sir Theodore, 154, 161, 213, 214

Marx, Karl, 319

Mary I, 116, 207

Mary of Cambridge, Princess, 277

Mason, James Murray, 419

Maximilian, Archduke, 381, 413

Mazzini, Joseph, 319

Mecklenburg-Strelitz, Grand Duchess of *see* Augusta of Cambridge

Mecklenburg-Strelitz, Grand Duke of, 382

Meerut, 369, 371

Mehemet Ali, 237–8, 300

Melbourne, William Lamb, 2nd Viscount, 48, 63, 65, 66, 69, 79, 89, 91, 104, 106, 114, 126, 145, 151, 170, 179, 192, 194, 197, 201, 208, 225, 227, 237, 300, 301, 302; not in favour of Dutch marriage for V, 76–7; as leader of Whigs, 82; announces V's accession, 83; at V's first Council, 84, 86–7; comforts V over scenes with mother, 92–3, 110, 167; relationship with V, 93, 98–9, 100, 215–16; youth and career, 94–7; and V's Civil List, 108–9; at V's Coronation, 124–5; and Flora Hastings affair, 129, 130, 133–6, 137, 138, 139, 140; resignation, 141, 142, 143; and Bedchamber crisis, 144, 150, 198; return to power, 146; advises V to marry, 150; and A's annuity, religion and precedence, 172–4; and A's Household, 180–1; at V's marriage, 185, 186; defeat of government, 199, 202; final audience and farewell, 202; correspondence with V, 203–7, 284; gives advice to Peel, 203; decline and death, 214; refuses to intervene in Corn Law crisis, 262; advice on education of Prince of Wales, 293, 297

Mendelssohn, Felix, 226, 227, 275, 384

Mensdorff, Count Arthur, 155, 164

Menshikoff, Prince, 346

Mercer Elphinstone, Miss, 4, 6, 22
Metternich, Prince von, 30, 53, 206, 313, 319
Miguel, Dom, 72
Miraflores, Marquis de, 118
Montes, Lola, 308
Montgenet, Comtesse de *see* St Laurent, Mme Julie
Montpensier, Duke of, 243, 253, 257, 304, 305–6, 310
Morning Chronicle, The, 23, 214, 257, 303
Morning Herald, The, 348, 350
Morning Post, The, 136, 138–9, 236
Morton, Sir William, 34
Mulgrave, Lady *see* Normanby, Lady
Murray, Lady Augusta, 19, 36
Murray, Sir Charles, 113, 147, 223

Nana Sahib, 372
Napoleon, 118, 242, 346, 359, 363, 397
Napoleon III, 376, 395; as Prince Louis Napoleon, *coup d'état*, 323; President of French Republic, 336; Emperor, 345; and Crimean War, 345, 349, 356, 366–7; visits England, 358; effect on V, 359–60; attempts on life, 359, 387; discussions with Palmerston, 360–1; entertains V and A, 362–5; at Osborne, 381; signs armistice between France and Austria, 397
Nash, John, 102, 106
Nemours, Duke of, 53, 76, 239, 309, 311, 318
Nemours, Victoire, Duchess of, 163, 239, 309, 310, 311
Nesselrode, Count, 251
Newcastle, Duke of, 352, 399
Newman, Cardinal, 172, 325
Nicholas I, Tsar of Russia, 320, 357; visits England, 249–50, 282; and Crimean War, 345, 346, 351; death, 356

Nield, John Camden, 343
Nightingale, Florence, 354–5
Normanby, Lady, 111, 145, 188, 189, 200
Normanby, Lord, 170, 310, 323
Northumberland, Duchess of, 59, 61, 63, 168

Observer, The, 336, 338, 342
O'Connell, Daniel, 96, 251–2
O'Connor, Feargus, 316
Oldenburg, Catherine, Grand Duchess of, 22
Orange, Prince of, 2, 3, 4, 76, 77, 113, 401
Orléans, Duchess of, 241, 243, 310
Orléans, Duke of, 75–6, 239
Orsini, Felici, 387
Osborne House, 261, 317, 381, 382, 408, 410, 412; bought by A, 283; new building of, 284–5
Otto of Greece, 320
Oxford, Edward, 221
Oxford Movement, 325
Oxford University, 97; Prince of Wales at, 390, 400

Pacifico, Don, 320
Palmella, Duke de, 118
Palmerston, Henry Temple, 3rd Viscount, 53, 73, 97, 106, 113, 198, 214, 302, 369, 380, 410; and Eastern Question, 238; at Foreign Office, 264, 272, 303; advises V on foreign affairs, 299; character, 300; in conflict with V, 300–1, 313–15, 323–4; on poverty of French royal family, 310–11; Don Pacifico affair, 320–1; Haynau and Kossuth affairs, 322–3; returns to Home Office, 343; and Crimean War, 347, 360–1, 366; as Prime Minister, 355, 356; discussions with Napoleon III, 360–1; V's assessment of, 367; and Indian

Mutiny, 371; Vicky's engagement, 377; at Vicky's wedding, 384; resignation, 387, 388; premier again, 397; and Trent affair, 419; worry at A's fatal illness, 420, 421, 423

Panam, Pauline, 153

Paris, Count of, 308, 310

Parkes, Dr Edmund, 422

Paxton, Joseph, 247, 331, 339

Pedro IV of Portugal, 72–3

Pedro V of Portugal, 416

Peel, Sir Robert, 25, 108, 109, 170, 176, 177, 206, 207, 208, 220, 232, 234, 300, 301, 303; as Leader of Tories, 82, 84; Prime Minister, 195–6; and Bedchamber crisis, 142–5, 198; and Regency Bill, 192; and new Household crisis, 199, 201; again premier, 203–4; and attempts on V's life, 220, 221, 222–3; and income tax, 229–30; and repeal of Corn Laws, 259–61, 266, 267, 268; and Irish issue, 259; resigns, 261; relationship with A, 261–2; target for assassination, 263; again Prime Minister, 264–5, 267; resignation, 269; characteristics of, 270–1; death of, 272, 330; recommends purchase of Osborne, 283; and Spanish marriages, 304; supports A over Great Exhibition, 328

Philip of Spain, 207

Philippe Égalité, 237

Phipps, Sir Charles, 421, 423, 424, 425

Pius IX, Pope, 319, 325

Pluton (French ship), 240, 244

Pomare, Queen of Tahiti, 252

Ponsonby, Henry, 380

Portman, Lady, 111, 129, 130, 131–2, 134, 139

Portman, Lord, 134, 139

Portugal, 72–3, 82, 118, 306, 314, 416

Pritchard, George, 252–3

Punch, 257, 331, 378 .

Pusey, Dr Edward, 172, 325

Putbus, Prince of, 118

Quarterly Review, The, 102

Queen's House *see* Buckingham Palace

Quetelet, M., 157

Raglan, Lord, 349, 352, 353

Raikes, Thomas, 119, 239, 240; his *Journal*, 119

Rea (Clerk of Works), 110

Reform Bills, 60, 82, 97, 201, 228

Rhodes James, Robert, 143, 153, 156, 159, 160, 166, 302

Roberts, Lord, 370

Roebuck, John Arthur, 349, 355, 381

Roebuck, Lord, 321, 327

Rolle, Lord, 126

Rosebery, Lord, 235

Rosenau, the (A's birthplace), 152, 249, 256

Royal George (ship), 234

Royal Marriages Act (1772), 19

Russell, John Scott, 329

Russell, Lord John, 141, 170, 174–5, 177, 200, 214, 292, 300, 303, 306, 314, 350, 352, 419; and Eastern Question, 238; and repeal of Corn Laws, 260; invited to form Government, 261–2; fails, 264; Prime Minister on death of Peel, 272; agrees to asylum for Louis Philippe, 310; and Portugal, 315; Don Pacifico affair, 320–1; and Kossuth affair, 323; demands Palmerston's resignation, 324; Government defeated, 324, 327; and 'papal aggression', 326; again Prime Minister, 327

Russell, Lord William, 79

Russell, William Howard, 354

St James's Palace, 2, 51, 59, 99, 101, 103, 104, 189; V's marriage in, 183–5, 186; Princess Royal's wedding at, 383

St Laurent, Mme Julie, 18, 23

St Stephens (poem), 97

Saxony, King of, 249

Schindler, Captain, 56–7

Scott, Sir Walter, 52, 236, 298

Scutari, 354

Sebastopol, 351, 352, 353, 356, 360, 362, 365, 366, 376

Sedgwick, Professor, 246

Selim Pasha, 351

Seymour, Sir Hamilton, 314–15

Shrewsbury, John Talbot, 16th Earl of, 120

Sibthorp, Colonel Charles, 176, 177, 332

Sidmouth, 33, 34

Sidmouth, Henry Addington, 1st Viscount, 7

Simpson, Dr James Young, 276

Sims, Dr, 8

Sinope, 347, 351

Slidell, John, 419

Solferino, 397

Solms-Braunfels, Prince Frederick of, 18

Somerset House, 101, 329

Sophia, Princess, 37, 40, 44, 186, 279

Sophia of Gloucester, Princess, 22, 186

Sotomayor, Duke of, 314

Soult, Marshal, 118–19

Southey, Mrs (nurse), 210

Spaeth, Baroness, 38–9

Spectator, The, 333, 349

Spencer, Earl, 218

Spring Rice, Miss Mary, 128

Spring Rice, Thomas, 109

Standard, The, 260

Stanhope, Lady Wilhelmina *see* Cleveland, Wilhelmina, Duchess of

Stanley, Frederick, 380

Stanley, Lady Eleanor, 244, 245, 276, 282

Stanley of Alderley, Edward 2nd Baron, 320

Stevenson, Mrs (wife of American Ambassador), 189

Steward, Thomas, 48, 49

Stockmar, Christian, Baron, 6, 14, 89, 93, 112, 113, 224, 401, 410; at Charlotte's death, 9; becomes Leopold's agent, 10; on Duke of York, 16; at Sidmouth, 34; cousin of Caroline Bauer, 42, 43; on Conroy, 57, 129, 130; 'good faithful Stockmar', 87; supports V's resistance to mother, 88; used as intermediary by Conroy, 90; praises Melbourne, 95; and Flora Hastings affair, 129–30; opinion of Albert, 156–7, 162–3; in Italy with A, 161–2; told of engagement by V and A, 166; on Tory prejudice against A as a foreigner, 170, 171; and Regency Bill, 192; return to Coburg, 193; correspondence with A, 193, 196, 209, 242, 248, 255, 265, 312, 318, 330, 336, 339, 346, 376, 388; and Crimean War, 347; V and A visit, 402, 403; questions deep Court mourning, 413

Stopford, Lady Mary, 128

Strachey, Lytton, 152, 205

Stratford de Redcliffe, Viscount, 346

Stroganoff, Count, 118, 127

Sumner, Holme, 21

Sun, the, 236

Surrey, Lord (later 13th Duke of Norfolk), 126

Sussex, Augustus, Duke of, 25, 32, 81; character, 19; at Kensington Palace, 36–7; officially announces death of William IV to V, 83; as Privy Councillor, 84; and A's precedence, 173; gives V away in marriage, 185, 186; suggested as

co-Regent with A, 192; godfather to Princess Royal, 197; burial at Kensal Green, 226
Sutherland, Duchess of, 111, 119, 200
Sutherland, Duke of, 118

Tahiti, 252–3
Talbot, Lady Mary, 120
Talleyrand, 113
Tamburini, Antonio, 74, 104
Tascher de la Pagerie, Count Charles, 358
Tavistock, Marchioness (later Duchess of Bedford), 111, 129, 134
Tavistock, Marquess of (later Duke of Bedford), 134, 139
Taylor, A. J. P., 345
Taylor, Sir Herbert, 76, 89
Teesdale, Major Christopher, 388
Thierry, General, 310
Thiers, Adolphe, 237, 238
Thynne, Lord John, 125
Times, The, 138, 185, 207, 257, 378, 381; approves of Kent marriage, 24; reproves Duchess of Kent, 60–1; against early betrothal for V, 75; on William IV, 80; attacks Conroy, 110; A 'too young' on marriage, 171; for repeal of Corn Laws, 260; on Peel's remoteness, 267; on French 'perfidy', 306; on Chartists, 318; attacks Great Exhibition, 330; W. H. Russell as correspondent for, 354
Torrington, Lord, 182, 417
Trapain, Count of, 304
Trent incident, 419
Tubeuf, Polyxene von, 34
Turgot, M., 323
Tuscany, Duke of, 319
Tylney-Long, Miss, 22

United States of America, 398, 399, 419

Valletort, Lord, 388
Victor of Hohenlohe-Langenburg, Prince, 412
Victor Emmanuel of Sardinia (later King of Italy), 313
Victoire of Saxe-Coburg *see* Kent, Victoire, Duchess of
Victoria, Princess Royal (Vicky), 156, 254, 274, 424; birth, 195; christening, 197–8; ill-health, 210–11; precosity, intelligence and bond with father, 276–8, 392; first public engagement, 282; religious education, 293–4; attends opening of Great Exhibition, 334; meets Emperor of France, 358, 359; accompanies parents to France, 362, 365; betrothal, 376–7; dowry approved by Parliament, 381; wedding, 383–4; leaves for Germany, 385; pregnancy, 395; difficult birth of William II, 396–7; visits England, 398; vets suitors for Alice, 401; birth of Charlotte and parents visit, 402; chooses Princess Alexandra for Bertie, 404, 415; death of King of Prussia, 405–6; unable to travel to father's deathbed, 424
Victoria, Queen, 10, 14, 38, 39, 40; line of succession and birth, 26, 31, 32; christening, 32–3; at Sidmouth, 33; death of father, 34; Leopold as father figure, 41, 43, 44; visits George IV, 45, 46; education and upbringing at Kensington, 47–54; 'Kensington system', 55–7, 70; fondness for Queen Adelaide, 57–8; accepted as heiress presumptive, 58–60; prevented from attending William IV's Coronation, 60–1; series of 'progresses', 61–2, 65; begins journal, 61–2, 86; confirmation, 63–4; poor health at Ramsgate, 66;

upset at mother's quarrel with
William, 67–8; capacity for love
and friendship, 70; comes of age,
70; Feodora's visit, 70;
correspondence with Leopold,
71–4, 80, 86, 92, 112, 146, 153,
191–2, 202, 206, 209, 229, 231, 239,
250, 272, 309, 328, 350, 372, 396,
409, 411; interest in Spanish and
Portuguese affairs, 72–3;
enjoyment of theatre and singing,
74–5; love of animals, 75; visits
Ascot races, 75; question of
marriage, 75–9; visit of Princes of
Orange and Princes of Coburg,
77–8; attracted to A, 78;
undaunted by prospect of
becoming Queen, 80; accession, 81;
first Privy Council, 82–5;
William's earlier desire to change
her name, 85; rejects brother's
intervention between V and
Duchess, 89; hatred of Sir John
Conroy unabated and further
scenes with mother over him, 91–3;
relationship with Melbourne, 93,
98–9, 100; proclaimed Queen, 99;
dissolves Parliament, 100;
enjoyment of personal success, 101;
moves to Buckingham Palace,
103–4; love of dance, 104–5;
pleasure in riding, 106; debts of
parents, 109–10; Household
appointments, 111; learns business
of government, 112; Coronation,
115–27; and Flora Hastings affair,
128–38, 150; hissed at Ascot, 138;
and Bedchamber affair, 140,
143–5, 150, 170; visit of Grand
Duke Alexander, 148–9; wish to
delay marrying, 149–51, 158;
impatience with Melbourne, 151;
'growing disinclination to
business', 152; correspondence
with A, 159–61, 163, 168–9;

impressions of A, 164; proposes to
him, 164; and question of A's
religion, 171–2; difficulties over
precedence, 173–4; his annuity
debated in Parliament, 174–5,
176–8; against peerage for A,
178–80; and A's Household, 180;
strained relations with Leopold,
180–1; wedding plans, 181–2;
marriage, 183–8; 'vein of iron',
189, 217; jealous of rights as
sovereign, 190–1; pregnancy, 191;
dislike of child-bearing, 191, 393;
birth of Princess Royal (Vicky),
195; new Household crisis,
199–201; farewell to Melbourne
and correspondence with, 202–6;
birth of Prince of Wales (Bertie),
207; quarrels with A over Lehzen,
209–12; A's influence on, 215–16;
improved relations with mother,
216; and education of children,
216–18; assassination attempts on,
220–3; spontaneity and simplicity,
224, 275; attitude towards religion,
225–6, 236; artistic
accomplishments, 226–7; social
conscience, 228–9, 316; begins to
share power with A, 231–3; first
visit to Scotland, 235–7; invited to
France, 237; visits French royal
family, 241–4; and Spanish
marriages, 244, 257, 304–6; visits
Belgium, 245; new esteem for Peel,
246–7, 265, 270; birth of Prince
Alfred (Affie), 251; visit of Louis
Philippe, 252–4; complex
relationship with children, 275–6,
277–8, 392–3; given chloroform at
Leopold's birth, 276; on Prince of
Wales, 279; visit to Ireland, 282–3;
first night at Osborne, 286; buys
Balmoral, 288–92; views on
education, 293–4; conflict with
Palmerston, 300–1, 313–15, 320,

322, 323, 324; relations with
Aberdeen, 302; supervision of
foreign affairs, 303; and Portugal,
307; affords Louis Philippe asylum,
309–10; birth of Princess Louise,
309; sadness at death of Queen
Louise, 312; against Italian
independence, 314–15;
'extraordinary proceeding of Pope',
325–6; and Papal aggression,
326–7; concern for A's health, 330,
418, 422; visits to Crystal Palace,
331, 332, 333, 335; opening of
Great Exhibition, 333–4; grief at
death of Wellington, 341; lays
foundation stone at Balmoral, 343;
and Crimean War, 347, 351–2,
353–6, 361, 365; indignation at
attacks on A, 350; obliged to
appoint Palmerston Prime
Minister, 355; visit of Emperor of
France, 357–60; his effect on V,
359–60; distributes war medals,
361; visit to France, 362–5;
assessment of Palmerston, 367; and
Indian Mutiny, 371, 372; assumes
government of India, 374–5; and
Vicky's betrothal, 376–7, 381;
creates A Prince Consort, 382–5;
misses A's absence less, 391–2; and
domestic friction, 392–4; visits
Cherbourg, 394–5; birth of first
grandchild, 396–7; letters to Vicky,
395, 396, 399, 400, 401, 407, 410,
411, 412, 418; visit to Coburg and
Vicky, 402–3; and Alice's
engagement, 403; candidates for
Bertie's hand, 404; death of mother
and grief for, 408–13; visits Ireland
again, 413–14; expeditions from
Balmoral, 414–15; and Bertie's
meeting with Alix, 416; *Trent* affair,
419; at A's bedside, 423–5; his
death, 425; 'There is no-one to call
me Victoria now', 425

Victoria and Albert (yacht), 240, 244
Vienna, Congress of (1815), 53
Villiers, Charles, 259

Walewski, Count, 323, 366, 387
Wallenstein, Prince, 307
Waterloo, battle of (1815), 38, 118
Watson, Dr, 423
Wellesley, Hon Gerald, Dean of
    Windsor, 388
Wellington Duke of, 15, 45, 169, 170,
    186, 232, 240, 253, 269, 282, 335,
    336, 346; on George III's sons, 22;
    attends V's birth, 26; and Duchess
    of Kent's aims at precedence, 58; at
    V's first Council, 84; at V's
    Coronation, 118, 125; tries to
    reconcile V & Duchess, 134, 136;
    refuses to form Government,
    141–2, 143; question of A's
    Protestantism, 172–3; at V's
    marriage, 184; at Princess Royal's
    christening, 197; in Peel's
    Government, 203; attends birth of
    Prince of Wales, 207; plans defence
    of British Isles, 301; and security
    measures for Chartist meeting, 317;
    advises V to recall Lord John
    Russell, 327; death of, 328, 340,
    349; state funeral, 341–3
Westall, Richard, 50, 227
Westminster Abbey, 115, 119; V's
    Coronation in, 120–1, 122–6
Wharncliffe, Lord, 170
Wheeler, Sir Hugh, 372
Whewell, Dr, 246, 400
Wiechmann, Baron, 157
Wilkes, John, 122
William, Duke of Gloucester (son of
    Queen Anne), 207
William, Prince of Prussia, later
    Emperor William I, 79, 255, 313,
    332, 333, 377, 407
William I of Holland, 114
William II, later Kaiser, 396–7, 402

William IV, 13, 103, 104, 105, 117, 300; liaison with Mrs Jordan, 17; marriage grant, 20–2; search for wife, 22; marriage, 24, 183; death of daughters, 31; accession, 53; character, 57; calls new Parliament, 58; recommends increased allowances for V and Duchess of Kent, 59; Coronation, 60–1, 117, 119, 125; annoyance at V's 'progresses', 62, 64–7; offers Duchess of Kent Kew Palace, 62–3; disagrees with Duchess over V's confirmation, 63–4; attachment to V, 67; publicly insults Duchess, 67–8; offers income and separate establishment to V, 69; declining health, 76; invites Princes of Orange to visit, 71; death, 79, 81, 90, 103, 159; evaluation of, 80; his desire to change V's name, 85–6; dismisses Whigs, 95–6; offers Buckingham Palace to Lords and Commons, 102
William of Lowenstein, Prince, 161, 189
William of Orange, Prince, 76, 77
William of Orange, Prince, 401
Williamson, Lady, 188
Willoughby d'Eresby, Lady, 188
Willoughby d'Eresby, Lord, 125, 325
Wilson, Archdale, 371
Wilton, Lord, 247
Windsor Castle, 14, 67, 86, 99, 101, 111, 168, 195, 204, 224, 225, 227,

239, 262, 300, 416, 418; Duke of Kent buried at, 35; V's first visit to, 45; death of William IV at, 81; George IV's reconstruction of, 102, 105; visitors at, 105–6; lack of security at, 146; Ernest and A's visit, 164; V proposes to A at, 165; their honeymoon at, 186–7; King of Saxony and Tsar Nicholas at, 249–50; mismanagement of, 219; Louis Philippe invested with Garter at, 254; Princess Royal's honeymoon at, 384–5; confirmation of Prince of Wales at, 388; Empress Eugenie visits incognito, 403; Duchess of Kent buried at, 411; death of Prince Consort at, 425
Winterhalter, Franz, 227, 286, 358
Wiseman, Cardinal, 325, 326
Wood, Charles, 380
Woodham-Smith, Cecil, 46, 47, 56, 129, 132, 417
Wyckham, Miss, 22
Wylde, Colonel, 221
Wyse, Mr, 320

York, Frederica, Duchess of, 16–17, 30
York, Frederick, Duke of, 5, 11, 16, 20, 27, 31, 32, 37, 44

Zavellos, General, 320